# Vital Issues in the Inerrancy Debate

# Vital Issues in the Inerrancy Debate

General Editor
F. DAVID FARNELL

Associate Editors
NORMAN L. GEISLER
JOSEPH M. HOLDEN
WILLIAM C. ROACH
PHIL FERNANDES

Foreword by
PAIGE PATTERSON

WIPF & STOCK · Eugene, Oregon

VITAL ISSUES IN THE INERRANCY DEBATE

Copyright © 2015 Wipf and Stock Publishers. All rights reserved. Except for brief quotations in critical publications or reviews, no part of this book may be reproduced in any manner without prior written permission from the publisher. Write: Permissions, Wipf and Stock Publishers, 199 W. 8th Ave., Suite 3, Eugene, OR 97401.

Wipf & Stock
An Imprint of Wipf and Stock Publishers
199 W. 8th Ave., Suite 3
Eugene, OR 97401

www.wipfandstock.com

ISBN 13: 978-1-4982-3724-6

Manufactured in the U.S.A. 01/13/2016

To . . .

Dr. Norman L. Geisler

*The Great Christian Apologist of the Twentieth and Twenty-First Century*

The contributors to *Vital Issues* would like to acknowledge their debt of gratitude to Norman L. Geisler. Dr. Geisler has dedicated his whole career in theological studies to a fearless defense of the inerrancy of God's Word. His love for God's Word is very evident in his stand for an apologetic presentation of defense to all those who have contributed to this work.

He has unwaveringly stood firm in his commitment to the historic, orthodox position of inerrancy as a foundational doctrine of the Christian faith. His commitment has often been praised for its boldness and fearlessness. That commitment has also been a lightning rod of opposition.

Yet, what stands out most clearly to us, is his willingness to endure . . .

"In the Defense and Confirmation of the Gospel" (Phil 1:7)

His example has encouraged us all for the same.

As Paul echoed . . .

2 Timothy 2:2

"The things which you have heard from me in the presence of many witnesses, entrust these to faithful men who will be able to teach others also."

Dave Farnell
Joseph Holden
Bill Roach
Phil Fernandes
Shawn Nelson
Chris Haun
Bob Wilkin

# Contents

*Contributors* | xi
*Foreword by Paige Patterson* | xiii
*Preface* | xv

## Part 1—Inerrancy Defined

Chapter 1
**The Historic Documents of the International Council on Biblical Inerrancy** | 3
—NORMAN L. GEISLER

Chapter 2
**What Is Inerrancy and Why Should We Care?** | 20
—NORMAN L. GEISLER AND SHAWN NELSON

Chapter 3
**A Voice from a New Generation: What's at Stake?** | 24
—SHAWN NELSON

Chapter 4
**Evangelical Mentoring: The Danger from Within** | 39
—F. DAVID FARNELL, PHD

Chapter 5
**Review of *Five Views on Biblical Inerrancy*,
edited by J. Merrick and Stephen Garrett** | 60
—NORMAN L. GEISLER

Chapter 6
**The 2015 Shepherds' Conference on Inerrancy** | 99
—WILLIAM C. ROACH

Chapter 7
**Interview with Paige Patterson on the Importance of Inerrancy** | 106
—WILLIAM C. ROACH

Chapter 8
**Do You Have to Be a Calvinist to Believe in Inerrancy? | 109**
 —NORMAN L. GEISLER

## Part 2—Inerrancy Defended

Chapter 9
**"It's Just a Matter of Interpretation, Not of Inerrancy": Examining the Relation between Inerrancy and Hermeneutics | 115**
 —NORMAN L. GEISLER

Chapter 10
**Biblical Inerrancy, Inductive or Deductive Basis: A Response to William Lane Craig | 132**
 —NORMAN L. GEISLER

Chapter 11
**Early Twentieth Century Challenges to Inerrancy | 145**
 —F. DAVID FARNELL

Chapter 12
**Early Twenty-First-Century Challenges to Inerrancy | 162**
 —F. DAVID FARNELL

Chapter 13
**The Resurgence of Neo-Evangelicalism: Craig Blomberg's Latest Book and the Future of Evangelical Theology | 208**
 —WILLIAM C. ROACH

Chapter 14
**The Battle for the Bible Begins Anew | 240**
 —PHIL FERNANDES

Chapter 15
**Inerrancy as a Litmus Test of Evangelical Orthodoxy? Clarifications on Carl F. H. Henry's View | 248**
 —CHRISTOPHER T. HAUN

Chapter 16
**Can We Still Believe Critical Evangelical Scholars? The Danger from Within | 254**
 —F. DAVID FARNELL

Chapter 17
**The "Magic" of Historical Criticism | 279**
 —F. DAVID FARNELL

Chapter 18

**Part One: A Critical Evaluation of Robert H. Gundry's Westmont College Lecture, "Peter: False Disciple and Apostate according to Saint Matthew"** | 321

—F. DAVID FARNELL

Chapter 19

**Part Two: A Critical Evaluation of Robert H. Gundry's Westmont College Lecture, "Peter: False Disciple and Apostate According to Saint Matthew" (and Now Recently Released Book)** | 339

—F. DAVID FARNELL

Chapter 20

**A Critical Review of Donald Hagner's "Ten Guidelines for Evangelical Scholarship"** | 347

—F. DAVID FARNELL AND NORMAN L. GEISLER

Chapter 21

**On Licona Muddying the Waters of the Chicago Statements of Biblical Inerrancy and Hermeneutics** | 365

—NORMAN L. GEISLER

Chapter 22

**The Early Church Fathers and the Resurrection of the Saints in Matthew 27:51–54** | 375

—NORMAN L. GEISLER

Chapter 23

**Can We Still Believe in the Bible?** | 388

—NORMAN L. GEISLER

Chapter 24

**ICBI Inerrancy Is Not for the Birds** | 403

—JOSEPH M. HOLDEN

Chapter 25

**Contemporary Evangelical NT Genre Criticism: Opening Pandora's Box?** | 406

—JOSEPH M. HOLDEN

Chapter 26

**Book Review: Craig Blomberg's *Can We Still Believe the Bible?*** | 410

—JOSEPH M. HOLDEN

Chapter 27

**Book Review: *The Lost World of Adam and Eve*** | 430

—NORMAN L. GEISLER

Chapter 28
**An Exposition and Refutation of the Key Presuppositions of Contemporary Jesus Research** | 447
—PHIL FERNANDES

Chapter 29
**Redating the Gospels** | 466
—PHIL FERNANDES

Chapter 30
**Misinterpreting J. I. Packer on Inerrancy and Hermeneutics** | 489
—WILLIAM C. ROACH AND NORMAN L. GEISLER

Chapter 31
**Can We Still Trust New Testament Professors?** | 494
—BOB WILKIN

Chapter 32
**Did Roman Christians Detect the Influence of Roman Historiography in Matthew 27:45–54?** | 501
—CHRISTOPHER T. HAUN

Epilogue
**Historical Criticism vs. Grammatico-Historical: *Quo Vadis* Evangelicals?** | 516
—F. DAVID FARNELL

APPENDIX: Statements on the Importance of Inerrancy from Prominent Christian Leaders | 529

*Bibliography* | 541
*Person and Subject Index* | 559
*Scripture Index* | 563

# Contributors

General Editor: F. David Farnell, PhD, Professor of New Testament at The Master's Seminary, Sun Valley, CA. His publications include *The Jesus Crisis*, *The Jesus Quest*, and *Three Views on the Origins of the Synoptic Gospels*.

Associate Editor: Norman L. Geisler, PhD, Chancellor of Veritas Evangelical Seminary; Distinguished Professor of Theology and Apologetics; Occupant of the Norman L. Geisler Chair of Christian Apologetics.

Associate Editor: *Joseph M. Holden*, PhD, President of Veritas Evangelical Seminary, Santa Ana, CA. His publications include *The Popular Handbook of Archaeology and the Bible*; *Charts of Apologetics and Christian Evidence*; *Living Loud: Defending Your Faith*; and *The Apologetics Study Bible: Bones and Dirt*.

Associate Editor: *William C. Roach*, PhD, is the senior-editor of the *Journal of the International Society of Christian Apologetics* and adjunct professor at The College at Southeastern in Wake Forest, NC, and Capital Theological Seminary in Washington, DC. Dr. Roach has authored numerous articles and book chapters, including *Hermeneutics as Epistemology: A Critical Assessment of Carl F. H. Henry's Epistemological Approach to Hermeneutics* and has coauthored the book *Defending Inerrancy*. He also regularly contributes articles to the website www.defendinginerrancy.com and operates a blog titled *Confessions of a Theologian*.

Associate Editor: *Robert Wilkin*, PhD, is President of Grace Evangelical Society. He has written four books, *Confident in Christ*; *The Road to Reward*; *Secure and Sure*; and *The Ten Most Misunderstood Words in the Bible*. He also was the editor and a contributor to the two-volume Grace New Testament Commentary and is a contributor to *Four Views on the Role of Works at the Final Judgment*.

Associate Editor: *Phil Fernandes*, PhD, President of the Institute of Biblical Defense and Pastor of Trinity Bible Fellowship in Bremerton, WA. His recent publications include *The Atheist Delusion: A Christian Response to Christopher Hitchens and Richard*

*Dawkins* and *Hijacking the Historical Jesus: Answering Recent Attacks on the Jesus of the Bible.*

Contributor: Shawn Nelson holds a BA in Biblical Studies and is President of Geeky Christian, a nonprofit ministry dedicated to reaching the next generation with the Gospel through technology. Shawn's books include *Romans in Logical Form* and *Evidence of an Early New Testament Canon*. More info regarding his ministry can be found at www.geekychristian.com.

Contributor: Christopher Travis Haun is a Master's Degree candidate at Veritas Evangelical Seminary, Santa Ana, CA. He is an Editorial Associate at Bastion Books, a Technical Assistant to Norman Geisler International Ministries, and a contributor to *Journal of the International Society of Christian Apologetics*.

# Foreword

Mark Twain was not a theologian, but he was a shrewd observer of life on the Mississippi River. And one thing that you never read in his novels is a pericope about a loosely tethered boat slipping the knot and drifting upriver to some mysterious location. As certain as anything in this life can be, all that is adrift on the mighty Mississippi is headed south. If you want to go upriver there must be deliberate propulsion and guidance. Such an observation requires only the opportunity to reflect for a few days on the flow of the river. Only a fool would attempt to sustain the case that things quite frequently drift upriver.

Norman Geisler and F. David Farnell, together with a cast of highly credible thinkers, understand that pedestrian avowal and know that the same forces are at work in theology. *Vital Issues in Inerrancy* is the resulting volume unveiling the sorrowful journey of dozens of "theological boats" that have slipped their logical and spiritual knots and are now drifting south on the "River of Doubt." The authors reset this strategic doctrine, setting the parameters both for what qualifies and for what does not meet the standards for biblical inerrancy.

But why is such a book necessary. Isn't this thrashing the proverbial dead horse? When the International Council on Biblical Inerrancy (ICBI) was functioning in the late '70s and '80s, there was a lively discussion among the members of the board about the future of the organization. Some saw the need for the organization to exist in perpetuity. Others of us feared the prospects of an organization that could become another parachurch ministry furthering the departure of talent and resources from the local churches in America. We suggested a ten-year limitation with a sunset clause in place to guarantee a concluding date. An incredible number of critical texts penned during those ten years contributed heavily to the reversals in the Missouri Synod Lutheran Church and most dramatically in the Southern Baptist Convention.

While I remain confident that a limited period was appropriate, the volume that you hold in your hand or view on the screen is a testimony to two things. First, the ICBI shut down, but the need for continued vigilance is unmitigated. Second, the amazing tendency on the part of "evangelical scholars" to follow the line of least resistance and drift away from biblical theology is continuing to the sorrow of the church of God. I used the word "amazing" because the history of the effects of biblical scholarship hinged to historical-critical interpretation is the history of decimated congregations and evangelistic and mission stagnation. This is so obvious as to need no elucidation.

Regrettably, the younger generation does not read nearly as prolifically as former generations. So most are simply unaware of Gerhard Maier's *The End of the Historical-Critical Method*. They have not read the arresting articles from Norm Geisler's 1979 edited volume titled *Inerrancy*. They remain blissfully unaware of Laird Harris's work on *Inspiration and Canonicity of the Bible*. Although the book is actually concise enough for anyone to read, few have heard of the early Clark Pinnock's magnificent 1967 treatment of *A Defense of Biblical Infallibility*. D. A Carson and John Woodbridge examined *Scripture and Truth* in 1983, but a fair number of the young future pastors were just being born about that time. And hardly any of the younger set has carefully considered Carl F. H. Henry's fifteen wonderfully crafted theses articulated convincingly in the first sixteen pages of *God, Revelation and Authority*, vol. 2. In my own Southern Baptist denomination, there is little consciousness of editors Robison B. James and David S. Dockery's revealing work *Beyond the Impasse?* which contrasts the difference in believing and unbelieving perspectives with clarity. And, of course, this is to name but a few of the convincing tomes penned on this subject.

There are better reasons to revisit the subject. The earliest attack in Eden appears to be directed at the possibility that God had spoken a clear, definitive, cogent, and permanent word: "Has God said?" What began there continues relentlessly through the ages, whether it be an early attack on the historicity of Daniel by Porphyry or the most recent attack on the historicity of Matthew 27:52–53 by Michael Licona in *The Resurrection of Jesus (2010)*. *Of course, Licona wants to have his cake and eat it also, but the verse cannot at the same moment both describe a reality and be dismissed as Midrash. The point is that every generation has to answer this issue for itself. This current treatise engages the postmodern with the claims of inerrancy and documents in a kind but firm way those evangelical voices damaged by compromise with the culture and the academy.*

*All associated with this book wish that it were not necessary. Like Jude, they would much rather have written concerning "our common salvation." Unfortunately, in every generation, Satan must attack the doctrines of revelation, creation, the person and work of Christ, and the consummation of the kingdom. If these doctrines are allowed to stand as believed and taught by the apostles, then Satan's efforts to destroy the church surely fail. The authors of this volume understand that they must contend for the faith once delivered to the saints. And that faith begins with a sure and certain word from God.*

*May God be pleased to bless these pages for the edification of the young church today. And may the end result be the opportunity for all seven billion of this world's teeming population to hear the message of the unsearchable riches of Christ.*

Paige Patterson, President
Southwestern Baptist Theological Seminary
Ft. Worth, Texas

# Preface

The contributors to *Vital Issues in the Inerrancy Debate* would like to acknowledge especially the hundreds of courageous men and women of the International Council of Biblical Inerrancy who assembled in Chicago some thirty-five years ago and forged the watershed documents of the Chicago Statements on Biblical Inerrancy (1978) and Hermeneutics (1982). These biblical scholars and pastors from all over the world, assembled three times over a ten-years period to leave a testimony of the (1) absolute inerrancy of God's Word, (2) the orthodox meaning and nature of the term, as well as (3) issue a stern warning to future generations of the acute danger and consequences of its abandonment by God's faithful. They were all direct witnesses to what shook the church in the earlier parts of the twentieth century when inerrancy was abandoned. They left marvelous documents that would witness to inerrancy as foundational to all other truths of Christianity as expressed in the Old and New Testaments. Inspiration and inerrancy, to them, were the bedrock foundation for all other doctrines of Christianity, without which foundation, no truth claims exist for Christianity. Many of these have gone to be with the Lord since the original signing of these declarations. Yet, they have left for us a marvelous, sustaining testimony to the need for faithfulness to God's Word and inerrancy as the "watershed" issue for our time.

Many troubling events preceded the Chicago Statements. At the turn of the twentieth century, mainline denominations redefined the term "infallibility" from its traditional, orthodox meaning to the idea that while the Scripture was "infallible" only in faith and practice, the Old and New Testaments contained errors in history, geography, science and origins. Bible-believing people America broke away from these mainline denominations and formed their own schools and seminaries. The term "inerrancy" or "without any error" became the watchword used to distinguish the redefining in meaning of the former word, "infallibility." Sadly, while both terms really mean the same, now a distinction is maintained by the faithful to prevent any misunderstanding that God's Word is true in all matters that it addresses, i.e., "Your Word is Truth" (John 17:17).

Not only did mainline denominations redefine "infallibility" to include "errancy" but also adopted a qualitatively different hermeneutic to interpret Scripture that is directly associated with an assault on the foundational truths in God's Word.

## Preface

A departure from grammatico-historical hermeneutics adopted by ICBI preceded the redefining of the term "infallibility." This plain, normal sense of Scripture, maintained by grammatico-historical exegesis, was abandoned to meet the popular theological and scientific fads developing in the nineteenth and twentieth centuries. Although these fads were ever fleeting and changing, waxing and waning, the church abandoned the plain sense of Scripture so that the Scripture could be remolded for current thought that often stood diametrically opposed to the plain, normal sense. Indeed, the historical-critical method adopted by mainline denominations was a direct cause for their need to redefine the term "infallibility," for the plain, normal sense could not be forced to accommodate modern philosophies. Historical-critical ideologies directly influenced the adoption of many philosophies and "isms" that denigrated the truths of Scripture maintained by orthodox Christianity from its foundations in the first century. Historical-criticism became the dissolvent that could make the Scripture pliable to modern sensibilities, rather than a trust in the timeless truth of God's Word. The Bible was remolded rather than rejecting the ideologies that were hostile to God's Word. In sum for this early period, (1) the adoption of historical criticism and (2) redefining of "infallibility" to exclude inerrancy resulted in the creation of new churches and schools among the faithful in the churches of America.

Sadly, in the 1950s and 1960s of the twentieth century, the very same adoption of (1) historical-critical ideologies and (2) the redefining of the term "inerrancy" began among those who had withdrawn at the turn of the century. A battle for the Bible was occurring again. The lessons of history had not been learned. The faithful descendants of those who had withdrawn from mainline denominations rallied in Chicago for ten years to stem the tide that was once again occurring. They carefully formulated the Chicago Statements on Inerrancy and Hermeneutics in hopes of stemming the tide and guide the faithful away from the spiritual disaster that was forming. The Chicago Statements championed (1) grammatico-historical hermeneutics (e.g., CSBI art. XVIII) and (2) set forth the orthodox meaning of inerrancy maintained since the nascent beginnings of the early church.

Since the signing of the Chicago Statements, troubling signs have once again been appearing in recent years among many Neo-Evangelicals who either did not fight the battles for the inerrancy of Scripture as did the Council or who do not remember the troubling times that caused their development. The nature and definition of "inerrancy" are now being challenged and/or redefined from the orthodox position to include ideas of fallibility once again. *History is being forgotten* and Evangelicals are showing the need once again for sounding the alarm for *Defending Inerrancy*. Historical criticism now dominates among schools and churches that broke away in the earlier, academic prestige and fads in scholarship now hold as watchwords instead of faithfulness of God's inerrant Word. The contributors to this volume pray that the Lord will raise up a new generation of Evangelicals with the spiritual fervency of the

*Preface*

*International Council* to uphold the inerrancy of God's Word: Isaiah 40:8—"*The grass withers, the flower fades, But the word of our God stands forever*" (Isa 40:8).

Earnestly contending for the faith delivered once and for all to God's people . . . (Jude 3).

F. David Farnell
Norman L. Geisler
Joseph P. Holden
William C. Roach
Phil Fernandes,
Shawn Nelson
Chris T. Haun
Robert Wilkins

# Part 1

# Inerrancy Defined

At the beginning of the twenty-first century, prominent Neo-Evangelicals are actively involved in an attempt to redefine the term "inerrancy" away from the historic, orthodox position of the church through its history. Theological liberals in the early twentieth century did the very same thing to the term "infallibility." Infallibility lost its meaning and became a meaningless term.

The same is now being done with "inerrancy" in the evangelical camp by historical-critical evangelicals. This section sounds forth the warning to God's people of those evangelicals who are attempting to redefine the term "inerrancy." It also explains its historic, orthodox meaning and characteristics held from the earliest foundations with special attention given to the historic International Council on Biblical Inerrancy and its Chicago Statements (1978) on Biblical Inerrancy and Hermeneutics (1982) developed to combat such a drift.

# Chapter 1

# The Historic Documents of the International Council on Biblical Inerrancy[1]

## NORMAN L. GEISLER

It is a fact of human experience that when the living eyewitnesses to events die off, the process of developing myths about these events is often accelerated. So, as one of the three living framers of the Chicago Statements on inerrancy and hermeneutics, it seemed good to put the first two statements and their official commentaries in one inexpensive and universally accessible source, entitled *Explaining Biblical Inerrancy: Official Commentary on the ICBI Statements* (2013).[2]

### FOUR FUNDAMENTAL ICBI DOCUMENTS

There were four ICBI documents on the meaning of inerrancy: (1) The Chicago Statement on Biblical Inerrancy (by the ICBI drafting committee, 1978); (2) The Commentary on the Chicago Statement on Biblical Inerrancy, by Dr. Sproul; (3) The Chicago Statement on Biblical Hermeneutics (by the ICBI drafting committee, 1982); (4) The Commentary on the Chicago Statement on Biblical Hermeneutics, by Dr. Geisler. These four documents are reproduced here in the combined version that was produced in 2013.[3]

---

1. Chapter 1 of *Vital Issues in the Inerrancy Debate* is mostly a reproduction of Norman L. Geisler's introduction to *Explaining Biblical Inerrancy*. The editors of this volume believe that it serves as a very appropriate introduction to *Vital Issues in the Inerrancy Debate*. See Geisler, introduction to *Explaining Biblical Inerrancy*, 6–14.

2. This updated, combined version of the *Official Commentary on the ICBI Statements* may be obtained at www.bastionbooks.com. See also Geisler and Roach, *Defending Inerrancy*.

3. This commentary only contains the heart of the first and second Chicago statements, the articles

Part 1—Inerrancy Defined

Dr. R. C. Sproul was not just a signer of the three ICBI statements. He was also the original framer of the affirmations and denials of the Chicago Statement on Biblical Inerrancy, the president of the ICBI during its tenure, and the author of the official commentary on the Chicago Statement on Biblical Inerrancy. Dr. Sproul wrote *Explaining Inerrancy: A Commentary* (International Council on Biblical Inerrancy) in 1980.

Dr. Norman Geisler was a signatory of the ICBI statements, a member of the ICBI drafting committee, the general editor of all the books published by ICBI, and the author of the official booklet explaining the second Chicago Statement, titled *Explaining Hermeneutics: A Commentary on the Chicago Statement on Biblical Hermeneutics* (International

Council on Biblical Inerrancy, 1983).

## OTHER IMPORTANT ICBI BOOKS

In addition, official ICBI books were produced on these two statements. On the first statement (1978), the book titled *Inerrancy* was produced, consisting of chapters by ICBI conference scholars and edited by Norman L. Geisler. Also, there was *Hermeneutics, Inerrancy, and the Bible* (Zondervan, 1984), edited by Earl Radmacher and Robert Preus, consisting of papers from the ICBI hermeneutics summit in 1982. Gordon Lewis and Bruce Demarest put together *Challenges to Inerrancy: A Theological Response* (Moody, 1984). Another ICBI book on the meaning of inerrancy was produced, titled *Biblical Errancy: An Analysis of Its Philosophical Roots* (Zondervan, 1981), and was edited by Norman L. Geisler. The final book of the ICBI series was on the application of inerrancy. It was edited by Kenneth S. Kantzer and titled *Applying the Scriptures* (Zondervan, 1987).

## WHY THE ICBI VIEW ON INERRANCY IS SO IMPORTANT

As evangelicals we recognize that no extra-biblical statements or creeds are infallible. Only the Bible is infallible. Nonetheless, some doctrinal statements are very important. The ICBI statements fall into this category for many reasons. First, they stand in continuity with the historic orthodox view of Scripture.[4] Second, it was put together by an international group of some three hundred evangelical scholars, not by an individual or mere handful of persons. Third, it has been adopted (in 2003) as a guide in understanding inerrancy by the largest group of evangelical scholars in the world, the Evangelical Theological Society. Fourth, its views were adopted by one of

---

of affirmation and denial. The summary statements and the excellent short expositions that are normally included in those statements have not been included. The full statements can be viewed at http://library.dts.edu/Pages/TL/Special/ICBI.shtml.

4. See Hannah, *Inerrancy and the Church.*

the largest protestant denominations in the world (the Southern Baptist Convention) in a landmark turnaround which saved them from drifting into liberalism. Finally, it has become the standard view of evangelicalism in America on this topic, having been officially or unofficially widely adopted as the guideline on the meaning of the inspiration and inerrancy of the Bible in numerous schools, churches, and Christian organizations.

## PURPOSES OF THIS BOOK

As general editor of the International Council of Biblical Inerrancy (ICBI) books, a member of the ICBI drafting committee, and the author of the ICBI official commentary on the ICBI hermeneutics statement, my purpose in this combined commentary is twofold. First, my desire is to make all four foundational ICBI documents available in one volume for this and future generations to study. Second, I hope this will help dispel some contemporary misinterpretations of what the ICBI framers meant by inerrancy. There are several issues to which we wish to draw attention.

## MISUNDERSTANDING ABOUT THE MEANING OF THE CONCEPT OF "TRUTH" IN THE ICBI STATEMENTS

One of the most important misunderstandings of the ICBI statements occurs on what the framers meant by the biblical view of truth mentioned in article XIII of the Chicago Statement on Biblical Inerrancy (1978). It reads, "We deny that it is proper to evaluate Scripture according to standards of truth and error that are alien to its usage or purpose." Some mistakenly took this to justify an intentionalist view of truth and inerrancy which states that the Bible is only true in what it *intends* to affirm, not necessary in all that it *actually* affirms. But this is contrary to what the ICBI framers meant by inerrancy, as is revealed in its official commentary on those very articles. ICBI declared explicitly, "When we say that the truthfulness of Scripture ought to be evaluated according to its own standards that means that . . . *all the claims of the Bible must correspond with reality*, whether that reality is historical, factual or spiritual."[5] It adds, "*By biblical standards of truth and error is meant the view used both in the Bible and in everyday life, viz., a correspondence view of truth.*[6] This part of the article is directed toward those who would redefine truth to relate merely to redemptive intent, the purely personal, or the like, rather than to mean that which corresponds with reality."

---

5. Sproul, *Explaining Inerrancy*, 48.
6. Ibid.

Part 1—Inerrancy Defined

## MISUNDERSTANDING ABOUT THE FUNCTION OF GENRE IN SCRIPTURE

The second major misinterpretation of the ICBI statements centers on the use of genre in the interpretation of Scripture. Article XVIII of the Chicago Statement on Biblical Inerrancy (1978) reads: "We affirm that the text of Scripture is to be interpreted by grammatico-historical exegesis, *taking account of its literary forms and devices*, and that Scripture is to interpret Scripture" (emphasis added). Likewise, article XIII asserts, "We affirm that awareness of the literary categories, formal and stylistic, of the various parts of Scripture is essential for proper exegesis, and hence *we value genre criticism* as one of the many disciplines of biblical study" (emphasis added). Article XV adds, "We affirm the necessity of interpreting the Bible according to its literal, or normal sense. . . . Interpretation according to the literal sense *will take account of all figures of speech and literary forms found in the text*" (emphasis added).[7]

From these statements some evangelical scholars have claimed ICBI blessing on the view that one can determine the meaning of a biblical text by first making a list of the kinds of genre from external sources and then applying what they believe is the appropriate genre to the Scriptures. However, the view that genre determines meaning is not only contrary to what the ICBI framers meant, but it also suffers from a logical mistake. In order to discover the genre of a particular text, one must already have a developed a genre theory. But a genre theory comes from studying and comparing individual texts of the Bible by means of the "grammatico-historical" method of interpretation which the ICBI framers were committed to from the beginning.[8] But if externally determined genre governs the meaning of the biblical text, then this scenario is impossible. The interpreter must know the genre before he knows the text. But this is tantamount to imposing genre expectations upon the text. In hermeneutics, this is labeled *eisegesis* (reading meaning into the text), rather an *exegesis* (reading meaning out of the text)! So, this widely used method of genre determination is contrary to the ICBI understanding of inerrancy.

## MISUNDERSTANDING OF THE HISTORICAL NATURE OF BIBLICAL NARRATIVES

From the beginning, ICBI spelled out its commitment to the historicity of the biblical narratives. Article XVIII of the Chicago Statement on Biblical Inerrancy (1978) reads, "We deny the legitimacy of any treatment of the text or quest for sources lying behind it that leads to relativizing, *dehistoricizing*, or counting its teaching, or rejecting its claim to authorship" (emphasis added). The ICBI position became even more explicit

---

7. Also see Osborne, Allen, and Scaer, "Genre Criticism," in *Hermeneutics, Inerrancy and the Bible*, 165–216.

8. See "Chicago Statement on Biblical Inerrancy" [hereafter CSBI], art. 18.

in its Chicago Statement on Biblical Hermeneutics (1982). Article XIII declares, "*We deny that generic categories which negate historicity may rightly be imposed on biblical narratives* which present themselves as factual." Article XIV goes on to say, "*We deny that any event, discourse or saying reported in Scripture was invented by the biblical writers* or by the traditions they incorporated" (emphasis added).

The Chicago Statement on Biblical Inerrancy is clear on this issue: "We affirm the propriety of using inerrancy as a theological term with reference *to the complete truthfulness of Scripture*" (art. XIII). "We affirm that inspiration, though not conferring omniscience, *guaranteed true and trustworthy utterance on all matters of which the biblical authors were moved to speak and write*" (art. IX). "*We affirm that Scripture in its entirety is inerrant, being free from all falsehood, fraud, or deceit*. We deny that biblical infallibility and inerrancy are limited to spiritual, religious, or redemptive themes, exclusive of assertions in *the fields of history and science*" (art. XII). "We affirm the propriety of using inerrancy as a theological term with reference to *the complete truthfulness of Scripture*" (art. XII).

The ICBI commentary adds, "Though the Bible is indeed *redemptive* history, it is also redemptive *history*, and this means that the acts of salvation wrought by God actually occurred in the space-time world" (art. XII). With regard to the historicity of the Bible, article XIII in the commentary points out that we should not "take Adam to be a myth, whereas in Scripture he is presented as a real person." Likewise, it affirms that we should not "take Jonah to be an allegory when he is presented as a historical person and [is] so referred to by Christ." It adds, "We further deny that scientific hypotheses about earth history may properly be used to overturn the teaching of Scripture on creation and the flood" (art. XII). In short, the ICBI framers believed that using genre to deny any part of the historicity of the biblical record was a denial of inerrancy.

## MISUNDERSTANDING ABOUT THE RELATION OF HERMENEUTICS AND INERRANCY

Another misunderstanding is the claim that the ICBI view is that inerrancy is hermeneutic and inerrancy are to be totally separated. In short, they claim that inerrancy simply affirms that whatever the Bible affirms is true, but only hermeneutics can inform us as to what the Bible is actually affirming. That is to say, it is just a matter of interpretation of the text and not a question of inerrancy. It is wrongly thought by some that ICBI made no specific claims on what the biblical text means or on whether the biblical narrative is historical as long as they believe that the text is inerrant—whatever it may mean. However, this is clearly not the case for many reasons:

Part 1—Inerrancy Defined

## The Total Separation of Hermeneutics and Inerrancy Is Not Logically Necessary

The ICBI framers foresaw this issue and spoke to it clearly. In brief, the ICBI response is that hermeneutics and inerrancy are *formally distinct*, but when it comes to the inerrancy of the Bible they are *actually inseparable*. For example, Siamese twins with two heads and only one heart are inseparable but not identical. Apart from death, our soul and body are inseparable, but they are not identical. Hence, the charge that inerrancy and hermeneutics are identical does not necessarily follow logically.

A bifurcation of hermeneutics from inerrancy is empty, vacuous, and meaningless. This innovative view of the ICBI statements on inerrancy amounts to saying that the Bible is not teaching that anything is actually true. However, the ICBI statements repeatedly affirm that everything the Bible affirms is completely true. The Chicago Statement makes "*reference to the complete truthfulness of Scripture*" (art. XIII). It insists that it is "*trustworthy utterance on all matters of which the biblical authors were moved to speak and write*" (art. IX). But these would be senseless claims, if the Bible was not really making any claims about reality. So, the claim to inerrancy entails a certain kind of understanding of what the Bible means, namely, a historical-grammatical understanding of the text. This, along with the correspondence view of truth (see above) negate the claim that inerrancy as such is merely a vacuous claim that amounts to saying, "If the Bible is claiming that anything is true, then it is actually true, but inerrancy is not really claiming anything is actually true. Only hermeneutics can fill in this void." On the contrary, both the correspondence view of truth and the historical-grammatical view of interpretation demand that the doctrine of inerrancy as embraced by ICBI is claiming that the belief in biblical inerrancy entails actual truths about reality.

The ICBI Chicago Statement on inerrancy includes a statement on the literal historical-grammatical hermeneutics. As noted above, article XVIII reads: "We affirm that the text of Scripture is to be interpreted by grammatico-historical exegesis . . ." There are very good reasons for including this statement on hermeneutics in an evangelical inerrancy statement. For one thing, there would be no doctrine of inerrancy were it not for the historical-grammatical hermeneutic by which we derive inerrancy from Scripture. For another, the term "evangelical" implies a certain doctrinal stand on essential doctrines, including the inspiration of Scripture, the virgin birth, the deity of Christ, his atoning death, and his bodily resurrection. These doctrines expressed in the early creeds of Christendom are derived from Scripture by the historical-grammatical hermeneutic. Without it there would be no "evangelical" or "orthodox" creeds or orthodox beliefs in accord with them. Thus, the ICBI evangelical view of inerrancy is wedded with a literal method of interpretation that affirms truth about the real world.

## The ICBI Claim to Inerrancy Involved a Claim to Objective Truth about Reality

Since ICBI embraced a correspondence view of truth which affirms that truth corresponds with reality, then when we say the Bible is completely true the statement cannot be empty. It must refer to some reality beyond itself. This is why ICBI included a statement about the literal historical-grammatical interpretation of the Bible as part of its articles about the meaning of inerrancy. Article XVIII says: "We affirm that the text of Scripture is to be interpreted by grammatico-historical exegesis . . ." In short, there is an overlap between inerrancy and hermeneutics because inerrancy is not an empty claim. It is a claim that involves the assertion that an inerrant Bible is actually true in all that it affirms. And this truth corresponds literally to the reality about which it speaks. This is not to say that Bible does not use figures of speech for article XVIII clearly allows "taking account of literary forms and devices." It means that there is some literal referent for these figures of speech. Thus, inerrancy is not claiming that "if the Bible is making a truth claim, then that truth claim must be true." Rather, inerrancy claims that "the Bible is making truth claims, and they are all true." Since truth is what corresponds to reality, to say the Bible is inerrant is to say that all of its claims correspond to reality. In this way there is a marriage, not a divorce, between inerrancy and the literal method of interpreting the Bible. This disjunction between hermeneutics and inerrancy is an example of "methodological unorthodoxy."[9] If it were true, then one could completely allegorize the Bible—denying the literal virgin birth, physical resurrection of Christ, and everything else—and still claim that they held to the inerrancy of the Bible. This would mean that someone like Mary Baker Eddy (the founder of the Christian Science cult) could, even with a totally allegorical method, affirm that the ICBI statements on inerrancy are true, even though she does not believe in any evangelical doctrine, including the inspiration of Scripture. It would also mean that someone could use a so-called Averronian method of "double truth" and still hold to an ICBI view of inerrancy. But it makes no sense to claim that the Bible is completely true in all that it affirms and yet deny that it affirms certain specific doctrines. In addition to unorthodox doctrines, there are also unorthodox methods. Historical-grammatical hermeneutics is an orthodox method accepted by ICBI. An allegorical method is an unorthodox method. Likewise, New Testament scholars who deny the historicity of sections of the Gospel narratives are acting contrary to the meaning of the ICBI framers.

## The Separation Is Explicitly Contrary in Spirit and in Letter to the ICBI

The preface to the Chicago Statement on Biblical Hermeneutics made it clear that the ICBI framers saw hermeneutics as being inseparably connected to inerrancy. It says:

---

9. We first addressed this issue in the *Journal of the Evangelical Theological Society* (*JETS*) in 1983. See http://normangeisler.net/articles/Bible/Inspiration-Inerrancy/methodological-unorthodoxy.htm.

## Part 1—Inerrancy Defined

The work of Summit I had hardly been completed when it became evident that there was yet another major task to be tackled. While we recognize that belief in the inerrancy of Scripture is basic to maintaining its authority, the values of that commitment are only as real as one's understanding of the meaning of Scripture. Thus, the need for Summit II. For two years plans were laid and papers were written on themes relating to hermeneutical principles and practices.[10]

The very fact that there was a second ICBI summit is a clear indication of how the ICBI framers and signers judged this matter. The second ICBI summit is an expansion and elaboration of article XVIII from the statement produced by the first ICBI Summit.

## CONCLUDING COMMENTS

It is hoped that providing the primary sources for the ICBI view on inerrancy will help clarify these and other issue at stake in the current inerrancy debates. While every scholar is free to mean by inerrancy whatever he or she desires it to mean, no one is free to dictate to the ICBI framers what they meant by inerrancy. This is particularly true of those who subscribe to the grammatico-historical method of interpretation, as the ICI framers did. For if a document should be interpreted in accord with the expressed intentions of an author, then there are stated limits (as shown above) on what inerrancy covers or does not cover.

Failing to follow this path gave rise to an acute problem in the Evangelical Theological Society (ETS). The issue surfaced in 1976 when the ETS Executive Committee confessed that "some of the members of the Society have expressed the feeling that a measure of intellectual dishonesty prevails among members who do not take the signing of the doctrinal statement seriously." Other "members of the Society have come to the realization that they are not in agreement with the creedal statement and have voluntarily withdrawn. That is, *in good conscience* they could not sign the statement."[11] Later, an ETS ad hoc committee recognized this problem when it posed the proper question: *"Is it acceptable for a member of the society to hold a view of biblical author's intent which disagrees with the Founding Fathers and even the majority of the society, and still remain a member in good standing?"*[12] Failing to say "no" is not only contrary to the expressed "intention of the author" view, but it opens the door for a deconstructionist and reconstructionist view of doctrinal statements like those of the ICBI. It is hoped that these primary ICBI sources contained in this book can help avoid this problem among those who claim to subscribe to biblical inerrancy. Since the three

---

10. See International Council on Biblical Inerrancy, "Chicago Statement on Hermeneutics," para. 2l (emphasis added).

11. 1976 ETS Minutes, emphasis added.

12. In 1983 ETS minutes.

living framers of the ICBI statements (Sproul, Packer, and I) concur on these matters, it would be as presumptuous to reject this official understanding of the ICBI statement on these matters as it would be for a liberal judge to reject the meaning of Madison, Washington and Adams on the First Amendment to the US Constitution.

## THE CHICAGO STATEMENT ON BIBLICAL INERRANCY (1978)

### Articles of Affirmation and Denial

| ARTICLE | AFFIRMATION AND DENIALS |
|---|---|
| Article I | *We affirm* that the Holy Scriptures are to be received as the authoritative Word of God.<br><br>*We deny* that the Scriptures receive their authority from the church, tradition or any other human source. |
| Article II | *We affirm* that the Scriptures are the supreme written norm by which God binds the conscience, and that the authority of the church is subordinate to that of Scripture.<br><br>*We deny* that church creeds, councils or declarations have authority greater than or equal to the authority of the Bible. |
| Article III | *We affirm* that the written Word in its entirety is revelation given by God.<br><br>*We deny* that the Bible is merely a witness to revelation, or only becomes revelation in encounter, or depends on the responses of men for its validity. |
| Article IV | *We affirm* that God who made mankind in his image has used language as a means of revelation.<br><br>*We deny* that human language is so limited by our creatureliness that it is rendered inadequate as a vehicle for divine revelation.<br><br>*We further deny* that the corruption of human culture and language through sin has thwarted God's work of inspiration. |
| Article V | *We affirm* that God's revelation in the Holy Scriptures was progressive.<br><br>*We deny* that later revelation, which may fulfill earlier revelation, ever corrects or contradicts it.<br><br>*We further deny* that any normative revelation has been given since the completion of the New Testament writings. |

## Part 1—Inerrancy Defined

| | |
|---|---|
| Article VI | *We affirm* that the whole of Scripture and all its parts, down to the very words of the original, were given by divine inspiration.<br><br>*We deny* that the inspiration of Scripture can rightly be affirmed of the whole without the parts, or of some parts but not the whole. |
| Article VII | *We affirm* that inspiration was the work in which God by His Spirit, through human writers, gave us His Word. The origin of Scripture is divine. The mode of divine inspiration remains largely a mystery to us.<br><br>*We deny* that inspiration can be reduced to human insight, or to heightened states of consciousness of any kind. |
| Article VIII | *We affirm* that God in His work of inspiration utilized the distinctive personalities and literary styles of the writers whom He had chosen and prepared.<br><br>*We deny* that God, in causing these writers to use the very words that He chose, overrode their personalities. |
| Article IX | *We affirm* that inspiration, though not conferring omniscience, guaranteed true and trustworthy utterance on all matters of which the biblical authors were moved to speak and write.<br><br>*We deny* that the finitude or fallenness of these writers, by necessity or otherwise, introduced distortion or falsehood into God's Word. |
| Article X | *We affirm* that inspiration, strictly speaking, applies only to the autographic text of Scripture, which in the providence of God can be ascertained from available manuscripts with great accuracy.<br><br>*We further affirm* that copies and translations of Scripture are the Word of God to the extent that they faithfully represent the original.<br><br>*We deny* that any essential element of the Christian faith is affected by the absence of the autographs.<br><br>*We further deny* that this absence renders the assertion of biblical inerrancy invalid or irrelevant. |

| | |
|---|---|
| Article XI | We *affirm* that Scripture, having been given by divine inspiration, is infallible, so that, far from misleading us, it is true and reliable in all the matters it addresses.<br><br>We *deny* that it is possible for the Bible to be at the same time infallible and errant in its assertions. Infallibility and inerrancy may be distinguished, but not separated. |
| Article XII | We *affirm* that Scripture in its entirety is inerrant, being free from all falsehood, fraud or deceit.<br><br>We *deny* that biblical infallibility and inerrancy are limited to spiritual, religious or redemptive themes, exclusive of assertions in the fields of history and science.<br><br>We further deny that scientific hypotheses about earth history may properly be used to overturn the teaching of Scripture on creation and the flood. |
| Article XIII | We *affirm* the propriety of using inerrancy as a theological term with reference to the complete truthfulness of Scripture.<br><br>We *deny* that it is proper to evaluate Scripture according to standards of truth and error that are alien to its usage or purpose.<br><br>We *further deny* that inerrancy is negated by biblical phenomena such as a lack of modern technical precision, irregularities of grammar or spelling, observational descriptions of nature, the reporting of falsehoods, the use of hyperbole and round numbers, the topical arrangement of material, variant selections of material in parallel accounts, or the use of free citations. |
| Article XIV | We *affirm* the unity and internal consistency of Scripture.<br><br>We *deny* that alleged errors and discrepancies that have not yet been resolved vitiate the truth claims of the Bible. |
| Article XV | We *affirm* that the doctrine of inerrancy is grounded in the teaching of the Bible about inspiration.<br><br>We *deny* that Jesus' teaching about Scripture may be dismissed by appeals to accommodation or to any natural limitation of His humanity. |

## Part 1—Inerrancy Defined

| | |
|---|---|
| *Article XVI* | *We affirm* that the doctrine of inerrancy has been integral to the Church's faith throughout its history.<br><br>*We deny* that inerrancy is a doctrine invented by Scholastic Protestantism, or is a reactionary position postulated in response to negative higher criticism. |
| *Article XVII* | *We affirm* that the Holy Spirit bears witness to the Scriptures, assuring believers of the truthfulness of God's written Word.<br><br>*We deny* that this witness of the Holy Spirit operates in isolation from or against Scripture. |
| *Article XVIII* | *We affirm* that the text of Scripture is to be interpreted by grammatico-historical exegesis, taking account of its literary forms and devices, and that Scripture is to interpret Scripture.<br><br>*We deny* the legitimacy of any treatment of the text or quest for sources lying behind it that leads to relativizing, dehistoricizing, or discounting its teaching, or rejecting its claims to authorship. |
| *Article XIX* | *We affirm* that a confession of the full authority, infallibility and inerrancy of Scripture is vital to a sound understanding of the whole of the Christian faith.<br><br>*We further affirm* that such confession should lead to increasing conformity to the image of Christ.<br><br>*We deny* that such confession is necessary for salvation. However, we further deny that inerrancy can be rejected without grave consequences, both to the individual and to the church. |

# THE CHICAGO STATEMENT ON BIBLICAL HERMENEUTICS

## Articles of Affirmation and Denial (1982)

| Article | Affirmation and Denial |
|---|---|
| *Article I* | *We affirm* that the normative authority of Holy Scripture is the authority of God Himself, and is attested by Jesus Christ, the Lord of the Church.<br><br>*We deny* the legitimacy of separating the authority of Christ from the authority of Scripture, or of opposing the one to the other. |

| | |
|---|---|
| *Article II* | *We affirm* that as Christ is God and Man in one Person, so Scripture is, indivisibly, God's Word in human language.<br><br>*We deny* that the humble, human form of Scripture entails errancy any more than the humanity of Christ, even in His humiliation, entails sin. |
| *Article III* | *We affirm* that the person and work of Jesus Christ are the central focus of the entire Bible.<br><br>*We deny* that any method of interpretation which rejects or obscures the Christ-centeredness of Scripture is correct. |
| *Article IV* | *We affirm* that the Holy Spirit who inspired Scripture acts through it today to work faith in its message.<br><br>*We deny* that the Holy Spirit ever teaches to any one anything which is contrary to the teaching of Scripture. |
| *Article V* | *We affirm* that the Holy Spirit enables believers to appropriate and apply Scripture to their lives.<br><br>*We deny* that the natural man is able to discern spiritually the biblical message apart from the Holy Spirit. |
| *Article VI* | *We affirm* that the Bible expresses God's truth in propositional statements, and we declare that biblical truth is both objective and absolute. We further affirm that a statement is true if it represents matters as they actually are, but is an error if it misrepresents the facts.<br><br>*We deny* that, while Scripture is able to make us wise unto salvation, biblical truth should be defined in terms of this function. We further deny that error should be defined as that which willfully deceives. |
| *Article VII* | *We affirm* that the meaning expressed in each biblical text is single, definite, and fixed.<br><br>*We deny* that the recognition of this single meaning eliminates the variety of its application. |

# Part 1—Inerrancy Defined

| | |
|---|---|
| Article VIII | *We affirm* that the Bible contains teachings and mandates which apply to all cultural and situational contexts and other mandates which the Bible itself shows apply only to particular situations.<br><br>*We deny* that the distinction between the universal and particular mandates of Scripture can be determined by cultural and situational factors.<br><br>*We further deny* that universal mandates may ever be treated as culturally or situationally relative. |
| Article IX | *We affirm* that the term hermeneutics, which historically signified the rules of exegesis, may properly be extended to cover all that is involved in the process of perceiving what the biblical revelation means and how it bears on our lives.<br><br>*We deny* that the message of Scripture derives from, or is dictated by, the interpreter's understanding. Thus we deny that the "horizons" of the biblical writer and the interpreter may rightly "fuse" in such a way that what the text communicates to the interpreter is not ultimately controlled by the expressed meaning of the Scripture. |
| Article X | *We affirm* that Scripture communicates God's truth to us verbally through a wide variety of literary forms.<br><br>*We deny* that any of the limits of human language render Scripture inadequate to convey God's message. |
| Article XI | *We affirm* that translations of the text of Scripture can communicate knowledge of God across all temporal and cultural boundaries.<br><br>*We deny* that the meaning of biblical texts is so tied to the culture out of which they came that understanding of the same meaning in other cultures is impossible. |
| Article XII | *We affirm* that in the task of translating the Bible and teaching it in the context of each culture, only those functional equivalents that are faithful to the content of biblical teaching should be employed.<br><br>*We deny* the legitimacy of methods which either are insensitive to the demands of cross-cultural communication or distort biblical meaning in the process. |

| | |
|---|---|
| Article XIII | *We affirm* that awareness of the literary categories, formal and stylistic, of the various parts of Scripture is essential for proper exegesis, and hence we value genre criticism as one of the many disciplines of biblical study.<br><br>*We deny* that generic categories which negate historicity may rightly be imposed on biblical narratives which present themselves as factual. |
| Article XIV | *We affirm* that the biblical record of events, discourses and sayings, though presented in a variety of appropriate literary forms, corresponds to historical fact.<br><br>*We deny* that any such event, discourse or saying reported in Scripture was invented by the biblical writers or by the traditions they incorporated. |
| Article XV | *We affirm* the necessity of interpreting the Bible according to its literal, or normal, sense. The literal sense is the grammatical-historical sense, that is, the meaning which the writer expressed. Interpretation according to the literal sense will take account of all figures of speech and literary forms found in the text.<br><br>*We deny* the legitimacy of any approach to Scripture that attributes to it meaning which the literal sense does not support. |
| Article XVI | *We affirm* that legitimate critical techniques should be used in determining the canonical text and its meaning.<br><br>*We deny* the legitimacy of allowing any method of biblical criticism to question the truth or integrity of the writer's expressed meaning, or of any other scriptural teaching. |
| Article XVII | *We affirm* the unity, harmony, and consistency of Scripture and declare that it is its own best interpreter.<br><br>*We deny* that Scripture may be interpreted in such a way as to suggest that one passage corrects or militates against another. We deny that later writers of Scripture misinterpreted earlier passages of Scripture when quoting from or referring to them. |

## Part 1—Inerrancy Defined

| | |
|---|---|
| Article XVIII | *We affirm* that the Bible's own interpretation of itself is always correct, never deviating from, but rather elucidating, the single meaning of the inspired text. The single meaning of a prophet's words includes, but is not restricted to, the understanding of those words by the prophet and necessarily involves the intention of God evidenced in the fulfillment of those words.<br><br>*We deny* that the writers of Scripture always understood the full implications of their own words. |
| Article XIX | *We affirm* that any preunderstandings which the interpreter brings to Scripture should be in harmony with scriptural teaching and subject to correction by it.<br><br>*We deny* that Scripture should be required to fit alien preunderstandings, inconsistent with itself, such as naturalism, evolutionism, scientism, secular humanism, and relativism. |
| Article XX | *We affirm* that since God is the author of all truth, all truths, biblical and extra-biblical, are consistent and cohere, and that the Bible speaks truth when it touches on matters pertaining to nature, history, or anything else.<br><br>*We further affirm* that in some cases extra-biblical data have value for clarifying what Scripture teaches, and for prompting correction of faulty interpretations.<br><br>*We deny* that extra-biblical views ever disprove the teaching of Scripture or hold priority over it. |
| Article XXI | *We affirm* the harmony of special with general revelation and therefore of biblical teaching with the facts of nature.<br><br>*We deny* that any genuine scientific facts are inconsistent with the true meaning of any passage of Scripture. |
| Article XXII | *We affirm* that Genesis 1–11 is factual, as is the rest of the book.<br><br>*We deny* that the teachings of Genesis 1–11 are mythical and that scientific hypotheses about earth history or the origin of humanity may be invoked to overthrow what Scripture teaches about creation. |
| Article XXIII | *We affirm* the clarity of Scripture and specifically of its message about salvation from sin.<br><br>*We deny* that all passages of Scripture are equally clear or have equal bearing on the message of redemption. |

| | |
|---|---|
| *Article XXIV* | *We affirm* that a person is not dependent for understanding of Scripture on the expertise of biblical scholars.<br><br>*We deny* that a person should ignore the fruits of the technical study of Scripture by biblical scholars. |
| *Article XXV* | *We affirm* that the only type of preaching which sufficiently conveys the divine revelation and its proper application to life is that which faithfully expounds the text of Scripture as the Word of God.<br><br>*We deny* that the preacher has any message from God apart from the text of Scripture. |

Chapter 2

# What Is Inerrancy and Why Should We Care?

## NORMAN L. GEISLER AND SHAWN NELSON

It has been said that a table must have at least three legs to stand. Take away any of the three legs and it will surely topple. In much the same way, the Christian faith stands on three legs. These three legs are the inspiration, infallibility, and inerrancy of Scripture. Take away one and, like the table, the divine authority of the Christian faith will surely topple. These three "in's" complement each other, yet each expresses a slightly different distinction in our understanding of Scripture.

*Inspiration.* The first "in" is inspiration which deals with the origin of the Bible. Evangelicals believe that "God breathed out" the words of the Bible using human writers as the vehicle. Paul writes, "All Scripture is inspired by God (literally "is God-breathed") and profitable for teaching, for reproof, for correction, for training in righteousness; so that the man of God may be adequate, equipped for every good work" (2 Tim 3:16–17).[1]

*Infallibility.* The next "in," infallibility, speaks to the authority and enduring nature of the Bible. To be infallible means that something is incapable of failing and therefore is permanently binding and cannot be broken. Peter said "the word of the Lord endures forever" (1 Pet 1:23–25) and therefore its authority cannot be broken. When addressing a difficult passage, Jesus said, "the Scripture cannot be broken" (John 10:34–35). In fact, he said, "not the smallest letter or stroke shall pass from the Law until all is accomplished" (Matt 5:18). These speak to the Bible's infallibility.

*Inerrancy.* The last "in," inerrancy, simply means that the Bible is without error. It is a belief in the "total truthfulness and reliability of God's words."[2] Jesus said, "Your word is truth" (John 17:17). This inerrancy isn't just in passages that speak about

---

1. All Scripture quotes are taken from the NASB unless otherwise specified.
2. Grudem, *Systematic Theology*, 90.

salvation, but also applies to all historical and scientific statements as well. It is not only accurate in matters related to faith and practice, but it is accurate and without error regarding any statement, period (John 3:12).

## BUT IS IT REALLY IMPORTANT?

Yes, inerrancy is extremely important because: (1) it is attached to the character of God; (2) it is taught in the Scriptures; (3) it is the historic position of the Christian church; and (4) it is foundational to other essential doctrines.

### 1. It Is Based on the Character of God

Inerrancy is based on the character of God who cannot lie (Heb 6:18; Titus 1:2). God cannot lie intentionally because he is an absolute moral law-giver. He cannot err unintentionally because he is omniscient. And if the Bible is the written Word of God (and it is), then it is without error.

### 2. It Was Taught by Christ and the Apostles

Inerrancy was taught by Christ and the apostles in the New Testament. This should be our primary basis for believing it. B. B. Warfield said, "We believe this doctrine of the plenary inspiration of the Scriptures primarily because it is the doctrine which Christ and his apostles believed, and which they have taught us."[3]

To quote Jesus himself, "The Scripture cannot be broken" (John 10:35) and "until heaven and earth pass away, not the smallest letter or stroke shall pass from the Law until all is accomplished" (Matt 5:18).

### 3. It Is the Historic Position of the Church

Inerrancy is the historic position of the Christian church. ICBI produced a whole book demonstrating this point.[4] As Al Mohler pointed out, even some errantists have agreed that inerrancy has been the standard view of the Christian church down through the centuries. He cites the Hanson brothers, Anthony and Richard, Anglican scholars, who said,

> The Christian Fathers and the medieval tradition continued this belief [in inerrancy], and the Reformation did nothing to weaken it. On the contrary, since for many reformed theologians the authority of the Bible took the place which the Pope had held in the medieval scheme of things, the inerrancy of

3. Warfield, *Inspiration and Authority of the Bible*, 128.
4. See Hannah, *Inerrancy and the Church*, ix.

the Bible became more firmly maintained and explicitly defined among some reformed theologians than it had even been before.[5]

They added, "The beliefs here denied [inerrancy] have been held by all Christians from the very beginning until about a hundred and fifty years ago."[6]

### 4. It Is Fundamental to All Other Doctrines.

Inerrancy is foundational to all other essential Christian doctrines. It is granted that some other doctrines (like the atoning death and bodily resurrection of Christ) are more essential to salvation. However, all soteriological (salvation-related) doctrines derive their divine authority from the divinely authoritative Word of God. So, epistemologically (in a knowledge-related sense), the doctrine of the divine authority and inerrancy of Scripture is the fundamental of all the fundamentals. And if the fundamental of fundamentals is not fundamental, then what is fundamental? Fundamentally nothing! Thus, while one can be saved without believing in inerrancy, the doctrine of salvation has no divine authority apart from the infallibility and inerrancy of Scripture.

## IT IS AN ESSENTIAL

Inerrancy deserves high regard among evangelicals and has rightly earned the status of being essential (in an epistemological sense) to the Christian faith. Thus, to reduce inerrancy to the level of nonessential or even incidental to the Christian faith, reveals ignorance of its theological and historical roots and is an offense to its watershed importance to a consistent and healthy Christianity. Inerrancy simply cannot be rejected without grave consequences, both to the individual and to the church.

## IT IS UNDER ATTACK . . . RIGHT NOW!

The International Council on Biblical Inerrancy (ICBI) was founded in 1977 specifically over concerns about the erosion of inerrancy. Christian leaders, theologians, and pastors assembled together three times over the course of a decade to address the issue. At the first meeting, a doctrinal statement was jointly created titled "The Chicago Statement on Biblical Inerrancy." This document has been described as "a landmark church document" created "by the then largest, broadest, group of evangelical protestant scholars that ever came together to create a common, theological document in the twentieth century. It is probably the first systematically comprehensive, broadly

---

5. Hanson and Hanson, *Bible without Illusions*, 51–52; Mohler, "When the Bible Speaks," 40–41.
6. Hanson and Hanson, *Bible without Illusions*, 13.

based, scholarly, creed-like statement on the inspiration and authority of Scripture in the history of the church."[7]

Despite this modern safeguard, in 2010, Dr. Mike Licona, an evangelical professor, wrote a book titled *The Resurrection of Jesus: A New Historiographical Approach*. In this book, he suggested that the account of the resurrected saints walking through the city might be "apocalyptic imagery" (Matt 27:51–53).[8] In other words, he suggested that the event did not actually happen, but that it was lore or legend. Subsequently, Licona resigned from his position with the Southern Baptists and at Southern Evangelical Seminary. What followed is rather alarming. Incredibly, some notable evangelical scholars began to express their support for Licona's view, considering it consistent with a belief in inerrancy.

## SCHOLARS TRYING TO REDEFINE INERRANCY

Of course, in order to defend Licona's view they had to redefine inerrancy to include what were previously considered to be errors. Some did this by misinterpreting inerrancy as expressed by the ICBI framers.

Since 2011, more alarming statements from Licona have surfaced, including: (1) A denial of the historicity of the mob falling backward at Jesus' claim "I am he" in John 18:4–6 as a "candidate for possible embellishment";[9] (2) A denial of the historicity of the angels at the tomb recorded in all four Gospels (Matt 28:2–7; Mark 16:5–7; Luke 24:4–7; John 20:11–14), as "we may also be reading poetic language or legend at certain points, such as . . . the angel(s) at the tomb";[10] (3) A denial of the accuracy of the Gospel of John by claiming it says Jesus was crucified on the wrong day;[11] (4) A claim that the gospel genre is Greco-Roman biography which he says is a "flexible genre" in which "it is often difficult to determine where history ends and legend begins."[12] Amazingly, these views continue to gain support among the evangelical community.

These are the professors of some of the finest evangelical schools in the nation, who are responsible for training the pastors of today and future generations, and they are saying that they are comfortable with these verses not being factual. This is an outright departure from the historic definition of inerrancy.

---

7. Dallas Theological Seminary, "Records of the International Council on Biblical Inerrancy."
8. Licona, *Resurrection of Jesus*, 548–53, 701.
9. Ibid., 306n114.
10. Ibid., 185–86.
11. See Ehrman and Lincona, debate at Southern Evangelical Seminary.
12. Licona, *Resurrection of Jesus*, 34.

Chapter 3

# A Voice from a New Generation
## What's at Stake?

SHAWN NELSON

### A HISTORY OF ATTACK

With the Bible having been under attack now for a few hundred years, it might seem rather uneventful when a new battle for the Bible emerges. Recently, however, a new battle for the Bible has begun and this one indeed is worthy of sounding the war cry. What is unusual about this most recent attack is not that it started *from within* the camp—that's how many battles within the church have begun. But it is *how quickly* our leaders have jumped ship—and what little fight they put up! The very generals who were supposed to protect us have willingly handed the troops over to the enemy before the skirmish had even begun!

This most recent battle I am referring to began with a seminary professor named Dr. Mike Licona. In 2010, Licona wrote a book titled *The Resurrection of Jesus: A New Historiographical Approach*. In his book, he suggested that the account of the resurrected saints mentioned in Matthew 27:51–53 did not actually happen but that it might be apocalyptic imagery, lore, or legend.[1]

As to be expected, some notable evangelical theologians began to cry foul, in particular Dr. Norman Geisler, who addressed an open letter to Licona, charging him

---

1. Licona, *Resurrection of Jesus*, 548, 552.

with violating the inerrancy of Scripture.[2] Licona left his position with the Southern Baptists and with Southern Evangelical Seminary Home Mission Board. Yet what followed is rather alarming. Incredibly, many notable evangelical scholars began to express *their support* for Licona. Drs. Craig Blomberg at Denver Seminary, William Lane Craig at Talbot School of Theology, Gary Habermas at Liberty University, Daniel B. Wallace at Dallas Theological Seminary, J. P. Moreland at Talbot School of Theology, W. David Beck at Liberty University, James Chancellor at Southern Baptist Theological Seminary, Jeremy A. Evans at Southeastern Baptist Theological Seminary, Craig S. Keener at Asbury Theological Seminary, Douglas J. Moo at Wheaton College, Heath A. Thomas at Southeastern Baptist Theological Seminary, William Warren at New Orleans Baptist Theological Seminary, and evangelical historian Edwin M. Yamauchi *all voiced their support* for Licona by countersigning an open letter in response to Geisler.[3]

These clearly stated that they were aware of Licona's position concerning the resurrected saints: "He proposes that the report may refer to a literal/historical event, a real event partially described in apocalyptic terms, or an apocalyptic symbol" and furthermore, "we are in firm agreement that it is compatible with biblical inerrancy, despite objections to the contrary."[4] In other words, they were *perfectly comfortable* with the possibility that the account might not be factual history but could be an "apocalyptic symbol."

What's alarming is that these are the professors of some of the finest evangelical schools in the nation, who are responsible for training the pastors of today and future generations, and they stated that they were comfortable with this one verse not being factual. Some say, "So what! Why is this such a big deal?" Here is why.

## THE THREE "IN'S"

It's been said that a table must have at least three legs to be able to stand. Take away any of the three legs and it will surely topple. In much the same way, the authority of the Christian faith stands on three legs. These three legs are the inspiration, infallibility, and inerrancy of Scripture. These three "in's" complement each other, yet each expresses a slightly different distinction in our understanding of Scripture. Each concept in and of itself is important, yet they all depend on the other. Take away one and, like the table, the Christian faith will surely topple.

The first "in" is inspiration, and deals with the origin of the Bible. Evangelicals believe that "God breathed out" the words of the Bible, using human writers as the vehicle. The human writers were not inspired, like we might say today of a rock star, "He was inspired when he wrote that song." Rather, inspiration speaks to the writings

2. See Mohler, "Devil Is in the Details."
3. See Credo House Ministries, "Michael Licona Response to Norm Geisler."
4. Ibid.

themselves—that the writings, not the people, were inspired, or "breathed out by God." That is how they originated. This concept comes from 2 Timothy 3:16–17 where it says that "all Scripture is inspired by God and profitable for teaching, for reproof, for correction, for training in righteousness; so that the man of God may be adequate, equipped for every good work."[5]

The next "in," infallibility, speaks to the authority and enduring nature of the Word. To be infallible means that something is incapable of failing, and therefore is binding and cannot be broken. This is a fitting description. First Peter 2:23–25 says, "For you have been born again not of seed which is perishable but imperishable, *that is*, through the living and enduring word of God. For, 'all flesh is like grass, and all its glory like the flower of grass. The grass withers, and the flower falls off, but the Word of the Lord endures forever.' And this is the word which was preached to you." Here, it says that it endures without end, and as we have seen from the 2 Timothy 3:16–17 passage, it has all authority. This authority of Scripture cannot be broken. Jesus affirmed this in John 10:34–35. In addressing a difficult passage, he said, "The Scripture cannot be broken." In fact, he also said, "For truly I say to you, until heaven and earth pass away, not the smallest letter or stroke shall pass from the Law until all is accomplished" (Matt 5:18). What is important to understand is that there is a distinction between inspiration being the origin of the Bible—that it was "God breathed"—and infallibility being that it cannot be broken and thus has all authority. Yet, they are closely related and each depends on the other.

The same is true for the last "in," inerrancy. Inerrancy simply means that the Bible is without error. It's a belief in the "total truthfulness and reliability of God's words."[6] This isn't just in passages that speak about salvation, but also applies to all historical and scientific statements as well. It is not only accurate in matters related to faith and practice, but it is accurate and without error regarding any statement, period. It rejects any notion that the biblical writers "meant well" but ultimately misrepresented the truth.

At first glance, it would make sense that if the Bible originated from God and contains all authority and cannot be broken then it *must* be without error. So why is there a debate over inerrancy today? When did this debate begin? Why do some Christians believe that the Bible can contain errors? And ultimately, what does this do to our ability to understand anything about God?

---

5. The phrase "given by inspiration of God" is the single Greek word θεόπνευστος (*theopneustos*) and means quite literally "God breathed." That is a great description of Scripture—that it is breathed out by God. The word θεόπνευστος is also translated "by inspiration" and forms the basis of the evangelical concept of inspiration. Because it is God-breathed, it is authoritative, and profitable for reproof and instruction. The basis for its authority is that it is breathed out or inspired by God who cannot error, and therefore all of it is without error.

6. Grudem, *Systematic Theology*, 90.

## WHAT STARTS WELL DOESN'T ALWAYS END WELL

To those of us born into this controversy, it can feel as though the inerrancy debate has been around forever, but it hasn't. It might come as a surprise to some that it's a relatively new issue. Author and scholar Harold Lindsell stated, "Apart from a few exceptions, the church through the ages has consistently believed that the entire Bible is the inerrant or infallible Word of God."[7] It's clear that the early church received the New Testament writings as inspired writings, and that they ascribed the same authority to them as they did to the Old Testament Scriptures. This recognition of authority continued throughout church history up until a couple hundred years ago, until inerrancy gave way to new "scientific" thought, at which time the possibility of error was entertained, and the entire biblical foundation unraveled into the mess we have today. Let us briefly survey what some of the church fathers had to say on this important subject up through the Middle Ages beginning with the apostolic fathers.

The apostolic fathers are the generation of believers who had personal contact with Jesus' twelve apostles (ca. AD 70–ca. 150). We have many of their writings which can help to shed light on what the early church believed. In these writings, many references can be found which speak to the fact that these early church fathers believed in the inspiration, infallibility, and inerrancy of Scripture. While they did not specifically use these terms (they would be developed much later), it is clear that they believed what they teach.

Clement of Rome (ca. AD 95) said to his readers: "You have looked into the holy scriptures, which are true, which were given by the Holy Spirit. You know that nothing unrighteous or falsified is written in them" (1 Clem 45:2–3).[8] In speaking about Paul's writings, Clement said, "Truthfully [lit. 'by truth'] he wrote to you in the Spirit" (1 Clem 47:3).[9] Polycarp, a disciple of the Apostle John, also affirmed Paul's writings when he said that Paul "taught the word of truth accurately and reliably" and since they had this teaching (his letters) they were to "examine them" (Pol. *Phil.* 3:2–3).[10]

There are many other writings, including those of Pseudo-Barnabas,[11] Papias, Ignatius of Antioch, the Shepherd of Hermas, the Didache, and the Epistle to Diognetus which clearly show the early church held to inspiration, infallibility and inerrancy. "Taken together, this important early material demonstrates that by about AD 150 the early church, both East and West, accepted the New Testament claim for divine inspiration. The Fathers looked upon those books with the same high regard as the

---

7. Lindsell, *Battle for the Bible*, 42–43.
8. Brannan, *Apostolic Fathers*.
9. Ibid.
10. Ibid.
11. Pseudo-Barnabas is so named because it was initially believed to be written by the wrong person.

## Part 1—Inerrancy Defined

New Testament writers did the Old Testament Scriptures, namely, as the inspired, authoritative, and absolutely true Word of God."[12]

This belief continued throughout the Ante-Nicene and Nicene Fathers periods (ca. AD 150–ca. 350). Justin Martyr said of the Scriptures that "when you hear the utterances of the prophets spoken as it were personally, you must not suppose that they are spoken by the inspired themselves, but by the Divine Word who moves them."[13] Irenaeus, interestingly enough, had personal contact with Polycarp who was a disciple of the Apostle John. He made a profound statement about the reliability of Scripture when he wrote how "the only true and life-giving faith" was "received from the apostles and imparted to her sons. For the Lord of all gave to His apostles the power of the Gospel, through whom also we have known the truth, that is, the doctrine of the Son of God."[14] He further said these writings were above all falsehood:

> Since, therefore, the tradition from the apostles does thus exist in the church, and is permanent among us, let us revert to the scriptural proof furnished by those apostles who did also write the Gospel, in which they recorded the doctrine regarding God, pointing out that our Lord Jesus Christ is the truth, and that no lie is in him. . . . The apostles, likewise, being disciples of the truth, are above all falsehood; for a lie has no fellowship with the truth.[15]

Another father, Clement of Alexandria, said he had successfully "demonstrated that the Scriptures which we believe are valid from their omnipotent authority," and therefore should be used to combat all heresies. He then goes on to name those Scriptures as that which is "preached by the law and the prophets, and besides by the blessed gospel."[16]

Nearly all of the other Fathers held to the inspiration/inerrancy of Scripture, including Tatian, Tertullian, Hippolytus, Origen, Cyprian, Eusebius of Caesarea, Athanasius of Alexandria, and Cyril of Jerusalem.[17] Not surprisingly, this view continued through the great medieval church teachers (ca. 350–ca. 1350). Jerome believed Paul was a chosen vessel "assuredly because he is a repertory of the Law and of the holy scriptures."[18] Augustine, considered by many to be one of the greatest theologians of all time, stated the following:

> For I confess to your Charity that I have learned to yield this respect and honour only to the canonical books of Scripture: of these alone do I most firmly believe that the authors were completely free from error. And if in these

---

12. Geisler, *Systematic Theology*, 1:284.
13. First Apology 36.
14. *Against Heresies* 3, preface to ch. 1.
15. Ibid. 3.5.1.
16. *Strom.* 4.1.
17. Geisler, *Systematic Theology*, 1:284–88.
18. Schaff and Wace, *Nicene and Post-Nicene Fathers*, 2nd ser., 6:98.

writings I am perplexed by anything which appears to me opposed to truth, I do not hesitate to suppose that either the manuscript is faulty, or the translator has not caught the meaning of what was said, or I myself have failed to understand it. As to all other writings, in reading them, however great the superiority of the authors to myself in sanctity and learning, I do not accept their teaching as true on the mere ground of the opinion being held by them; but only because they have succeeded in convincing my judgment of its truth either by means of these canonical writings themselves, or by arguments addressed to my reason. I believe, my brother, that this is your own opinion as well as mine. I do not need to say that I do not suppose you to wish your books to be read like those of prophets or of apostles, concerning which it would be wrong to doubt that they are free from error.[19]

It was during this same period that the Council of Laodicea (AD 363), the Council of Hippo (AD 393), and the Council of Carthage (AD 397) affirmed the books of the Bible as being authoritative in nature, consistent with the admonition from 2 Timothy 3:16–17 that the Bible, since it is "God-breathed," is the absolute authority for conduct, binding, infallible, and able to lead into all truth.

This view prevailed throughout the medieval period, and can be seen in teachings of another prominent theologian, Thomas Aquinas (ca. 1225–1274), who stated, "It is unlawful to hold that any false assertion is contained either in the Gospel or in any canonical Scripture, or that the writers thereof have told untruths, because faith would be deprived of its certitude which is based on the authority of Holy Writ."[20] Additionally he said, "A true prophet is always inspired by the Spirit of truth, in whom there is no falsehood, wherefore he never says what is not true,"[21] and, "it is plain that nothing false can ever underlie the literal sense of Holy Writ."[22] He also affirms that he agreed with Augustine when he said, "Only those books of Scripture which are called canonical have I learned to hold in such honor as to believe their authors have not erred in any way in writing them."[23]

What are we to make of all of this? If the apostolic fathers who had personal contact with the New Testament apostles, the early church fathers, and the medieval church teachers all held to an inerrant view of Scripture, when and how did the idea that the Bible could contain errors creep into the church? And why are some evangelical theologians tempted to depart from this historical view today?

---

19. Augustine, *Confessions and Letters*, 350.
20. Aquinas, *Summa Theologica* (Bellingham, WA: Logos, 2009), *STh.*, II-II q.110 a.3 resp.
21. Ibid., II-II q.172 a.6 ad.2.
22. Ibid., I q.1 a.10 ad.3–2.
23. Ibid., I q.1 a.8 ad.2.

Part 1—Inerrancy Defined

## INFLUENCES LEADING TO THE EROSION OF INERRANCY

The philosophical influences of the Enlightenment are to blame for undermining inerrancy. The first influence that led to modern criticism of the Bible was *inductivism*, led by Francis Bacon (1561–1626). Bacon began his life as a devout Anglican. During the ascension of King James to power Bacon began to question the extent of learning and our ability to understand. He proposed a new approach for truth based on experimentation and inductive reasoning.[24] This marked the beginning of the movement that ultimately would seek to remove the Bible from the pursuit of science and understanding. While Bacon himself remained a devote Christian until his death, his inductive approach would ultimately be the spark of the beginning of the Enlightenment.[25]

What followed was *materialism* (Thomas Hobbes, 1588–1679). Materialism held that everything is finite, there is no infinite. In other words, what we see in this universe is all there is; there can be no spiritual world beyond our physical universe.

This was quickly followed by *antisupernaturalism* (Benedict Spinoza, 1632–1677). If materialism is true, then there is no God, no heaven, and no hell—nothing supernatural. The Bible needed to be rethought of in light of this new "truth." The demon possessed of Scripture became madmen. Jesus could not have really risen from the dead, but his disciples merely believed that he rose from the dead, and so on. This "rethinking" of Scripture was the beginning of higher criticism of the Bible.

*Antisupernaturalism* led to *skepticism* (David Hume, 1711–1776). Hume became famous for his argument against the credibility of miracles. The gist of his argument was that miracles are a violation of the fixed laws of nature, that there is far greater evidence for the continuity of natural law, and as such, a wise man should base belief on that which has greater evidence. Hume's argument was and has since been *the* intellectual argument against miracles, and while the argument is surprisingly weak, it has yielded disastrous results for the Christian faith, as we shall see.

Next came *agnosticism* (Immanuel Kant, 1724–1804). With miracles "proven" to be impossible and the Bible downgraded to a fairytale, what was left is agnosticism—that there probably is a God, but we cannot really know anything about him. Kant's concept was the logical conclusion to the line of philosophical ideas preceding him. His conclusion was that science is possible because it deals with the observable world, but we simply do not and cannot know what lies beyond that.

Finally, we arrived at *evolutionism* (Charles Darwin, 1809–1882). Darwin attempted to remove the last remaining weapon in Christendom's war chest—the

---

24. Galli and Olsen, *131 Christians Everyone Should Know*, 354.

25. It is worthy of noting that Francis Bacon actually believed strongly that the use of rationality and his inductive approach would lead one to conclude that God exists. His high regard for both science and the Bible can be seen in his statement: "There are two books laid before us to study, to prevent our falling into error; first, the volume of Scriptures, which reveal the will of God; then the volume of the Creatures, which express his power." See Morris, "Sir Francis Bacon," in *Men of Science*.

argument that complex life requires a Creator. Darwin's theory of natural selection was a solution that did not require a supernatural origin. Life could have arisen spontaneously, and through natural processes over time; it could have evolved into higher, more organized and better adapted life forms apart from a divine Creator—a theory which was accepted with open arms.

Thus, in just a few hundred years, the biblical worldview had been completely overturned. The book which was once thought to be without error, unable to be broken, and the final absolute authority for the church, was now "proven" riddled with mistakes, legend, and superstition. Yet, Christianity continued—with a serious problem. With all of this "new truth" from the Enlightenment, what did real Christians who wanted to follow Jesus Christ do with the Bible? As we will see, many compromised.

## A SMORGASBORD OF BIBLICAL VIEWS

There are four major views of Scripture that came in the wake of these destructive philosophies and these views remain today. We have the *evangelical, liberal, Neo-Orthodox* and *Neo-Evangelical* views of Scripture. The first is the early historical position, and the last three are concessions based on the "new truth" of so-called scientific advancement.

The *evangelical* view of Scripture is that the Bible *is* the Word of God. This would include belief in the three "in's" discussed earlier—belief in the inspiration, infallibility, and inerrancy of the Bible. Evangelicals also hold to *sola Scriptura*, that famous Reformation doctrine which states that Bible alone is authoritative (as opposed to the pope, or apostolic tradition), and the concept of the preservation of the Bible.

*Liberalism* believes that the Bible *contains* the Word of God. On one hand liberals believe that the Bible contains errors, that the human authors often made mistakes and misrepresentations about the truth, that the written record is corrupt, that commonly believed authors of various books did not actually author those books, and so forth. Yet, on the other hand, liberals believe that there is still some truth to be discovered in the pages of Scripture. They embrace higher criticism to help identify truth from error.

The *Neo-Orthodox* position is closely related and asserts that the Bible *becomes* the Word of God. Even though the Bible is considered to be errant, the voice of God can be heard through a personal encounter with Jesus Christ. It becomes necessary to try to distinguish between the voice of God and the voice of man. Like the liberal view, this view also embraces higher criticism of the Bible to determine what is true and what is not.

In these ways, some Christians have attempted to find ways to cope with the "new truth" gained through the Enlightenment. They believe that a fallible Bible is perfectly compatible with Christianity. However, this is wrong, and the evangelical would do well to avoid making similar concessions. Here's why.

Part 1—Inerrancy Defined

## INERRANCY WAS THE FIRST LEG TO FALL

Earlier, we looked at how the Christian faith can be likened to a table standing on the three legs of inspiration, infallibility, and inerrancy. What is clear in our review of the Enlightenment is that inerrancy was the *first* leg to fall. Beginning with Hobbes, Spinoza, Hume and the like, we see this line of reasoning develop: (1) miracles are not possible; (2) there is no supernatural (everything is natural); (3) the Bible is wrong when it talks about these things (not inerrant); (4) it cannot have originated from a perfect being (not inspired); and (5) it therefore is not absolutely divinely authoritative and not binding (not infallible).

## WHERE DOES IT END?

The problem is once the floodgate opens, where does it end? When a passage is determined to not be possible and is stripped of its supernatural strength, the only conclusion is that the biblical authors made a mistake. Inerrancy falls, followed by inspiration and infallibility. Once allowance is made in one passage on the basis of it sounding like lore, legend, or too great of a miracle, what prevents us from erasing other passages? Some might say this is a "slippery slope" argument. However, it should not be quickly dismissed. If an accountant claimed to be divinely infallible and inerrant but made one mistake, then we have reason to not trust the accountant's infallibility claim in anything they said. Likewise, if the Bible claims to be the infallible/inerrant Word of God and makes one mistake, then we cannot trust it as infallible and inerrant in *anything* it says. We would have good reason to question whether *any* passage has divine authority.

Once a concession is made about a passage being lore or nonfactual, the Pandora's Box of doubt is opened on the entire Gospel record. Indeed, in the recent case of the reevaluation of the account of the resurrected saints in Matthew 27, it led to the reevaluation of other significant passages as well. In addition to denying the physical resurrection of the saints, Licona goes on to further assert the following: (1) The denial of the historicity of the mob falling backward at Jesus claim "I am he" in John 18:4–6;[26] (2) A denial of the historicity of the angels at the tomb recorded in all four Gospels (Matt 28:2–7; Mark 16:5–7; Luke 24:4–7; John 20:11–14;[27] (3) The claim that the gospel genre is Greco-Roman biography which he says is a "flexible genre" in which "it is often difficult to determine where history ends and legend begins";[28] (4) Additionally, in a debate with Bart Ehrman at Southern Evangelical Seminary in the spring of 2009, Licona asserted concerning the day Jesus was crucified: "I think that

---

26. Licona, *Resurrection of Jesus*, 306n114.
27. Ibid., 185–86.
28. Ibid., 34.

John probably altered the day in order for a theological—to make a theological point there."[29]

## IS MIKE LICONA THE NEXT BART EHRMAN?

It appears that Licona might well be on his way to becoming the next Bart Ehrman, with an impressive list of evangelical scholarship following closely behind.

Who is Bart Ehrman and why is he important to this discussion? Bart Ehrman serves as a warning sign of what can happen to evangelicals who are tempted to dismiss difficult passages in the biblical text. In Ehrman's story we see that when it is carried to its logical conclusion, one denial ultimately ends in a complete denial of the Christian faith, leaving the former believer in a miserable state of agnosticism.

Ehrman began as a typical evangelical Christian. He encountered the gospel while in high school at a Campus Life Youth for Christ club where he made a decision to become born again. As a new Christian, Ehrman displayed passion and zeal for the Lord, and held a fundamental, evangelical view of Scripture. He believed that the Bible was authoritative, without error, and was committed to studying it as such by enrolling at Moody Bible Institute to study biblical theology, eventually transferring, and then graduating from Wheaton College. He then enrolled at Princeton Theological Seminary for higher education.

It was at Princeton that Ehrman's perspective on the Bible changed. It all came down to a term paper surrounding a challenging passage in Mark 2. In the passage where Jesus says David went in and ate the showbread, Mark says Abiathar was high priest (Mark 2:26) while the verse Mark was quoting from (1 Sam 21:1–6) seems to suggest that Ahimelech was high priest—how can this be if the Bible is without error?[30] Ehrman filled up his term paper with "a long and complicated argument" on how to resolve this difficulty. And he assumed that his professor would appreciate his hard work in resolving it. But in his Ehrman's own words:

> At the end of my paper he made a simple one-lined comment that for some reason went straight through me. He wrote: "Maybe Mark just made a mistake." I started thinking about it, considering all the work I had put into the paper, realizing that I had had to do some pretty fancy exegetical footwork to get around the problem, and that my solution was in fact a bit of a stretch. I finally concluded, "Hmm . . . maybe Mark *did* make a mistake."[31]

Here's what happened next:

> Once I made that admission, the floodgates opened. For if there could be one little, picayune mistake in Mark 2, maybe there could be mistakes in other

---

29. Geisler, "Licona's Denial of Inerrancy."
30. There are many satisfactory resolutions to this passage.
31. Ehrman, *Misquoting Jesus*, 9.

places as well. Maybe, when Jesus says later in Mark 4 that the mustard seed is "the smallest of all seeds on the earth," maybe I don't need to come up with a fancy explanation for how the mustard seed is the smallest of all seeds when I know full well it isn't. And maybe these "mistakes" apply to bigger issues. Maybe when Mark says that Jesus was crucified the day *after* the Passover meal was eaten (Mark 14:12; 15:25) and John says he died the day *before* it was eaten (John 19:14)—maybe that is a genuine difference. Or when Luke indicates in his account of Jesus' birth that Joseph and Mary returned to Nazareth just over a month after they had come to Bethlehem (and performed the rites of purification; Luke 2:39), whereas Matthew indicates they instead fled to Egypt (Matt 2:19–22)—maybe that is a difference. Or when Paul says that after he converted on the way to Damascus he did *not* go to Jerusalem to see those who were apostles before him (Gal 1:16–17), whereas the book of Acts says that that was the first thing he did after leaving Damascus (Acts 9:26)—maybe that is a difference.[32]

The concession that there might be one little error in Mark 2 turned Ehrman into a full-fledged liberal. He eventually became an agnostic. And this is the point—if we allow even one little error in the biblical text, *nothing* can have divine certainty in the biblical text, and the very foundation of Christianity crumbles. But why must it end this way?

## THE BIBLE IS THE ONLY SPECIAL REVELATION WE HAVE

An attack on biblical inerrancy is an attack on special revelation. There are only two avenues whereby we can know truth. The first is general revelation and the second is special revelation. Through general revelation we can know *some things* about God. Using rationality and reason, we understand that there must be a creator and designer of this vastly complex universe. We can also clearly understand that there is an absolute moral law. We know right from wrong by our own reaction when wrong is done to us, and we intuitively know we should not treat people this way.[33] However, there is a limit to what we can know about God through logic, rational senses, and reason.

This is why special revelation is important. While we're limited with general revelation, we can know *everything* God has chosen to reveal to us through special revelation. Through special revelation, we learn of the truths of (1) the tri-unity of God; (2) the virgin birth of Christ; (3) the deity of Christ; (4) the all-sufficiency of Christ's atoning sacrifice for sin; (5) the physical and miraculous resurrection of Christ; (6) the necessity of salvation by faith alone through God's grace alone based on the work

---

32. Ibid., 9–10.

33. The Bible validates general revelation. Paul says mankind clearly perceives God but doesn't receive him (Rom 1:18–22) and later says that mankind has the work of the moral law on their hearts, so they are without excuse (Rom 2:14–16).

of Christ alone; (7) the physical bodily return of Christ to earth; (8) the eternal conscious bliss of the saved; and (9) the eternal conscious punishment of the unsaved.[34]

The Bible is the only record of special revelation we have. If we remove special revelation all we are left with is general revelation. All we would know is that there is some kind of God who gave us moral law, and we individually have failed to keep it. We would be incapable of knowing this God, reminded constantly of our own failure to please him, uncertain of our past or our future, living out our days in a wretched state of miserable ignorance, until we cross the void into the unknown. What a horrible state of existence!

And it all begins with making a simple concession that the Bible contains one little error, just like Ehrman did, and just like Licona and others are now doing. If history repeats itself, with further reasoning, they may very well end up agnostics. Of course, it doesn't always end this way, but it certainly is the *logical* conclusion. Consider the following hypothetical argument.

## BASIC LOGICAL ARGUMENT

If we accept that the Bible contains error, what we are saying is this: some amount from 0.001 to 100 percent would be error.[35] The amount would be unknown; it could be *slightly* in error or *all of it* could be in error.

There would then be a problem with our basis for doctrinal truth. We could not be *absolutely certain* about anything we hope in as Christians since these are only known through special revelation: Jesus' sinless life and qualifications for being a substitutionary sacrifice for sin, salvation by faith in the finished work of Christ alone, hope of the second coming, eternal conscious bliss of the saved, etc. We would only be certain of what comes through general revelation: that there is a God and that we have failed to keep his moral law.

There would be a problem with the basis for what is authoritative. What is false (error) does not correspond to reality and therefore cannot be divinely authoritative. Only what is true (what actually corresponds to reality) can be divinely authoritative. Errancy asserts that 0 percent to 99.999 percent is true.[36] Therefore only some unknown amount—0 percent, 10 percent, 40 percent, 90 percent—would be divinely authoritative. Under this framework who determines which parts—if any—are authoritative? On what basis would we know *for certain* that any passage is binding? How could we possibly know whether the Bible is expressing the mere opinion of men or the absolute will of God? We would not be able to know for sure.

---

34. These along with inspiration are the beliefs that define an evangelical Christian. See Geisler, *Systematic Theology*, 1:15.

35. The zero before the trailing one is infinitely-repeated (e.g., 0.00000000000000000001 percent).

36. The trailing nine is infinitely-repeated (e.g., 99.99999999999999999999 percent).

## Part 1—Inerrancy Defined

There would be a problem with Jesus Christ. Jesus not only claimed to be God[37] but he asserted that 100 percent of the Bible in his day was divinely authoritative (without error).[38] He said that future revelation coming through his apostles would be "all truth" revelation from the Father.[39] God cannot unintentionally err since God is omniscient (knows all things). Neither can God intentionally err since this is deception—and a morally perfect being cannot deceive. Therefore if Jesus were to err (intentionally or unintentionally) he could not be God.

There would also be a problem with our salvation. If Jesus Christ *accidently* made false truth claims he would no longer be perfect; if he deceived *intentionally* he would be a sinner. In either case he would not be the perfect Lamb of God whose sacrifice took away the sin of the world since he would not have been sinless and without blemish (John 1:29; 1 Pet 1:19). Therefore we would still be in our sins.

Taken to its absolute logical conclusion, if we accept a Bible with error then we jettison our basis for doctrinal truth. We would have reason to question the nature of God (the Trinity), the efficacy of our salvation, and the legitimacy of the authority of *any* passage of Scripture. In short, Christians could rightly question anything and everything. The only things we could know *for certain* are that we are moral lawbreakers who cannot know whether we truly know God at all (agnosticism). This is precisely

---

37. Jesus claimed to be the Messiah who was to be God (Ps 110:1; Isa 51:11; Zeph 3:14–15; Isa 9:6; Ps 45:6; Isa 42:10; Zeph 3:17; Zech 2:10; 9:9; Ezek 37:27; Lev 26:12; Ps 68:18; Zech 12:10; John 4:25–26; Matt 14:61–62); his disciples claimed Jesus was God (John 1:1; Col 1:15; 2:9; Phil 2:6; Heb 1:3, 8–9, 10–12); Jesus claimed to be God (John 8:58; Mark 2:5–7; John 5:23).

38. Jesus affirmed that the Bible of his day, the Old Testament, was the Word of God. He held that the Old Testament is divinely authoritative (Matt 4:4, 7, 10), imperishable (Matt 5:17–18), infallible (John 10:35), inerrant (without error; Matt 22:29), is historically reliable (Matt 12:40; 24:37–38), scientifically accurate (Matt 19:4–5) and had ultimate supremacy (Matt 15:3, 6). Jesus applied his view of Scripture to the Old Testament as a whole, calling it "the Word of God" (John 10:35), "the Scriptures" (John 5:39) and "Your (Jewish) Law" (John 10:34). He indicated that everything from start to finish was to be considered Scripture ("From Abel to Zechariah," Matt 23:35). He cited from all sections of the Old Testament, from Moses through the Prophets (Matt 5:17; 7:12; Luke 16:31; 24:27, 44). See Geisler and Nelson, *Evidence of an Early New Testament Canon*, Kindle locations 125–26.

39. Jesus promised new revelation through his apostles. He promised that after his ascension there would be the giving of new revelation to his apostles. He declared, "The Helper, the Holy Spirit, whom the Father will send in my name, he will teach you all things and bring to your remembrance all that I have said to you" (John 14:26). He added, "I still have many things to say to you, but you cannot bear them now," he said. "However, when He, the Spirit of truth, has come, He will guide *you* into *all truth*" (John 16:12–13), Jesus was speaking at the time to his twelve apostles (cf. John 17:9, 20). He promised that *these* apostles would receive "all truth" revelation. This revelation would be clearer than any revelation Jesus had already given them ("I will no longer speak to you in figurative language, but I will tell you plainly about the Father," John 16:25). The question must be asked: *What else could Jesus have been referring to but the New Testament?* The New Testament writings are the *only* writings we have ever seen from these apostles. Therefore it is perfectly reasonable to believe that these very New Testament writings are the inspired "all truth" revelation Jesus promised. If Jesus had a high view of Old Testament *written* revelation (and he did; see above) he certainly would have a high view of this future "all truth" *written* revelation. In this way Jesus affirmed *beforehand* that the New Testament was coming—and that it would be just as authoritative as Old Testament. See Geisler and Nelson, *Evidence of an Early New Testament Canon*, Kindle locations 133–50.

where the philosophers of the Enlightenment have led us as a society, precisely where Bart Ehrman has ended up personally, and where Mike Licona and others who adopt his methodology may very well end up over time.

## PREVENTING TRUTH DECAY

What can be done to prevent "truth decay?" Thankfully, steps have already been taken to ensure that the evangelical view of Scripture is upheld for generations to come. The International Council on Biblical Inerrancy (ICBI) was founded in 1977 specifically over concerns of the erosion of biblical inerrancy. Christian leaders, theologians, and pastors assembled together three times over the course of a decade to address the issue. At the first meeting a doctrinal statement was jointly created, titled "The Chicago Statement on Biblical Inerrancy," which clearly defined biblical inerrancy. This document has been described as "a landmark church document" created by the then largest, broadest group of evangelical protestant scholars that ever came together to create a common, theological document in the twentieth century. It is probably the first systematically comprehensive, broadly based, scholarly, creed-like statement on the inspiration and authority of Scripture in the history of the church.[40] All who hold a high, inerrant view of Scripture would do well to read, understand, affirm and promote the points touched upon in this document.

## CALLING A SPADE A SPADE

However, it would appear that simply having a document like the Chicago Statement on Biblical Inerrancy is not enough. It must be enforced, so to speak. Anybody who has children knows that it is not enough to simply have rules around the house. These rules must be enforced. Otherwise the children behave as if there are no rules at all and there is chaos and disorder.

In conclusion, the concern is that we are now seeing within certain evangelical academic circles a departure from the traditional view of inerrancy yet once again. And the rules *must* be enforced. If Dr. Mike Licona (who is now at Houston Baptist University) and those who support him want to believe that there is legend and lore in the Gospel records, and that the records are not 100 percent factual, fine. But they should not be allowed to present this as if it is inerrancy. Call it what it is, but don't call it evangelical. It is really a Neo-Evangelical view. It is time for seminary leaders and the evangelical community to take a stand lest we see further erosion. In the words of the Chicago Statement on Biblical Inerrancy:

> We see it as our timely duty to make this affirmation in the face of current lapses from the truth of inerrancy among our fellow Christians and

---

40. See "Records of the International Council on Biblical Inerrancy."

## Part 1—Inerrancy Defined

misunderstanding of this doctrine in the world at large.... We offer this Statement in a spirit, not of contention, but of humility and love, which we purpose by God's grace to maintain in any future dialogue arising out of what we have said. We gladly acknowledge that many who deny the inerrancy of Scripture do not display the consequences of this denial in the rest of their belief and behavior, and we are conscious that we who confess this doctrine often deny it in life by failing to bring our thoughts and deeds, our traditions and habits, into true subjection to the divine Word.[41]

May God help us to this end, for inerrancy is the foundation of everything.

---

41. CSBI.

# Chapter 4

# Evangelical Mentoring
## The Danger from Within

F. DAVID FARNELL, PHD

It is enough for the disciple that he become like his teacher, and the slave like his master.
(MATT 10:25)

### INTRODUCTION: MENTORING MATTERS!

This article is not so much about methods of mentoring as it is about *the consequences of mentoring*. Mentoring has at its core that of training disciples for the glory of Jesus Christ. When Jesus pronounced the Great Commission, discipleship or mentoring was at its core ("make disciples," Matt 28:19–20). He commanded his followers to mentor or make disciples of all nations. The content of mentoring was to be that of his teaching ("teaching them to observe all the things that I have commanded you," Matt 28:20) as well as that of conforming to his person, i.e., Jesus' disciples were to be like him ("It is enough for the disciple that he become like his teacher, and the slave like his master," Matt 10:25). The Scripture contains a promise that when Jesus returns his true disciples will be conformed to his image: "We know that when He appears, we will be like Him, because we will see Him just as He is" (1 John 3:2).

Mentoring or discipleship has a special, sharp focus in the church of Jesus Christ. According to Paul, pastors and teachers are to equip the saints for ministry (Eph 4:11–12) until we are all conformed or matured to the image of Christ: "until we all attain to the unity of the faith, and of the knowledge of the Son of God, to a mature man, to the measure of the stature which belongs to the fullness of Christ. *As a result, we are no longer to be children, tossed here and there by waves and carried about by every wind of doctrine, by the trickery of men, by craftiness in deceitful scheming*; but speaking the truth in love, we are to grow up in all *aspects* into Him who is the head, *even* Christ" (Eph 4:13–16). Discipleship has a primary *goal of maturity in the Christian faith* (1) toward Christ-likeness and (2) maturing believers in "healthy teaching" (sound or "healthy" doctrine) so that they are strengthened in their Christian beliefs (i.e., doctrine) with the result that they can withstand the onslaught of false doctrine. For Paul reminds us not only can there be "sound" or "healthy doctrine" but also "false doctrine" ("teaching strange" or "heterodox" doctrine, 1 Tim 1:3) that he also characterized as "doctrines of demons" that bring harm to Jesus' church (1 Tim 4:1).

Peter reminds us that leaders in Christ's church, his body, are the under-shepherds who are to disciple his flock until he returns (1 Pet 5:1–4). Hebrews reminds all those who assume leadership positions in the church as "those who will give an account" to the Lord at judgment for their discipling of his people (Heb 13:17). Perhaps Jesus' half-brother James issued the most solemn warning about those who would disciple, train, mentor Jesus' flock: "Let not many *of you* become teachers, my brethren, knowing that as such we will incur a stricter judgment" (Jas 3:1) that echoes Jesus' words that "to whom much is given, much is required" (Luke 12:48). Particular with James is the focus upon the damage that the tongue (teaching) of the teacher can do when misused, for the source of the tongue James ascribes to "hell" ("gehenna," Jas 3:6) itself when it does things that damage God's flock as a result of bad mentoring.

Why state the obvious about mentoring? The context of Christian education, training of men and women for serving Jesus Christ, is especially where mentoring and discipleship comes to great prominence, especially among evangelicals who profess some form of faithfulness to God's Word. Christian education can be used to strengthen God's church or it can also become a means to damage God's flock.

## MENTORING CAN PRODUCE DISCIPLES TWICE AS MUCH A SON OF HELL AS THEIR TEACHER!

Jesus excoriated the Pharisees of the day, for their teaching or mentoring produced a radicalizing of their teaching or doctrine among their students, "Woe to you, scribes and Pharisees, hypocrites, because you travel around on sea and land to make one proselyte; and when he becomes one, you make him twice as much a son of hell as yourselves" (Matt 23:15). Perhaps above many in Judaism, the Pharisees recognized the importance of mentoring but were neglectful of its consequences. Jesus keenly observed the students whom the Pharisees mentored and understood very well the influence that this mentoring had on their students. In short, the impact of the false teaching of the Pharisees radicalized the "next generation" of their disciples. The oral law of the Pharisees serves as a primary example. Their oral law taught that the oral word of the scribes ("doctrines of men") had been used to nullify the Word of God, for Jesus applied Isaiah 29:13, "but in vain do they worship me, teaching as doctrines the precepts of men." This oral law (i.e., Mishnah) became so radicalized in Second Temple Judaism that the Talmud (the oral law that was eventually written down) asserted that scribes could overturn the written Word of God. The following assertions, taken from the Soncino Unabridged Talmud (Baylonian) used in mentoring among these rabbinical students, are merely a few surprising examples:

- It is more wicked to question the words of the rabbis than those of the Torah: "My son, be more careful in [the observance of] the words of the Scribes than in the words of the Torah, for in the laws of the Torah there are positive and negative precepts; but, as to the laws of the Scribes, whoever transgresses any of the enactments of the Scribes incurs the penalty of death" (Babylonian Talmud Mas. Eiruvin 21b).

- A rabbi debates God and defeats him. God admits the rabbi won the debate: "R. Nathan met Elijah and asked him: What did the Holy One, Blessed be He, do in that hour—He laughed [with joy], he replied, saying 'My sons have defeated Me, My sons have defeated Me'" (Mas. Baba Metzia 59b).

- The prophet Isaiah was justifiably killed for stating that the Israelites had unclean lips: "When the saw reached his mouth he died [and this was his penalty] for having said, 'And I dwell in the midst of a people of unclean lips'" (Babylonian Talmud Yevamoth 49b).

- No merit in studying the Old Testament Scripture but great merit in studying the Talmud or oral rabbinical traditions: "Our rabbis taught: They who occupy themselves with the Bible (alone) are but of indifferent merit; with Mishnah, are indeed meritorious, and are rewarded for it; with Gemara—there can be nothing more meritorious. Yet always run to the Mishna more than to the Gemara" (Babylonian Talmud Mas. Baba Metzia 33a).

- Rabbis may overturn the written OT words of God. Several places throughout Talmudic literature, we are told of the principle that the Rabbis have the ability to "uproot" directives from the Torah (Babylonian Talmud Mas. Yevamot 89b–90b).

The point here is that the Pharisees, while perhaps starting out well in their history, radicalized, departed from God's written Word, disrespected it for their oral traditions, and then radicalized their students through their teachings, and those radicalized further radicalized others until the authority of the written Word was entirely rejected. This tragic state of affairs in mentoring reveals tragic results.

Mentoring by Christians cannot absolve itself of similar tragic mistakes, for similar ideas have been advocated whereby the Word of God is overridden for the sake of traditions of men as well as philosophy (Col 2:8). Jesus excoriated the Judaism of his day (Matt 15:1–9; 23:1–33) and was the greatest advocate for return to the commandments of God. For this reason, evangelicals who attempt to place Jesus under the confines of Second temple Judaism do so by invalidating Jesus' teaching on the primacy of God's Word and the need to avoid the traditions of men as so evidenced in the corruption of Judaism in his day.

The New Testament writers made clear that faithfulness to New Testament teaching is paramount in mentoring. Paul wrote that faithful men are to instill faithfulness, not radicalized teaching, into their mentoring ministry of future generations: 2 Timothy 2:2—"the things which you have heard from me in the presence of many witnesses, entrust these to faithful men who will be able to teach others also"; and Titus 1:9—"holding fast the faithful word which is in accordance with the teaching, so that he will be able both to exhort in sound doctrine and to refute those who contradict." Consistent faithfulness to God's Word is always the goal of Christian mentoring. This stipulation is why Paul urged Christian leaders, mentors, teachings, disciplers to "preach the Word" and avoid the "strange" doctrines of men (1 Tim 1:3), i.e., doctrine that is not plainly, normally expressed in the New Testament writers, for as John the Apostle also noted those who abide in fellowship or agreement with apostolic teaching abide in fellowship also with the Father and Son (1 John 1:3–4). Those who leave orthodox Christianity and its teachings demonstrate their apostate position (1 John 2:19—"they went out from us, but they were not *really* of us; for if they had been of us, they would have remained with us; but *they went out,* so that it would be shown that they all are not of us"). To depart from sound doctrine or apostolic teaching is to demonstrate false discipleship (cp. Acts 20:28–31—"Be on guard" against false teachers).

## DO THEY TRULY, REALLY STILL BELIEVE?

Why this kind of introduction? A recent book by Zondervan, *I (Still) Believe* (2015), edited by John Byron (Professor of New Testament, Ashland Theological Seminary) and Joel N. Lohr (Dean of Religious Life and Associate Professor of Practice, University of the Pacific), serves as a timely warning about the importance of discipleship and radicalization of disciples in Christian circles. It speaks to mentoring and discipleship and the training of the "next generation" of preachers and teachers in the evangelical church. Evangelical churches and schools serve as primary training centers for future generations. Indeed, evangelical churches and their denominational, and nondenominational, schools are *the primary foci* for training the future trainers of congregations in Christian doctrine, i.e., pastors. They produce the "next generation" of Christian scholars, i.e., trainers of these pastors, who will move into these evangelical churches, train disciples, who in turn, will become the trainers in their schools and colleges for each successive generation. The impact of mentoring is unquestionably enormous for evangelicals who set themselves forth as a "faithful" remnant among the professing church as a whole. However, what this current article and writer contends is that mentoring in evangelical circles has too many frequent examples of tragically bad mentoring that has lead to tragically bad results in the mentoring of future generations.

The book is dedicated as follows: "For all who have struggled, wrestled, been discouraged, lamented, lost hope, wanted to give up, wondered if it all made sense, but still believe." So its focus is on those who struggle about their Christian faith and its teachings. In turn, it gives the spiritual testimony of eighteen Christian scholars who have mentored countless others in their Christian faith but who have faced their own doubts about the Old and New Testament. The book's editors correctly recognize the importance of mentorship, "Like many students, our professors made quite an impression on us."[1] "When we became graduate students the relationships grew deeper, and their influence only intensified."[2] Thus, evangelical churches and schools have enormous influence on the spiritual state of God's people through the mentors that disciple future generations, as is evidenced in all eighteen of these testimonies in the book. The editors decided to put together in this work "a book of professors' autobiographies."[3] "We loved and admired our professors and wanted to learn more about them."[4] "We wanted to learn about their struggle, their pains, their sorrows, but also their joys, reasons for hope, and what brought them fulfillment in life."[5] They go on to note something very strategic as their plans developed and the importance of the mentors in their training, "The more we talked about possible themes the more that faith and scholarship came to the fore . . . we found ourselves talking again and again about how our own work as scholars of biblical literature affected our lives as people of faith . . . we couldn't help but be reminded that our lives in the church and as people of faith did affect our scholarship . . . given that we regularly encountered stories in popular books and other media of prominent Bible scholars who left the faith as a result of their scholarship, and personally knew others who journeyed similar paths, away from faith, was their more to this story?"[6]

The editors decided to form a collection of "life stories by a diverse group of prominent—indeed some of the most influential and popular—Bible scholars."[7] They

1. Byron and Lohr, *I (Still) Believe*, 11.
2. Ibid.
3. Ibid.
4. Ibid.
5. Ibid.
6. Ibid., 12.
7. Ibid.

continue, "All of them [i.e., the featured scholars' life stories] explore how faith and biblical scholarship intersect, each in their own way. All of them engage with the ever-important question of how serious study of the Bible affects, whether to threaten or enhance (or both), one's faith."[8] Importantly, therefore, the book reveals the impact and importance that these mentors have had upon the live of other students and how these featured mentors were influenced by their own education and mentors that mentored them—i.e., "one area in which it seems our contributors are almost completely unanimous was in their indebtedness to their own professors, teachers in whose footsteps they followed."[9] The goal of the editors compilation of these "testimonies" is stated as to strengthen other mentors: "The essays you are about to read have strengthened our walks and blessed our way. We hope they strengthen and bless you too."[10] They above all "hope this collection brings glory and honor to the One who lives and reigns with God the Father."[11]

In evaluating this work, the present writer was not strengthened in his faith or blessed. To put it bluntly, many of the scholars featured revealed a shocking departure from a faithful teaching of God's Word. What is revealed, perhaps inadvertently in this work, is how far afield many who train our future generations have gone from teaching trust and confidence in God's Word, and instead, have sown seeds of doubt and uncertainty in the future generations that God has placed under their sphere of influence. Instead of faithfulness, a strong tendency to the exaltation of scholarship over the Lordship of God and his Word is shown to be pervasive in some of these testimonies. The book's goal, to bring "glory and honor" to God, fails miserably among some of these testimonies, since they reveal a high-handed rejection of God's sovereignty over his Word, i.e., what God plainly says is not what he really means or cannot really be trusted. Many of these evangelical mentors were mentored or influenced by others who were either completely unbelievers in secular university who raise up great doubt in them through their instruction under them or by other evangelicals who were experiencing great crisis of doubt themselves. These influences were then passed on to others sitting in evangelical churches, colleges and seminaries. While perhaps not all these testimonies contained in the book were entirely negative in the impact of mentoring, a significant portion of these testimonies leave the reader with the startling conclusion that evangelicals are in trouble not merely because of the influence of the world from the outside but also because of an infiltration of a negative influence in mentoring in the church from within.

Due to space limitations, four examples must suffice. The readers of this review are encouraged to examine the other testimonies in the work. One must note that this article is in no way questioning the *renowned scholarship* of those being reviewed, but

---

8. Ibid., 13.
9. Ibid., 14.
10. Ibid., 16.
11. Ibid.

what is being questioned is the startlingly negative potential impact of what they teach (content of the teaching) to those who were influenced by them under their ministry in the church or classroom as disciples (future pastors and educators) of God's people, especially as centering on the how they influenced minds regarding the trustworthiness and integrity of God's Word. The point being driven home in this review is that mentoring among evangelicals is crucial and that mentoring is not being examined carefully or closely by evangelicals as a whole.

## Example Number One: Donald Hagner—Historical Criticism and the Wondrous Freedom from Any Ideas of the Inerrancy God's Word

Hagner's testimony brings into sharp focus the current state of mentoring at many evangelical seminaries. Although he attended a variety of Lutheran and "fundamentalist" churches in his youth, Hagner relates that "philosophy could be dangerous to your faith," so that by his junior year at Northwestern University, on a music scholarship, "I was calling myself an agnostic. . . . My faith was easily demolished. I was in fact defenseless. . . . I was a lapsed Christian."[12] Fortunately, a Christian reached out to Hagner, and "I began to reconsider Christianity" so that "at the end of my four year stint in the band I was back on tract and decided to go to seminary."[13] He enrolled at Covenant Seminary, but he found it "academically rather disappointing."[14] Why? He relates the reason, "There was no encouragement of critical thinking"[15] and "the seminary seemed to reflect a fortress mentality."[16] Perhaps, however, the following quote, clearly expresses the mentoring that Hagner provided to his students (and readers): "The seminary's [Covenant] stance on inerrancy had a paralyzing effect when it came to biblical scholarship. Serious work with the text had to yield to forced harmonization."[17] Instead, Hagner found a blessing in "critical approaches to the Bible, which can be intrinsically risky to the believer."[18] He believes that these critical approaches can be "purged from its unjustifiable presuppositions" and "no ultimate threat to the believer" (108). In terms of inspiration, Hagner maintains that "conservatives" "welcome criticism [of Scripture] and be willing to join in it."[19] For Hagner, "that the Bible claims inspiration is patent. The problem is to determine the nature of that inspiration in light of the phenomena therein." He outright rejects the deductive approach to inspiration that would assert that "the Bible is the word of God;

12. Hagner, "Faith, Historical Criticism, and the Grace of God," 106–7.
13. Ibid., 107.
14. Ibid.
15. Ibid.
16. Ibid.
17. Ibid.
18. Ibid., 108.
19. Ibid.

## Part 1—Inerrancy Defined

God does not lie, therefore there are no 'errors' in the Bible,"[20] since such a criteria "results often in the imposing our own criteria upon the Scripture (a particular level of exactness of detail in chronological numbers, Synoptic agreement, and so forth) that may have been no concern to the original authors."[21] He admits, however, that because of the "critical method" that he favors, "many, including friends of mine, have lost their faith when they encountered critical thinking from their professors."[22] However, Hagner especially blames "fundamentalist contexts" for loss of faith instead: "Some who have lost their faith through their studies are often driven away from believing by fundamentalist contexts which allowed them no alternative between, on the one hand, a closed-minded, clench-fisted, fear-ridden mentality and, on the other, outright unbelief, whether agnostic or atheistic."[23]

Apparently, Hagner believes in a "goldilocks" position of some kind of partial belief in Scripture. He praises Fuller Theological Seminary where he taught for so many years, for dropping in 1972 the language in the doctrinal commitment of "'free from error in the whole and in part' from its description of Scripture."[24] He prefers the idea that Scripture is a "trustworthy record," "given by divine inspiration," and is "the only infallible rule of faith and practice."[25] He rejects the term "inerrancy" because it functions as a "shibboleth" that in his mind has little apparent meaning, i.e., the word "'inerrancy' is difficult to define." He does not find the word "inerrant" as "helpful" in describing Scripture. Instead, he accepts that inerrancy would only be applied to intention of the author, "I accepted inerrancy only in terms of the intention of the authors, and not as determined by criteria external to the text itself."[26] He especially reacts to Harold Lindsell, also a Fuller professor, whose view of inerrancy he describes as "flat-footed, literalistic interpretation that refuses to face the reality of Scripture as God has given it to us."[27] He especially criticizes Lindsell for not recognizing the Scripture as "the words of human beings."[28] Instead, Hagner likes "open inerrancy" as a term that apparently allows for errors in the Bible as "breathing room for the scholar to deal with the actual phenomena . . . in the Scripture."[29]

Yet, Hagner ironically has a patent ignorance of the Chicago Statement on Inerrancy.[30] He erroneously ascribes to the Chicago Statement as agreeing with his position

20. Ibid., 108–9.
21. Ibid., 109.
22. Ibid.
23. Ibid.
24. Ibid.
25. Ibid., 109–10.
26. Ibid., 110.
27. Ibid.
28. Ibid.
29. Ibid., 111.
30. Ibid.

by citing ICBI article XIII, "We deny that it is proper to evaluate Scripture according to standards of truth and error that are alien to its original purpose." However, R. C. Sproul, a founding member of ICBI on inerrancy, noted regarding the committee's formulation of this article the exact opposite intent of Hagner's application,

> By biblical standards of truth and error is meant the view used both in the Bible and in everyday life, viz., a correspondence view of truth. This part of the article is directed toward those who would redefine truth to relate merely to redemptive intent, the purely personal or the like, rather than to mean that which corresponds with reality. For example, when Jesus affirmed that Jonah was in "the belly of the great fish" this statement is true, not simply because of the redemptive significance the story of Jonah has, but also because it is literally and historically true. The same may be said of the New Testament assertions about Adam, Moses, David and other Old Testament persons as well as about Old Testament events.[31]

The correspondence view of truth that is anchored to this statement would immediately rule out the kind of biblical interpretation or "historical criticism" that Hagner advocates, for it affirms the plain, normal sense of Scripture as the meaning of the passage by referencing the "correspondence view of truth," i.e., the Bible.

In contrast, using historical-critical ideology, Hagner maintains that in his Word commentary on Matthew (*Matthew 1–13*) regarding the infancy narratives, he "decided not to defend the historicity of each event and each detail of each event"[32] Instead, he "took as a beginning presupposition that every pericope has a historical core that was transmitted carefully, but also worked with creatively by the evangelist," preferring Birger Gerhadsson's approach, who mentored Hagner during a sabbatical, wherein was advocated "a middle way between belief in inerrant documents immune from critical judgment and the skepticism of more radical criticism."[33] Hagner asserts that "I discovered further that my faith in the basic reliability of the Gospels is not undermined if, in a few rare instances, I may suspect the actual historicity of a report."[34] For Hagner, such assertions as the resurrection of the saints in Matthew 27:51–54 was not an actual, historical event: "I could not convince myself that the narrative of the resurrected saints who walked into Jerusalem and were seen by many (27:51–54) was an actual occurrence.[35] Hagner asserts that the resurrection of saints at Jesus' death did not occur historically. For Hagner, the earliest Christians interpreted the open tombs, that were really caused by an earthquake, mistakenly as resurrection. "In my opinion the evangelist was handing down a piece of tradition that originated with the

---

31. ICBI, *Commentary on Inerrancy*, Sproul, 50.
32. Ibid., 112.
33. See Gerhardsson, *Reliability of the Gospel Tradition*, 86–87.
34. Hagner, "Faith, Historical Criticism, and the Grace of God," 112.
35. Ibid.

earthquake that took place at the death of Jesus. It was the sight of open tombs that made the Christians think of resurrection, anticipating the imminent resurrection of Jesus, that produced this theologically [*but* not historically] correct story."[36] Yet, one wonders about Hagner's logic here since he believes the early Christians were mistaken about the resurrection of the saints, what stops this kind of logic from being applied to Jesus' resurrection in that the earliest Christians mistook the rolled away stone for the resurrection of Jesus and that his alleged appearances were figments of imagination like he contends for the saints who appeared to many.

Hagner also believes that Jesus' disciples also misunderstood and misapplied the "imminence sayings" in Matthew. He argues, "As I tried to make sense of the various eschatological sayings in Matthew, only one answer seemed to make all the data understandable. The imminence sayings concerning the coming of the Son of Man (10:23; 16:28; 24:34) all refer to the fall of Jerusalem, but because the disciples could not separate the destruction of the temple from the coming of the end of the age (see 24:3), the imminence because attached also to the end of the age. May not the disciples be excused for being a little confused on eschatology (as in Acts 1:6–7)."[37]

One is left wondering with Hagner's historical-critical approach, where this "confusion" beings and ends, leaving one absolutely confused as to what to trust about their understanding of future events in other portions of the New Testament and not merely here, i.e., Hagner's logic cannot be limited to a few instances of his choosing! Hagner insists, however, that "these conclusions do not undermine my strong conviction concerning *the overall* [emphasis added] reliability and inspiration of the Gospels nor of the truth of Christianity. Grant me a historical core, and I can be content with approximations and interpretations. I do not need the ipsissima verba, the precise word of Jesus . . . it is sufficient to have the ipsissima vox, a re-expression of what he said, and even in highly interpreted form . . . under the inspiration of writers and their circle. Truthful narratives are possible without exact words or exactly accurate accounts."[38] Thus, for Hagner, his view of inspiration allows for discrepancies and errors due to human involvement in their composition because "God . . . was pleased to give us Scripture via the words of human authors."[39]

Moreover, Hagner affirms that the Chicago Statements advocated "historical-grammatical" criticism of the Bible that affirms the plain, normal sense of Scripture rather than Hagner's "historical-critical" approach: On the contrary, both the correspondence view of truth and the historical-grammatical view of interpretation demand that the doctrine of inerrancy as embraced by ICBI is claiming that the belief in biblical inerrancy entails actual truths about reality.[40]

---

36. Ibid., 112–13.
37. Ibid., 113.
38. Ibid.
39. Ibid.
40. ICBI, *Commentary on Inerrancy*, Sproule, 11.

In spite of these negations of the historicity or factuality of the Gospel content and his being mentored by more liberal-leaning Tübingen scholars like Hengel, Hofius and Stuhlmacher during a sabbatical, Hagner was "won over" to these professors' "*scholarship and faith*" due to the "convincing power and plausibility of their credible work, their reverence for Scripture, and their confidence that scholarship that was superior to that of liberals vindicated the faith of their church."[41] One is left wondering about Hagner's assertions here; specifically one is left with the impression that in Hagner's way of thinking anyone who fully trusted the Scripture in its content, as the three hundred ICBI theologians did, would not be true scholars in Hagner's assessment. They would be considered more naïve simpletons who failed to appreciate the superior critical judgment of historical critics.

He alleges that "practitioners of the critical method should therefore be prime models of humility."[42] The reader of his article, however, is not given that impression of Hagner's assessment of himself since a very strong underlying tone is his hubris in being a judge of Scripture; a final arbiter of what can and cannot be accepted in Scripture as to its truthworthiness, integrity, historicity and meaning. Hagner presides as judge, i.e., "lord," over Scripture, rather than allowing Scripture to stand as judge in its plain, normal sense over the actions of Hagner's interpretive ploys. This arrogance is demonstrated when Hagner affirms, with George Ladd, the impossibility of any certainty in knowledge of the contents of Bible ("authority of the Bible as the Word of God is not dependent upon infallible certainty in all matters of history and criticism").[43] Apparently, for Hagner and Ladd, God's communication of truth has the limitations of doubt and uncertainty that cannot be overridden due to the human content of the work. Hagner continues to note that "I have . . . had doubts about the truth of Christianity now and then. . . . When I have been tempted to doubt the truth of Christianity I have discovered that I really cannot."[44] Apparently, for Hagner some type of personal, existential affirmation, in spite of his historical-critical approach to negating portions of Scripture, compel his belief that Christianity is true, for he confesses that his confidence lies in his "historical reasoning . . . [but] it does not amount to absolute proof [since] nothing can be proved absolutely."[45] Apparently, this lack of certainty applies to Scripture for Hagner.

In sum, what has disciples who learned under Hagner's mentorship come to learn about Scripture? They are seeded in thought with a profound sense of doubt and uncertainty in God's Word but also profound sense of the certainty of historical-criticism to evaluate the Bible.

---

41. Hagner, "Faith, Historical Criticism, and the Grace of God," 113.
42. Ibid., 114.
43. Ibid., 114–15; cf. Ladd, *New Testament and Criticism*, 17.
44. Hagner, "Faith, Historical Criticism, and the Grace of God," 115.
45. Ibid.

Part 1—Inerrancy Defined

## Example Number Two: Bruce Waltke—Historical Criticism of Sources and Scientism of Evolution Override the Plain, Norman Meaning

Another scholar addressed in the work is Bruce K. Waltke. Waltke affirms, "My faith in the inerrancy of Scripture as to its Source and its infallibility as to its authority for faith and practice was firmly rooted in my formative years."[46] This is well and good. Please notice, however, that Waltke appears to limit inerrancy/infallibility to "faith and practice." Although a Christian at a very young age due to the influence of his mother, he reveals that his college years were filled with doubt and uncertainty while studying history and philosophy (e.g., Voltaire and Rousseau). While he overcame his crisis of faith, he still continued with "doubt about my inherited high view of the Bible's inspiration."[47] For him, such uncertainty was "fueled by the Bible's apparent contradictions; by its numerous textual variants in ancient Hebrew manuscripts and versions of the Bible; by questions of higher criticism . . . and by the fossil record, which calls into question the historical reliability of Genesis 1."[48]

In terms of Bible discrepancies, he believes that "most" but "not all" can be eliminated (242). Attending Harvard, however, for his doctorate, he confronted "intellectual problems to my faith" (243). He notes, "Harvard emphasized their similarity [between the OT and ancient Near Eastern literatures], and this similarity makes the Bible appear to be a very human—not a divinely inspired—book. The cosmology of Genesis 1 is similar to pagan cosmologies of the biblical Word; Moses' book of the covenant at some points repeats word-for-word the Code of Hamurabi; the war annals of the historical book resemble those of the pagans; David's psalms are similar to Sumerian, Akkadian, and Canaanite hymns."[49]

The good news is that Waltke believes his faith was still intact. He praises his "Harvard professors, who accepted me graciously and honed me into a scholar."[50] Yet their influence upon him was apparently profound. He now believes in a form of documentary hypothesis rather than Mosaic, eyewitness authorship. He admits that now he does not hold to the Mosaic authorship of the Pentateuch: "During my career I rethought the authorship of the Pentateuch. Changes in the divine name . . . of vocabulary and style . . . of theological perspective strongly argue that the Pentateuch is composed of at least three sources documents" (i.e., J, P, D). Thus, he adopts the idea that "the scientific evidence that the Pentateuch is composed of documents is compelling."[51] He also believes that Deuteronomy's "canonical form" is "a postexilic work that recounts the history of Moses' writing the book of the law." He sums

---

46. Waltke, "Why I Have Kept the Faith," 237.
47. Ibid., 239.
48. Ibid., 239–40.
49. Ibid., 243–44.
50. Ibid., 245.
51. Ibid., 247.

up that "I accept the documentary hypothesis, but I do not accept *the* documentary hypothesis of Wellhausen."[52] Moreover, he believes that the book of Isaiah had at least two authors, "conservative response [to multiple Isaiah authorship] has been overreactionary,"[53] and "as Jesus blends Elijah with John the Baptist, the book of Isaiah blends Isaiah with his disciple."[54]

He sums up his position by affirming, "I am not a Fundamentalist, who stands upon the Word of God, convinced that the preconceived interpretations of my tradition are right or that my interpretations are inerrant."[55] As such, he regards the early chapters of Genesis "as recounting real history in the garb of the ancient Near Eastern mythological imagery, and so interpret the fossil record with mainstream science. I believe *that* theistic evolution is a possible synthesis of Scripture and science, but I do not believe *in* theistic evolution."[56] One wonders, however, where Genesis as "Near Eastern mythological imagery," as Waltke asserts, begins and ends as myth, i.e., what can be truly understood as historical in the account at all.

He concludes that "I hope that those who plan on an academic career in biblical studies will find these reflections on apologetics and biblical criticism helpful to their faith in the Bible's inspiration and authority."[57] Oddly, how could a student being mentored under Waltke's approach in thinking ever being strengthened in faith? Waltke has called into question large parts of the Old Testament in terms of historicity, factuality and authorship. Prophecy as supernatural has been discounted in seeing two Isaiahs. The student under his mentorship would most likely be filled with doubts about the assuredness of God's Word. His education has enlightened him to place the burden on proof on Scripture, i.e., doubt.

## Example Number Three: Jimmy Dunn—Searching for Jesus with Doubt and Uncertainty as Prime Virtues Directed against God's Word

Another mentor featured is that of James D. G. Dunn, who titles his testimony "In Quest of Truth."[58] Dunn was mentored by C. F. D. Moule at Cambridge as well as Tyndale House.[59] While he began under a conservative bent as "one of the leaders of a conservative evangelical faction" in Glascow and Trinity College, Dunn relates that "probing questions below the surface of faith began to predominate."[60] An

52. Ibid.
53. Ibid.
54. Ibid.
55. Ibid., 247–48.
56. Ibid., 248.
57. Ibid., 249.
58. Dunn, "In Quest of Truth," 55.
59. Ibid., 57.
60. Ibid.

## Part 1—Inerrancy Defined

"international group of evangelical New Testament postgraduates who came together in Cambridge a that time began to hold regular meetings to explore how their historical and theological explanations were affecting their overview of Scripture."[61] Dunn began to break "a previous unwillingness to question the infallibility of the Bible" through his doubts about the authorship of 2 Peter as not being written by the historical apostle.[62] He decided that such questions did not set him on a "slippery slope, down to which you would slide unavoidably into unbelief."[63] He also prided himself on being able to distinguish "things that really mattered from those which mattered less or not much at all."[64] Further, he asserts that "one could see Scripture though which God speaks without making that dependent on Scripture as infallible."[65] He no longer made his faith "depend on minor matters of detail . . . [when] could already see clearly, was likely to prove disastrous when some detail proved to be questionable."[66] He kept the focus of faith on "the primary points in biblical passages . . . and fellowship could extend across a wide range of faith tradition."[67] He does not specify the criteria by which he would determine "primary points" from minor ones in the biblical data or what the cumulative impact of increasingly numerous "minor" points would do to his conceptions of trust in God's Word.

His research in publishing lead him to "turn to explore what was primary and what was secondary in the Christian faith."[68] He appreciated his discussion groups that he had experienced at Cambridge where "we could be totally honest—not least about doubts, questions, and failures—and still be fully accepted."[69] He "came to the conclusion of the centrality of Christ (one might say the sole centrality of Christ) for the Christian faith and the beginnings of Christianity . . . how the doctrine of the incarnation came about."[70] He insists "that one should read the New Testament's Christological statements without using the spectacles of later church doctrine, but also that the relevant New Testament passages were not already fixed in meaning, but were expressing the developing understanding of first Christians."[71] For Dunn, "holding together the man Jesus and the Christ of God has never been easy!"[72]

---

61. Ibid.
62. Ibid.
63. Ibid.
64. Ibid.
65. Ibid.
66. Ibid., 58.
67. Ibid.
68. Ibid., 60.
69. Ibid.
70. Ibid., 61.
71. Ibid., 61.
72. Ibid.

At his tenure at the University of Durham, Dunn became a strong advocate for the New Perspective on Paul wherein he went against the Reformation perspective, arguing that danger existed in the Reformation position since Paul was "much more positive" "on the Judaism of his upbringing" than was the Reformation position of "anti-Judaism."[73] He relates also that "with my personal evangelical history, the issue of the authority of Scripture was never far from me, from my more conservative days in Glasgow through the deepening of insight and discussion in Cambridge and thereafter."[74] Dunn came to the position that "Christian fundamentalism" displayed "narrowness."[75] In turn, he began to engage in advocating a third "search" for what is now termed the "historical Jesus."[76]

One work that he engaged in deserves special attention, that he titled *Jesus Remembered* (Eerdmans, 2003). To this present writer, it is this book that clearly delineates Dunn's departure from his alleged label as a leader of "a conservative evangelical faction."[77] In Dunn's work *Jesus Remembered* (2003), he states that third questers consider the neglect of the "Jewishness of Jesus" as "the most blatant disregard of history in the quest."[78]

The following analysis is derived from this reviewer's analysis of evangelical questing in *The Jesus Quest the Danger from Within*, 392–95, and the reader is encouraged to read the original article for a fuller presentation of the issue. For Dunn, those who seek knowledge of Jesus' life at best can hope for "probability, not certainty" when examining the Gospel accounts. He makes his own critical distinction between event, data, and fact in the formulation of historical events in the canonical Gospels:

> All the historian has available are the "data" which have come down through history—personal diaries, reminiscences of eyewitnesses, reports constructed from people who were present, perhaps some archaeological artifacts, as well as circumstantial data about climate, commercial practice, and laws of the time. . . . From these the historian attempts to reconstruct "facts." The facts are not to be identified as data; they are always an *interpretation* [italics in original] of the data. Nor should the fact be identified with the event itself, though it will always be in some degree of approximation to the event. Where the data are abundant and consistent, the responsible historian may be confident of achieving a reasonably close approximation. Where they are much more fragmentary and often inconsistent, confidence in achieving a closes approximation is bound to be much less. It is for this reason that the critical scholar

---

73. Ibid., 63, cf. also a sharp critique of the *New Perspective on Paul* (by Dunn et al.) by F. David Farnell, "The Problem of Philosophy in New Testament Studies," in *Jesus Quest*, 86–142.

74. Ibid.

75. Ibid., 64.

76. Ibid., 66.

77. Ibid., 67.

78. Dunn, *Jesus Remembered*, 92.

learns to make carefully graded judgments which reflect the quality of the data—almost certain (never simply "certain"), very probable, probable, likely, possible, and so on. In historical scholarship the judgment "probable" is a very positive verdict. And given that more data always emerge—in ancient history, a new inscription or, prize of prizes, a new cache of scrolls or documents—any judgment will have to be provisional, always subject to the revision necessitated by new evidence or by new ways of evaluating the old evidence.[79]

For Dunn, "'facts' properly speaking are always and never more than interpretations of the data. . . . The Gospel accounts are themselves such data or, if you like hard facts. But the events to which the Gospels refer are not themselves 'hard facts'; they are facts only in the sense that we interpret the text, together with such other data as we have, to reach a conclusion regarding the events as best we are able."[80] Dunn defines the Gospel "facts" as "interpretations of the data" regarding the events to which they refer. They do not have certainty since they are mediated through the evangelists' interpretation of those events and "the possibility that later faith has in some degree covered over the historical actuality cannot be dismissed as out of the question." The consequence of his thinking is that "historical methodology can only produce probabilities, the probability that some event took place in such circumstances being greater or smaller, depending on the quality of the data and the perspective of the historical enquirer."[81]

At best, to Dunn, the Gospels may give probabilities, but certainty is not a factor in historiography. In references to miracles, Dunn relates,

> It was the Enlightenment assumption that necessary truths of reason are like mathematical axioms, and that what is in view is the certain QED of mathematical proof that has skewed the whole question. But faith moves in a totally different realm from mathematics. The language of faith uses words like "confidence" and "assurance" rather than "certainty." Faith deals in trust, not in mathematical calculations, nor in a "science" which methodologically doubts everything which can be doubted. Nor is it to be defined simply as "assent to propositions as true" (Newman). Walking "by faith" is different from walking "by sight" (2 Cor. 5:7). Faith is commitment, not just conviction.[82]

To Dunn, "it is the 'lust for certainty' which leads to fundamentalism's absolutizing of its own faith claims and dismissal of others."[83] In chastising evangelicals for their greater certainty regarding the Gospels and their supernatural elements, he relates that only probability—not certainty—is the stinging "nettle" that evangelical Chris-

---

79. Ibid, 102–3.
80. Dunn, "Response to Darrell Bock," in *Historical Jesus: Five Views*, 299.
81. Ibid., 299–300.
82. Dunn, *Jesus Remembered*, 104.
83. Ibid.

tians must grasp, qualifying his remark by noting that "genuinely critical historical inquiry is necessary if we are to get as close to the historical as possible. *Critical* [italics in original] here, and this is the point, should not be taken to mean negatively critical, hermeneutical suspicion, or dismissal of any material that has overtones of Easter faith. It means, more straightforwardly, a careful scrutiny of all the relevant data to gain as accurate or as historically responsible a picture as possible."[84] Dunn notes, "In a day when *evangelical*, and even *Christian* [italics in original], is often identified with a strongly right-wing, conservative and even fundamentalist attitude toward the Bible, it is important that responsible evangelical scholars defend and advocate such critical historical inquiry."[85] In this way, for Dunn, the term "evangelical (not to mention Christian) can again become a label that men and women of integrity and good will can respect and hope to learn from more than most seem to do today."[86] Apparently, anyone who holds to certainty regarding such miracles as Christ's resurrection moves into this criticism by Dunn. As to the greatest event in the Gospels, the resurrection of Jesus (Acts 1:3), Dunn, comparing the Passion accounts in the Gospels to that of Second Temple Judaism's literature, relates that Jesus' hope for resurrection reflected more of the ideas of Second Temple Judaism's concept of vindication hope of a general and final resurrection: "The probability remains, however, that any hope of resurrection entertained by Jesus himself was hope to share in the final resurrection."[87] For Dunn, Jesus had in mind that "his death would introduce the final climactic period, to be followed shortly ('after three days'?) by the general resurrection, the implementation of the new covenant, and the coming of the kingdom."[88] Yet, even to speculate this much on the resurrection, he turns negative: "To be even able to say as much is to say more than historical questers have usually allowed."[89] For Dunn, any proof of Jesus' resurrection centers in the "impact made by Jesus as it impressed itself into the tradition." This "impact summarized in the word 'resurrection' . . . requires us to concede that there was a something which happened 'on the third day' which could only be apprehended/conceptualized as 'resurrection.'"[90] Dunn summarizes his thinking on data and facts regarding the resurrection:

> The resurrection certainly cannot be numbered among the data which have come down to us. Nor can we speak of empty tomb and resurrection appearances as data. The data are *reports* [italics in original] of empty tomb and of seeing/visions of Jesus. If historical facts are *interpretations* [italics in original] of the data, then the historical facts in this case, properly speaking, are

84. Dunn, "Response to Darrell Bock," in *Historical Jesus: Five Views*, 300.
85. Ibid., 300.
86. Ibid.
87. Dunn, *Jesus Remembered*, 821–24 (824).
88. Ibid., 824.
89. Ibid.
90. Ibid., 876.

at best the fact of the empty tomb, and the fact that disciples saw Jesus. The conclusion, "Jesus has been raised from the dead," is further interpretation, an interpretation of interpreted data, an interpretation of the facts. The resurrection of Jesus, in other words, is at best a second order "fact," not a first order "fact"—an interpretation of an interpretation.[91]

Dunn's thinking here reflects the skepticism of Hume as well as Kant, having praised the former by stating, "As David Hume had earlier pointed out, it is more probable that the account of a miracle is an untrue account than the miracle recounted actually took place."[92] Therefore Jesus being raised from the dead was possibly just an interpretation by the first disciples. For Dunn, this is why the resurrection of Jesus is so "problematic" for the twenty-first century quester:

> The conclusion that "God has raised Jesus from the dead," as a conclusion of the quest, is a further act of interpretation—again, an interpretation (evaluation) of the first-century interpretation (evaluation) of the first-century interpretation . . . that departure from this life (death) can be described as a historical event, whereas entry on to some further existence can hardly be so described—it can be seen just how problematic it is to speak of the resurrection of Jesus as historical.[93]

Dunn also describes the term "resurrection" as a "metaphor" wherein he says that "the power of a metaphor is the power 'to describe a reality inaccessible to direct description' (Ricoeur), 'reality depicting without pretending to be directly descriptive' (Martin Soskice)." Thus in Dunn's thinking it defines an undefinable something—"*something which could not otherwise be said*" (italics in original). Furthermore, "to translate 'resurrection' into something more 'literal' is not to translate it but to abandon it" and, he notes,

> Christians have continued to affirm the resurrection of Jesus, as I do, not because they know what it means. Rather, they do so because, like the affirmation of Jesus as God's Son, "the resurrection of Jesus" has proved the most satisfying and enduring of a variety of options, all of them inadequate in one degree or other as human speech, to sum up the impact made by Jesus, the Christian perception of his significance. . . . In short, the "resurrection of Jesus" is not so much a criterion of faith as a paradigm for hope.[94]

If one applied this same logic to Dunn's writing, then the data of his writing are merely interpreted facts of what Dunn certainly intended to express, and therefore, no one can be certain as to what Dunn meant except that what he says is a metaphor for

---

91. Ibid., 877.
92. Ibid., 103–4.
93. Ibid., 877.
94. Ibid., 878–79.

what he meant because it is beyond anyone's true comprehension to discern the intentions only understood by Dunn himself. Thus Dunn offers us, as he did with Paul, "a new perspective on the Jesus tradition."[95]

## Example Number Four: Scot McKnight—Scholarship Reigns over Lordship and the Inerrancy of Scripture

One other example of scholar mentioned in this sampling from *I (Still) Believe* who mentored students is that of Scot McKnight. Being associated in his youth with a baptistic background ("my father was a deacon at First Baptist Church"), McKnight relates that "as a child I was saved one night kneeling at a chair with my mother and father."[96] He later would experience what he termed a "rededicated" life because of a "backslidden" condition.[97] After rededicating his life, he "was given a voracious desire to study and know the Bible, to comprehend theology, and to become a teacher someday."[98] McKnight admits, however, that

> in my junior and senior year I became embittered about fundamentalism, and the leading impulse was the work of Francis Schaeffer. Ironically, Francis Schaeffer was a fundamentalist but was also critical of the shallowness of the American evangelical church. At that time I had not known the difference between an evangelical and a fundamentalist but a summer missionary experience in Austria with reading people like John Stott led me to see that I was an evangelical and no longer a fundamentalist. I became critical of fundamentalism enough that there were times when I was no longer sure what I believed. Seminary and later doctoral studies helped me sort out my faith.[99]

He attended Trinity Evangelical Divinity School where he came under the influence of such mentors as Murray Harris, Douglas Moo, and Grant Osborne, to name only a few. He notes that "it was at Trinity, under the tutelage of Walter Liefield and Grant Osborne, that I fell in love with Jesus and it was during that time my faith was formed christocentrically. Prior to that time my faith was fundamentalistic, systematic, and reactive. During those days I found what needs to be at the center of Christian faith: God in Christ."

Nottingham University accepted him as a doctoral student, where James D. G. Dunn "admitted me and became both a wonderful mentor to my research and now a friend (even if he will always be my Doktorvater)."[100] Later he would replace

---

95. Ibid., 881.
96. McNight, "Man of Two Places," 160.
97. Ibid., 161.
98. Ibid.
99. Ibid., 162–63.
100. Ibid., 164.

Wayne Grudem at Trinity as a New Testament professor.[101] He now teaches at Northern Seminary.[102]

He admits that "first as a college student, but then even more in my seminary education and especially in my doctoral studies, minute comparison of the Synoptic Gospels shook what I had been taught about the doctrine of Scripture."[103] He notes that he now believes that the OT and NT is "not one self-contained text added to the previous but one text interacting—sometimes agreeing, sometimes even disagreeing, but often expanding and adjusting and renewing the previous texts. God's inspiration then is at work in a history and a community expressed by an author for a given moment."[104] He continues, "This experience of underlining the Synoptics one word and one line after another led me to think that the words like 'inerrancy' are inadequate descriptions of what is going on in the Bible. I have for a long time preferred the word 'true' or 'truth.' The Bible is God's true and living Word is far more in line with the realities of the Bible itself than the political term that have arisen among evangelicals in the twentieth century."[105] As a result, he joined into the third search for the "historical Jesus" but has now rejected it because "historical Jesus studies yields limited conclusions. . . . . I can prove that Jesus died but I can never prove that he died *for my sins*; I can prove that Jesus asserted that he would be raised from the dead but I can never prove he rose *for my justification*; the historical method can only do so much."[106] He asserts that the church "*does not need historical Jesus studies.*"[107] Also, he relates that "I have come to the conclusion that the Gospels are the church's portrait of Jesus, and that portrait is what the church needs most."[108] He considers Jimmy Dunn's *Jesus Remembered* as a very good example of good research.

He concludes that in his experience, "many former believers walk away more often [from the Christian faith] because of superficial theology of Scripture they are taught in conservative circles. Or because they have combined that kind of Scripture theory with a sudden encounter with the science of evolution . . . but when someone is reared in the faith to think it is all or nothing and that Genesis 1–3 describe the world about 6,000 or 10,000 or 20,000 years ago and they suddenly learn that the universe is 14.5 billion years old and that our DNA emerges out of hominid ancestors way more than even 20,000 their entire faith can be turned inside out." And again, "I am grateful that I learned about science from some theologians who did not diminish science,

---

101. Ibid., 165.
102. Ibid., 166.
103. Ibid., 167.
104. Ibid.
105. Ibid., 167–68.
106. Ibid., 168.
107. Ibid., italics in original.
108. Ibid.

as it often is in some conservative circles, but who slowly and patiently worked out theology in conversation with science."[109]

When he is often asked to address Christians who are losing their faith, he tries is to "distance their faith from what they have learned, from the theology that they have embraced, and to try to get them to think about Jesus—the Jesus of the Gospels—what he taught, what he did, what he reveals about God, and if he is God, what he reveals God to be like."[110]

## CONCLUSION: THE NEED FOR REPENTANCE BY SOME EVANGELICAL SCHOLARS

This article began by noting that Jesus called the Pharisees "sons of hell" (gehenna) because they overturned the Word of God for their traditions. The educated rabbis taught the teaching of men and nullified the Word of God. What these sampling of testimonies from *I (Still) Believe* has demonstrated the very same approach among Christian "rabbis" or "teachers." They have used historical criticism ("teaching of men") to negate the plain, normal sense of God. These evangelical historical-critical scholars overturn the Word like the rabbis of Judaism.

Just like the rabbis, they have questioned God's Word and "defeated God" as not being able to guarantee the absolute truth of his Word. What kind of God do they imagine that they confess to serve that cannot preserve the factuality, integrity and historical veracity of his Word? Their God is weak, subject to the vascilations of human weakness that apparently their God cannot overcome when he inspired his inerrant Word, a term that they reject as liberating. They revile those who reject inerrancy and inspiration of God's Word in an orthodox sense and refuse to give in to "scientific thinking." They consider themselves to be the arbiters of what can and cannot be accepted as historical, factual and actual in God's Word. *How many students have they trained* who will become more radical than their teachers, just like Jesus said of the Pharisees? They spread doubt and uncertainty about the written word, all the while, confirming the certainty of their teachings and conclusions. The Word of God is the clear looser in their approaches. Their kind of apologetic "defense" actually is a clever undermining and attack on God's nature and God's Word.

The question left unanswered in this book regarding many of these evangelical scholars from a variety of Christian schools and seminaries is left hanging: Do they *really, truly still believe*? The evidence from their own testimony leaves that answer in grave doubt, at least as far as the full inerrancy of the Bible is concerned. How many preachers and future teachers have been infected and will be infected in the future with such doubts by these mentors? No wonder Jesus said, "When the Son of Man comes, will He find *the faith* upon the earth?" (Luke 18:8).

109. Ibid., 170.
110. Ibid., 171.

Chapter 5

# Review of *Five Views on Biblical Inerrancy*, edited by J. Merrick and Stephen Garrett[1]

NORMAN L. GEISLER

## INTRODUCTION

The Zondervan general editor of the Counterpoints series, Stanley Gundry, together with his chosen editors, J. Merrick and Stephen Garrett, have produced a provocative book on *Five Views on Biblical Inerrancy* (2013). The five scholar participants are Albert Mohler, Peter Enns, Kevin Vanhoozer, Michael Bird, and John Franke. This Counterpoints series has produced many stimulating dialogues on various topics, and they no doubt intended to do the same on this controversial topic of inerrancy. However, there is a basic problem in the dialogue format as applied to biblical inerrancy.

### There Is Madness in the Method

The "dialogue" method works well for many intramural evangelical discussions like eternal security, the role of women in the ministry, and the like. However, when it is applied to basic issues which help define the nature of evangelicalism, like the nature of Scripture, the method has some serious drawbacks. For if inerrancy is a doctrine that is essential to consistent evangelicalism, as most evangelicals believe that it is, then it seems unfitting to make it subject to the dialogue method for two reasons. First, for many evangelicals the issue of inerrancy is too important to be "up for grabs"

---

1. All references to *Five Views on Biblical Inerrancy* are distinguished in this chapter by name of the contributor rather than by each individual contributor's article title.

on the evangelical dialogue table. Second, just by providing non-inerrantists and anti-inerrantists a "seat at the table" gives a certain undeserved legitimacy to their view. If, as will be shown below, the non-inerrancy view is not biblical, essential, or in accord with the long history of the Christian church, then the dialogue method fails to do justice to the topic because it offers an undeserved platform to those who do not really believe the doctrine. To illustrate, I doubt if one were setting up a conference on the future of Israel that he would invite countries who don't believe in the existence of Israel (like Iran) to the table.

## Stacking the Deck

Not only can the staging of the inerrancy discussion in the *Five Views* book be challenged, but so can the choice of actors on the stage. For the choice of participants in this *Five Views* "dialogue" did not fit the topic in a balanced way. Since the topic was inerrancy and since each participant was explicitly asked to address the Chicago Statement on Biblical Inerrancy (CSBI), the choice of participants was not appropriate. For only one participant (Al Mohler) states his unequivocal belief in the CSBI view of inerrancy produced by the International Council on Biblical Inerrancy (ICBI). Some participants explicitly deny inerrancy.[2]

Others prefer to redefine the CSBI statement before agreeing with it. Still others claim to agree with it, but they do so based on a misunderstanding of what the framers meant by inerrancy, as will be shown below.

What is more, an even greater problem is that none of the framers of the CSBI, whose statement was being attacked, were represented on the panel. Since three of them (J. I. Packer, R. C. Sproul, and N. L. Geisler) are still alive and active, the makeup of the panel was questionable. It is like convening a panel on the First Amendment to the US Constitution while Washington, Adams, and Madison were still alive but not inviting any of them to participate! Further, only one scholar (Al Mohler) was unequivocally in favor of the CSBI view and some were known to be unequivocally against it (like Peter Enns). This is loading the dice against positive results. So, with a stacked deck in the format and the dice loaded in the choice of participants, the probabilities of a positive result were not high, and understandably the result confirms this anticipation.

## UNDERSTANDING INERRANCY

To be sure, whether inerrancy is an essential doctrine is crucial to the point at hand. In order to answer this question more fully, we must first define inerrancy and then evaluate its importance.

---

2. E.g., Enns, *Five Views*, 83–116.

Part 1—Inerrancy Defined

## Definition of Inerrancy

Unless otherwise noted, when we use the word "inerrancy" in this article, we mean inerrancy as understood by the ETS framers and defined by the founders of the CSBI, namely, what is called total or unlimited inerrancy. The CSBI defines inerrancy as *unlimited* inerrancy, whereas many of ETS participants believe in *limited* inerrancy. Unlimited inerrancy affirms that Bible is true on whatever subject is speaks—whether it is redemption, ethics, history, science, or anything else. Limited inerrancy affirms that the Bible's inerrancy is limited to redemptive matters.

The Evangelical Theological Society (ETS), the largest of any society of its kind in the world, with some three thousand members, began in 1948 with only one doctrinal statement: "The Bible alone and the Bible in its entirety is the Word of God written, and therefore inerrant in the autographs." After a controversy in 2003 (concerning Clark Pinnock's view) which involved the meaning of inerrancy, the ETS voted in 2004 to accept "the CSBI as its point of reference for defining inerrancy."[3] It states: "For the purpose of advising members regarding the intent and meaning of the reference to biblical inerrancy in the ETS Doctrinal Basis, the Society refers members to the Chicago Statement on Biblical Inerrancy (1978)."[4] So, for the largest group of scholars believing in inerrancy the officially accepted definition of the term "inerrancy" is that of the CSBI.

The CSBI supports unlimited or total inerrancy, declaring: "The holy Scripture . . . is of divine authority in all matters upon which it touches."[5] Also, "We deny that biblical infallibility and inerrancy are limited to spiritual, religious, or redemptive themes, exclusive of assertions in the fields of history and science."[6] It further declares that: *"The authority of Scripture is inescapably impaired if this total divine inerrancy is in any way limited or disregarded, or made relative to a view of truth contrary to the Bible's own."*[7] As we shall see below, unlimited inerrancy has been the historic position of the Christian church down through the centuries. Thus, the history supporting the doctrine of inerrancy is supporting unlimited inerrancy.

## The Importance of Inerrancy

The question of the importance of inerrancy can be approached both doctrinally and historically. Doctrinally, inerrancy is an important doctrine because: (1) it is attached to the character of God; (2) It is foundational to other essential doctrines; (3) it is taught in the Scriptures; and (4) it is the historic position of the Christian church.

---

3. Garrett with Merrick, "Opening Lines of Communication," 311.
4. Ibid.
5. "Short Statement," 2.
6. CSBI, art. XII.
7. "Short Statement," 5, emphasis added.

## The Doctrinal Importance of Inerrancy

First of all, as the ETS statement declares, inerrancy is based on the character of God who cannot lie (Heb 6:18; Titus 1:2). For it affirms that the Bible is "inerrant" because (note the word "therefore") it is the Word of God. This makes a direct logical connection between inerrancy and the truthfulness of God.

Second, inerrancy is fundamental to all other essential Christian doctrines. It is granted that some other doctrines (like the atoning death and bodily resurrection of Christ) are more essential to salvation. However, all soteriological (salvation-related) doctrines derive their divine authority from the divinely authoritative Word of God. So, in an epistemological (knowledge-related) sense, the doctrine of the divine authority and inerrancy of Scripture is the fundamental of all the fundamentals. And if the fundamental of fundamentals is not fundamental, then what is fundamental? Fundamentally nothing! Thus, while one can be saved without believing in inerrancy, the doctrine of salvation has no divine authority apart from the infallibility and inerrancy of Scripture. This is why Carl Henry (and Al Mohler following him) affirmed correctly that while inerrancy is not necessary to evangelical *authenticity*, it is nonetheless, essential to evangelical *consistency*.[8]

Third, B. B. Warfield correctly noted that the primary basis for believing in the inerrancy of Scripture is that it was taught by Christ and the apostles in the New Testament. And he specified it as unlimited inerrancy,[9] Warfield declared: "We believe in the doctrine of plenary inspiration of the Scriptures primarily because it is the doctrine of Christ and his apostles believed, and which they have taught us."[10] John Wenham in *Christ and the Bible* amply articulated what Christ taught about the Bible, including its inerrancy, for Wenham was one of the international signers of the 1978 *Chicago Statement on Biblical Inerrancy*.[11] Indeed, to quote Jesus himself, "The Scripture cannot be broken" (John 10:35) and "not the smallest letter or stroke shall pass from the Law until all is accomplished" (Matt 5:18). A more complete discussion of what Jesus taught about the Bible is found in chapter 16 of our *Systematic*.[12]

Fourth, inerrancy is the historic position of the Christian church. As Al Mohler pointed out,[13] even some inerrantists have agreed that inerrancy has been the standard view of the Christian church down through the centuries. He cites the Hanson brothers, Anthony and Richard, Anglican scholars, who said, "The Christian Fathers and the medieval tradition continued this belief [in inerrancy], and the Reformation did nothing to weaken it. On the contrary, since for many reformed theologians the

---

8. Mohler, *Five Views*, 29, emphasis added.
9. Warfield, *Inspiration*, 128.
10. Ibid., 128; cited by Mohler, *Five Views*, 42.
11. See Geisler and Roach, *Defending Inerrancy*, 348.
12. Geisler, *Systematic Theology*, 1:266–81.
13. Mohler, *Five Views*, 48–49.

## Part 1—Inerrancy Defined

authority of the Bible took the place which the Pope had held in the medieval scheme of things, the inerrancy of the Bible became more firmly maintained and explicitly defined among some reformed theologians than it had even been before."[14] They added, "The beliefs here denied [viz., inerrancy] have been held by all Christians from the very beginning until about a hundred and fifty years ago."[15]

Inerrancy is a fundamental doctrine since it is fundamental to all other Christian doctrines which derive their authority from the belief that the Bible is the infallible and inerrant Word of God. Indeed, like many other fundamental doctrines (e.g., the Trinity), it is based on a necessary conclusion from biblical truths. The doctrine of inerrancy as defined by CSBI is substantially the same as the doctrine held through the centuries by the Christian church (see discussion below). So, even though it was never put in explicit confessional form in the early church, nevertheless, by its nature as derived from the very nature of God and by its universal acceptance in the Christian church down through the centuries, it has earned a status of tacit catholicity (universality). It thus deserves high regard among evangelicals and has rightly earned the status of being essential (in an epistemological sense) to the Christian faith. Thus, to reduce inerrancy to the level of nonessential or even incidental to the Christian faith, reveals ignorance of its theological and historical roots and is an offense to its watershed importance to a consistent and healthy Christianity. As the CSBI statement declares: "However, we further deny that inerrancy can be rejected without grave consequences, both to the individual and to the church."[16]

## UNJUSTIFIED ASSUMPTIONS ABOUT INERRANCY

A careful reading of the *Five Views* dialogue reveals that not only were the dice loaded against the CSBI inerrancy view by format and by the choice of participants, but there were several anti-inerrancy presuppositions employed by one or more of the participants. One of the most important is the nature of truth.

### The Nature of Truth

The framers of the CSBI strongly affirmed a correspondence view of truth. This is not so of all of the participants in the *Five Views* dialogue. In fact there was a major misreading by many non-inerrantists of article XIII which reads in part: "We deny that it is proper to evaluate Scripture according to standards of truth and error that are alien to its usage or purpose." Some non-inerrantists were willing to subscribe to the CSBI based on their misinterpretation of this statement. Franke claims that "this opens up a vast arena of interpretive possibilities with respect to the 'usage or purpose'

---

14. Hanson and Hanson, *Bible Without Illusions*, 51–52; cited by Mohler, *Five Views*, 41.
15. Ibid., 13.
16. CBSI, art. XIX.

of Scripture in relation to standards of 'truth or error.'"[17] Another non-inerrantist (in the CSBI sense), Clark Pinnock, put it this way: "I supported the 1978 'Chicago Statement on the International Council on Biblical Inerrancy,'" noting that it "made room for nearly every well-intentioned Baptist."[18]

However, the framers of the CSBI anticipated this objection, and R.C. Sproul was commissioned to write an official ICBI commentary on the Chicago Statement which, straight to the point in article XIII, reads: "'*By biblical standards of truth and error' is meant the view used both in the Bible and in everyday life, viz., a correspondence view of truth.* This part of the article is directed at those who would redefine truth to relate merely to redemptive intent, the purely personal, or the like, rather than to mean that which corresponds to reality." Thus, "all the claims of the Bible must correspond with reality, whether that reality is historical, factual, or spiritual."[19] So, non-inerrantists, like Pinnock and Enns, misunderstand the Chicago Statement which demands that truth be defined as correspondence with reality. This is important since to define it another way, for example, in terms of redemptive purpose, is to open the door wide to a denial of the factual inerrancy of the Bible as espoused by CSBI.

## Purpose and Meaning

Another serious mistake of some of the non-inerrantists in the *Five Views* dialogue is to believe that purpose determines meaning. This emerges in several statements in the book and elsewhere. Vanhoozer claims "I propose that we identify the literal sense with the illocutionary act the author is performing."[20] The locutionary act is *what* the author is saying, and the illocutionary act is *why* (purpose) he said it. The *what* may be in error; only the *why* (purpose) is without error. This is why Vanhoozer comes up with such unusual explanations of biblical texts. For example, when Joshua commanded the sun to stand still (Josh 10), according to Vanhoozer, this does not correspond to any actual and unusual phenomena involving an extra day of daylight. Rather, it simply means, as he believes that the purpose (illocutionary act) indicates, that Joshua wants "to affirm God's covenant relation with his people."[21] Likewise, according to Vanhoozer, Joshua is not affirming the literal truth of the destruction of a large walled city (Josh 6). He contends that "simply to discover 'what actually happened'" is to miss the main point of the discourse, which is to communicate a theological interpretation of what happened (that is, God gave Israel the land) and

---

17. Franke, *Five Views*, 264.
18. Pinnock, *Scripture Principle*, 266.
19. See Geisler and Roach, *Defending Inerrancy*, 31, emphasis added.
20. Vanhoozer, *Five Views*, 220.
21. Vanhoozer, *Drama of Doctrine*, 106.

to call for right participation in the covenant."²² That is why Joshua wrote it, and that alone is the inerrant purpose of the text.

However, as we have explained in detail elsewhere, purpose does not determine meaning.²³ This becomes clear when we examine crucial texts. For example, the Bible declares, "Do not cook a young goat in its mother's milk" (Exod 23:19). The meaning of this text is very clear, but the purpose is not, at least not to most interpreters. Just scanning a couple commentaries from off the shelf reveals a half dozen different guesses as to the author's purpose. Despite this lack of unanimity on what the purpose is, nonetheless, virtually everyone understands what the meaning of the text is. An Israelite could obey this command, even if he did not know the purpose for doing so (other than that God had commanded him to do so). So, knowing meaning stands apart from knowing the purpose of a text. For example, a boss could tell his employees, "Come over to my house tonight at 8 PM." The meaning (what) is clear, but the purpose (why) is not. Again, understanding the meaning is clear apart from knowing the purpose.

This does not mean that knowing the purpose of a statement cannot be interesting and even enlightening. If you knew your boss was asking you to come to his house because he wanted to give you a million dollars, that would be very enlightening, but it would not change the meaning of the statement to come over to his house that night. So, contrary to many non-inerrantists, purpose does not determine meaning. Further, with regard to biblical texts, the meaning rests in *what* is affirmed, not in *why* it is affirmed. This is why inerrantists speak of propositional revelation and many non-inerrantists tend to downplay or deny it.²⁴ The meaning and truth of a proposition (affirmation or denial about something) is what is inspired, not in the purpose. Inerrancy deals with truth, and truth resides in propositions, not in purposes.

At the CSBI conference on the meaning of inerrancy (1982), Carl Henry observed the danger of reducing inerrancy to the purpose of the author, as opposed to the affirmations of the author as they correspond with the facts of reality. He wrote: "Some now even introduce authorial intent or cultural context of language as specious rationalizations for this crime against the Bible, much as some rapist might assure me that he is assaulting my wife for my own or for her good. They misuse Scripture in order to champion as biblically true what in fact does violence to Scripture."²⁵ This is precisely what has happened with some of the participants in the *Five Views* book when they reduced meaning to purpose and then read their own extra-biblical speculations into the author's supposed intention or purpose. This will be discussed more when the genre presupposition is discussed below.

---

22. Vanhoozer, *Five Views*, 228.
23. Geisler, *Systematic Theology*, 1:137–59.
24. Vanhoozer, *Five Views*, 214.
25. Henry, "Bible and the Conscience of Our Age," 917.

Limited inerrantists and non-inerrantists often take advantage of an ambiguity in the word "intention" of the author in order to insert their own heterodox views on the topic. When traditional unlimited inerrantists use the phrase "intention of the author" they use it in contrast to those who wish to impose their own meaning on the text in contrast to discovering what the biblical author intended by it. So, what traditional unlimited inerrantists mean by "intention" is not purpose (why) but *expressed intention* in the text, that is, its meaning. They were not asking the reader to look for some *unexpressed intention* behind, beneath, or beyond the text. Expressed intention refers to the meaning of the text. And it would be better to use the word *meaning* than the world *intention*. In this way the word *intention* cannot be understood as *purpose* (why), rather than *meaning* or expressed intention (what) which is found in the text. To put it simply, there is a *meaner* (author) who expresses his *meaning* in the text so that the reader can know what is *meant* by the text. If one is looking for this objectively expressed meaning (via historical-grammatical hermeneutics) it limits the meaning to the text and eliminates finding the meaning beyond the text in some other text (i.e., in some alien extra-biblical genre).

Mike Licona is a case in point. He redefines "error" to include genre that contains factual errors. He claims that "intentionally altering an account" is not an error but is allowed by the Greco-Roman genre into which he categorizes the Gospels, insisting that a CSBI view cannot account for all the data.[26]

## PROPOSITIONAL REVELATION

It is not uncommon for non-inerrantists to attempt to modify or deny propositional revelation. Vanhoozer cites John Stott as being uncomfortable with inerrancy because the Bible "cannot be reduced to a string of propositions which invites the label truth or error."[27] Similarly, he adds, "Inerrancy pertains directly to assertions only, not to biblical commands, promises, warnings, and so on. We would therefore be unwise to collapse everything we want to say about biblical authority into the nutshell of inerrancy."[28]

Carl Henry is criticized by some for going "too far" in claiming that "the minimal unit of meaningful expression is a proposition" and that only propositions can be true or false.[29] However, it would appear that it is Vanhoozer's criticisms that go too far. It is true that there are more than propositions in the Bible. All propositions are sentences, but not all sentences are propositions, at least not directly. However, the CSBI inerrantist is right in stressing propositional revelation. For only propositions express truth and inerrancy is concerned with the truthfulness of the Bible. Certainly,

---

26. MP3 recording of his 2013 ETS lecture.
27. Vanhoozer, *Five Views*, 200.
28. Ibid., 203.
29. Ibid., 214.

there are exclamations, promises, prophecies, interrogations, and commands that are not formally and explicitly propositions. But while not all of the Bible is propositional, most of the Bible is propositionalizable. And any text in the Bible which states or implies a proposition can be categorized as propositional revelation. And inerrantists claim that all propositional revelation is true. That is to say, all that the Bible affirms to be true (directly or indirectly) is true. And all that the Bible affirms to be false is false. Any attack on propositional revelation that diminishes or negates propositional truth has denied the inerrancy of the Bible. Hence, inerrantists rightly stress propositional revelation.

The fact that the Bible is many more things than inerrant propositions is irrelevant. Certainly, the Bible has other characteristics, such as infallibility (John 10:35), immortality (Ps 119:160), indestructibility (Matt 5:17–18), indefatigability (it cannot be worn out—Jer 23:29), and indefeasibility (it cannot be overcome—Isa 55:11), but these do not diminish the Bible's inerrancy (lack of error). In fact, if the Bible were not the inerrant Word of God, then it would not be all these other things. They are complementary, not contradictory to inerrancy. Likewise, the Bible has commands, questions, and exclamations, but these do not negate the truth of the text. Instead, they imply, enhance, and compliment it.

## Accommodationism

Historically, most evangelical theologians have adopted a form of divine condescension to explain how an infinite God could communicate with finite creatures in finite human language. This is often called analogous language.[30] However, since the word "accommodation" has come to be associated with the acceptance of error, we wish to distinguish between the legitimate evangelical teaching of God's *adaptation to human finitude* and the illegitimate view of non-inerrantists who assert God's *accommodation to human error*. It appears that some participants of the inerrancy dialogue fit into the latter category. Peter Enns believes that accommodation to human error is part of an Incarnational Model which he accepts. This involves writers making up speeches based on what is not stated but is only thought to be "called for," as Greek historian Thucydides admitted doing.[31] This accommodation view also allows for employing Hebrew and Greco-Roman literary genres which include literature with factual errors in them.[32] The following chart draws a contrast between the two views:

| Adaptation View | Accommodation View |
|---|---|
| God adapts to finitude | God accommodates to error |
| Bible uses analogous language | Bible uses equivocal language |

30. See Geisler, *Systematic Theology*, 1:137–59.
31. Enns, *Five Views*, 101–2.
32. Ibid., 103.

| Bible stories are factual | Some stories are not factual |

Peter Enns believes that "details" like whether Paul's companions heard the voice or not (Acts 9, 22) were part of this flexibility of accommodation to error. In brief, he claims that "biblical writers shaped history creatively for their own theological purposes."[33] Recording "what happened" was not the "primary focus" for the book of Acts but rather "interpreting Paul for his audience."[34] He adds, "Shaping significantly the portrayal of the past is hardly an isolated incident here and there in the Bible; it's the very substance of how biblical writers told the story of their past."[35] In brief, God accommodates to human myths, legends, and errors in the writing of Scripture. Indeed, according to some non-inerrantists like Enns, this includes accommodation to alien worldviews.

However, ETS/CSBI inerrantists emphatically reject this kind of speculation. The CSBI declares: "We affirm the unity and internal consistency of Scripture."[36] Further, "We deny that Jesus' teaching about scripture may be dismissed by appeals to accommodation or to any natural limitation of His humanity." "We affirm that inspiration, though not conferring omniscience, guaranteed true and trustworthy utterances on all matters of which the biblical authors were moved to speak and write. We deny that finitude or fallenness of these writers, by necessity or otherwise, introduced distortion or falsehood into God's Word."[37] Also, "We deny that human language is so limited by our creatureliness that it is rendered inadequate as a vehicle for divine revelation. We further deny that the corruption of human culture and language through sin has thwarted God's work in inspiration."[38]

## Reasons to Reject the Accommodation to Error View

There are many good reasons for rejecting the non-inerrantist accommodation to error theory. Let's begin with the argument from the character of God.

First, it is contrary to the nature of God as truth that he would accommodate to error. Michael Bird states the issue well, though he wrongly limits God to speaking on only redemptive matters. Nevertheless, he is on point with regard to the nature of inerrancy in relation to God. He writes: "God identifies with and even invests his own character in his Word. . . . The accommodation is never a capitulation to error. God does not speak erroneously, nor does he feed us with nuts of truth lodged inside

33. Ibid., 100.
34. Ibid., 102.
35. Ibid., 104.
36. CBSI, art. XIV.
37. Ibid., art. IX.
38. Ibid., art. IV.

shells of falsehood."[39] He cites Bromley aptly, "It is sheer unreason to say that truth is revealed in and through that which is erroneous.[40]

Second, accommodation to error is contrary to the nature of Scripture as the inerrant Word of God. God cannot err (Heb 6:18), and if the Bible is his Word, then the Bible cannot err. So, to affirm that accommodation to error was involved in the inspiration of Scripture is contrary to the nature of Scripture as the Word of God. Jesus affirmed that the "Scripture" is the unbreakable Word of God (John 10:34–35) which is imperishable to every "iota and dot" (Matt 5:18). The New Testament authors often cite the Old Testament as what "God said" (cf. Matt 19:5; Acts 4:24–25; 13:34–35; Heb 1:5–7). Indeed, the whole Old Testament is said to be "God-breathed" (2 Tim 3:16). Bird wrongly claimed "God directly inspires persons, not pages."[41] In fact, the New Testament only uses the word "inspired" (*theopneustos*) once (2 Tim 3:16) and it refers to the *written* Scripture (*grapha*, writings). The writings, not the writers, are "breathed out" by God. To be sure, the writers were "moved by" God to write (2 Pet 1:20–21), but only what they *wrote* as a result was inspired. So if the Scriptures are the very *writings* breathed out by God, then they cannot be errant since God cannot err (Titus 1:2).

Third, the accommodation to error theory is contrary to sound reason. Anti-inerrantist Peter Enns saw this logic and tried to avoid it by a Barthian kind of separation of the Bible from the Word of God. He wrote, "The premise that such an inerrant Bible is the only kind of book God would be able to produce . . . strikes me as assuming that God shares our modern interest in accuracy and scientific precision, rather than allowing the phenomena of Scripture to shape our theological expectations."[42] But Enns forgets that any kind of error is contrary, not to "modern interest" but to the very nature of the God as the God of all truth. So, whatever nuances of truth there are which are borne out by the phenomena of Scripture cannot, nevertheless, negate the naked truth that God cannot err, nor can his Word. The rest is detail.

## The Lack of Precision

The doctrine of inerrancy is sometimes criticized for holding that the Bible always speaks with scientific precision and historical exactness. But since the biblical phenomena do not support this, the doctrine of inerrancy is rejected. However, this is a straw man argument. For the CSBI states clearly: "We further deny that inerrancy is negated by biblical phenomena such as a lack of modern technical precision . . . including 'round numbers' and 'free citations'" (CSBI, art. XIII). Vanhoozer notes that Warfield and Hodge[43] helpfully distinguished "accuracy" (which the Bible has) from

---

39. Bird, *Five Views*, 159.
40. Ibid., citing Bromiley, "Authority of Scripture," 22.
41. Bird, *Five Views*, 164.
42. Enns, *Five Views*, 84.
43. Hodge and Warfield, *Inspiration*, 42.

"exactness of statement" (which the Bible does not always have).⁴⁴ This being the case, this argument does not apply to the doctrine of inerrancy as embraced by the CSBI since it leaves room for statements that lack modern "technical precision." It does, however, raise another issue, namely, the role of biblical and extra-biblical phenomena in refining the biblical concept of truth.

With regard to the reporting of Jesus' words in the Gospels, there is a strong difference between the inerrantist and non-inerrantist view, although not all non-inerrantists in the *Five Views* book hold to everything in the "non-inerrantist" column:

## Use of Jesus' Words and Deeds in the Gospels

| Inerrantist View | Non-Inerrantist View |
| --- | --- |
| Reporting them | Creating them |
| Paraphrasing them | Expanding on them |
| Changing their form | Changing their content |
| Grammatically editing them | Theologically redacting them |

Inerrantists believe that there is a significant difference between *reporting* Jesus words and *creating* them. The Gospel writings are based on eyewitness testimony, as they claim (cf. John 21:24; Luke 1:1–4) and as recent scholarship has shown.⁴⁵ Likewise, they did not put words in Jesus' mouth in a theological attempt to interpret Jesus in a certain way contrary to what he meant by them. Of course, since Jesus probably spoke in Aramaic (cf. Matt 27:46) and the Gospels are in Greek, we do not have the exact words of Jesus (*ipsissima verba*) in most cases, but rather an accurate rendering of them in another language. But for inerrantists the New Testament is not a reinterpretation of Jesus' words; it is an accurate translation of them. Non-inerrantists disagree and do not see the biblical record as an accurate report but as a reinterpreted portrait, a literary creation. This comes out clearly in the statement of Peter Enns that conquest narratives do not merely "report events."⁴⁶ Rather, "Biblical history shaped creatively in order for the theological purposes" to be seen.⁴⁷

Vanhoozer offers a modified evangelical version of this error when he speaks of not "reading Joshua to discover 'what happened'[which he believes] is to miss the main point of the discourse, which is to communicate a theological interpretation of what happened (that is, God gave Israel the land) and to call for right participation in the covenant."⁴⁸ So, the destruction of Jericho (Josh 6), while not being simply a "myth" or "legend," Vanhoozer sees as an "artful narrative testimony to an event that

---

44. Vanhoozer, *Five Views*, 221.
45. See Bauckham, *Jesus and the Eyewitnesses*.
46. Enns, *Five Views*, 108.
47. Ibid.
48. Vanhoozer, *Five Views*, 228.

happened in Israel's past."⁴⁹ A surface reading of Vanhoozer's view here may appear to be orthodox, until one remembers that he believes that only the "main point" or purpose of a text is really inerrant, not what it affirms. He declares, "I propose that we identify the literal sense with the illocutionary act an author is performing."⁵⁰ That is, only the theological purpose of the author is inerrant, not everything that is affirmed in the text (the locutionary acts). He declared elsewhere, "The Bible is the Word of God (in the sense of its illocutionary acts)."⁵¹

The implications of his view come out more clearly in his handling of another passage, namely, Joshua 10:12: "Sun, stand still . . ." This locution (affirmation) he claims is an error. But the illocution (purpose of the author) is not in error—namely, what God wanted to say through this statement which was to affirm his redemptive purpose for Israel.⁵² This is clearly not what the CSBI and historic inerrancy position affirms. Indeed, it is another example of the fallacious "purpose determines meaning" view discussed above and rejected by CSBI.

## The Role of Biblical and Extra-Biblical Data

The claim that in conflicts between them one should take the Bible over science is much too simplistic. Space does not permit a more extensive treatment of this important question which we have dealt with more extensively elsewhere.⁵³ Al Mohler was taken to task by Peter Enns for his seemingly *a priori* biblical stance that would not allow for any external evidence to change ones view on what the Bible taught about certain scientific and historical events.⁵⁴ Clearly the discussion hinges on what role the external data have (from general revelation) in determining the meaning of a biblical text (special revelation).

For example, almost all contemporary evangelicals scholars allow that virtually certain scientific evidence from outside the Bible shows that the earth is round, and this must take precedence over a literalistic interpretation of the phrase "four corners of the earth" (Rev 20:8). Further, interpretation of the biblical phrase "the sun set" (Josh 1:4) is not be taken literalistically to mean the sun moves around the earth. Rather, most evangelical scholars would allow the evidence for a heliocentric view of modern astronomy (from general revelation) to take precedence over a literalistic pre-Copernican geocentric interpretation of the phrase the "sun stood still" (Josh 10:13).

On the other hand, most evangelicals reject the theistic evolutionary interpretation of Genesis 1-2 for the literal (not literalistic) interpretation of the creation of life

49. Ibid.
50. Ibid., 220.
51. Vanhoozer, *First Theology*, 195.
52. Vanhoozer, *Lost in Interpretation*, 138.
53. See Geisler, *Systematic Theology*, 1:64–80; 205–26.
54. Mohler, *Five Views*, 51, 60.

and of Adam and Eve. So, the million-dollar question is: when does the scientist's interpretation of general revelation take precedence over the theologian's interpretation of special revelation?

Several observations are in order on this important issue. First, there are two revelations from God, general revelation (in nature) and special revelation (in the Bible), and they are both valid sources of knowledge. Second, their domains sometimes overlap and conflict, as the cases cited above indicate, but no one has proven a real contradiction between them. However, there is a conflict between some *interpretations* of each revelation. Third, sometimes a faulty interpretation of special revelation must be corrected by a proper interpretation of general revelation. Hence, there are few evangelicals who would claim that the earth is flat, despite the fact that the Bible speaks of "the four corners of the earth" (Rev 20:8) and that the earth does not move: "The world is established; *it shall never be moved*" (Ps 93:1, emphasis added).

However, most evangelical theologians follow a literal (not literalistic) understanding of the creation of the universe, life, and Adam (Gen 1:1, 21, 27) over the Darwinian macroevolution model. Why? Because they are convinced that the arguments for the creation of a physical universe and a literal Adam outweigh the Darwinian speculations about general revelation. In brief, our understanding of Genesis (special revelation) must be weighed with our understanding of nature (general revelation) in order to determine the truth of the matter.[55] It is much too simplistic to claim one is taking the Bible over science or science over the Bible—our understanding about both are based on revelations from God, and their interpretations of both must be weighed in a careful and complimentary way to arrive at the truth that is being taught on these matters.

To abbreviate a more complex process which is described in more detail elsewhere:[56] (1) we start with an *inductive* study of the biblical text; (2) we make whatever necessary *deduction* that emerges from two or more biblical truths; (3) we do a *retroduction* of our discovery in view of the biblical phenomena and external evidence from general revelation; and then (4) we draw our final *conclusion* in the nuanced view of truth resulting from this process. In brief, there is a complimentary role between interpretations of special revelation and those of general revelations. Sometimes, the evidence for the interpretation of one revelation is greater than the evidence for an interpretation in the other, and vice versa. So, it is not a matter of taking the Bible over science, but when there is a conflict, it is a matter of taking the interpretation with the strongest evidence over the one with weaker evidence.

---

55. See Geisler, *Systematic Theology*, 1:64–80; 205–26.
56. Ibid.

Part 1—Inerrancy Defined

## The Role of Hermeneutics in Inerrancy

The ICBI (International Council on Biblical Inerrancy) framers of the "Chicago Statement on Biblical Inerrancy" (CSBI) were aware that, while inerrancy and hermeneutics are *logically distinct*, hermeneutics cannot be *totally separated* from inerrancy. It is for this reason that a statement on historical-grammatical hermeneutics was included in the CSBI presentation (1978). Article XVIII reads: "We affirm that the text of Scripture is to be interpreted by the grammatico-historical exegesis, taking account of its literary forms and devices, and that Scripture is to interpret Scripture. We deny the legitimacy of any treatment of the text or quest for sources lying behind it leads to relativizing, *dehistoricizing*, or discounting its teaching, or rejecting its claim to authorship" (emphasis added).

The next ICBI conference after the CSBI in 1978 was an elaboration on this important point in the hermeneutics conference (of 1982). It produced both a statement and an official commentary as well. All four documents are placed in one book, titled *Explaining Biblical Inerrancy: Official Commentary on the ICBI Statements*.[57] These four statements contain the corpus and context of the meaning of inerrancy by nearly three hundred international scholars on the topic of inerrancy. Hence, questions about the meaning of the CSBI can be answered by the framers in the accompanying official ICBI commentaries.

Many of the issues raised in the *Five Ways* are answered in these documents. Apparently, not all the participants took advantage of these resources. Failure to do so led them to misunderstand what the ICBI framers mean by inerrancy and how historical-grammatical hermeneutics is connected to inerrancy. So-called genre criticism of Robert Gundry and Mike Licona are cases in point.

## The Role of Extra-Biblical Genre

Another aspect of non-inerrantist's thinking is genre criticism. Although he claims to be an inerrantist, Mike Licona clearly does not follow the ETS or ICBI view on the topic. Licona argues that "the Gospels belong to the genre of Greco-Roman biography (*bios*)" and that "*Bioi* offered the ancient biographer great flexibility for rearranging material and inventing speeches . . . , and the often include legend."[58] But, he adds "because *bios* was a flexible genre, it is often difficult to determine where history ends and legend begins."[59] This led him to deny the historicity of the story of the resurrection of the saints in Matthew 27:51–53,[60] and to call the story of the crowd

---

57. *Explaining Biblical Inerrancy: Official Commentary on the ICBI Statements* (2013). Available at www.BastionBooks.com.

58. Licona, *Resurrection of Jesus*, 34.

59. Ibid.

60. Ibid., 527–28; 548; 552–53.

falling backward when Jesus claimed "I am he" (John 14:5–6) "a possible candidate for embellishment,"[61] and the presence of angels at the tomb in all four Gospels may be "poetic language or legend."[62]

Later, in a debate with Bart Ehrman at Southern Evangelical Seminary in the spring of 2009, Licona claimed there was a contradiction in the Gospels as to the day of Jesus' crucifixion. He said, "I think that John probably altered the day [of Jesus' crucifixion] in order for a theological—to make a theological point here." Then in a professional transcription of a YouTube video on November 23, 2012,[63] Licona affirmed the following: "So *um this didn't really bother me in terms of if there were contradictions in the Gospels. I mean I believe in biblical inerrancy but I also realized that biblical inerrancy is not one fundamental doctrines of Christianity. The resurrection is. So if Jesus rose from the dead, Christianity is still true even if it turned out that some things in the Bible weren't. So um it didn't really bother me a whole lot even if some contradictions existed*" (emphasis added).

This popular Greco-Roman genre theory adopted by Licona and others is directly contrary to the CSBI view of inerrancy as clearly spelled out in many articles. First, article XVIII speaks to it directly: "*We affirm that the text of Scripture is to be interpreted by grammatico-historical exegesis, taking account of its literary forms and devices, and that Scripture is to interpret Scripture.*"[64] But Licona rejects the strict "grammatico-historical exegesis" where "Scripture is to interpret Scripture" for an extra-biblical system where Greco-Roman genre is used to interpret Scripture. Of course, "Taking account" of different genres within Scripture, like poetry, history, parables, and even allegory (Gal 4:24), is legitimate, but this is not what the use of extra-biblical Greco-Roman genre does. Rather, it uses extra-biblical stories to determine what the Bible means, even if using this extra-biblical literature means denying the historicity of the biblical text.

Second, the CSBI says emphatically that "we deny the legitimacy of any treatment of the text or quest for sources lying behind it that leads to relativizing, *dehistoricizing*, or discounting its teaching, or rejecting its claim to authorship."[65] But this is exactly what many non-inerrantists, like Licona, do with some Gospel events. The official ICBI commentary on this article adds, "*It is never legitimate, however, to run counter to express biblical affirmations.*"[66] Further, in the ICBI commentary on its 1983 Hermeneutics Statement on inerrancy, it adds, "*We deny that generic categories which negate historicity may rightly be imposed on biblical narratives which present themselves as factual. Some, for instance, take Adam to be a myth, whereas in Scripture he is presented*

---

61. Ibid., 306.
62. Ibid., 185–86.
63. See "Mike Licona Discusses What Makes a Bible Contradiction."
64. Emphasis added.
65. CBSI, art. XVIII, emphasis added.
66. Packer, *Explaining Biblical Inerrancy*, 60.

*as a real person. Others take Jonah to be an allegory when he is presented as a historical person and [is] so referred to by Christ."*[67] Its comments in the next article (art. XIV) add, *"We deny that any event, discourse or saying reported in Scripture was invented by the biblical writers or by the traditions they incorporated."*[68] Clearly, the CSBI fathers rejected genre criticism as used by Gundry, Licona, and many other evangelicals.

Three living eyewitness framers of the CSBI statements (Packer, Sproul, and Geisler) confirm that authors like Robert Gundry were in view when these articles were composed. Gundry had denied the historicity of sections of the Gospel of Matthew by using a Hebrew "midrashic" model to interpret Matthew.[69] After a thorough discussion of Gundry's view over a two year period and numerous articles in the ETS journal, the matter was peacefully, lovingly, and formally brought to a motion by a founder of the ETS, Roger Nicole, in which the membership by an overwhelming 74 percent voted and asked Gundry to resign from the ETS. Since Licona's view is the same in principle with that of Gundry's, the ETS decision applies equally to his view as well.

Mike Licona uses a Greco-Roman genre to interpreting the Gospels, rather than Jewish midrash which Gundry used. The Greco-Roman genre permits the use of a contradiction in the Gospels concerning the day Jesus was crucified. However, the ICBI official texts cited above reveal that the CSBI statement on inerrancy forbids "dehistoricizing" the Gospels.[70] Again, living ICBI framers see this as the same issue that led to Gundry's departure from ETS. When asked about the orthodoxy of Mike Licona's view, CSBI framer R.C. Sproul wrote: "As the former and only President of ICBI during its tenure and as the original framer of the Affirmations and Denials of the Chicago Statement on Inerrancy, *I can say categorically that Dr. Michael Licona's views are not even remotely compatible with the unified Statement of ICBI.*"[71]

The role of extra-biblical genre in Gospel interpretation can be charted as follows:

## *The Use of Extra-Biblical Genre*

| Legitimate Use | Illegitimate Use |
|---|---|
| A material cause | The formal cause |
| Help provide parts | Determine the whole |
| Illuminates significance | Determines meaning |

---

67. "Chicago Statement on Biblical Hermeneutics," art. XIII, emphasis added; Geisler and Sproul, *Explaining Hermeneutics*, 74.
68. Ibid., 75.
69. See Mohler on Franke, *Five Views*, 294.
70. CSBI, art. XVIII.
71. Personal correspondence between Packer and Geisler, May 22, 2012, emphasis added.

The formal cause of meaning is in the text itself (the author is the efficient cause of meaning). No literature or stories outside the text are hermeneutically determinative of the meaning of the text. The extra-biblical data can provide understanding of a part (e.g., a word), but it cannot decide what the meaning of a whole text is. Every text must be understood only in its immediate or more remote contexts. Scripture is to be used to interpret Scripture.

Of course, as shown above, general revelation can help modify our understanding of a biblical text, for the scientific evidence based on general revelation demonstrates that the earth is round and can be used to modify one's understanding of the biblical phrase "four corners of the earth." However, no Hebrew or Greco-Roman literature genre should be used to determine what a biblical text means since it is not part of any general revelation from God, and it has no hermeneutical authority.

Further, the genre of a text is not understood by looking outside the text. Rather, it is determined by using the historical-grammatical hermeneutic on the text in its immediate context, and the more remote context of the rest of Scripture to decide whether it is history, poetry, parable, an allegory, or whatever.

Furthermore, similarity to any extra-biblical types of literature does not demonstrate identity with the biblical text, nor should it be used to determine what the biblical text means. For example, the fact that an extra-biblical piece of literature combines history and legend does not mean that the Bible also does this. Nor does the existence of contradictions in similar extra-biblical literature justify transferring this to biblical texts. Even if there are some significant similarities of the Gospels with Greco-Roman literature, it does not mean that legends should be allowed in the Gospels since the Gospel writers make it clear that they have a strong interest in historical accuracy by an "orderly account" so that we can have "certainty" about what is recorded in them (Luke 1:1–4). And multiple confirmations of geographical and historical details confirm that this kind of historical accuracy was achieved.[72]

## The Issue of Gospel Pluralism

Another associated error of some non-inerrantism is pluralism. Kenton Sparks argues that the Bible "does not contain a single coherent theology but rather numerous theologies that sometimes stand in tension or even contradiction with one another."[73] So, God accommodates himself and speaks through "the idioms, attitudes, assumptions, and general worldviews of the ancient authors."[74] But he assures us that this is not a problem, because we need to see "God as so powerful that he can overrule ancient human error and ignorance, [by contrast] inerrancy portrays as weak view of God."[75]

---

72. See Hemer, *Book of Acts*.
73. Sparks, *God's Word in Human Words*, 301; cited by Mohler, *Five Views*, 55.
74. Enns, *Five Views*, 87.
75. Ibid., 91.

## Part 1—Inerrancy Defined

However, it must be remembered that contradictions entail errors, and God cannot err.

By the same logical comparison, Christ must have sinned. For if the union of the human and divine in Scripture (God's written Word) necessarily entails error, then by comparison the union of the human and divine in Christ must result in moral flaws in him. But the Bible is careful to note that, though Christ, while being completely human, nonetheless, was without sin (Heb 4:15; 2 Cor 5:21). Likewise, there is no logical or theological reason why the Bible must err simply because it has a human nature to it. Humans do not always err, and they do not err when guided by the Holy Spirit of Truth who cannot err (John 14:26; 16:13; 2 Pet 1:20-21). A perfect Book can be produced by a perfect God through imperfect human authors. How? Because God can draw a straight line with a crooked stick! He is the ultimate cause of the inerrant Word of God; the human authors are only the secondary causes.

Enns attempts to avoid this true incarnational analogy by arguing the following: (1) This reasoning diminishes the value of Christ's Incarnation. He tried to prove this by noting that the Incarnation of Christ is a unique "miracle."[76] However, so is the union of the human and divine natures of Scripture miraculous (2 Sam 23:2; 2 Pet 1:20–21). In effect, Enns denies the miraculous nature of Scripture in order to exalt the miraculous nature of the Incarnation of Christ. (2) His comparison with the Quran is a straw man because it reveals his lack of understanding of the emphatic orthodox denial of the verbal dictation theory claimed by Muslims for the Quran, but denied vigorously by orthodox Bible scholars about the Bible. (3) His charge of "bibliolatry" is directly opposed to all evangelical teaching that the Bible is not God and should not be worshiped.

Of course, Christ and the Bible are not a *perfect* analogy because there is a significant difference: Christ is God, and the Bible is not. Nonetheless, it is a *good* analogy because there are many strong similarities: (1) both Christ and the Bible have a divine and human dimension; (2) both have a union of the two dimensions; (3) both have a flawless character that in Christ is without sin and in the Bible is without error; and (4) both are the Word of God, one the written Word of God and other the incarnate Word of God. Thus, a true incarnational analogy calls for the errorlessness of the Bible, just as it calls for the sinlessness of Christ.

## The Acceptance of Conventionalism

Some non-inerrantists hold the self-defeating theory of meaning called conventionalism. Franke, for example, argues that "since language is a social construct . . . our words and linguistic conventions do not have timeless and fixed meanings."[77] There

---

76. Ibid., 298.
77. Franke, *Five Views*, 194.

are serious problem with this view which Franke and other contemporary non-inerrantists have adopted.

Without going into philosophical detail, the most telling way to see the flaws of this view is to reflect on its self-defeating nature. That is, it cannot deny the objectivity of meaning without making an objectively meaningful statement. To claim that all language is purely conventional and subjective is to make a statement which is not purely conventional and subjective. In like manner, when Franke claims that truth is perspectival,[78] he seems to be unaware that he is making a non-perspectival truth claim. This problem is discussed more extensively elsewhere.[79] We would only point out here that one cannot consistently be an inerrantist and a conventionalist. For if all meaning is subjective, then so is all truth (since all true statements must be meaningful). But inerrancy claims that the Bible makes objectively true statements. Hence, an inerrantist cannot be a conventionalist, at least not consistently.

## The Issue of Foundationalism

The CBSI statement is taken to task by some non-inerrantists for being based on an unjustified theory of foundationalism. Franke insists that "the Chicago Statement is reflective of a particular form of epistemology known as classic or strong foundationalism."[80] They believe that the Bible is "a universal and indubitable basis for human knowledge."[81] Franke believes that: "The problem with this approach is that it has been thoroughly discredited in philosophical and theological circles."[82]

In response, first of all, Franke confuses two kinds of foundationalism: (1) deductive foundationalism, as found in Spinoza or Descartes where all truth can be deduced from certain axiomatic principles. This is rejected by all inerrantist scholars I know and by most philosophers; (2) However, reductive foundationalism which affirms that truths can be reduced to or are based on certain first principles like the Law of Noncontradiction is not rejected by most inerrantists and philosophers. Indeed, first principles of knowledge, like the Law of Non-contradiction, are self-evident and undeniable. That is, the predicate of first principles can be reduced to it subject, and any attempt to deny the Law of Non-contradiction uses the Law of Non-contradiction in the denial. Hence, the denial is self-defeating.

Second, not only does Franke offer no refutation of this foundational view, but any attempted refutation of it self-destructs. Even so-called "post-foundationalists" like Franke cannot avoid using these first principles of knowledge in their rejection of foundationalism. So, Franke's comment applies to deductive foundationalism but

78. Ibid., 267.
79. Geisler, *Systematic Theology*, 98–108.
80. Franke, *Five Views*, 261.
81. Ibid.
82. Ibid., 262.

## Part 1—Inerrancy Defined

not to reductive foundationalism as held by most inerratists. Indeed, first principles of knowledge, including theological arguments, are presupposed in all rational arguments, including theological arguments.

Third, Franke is wrong in affirming that all inerrantists claim that "Scripture is the true and *sole* basis for knowledge on all matters which it touches."[83] Nowhere does the CSBI statement or its commentaries make any such claim. It claims only that the "Scriptures are the supreme *written* norm" "in all matters on which it touches."[84] Nowhere does it deny that God has revealed himself outside his written revelation in his general revelation in nature, as the Bible declares (Rom 1:1-20; Ps 19:1; Acts 14, 17).

As for "fallibilism" which Franke posits to replace foundationalism, CSBI explicitly denies creedal or infallible basis for its beliefs, saying, "We do not propose this statement be given creedal weight."[85] Furthermore, "We deny creeds, councils, or declarations have authority greater than or equal to the authority of the Bible."[86] So, not only do the ICBI framers claim their work is not a creed nor is it infallible, but they claim that even the Creeds are not infallible. Further, it adds. "We invite response to this statement from any who see reason to amend its affirmations about Scripture by the light of Scripture itself, under whose infallible authority we stand as we speak."[87] In short, while the doctrine of inerrancy is not negotiable, the ICBI statements about inerrancy are revisable. However, to date, no viable revisions have been proposed by any group of scholars such as those who framed the original CSBI statements.

## Dealing with Bible Difficulties

As important as the task may be, dealing with Bible difficulties can have a blinding effect on those desiring the clear truth about inerrancy because they provide a temptation not unlike that of a divorce counselor who is faced with all the problems of his divorced counselees. Unless, he concentrates on the biblical teaching and good examples of many happy marriages, he can be caught wondering whether a good marriage is possible. Likewise, one should no more give up on the inerrancy (of God's special revelation) because of the difficulties he finds in explaining its consistency than he should give up on the study of nature (God's general revelation) because of the difficulties he finds in it.

There are several reasons for believing that both of God's revelations are consistent: First, it is a reasonable assumption that the God who is capable of revealing himself in both spheres is consistent and does not contradict himself. Indeed, the Scriptures exhort us to "Avoiding . . . opposing arguments" (ἀντιθέσεις—1 Tim 6:20).

---

83. Ibid., emphasis added.
84. CSBI, art. II, and "Short Statement," emphasis added.
85. CSBI, preamble.
86. CSBI, art. II.
87. CSBI, preamble.

Second, persistent study in both spheres of God's revelations, special and general revelation (Rom 1:19-20; Ps 19:1), have yielded more and more answers to difficult questions. Finally, contrary to some panelists who believe that inerrancy hinders progress in understanding Scripture,[88] there is an investigative value in assuming there is no contradiction in either revelation, namely, it prompts further investigation to believe that there was no error in the original. What would we think of scientists who gave up studying God's general revelation in nature because they have no present explanation for some phenomena? The same applies to Scripture (God's special revelation). Thus, assuming there is an error in the Bible is no solution. Rather, it is a research stopper.

Augustine was right in his dictum.[89] There are only four alternatives when we come to a difficulty in the Word of God: (1) God made an error, (2) the manuscript is faulty, (3) the translation is wrong, or (4) we have not properly understood it. Since it is an utterly unbiblical presumption to assume the first alternative, we as evangelicals have three alternatives. After over a half century of studying nearly one thousand such difficulties,[90] I have discovered that the problem of an unexplained conflict is usually the last alternative—I have not properly understood.

That being said, even the difficult cases the participants were asked to respond to are not without possible explanations. In fact, some of the participants, who are not even defenders of inerrancy, offered some reasonable explanations.

## Acts 9 and 22

As for the alleged contradiction in whether Paul's companions "heard" (Acts 9:4) and did not "hear" (Acts 22:9) what the voice from heaven said, two arguments should be noted. First, a resolution is found in the cases used in each instance with the verb ἀκούω ("hear"). When the genitive case (τῆς φωνῆς) is used (i.e., Acts 9:7) with this verb it means to "hear a sound of a voice," but when the accusative is used (φωνὴν in Acts 22:9) it signifies to understand cognitively what the sound was indicating. The Greek case form used with "hear" is strategic. Thus, Paul's companions in Acts 9:7 heard the sound of a voice speaking to Paul (ἀκούοντες τῆς φωνῆς—use of genitive case), while in Acts 22:9 the idea is conveyed with the accusative case (τὴν δὲ φωνὴν οὐκ ἤκουσαν—use of accusative case) that they did not understand the substance of what the voice was communicating."[91] Long ago, the Greek grammarian Robertson noted that "The accusative case (case of extent) accents the intellectual apprehension of the sound, while the genitive, while the genitive (specifying case) calls attention to the sound of the voice without accenting the sense. The word ἀκούω ("hear")

---

88. Franke, *Five Views*, 278.
89. Augustine, *Letter to Jerome* 82.3; cited by Vanhoozer, *Five Views*, 235.
90. See Geisler and Howe, *Big Book of Bible Difficulties*.
91. Vanhoozer, *Five Views*, 229.

itself has two senses which fall in well this case-distinction, one 'to hear,' the other 'to understand.'"[92]

Second, we have exactly the same experience with the word "hear" today. In fact, at our house, hardly a day or two goes by without either my wife or I saying from another room, "I can't hear you." We heard their voice, but we did not understand what they said.

One thing is certain, we do not need contorted attempts to explain the phenomenon like Vanhoozer's suggestion that this conflict serves "Luke's purpose by progressively reducing the role of the companions, eventually excluding them altogether from the revelatory event."[93] It is totally unnecessary to sacrifice the traditional view of inerrancy with such twisted explanations.

*Joshua 6*

This text records massive destruction of the city with its large walls falling down, which goes way beyond the available archaeological evidence. Peter Enns insists that "the overwhelmingly dominant scholarly position is that the city of Jericho was at most a small settlement and without walls during the time of Joshua."[94] He concludes that "these issues cannot be reconciled with how inerrancy functions in evangelicalism as articulated in the CSBI."[95] He further contends that the biblical story must be a legendary and mythological embellishment.[96]

In response, it should be noted that: (1) This would not be the first time that the "dominant scholarly position" has been overturned by later discoveries. The charge that there was no writing in Moses's day and that the Hittites mentioned in the Bible (Gen 26:34; 1 Kgs 11:1) never existed, are only two examples. All scholars know that both of these errors were subsequently revealed by further research. (2) There is good archaeological evidence that other events mentioned in the Bible did occur as stated. The plagues on Egypt and the destruction of Sodom and Gomorrah are examples in point. The first fits well with the Uperwer Papyrus and the second with the recent discoveries at the Tall el Hamman site in Jordan.[97]

Indeed, Enns admits that the Joshua description of some other cities around Jericho fits the archaeological evidence.[98] He even admits that "a trained archaeologist and research director" offers a minority view that fits with the Joshua 6 record,[99] only

92. Robertson, *Grammar*, 506.
93. Vanhoozer, *Five Views*, 230.
94. Enns, *Five Views*, 93.
95. Ibid., 92.
96. Ibid., 96.
97. Holden and Geisler, *Popular Handbook of Archaeology*, 214–24.
98. Enns, *Five Views*, 98.
99. Ibid., 94.

the alleged time period is different. However, since the dating issue is still unresolved by scholars, a date that fits the biblical record is still possible.

The fact that the belief in the full historicity of Joshua 6 is in the minority among scholars poses no insurmountable problem. Minority views have been right before. Remember Galileo? As for the alleged absence of evidence for a massive destruction of a walled city of Jericho, two points are relevant: (1) the absence of evidence is not necessarily the evidence of absence since other evidence may yet be found; (2) the main dispute is not over whether something like the Bible claimed to have happened actually did happen to Jericho, but whether it happened at the alleged time. However, the dating of this period is still disputed among scholars. Hence, nothing like "overwhelmingly" established evidence has disproven the biblical picture of Joshua 6. Certainly there is no real reason to throw out the inerrantist's view of the historicity of the event. On the contrary, the Bible has a habit of proving the critics wrong.

## Deuteronomy 20 and Matthew 5

Again, this is a difficult problem, but there are possible explanations without sacrificing the historicity and inerrancy of the passages. The elimination of the Canaanites and the command to love one's enemies are not irreconcilable. Even Enns, no friend of inerrancy, points out that an "alternate view of the conquest that seems to exonerate the Israelites,"[100] noting that the past tense of the Leviticus statement that "the land vomited [past tense] out its inhabitants" (Lev 18:25) implies that "God had already dealt with the Canaanite problem before the Israelites left Mt. Sinai."[101]

But even the traditional view that Israel acted as God's theocratic agent in killing the Canaanites poses no irreconcilable problem for many reasons. First of all, God is sovereign over life and can give and take it as he wills (Deut 32:39; Job 1:21). Second, God can command others to kill on his behalf, as he did in capital punishment (Gen 9:6). Third, the Canaanites were wildly wicked and deserved such punishment (cf. Lev 18). Fourth, this was a special theocratic act of God through Israel on behalf of God's people and God's plan to give them the Holy Land and bring forth the Holy One (Christ), the Savior of the world. Hence, there is no pattern or precedent here for how we should wage war today. Fifth, loving our enemy who insults us with a mere "slap on the right cheek" (Matt 5:39) does not contradict our killing him in self-defense if he attempts to murder us (Exod 22:2), or engaging him in a just war of protecting the innocent (Gen 14). Sixth, God gave the Canaanites some four hundred years (Gen 15:13-15) to repent before he found them incorrigibly and irretrievably wicked and wiped them out. Just as it is sometimes necessary to cut off a cancerous limb to save one's life, even so God knows when such an operation is necessary on a nation which has polluted the land. But we are assured by God's words and actions elsewhere that

---

100. Ibid., 108.
101. Ibid.

Part 1—Inerrancy Defined

God does not destroy the righteous with the wicked (Gen 18:25). Saving Lot and his daughters, Rahab, and the Ninevites are examples.

As for God's lovingkindness on the wicked non-Israelites, Nineveh (Jonah 3) is proof that God will save even a very wicked nation that repents (cf. 2 Pet 3:9). So, there is nothing in this Deuteronomy text that is contradictory to God's character as revealed in the New Testament. Indeed, the judgments of the New Testament God are more intensive and extensive in the book of Revelation (cf. Rev 6-19) than anything in the Old Testament.

## RESPONDING TO ATTACKS ON INERRANCY

We turn our attention now to some of the major charges leveled against CSBI inerrancy. We begin with two of the major objections: It is not biblical and it is not the historical view of the Christian church. But before we address these, we need to recall that the CSBI view on inerrancy means *total* inerrancy, not *limited* inerrancy. Total or unlimited inerrancy holds that the Bible is inerrant on both redemptive matters and all other matters on which it touches, and limited inerrancy holds that the Bible is only inerrant on redemptive matters but not in other areas such as history and science. By "inerrancy" we mean total inerrancy as defined by the CSBI.

### The Charge of Being Unbiblical

Many non-inerrantists reject inerrancy because they claim that it is not taught in the Bible as the Trinity or other essential doctrines are. But the truth is that neither one is taught formally and explicitly. Both are taught in the Bible only implicitly and logically. For example, nowhere does the Bible teach the formal doctrine of the Trinity, but it does teach the premises which logically necessitate the doctrine of the Trinity. And as the *Westminster Confession of Faith* declares, a sound doctrine must be "either set down in Scripture, or by good and necessary consequences may be deduced from Scripture."[102] Both the Trinity and inerrancy of Scripture fall into the latter category. Thus, the Bible teaches that there are three Persons who are God: the Father, the Son, and the Holy Spirit (Matt 29:18-20). Furthermore, it teaches that there is only one God (1 Tim 2:5). So, "by good and necessary consequences" the doctrine of the Trinity may be deduced from Scripture.

Likewise, while inerrancy is not formally and explicitly taught in Scripture, nonetheless, the premises on which it is based are taught there. For the Bible teaches that God cannot err, and it also affirms that the Bible is the Word of God. So "by good and necessary consequences [the doctrine of inerrancy] may be deduced from Scripture."

---

102. Ch. 1, art. VI.

Of course, in both cases the conclusion can and should be nuanced as to what the word "person" means (in the case of the Trinity), and what the word "truth" means (see below) in the case of inerrancy. Nevertheless, the basic doctrine in both cases is biblical in the sense of a "good and necessary consequence" of being logically "deduced from Scripture."

## The Charge of Being Unhistorical

Many non-inerrantists charge that inerrancy has not been the historic doctrine of the church. Some say it was a modern apologetic reaction to Liberalism. Outspoken opponent of inerrancy, Peter Enns, claims that "'inerrancy,' as it is understood in the evangelical and fundamentalist mainstream, has not been the church's doctrine of Scripture through its entire history; Augustine was not an 'inerrantist.'"[103] However, as the evidence will show, Enns is clearly mistaken on both counts. First of all, Augustine (fifth century) declared emphatically, "I have learned to yield respect and honour only to the canonical books of Scripture: of these alone do I most firmly believe that the authors were completely free form error."[104]

Furthermore, Augustine was not alone in his emphatic support of the inerrancy of Scripture. Other Fathers both before and after him held the same view. Thomas Aquinas (thirteenth century) declared that "it is heretical to say that any falsehood whatever is contained either in the gospels or in and canonical Scripture."[105] For "a true prophet is always inspired by the Spirit of truth in whom there is no trace of falsehood, and he never utters untruths."[106]

The Reformer Martin Luther (16th c.) added, "When one blasphemously gives the lie to God in a single word, or say it is a minor matter . . . one blasphemes the entire God."[107] "Indeed, whoever is so bold that he ventures to accuse God of fraud and deception in a single word . . . likewise certainly ventures to accuse God of fraud and deception in all His words. Therefore it is true, absolutely and without exception, that everything is believed or nothing is believed."[108]

John Calvin agreed with his predecessors, insisting that "the Bible has come down to us from the mouth of God.[109] Thus "we owe to Scripture the same reverence which we owe to God; because it has proceeded from him alone. . . . The Law and the Prophets are . . . dictated by the Holy Spirit."[110] Scripture is "the certain and unerring

---

103. Enns, *Five Views*, 181.
104. Augustine, *Letters*, 82, 3.
105. Aquinas, "Exposition on Job 13," lect. 1.
106. Aquinas, *Summa Theologica*, 2a2ae, 172, 6ad 2.
107. Luther, *Works*, 37:26.
108. Cited in Reu, *Luther and the Scriptures*, 33.
109. Calvin, *Institutes*, 1.18.4.
110. Urquhart, *Inspiration and Accuracy*, 129-30.

rule."¹¹¹ He added that the Bible is "a depository of doctrine as would secure it from either perishing by neglect, vanishing away amid errors, of being corrupted by the presumptions of men."¹¹²

Furthermore, it is nit-picking to claim, as some non-inerrantists suggest,¹¹³ that the church fathers did not hold precisely the same view of Scripture as contemporary evangelicals. Vanhoozer claims they are "not quite the same."¹¹⁴ Bird asserted, "The biggest problem I have with the AIT [American Inerrancy Tradition] and the CSBI [Chicago Statement on Biblical Inerrancy] are their lack of catholicity. What Christians said about inerrancy in the past might have been similar to the AIT and CSBI, but they were never absolutely the same!"¹¹⁵ However, identical twins are not absolutely the same in all "details," but, like the doctrine of inerrancy down through the years, both are *substantially* the same. That is, they believed in total inerrancy of Scripture, that it is without error in whatever it affirms on any topic.

The basic truth of inerrancy has been affirmed by the Christian church from the very beginning. This has been confirmed by John Hannah in *Inerrancy and the Church*. Likewise, John Woodbridge provided a scholarly defense of the historic view on inerrancy, *Biblical Authority and Interpretation of the Bible: A Critique of the Rogers/McKim Proposal*, that Rogers never even attempted to refute. Neither Rogers nor anyone else has written a refutation of the standard view on inerrancy, as defended by Woodbridge, expressed in the ETS, and explained by the ICBI.

Of course, other difficulties with the historic doctrine of inerrancy can be raised, but B. B. Warfield summed up the matter well, claiming: "The question is not whether the doctrine of plenary inspiration has difficulties to face. The question is, whether these difficulties are greater than the difficulty of believing that the whole church of God from the beginning has been deceived in her estimate of Scripture committed to her charge—are greater than the difficulties of believing that the whole college of the apostles, yes and of Christ himself at their head were themselves deceive as to the nature of those Scripture."¹¹⁶

## The Charge of the "Slippery Slope Argument"

An oft repeated charge against inerrancy is that it is based on a "slippery slope" argument that it should be accepted on the basis of what we might lose if we reject it.¹¹⁷ The charge affirms that if we give up the inerrancy of the Bible's authority on historical

---

111. Calvin, *Commentaries*, Ps 5:11.
112. Calvin, *Institutes*, 1.6.3.
113. Franke, *Five Views*, 261.
114. Vanhoozer, *Five Views*, 73.
115. Bird, *Five Views*, 67.
116. Warfield, *Inspiration and Authority of the Bible*, 128; cited by Mohler, *Five Views*, 42.
117. Enns, *Five Views*, 89.

or scientific areas, then we are in danger of giving up on the inerrancy of redemptive passages as well. In brief, it argues that if you can't trust the Bible in all areas, then you can't trust it at all. Enns contends this is "an expression of fear," not a valid argument but one based on "emotional blackmail."[118] Franke states the argument in these terms: "If there is a single error at any place in the Bible, [then] none of it can be trusted."[119]

One wonders whether the anti-inerrantist would reject Jesus' arguments for the same reason when he said, "If I have told you earthly things and you do not believe, how can you believe if I tell you heavenly things" (John 3:12)? The truth is that there are at least two different forms of the "slippery slope" reasoning: one is valid and the other is not. It is not valid to argue that if we don't believe everything one says, then we cannot believe anything he says. For example, the fact that an accountant makes an occasional error in math does not mean that he is not reliable in general. However, if one claims to have divine authority, and makes one mistake, then it is reasonable to conclude that nothing he says has divine authority in it. For God cannot make mistakes, therefore, anyone who claims to be a prophet of God who does make mistakes (cf. Deut 18:22) cannot be trusted to be speaking with divine authority on anything (even though he may be right about many things). So, it is valid to say, if the Bible errs in anything, then it cannot be trusted to be the inerrant Word of God in anything (no matter how reliable it may be about many things).

## The Charge of Being Parochial

Vanhoozer poses the question: "Why should the rest of the world care about North American evangelicalism's doctrinal obsession with inerrancy?"[120] There are no voices from Africa, Asia, or South America that had "any real input into the formation of the CSBI."[121] "Indeed, it is difficult to attend a meeting of the Evangelical Theological Society and not be struck by the overwhelming white and male group it is."[122]

However, "It is a genetic fallacy to claim that the doctrine of inerrancy can't be right because it was made in the USA."[123] While it is true that "in the abundance of counselors there is wisdom" (Prov 11:14), it is not necessarily true that universality and inter-ethnicity is more conducive to orthodoxy. Would anyone reject Newton's Laws simply because they came from a seventeenth-century Englishman? Vanhoozer rightly asks, "Is it possible that the framers of the Chicago statement, despite the culturally conditioned and contingent nature of the North American discussion, have discovered a necessary implication of what Christians elsewhere might have to say

118. Ibid.
119. Franke, *Five Views*, 262.
120. Vanhoozer, *Five Views*, 190.
121. Franke, *Five Views*, 194.
122. Ibid., 195.
123. Vanhoozer, *Five Views*, 190.

about Scripture's truth?"[124] "Is it not possible that inerrancy represents a legitimate development of the doctrine of Scripture that arose in response to the needs and challenges of our twentieth-century context? I don't see why not."[125]

The early Christian Creeds on the deity of Christ and the Trinity were all time-bound, yet they rightly attained the status of a Creed—an enduring and universal statement which is accepted by all major sections of Christendom. Although the CSBI statement does not claim creedal status, nonetheless, being time-bound does not hinder its deserved wide representation and acceptance in historic evangelical churches.

Franke claims that one of the problems with claiming inerrancy as a universal truth is that "it will lead to the marginalization of other people who do not share in the outlooks and assumptions of the dominant group. Inerrancy calls on us to surrender the pretensions of a universal and timeless theology."[126] However, he seems oblivious to the universal and timeless pretension of his own claim. As a truth claim, the charge of parochialism is self-defeating since it too is conditioned by time, space, and ethnic distinctiveness. Indeed, it is just another form of the view that all truth claims are relative. But so is that claim itself relative. Thus, the proponent of parochialism is hanged on his own gallows.

## The Charge of Being Unethical

The alleged unethical behavior of inerrantists seems to have been the hot-button issue among most of the participants in the dialogue, including the editors. They decry, sometimes in strong terms, the misuse of inerrancy by its proponents. In fact, this issue seems to simmer beneath the background of the anti-inerrancy discussion as a whole, breaking forth from time-to-time in explicit condemnation of its opponents. In fact, the editors of the *Five Views* book appear to trace the contemporary inerrancy movement to this issue.[127]

Both the editors and some participants of the *Five Views* book even employ extreme language and charges against the inerrancy movement, charging it with evangelical "fratricide."[128] The word "fratricide" is repeated a few pages later.[129] Three participants of the dialogue (Franke, Bird, and Enns) seem particularly disturbed about the issue, along with the two editors of the book. They fear that inerrancy is used as "a political instrument (e.g., a tool for excluding some from the evangelical

---

124. Ibid.
125. Ibid., 191.
126. Ibid., 279.
127. See Merrick, *Five Views*, 310.
128. Ibid.
129. Ibid., 317.

family)"[130] in an "immoral" way[131] They speak of times "when human actions persist in ways that are ugly and unbecoming of Christ."[132]

Enns, for example, speaks strongly to the issue, chiding "those in positions of power in the church . . . who prefer coercion to reason and demonize to reflection."[133] He adds, "Mohler's position (the only one explicitly defending the CSBI inerrancy view) is in my view intellectually untenable, but wielded as a weapon, it becomes spiritually dangerous."[134] He also charges inerrantists with "manipulation, passive-aggressiveness, and . . . emotional blackmail."[135] Further, he claims that "inerrancy regularly functions to short-circuit rather than spark our knowledge of the Bible."[136] In spite of the fact that he recognizes that we cannot "evaluate inerrancy on the basis of its abusers," Enns hastens to claim that "the function of inerrancy in the funamentalist and evangelical subculture has had a disturbing and immoral partnership with power and abuse."[137]

Franke joins the chorus against inerrantists more softly but nonetheless strongly expresses his disappointment, saying, "I have often been dismayed by many of the ways in which inerrancy has commonly been used in biblical interpretation, theology, and the life of the church . . . Of even greater concern is the way in which inerrancy has been wielded as a means of asserting power and control" over others.[138]

## A Response to the Ethical Charges

Few widely read scholars will deny that some have abused the doctrine of inerrancy. The problem is that while we have a perfect Bible, there are imperfect people using it—on both sides of the debate.

### Misuse Does Not Bar Use

However, the misuse of a doctrine does not prove that it is false. Nor does the improper use of Scripture prove that there is no proper way to use it. Upon examination of the evidence, the abuse charge against inerrantists is overreaching. So far as I can tell, virtually all the scholars I know in the inerrancy movement were engaged in defending inerrancy out of a sincere desire to preserve what they believed was an important part

---

130. Vanhoozer, *Five Views*, 302.
131. Enns, *Five Views*, 292.
132. Merrick, *Five Views*, 317.
133. Enns, *Five Views*, 60.
134. Ibid.
135. Ibid., 89.
136. Ibid., 91.
137. Ibid., 292.
138. Franke, *Five Views*, 259.

of the Christian faith. Often those who speak most vociferously about the errors of another are unaware of their own errors. Ethics is a double-edged sword, as any neutral observer will detect in reading the above ethical tirade against inerrantists. Certainly, the charges by non-inerrantists are subject to ethical scrutiny themselves. For example, is it really conducive to unity, community, and tranquility to charge others with a form of evangelical fratricide, a political instrument for excluding some from the evangelical family, ugly and unbecoming of Christ, a means of asserting power and control, a means of coercion, spiritually dangerous, manipulation, a passive-aggressiveness attack, emotional blackmail, and a disturbing and immoral partnership with power and abuse? Frankly, I have never seen anything that approaches this kind of unjustified and unethical outburst coming from inerrancy scholars toward those who do not believe in the doctrine. So, as far as ethics is concerned, the charge of abuse looks like a classic example of the kettle calling the pot black!

## The Log in One's Own Eye

Non-inerrantists are in no position to try to take the ethical speck out of the eye of inerrantists when they have an ethical log in their own eye. Harold Lindsell pointed out in *The Battle for the Bible* the ethical inconsistency of the Fuller faculty in voting inerrancy out of their doctrinal statement which they had all signed and was still in effect when they were voting it out of existence.[139] But how could they be against it, if they were on record as being for it. We know they were for it *before* they were against it, but how can they be against it *when* they were for it? Is there not an ethical commitment to keep a signed document? When one comes to no longer believe in a doctrinal statement he has signed, then the ethical thing to do is to resign one's position. Instead, at Fuller, in ETS, and in organization after organization, those who no longer believe what the framers meant will stay in the group in an attempt to change the doctrinal statement to mean what they want it to mean. This is a serious ethical breach on the part of non-inerrantists.

Let me use an illustration to make the point. If one sincerely believes in a flat earth view and later comes to change his mind, what it the ethical thing to do? It is to resign and join the Round Earth Society. To stay in the Flat Earth Society and argue that (1) it all depends on how you define flat; (2) from my perspective it looks flat; (3) I have a lot of good friends in the Flat Earth Society with whom I wish to continue fellowship, or (4) the Flat Earth Society allows me to define "flat" the way I would like to do so—to do any of these is disingenuous and unethical. Yet it is what happened at Fuller and is currently happening at ETS and in many of our Christian institutions today.

---

139. See Lindsell, *Battle for the Bible*, 106–21 (note especially Lindsell's criticism of Ladd who signed the inerrancy doctrinal statement for years then repudiated it once Fuller questioned and rejected the doctrine, 114–15); cf. Ladd, *New Testament and Criticism*, 16–18.

An important case in point was in 1976 when the ETS Executive Committee confessed that "some of the members of the Society have expressed the feeling that a measure of *intellectual dishonesty prevails among members who do not take the signing of the doctrinal statement seriously*." Later, an ETS ad hoc committee recognized this problem when it posed the proper question in 1983: "*Is it acceptable for a member of the society to hold a view of biblical author's intent which disagrees with the Founding Fathers and even the majority of the society, and still remain a member in good standing?*" (emphasis added). The society never said no, leaving the door open for non-inerrantists to come in. This left a society in which the members could believe anything they wished to believe about the inerrancy statement, despite what the framers meant by it.

The ETS Committee further reported that other "members of the Society have come to the realization that they are not in agreement with the creedal statement and have voluntarily withdrawn. That is, *in good conscience* they could not sign the statement" (1976 Minutes, emphasis added). This is exactly what all members who no longer believed what the ETS framers believed by inerrancy should have done. A member who is now allowed to sign the ETS statements but "disagrees with the Founding Fathers" is not acting in "good conscience." Thus, it is only a matter of time before the majority of the members disagree with the ETS Founders, and the majority of the Society then officially deviates from its founding concept of inerrancy. As someone rightly noted, most religious organizations are like a propeller-driven airplane: they will naturally go left unless you deliberately steer them to the right.

## No Evidence for Any Specific Charges Ever Given

The *Five Views* dialogue book contains many sweeping claims of alleged unethical activity by inerrantists, but no specific charges are made against any individual, nor is any evidence for any charges given. Several points should be made in response.

First, even secular courts demand better than this. They insist on due process. This means that: (1) Evidence should be provided that any persons who have allegedly violated an established law. This is particularly true when the charge is murder of a brother!—"fratricide." In the absence of such evidence against any particular person or group, the charge should be dropped, and the accusers should apologize for using the word or other words like demonize, blackmail, or bullying. (2) Specifics should be given of the alleged crime. Who did it? What did they do? Does it match the alleged crime? The failure of non-inerrantists to do this is an unethical, divisive, and destructive way to carry on a "dialogue" on the topic, to say nothing of doing justice on the matter. Those who use such terms about other brothers in Christ, rather than sticking to the issue of a valid critique of deviant views, are falling far short of the biblical exhortation to speak the truth in love (Eph 4:15).

Part 1—Inerrancy Defined

## The Robert Gundy Case

The so-called "Gundry—Geisler" issue is a case in point. First, ethical charges by non-inerrantists reveal an offensive bias in narrowing it down to one inerrantist in opposition to Gundry when in fact there were was a massive movement in opposition to Gundry's position, including founders of ETS. Indeed, the membership vote to ask him to leave the society was an overwhelming 74 percent. Even though I was an eyewitness of the entire process, I never observed hard feelings expressed between Gundy and those asking for his resignation before, during, or after the issue.

Long-time dean of Trinity Evangelical Divinity School, Dr. Kenneth Kantzer, was the first one to express concern about the issue to me. An ETS founder, Roger Nicole, made the motion for Gundry's resignation with deep regret. Knowing I was a framer of the CSBI statement, Gundry personally encouraged me to enter the discussion, saying, he did not mind the critique of his view because he had "thick skin" and did not take it personally. So, to make charges of ethical abuse against those who opposed Gundry's "dehistoricizing"[140] of the Gospel record is to turn an important doctrinal discussion into a personal attack and it is factually unfounded and ethically unjustified.

Second, the CSBI principles called for an ethical use of the inerrancy doctrine. CSBI framers were careful to point out that "Those who profess faith in Jesus Christ as Lord and Savior are called to show the reality of their discipleship humbly and faithfully obeying God's written Word. To stray from Scripture in faith or conduct is disloyalty to our Master."[141] They also acknowledged that "submission to the claims of God's own Word . . . marks true Christian faith."[142] Further, "those who confess this doctrine often deny it in life by failing to bring our thoughts and deeds, our traditions and habits, into true subjection to the Divine Word."[143] The framers of CSBI added, "We offer this statement in a spirit, not of contention, but of humility and love, which we purpose by God's grace to maintain in any future dialogue arising out of what we have said."[144] To my knowledge, the ETS procedure on the Gundry issue was in accord with these principles, and none of the participants of the *Five Views* book provided any evidence that anyone violated these procedures.

Third, in none of the ETS articles, papers, or official presentations was Robert Gundry attacked personally or demeaned. The process to ask him to resign was a lawful one of principle and not a personal issue, and the parties on both sides recognized and respected this distinction. Anyone who had any evidence to the contrary should have come forward a long time ago or forever held his peace.

140. CSBI, art. XVIII.
141. CSBI, preamble.
142. Ibid.
143. Ibid.
144. Ibid.

Fourth, as for all the parties on the inerrancy discussion over Gundry's views, I know of none who did not like Gundry as a person or did not respect him as a scholar, including myself. In fact, I later invited him to participate with a group of New Testament scholars in Dallas (which he accepted), and I have often cited him in print as an authority on the New Testament and commended his excellent book defending, among other things, the physical nature of the resurrection body.[145]

Fifth, the decision on Gundry's views was not an unruly act done in the dark of night with a bare majority. It was done by a vast majority in the light of day in strict accordance with the rules stated in the ETS policies. It was not hurried since it took place over a two year period. It involves numerous articles *pro* and *con* published in the ETS journal (JETS) as well as dozens of ETS papers and discussions. In short, it was fully and slowly aired in an appropriate and scholarly manner.

Sixth, the final decision was by no means a close call by the membership. It passed with a decisive majority of 74 percent of the members. So, any charge of misuse of authority in the Gundry case is factually mistaken and ethically misdirected.

Since there are no real grounds for the ethical charges against those who opposed Gundry's views on inerrancy, one has to ask why the non-inerrantists are so stirred up over the issue as to make excessive charges like blackmail, demonize, or fratricide? Could it be that many of them hold similar views to Gundry and are afraid that they may be called on the carpet next? As the saying goes, when a stone is tossed down an alley, the dog that squeals the loudest is the one that got hit! We do know this: there is some circumstantial evidence to support this possibility, for many of the most vociferous opponents are the ones who do not accept the ICBI statement on inerrancy or they called for either modification or destruction of it. For example, Enns argues, "Inerrancy should be amended accordingly or, in my view, scrapped altogether."[146] But it has been reported that he himself left Westminster Theological Seminary under a cloud involving a doctrinal dispute that involved inerrancy. And as fellow participant of the *Five Ways* book, John Franke, put it: "His title makes it clear that after supporting it [inerrancy] for many years as a faculty member at Westminster Theological Seminary. . . . In reading his essay, I can't shake the impression that Enns is still in reaction to his departure from Westminster and the controversy his work has created among evangelicals."[147]

Putting aside the specifics of the Gundry case, what can be said about ethics of inerrantists as charged by the participants of the *Five Views* dialogue? Allow me to respond to some specific issues that have been raised against inerrancy by non-inerrantists.

---

145. Gundry, *Sōma in Biblical Theology*.
146. Enns, *Five Views*, 84.
147. Franke, *Five Views*, 137.

Part 1—Inerrancy Defined

## Does the Abuse of Inerrancy Invalidate the Doctrine of Inerrancy?

Most scholars on both sides of this debate recognize that the answer is "No." Abusing marriage does not make marriage wrong. The evil use of language does not make language evil. And abusing inerrancy by some does not make it wrong for all to believe it. Even if one would speak truth in an unloving way, it would not make it false. Likewise, one can speak error in a loving way, but it does not make it true. Of course, we should always try to "speak the truth in love" (Eph 4:15). But when the truth is not spoken in love it does not transform the truth into an error. Accordingly, Vanhoozer rightly wondered whether "Enns, too quickly identifies the concept of inerrancy itself with its aberrations and abuses."[148]

## Is Animated Debate Necessarily Contrary to Christian Love?

Even the editors of the *Five Ways* book, who spent considerable time promoting harmony in doctrinal discussions, admit that the two are not incompatible. They claim: "There is a place for well-reasoned, lucid, and spirited argumentation."[149] They add, "Certainly, debate over concepts and ideas involve[s] description, analysis, and clear reasoning."[150] Indeed, the Apostle Paul "reasoned' with the Jews from the Scriptures (Acts 17:2) and tried to "persuade Jews and Greek" (Acts 18:4). He taught church leaders "to rebuke" those who contradict sound doctrine (Titus 1:9). Jude urged believes to "contend for the faith" (v. 3). In view of Peter's defection, Paul "opposed him to his face" (Gal 2:11). Indeed, Paul and Barnabas "had no small dissension and debate" with the legalists from Judea (Acts 15:2). Sometimes, a refutation or even a rebuke is the most loving thing one can do to defend the truth.

Our supreme example, Jesus, certainly did not hesitate to use strong words and to take strong actions against his opponent's views and actions (Matt 23; John 2:15-17). There are in fact times when a vigorous debate is necessary against error. Love—tough love—demands it. All of these activities can occur within the bound of Christian. John Calvin and Martin Luther were certainly no theological pansies when it came to defending the truth of the Christian faith. But by the standards of conduct urged by non-inerrantists, there would have been no orthodox creeds and certainly no Reformation. And should any knowledgeable evangelical charge the Reformers with being unethical because they vigorously defended Scripture or salvation by faith alone? Of course not!

---

148. Vanhoozer, *Five Views*, 302.
149. Merrick, *Five Views*, 312.
150. Ibid., 316.

## Should Unity Be Put Above Orthodox?

One of the fallacies of the anti-inerrancy movement is the belief that unity should be sought at all cost. Apparently no one told this to the Apostle Paul who defended Christianity against legalism or to Athanasius who defended the deity of Christ against Arius, even though it would split those who believed in the deity of Christ from those, like Arius and his followers, who denied it. The truth is, when it comes to essential Christian doctrine, it would be better to be divided by the truth than to be united by error. If every doctrinal dispute, including those on the Trinity, deity of Christ, and inspiration of Scripture, used the unity over orthodoxy principle that one hears so much about in current inerrancy debate, then there would be not much orthodox Christian faith left. As Rupertus Meldinius (d. 1651) put it, "In essentials, unity; in non-essentials, liberty, and in all things, charity," but as we saw above, the inerrancy of Scripture is an essential doctrine of the Christian faith because all other doctrines are based on it. So, it is epistemologically fundamental to all other biblical teachings.

## Is It Improper to Place Scholarly Articles on the Internet?

Some have objected to carrying on a scholarly discussion on the Internet, as opposed to using scholarly journals. My articles on Mike Licona's denial of inerrancy were subject to this kind of charge.[151] However, given the electronic age in which we live, this is an archaic charge. Dialogue is facilitated by the Internet, and responses can be made much more quickly and by more people. Further, much of the same basic material posted on the Internet was later published in printed scholarly journals.

In a November 18, 2012 paper for the Evangelical Philosophical Society, Mike Licona speaks of his critics saying "bizarre" things like "bullying" people around, of having "a cow" over his view, and of engaging in a "circus" on the Internet. Further, he claims that scholarly critics of his views were "targeting" him and "taking actions against" him. He speaks about those who have made scholarly criticisms of his view as "going on a rampage against a brother or sister in Christ." And he compares it to the statement of Ammianus Marcellinus who wrote, "no wild beasts are such dangerous enemies to man as Christians are to one another." Licona complained about critics of his view, saying, "I've been very disappointed to see the ungodly behavior of a few of my detractors. The theological bullying, the termination and internal intimidation put on a few professors in SBC . . . all this revealed the underbelly of fundamentalism." He charged that I made contacts with seminary leaders in an attempt to get him kicked out of his positions on their staff. The truth is that I made no such contacts for no such purposes. To put it briefly, it is strange that we attack those who defend inerrancy and defend those who attack inerrancy.

---

151. See www.normgeisler.com/articles.

While it is not unethical to use the Internet for scholarly articles, it wrong to make the kind of unethical response that was given to the scholarly articles such as that in the above citations. Such name-calling has no place in a scholarly dialogue. Calling the defense of inerrancy an act of "bullying" diminishes their critic, not them. Indeed, calling one's critic a "tar baby" and labeling their actions as "ungodly behavior" is a classic example of how not to defend one's view against its critics.

What is more, while Licona condemned the use of the Internet to present scholarly critiques of his view as a "circus," he refused to condemn an offensive YouTube cartoon produced by his son-in-law and his friend that offensively caricatured my critique of his view as that of a theological "Scrooge." Even Southern Evangelical Seminary (where Licona was once a faculty member before this issue arose) condemned this approach in a letter from the Office of the President, saying, "We believe this video was totally unnecessary and is in extremely poor taste."[152] One influential alumnus wrote the school, saying, "It was immature, inappropriate and distasteful" and recommended that "whoever made this video needs to pull it down and apologize for doing it."[153] The former president of the SES student body declared: "I'll be honest that video was outright slander and worthy of punishment. I was quite angry after watching it."[154] This kind of unapologetic use of the Internet by those who deny the CSBI view of inerrancy of the Bible is uncalled for and unethical. It does the perpetrators and their cause against inerrancy no good.

## Is Disciplinary Action Sometimes Called For in Organizations like ETS?

"Judge not" is a mantra of our culture, and it has penetrated evangelical circles as well. But ironically, even that statement is a judgment. Rational and moral people must make judgments all the time. This is true in theology as well as in society. Further, discipline on doctrinal matters is not unprecedented in ETS. Indeed, the ETS By Laws provide for such action, saying: "A member whose writings or teachings have been challenged at an annual business meeting as incompatible with the Doctrinal Basis of the Society, upon majority vote, shall have his case referred to the executive committee, before whom he and his accusers shall be given full opportunity to discuss his views and the accusations. The executive committee shall then refer his case to the Society for action at the annual business meeting the following year. A two-thirds majority vote of those present and voting shall be necessary for dismissal from membership."[155] This procedure was followed carefully in the Robert Gundry case.

---

152. Letter, December 9, 2011.
153. Letter, December 21, 2011.
154. Letter, December 17, 2011.
155. Art. 4, sect. 4.

In point of fact, the ETS has expressed an interest in monitoring and enforcing its doctrinal statement on inerrancy from the beginning. The official ETS minutes record the following:

1. In 1965, ETS Journal policy demanded a disclaimer and rebuttal of Dan Fuller's article denying factual inerrancy published in the ETS *Bulletin*. They insisted "that an article by Dr. Kantzer be published simultaneously with the article by Dr. Fuller and that Dr. Schultz include in that issue of the *Bulletin* a brief explanation regarding the appearance of *a view point different from that of the Society*."

2. In 1965, speaking of some who held "Barthian" views of Scripture, the minutes of the ETS Executive Committee read: "President Gordon Clark invited them to leave the society."

3. The 1970 Minutes of ETS affirm that "Dr. R. H. Bube for three years signed his membership form with a note on his own interpretation of infallibility. The secretary was instructed to point out that "*it is impossible for the Society to allow each member an idiosyncratic interpretation of inerrancy, and hence Dr. Bube is to be requested to sign his form without any qualifications*, his own integrity in the matter being entirely respected" (emphasis added). This reveals efforts by ETS to protect and preserve the integrity of its doctrinal statement.

4. In 1983, by a 74-percent majority vote of the membership, Robert Gundry was asked to resign from ETS for his views based on Jewish midrash genre by which he held that sections of Matthew's Gospel were not historical, such as the story of the magi (Matt 2:1–12).

5. In the early 2000s, while I was still a member of the ETS Executive Committee, a majority voted not to allow a Roman Catholic to join ETS largely on the testimony of one founder (Roger Nicole) who claimed that the ETS doctrinal statement on inerrancy was meant to exclude Roman Catholics.

6. In 2003, by a vote of 388 to 231 (nearly 63 percent) the ETS expressed its position that Clark Pinnock's views were contrary to the ETS doctrinal statement on inerrancy. This failed the needed two-third majority to expel him from the society, but it revealed a strong majority who desired to monitor and enforce the doctrinal statement.

Finally, preserving the identity and integrity of any organization calls for doctrinal discipline on essential matters. Those organizations which neglect doing this are doomed to self-destruction.

## Should an Inerrantist Break Fellowship with a Non-Inerrantist over Inerrancy?

The ICBI did not believe that inerrancy should be a test for evangelical fellowship. It declared: "We deny that such a confession is necessary for salvation."[156] And "we

---

156. CSBI, art. XIX.

do not propose that his statement be given creedal weight."[157] In short, it is not a test of evangelical *authenticity*, but of evangelical *consistency*. One can be saved without believing in inerrancy. So, holding to inerrancy is not a test of *spiritual fellowship*; it is a matter of *theological consistency*. Brothers in Christ can fellowship on the basis of belonging to the same spiritual family, without agreeing on all non-salvific doctrines, even some very important ones like inerrancy. In view of this, criticizing inerrantist of evangelical "fratricide" seriously misses the mark and itself contributes to disunity in the body of evangelical believers. Indeed, in the light of the evidence, the ethical charge against inerrantists seriously backfired.

## CONCLUSION

In actuality, the *Five Views* book is basically a two views book: only one person (Al Mohler) unequivocally supports the standard historic view of total inerrancy expressed in the Chicago Statement on Biblical Inerrancy (CSBI), and the other four participants do not. They varied in their rejection from those who presented a more friendly tone, but undercut inerrancy with their alien philosophical premises (Kevin Vanhoozer) to those who are overtly antagonistic to it (Peter Enns).

There was little new in the arguments against the CSBI view of total inerrancy, most of which has been responded to by inerrantists down through the centuries into modern times. However, a new emphasis did emerge in the repeated charge about the alleged unethical behavior of inerrantists. But, as already noted, this is irrelevant to the truth of the doctrine of inerrancy. Further, there is some justification for the suspicion that attacks on the person, rather than the issue, are because non-inerrantists are running out of real ammunition to speak to the issue itself in a biblical and rational way.

In short, after careful examination of the *Five Views* book, the biblical arguments of the non-inerrantists were found to be unsound, their theological arguments were unjustified, their historical arguments were unfounded, their philosophical arguments were unsubstantiated, and their ethical arguments were often outrageous. Nevertheless, there were some good insights in the book, primarily in Al Mohler's sections and from time to time in the other places, as noted above. However, in its representation of the ETS/ICBI view of total inerrancy, the book was seriously imbalanced in format, participants, and discussion. The two professors who edited the book (J. Merrick and Stephen Garrett) were particularly biased in the way the issue was framed by them, as well in many of their comments.

---

157. CSBI, preamble.

Chapter 6

# The 2015 Shepherds' Conference on Inerrancy[1]

WILLIAM C. ROACH

The recent Conference on Inerrancy hosted by John MacArthur and The Master's Seminary (March 3–8, 2015) was an important event in the life of contemporary evangelicalism. Evangelical leaders from around the country and the world convened upon Los Angeles, California, to discuss the importance of the famous Chicago Statement on Biblical Inerrancy for twenty-first-century evangelicalism and the church international. Unashamedly the speakers made one point clear: If evangelicalism is going to have a continued effect for Christ in our lives, we must remain wholeheartedly committed to the inerrancy of Scripture and unashamed to preach the Bible as God's Holy Word. The conference adds a significant second voice to a reaffirmation of this historic statement. Joining with DefendingInerrancy.com, which has already collected nearly fifty thousand names in support of the total inerrancy of Scripture, a powerful voice is now being raised for this generation in defense of Holy Scripture.[2]

Following events of this significance always calls for reflection. The watching world and church sometimes need to be reminded of the importance of the event and the details of the issue. With that caveat in place, in what follows I am going to very briefly lay out five of the most pressing issues facing the inerrancy of Scripture, and how this movement for Inerrancy is a much-needed event in the life of evangelicalism.

---

1. Note: Video for The Master's Seminary 2015 Inerrancy Summit discussed in this article can be found at https://vimeo.com/channels/887255.

2. http://defendinginerrancy.com/signatures.

Part 1—Inerrancy Defined

## 1. AUTHORITY AND TRADITION

Simply put, the Bible is first and foremost a *divine book*. God is the primary cause of Scripture and for that reason, the Bible carries with it divine authority. The framers of the Chicago Statement sought to articulate a thoroughgoing Protestant declaration on the nature of the Scriptures. The official commentary states, "This article [i.e., Art. I], as well as Article II, makes the statement clearly a Protestant one. Though it is true that that Roman Catholic Church has consistently and historically maintained a high view of the inspiration of Holy Scripture, there remains the unresolved problem of the uniqueness and sufficiency of biblical authority for the church."[3] Therefore, article I claims, "*We affirm* that the Holy Scriptures are to be received as the authoritative Word of God. *We deny* that the Scriptures receive their authority from the church, tradition, or any other human source."

Immediately, one should contrast the two sources: divine versus human. The reason evangelicals affirm the sole authority of the Scriptures is because the Bible, and the Bible *alone*, has divine origin; hence, it has divine authority and is able to bind the conscience in matters of faith and practice. Tradition, in contra-distinction to Catholic claims, has a human origin; consequently, it does not have the absolute authority to bind the conscience in matters of faith and practice. Roman Catholics believe both the Scriptures and tradition are able to bind the conscience. But in making that claim, they are by necessity admitting the Scriptures are not the supreme *written* norm, and denying that the church is subordinate to the Scriptures. On the other hand, Protestants are clear that Scripture and Scripture *alone*, is the supreme written norm that binds the conscience.

Evangelicals need to be clear to address the fact that we are not Roman Catholics, nor should we try to act like there is some sort of ecumenical unity between Protestants and Catholics on this matter (or a host of other matters). The absolute authority and sufficiency of Scripture was the formal cause of the Reformation, and now is not the time for Protestants to quit protesting against Rome's claims about the theoretical equal authority of tradition and Scripture, and the practical authority tradition takes over Scripture in their system. Indeed, we still stand with the Reformed churches, who claim that tradition has ministerial authority over the body of Christ, not magisterial authority.

## 2. REVELATION AND THE INERRANCY OF THE WHOLE

The Scriptures *are* a revelation given to us by God. The Scriptures *are not* a witness to revelation, nor do they require response to *become* revelation, nor do they merely *contain* revelation. Instead, they *are* revelation. Several theologians throughout the years have denied that the Bible is objectively given revelation. They claim revelation

---

3. Sproul, *Explaining Inerrancy*, 25.

requires the written Scriptures plus something else (e.g., dynamic response, perlocutionary effect, and so forth). These views have commonly been labeled as existential or neo-Orthodox approaches to Scriptures.

The Chicago Statement thoroughly sought to withstand these types of claims, maintaining as seen in article III, "*We deny* that the Bible is merely a witness to revelation, or only becomes revelation in encounter, or depends on the responses of men for its validity." Consequently, they stated, "*We affirm* that the written Word in its entirety is revelation given by God."

Evangelical theologians as of late, however, have developed an infatuation with neo-Orthodoxy. They maintain alongside Barth that the Bible can be the revelation of God and contain the admixture of error. They are not bothered when theologians claim the Scriptures are generally true, even though they contain the admixture of error. All that matters, so they maintain, is the general message of Scripture be true, not the finer historical points and details.

Carl Henry was right when he claimed, "Revelation is a divinely initiated activity, God's free communication by which he alone turns his personal privacy into a deliberate disclosure of his reality."[4] In addition, "The nature, content, and variety [of revelation] are exclusively God's determination."[5] In other words, the source of revelation is God. God's character and nature determine the character and nature of Scripture—not humanity, ancient Near Eastern cultural customs, or so-called acceptable historical and biographical practices.

Basic to each pronouncement of Scripture is that God is the sole source, ultimate originator and determiner of revelation. God's pronouncements rightly represent God's nature; Scripture is a pronouncement of God; therefore, Scripture rightly represents God's nature. In the final analysis, then, an attack on the total truthfulness of the Bible, or claiming the Scriptures contain truth with the admixture of error, is an attack on the character of God and the purity of his nature. Can God lie? May it never be!

## 3. THE NATURE OF TRUTH AND ACCOMMODATION

If God is the *ultimate source* of Scripture, and the *determiner* of revelation, and the *basis* for all scriptural truth claims rest upon his *nature*; and if it be admitted that humanity is *depraved*, and that the world has been plunged into *sin*, so that our *minds*, *culture*, *society*, etc. are *fallen*; then one would be correct to say there is a cosmic battle between the truth claims of God's divine revelation and the truth claims of humanity, society, and culture.

Clearly the history of redemption insists that humanity lives in constant rebellion against God. Truly there is no one who seeks God, no, not one! All have turned away from him. All are living idol-making factories. Each of us and every society have

4. Henry, *God, Revelation, and Authority*, 2:8.
5. Ibid., 2:9.

been plagued by the social and noetic effects of sin. Consequently, there are cultural ideals and claims that mount up against the truth claims of God.

Sometimes these claims assert that we can become like God. Other times they claim God did not fashion the world in a particular way, whether it be the construction of the cosmos or the actual inherent value of humanity. Still, further, there are times when humanity claims that God's pronouncements are not true or that Jesus and Paul were merely flawed and errant men. Sadly, whether it be through the influence of major political or religious leaders, or the prodding of an influential parent, or the instruction of an influential teacher; each of us are prone to distort the truth and believe that lies actually corresponds to reality, the scriptural reality included.

The scholarly effect of this distortion of reality is known as accommodation. Academia insists that Scripture cannot be making timeless truth claims because they are restricted by natural and finite limitations. Subsequently, many of these academics claim the Scriptures merely reflect the cultural *milieu* and the customs of the people. Therefore, it is the task of the scholar to recognize these erred reflections and to sort out the wheat from the chaff, the true from the speculative, the real from the falsely claimed. In effect, culture and society serve as the *determiner* of revelation and the *corrector* of scriptural claims.

For example, scholars claim research indicates humanity is merely the byproduct of evolution or that Adam is merely a hominoid representative for the rest of humanity. Others will claim Jesus was merely reflecting the cultural customs of his day, or Paul was merely a pre-literate man saturated in the false views of his day; therefore, he was not really qualified to speak about the historical Adam or the truthfulness of gender roles.

Fundamental to this errant thesis is the claim that God is *not* the source and determiner of all revelation. But what is also fundamental to the Bible's clear teaching is that the Scriptures serve to confront and correct all other worldviews. So the practical effects being, if Scripture and any other worldview or truth claims conflict, one who submits to the authority of Scripture must submit to the Bible's truth claims. In the final analysis—we are to use Scripture as a weapon to confront the errant views of opposing worldviews (for it is the instrument by which we tear down intellectual and moral strongholds)—we are not to allow speculative and errant worldviews to confront and attack the biblical worldview or the Scriptures. May the Word of the Lord stand forever!

## 4. HERMENEUTICS AND INERRANCY

*Some* battles for the Bible are actually battles for *the Bible*. *Some* battles for the Bible are actually battles for *one's interpretation* of the Bible. Consequently, *some* interpretations of the Bible *do not* undermine the total truthfulness of the Bible; while *some* interpretations *do* undermine the total truthfulness of the Bible. In other words, each group *approaches* the Bible, and each group interprets the Bible. But not all approaches uphold the total truthfulness of Scripture and consequently, some can actually undermine the inerrancy of the Bible by the way they handle the text of Holy Scripture.

Many evangelicals today are asking: Is inerrancy a hermeneutic? The short answer is, yes! The Chicago Statement on Biblical Inerrancy clearly believed *only* the grammatical-historical approach to Scripture methodologically and *consistently* upholds and affirms the inerrancy of the Bible. Article XVIII states: "*We affirm* that the text of Scripture is to be interpreted by grammatico-historical exegesis, taking account of its literary forms and devices, and that Scripture is to interpret Scripture. *We deny* the legitimacy of any treatment of the text or quest for sources lying behind it that leads to relativizing, dehistoricizing, or discounting its teachings, or rejecting its claims to authorship."

Some believe the classic-evangelical insistence upon the grammatico-historical interpretation of Scripture is nothing more than wooden-headed literalism. They claim evangelicals cannot distinguish between different literary styles and resort to ridicule rather than rationally engage the issue.

One thing that needs to be remembered is that all of the arguments raised against the inerrancy of Scripture are really old arguments dressed in contemporary clothing. Carl Henry addressed a similar issue in his day. Henry recognized some evangelicals might be inconsistent with the literal method; however, that is not an argument against the method *per se*, but the *use* or *abuse* of the method. He also notes it was not evangelicalism that first subverted a literal interpretation to modernism, but neo-Protestantism by labeling the miracle claims of Scripture as legend and myth. Henry suggests the best way to know whether the author intends for the text to be taken literally or figuratively is from the context of the passage. He warns his readers, noting,

> Evaluation of an author's intention can, of course, be manipulated by critical presuppositions . . . Surely writers who use sayings or events for apologetic purposes need not require or presuppose the nonfactuality of those sayings or events. Yet Barr proposes that we take "very seriously" what is nonfactual, and dignifies this approach as literal interpretation.[6]

Henry believes individuals attempt to escape the literal method by examining the authors supposed intention, when in reality they repudiate the literal interpretation of the Bible and use authorial intention to gut the Scriptures of their literal meaning. He concludes that this new "literal method" used by these Neo-Evangelicals (e.g., individuals going beyond the tenets of historic or classical evangelicalism), is a result of their disdain for the inspiration of the Scriptures. Furthermore, when they do make use of a "literal" interpretation, they do so upon the premise that the Bible is not historically and factually accurate.

---

6. Henry, *God, Revelation and Authority*, 4:127–28.

Part 1—Inerrancy Defined

## 5. HEALTH OF THE CHURCH

Ideas have consequences. Truth matters. And the idea about the total truthfulness of Scripture matters, bearing eternal consequences for the health of the church and the lives of individuals worldwide.

Francis Schaeffer reminds us, "We have seen then that as Bible-believing Christians we are locked in a battle in the arena of ideas. But in the area of actions there is a direct parallel. Ideas are never neutral and abstract. Ideas have consequences in the way we live and act, both in our personal lives and in the culture as a whole."[7]

One must ask: Can one really expect Christians worldwide to remain true to the message and ethic of Jesus Christ if they no longer believe in the total truthfulness of Scripture? Ideas have consequences. If the battle for the Bible is really the watershed for evangelical identity and consistency, one might rightly ask: Can one really expect individual Christians to not bend the Bible in their individual theological beliefs and moral lives if the Scriptures are no longer completely true? Ideas have consequences.

If we no longer have an inerrant Bible, divine promises lack all assurance and moral imperatives cease to bind the conscience. If we no longer have an inerrant Bible, preaching becomes null and void, for the preacher is merely communicating one man's interpretation of a pre-historic individual who happened to write down his thoughts over two-thousand years ago.

The mark of our age is that society holds all of its beliefs tentatively and seeks to reevaluate religious claims daily. Sadly evangelicals are not inoculated to this trend, and some are starting to reevaluate the practical effects of denying the inerrancy of Scripture. Unfortunately, many evangelicals have neglected to heed the voice of their twentieth-century prophet Francis Schaeffer, who warned of this very thing. He warned of the practical effects of denying the inerrancy of Scripture for both evangelicalism and culture. Schaeffer warns that if we give up the Bible's own self-testimony and Jesus' claims for the Scriptures, we will no longer be the redeeming salt for our culture or faithful witnesses of Jesus Christ. Schaeffer goes on to note, saying:

> Here then is the watershed of the evangelical world. We must say most lovingly but clearly: evangelicalism is not consistently evangelical unless there is a line drawn between those who take a view of Scripture and those who do not. But remember that we are not just talking about an abstract theological doctrine. It makes little difference in the end if Scripture is compromised by theological infiltration from the surrounding culture. It is the obeying of Scripture which is the watershed—obeying the bible equally in doctrine and in the way we live in the full spectrum of life.[8]

---

7. Shaeffer, *Complete Works*, 4:315.
8. Ibid., 343.

Let's consider the battle that we're in as evangelical Christians. God's Word will never pass away, but the history of redemption since the foundation of the world indicates that men will either blatantly rebel against the text of Scripture, or they will try to hide it under the bushel of profound intellectual and speculative theories.

The implications of these efforts for the doctrine of inerrancy, calls for us to consider the nature and authority of Scripture, alongside the proper function of Christ's church and the practice of truth by Christians. We at DefendingInerrancy.com join with MacArthur and the TMS Conference on Inerrancy in support of the landmark statements of the International Council on Biblical Inerrancy in defense of this historic doctrine.

## Chapter 7

# Interview with Paige Patterson on the Importance of Inerrancy[1]

### WILLIAM C. ROACH

*Roach*: Recently Baptist Press claimed that inerrancy provided the necessary bedrock to revive the denomination from aberrant theological views. Can you elaborate upon the role inerrancy played in the Conservative Resurgence?

*Patterson*: The theological slippage in the Southern Baptist Convention was widespread and target rich. However, it occurred to those of us in leadership that there was a certain sense in which the whole of it could be reduced to one issue. We believed that the overwhelming majority of Southern Baptists believed in the inerrancy of God's Word. Furthermore, we felt that this was an issue that easily could be explained to the vast majority of people. In addition, the same people who were propagating other forms of heresy invariably had a problem with the truthfulness of God's Word. Consequently, we made our decision to pursue one subject and basically to refuse to be sidetracked onto others. By making the epistemological issue of inerrancy of the Word of God primary, we were able to secure the following of the vast majority of the people in the Southern Baptist Convention. When we then voted on the Baptist Faith and Message 2000 with the major changes to strengthen the doctrine of Holy Scripture, 98 percent of the convention messengers voted in support of that revised confession. Consequently, clearly the doctrine of the inerrancy of Scripture was the primary focus of the Conservative Resurgence; and, as we had expected, the other doctrines of the church fell quickly in line once that was accepted by the convention.

---

1. Editor's note: Paige Patterson, president of Southwestern Baptist Theological Seminary, discusses the role inerrancy played in the Conservative Resurgence in the Southern Baptist Convention, with *Defending Inerrancy* contributing editor William Roach.

*Roach*: Some people who opposed the Conservative Resurgence claimed that inerrancy has not always been the historic Baptist view. How well do you think inerrancy represents the historic Baptist view of the Bible?

*Patterson*: Some during the Conservative Resurgence argued that inerrancy was not always the historic view of the Bible among Baptist people. However, in the 1980s Drs. L. Russ Bush and Tom Nettles, then both on the faculty of Southwestern Baptist Theological Seminary, published a book entitled *Baptists and the Bible*.[2] Basically, they simply demonstrated in the book that while not all Baptists in history held to the inerrancy of God's Word, the overwhelming majority of Baptists did hold to the inerrancy of the Bible. From the time of the publication of that book until now, no one has again dared to challenge the view that most Baptists—and just about all of Baptist leadership—in the history of Baptists and the Anabaptist people, held diligently to the inerrancy of God's Word.

*Roach*: How do you think the Chicago Statement on Biblical Inerrancy has influenced the Southern Baptist Convention's view of the inerrancy of Scripture?

*Patterson*: The Chicago Statement on Biblical Inerrancy had no effect at all on Southern Baptists' commitment to the inerrancy of God's Word. Such a commitment had a long history prior to the Council on Biblical Inerrancy's founding. However, the International Council on Biblical Inerrancy and the subsequent Chicago Statement on Biblical Inerrancy did have a profound effect in strengthening many Southern Baptists. My contention would be that what was going on in the Southern Baptist Convention at the same time that the International Council on Biblical Inerrancy was doing its work provided mutual help for the two entities. On the one hand, the Southern Baptists provided the people power in support of the International Council on Biblical Inerrancy while, on the other hand, the large number of tremendously helpful books and articles that came from the International Council on Biblical Inerrancy provided Southern Baptist people with the ammunition they needed to fight their battle. Consequently, even though I served on the Council on Biblical Inerrancy, I can also say that as a Southern Baptist, I am grateful to God for the monumental contribution that was made by the International Council.

*Roach*: What's the importance of inerrancy for a pastor to maintain a thriving pulpit ministry?

*Patterson*: The simple truth is that if a man does not believe that God has spoken a sure and certain word, then when he enters the pulpit and gives a sermon, the very best that he has to offer is a moral platitude of some variety, calling on human beings to a more noble existence; but even then he cannot be sure that what he says is true. The only way to have a thriving pulpit ministry and a growing church that is uniquely

---

2. Bush and Nettles, *Baptists and the Bible*.

blessed of God is to have a pastor opening God's Word as the final adjudication of all matters of human life and eternity. With charisma, one can build a large congregation if it's located in the right place, but it is impossible to build saintly lives without the highest conceivable view of God's Word.

*Roach*: How has the inerrancy of Scripture encouraged missions to thrive in the Southern Baptist Convention?

*Patterson*: Well, today Southern Baptists maintain almost five thousand missionaries ministering for Christ in 132 countries of the world. Actually, there is ministry considerably beyond that, but these are the ones who are publically identifiable. It is conceivable that Southern Baptists could have yielded that many missionaries just based on the amount of money that was available, but they certainly would not under any circumstances be as effective as they are now. The result of taking the seminaries back to Christ and to the highest commitment to the Scriptures has resulted in the deluge of godly missionaries who believe that the Bible is the inerrant Word of God. Consequently, these are given courage to go to the most forbidding places on the earth and risk everything for the cause of Christ. Any lesser view of Scripture and confidence in the inerrancy of God's Word would never produce such a missionary.

*Roach*: As a seminary president, how does the doctrine of inerrancy shape your view of evangelical theological education?

*Patterson*: The greatest miracle of God in the Conservative Resurgence in the Southern Baptist Convention is that when we began the movement in 1979, I could identify only sixteen inerrantists teaching on the faculties of our six seminaries. Most of these did not take an open stand. There are a few to whom I've never talked; so possibly there were a very few more than sixteen, but those are the ones I know and can count. Today, thirty-five years later, the incredible and unbelievable has happened under the leadership of our Lord. We have six seminaries boasting a total full-time faculty of more than two hundred; and to my knowledge, there is not a single one who is not a biblical inerrantist. On top of that, all six seminary presidents are inerrantists. In addition to that, all six are outspoken inerrantists who make it crystal clear that biblical inerrancy is the epistemological position of the particular seminary they serve. The full impact of this, and even the recognition of it, has been slow to come, but in fact, that is what has happened. Among the first questions I ask any candidate for our faculty is for his view of the Bible. If he does not state a clear view of the inerrancy of God's Word, then there is no chance that he will have a position at Southwestern Baptist Theological Seminary. Consequently, I would have to say that the doctrine of the inerrancy of God's Word has had a profound impact on all of our seminaries.

Chapter 8

# Do You Have to Be a Calvinist to Believe in Inerrancy?

## NORMAN L. GEISLER

### INTRODUCTION

Many leaders in the modern inerrancy movement are strong Calvinists. From this some have inferred that inerrancy is a uniquely Calvinistic doctrine. They claim that the prime movers on International Council on Biblical Inerrancy (1978–1989) were strong Calvinists. This is true, however the ICBI was not exclusively made up of strong Calvinists and they were by no means the beginning of the inerrancy movement. In fact, the doctrine of inerrancy was held by the early church fathers and on through Augustine, Anselm, and Aquinas. So, it is historically inaccurate to claim that inerrancy originated with Calvinism.

### MEDIEVAL CHURCH INERRANTISTS

Belief in inerrancy of Scripture has been the standard view of orthodox Christianity from the beginning,[1] long before there were Calvinists in name or doctrine. St Augustine (fourth century AD) held to the inerrancy of Scripture, proclaiming that "when they write that he has taught and said . . . the members put down what they had come to know at the dictation of the Head. Therefore whatever he wanted us to read concerning his words and deeds, he commanded the disciple, his hands, to write. Hence one cannot but receive what he reads in the Gospels, though written by the

---

1. Hannah, *Inerrancy and the Church*.

very hand of the Lord Himself."[2] He added that "by the admission of a falsehood here, the authority of the Holy Scripture given for the faith of all coming generations is to be made wholly uncertain and wavering."[3]

As for alleged errors in the Bible, he declared emphatically that "it is not allowable to say, the author of this books is mistaken." No error can be in the original text which was breathed out by God. Rather, said Augustine, "either the manuscript [copy] is faulty, or the translation is wrong, or you have misunderstood."[4]

## THE REFORMERS ON INERRANCY

Space only allows comment on the two major reformers. Martin Luther (d. 1546) declared, "The Scriptures, although they were written by men, are neither of men nor from men but from God."[5] He added, "I have learned to ascribe this honour (namely the infallibility) only to books which are termed canonical, so that I confidently believe that not one of their authors erred."[6] Luther went so far as to assert that "whoever is so bold that he ventures to accuse God of fraud and deception in a single word blasphemes God."[7]

John Calvin (d. 1564) also defended the full inerrancy of Scripture, saying, "Nor is it sufficient to believe God is true, and cannot lie or deceive, unless you feel firmly persuaded that every word which proceeds from him is sacred, inviolable truth."[8] For the writers of Scripture were "sure and authentic amanuenses of the Holy Spirit; and, therefore, their writings are regarded as the oracles of God."[9]

The truth is that on crucial points of Five-Point Calvinism (like Limited Atonement) up to the time of Calvin there were no strong Calvinists among the great leaders of the church, with the exception of the late Augustine.[10]

## OLD PRINCETON CALVINISTS ON INERRANCY

Much of the impetus for giving Calvinism credit for the doctrine of inerrancy is taken from the Old Princetonians, B. B. Warfield and A. A. Hodge, who provided a strong defense of inerrancy just before the turn of the century. Their books did indeed serve as a confirmation of the doctrine of inerrancy in the twentieth century. And they

2. Augustine, *Harmony of the Gospels*, 1.35.54.
3. Augustine, *Letters*, 40.3.5.
4. Augustine, *Against Faustus*, 11.5.
5. Luther, *Works*, 35:153.
6. Cited by Reu, *Scriptures*, 17.
7. Luther, *Works*, 37:26.
8. Calvin, *Institutes*, 3.2.6.
9. Ibid., 4.8.9.
10. See Geisler, *Chosen but Free*, appendix 3.

were definitely Calvinists, and they spearheaded the movement to preserve the belief in doctrine of inerrancy.[11] They wrote, "The New Testament writers continually assert the Scriptures of the Old Testament . . . *are the word of God*. What their writers said God said."[12] This means that "the Holy Spirit was present . . . and everywhere securing the errorless expression in language of the thought designed by God."[13] However, "We do not assert that the common text, but only that the original autographic text was inspired."[14]

It is also true that many of the leaders of the later ICBI inerrancy movement were strong Calvinists. John Gerstner, R.C. Sproul, James Boice, J. I. Packer, and Roger Nicole come to mind. However, not all ICBI leaders were strong Calvinists. Earl Radmacher, Harold Hoehner, Bill Bright, Walter Kaiser, and myself come to mind. The truth be told, if all noses were counted, a majority of those who signed and/or supported the famous Chicago Statement on Biblical Inerrancy (1978) were not strong Calvinists. They were either moderate Calvinists, so-called "Cal-minians," Arminians, Wesleyans, or some other label. This would include a majority of the Southern Baptist leaders (like W. A. Criswell, Paige Patterson, Richard Land, Rush Bush, and William E. Nix) and the majority of laypersons. It would also include others like Robert Preus and other Lutherans, J. P. Moreland, Josh McDowell, Kenneth Gangel, and many other Christian leaders.

Indeed, many ICBI leaders and signers would identify themselves as Arminians or Wesleyans. At least nine of them signed the ICBI Chicago Statement: Allan Coppedge, Wilbur Dayton, Ralph Earle, Eldon R. Fuhrman, Dennis F. Kinlaw, Daryl McCarthy. James Earl Massey, A. Skevington Wood, and Laurence W. Wood.[15] Indeed, McCarthy later was chosen by ICBI leaders to write the chapter on the Wesleyan view on inerrancy in the ICBI sponsored book on the topic.[16]

## A STATEMENT OF THE WESLEYAN (ARMINIAN) VIEW ON INERRANCY

John Wesley wrote: "The Scripture therefore of the Old and New Testament is a most solid and precious system of Divine truth. Every part thereof is worthy of God; and all together are one entire body, wherein is no defect, nor excess."[17] He added, "The Proverbs of Solomon . . . were the dictates of the Spirit of God in Solomon; so

---

11. See their book *Inspiration*, 1881.
12. Ibid., 29.
13. Ibid., 17.
14. Ibid.
15. Reasoner, *Importance of Inerrancy*, 64.
16. Hannah, *Inerrancy and the Church*.
17. Wesley, preface to *Explanatory Notes*, 5.

that it is by Solomon that he speaks."[18] Also, he said, the Bible is "the only standard of truth."[19] He would not allow any error in the Bible, saying, "Nay, will not the allowing there is any error in Scripture, shake the authority of the whole."[20] British Wesleyan theologian Adam Clarke wrote, "Men may err, but the Scriptures cannot: for it is the Word of God himself, who can neither mistake, deceive, nor be deceived."[21] Wesley himself said emphatically, "Nay, if there be any mistake in the Bible there may well as be a thousand. If there be one falsehood in that book, it did not come from the God of truth."[22]

## CONCLUSION

The doctrine of inerrancy does not belong to any one denomination or section of Christendom. It belongs to the whole church. It was articulated long before there were any Presbyterians or Methodists by Early Fathers, St. Augustine, and Thomas Aquinas. John Calvin held it, but so did so did John Wesley, and, as noted, the ICBI affirmation of it (1978) was signed by many Wesleyans. In fact one Wesleyan scholar, Daryl McCarty, wrote the article on the Wesleyan view of inerrancy for the official ICBI book on the topic edited by John Hannah, *Inerrancy and the Church*. Inerrancy is not uniquely Presbyterian or Baptist. Inerrancy is neither a late nor a denominational doctrine. It is not provincial but universal. It is the foundation for every group that names the name of Christ and, as the psalmist said, "If the foundation is destroyed, then what shall the righteous do" (Ps 11:3)?

---

18. Ibid., 3:1830.
19. Wesley, *Bicentennial Edition of the Works of John Wesley*, 13:137.
20. Ibid., 11:504.
21. Clarke, *Miscellaneous Works*, 12:132.
22. Wesley, *Journals*, 24 July 1776.

# Part 2

# Inerrancy Defended

This section identifies many of the prominent Neo-Evangelical scholars who are now moving away from an orthodox view of inerrancy toward redefining the term in aberrant ways. It also highlights the various ideological methods and artifice that are now being employed by these critical evangelical scholars that are causing this change in meaning. These articles present not only a rigorous defense of the biblical, orthodox understanding of inerrancy but also a sound refutation of the ideas of those attempting to change its meaning . . .

Jude 3—"Contend earnestly for the faith which was once for all handed down to the saints."

Chapter 9

# "It's Just a Matter of Interpretation, Not of Inerrancy"

Examining the Relation between Inerrancy and Hermeneutics

NORMAN L. GEISLER

## INTRODUCTION

A current argument for broadening the traditional meaning of inerrancy is: "It's just a matter of interpretation, not of inerrancy." This is used to justify the acceptance of views that have been traditionally rejected by inerrantists. For example, Jack Rogers of Fuller Seminary held that the Bible is wholly true. He even went so far as to say that he was "in agreement with the view of inerrancy set forth in the Chicago Statement on Biblical Inerrancy [1978]."[1] Yet he allowed for there to be factual mistakes in the Bible.[2] How so? Because when examining the biblical text according to his "the intention of the author" view, he insisted that the biblical authors did not intend to mislead the reader, even when they said that some things are factually incorrect.

Likewise, Robert Gundry justified his "dehistoricizing" of sections of Matthew (e.g., the visit of the magi) by claiming he believed in the inerrancy of the whole Bible, including that text on the magi in Matthew 2, but that it was not to be interpreted

---

1. Kantzer, "Rhetoric about Inerrancy," 18.
2. Rogers and McKim, *Authority and Interpretation of the Bible*, 31, 65, 384–85, 389–93; 432–35.

literally.³ So, he claimed this was not denying the inerrancy of Matthew 2 since it was only a matter of interpretation, not one of inspiration.

Similarly, Mike Licona claims to believe in the inerrancy of the Bible (including Matthew), even though he affirms that it would not be contrary to inerrancy to view the resurrection of the saints in Matthew 27:51–54 as "poetic" or a "legend"⁴ claiming that in that kind of Greco-Roman genre "it is often difficult to determine where history ends and legend begins."⁵ Indeed, he goes so far as to claim that even a literal contradiction in the Gospel record⁶ could be consistent with a belief in inerrancy, since the kind of genre used in the Gospels allows for both of these texts to be true, even though they contradict each other.⁷

According to this view, challenging the meaning of a biblical narrative (as to whether it is historical) does not call inspiration into question; is simply a matter of interpretation. By this kind of separation of inspiration and inerrancy, one can hold that the entire Bible is inspired, even though there may be errors in given passages. Clearly, this leaves a lot more latitude for errors than the traditional view does. However, there are serious problems with the suppositions involved in such a procedure. We will examine several of these faulty assumptions now.

## EXAMINING THE ASSUMPTIONS OF THE DENIAL OF TRADITIONAL INERRANCY

Assumption 1: Inspiration and interpretation are totally separate matters.

This view of the separation of inspiration and interpretation is open to serious challenge. For if inspiration and inerrancy are totally separate, then the Bible could be inerrant, even if it affirmed nothing. But this is absurd. The fact is that inspiration cannot be totally separated from inerrancy. If it could, then logically no text of Scripture would have any meaning. It would be totally vacuous. Inerrancy would be affirming nothing in the biblical text. But something has to be affirmed (or denied) in order for there to be meaning and truth, for a statement is meaningful only if it is either true or false. And it is true or false only if it either affirms or denies something. But, as Aristotle noted, truth is what corresponds to the facts. For "to say of what is that it is not, or of what is not that it is, is false."⁸ Aquinas concurred, saying, "Truth is defined by the conformity of the intellect and the thing and hence to know this conformity

---

3. Gundry, "Theological Postscript," 623–47.

4. Licona, *Resurrection of Jesus*, 548, 553.

5. Ibid., 34.

6. In a transcript of the debate with Bart Ehrman (spring 2009) Licona said, "I think that John probably altered the day [of Jesus' crucifixion] in order for a theological—to make a theological point there. But that does not mean that Jesus wasn't crucified."

7. See Geisler, "Mike Licona Admits Contradictions."

8. Aristotle, *Metaphysics* 7.6.25.

is to know truth."⁹ Modern philosopher G. E. Moore agreed, writing, "To say that this belief is true, is to say that there is in the Universe a fact to which it corresponds; and to say that it is false is to say that there is not in the Universe any fact to which it corresponds."[10]

So, if the Bible has any meaning whatsoever, then it must be affirming or denying something. And, if it has any truths, then it must have affirmations or denials to which its statements correspond. So, its truthfulness (inerrancy) cannot be maintained totally apart from its affirmations (and denials). So, while inspiration and inerrancy are logically distinct, nonetheless, they are not actually separable.

## Assumption 2: The Bible could be inerrant, even if its interpretations were completely allegorical.

All sides of the debate agree that there is poetry (psalms), parable (Matt 13), and allegory (Gal 4:24) in the Bible. If so, then some critics argue that it is possible that any given passage (and by logical extension all passages) could be taken allegorically. After all, if inspiration and inerrancy are totally separate issues, then all passages could be taken allegorically (i.e., nonliterally). Hence, it is possible that nothing in the Bible is literally true, including the story of the magi (Matt 2) and the resurrection of the saints (Matt 27).

Indeed, both Robert Gundry and Mike Licona have admitted this possibility. When Gundry was asked whether he would vote "yes" on Christian Science founder Mary Baker Eddy (who totally allegorized the Bible) to be a member of the Evangelical theological Society (ETS), if she sincerely accepted its doctrinal statement on inerrancy, Gundry said, "I would vote yes . . ."![11] Likewise, when Licona was interrogated by the Southern Evangelical Seminary (SES) faculty about his views, he said "that if someone interpreted the resurrection accounts as metaphor and therefore denied the historicity of the Gospel accounts that would not contradict inerrancy." That faculty examiner exclaimed, "That was unbelievable."[12] Shocking as this may seem, it is a logical extension of the view that inspiration and inerrancy are totally separate issues. That is to say, the Bible could be entirely inerrant without anything in it being actually true.

Even Paul Tillich admits that God-talk could not be totally symbolic, for there could be no negation of a literal truth, if there were no preceding affirmation to be negated. Something has to be literally true. Tillich believed that the statement that God is "Being" or "the Ground of Being" or, better, "Being Itself" was literally true.[13] In-

---

9. Aquinas, *Summa Theologica* 1.16.
10. Moore, *Some Main Problems in Philosophy*, 279.
11. Geisler, "Methodological Unorthodoxy," 87–94.
12. Thomas Howe, letter to Norman Geisler, September 22, 2014.
13. Tillich, *Ultimate Concern*, 46.

deed, logic demands that not every statement about God (or reality) can be nonliteral. Something has to be literally true before one can know that something else is not-literal. Every negation of knowledge presupposes some positive knowledge. Even the Neoplatonic mystic Plotinus (third century AD) admitted, "It is impossible to say, 'Not that' if one is utterly without experience or conception of the 'That.'"[14]

Likewise, inspiration and inerrancy cannot be totally separated. To assume they can be is logically incoherent. Yet both Gundry and Licona, and other Neo-Evangelicals following them, argue that they can be totally separated. Thus, the basic premise behind this view is incoherent. Something has to be known to be literally true in order for us to know that something else is not literally true. Everything cannot be purely symbolic. The Bible must be actually making some literal truth claim before we can say it is inerrant.

## Assumption 3: Since interpretation is an entirely separate issue from inerrancy, the real issue is one of interpretation, not one of inerrancy.

It is argued that if interpretation is an entirely separate issue from inerrancy, then all the debates about inerrancy boil down to a matter of interpretation. But since there are many different and legitimate ways to interpret a biblical text, then the inerrancy issue becomes one of how one interprets the Bible.

In response, inerrancy and interpretation are not totally separate matters. Inerrancy implies a certain way to interpret the Bible. For even the statement that "the Bible is inerrant (without error)" involves an interpretation of some facts. Otherwise how could one know it was without error, unless he knew what was true (that is, what corresponds to the facts). As already noted, one cannot know what is not true, unless he first knows what is true. But this is only possible if one has a proper understanding of the facts. Thus, inerrancy and interpretation are inseparably connected. Otherwise, the very statement that "the Bible is without error" would mean no more than, "If anything is true in the Bible, then the Bible is true on this matter."

However, this is a hypothetical and vacuous statement, and it is clearly not what confessors of inerrancy mean when they claim "the Bible is completely without error." What they mean is that "all of the many things the Bible does affirm as true are true." In other words, inerrancy confessions are confessions of truth in the Bible—all the truth of the Bible.

Even in its landmark Statement on Biblical Inerrancy (1978), the ICBI framers recognized the connection between inspiration and interpretation by its article XIII: "We affirm that the text of Scripture is to be interpreted by grammatico-historical exegesis . . ." Thus, "all the claims of the Bible must correspond with reality, whether that

---

14. Plotinus, *Enneads*, 6.7.29.

reality is historical, factual, or spiritual."[15] Without the historical-grammatical (literal) interpretation of the Bible, one could not even embrace the doctrine of inerrancy.

This leads to another problem with the total separation of inspiration and inerrancy. So, the ICBI statement on inerrancy includes a statement on the historical-grammatical method by which even that statement on inerrancy should be understood. And it looks forward to a fuller statement on the relation between interpretation and inerrancy which followed (in 1982).

Some have taken a statement by J. I. Packer out of context to support their view that inerrancy and interpretation are totally separate issues. In responding to what he believed were extreme literalistic interpretations, Packer said that "the questions of inerrancy and interpretation must be kept separate."[16]

However, first of all, in context Packer is speaking about issues like "Calvinists and evangelical Arminians [who] have significantly different hermeneutics."[17] Or, about "some [who] find in Scripture wonderful anticipations of modern physics, geology, medicine and all kinds of technology."[18] Second, Packer affirms that inerrancy commits us to "Scripture, rightly interpreted,"[19] thus affirming a connection between inerrancy and a correct interpretation of Scripture. Third, Packer was a framer of the ICBI "Chicago Statement" (1978) on inerrancy view which declares that: "We affirm that the text of Scripture is to be interpreted by the grammatico-historical exegesis."[20] Finally, with regard to denying the historicity of narratives in the Gospels, Packer asserted, "We deny the legitimacy of any treatment of the text or quest for sources lying behind it that leads to relativizing, *dehistoricizing* [emphasis added], or discounting its teaching."[21] Indeed, Packer spoke specifically to the issue of Mike Licona's questioning the historicity of the resurrection of the saints after Jesus' resurrection (Matt 27), asserting: "As a framer of the ICBI statement on biblical inerrancy who once studied Greco-Roman literature at an advanced level, I judge Mike Licona's view that . . . details of their narratives may be regarded as legendary and factually erroneous, to be both academically and theological unsound."[22] Another ICBI framer, R.C. Sproul, wrote, "I can say categorically that Mr. Michael Licona's views are not even remotely compatible with the unified Statement of ICBI."[23]

---

15. CSBI, art. XII.
16. Packer, *Beyond the Battle for the Bible*, 144–46.
17. Ibid.
18. Ibid.
19. Ibid.
20. CSBI, art. XVIII.
21. Ibid.
22. Letter to Norman L. Geisler, May 8, 2014.
23. Letter to Norman L. Geisler, May 22, 2012.

Therefore, in view of both the immediate and broader contexts of Packer's statement, there are no grounds to use it to deny that, while formally distinct, inerrancy and the historical-grammatical interpretation of Scripture are inseparable.

## Assumption 4: Truth is not that which corresponds with the facts.

The reason that many contemporary Bible critics can hold that the Bible is true, even if it is not literally true, is that they have rejected the correspondence view of truth in part or in whole, at least when it comes to some biblical texts. That is, they believe the Bible is true, even if it is sometimes mistaken. For "truth" in this sense does not have to correspond with the facts. Truth is found in intentions so that something can be mistaken but if stated with good intentions, then it is still true. So, if one holds to the redemptive intent of a text, even if there are mistakes in it, then it is still true.

However, according to this faulty view of truth, virtually every sincerely uttered statement (no matter how many errors are in it), would be true. Further, the denial of the correspondence view of truth assumes the correspondence view of truth. For the statement that "the correspondence view is not true" assumes that this statement corresponds with reality. In fact, the correspondence view of truth is the bedrock of all communication. Without it, communication is impossible. Finally, totally symbolic language, with no anchors in the real world, is not possible. We cannot know what is not-literal (i.e., is symbolic) unless we know what is literal. Thus, inerrancy (the total truthfulness of Scripture) makes no sense apart from a correspondence view of truth, for unless something corresponds to the facts it cannot be true. So, for anything—let alone everything—in the Bible to be true, it must be literally true, even if it utilizes symbols and figures of speech to express this literal truth. For instance, the devil is a literal (real) person, even if he is symbolized as a dragon (Rev 12:3), a serpent (Rev 12:9), and a lion (1 Pet 5:8).

Even statements that are symbolic presuppose a literal truth behind them by which we know the symbolic statement is not literal. So the literal truth is at the basis of all truth. Thus, without knowing the literal truth of the Bible we could not say it is inerrant. Ultimately, truth is anchored in some factual reality. Hence to confess the Bible is inerrant (completely true) is to confess that there is actual truth in it that corresponds to reality for this is what truth means. And a denial of the correspondence view of truth lies at the basis of the denial of the literal truth of the Bible.

ICBI made it very clear that its view of inerrancy entailed a correspondence view of truth. The original framer of the ICBI articles, R. C. Sproul, in his official ICBI commentary on the famous "Chicago Statement on Inerrancy" (1978) wrote: "By biblical standards of truth and error is meant the view used both in the Bible and in everyday life, viz., a correspondence view of truth."[24] It adds, "This part of the article

---

24. Sproul, *Explaining Inerrancy*, 50; CSBI, art. XIII.

is directed toward those who would redefine truth to relate merely to redemptive intent, the purely personal, or the like, rather than to mean that which corresponds with reality."[25] Likewise, the ICBI commentary on Hermeneutics (1983) adds: "We further affirm that a statement is true if it represents matters as they actually are, but is an error if it misrepresents the facts" (art. VI).

So inerrancy, as defined by ICBI, is based on a correspondence view of truth. But on this view of truth everything cannot be symbolic, for nothing can be taken symbolically unless one knows the literal truth of which it is symbolic (nonliteral). Correspondence with the literal facts demands a literal interpretation of the facts. Thus, the correspondence view of truth is at the basis of the belief that a biblical narrative should be taken literally.

## Assumption 5: Biblical narratives are not necessarily historical.

Another assumption of the critics contrary to the correspondence view of truth and the historical-grammatical interpretation is that the biblical narratives do not have the presumption of historicity. When it comes to historical matters, some contemporary critics (like Licona) argue that the biblical record makes no presumption of historicity, even in the narrative sections. That is, a biblical narrative is neutral with regard to its historicity. One must prove its historicity or non-historicity.

However, this is based on a faulty premise. For just as the undeniable correspondence view of truth presumes a literal truth at the basis of all truth claims, even so, the correspondence view of truth also assumes that a narrative is telling the literal truth the Gospel writers are reporting, not creating the events. But according to *Webster's New Twentieth Century Dictionary, Unabridged*, a "report" is "a statement of facts." Thus, those who deny the historicity of sections of the Gospels have denied the fact stated in the report. It is futile to say that Matthew does not report these events, for he reports them in the same sense that he reports other events (sometimes in the same chapter) that are taken to be literally true about what happened, unless it is proven to the contrary. Even as when speaking of persons and events in the present we assume a literal interpretation, likewise, when the Bible speaks of persons and events in the past, we presume it is to be understood literally, unless there are clear indications to the contrary. For truth is what corresponds to the facts. And literal truth implies some literal facts. So, truth about the past (i.e., history) should be understood to be literal, unless proven otherwise.

This is why the ICBI statement on inerrancy speaks of the fallacious procedure of "dehistoricizing" a record in the Gospel narrative (art. XVIII). This implies that it should have been taken historically and that it is presumptively wrong not to do so. However, this view is clearly contrary to the facts of the matter for several reasons.

25. Ibid.

## Part 2—Inerrancy Defended

First, ICBI adopted the "grammatical-historical" method of interpreting the Bible (art. XVIII). Further, this method, by its very name assumes the historicity of the biblical text. It is also called the "literal" method of interpretation from the Latin *Sensus Literalis*. Also, it applies the correspondence view of truth to the Genesis narrative which "affirms that Genesis 1–11 is factual, as is the rest of the book."[26] Finally, the ICBI official commentary defends the historicity of some of the most disputed Old Testament events. It says, "Some, for instance, take Adam to be a myth, *whereas he is presented as a historical person*. Others take Jonah to be an allegory when *he is presented as a historical person* and [is] so referred to by Christ."[27]

The emphasized words in the above citations give the key to what should be presumed to be literal or historical, namely, whatever is presented as literal or historical! This presumption can be overcome only if there are clear indications in the text or in other related texts to the contrary—or if some moral or logical law (like the law of non-contradiction) is being violated if it is taken literally. For example, the command to "cut off your hand" (Mark 9:43) to avoid sin—a violation of a moral law against mutilation. Or, "swallowing a camel" (Matt 23:24)—which is physically impossible.

Thus, those who deny the historicity of sections of the Gospels have denied the fact stated in the report. It is futile to say that Matthew does not report these events, for he reports them in the same sense that he reports other events (sometimes in the same chapter) that are taken to be literally true.

A popular way to state the literal hermeneutic illustrates this point, namely, "If the literal sense makes good sense, then seek no other sense lest it result in nonsense." Likewise, "if the literal sense does not make good sense (because it violates some moral, rational, or physical law), then seek some other sense lest it result in nonsense." To apply this to narrative texts, we could say that: "If the literal sense of a narrative makes good sense, then seek no other sense lest it result in nonsense." Likewise, "if the literal sense of a narrative does not make good historical sense (because it violates some moral, rational, or physical law), then seek some other sense lest it result in nonsense." In brief, unless there are clear indications to the contrary in a narrative text (which by its very nature as a narrative has the presumption of historicity), then it should be taken as literal history.

## Assumption 6: A proper hermeneutical method is neutral on the issue of inerrancy.

Another faulty premise in claiming separation of hermeneutics and inerrancy is the claim that there are no unorthodox methods of interpretation. Methods are hermeneutically and doctrinally neutral. By doctrine we mean what one believes, and by hermeneutical method we mean how one arrives at this belief. The question, then,

---

26. See Geisler and Sproul, *Explaining Hermeneutics*, 83; CSBH, art. XXII.
27. Ibid., art. XIII, emphasis added.

is this: can one's method be contrary to his doctrine? Can one deny *de facto* (in fact) what he affirms *de jure* (officially)? If so, then would not the methodology he utilizes undermine or negate the theology he confesses? Those who separate the two domains seem to think there is no connection when in actuality there is.

Take some examples from church history, such as the Averronian double-truth method.[28] Thirteenth-century followers of Averroes were condemned for holding a double-truth methodology whereby they could confess the truth of revelation at the same time they held truths of reason that contradicted it. Should an Averronian belong to an inerrancy society like ETS? That is, should one belong to ETS if he holds that the Bible is wholly true from the standpoint of faith, yet from the standpoint of reason he also holds many things to be true that contradict truths of Scripture? Indeed, using this methodology contradicts the theology (i.e., bibliology) he confesses. Despite the fact that they could confess revelation to be inerrant, Averronians held things to be true (by reason) that were contradictory to this revelation. Thus the alleged confession to inerrancy is actually negated by other beliefs, and the denial of inerrancy flows logically from their method.

How about the allegorical method of Origen? He professed the inspiration of the Bible, saying: "That this testimony may produce a sure and unhesitating belief, either with regard to what we have still to advance, or to what has been already stated, it seems necessary to show, in the first place, that the Scriptures themselves are divine, i.e., were inspired by the Spirit of God."[29]

On the other hand, Origen claimed that to take the story of Adam and Eve as literal is absurd. He believed this because he adopted an allegorical methodology. Thus, while he confesses a belief in total inerrancy, his actual beliefs (resulting from his allegorical method) do not conform to an adequate understanding of total inerrancy, for he denies the truth of some parts of Scripture. In short, his methodology undermines his bibliology. He claims to believe what the Bible presents as true, but as a matter of fact he does not believe everything the Bible says happened, actually happened.

The same logic could be applied to a modern allegorist, for example, the Christian Scientist religion. There is no reason that Christian Scientists (followers of Mary Baker Eddy) could not sincerely confess to believe the ETS or ICBI statements of inerrancy. Yet by their allegorical method they deny the deity of Christ, the historicity of the resurrection, and many other biblical teachings. So, in effect, they take away with their left hand (hermeneutically) what they confess with their right hand (bibliologically).

---

28. Although Averroes himself probably never held the "double-truth" method, nonetheless, in 1277 Siger of Brabant and his followers were condemned by the Church for teaching that "things are true according to philosophy but not according to the Catholic faith, as though there were two contradictory truths." See "Averroism," *ODCC*, 116.

29. Origen, *De Principiis* 4.1.1.

## Part 2—Inerrancy Defended

Three contemporary examples, Jack Rogers, Paul Jewett, and Robert Gundry, will make the point. Let's ask whether their methodology is consistent with their theology (particularly their bibliology). All three of these men profess to a belief that the Bible is the inspired Word of God. At least two of them deny that there are any errors in the Bible (Rogers and Gundry), and one of them (Gundry) once belonged to ETS.

Jack Rogers denied inerrancy by allowing for the possibility of factual mistakes in the Bible. He has a theological procedure that allows him to believe that the Bible is true, even though not all statements in Scripture need to represent things as they really are—that is, some statements in Scripture may be mistaken. But this disavows the classic statement of inspiration: "What the Bible says, God says." This means that the Bible could affirm what God denies. So if there is significant content in the ETS statement, then someone like Jack Rogers would not be consistent with the ETS confession on inerrancy.

Paul Jewett of Fuller Seminary was another case in point. Jewett claimed to believe in the inspiration of the Bible. He also acknowledged that the Apostle Paul affirmed that the husband is the head of the wife (1 Cor 11:3). However, he insisted that Paul was wrong here—that is, God does not affirm what the Apostle Paul affirms here. Indeed, God denies it, for according to Jewett, the truth of God is that the husband is not the head of the wife as Paul affirmed him to be.[30]

What implications does Jewett's view have for inerrancy? Simply this: He has denied in principle the classic statement of inerrancy: "What the Bible affirms, God affirms." For he believes this is a case where Scripture affirms as true that which is not true. If Jewett is right, then in principle when the interpreter discovers what the Bible is saying he must still ask one more very significant question: "Hath God said?" But that could only be determined by something that is outside the Bible. Thus, the Bible would not be the final authority for faith and practice.

In view of this denial that "what the Bible says, God says," Paul Jewett's view is inconsistent with that of ETS. So, despite Jewett's claim to orthodoxy he has a method that is inconsistent with his confession. What he gives with the right hand confessionally he takes away with the left hand hermeneutically. His unorthodox methodology belies his confession to orthodoxy (on the doctrine of Scripture). Indeed, he is methodologically unorthodox.

The case of Robert Gundry is interesting and more crucial because he not only confesses to inerrancy but he also belonged to ETS which affirmed inerrancy. Yet like the other examples he held a methodology that is inconsistent with the ETS doctrine of inerrancy. Thus, he was asked to resign from ETS by a vote of nearly three-quarters of its members (1983). In spite of this, a significant section of ETS now desires that Gundry be restored to ETS.

In many respects Gundry holds a limited form of the allegorical method. Like Origen, he confesses that the Bible is inspired. And, like Origen, when there are parts

---

30. Jewett, *Man as Male and Female*.

of the Bible that, if taken literally, seem to him to contradict other parts of Scripture, then Gundry rejects their literal truth and takes a kind of allegorical (i.e., midrashic) interpretation of them. For example, Matthew reports that wise men followed a star, conversed with Herod and the scribes, went to Bethlehem, and presented gifts to Christ. Gundry, however, denies that these were literal events. He denies that Jesus literally went up on a mountain to give the Sermon on the Mount as Matthew reports it, and so on. So while Gundry confesses to believe that the Bible is the inerrant Word of God, he denies that these events reported by Matthew are literally and historically true. And more recently Gundry claims that there can be contradictions in the Gospels. In a presentation at Westmont College on October 6, 2014, titled "Peter: A False Disciple and Apostate as Portrayed by Matthew," Gundry cites Aristotle, relating, "In his worked called, *Poetics*, Aristotle defended the right of poets to engage in factual inconsistencies if they were necessary to make the desired point."[31] However, this begs the question by assuming the Gospels are poetry, not history. Clearly they are written in narrative form, not poetical form.

But to deny that what the Bible reports in these passages actually occurred is in effect to deny that the Bible is wholly true. As the 1982 Chicago Statement on Hermeneutics declares, "We deny that any event, discourse or saying reported in Scripture was invented by the biblical writers or by the traditions they incorporated" (art. XIV). This is precisely what Gundry did—namely, he claimed that some events reported in Matthew did not actually occur but were invented by the Gospel writer.

Neither will it suffice to point out that Rogers and Jewett officially deny the classic formula of inerrancy—"What the Bible says, God says"—but that Gundry does not officially deny it, for Origen and Christian Scientists could hold this formula too. Denial of the formula renders one unorthodox, but affirmation of the mere formula does not necessarily make one's view orthodox.

Nor is it sufficient to point out that while others deny inerrancy *de jure*, Gundry does not. Gundry's is a *de facto* denial of inerrancy, for he denies that some events reported in Scripture did in fact occur. But the ETS statement insists that we believe the entire Bible is true.

Still, some may insist that the implied evangelical content as to what the Bible is affirming should not exclude those whose methods do not entail the denial of any major doctrine of Scripture. But Gundry affirms all major evangelical doctrines, such as the deity of Christ, his atoning death, his bodily resurrection, etc. Surely, then, Gundry's unorthodox methodology is not tantamount to unorthodoxy. Or is it? In response let us note several things.

First, the doctrine of the inspiration-inerrancy of Scripture is a major doctrine, and Gundry's method is a *de facto* denial of the doctrine of the inerrancy of Scripture. Inerrancy cannot be separated from inspiration. For a divinely inspired error is a contradiction in terms. Even if his method never leads him actually to a denial

---

31. See https://www.youtube.com/watch?v=QloN9EuOGXE.

of any other doctrine, it does deny one important doctrine, the doctrine of the inerrancy of Scripture. In fact, as far as ETS is concerned this is the only explicitly stated doctrine by which one is tested for membership. So Gundry's denial of the occurrence of some events reported in the gospel of Matthew is a denial of the ETS doctrine that all Scripture is true.

It is acknowledged that Jewett's methodology has yet to lead him actually to deny any major doctrine. However, the method itself leads logically to a denial of a major doctrine, i.e., the doctrine of Scripture. For Jewett's method denies the principle of inerrancy that "what the Bible says, God says." And even though Jewett did not apply his own implied principle ("What the Bible says, God does not necessarily say"), yet this does not mean it is not applicable elsewhere. The fact remains that the principle is applicable, and if it is applied it will lead logically to denial of another major doctrine. For example, if Paul can be wrong (because of his rabbinical training) in affirming the headship of the husband over the wife, then logically what hinders one from concluding that Paul is (or could be) wrong in the same verse when he affirms the headship of Christ over the husband? Or if rabbinical background can influence an apostle to affirm error in Scripture, then how can we trust his affirmations about the resurrection in the same book (e.g., 1 Cor 15)? After all, Paul was a Pharisee, and Pharisees believed in the resurrection. If he had been a Sadducee perhaps his view on the resurrection would have been different. How then can we be sure that Paul is not also mistaken here on the major doctrine of the resurrection? In fact, once one has separated what the author of Scripture says from what God says, then the Bible no longer has any divine authority in any passage.

Although Gundry does not apply his allegorical (midrashic) interpretation to any major doctrine, the midrash methodology is applicable nonetheless. For example, why should one consider the report of the bodily resurrection of the saints after Jesus' resurrection (Matt 27) allegorical and yet insist that Jesus' resurrection, which was the basis for it (cf. 1 Cor 15:23), was literal? By what logic can we insist that the same author in the same book reporting the same kind of event in the same language can mean spiritual resurrection in one case and literal bodily resurrection in another case? Does not Gundry's method lead (by logical extension) to a denial of major doctrines of Scripture? And if it does, then there seems to be no more reason for including Gundry in ETS than to include Origen, Rogers, or Jewett. They all do (or could) affirm the inerrancy of Scripture, and yet all have a method that actually negates or undermines inerrancy in some significant way.

Even if one could builds safeguards into the midrash method whereby all major doctrines are preserved from allegorization, there is another lethal problem with Gundry's view. The ETS statement on inerrancy entails the belief that everything reported in the Gospels is true ("the Bible in its entirety"). But Gundry believes that some things reported in Matthew did not occur (e.g., the story of the magi [chap. 2], the report of the resurrection of the saints [chap. 27], etc). It follows therefore that

Gundry does not really believe everything reported in the Gospels is true, despite his claim to the contrary. And this is a *de facto* denial of inerrancy.

It will not suffice to say that Matthew does not really report these events, for he reports them in the same sense that he reports other events that Gundry believes actually occurred. In fact, on his view, some stories that seem more likely candidates for midrash (for example, the appearance of angels to the Jewish shepherds in Luke 2) Gundry takes as literal, whereas the earthly pilgrimage of astrologers following a sign in the sky he takes as imaginary (i.e., midrash). Regardless, the fact of the matter is that Gundry denies that certain events reported in Scripture (Matthew) actually occurred. This means in effect that he is denying the truth of these parts of Scripture. And if he denies in effect that the Bible is true "in its entirety," then he has disqualified himself from ETS.

## AN APPLICATION OF THESE CONCLUSIONS

How do these conclusions apply to the account of the resurrection of the saints in Matthew 27:51–54? First of all, as shown above, since it is a narrative passage it has the presumption of historicity. Second, it has no indications in the text or in other texts that it would be absurd if taken literally. Third, it is given in connection with other historical events, such as the resurrection of Christ (Matt 28). Indeed, it is given as a consequence of Christ's resurrection, noting that they did not come out of tombs until "after his [Jesus'] resurrection" (Matt 27:53). Fourth, there are no literary or logical markers in the text to indicate it is not historical. Licona's claim that it is "poetical," a "legend," an "embellishment," and literary "special effects"[32] is completely without justification. It is written in straightforward narrative form without the use of symbols or other indicators that it should not be taken literally. Fifth, it is directly connected to the great historical event of the resurrection of Christ as a result and proof of it (Matt 27:53). Even Origen took it as "evidences of the divinity of Jesus."[33] Sixth, it is taken as literal by a virtually unbroken line of early Fathers from the second century on, including Irenaeus (b. 120), Tertullian (b. 160), Origen (b. 185), Cyril of Jerusalem (b.315), Augustine (b. 354), to say nothing of Thomas Aquinas (b. 1224), and John Calvin (b. 1509).[34]

The truth is that there is every indication in the passage that it is historical. Even the extra-textual argument that no other Gospel mentions the event fails since by that same logic one would have to reject much of the Gospels, including the visit of Nicodemus (John 3), the woman at the well (John 4), the healing of the invalid (John 5), the resurrection of Lazarus (John 11), the rich young ruler (Luke 18), and the story of Zacchaeus (Luke 19). Further, an event does not have to be recorded more than

---

32. Ibid. See also 306, 548, 552–53.
33. Origen, ibid., book II, chap. XXXVI, *Ante-Nicene Fathers*, 446.
34. See my article "What Did the Early Fathers Say?"

once in a reliable document to be true. Finally, the objection that it was a supernatural event does not disqualify it, for that is unjustified anti-supernaturalism. As C. S. Lewis put it, "If we admit God, must we admit Miracle? Indeed, indeed, you have no security against it. That is the bargain."[35] If God exists, miracles are possible. So, to deny miracles one would have to disprove God. For as long as it is possible that God exists, then it is possible that miracles can occur.

## AN OBJECTION CONSIDERED

Does not the above argument prove too much? Granted the finitude and fallibility of man, is it not a reasonable presumption that we are all inconsistent in our beliefs in some way or another? Therefore should we not all be excluded from ETS, ICBI, or other inerrancy affirming groups?

In response, there are several crucial differences between common inconsistency of belief and a conscious commitment to a methodology that undermines our important beliefs. First, the common inconsistencies with which we are all plagued are usually unconscious inconsistencies. When they are brought to our attention we work to eliminate them. On the other hand, a theological method such as Gundry's midrash or Licona's Greco-Roman genre method is a conscious commitment. Further, and more importantly, common inconsistencies are not recommended as a formal method by which we are to interpret Scripture. Hence they have no official didactic force. They do not purport to teach us how to discover the truth of Scripture. Gundry's method, however, entails a crucial truth claim. It claims that by using this method we will discover the truth that God is really affirming in Scripture. After all, Gundry's method proposes to tell us what it is that the Bible is actually saying and thus what God is actually saying. This makes a conscious commitment to a theological method a very serious matter, for a hermeneutical method purports to be the means by which we discover the very truth of God.

Further, there is another possible difference between common inconsistencies and the serious inconsistency in which these NT critics engage. The former do not necessarily lead logically to a denial of a major doctrine, but the latter can. As was noted earlier, unorthodoxy in methodology leads logically to unorthodoxy in theology. This is true regardless of whether the proponent of the method makes this logical extension himself. For example, a "double-truth" method or an allegorical method leads logically to a denial of the literal truth of Scripture.

Now let us consider the question: Is conscientious confession of the doctrine of inerrancy solely in terms of what the confessor takes it to mean sufficient grounds for determining orthodoxy on this doctrine? We suggest that the answer to this is negative for several reasons.

35. Lewis, *Miracles*, 109.

First, making conscientious confession of inerrancy the only test of orthodoxy is tantamount to saying that sincerity is a test for truth. But as is well known even the road to destruction is paved with good intentions (Prov 14:12).

Second, a statement does not mean what the *reader* takes it to mean to him. It means what the *author* meant by it. If this is not so, then a statement can mean anything the reader wants it to mean, including the opposite of what the author meant by it. If this were the case then Neo-Orthodox theologians and liberals could also belong to ETS, since many of them believe that the Bible is inerrant in some sense (usually in its purpose).

Third, no theological organization has integrity without some objective, measurable standard by which its identity can be determined. In the case of ETS the standard was the stated doctrine of inerrancy: "The Bible alone, and the Bible in its entirety, is the Word of God written and is therefore inerrant in the autographs." But if anyone can take this statement to mean that the Bible is true in any sense he wishes—as long as he believes it sincerely—then an inerrancy affirming organization has no doctrinal integrity.

Benedict Spinoza, a Jewish pantheist and anti-supernaturalist, denied virtually every major doctrine in the Bible. Nonetheless, he sincerely believed that he was orthodox and acting in accordance with Scripture. He wrote, "I am certified of this much: I have said nothing unworthy of Scripture or God's Word, and I have made no assertions which I could not prove by most plain argument to be true. I can therefore, rest assured that I have advanced nothing which is impious or even savours of impiety."[36]

So we must conclude that sincerity is an insufficient test for orthodoxy. In addition to sincerity there must also be conformity to some objective standard or norm for orthodoxy, for truth is conformity with reality. And without such conformity one is not truly orthodox, regardless of his confession to the contrary. Our Lord made it clear that mere confession of him was not enough, for he denied those who confessed "Lord, Lord" but did not "do the will of the Father" (Matt 7:21). Likewise, saying "I believe, I believe" (in total inerrancy) is not sufficient. One's beliefs must truly conform to the fact that all of Scripture is true before he is considered orthodox on this point. So it is not mere subjective confession but objective conformity that is the sufficient test for orthodoxy.

## CONCLUSION

We have shown that there are some hermeneutical methods (like the "double-truth" method and total allegorical method) that are inconsistent with a belief in the ETS statement on inerrancy. Given this, there is the question of where should we draw

---

36. Spinoza, *Theologico-Political Treatise*, 166.

the line and why should we draw it there? In the above discussion I have offered a criterion for drawing such a line—that is, for determining methodological unorthodoxy. Briefly it is this: Any hermeneutical or theological method the logically necessary consequences of which are contrary to or undermine confidence in the complete truthfulness of all of Scripture is unorthodox. The method can do this either *de jure* or *de facto*.

It seems to me that if we do not accept some such criterion we are admitting the emptiness of our confession of inerrancy. For if the ETS or ICBI inerrancy statements of faith do not exclude any particular belief about Scripture, then they include all beliefs about Scripture. And whatever says everything, really says nothing.

So, in order to preserve our identity and integrity as an evangelical group that confesses an inerrant Word from God, we must define the limits of a legitimate methodology.

One thing seems safe to predict: granted the popularity of evangelicalism and the degree to which the borders of legitimate evangelical methodology are now being pushed, a group will not long be "evangelical" nor long believe in inerrancy in the sense meant by the framers of that statement unless it acts consistently on this matter.

In short we would argue that, since methodology determines one's theology, unless we place some limits on evangelical methodology there will follow a continued broadening of the borders of "evangelical" theology so that the original word will have lost its meaning. After all, even Barth called his Neo-Orthodox view "evangelical." Is this what the word "evangelical" meant to the founders of ETS? Or have they already conceded so much to the "new hermeneutic" that it does not really matter what the words "evangelical" or "inerrant" meant to the authors of the statements, but only what they mean to us? On the other hand, if we reject this kind of subjective hermeneutic (and we most certainly should), then it behooves us to draw a line that will preserve our identity and integrity as an "evangelical" society. Such a line, we suggest, need not entail a change in (or addition to) our doctrinal statement but simply the explicit acknowledgment (perhaps in the by-laws) that the denial of the total truth of Scripture, officially or factually, *de jure* or *de facto*, *is* grounds for exclusion from ETS.

It is assumed, however, that a conscientious confession is a necessary condition for membership in an organization that confess inerrancy, even though it is not a sufficient condition. That truth involves conformity to reality we have argued elsewhere.[37]

The 1982 Chicago Statement on Hermeneutics has a clear and succinct statement on this point in article VI: "We affirm that the Bible expresses God's truth in propositional statements, and we declare that biblical truth is both objective and absolute. We further affirm that a statement is true if it represents matters as they actually are, but is an error if it misrepresents the facts. We deny that, while Scripture is able to make us wise unto salvation, biblical truth should be defined in terms of this function. We further deny that error should be defined as that which willfully deceives."

---

37. Geisler, "Concept of Truth," 327–39.

In brief, belief in biblical inerrancy is not just a matter of personal interpretation. It has an objective meaning given it by virtue of its adoption of the historical-grammatical interpretation. That is to say, it implies at its basis a literal interpretation of the history and events without which it would be meaningless.

Chapter 10

# Biblical Inerrancy, Inductive or Deductive Basis
## A Response to William Lane Craig

### NORMAN L. GEISLER

In a recent web post,[1] William Lane Craig defends a view of limited inerrancy in contrast to the historic view of unlimited inerrancy. Unlimited inerrancy contends that the Bible is inerrant on all matters it addresses, not only on redemptive matters but also on historical and scientific matters as well. By contrast, limited inerrancy claims that the Bible is only without error when speaking on matters of salvation. There are several related questions to this view that need to be examined. First of all, limited inerrantists contend that unlimited inerrancy is based on deductive logic, whereas their view is inductively based.

## DOES INERRANCY HAVE AN INDUCTIVE OR DEDUCTIVE BASIS?

Craig claims that biblical inerrancy "as he learned it" and as "most of its adherents today would defend it, is not arrived at *inductively*, but *deductively*." However, as we have shown elsewhere,[2] this is a false disjunction. While a deductive move is involved to form the conclusion, the biblical basis for inerrancy is a perfect (complete) induction which yields two premises: (1) The Bible teaches that God cannot err, and (2) The Bible is the Word of God. From this inductive basis it follows logically that the Bible

---

1. See Craig, "What Price Biblical Inerrancy." All quotes of Craig's discussion are taken from this article on his personal website, www.reasonablefaith.org.
2. Geisler, *Systematic Theology in One Volume*, 149–68.

claims to be the errorless Word of God. Since the Bible is a limited set of data, one can make a complete induction of all its contents. So, biblical inerrancy, as usually held, has an inductive basis, even though a deduction from the two inductive premises is involved. Further refinement in view of the biblical data also has an inductive basis in the text and is not imposed upon it from some deductive theological or philosophical basis, but comes from Scripture or from general revelation of God (e.g., Ps 19:1–6; Rom 1:19–20; 2:12–15). For example, while the Bible speaks of the "four corners of the earth" (Rev 7:1), we know by observation from general revelation that the world is round. This trumps any literalistic interpretation of the figure of speech about "four corners" of the earth used to support the Square Earth Society.

What the Bible *says* must be understood in the light of what the Bible *shows*. So, a more nuanced doctrine of inerrancy involves a refinement wherein inerrancy is understood in view of the phenomena of Scripture and the facts (not theories) of nature. For example, if the Bible shows that it uses round numbers, then the use of a round number will not be considered an error. For example, Luke asserts that Jesus was "*about* thirty years of age" (Luke 3:23) when he began his ministry. Likewise, when the Bible affirms in 2 Chronicles 4:2 that the circumference of the laver by the temple was three times the diameter, this too can be taken as approximate and not more precisely as 3.14159 . . . , etc. Also, when the Bible speaks in observational language of "sun rise" or "sun set" (Josh 1:4), as even meteorologists do today, this is not to be taken as unscientific. Nor should the sun "standing still" (Josh 10:13) be taken as unscientific but merely as the language of appearance in a prescientific age. Just how God did it is not known, but the same is true of other miracles.

This is why the International Council on Biblical Inerrancy (ICBI) was careful to define inerrancy in the light of the biblical phenomena, saying, "We further deny that inerrancy is negated by biblical phenomena such as a lack of modern technical precision, irregularities of grammar or spelling, observational descriptions of nature, the reporting of falsehoods, the use of hyperbole and round numbers, the topical arrangement of material, variant selections of material in parallel accounts, or the use of free citations."[3]

However, none of this negates the fact that the biblical doctrine of inerrancy is based on a perfect (complete) inductive study of the whole Bible which yields two premises from which the full inerrancy of the Bible necessarily follows.

## ARE ONLY INTENTIONS OF THE AUTHOR INERRANT BUT NOT ALL HIS AFFIRMATIONS?

The Craig article also speaks of the truth of inerrancy in terms of "the intention" of the author. This would seem to imply an intentionalist's view of truth, as opposed

---

3. CSBI, art. XIII.

to a correspondence view of truth.[4] He wrote, "We may need indeed to revise our understanding of what constitutes an error." Then he gives two illustrations: The first one is about the reference to the mustard seed, he says, "Jesus is not teaching botany."[5] Rather, Jesus "intends" to teach only about the kingdom of God. And inerrancy should be judged in terms of what the author intends to teach, not in terms of what he actually said. So, contrary to the correspondence view of truth, which affirms that a mistake (an affirmation that does not correspond with reality) is an error, the intentionalists view of truth asserts that only wrong *intentions* are errors, not wrong affirmations.

The ICBI framers clearly repudiated the intentionalist view of truth (in which only wrong intentions are errors) in favor of the correspondence view of truth (which cannot be denied without affirming it). For the claim that truth is not that which corresponds to the facts also claims to be a truth that corresponds to the facts. Contrary to a non-inerrantist misinterpretation of ICBI article XIII that denies the Bible should be evaluated according to "standards of truth and error that are alien to its usage or purpose,"[6] the official ICBI commentary on this article declares clearly: "'By biblical standards of truth and error' is meant . . . the correspondence view of truth." Further, the ICBI statement on inerrancy and hermeneutics declares: "We further affirm that a statement is true if it represents matters as they actually are, but an error is an error if it misrepresents the facts."[7] It adds, "We further deny that error should be defined as that which willfully deceives."[8] This article addresses any subtle attempt to redefine error as that which "misleads" (through deceptive intent) and not that which "misrepresents" the facts (regardless of intent). Otherwise, anyone can easily say the Bible never *misleads* but may have mistakes, fiction, legend, or error in it. The reason for this is obvious, namely, if only deliberate deceptions are errors, then every factually mistaken statement ever made with good intentions would be true. The next alarming statement is about genre which leads to our next point.

---

4. Limited inerrantists sometimes claim to hold a correspondence view of truth, but they modify it when it comes to biblical truth, transforming it into an intentional view when it comes to the inerrancy of the Bible.

5. In accordance with a correspondence view, inerrantists can point out that Jesus' statement is botanically correct since his affirmations is not about all seeds *in the world* but in context only about the smallest seed which a first-century farmer "took and sowed in his field" *in the Holy Land* (Matt 13:31, italics added).

6. CSBI, art. XIII.

7. Ibid., art. VI.

8. Ibid.

## ARE ONLY ESSENTIAL MATTERS INERRANT BUT NOT PERIPHERAL ONES?

Craig speaks of things affirmed in a biblical text (like the mustard seed is the smallest seed) as "incidental to the lesson" and, thus, the author can be in error or mistaken in peripheral matters without affecting the inerrancy of the text. He adds, "What matters is that the central idea is conveyed . . . but the surrounding details are fluid and incidental to the story." But this opens Pandora's hermeneutical box. For instance, in most cases the numerous references to angels in the Bible are incidental to the main message of the passage. So, by this logic we would have to conclude that almost nothing the Bible affirms about angels is without error (mistakes). Likewise, other doctrines of the Bible, even fundamental ones like the Trinity, that are not an essential part of what the author intended to teach, could also be in error. For there are few, if any passages whose direct purpose (intention) is to teach the doctrine of the Trinity. So, by this intentionalistic logic of distinguishing between what is incidental and what is essential in biblical affirmations, the inerrant canonical text is seriously shrunk to a size determined by the interpreter.

What is more, according to the intentionalist view, only essentials are inerrant. But much of the time there is really no objective way in the biblical text of determining what is and what is not inerrant, for there is often no objective way to differentiate the peripheral from the essential. This leads to another problem—the appeal to extra-biblical sources to determine what the Bible really intends to affirm and what it does not.

Craig uses the illustration of a joke to make his point. He wrote: "Observe how the central idea and especially the punch line are the same . . ." when the joke is retold. But "the variation [is] in secondary details." In like manner, he argues that what is important in the Bible is the essential point, not the details.

The problem with this illustration is that *the Gospels are no joke!* They claim to be serious and accurate history. Luke, for example, claims (Luke 1:1–4) to have "followed all things closely" and to be giving an "orderly account" that we may have "certainty concerning the things you have been taught" which was from "eyewitnesses." Historians have found that what Luke records in Acts (part 2 of his history of Luke–Acts—Acts 1:1; Luke 1:1) is minutely accurate in numerous details.[9] And since Matthew, Mark, and even John affirm the same basic truths (where they overlap with Luke), then this speaks in general of the historical accuracy of all the Gospels. Indeed, John claims to be based on eyewitness testimony (John 19:35; 21:24). And even some noted New Testament scholars are now speaking of the eyewitness basis of the Gospels.[10]

---

9. See Hemer, *Book of Acts*.
10. See Bauckham, *Jesus and the Eyewitnesses*.

Part 2—Inerrancy Defended

## DOES EXTRA-BIBLICAL GENRE DETERMINE MEANING?

Along with a number of other Neo-Evangelicals on inerrancy, Craig appeals to extra-biblical genre to determine the meaning of biblical text. With his colleague, Mike Licona, who appealed to Greco-Roman genre, Craig claims that "questions of genre will have a significant bearing on our answer to that question." But Licona's conclusions reveal just how dangerous it is to use extra-biblical genre as hermeneutically determinative of the meaning and truth of a biblical text. He wrote, "Greco-Roman biography . . . often include legend. Because *bios* was a flexible genre, it is often difficult to determine where history ends and legend begins."[11] Indeed, Licona affirmed that there is legend or poetry in the Gospels.[12] He even holds there is a contradiction in the Gospels (in a debate with Bart Ehrman at Southern Evangelical Seminary, spring 2009), but he denies that this affects the doctrine of inerrancy. He said, "I think that John probably altered the day [Christ was crucified] in order for a theological—to make a theological point there. But that doesn't mean that Jesus wasn't crucified." However, a divinely inspired error is a contradiction in terms since God cannot err (Heb 6:18). And an inerrant error is a logical impossibility! With regard to the genre view, the biblical text could still be reliable, but certainly not inerrant, thus placing the Bible on a level with every other book that partially contains the truth and is partially errant.

## COMPARING THE GOSPELS WITH GRECO-ROMAN GENRE

Further, the comparison of the Gospels with Greco-Roman biography is a false analogy. Of course, there are some similarities, but there are significant differences which break the alleged analogy.

First of all, the Gospels are accurate history based on eyewitness testimony that is completely true with a clear distinction between truth and fiction. They inform us about our eternal salvation through the incarnation, crucifixion, and physical resurrection of God-Incarnate. But Greco-Roman biography admittedly lacks these characteristics, containing legend, error, and often admittedly the inability to distinguish between legend and history.

Second, Licona contends that on this ground Greco-Roman genre allows for contradictions like this, and that the Gospels are written in Greco-Roman genre. However, this premise should be rejected, as most biblical scholars have through the ages until recent times.

Third, even if there are some similarities in form between the New Testament and Greco-Roman genre, the New Testament has a greater concern for historical truth (see Luke 1:1–4) because Christianity is a historical religion that stresses the

---

11. Licona, *Resurrection of Jesus*, 34.
12. Ibid., 306, 548, 552, 553.

real spatio-temporal physical appearance of the God-man in the flesh (John 1:14; cf. 1 John 4:2; 2 John 7).

Fourth, the Bible warns us "avoiding . . . opposing arguments of what is falsely called 'knowledge'" (1 Tim 6:20), not to attempt to explain them away on the grounds of extra-biblical genre. Literally, Paul forbids holding "anti-theses." For both cannot be true.

Fifth, the law of non-contradictions controls all thought and writing, taking precedence over any genre determinations. It is a literally undeniable principle of thought.

Sixth, extra-biblical genre should not be used to determine the meaning of a biblical text for this gives them more authority than the inspired text. Of course, as already noted, extra-biblical facts (not theories, legends, or literary genre), such as those found in general revelation, can and should be used to help interpret the Bible.

Seventh, using extra-biblical genre determinations is rejected by the ICBI understanding of inerrancy which was adopted by the ETS, the largest group of evangelical scholars in the world (see citations above).

The truth is that once one rejects the full correspondence view of truth and accepts the validity of Greco-Roman genre (as Licona and Craig do) or Hebrew midrash genre (as Robert Gundry did in his 1982 commentary on Matthew), then the biblical text itself is not the final authority for faith and practice. Rather, the final authority rests outside the biblical text in some fallible Greek or Hebrew genre. This is a dangerous, if not disastrous, move for an evangelical, for it forsakes the Bible as the final authority and opens the door for extra-biblical literary sources to determine the meaning and truth of Christian doctrine.

## IS INERRANCY AN ESSENTIAL BIBLICAL DOCTRINE?

Craig also claims that inerrancy is not an essential evangelical doctrine. Rather, he holds that Jesus' affirmation of inerrancy is a weak premise. He wrote, "At the center of our web of beliefs ought to be some core belief like the belief that God exists, with the deity and resurrection of Christ somewhere near the center. The doctrine of inspiration of Scripture will be somewhere further out and inerrancy even farther toward the periphery, as a corollary of inspiration." Thus, if inerrancy is denied, then it would not seriously affect any core Christian belief.

On the contrary, *epistemologically*, inerrancy is at the very foundation of every other Christian doctrine, since if the Bible is not the divinely authoritative basis for our beliefs, then we have no divine authority for any Christian doctrine. For all Christian doctrines are derived from the Bible. Of course, if the Bible is not inspired, there may be degrees of probability for believing these doctrines but there would be no divine authority for embracing them. So, in this sense inspiration-inerrancy is the divinely authoritative basis for whatever other Christian doctrines we believe.

Furthermore, as we showed elsewhere,[13] the logical order of beliefs should have truth as its basis; for unless truth is knowable we cannot know it is true that God exists. So, the logical order is as follows: (1) truth is knowable; (2) the opposite of truth is false; (3) God exists; (4) miracles are possible; (5) miracles can confirm a miracle; (6) the New Testament is historically reliable; (7) Jesus was confirmed by miracles to be God; (8) therefore, Jesus is God; (9) whatever Jesus as God teaches is true; (10) Jesus taught the Bible is the inspired-inerrant Word of God; (11) therefore, the Bible is the inspired-inerrant Word of God; (12) whatever is opposed to the teaching of the Bible is false. That is, essential Christianity is true, and whatever is opposed to its teachings is false.

Using the above logical steps, premises 3 and 6 are crucial. For if it is true that God exists, then miracles are possible. And if the New Testament is historically reliable and teaches that Jesus is God, then it follows that Jesus' teaching that the Bible is the inspired-inerrant Word of God is true. But, contrary to critics, denying inerrancy would not thereby disprove God, miracles, and the deity of Christ. The issue would be: did Jesus teach that the Bible was the inspired-inerrant Word of God (point 11)? If he did, then inerrancy is true. If he did not, then the question of inerrancy would be up for grabs, but the essential redemptive truths of Christianity (e.g., God, miracles, Christ's deity) would not thereby be in question. So, contrary to Craig's view, Christianity does not crumble if the traditional view of inerrancy is denied.

Nonetheless, inspiration and its concomitant doctrine of inerrancy are not subsidiary or peripheral matters. They are logically connected to the divine nature. For if the Bible is God's Word, then a divinely inspired error is a contradiction in terms. So, if the Bible is God's Word, and if God cannot error, then by necessity the Bible cannot error. Logic demands it. This is precisely what the ETS statement on inerrancy declares: "The Bible alone and the Bible in its entirety is the Word of God written, and therefore inerrant in the autographs" (notice the word "therefore"). Likewise, if the Bible is infallibly true, then there are no errors in it. For an infallibly true fallible statement is a contradiction. Thus, infallibility and inerrancy are logically and necessarily connected to divine inspiration.

## DOES THE CASE FOR CHRISTIANITY COLLAPSE IF AN ERROR IS FOUND IN THE BIBLE?

Closely associated with the previous point is Craig's answer to the question: Does the case for Christianity collapse if an error is found in the Bible? Allegedly, this is what happened to the former evangelical, now agnostic, Bart Ehrman. But Craig's

---

13. Geisler, *Christian Apologetics*, 293.

alternative to this objection gives away too much of the farm. First of all, it suggests that one may retreat from full inerrancy to limited inerrancy by claiming the Bible does not teach inerrantly about history and science (where these alleged errors occur). Rather, it is affirming only the redemptive core of truth, not the truth about peripheral areas. Second, on this view, if necessary, one can give up inerrancy without giving up Christianity because inerrancy is not an essential or core doctrine of the faith. It is only peripheral. Let's address both of these issues. The truth is, however, that many important Christian doctrines relating to salvation are inseparably connected with historical or scientific truths (e.g., creation, the virgin birth, and the death and resurrection of Christ).

Thus one cannot deny, for example, the historicity of Christ's death and resurrection without denying the salvation doctrines to which they are connected.

## THE MOVE TO LIMITED INERRANCY

Claiming that inerrancy is not an essential doctrine, but is only a peripheral teaching, is not a helpful move for evangelicalism for several reasons. First, this is contrary to the historic view of the Christian church which holds to inerrancy.[14]

Second, it gives up the historic doctrine of total inerrancy for limited inerrancy. Thus, it moves from the Evangelical view on inerrancy to the Neo-Evangelical view (see above).

Third, this is contrary to the ICBI statement on inerrancy which was also adopted by ETS, the largest scholarly group of inerrantists in the world. Of course, one can reject the meaning the framers gave these statements and reconstruct their own meaning, but this is contrary to sound hermeneutics which seeks the author's meaning of a text and makes the Bible into a nose of putty that can be molded by the reader in any direction he desires.

Fourth, this forsakes the objective meaning of the biblical text for purely subjective and personal wishes. But one cannot deny the objectivity of the text without the use of objective statements about it.[15]

Fifth, what is more, the move to the purely redemptive model of limited inerrancy places much of the Bible in an unfalsifiable category. For if only redemptive or spiritual truths are inerrant, then there are no scientific and historical matters which can be falsified. Here one is reminded of the response of the liberal theologian Paul Tillich when asked why he did not believe in the physical resurrection of Christ. He is alleged to have replied, "Because I do not want any of my New Testament scholar friends calling me and saying, 'Guess what Paulus, we have found the body of Jesus!'" Of course, if one does not believe anything that is falsifiable, then his beliefs cannot be falsified. But neither can it be verified.

14. Hannah, *Inerrancy and the Church*.
15. See Howe, *Objectivity in Hermeneutics*.

Part 2—Inerrancy Defended

This unfalsifiable retreat to limited inerrancy is unsatisfactory for many reasons. First of all, the Apostle Paul said, "If Christ has not been raised, your faith is worthless; you are still in your sins" (1 Cor 15:17). In other words, if the resurrection is disproven, Christianity would crumble. This is a bold claim that opens the door to falsification. Even those who reject full inerrancy but believe in the bodily resurrection of Jesus have to admit that the resurrection is open to falsification, and if it is falsified, then essential Christianity collapses. Further, did not Jesus connect the two when he said to Nicodemus, "If I told you earthly things and you do not believe, how will you believe if I tell you heavenly things" (John 3:12)?

## WHAT WOULD IT TAKE TO DISPROVE INERRANCY?

It would take a demonstrable error in an original text of Scripture or in a perfect copy of it. By error is meant something that is logically contradictory or else that does not correspond to the facts of the matter. But this is not as easy as it may seem for several reasons. First, one must demonstrate that we have an autographic text of the Bible (i.e., either an original manuscript or perfect copy of one). Currently, we do not have a verified original manuscript or even a perfect copy of one. However, it is possible that one may be found. So, if one were found with a demonstrable error in it, then inerrancy would be falsified. However, as long as it is *possible* that the original text did not have an error, it would not be *necessary* to give up inerrancy.

Furthermore, the error would have to be more than an alleged or apparent one; it would have to be an *actual* error. This means there are no *possible* explanations for the alleged error. This is not easy to do. What is more, the two premises from which we derive inerrancy are so firmly based that finding a real error is unlikely. For we would have to demonstrate that the Bible is not the Word of God and that God can err. This is why the dictum of St. Augustine stands firm: "If we are perplexed by any apparent contradiction in Scripture, it is not allowable to say, The author of this book is mistaken; but either [1] the manuscript is faulty, or [2] the translation is wrong, or [3] you have not understood."[16]

Having examined over the last fifty years nearly a thousand of these alleged errors in the Bible,[17] I can testify that I have not found any *real* errors, only difficulties with solutions varying from possible to probable. This includes all of the alleged errors taken as real error by contemporary critics of total inerrancy, even those that led some to deny inerrancy and become agnostic. There are possible, even plausible, answer to all of these difficulties and, therefore, no real compelling reason to give up inerrancy.

---

16. Augustine, *Reply to Faustus*, 11.5.
17. See Geisler and Howe, *Big Book of Bible Difficulties*.

## LICONA'S REAL ERROR

A case in point is the alleged "contradiction" offered by Mike Licona on the day of Jesus' crucifixion, comparing Mark 14:12 (which seems to indicate it was on Friday) and John 19:14 (which appears to point to Thursday).

However, upon closer examination, we discover that: "Preparation" (used to support the Thursday view in John 19:14) is a word used for "Friday," the day of preparation for a Sabbath or feast and not for Thursday. Thus, there is no contradiction with Mark. For the Bible says clearly that "since it was the day of preparation, and so the bodies would not remain on the cross on the Sabbath, the Jews asked Pilate . . ." (John 19:31; cf. Mark 15:42). Many noted New Testament scholars support this same conclusion. For example, A. T. Robertson declared, "That is, Friday of Passover week, the preparation day before Sabbath of Passover week (or feast)."[18] Further, D. A. Carson adds: "('Preparation') regularly refers to Friday—i.e., the Preparation of the Sabbath is Friday."[19] This being the case, there is no error in the biblical text; the error is in the misinterpretation of the text.

## IS THE EVANGELICAL VIEW ONE OF UNLIMITED OR LIMITED INERRANCY?

While Craig claims to believe in inerrancy, he has a diminished view of it and one that is contrary to the standard historical view propounded by ICBI and adopted by a vast majority of the three thousand–member Evangelical Theological Society (2006) as the guide for understanding the meaning of inerrancy. In fact, he seems to have moved from a belief in *unlimited* inerrancy to *limited* inerrancy. This is a substantial move from the historic Evangelical view to the contemporary Neo-Evangelical view. These two views can be contrasted as follows:

| Evangelical View | Neo-Evangelical View |
| --- | --- |
| Unlimited inerrancy | Limited inerrancy |
| Correspondence view of truth | Intentionalist view of truth |
| Without error in affirmations | Without error in intentions only |
| Without error in all matters | Without error only in essential matters |
| Error is a mistake | Error is a deception |
| Extra-biblical genre does not determine meaning | Extra-biblical genre determines meaning |

Finally, a comment is called for about my former mentor, dean, and colleague for some twenty years, Dr. Kenneth Kantzer. His name is used by Craig in association with a form of the Neo-Evangelical view of limited inerrancy. But make no mistake,

---

18. Robertson, *Word Pictures*, 5:299.
19. Carson, *Gospel according to John*, 603.

## Part 2—Inerrancy Defended

Kantzer was and remained a committed follower of the Warfield-Hodge view[20] of total inerrancy which is clearly opposed to the Craig-Licona view of limited inerrancy. He affirmed that "attempts to limit the truthfulness of inspired Scripture to 'faith and practice,' viewed as less than the whole of Scripture, or worse, to assert that it errs in such matters as history, or nature, depart not only from the Bible's representation of its own veracity, but also from the central tradition of the Christian churches."[21] In fact, it was because of Kantzer's view on inerrancy and his prompting that I got involved in the exposure of Robert Gundry's view on inerrancy which led to his resignation from membership in the Evangelical Theological Society by an almost three-quarter majority vote of the society.

As for Licona's similar view of extra-biblical genre, which Craig believes is compatible with inerrancy, the three living framers of the ICBI statements (R.C. Sproul, J. I. Packer, and myself) affirm that the Neo-Evangelical view of limited inerrancy is incompatible with the ICBI stance on unlimited inerrancy.

J. I. Packer wrote: "As a framer of the ICBI statement on biblical inerrancy who studied Greco-Roman literature at advanced level, I judge *Mike Licona's view* that, because the Gospels are semi-biographical, details of their narratives *may be regarded as legendary and factually erroneous, to be both academically and theologically unsound.*"[22]

R.C. Sproul wrote: "As the former and only president of ICBI during its tenure and as the original framer of the Affirmations and Denials of the Chicago Statement on Inerrancy, *I can say categorically that Mr. Licona's views are not even remotely compatible with the unified Statement of ICBI.*"[23]

The ICBI statements on inerrancy made it clear that they held to an unlimited view which claims the Bible is inerrant on whatever it affirms, including matters of history and science. Consider the following: "Holy Scripture, being God's own Word . . . is of infallible divine authority *in all matters upon which it touches.*"[24] Article I reads: "We affirm that inspiration . . . guaranteed true and trustworthy utterances *on all matters* of which the biblical authors were moved to speak and write." This includes matters of history and science for the ICBI framers who declared: "We affirm that Genesis 1–11 is factual, as is the rest of the book. We deny that the teachings of Genesis 1–11 are mythical, and scientific hypotheses about earth's history of the origin of humanity may be invoked to overthrow what Scripture teaches about creation."[25]

---

20. See Warfield, *Inspiration and Authority of the Bible*.
21. Kantzer and Henry, *Evangelical Affirmations*, 33.
22. Letter to Norman L. Geisler, May 8, 2014, emphasis added.
23. Letter to William C. Roach, May 22, 2012, emphasis added.
24. ICBI, "Short Statement," 2.
25. CSBH, art. XXII.

Further, "*We deny that biblical infallibility and inerrancy are limited to spiritual, religious or redemptive themes, exclusive of assertions in the fields of history and science.*"[26]

As for the use of extra-biblical genre, ICBI was equally clear: "We affirm that the text of Scripture is to be interpreted by grammatico-historical exegesis, taking account of its [the Bible's] literary forms [not extra-biblical forms] and devices, and that *Scripture is to interpret Scripture.*"[27] Extra-biblical genre and forms are not to be used to interpret Scripture, for "*we deny the legitimacy of any treatment of the text or quest for sources lying behind it that leads to relativizing, dehistoricizing,* or discounting its teaching, or rejecting its claim to authorship."[28]

So, clearly, ICBI affirmed unlimited inerrancy in contrast to the Licona-Craig view of limited inerrancy. And since unlimited inerrancy was the historic position of the Christian church,[29] it follows that the Craig-Licona version of limited inerrancy is not in accord with the historic position of the Christian church. Further, since the ICBI view was adopted by the Evangelical Theological Society (ETS) as a guide for understanding the meaning of inerrancy (2006), then the largest society of inerrantists in the world also affirms unlimited inerrancy. Likewise, since the Evangelical Philosophical Society was begun as a sub section of the Evangelical Theological Society and adopted its same inerrancy statement, this would include its constituency as well. To this list could be added the nearly three hundred scholars and leaders who signed the famous ICBI Chicago Statement. What is more, in 1989 over six hundred participants of the "Evangelical Affirmations" conference held at Trinity Evangelical Divinity School declared: "We affirm the complete truthfulness and the full and final authority of the Old and New Testament Scriptures as the Word of God written. . . . Attempts to limit the truthfulness of inspired Scripture to 'faith and practice,' viewed as less than the whole of Scripture, or worse, to assert that it errs in such matters as history, or nature, depart not only from the Bible's representation of its own veracity, but also from the central tradition of the Christian churches."[30] Likewise it would include the 2,300 participants of the Lausanne Conference in Switzerland in 1974 who signed the unlimited inerrancy statement on Scripture, saying, "We affirm the divine inspiration, truthfulness and authority of both Old and New Testament Scriptures in their entirety as the only written Word of God, *without error in all that it affirms*, and the only infallible rule of faith and practice."

Further, unlimited inerrancy is embraced by www.defendinginerrancy.com which now is approaching ten thousand signatures including some of the top Evangelicals in the world such as Billy Graham, Franklin Graham, Ravi Zacharias, John Ankerberg, Al Mohler, Paige Patterson, Erwin Lutzer, John Warwick Montgomery,

---

26. CSBI, art. XII, emphasis added.
27. CSBI, art. XVIII, emphasis added.
28. Ibid., emphasis added.
29. See Hannah, *Inerrancy and the Church*; and Woodbridge, *Biblical Authority*.
30. Kantzer and Henry, *Evangelical Affirmations*, 33.

and Robert Lightner. All of them affirmed the unlimited inerrancy statement which reads: "I affirm that the Bible alone, and in its entirety, is the infallible written Word of God in the original text and is, therefore, *inerrant in all that it affirms or denies on whatever topic it addresses*" (emphasis added). Thus evangelicalism is the rightful owner of unlimited inerrancy, and those professed evangelicals who modify it or limit it to redemptive matters are, at best, the rightful owners of the term Neo-Evangelical.

# Chapter 11

# Early Twentieth Century Challenges to Inerrancy

## F. DAVID FARNELL

### INTRODUCTION

Proverb: "Those who do not learn the lessons of history will repeat past errors."

This is the witness of *The Fundamentals* published in 1917[1] as to what went wrong in American churches and institutions compared to what is now happening in the twenty-first century:[2]

| Early Twentieth Century[A] | Early Twenty-First Century[B] |
|---|---|
| Loss of doctrine of infallibility among mainline denominations (i.e., errancy championed) | Redefining of doctrine of inerrancy to errancy among evangelicals |
| Higher Criticism devastates schools and churches; OT & NT assaulted as to their plain, normal, grammatico-historical sense | Historical (a.k.a Higher) Criticism devastates schools and churches; OT & NT assaulted as to their plain, normal, grammatico-historical sense |
| Teachers sent to American Ivy League, European Continental, German, and British schools to gain broader influence for institutions | Teachers sent to American Ivy League and European Continental, German, and British schools to gain broader influence for institutions |
| Failure traced to uncritical acceptance of philosophy that originated from Spinoza, the father of modern biblical criticism | Failure traced to uncritical acceptance of philosophy that originated from Spinoza, the father of modern biblical criticism |
| The witness of Genesis 1–11 and the Gospels discredited historically | The witness of Genesis 1–11 and the Gospels discredited historically |

    1. All quotes of *The Fundamentals* are from the original 4-vol. edition issued by the Bible Institute of Los Angeles in 1917.

    2. Both lists are essentially identical because the errors of the past frequently reappear in church history as is the case in the beginning of the twentieth century and now the twenty-first century.

| | |
|---|---|
| Rejection of Prophetic Books as non-supernatural, false writings updated by multiple sources and unknown editors | Rejection of Prophetic Books as non-supernatural, false writings updated by multiple sources and unknown editors |
| German- and British-trained evangelicals, and those influenced by them, in America redefine the doctrines of inspiration and inerrancy (William Sanday cited as example) | German- and British-trained evangelicals, and those influenced by them, in America redefine the doctrines of inspiration and inerrancy (many evangelicals cited as examples) |
| A call of alarm by the faithful to reject this direction and defend the faith | A call of alarm by the faithful to reject this direction and defend the faith |
| Inerrancy conferences & meetings formed during this time | Inerrancy conferences & meetings formed during this time (e.g., 2015) |
| *World Conference On Christian Fundamentals* (1919):<br><br>"The future will look back to the World Conference on Christian Fundamentals . . . as an event of more historical moment than the nailing up, at Wittenberg, of Martin Luther's ninety-five theses. The hour has struck for the rise of a new Protestantism. . . . But now the very denominations, blessed by the Reformation, are rapidly coming under the leadership of a new infidelity, known as 'Modernism,' the whole attitude of which is inimical both to the church and the Christ of God."[C]<br><br>*Postscript*: They eventually failed to hold the line. | What will be written about today's Christians as they look back on this time?<br><br>Who will hold the line on inerrancy and faithfulness in the twenty-first century? |

A. As outlined in The *Fundamentals*.

B. See Thomas and Farnell, Jesus Crisis, and Geisler *and Farnell, Jesus Quest, for evidence of the twenty-first-century failures in these very same areas. Ch. 6 will deal with the twenty-first-century notations listed here.*

C. Riley, "Great Divide," 27.

## THOSE WHO DO NOT LEARN FROM THE LESSONS OF HISTORY AT THE TURN OF THE TWENTIETH CENTURY . . .

In 1909, God moved two Christian laymen, wealthy California oil magnates who were brothers named Lyman and Milton Stewart, to set aside a large sum of money for issuing twelve volumes that would set forth the fundamentals of the Christian faith and which were to be sent free of charge to ministers of the gospel, missionaries, Sunday School superintendents, and others engaged in aggressive Christian work throughout the English-speaking world. A committee of twelve men who were known to be sound in the faith was chosen to have the oversight of the publication of these volumes. Entitled *The Fundamentals*, they were a twelve-volume set published between 1910 and 1915 that set presented the fundamentals of the Christian faith. Three million individual volumes were distributed. R. A. Torrey related his own personal knowledge and experience with these volumes in the following terms,

> Rev. Dr. A. C. Dixon was the first Executive Secretary of the Committee, and upon his departure for England Rev. Dr. Louis Meyer was appointed to take his place. Upon the death of Dr. Meyer the work of the Executive Secretary developed upon me. We were able to bring out these twelve volumes according to the original plan. Some of the volumes were sent to 300,000 ministers and missionaries and other workers in different parts of the world. On the completion of the twelve volumes as originally planned the work was continued through The King's Business, published at 536 South Hope St., Los Angeles, California. Although a larger number of volumes were issued than there were names on our mailing list, at last the stock became exhausted, but appeals for them kept coming in from different parts of the world.[3]

Its purpose was to combat the inroads of liberalism that had been experienced by the church during the latter half of the nineteenth and early twentieth centuries (1885–1910) with the denominational conflict that resulted (1910–1930). In essence, it was the early twentieth century's witness to future Christian generations of their scriptural beliefs as well as a record detailing a crisis in biblical belief and authority for their time, constituting a warning to future generations to avoid what they had experienced among the denominations of their day. During this time modernists, or what is now known as "critical scholarship," had refused to give voice to anything approaching the trustworthiness of Scripture. Conservatives were isolated and shunned within mainline denominations. They decided to fight back. The 1925 Scopes Trial regarding evolution also marked a watershed issue for fundamentalists during this period.[4] The New Testament Gospels were being dismissed as historically defective, resulting in what Schweitzer called the "quest" for the historical Jesus. Fundamentalists refused to participate in the First Search for the "historical Jesus," because they realized its *a priori* destructive presuppositional foundations and its intent to destroy the influence of the Gospels and Christianity on society.[5]

## Higher Criticism Devastates American Churches and Schools

In 1915, the Bible Institute of Los Angeles sponsored a four-volume edition of *The Fundamentals* that included all but a few of the original ninety articles. Again, Torrey, who served as the dean of the Bible Institute of Los Angeles from 1912 to 1924, as well

---

3. Torrey, preface to *Fundamentals*, vol. 1.
4. Marsden, *Understanding Fundamentalism and Evangelicalism*, 36–37.
5. For more information, see Farnell, "Searching for the 'Historical' Jesus," 361–420; Schweitzer, *Quest of the Historical Jesus*, 1968.

as the first pastor of the Church of the Open Door in downtown Los Angeles, gave the following information in the preface to the 1917 edition:

> As the fund [supplied by the Lyman brothers] was no longer available for this purpose, the Bible Institute of Los Angeles, to whom the plates were turned over when the Committee closed its work, have decided to bring out the various articles that appeared in The Fundamentals in four volumes at the cheapest price possible All the articles that appeared in The Fundamentals, with the exception of a very few that did not seem to be in exact keeping with the original purpose of The Fundamentals, will be published in this series.[6]

In this four-volume series, the following subjects were highlighted as problems that had plagued the church during that time. First and foremost was the very negative impact that higher criticism was having on Old and New Testament interpretation and inspiration in biblical training centers and churches of the day. The very first article in the four-volume series, "The History of the Higher Criticism," by Dyson Hague, set the tone for all the volumes and provided the overall context or framework for the rest of the articles. The fundamentalists who produced these volumes were not anti-critical in terms of scriptural issues, for they declared that the term can mean "nothing more than the study of the literary structure of the various books of the Bible. Now this in itself is most laudable. It is indispensable."[7] They were, however, very wary of the kind of criticism that scholarly endeavors might employ in analysis of the text with an anti-supernatural bias. While it embraced "a higher criticism which is reverent in tone and scholarly in work"[8] that dealt with "author, date, circumstances, and purpose of writing,"[9] it rejected higher criticism based on the facts that (1) its experts were without a true "spiritual insight," (2) were those who "go far in the realm of the conjectural," and (3) the dominant men of the movement were men with a strong bias against the supernatural," adding that "some of the men who have been the most distinguished in the higher critical movement have been men who have no faith in the God of the Bible, and no faith in either the necessity or the possibility of a personal supernatural revelation."[10] This form of higher criticism was penetrating the mainline American denominations and causing great problems in Christian seminaries and schools that were once faithful.

European critical scholarship received special negative targeting in Hague's opening article, calling the popular German theories of the day as "German Fancies" and "some of the most powerful exponents of the modern Higher Critical theories have been the Germans, and it is notorious to what length the German fancy can go

---

6. Torrey, preface to *Fundamentals*, vol. 1.
7. Hague, "History of the Higher Criticism," 1:9.
8. Ibid., 1:10.
9. Ibid., 1:9.
10. Ibid., 1:12–14.

in the direction of the subjective and of the conjectural. For hypothesis weaving and speculation, the German theological professor is unsurpassed."[11] Hague also commented that "German thinkers are men who lack in a singular degree the faculty of common sense and knowledge of human nature."[12] Hague noted that "the dominant minds [of higher criticism] which have led and swayed the movement, who made the theories that the others circulated, were strongly unbelieving."[13]

The article also centered the origin of this form of negative higher criticism impacting his day to scholarship of (1) the French-Dutch, (2) the Germans, and (3) the British-Americans.[14] He traced the beginnings of modern criticism on these groups for a marked influence away from the inspiration of Scripture, with Spinoza, the rationalist Dutch philosopher, as the father of modern biblical criticism. Hague insightfully noticed, "Spinoza was really the fountain-head of the movement and his line was taken in England by the British philosopher Hobbes. He went deeper than Spinoza, as an outspoken antagonist of the necessity and possibility of personal revelation."[15]

After spreading from Spinoza and Hobbes, he identified the strong German influence of his day that had spread to American schools and churches. Hague sounded the alarm over the latest or "third stage" of the higher critical movement in America which was the "British-American Critics" that were active in theological schools.[16] He noted a particularly alarming trend among these British and American scholars, a piety that was combined with radical European skepticism. He identified Robertson Smith, a Scotchman, as "a man of deep piety and spirituality," who "combined with a sincere regard for the Word of God a critical radicalism that was strangely inconsistent, as did the scholar "George Adam Smith, the most influential of the present leaders, a man of great insight and scriptural acumen who in his works . . . adopted some of the most radical and least demonstrable of the German theories."[17]

Hague saw three areas as core beliefs of the "Continental Critics" influencing America that "can be confidently asserted of nearly all": (1) denial of "the validity of miracle, and the validity of any miraculous narrative. What Christians consider to be miraculous they considered legendary or mythical"; (2) "they . . . denied the reality of prophecy and the validity of any prophetical statement"; and (3) they . . . denied the reality of revelation, in the sense in which it has ever been held by the universal Christian church. . . . Their hypotheses were constructed on the assumption of the falsity of Scripture."[18] Hague summed up the whole of the higher criticism assault

11. Ibid., 1:12.
12. Ibid.
13. Ibid., 1:14–15.
14. Ibid., 1:14.
15. Ibid., 1:15.
16. Ibid., 1:17.
17. Ibid., 1:18.
18. Ibid., 1:19–20.

on the church "in one word" as "rationalistic" and "men who had discarded belief in God and Jesus Christ Whom He had sent. The Bible, in their view, was a mere human product."[19] The crescendo of Hague's lament centered in the fact that their views "have so dominated modern Christianity and permeated modern ministerial thought."[20]

Hague analyzed "English-writing Higher Critics" as "a more difficult subject" because "the British-American Higher Critics represent a school of compromise," commenting that

> on the one hand they practically accept the premises of the Continental school with regard to the antiquity, authorship, authenticity, and origins of the Old Testament books. On the other hand, they refuse to go with the German rationalists in altogether denying their inspiration. They still claim to accept the Scriptures as containing a Revelation from God. But may they not hold their own peculiar views with regard to the origin and date and literary structure of the Bible without endangering their own faith or the faith of Christians? This is the very heart of the question.[21]

Hague also catalogued the impact of higher criticism on the discrediting of the Old Testament (e.g., the JEDP hypothesis) was rampant with its idea of unknown "redactors," noting that "in the redactory process no limit apparently is assigned by the critic to the work of the redactors [who compiled the Pentateuch]. . . . With an utterly irresponsibility of freedom it is declared that they inserted misleading statements with the purpose of reconciling incompatible traditions" expressed by "leading theological writers of and professors of the day."[22] Moreover, the entire Old Testament had been called into question, relating that "the time-honoring traditions of the Catholic Church are set at naught, and its thesis of the relation of inspiration and genuineness and authenticity derided," e.g., Deutero-Isaiah, Daniel as "purely pseudonymous" of the second century BC.

In reference to the New Testament, historical criticism's assault was just beginning:

> With regard to the New Testament: The English writing schools have hitherto confined themselves mainly to the Old Testament, but if Professor Sanday, who passes as a most conservative and moderate representative of the critical school, can be taken as a sample, the historical books are "yet in the first instance strictly historical, put together by ordinary historical methods, or, in so far as the methods on which they are composed, are not ordinary, due to the peculiar circumstances of the case, and not to influences, which need be specially described as supernatural."[23]

19. Ibid., 1:20.
20. Ibid., 1:21.
21. Ibid., 1:21–22.
22. Ibid., 1:24.
23. Ibid., 1:26.

Interestingly, Hague refers to the famous scholar William Sanday who would also rise to New Testament fame, especially in regard to the four-source synoptic hypothesis. The following is from the Bampton Lectures of 1893 on Inspiration at Oxford University where the full quote of Sanday is as follows:

> We observe too that the Historical Books of the New Testament, like those of the Old Testament, whatever the sanctity attaching to them from their contents, are yet in the first instance strictly histories, put together by ordinary historical methods, or in so far as the methods on which they are composed are not ordinary, due to rather their peculiar circumstances of the case, and not to influences, which need specially described as supernatural.[24]

Here, Sanday immediately reduces the inspired nature of the canonical Gospels and Acts as not being composed by any "supernatural" influences, confirming Hague's view of British scholarship as compromising on vital issues. Sanday's limited or inconsistent view of "inspiration" distinguished between the "Traditional" approach of inspiration as viewed by the faithful (i.e., deductive approach) preferring what he called the "inductive approach" to inspiration.[25] It also demonstrated that the last vestiges of the orthodox view of inspiration were rapidly disappearing from the British scene at the end of the nineteenth century. Sanday argued,

> To sum up then, we may compare the Traditional and Inductive theories of Inspiration thus. The inspiration implied by both is real and no fiction, a direct objective action of the Divine upon the human. Nay, in one sense, if the inductive conception of Inspiration is not more real than the other, it is at least more thoroughly realized, because it is not something which is simply taken for granted but comes freshly and spontaneously, in such a way that the mind can get a full and vigorous impression of it, from the study of the documents themselves. The danger of the traditional view is lest inspiration should be thought of as something dead and mechanical; when it is arrived at inductively it must needs be conceived as something vital and organic. It is a living product which falls naturally into its place in the development of the purpose of the Living God. It is not therefore in the least degree inferior in quality to traditional inspiration. So far as they differ it would be rather in quantity, inasmuch as on the inductive view inspiration is not inherent in the Bible as such, but is present in different books and parts of books in different degrees. More particularly on this view—and here is the point of greatest divergence—it belongs to the Historical Books rather as conveying a religious lesson than as histories, rather as interpreting than as narrating plain matter of fact. The crucial issue is that in this last respect they do not seem to be exempted from possibilities of error.[26]

24. Sanday, *Inspiration*, 399.
25. See Geisler, *Systematic Theology*, 1:205–26.
26. Sanday, *Inspiration*, 399–400.

## Part 2—Inerrancy Defended

From this Hague correctly concluded that Continental and British scholarship in his day were outside the realm of orthodoxy regarding inspiration: "The difficulty presents itself to the average man of today is this: How can these critics still claim to believe in the Bible as the Christian church has ever believed it?"[27] At best, scholarship in his day was claiming some form of partial inspiration with a redefinition of orthodox understanding of the concept that was held from the nascent church, arguing "their theory of inspiration must be, then, a very different one from that held by the average Christian" and "its most serious feature is this: It is a theory of inspiration that completely overturns the old-fashioned ideas of the Bible and its unquestioned standard of authority and truth. For whatever this so-called Divine element is, it appears quite consistent with defective argument, incorrect interpretation, if not what the average man would call forgery or falsification. It is, in fact, revolutionary."[28]

Hague viewed these ideas of higher criticism in his day as threatening "the Christian system of doctrine and the whole fabric of systematic theology."[29] He alluded to name-calling among advocates of historical criticism toward Bible-believing people as being "ignorant alarmists" and "obscurantists,"[30] yet noted that these critical scholars were "irreverent in spirit" and must "certainly be received with caution."[31]

Even more interesting, however, was his following comment about the views of the "younger men" in his generation of scholars toward higher criticism:

> There is a widespread idea especially among younger men that the critics must be followed, because their scholarship settles the questions. . . . There is also a widespread idea among the younger men that because scholars are experts in Hebrew that, therefore, their deductions as experts in language must be received. This, too, is a mistake. . . . If we have any prejudice, we would rather be prejudiced against rationalism. If we have any bias, it must be against a teaching which unsteadies the heart and unsettles faith. We prefer to stand with Our Lord and Savior Jesus Christ in receiving the Scriptures as the Word of God, without objection and without a doubt. A little learning and a little listening to rationalistic theorizers and sympathizers may incline us to uncertainty; but deeper study and deeper research will incline us, as it inclined other scholars, to the profoundest conviction of the authority and authenticity of the Holy Scriptures.[32]

Hague noted that the younger scholars insisted that the critical scholars be followed as the "experts." Repeatedly, Hague mentioned that name-calling by the young scholars toward more conservative, Bible-believing scholarship was being conducted.

27. Hague, "History of Higher Criticism," 1:27.
28. Ibid., 1:29–30.
29. Ibid., 1:32.
30. Ibid., 1:36–37.
31. Ibid., 1:37.
32. Ibid., 1:39.

He lamented that "the old-fashioned conservative views are no longer maintained by men with pretension to scholarship. The only people who oppose the higher critics views are the ignorant, the prejudiced, and the illiterate."[33] Yet, he crystalized the real cause of concern regarding the higher criticism of his day:

> What the conservative schools oppose is not Biblical criticism, but Biblical criticism by rationalists. They do not oppose the conclusions . . . because they [i.e., higher critics] are experts and scholars; they oppose them because the Biblical criticism of rationalists and unbelievers can be neither expert nor scientific. A criticism that is characterized by the most arbitrary conclusion from the most spurious assumptions has no right to the word scientific. And further. Their [the faithful of Hague's day] adhesion to the traditional views is not only conscientious but intelligent. They believe that the old-fashioned views are as scholarly as they are scriptural. It is the fashion in some quarters to cite the imposing list of scholars on the side of the German school, and to sneeringly assert that there is not a scholar to stand up for the old views of the Bible.[34]

Hague concluded his article by affirming that "we desire to stand with Christ and His Church. . . . A little learning, and a little listening to rationalistic theorizers and sympathizers may incline us to uncertainty; but deeper study and deeper research will incline us . . . to the profoundest conviction of the authority and authenticity of the Holy Scriptures, and to cry 'Thy word is very pure; therefore Thy servant loveth it.'"[35]

Hague's first article set the tone and direction for the entire rest of the four volumes of *The Fundamentals* of 1917. The first volume of the four issued in 1917 included the following subjects that upheld the factual, historical basis of the material in each Testament and revealed where higher critical attacks were occurring at the turn of the twentieth century. The names in parenthesis reveal the "roll-call of the faithful" who defended Scripture in the articles that are listed and provide the reader with a sweeping overview of the variegated assault from higher criticism within the church at the turn of the twentieth century. Sadly, *many orthodox English theologians participated in the articles, but as the twentieth century would progress, higher criticism's influence on the British Empire would render its national church and evangelistic influence almost completely null and void.*[36] When viewing the titles of these articles, the modern reader may be surprised to see how great an overlap there is between the inerrancy issues of the early twentieth century and the current inerrancy crisis. Here are the subjects of the first volume:

I. The History of Higher Criticism (Dyson Hague)

---

33. Ibid., 1:39–40.
34. Ibid., 1:40.
35. Ibid., 1:42.
36. Swanson, "Downgrade Controversy and Evangelical Boundaries," 229–98.

## Part 2—Inerrancy Defended

II. The Authorship of the Pentateuch (i.e., Denial of Mosaic Authorship) (George F. Wright)

III. The Fallacies of the Higher Criticism (Franklin Johnson)

IV. The Bible and Modern Criticism (F. Bettex)

V. The Holy Scriptures and Modern Negations (James Orr)

VI. Christ and Criticism (Robert Anderson)

VII. Old Testament Criticism and New Testament Christianity (W. H. Griffith Thomas)

VIII. The Tabernacle in the Wilderness: Did It Exist? (David Heagle)

IX. The Internal Evidence of the Fourth Gospel (G. Osborne Troop)

X. The Testimony of Christ to the Old Testament (William Caven)

XI. The Early Narratives of Genesis (James Orr)

XII. One Isaiah (George L. Robinson)

XIII. The Book of Daniel (Joseph D. Wilson)

XIV. The Doctrinal Value of the First Chapter of Genesis (Dyson Hague)

XV. Three Peculiarities of the Pentateuch which are Incompatible with the Graf-Wellhausen Theories of Its Composition (Andrew Craig Robinson)

XVI. The Testimony of the Monuments to the Truth of the Scriptures (George Frederick Wright)

XVII. The Recent Testimony of Archaeology to the Scriptures (M. G. Kyle)

XVIII. Science and the Christian faith (James Orr)

XIX. My Personal Experience with the Higher Criticism (J. J. Reeve)

The second volume of the four defended the following and revealed where other attacks on Scripture were occurring, especially against orthodox views of inspiration and theology:

## Inspiration

I. The Inspiration of the Bible—Definition, Extent and Proof (James M. Gray)

II. Inspiration (L. W. Marshall)

III. The Moral Glory of Jesus Christ, A Proof of Inspiration (William G. Moorehead)

IV. The Testimony of Scripture to Themselves (George S. Bishop)

V. Testimony of the Organic Unity of the Bible to Its Inspiration (Arthur T. Pierson)

VI. Fulfilled Prophecy a Potent Argument for the Bible (Arno C. Gaebelein)

VII. Life in the Word (Philip Mauro)

## Theology

VIII. Is There a God? (Thomas Whitelaw)

IX. God in Christ the Only Revelation of the Fatherhood of God (Robert E. Speer)

X. The Deity of Christ (Benjamin W. Warfield)

XI. The Virgin Birth of Christ (James Orr)

XII. The God-Man (John Stock)

XIII. The Person and Work of Jesus Christ (Bishop Nuelsen)

XIV. The Certainty and Importance of the Bodily Resurrection of Jesus Christ from the Dead (R. A. Torrey)

XV. The Personality and Deity of the Holy Spirit (R. A. Torrey)

XVI. The Holy Spirit and the Son of God (W. J. Erdman)

XVII. Observations on the Conversion and Apostleship of St. Paul (Lord Lyttelton)

XVIII. Christianity No Fable (Thomas Whitelaw)

The third volume of the four continued the defense of orthodox views of theology and evangelism against higher criticism's attacks as well as Roman Catholicism's infiltration:

I. The Biblical Conception of Sin (Thomas Whitelaw)

II. Paul's Testimony to the Doctrine of Sin (Charles B. Williams)

III. Sin and Judgment to Come (Robert Anderson)

IV. What Christ Teaches Concerning the Future Resurrection (William C. Proctor)

V. The Atonement (Franklin Johnson)

VI. At-One-Ment, By Propitiation (Dyson Hague)

VII. The Grace of God (C. I. Scofield)

VIII. Salvation by Grace (Thomas Spurgeon)

IX. The Nature of Regeneration (Thomas Boston)

X. Regeneration, Conversion, Reformation (George W. Lasher)

XI. Justification by Faith (H. C. G. Moule)

XII. The Doctrines that Must Be Emphasized in Successful Evangelism (I. W. Munhall)

XIII. Preach the Word (Howard Crosby)

XIV. Pastoral and Personal Evangelism, or Winning Men to Christ One by One (John Timothy Stone)

XV. The Sunday School's True Evangelism (Charles Gallaudet Trumbull)

XVI. The Place of Prayer in Evangelism (R. A. Torrey)

XVII. Foreign Missions, or World-Wide Evangelism (Robert E. Speer)

## Part 2—Inerrancy Defended

XVIII. A Message from Missions (Charles A. Bowen)

XIX. What Missionary Motives Should Prevail? (Henry W. Frost)

XX. Consecration (Henry W. Frost)

XXI. Is Romanism Christianity? (T. W. Medhurst)

XXII. Rome, the Antagonist of the Nation (J. M. Foster)

XXIII. The True Church (Bishop Ryle)

XXIV. The Testimony of Foreign Missions to the Superintending Providence of God (Arthur T. Pierson)

XXV. The Purpose of the Incarnation (G. Cambell Morgan)

XXVI. Tributes to Christ and the Bible by Brainy Men not Known as Active Christians

The final volume issued warnings to beware of philosophies, modern thought and "isms" that had infiltrated the thinking of the church:

## Modern Thought

I. Modern Philosophy (Philip Mauro)

II. The Knowledge of God (David James Burrell)

III. The Wisdom of This World (A. W. Pitzer)

IV. The Science of Conversion (H. M. Sydenstricker)

V. The Decadence of Darwinism (Henry H. Beach)

VI. The Passing of Evolution (George Frederick Wright)

VII. Evolution in the Pulpit (an Occupant in the Pew)

VIII. The Church and Socialism (Charles R. Erdman)

## "Isms"

IX. Millennial Dawn: A Counterfeit of Christianity (William H. Moorehead)

X. Mormonism: Its Origin, Characteristics and Doctrines (R. G. McNiece)

XI. Eddyism, Commonly Called "Christian Science" (Maurice E. Wilson)

XII. Modern Spiritualism Briefly Tested by Scripture (Algernon J. Pollock)

XIII. Satan and His Kingdom (Jessie Penn-Lewis)

## Further Testimony to the Truth

XIV. Why Save The Lord's Day (Daniel Hoffman Martin)

XV. Apologetic Value of Paul's Epistles (E. J. Stobo)

XVI. The Divine Efficacy of Prayer (Arthur T. Pierson)

XVII. The Proof of the Living God, as Found in the Prayer Life of George Muller, of Bristol (Arthur T. Pierson)

XVIII. Our Lord's Teaching about Money (Arthur T. Pierson)

XIX. The Scriptures (A. C. Dixon)

XX. What the Bible Contains for the Believer (George F. Pentecost)

XXI. The Hope of the Church (John McNicol)

XXII. The Coming of Christ (Charles R. Erdman)

XXIII. The Testimony of Christian Experience (E. Y. Mullins)

XXIV. A Personal Testimony (Howard A. Kelly)

XXV. A Personal Testimony (H. W. Webb-Peploe)

XXVI. The Personal Testimony of Charles T. Studd (Charles T. Studd)

XXVII. A Personal Testimony (Philip Mauro)

In sum, *The Fundamentals* constitute a startling witness left as a testimony by the faithful to the early twentieth-century church's experience of the attack on orthodox Protestant beliefs, conducted aggressively by higher criticism, liberal theology, Catholicism (also called Romanism in the work), socialism, Modernism, atheism, Christian Science, Mormonism, Millennial Dawn, Spiritualism, and evolutionism that had infiltrated its ranks and subsequently caused great damage within the church with regard to its vitality and theology. Above all, they left it as a warning to future generations in hopes of preventing a similar occurrence among God's people in the future.

In 1958, at its fiftieth-year celebration, the Bible Institute of Los Angeles, by then known as Biola College, published a new edition of *The Fundamentals*, called *The Fundamentals for Today*, supervised by Charles Lee Feinberg and a committee of professors from Talbot Theological Seminary.[37] This reissue consisted of sixty-four selected and updated articles from the original ninety whereby Biola College and the new Talbot Theological Seminary affirmed their commitment at that time to the founding fathers' views of the full inspiration and authority of both the Old and New Testaments.

## THE RESULTING CALL TO GOD'S PEOPLE TO GATHER IN DEFENSE OF THE FAITH

An immediate impact of *The Fundamentals* was the alerting of God's people regarding the worsening spiritual condition that the church was experiencing. God's people issued a call to assemble throughout America, rallying in defense of God's inerrant

---

37. Feinberg "updated" the original to *The Fundamentals for Today*, 1958. This book was updated again in 1990 to *The Fundamentals: The Famous Sourcebook of Foundational Biblical Truths*.

Word. Warren Wiersbe related, "At that time in history, Fundamentalism was become a force to reckon with, thanks to effective preachers, popular Bible conferences and the publications that taught 'the fundamentals' and also exposed the growing apostasy of that day. . . . It was a time of growth and challenge."[38] On May 25–June 1, 1919, six thousand Christians met in Philadelphia at the "World Conference on Christian Fundamentals." W. H. Griffith Thomas chaired the Resolutions Committee, while popular well-known fundamentalist preachers spoke for those days, such as W. B. Riley, R. A. Torrey, Lewis Sperry Chafer, James M. Gray, and William L. Pettingill. Delegates came from forty-two states in America, most of the Canadian provinces as well as seven foreign countries to rally against the infiltration of destructive higher criticism and liberalism of the day in the church. The Bible Conference Committee issued *God Hath Spoken*, a work that consisted of twenty-five addresses that were delivered at the conference and stenographically recorded for posterity. The work described two outstanding phenomena as leading to the assembly in Philadelphia in 1919 that are very telling:

> On the one hand, the Great Apostasy was spreading like a plague throughout Christendom. A famine was everywhere—"not a famine of bread, nor a thirst for water, but of hearing the words of Jehovah." Thousands of false teachers, many of them occupying high ecclesiastical positions, were bringing in damnable heresies, even denying the Lord "that bought them," and bringing upon themselves swift destruction. And many were following their pernicious ways, by reason of whom the way of truth was evil spoken of. The Bible was wounded in the house of its friends. The great cardinal doctrines of Scripture were set at naught. The Virgin Birth of our Lord, His Sacrificial Death and Bodily Resurrection, these and similar truths were rejected as archaic and effete. The Consensus of Scholarship, the Assured Results of Modem Research, New Light from Original Sources, the Findings of Science, all these high-sounding phrases, and others like them, became popular slogans calculated to ensnare the simple, and to deceive if possible the very elect. People generally accepted the so-called Findings of Science at their face value, never suspecting that they were only the inventions of "false apostles, deceitful workers, transforming themselves into the apostles of Christ." To "the man whose eyes are open," of course, all this was "no marvel; for Satan himself is transformed into an angel of light."[39]

> On the other hand, parallel with the deepening apostasy, and probably actually stimulated by it, there was a widespread revival—not a revival in the sense of great ingatherings resulting from evangelistic effort, but a revival of interest in, and hunger for, the Word of God. This hunger, I say, was probably

---

38. Wiersbe, foreword to *Fundamentals: The Famous Sourcebook*.
39. Bible Conference Committee, introduction to *God Hath Spoken*, 7–8.

stimulated by the apostasy; for what will increase hunger like a famine? The sheep of Christ began to look up to their Shepherd for food, even for "every word that proceedeth out of the mouth of God." Men and women began insistently to ask, "Hath God really spoken? And, if so, what hath He said? What saith the Scriptures?"[40]

This quote reveals that God's people realized the crisis, not only did the faithful write apologetic defenses against what was occurring, such as *The Fundamentals*, to expose the grave danger but they also gathered the faithful together in defense of the orthodox faith (Phil 1:3; Jude 3). W. B. Riley, a well-known Baptist leader of the time, declared in his sermon "The Great Divide, or Christ and the Present Crisis," that

> the future will look back to the World Conference on Christian Fundamentals . . . as an event of more historical moment than the nailing up, at Wittenberg, of Martin Luther's ninety-five theses. The hour has struck for the rise of a new Protestantism. . . . But now the very denominations, blessed by the Reformation, are rapidly coming under the leadership of a new infidelity, known as "Modernism," the whole attitude of which is inimical both to the church and the Christ of God.[41]

The assembly issued a doctrinal declaration as follows:

> Your committee on resolutions herewith submits the following report:
>
> We regard it timely and altogether essential that this World Conference on Christian Fundamentals in Philadelphia should give expression to the faith for which it stands and we unite in declaring the following as our Doctrinal Statement:
>
> > I. We believe in the Scriptures of the Old and New Testaments as verbally inspired of God, and inerrant in the original writings, and that they are the supreme and final authority in faith and life.
> >
> > II. We believe in one God, eternally existing in three persons, Father, Son and Holy Spirit.
> >
> > III. We believe that Jesus Christ was begotten by the Holy Spirit, and born of the Virgin Mary, and is true God and true man.
> >
> > IV. We believe that man was created in the image of God, that he sinned and thereby incurred not only physical death, but also that spiritual death which is separation from God, and that all human beings are born with a sinful nature, and, in the case of those who reach moral responsibility, become sinners in thought, word, and deed.

---

40. Ibid., 7–9.
41. Ibid., 27.

V. We believe that the Lord Jesus Christ died for our sins according to the Scriptures as a representative and substitutionary sacrifice; and that all who believe in Him are justified on the ground of his shed blood.

VI. We believe in the resurrection of the crucified body of our Lord, in His ascension into heaven, and in His present life there for us, as High Priest and Advocate.

VII. We believe in "that blessed hope," the personal, premillennial and imminent return of our Lord and Saviour Jesus Christ.

VIII. We believe that all who receive by faith the Lord Jesus Christ are born again of the Holy Spirit, and thereby become the children of God.

IX. We believe in the bodily resurrection of the just and the unjust, the everlasting blessedness of the saved, and the everlasting, conscious punishment of the lost."[42]

## DO GOD'S PEOPLE EVER LEARN FROM THE HISTORY OF PAST CHRISTIAN FAILURES?

As a result of such warnings, the faithful broke away from mainline denominations and established their own Bible colleges and seminaries to preserve a faithful remnant. In subsequent years, scores of Bible schools and seminaries were launched by fundamentalists across America during this period of denominational decay. Moody Bible Institute was founded in 1886 by evangelist Dwight L. Moody. Lyman Stewart funded the production of *The Fundamentals* which heralded the founding of the Bible Institute of Los Angeles. By 1912, Torrey, coming from Moody Bible Institute, became dean of the Bible Institute of Los Angeles. The warning of J. Gresham Machen that "as go the theological seminaries, so goes the church" struck deep at the heart of Bible-believing scholars everywhere: "Many seminaries today *are* nurseries of unbelief; and because they are nurseries of unbelief the churches that they serve have become unbelieving churches too. As go the theological seminaries, so goes the church."[43] In 1929, Machen was influential in founding Westminster Theological Seminary as a result of Princeton's direction.[44] Dallas Theological Seminary was founded in 1924[45] and Fuller Theological Seminary was founded in 1947 by Biola graduate Charles E. Fuller along with Harold Ockenga.[46] These are just a select few of the many schools

42. Ibid., 11–12.

43. Machen, *Christian Faith in the Modern World*, 65.

44. For a revealing look at Machen's struggle, see Machen, *Christianity and Liberalism*; Machen, *Virgin Birth of Christ*; Machen, *What Is Faith?*

45. For a recent recounting of the history of Dallas Theological Seminary, see Hannah, *Uncommon Union*.

46. For the history of Fuller, see Marsden, *Reforming Fundamentalism*.

founded by faithful men in this period. Many today in evangelicalism can trace their educational and denominational roots to this period of time wherein the church was in a period of severe decline among mainstream groups. Chapter 12 discusses the present crisis of the twenty-first century.

## Chapter 12

# Early Twenty-First-Century Challenges to Inerrancy

### F. DAVID FARNELL

The previous chapter reviewed the early twentieth century and historical criticism's devastating impact upon the inspiration and inerrancy of the Old and New Testaments. After this strategic withdrawal by fundamentalists of the first generation who fought the battle to preserve Scripture from the onslaught of historical criticism as well as its subsequent searching for the historical Jesus, subsequent generations from fundamentalist groups became discontent with their isolation from liberal-dominated mainstream biblical scholarship. They sought a wider influence with its accompanying prestige in the eyes of mainline academia, especially through sending their young scholars once again to American Ivy League, British, and Continental European schools. Marsden centers this central thought on the transformation of Fuller Theological Seminary from one that had "fundamentalist" leanings toward separation to becoming that of a broadly defined, influential seminary in the nation, "Henry and Ockenga were zeroing in on what they saw as a major weakness in fundamentalism. The fundamentalist preoccupation with separation both ecclesiastically and in personal mores had cut the group off from any real social impact."[1] This desire for wide influence would eventually impact hiring decisions by Fuller Seminary to seek candidates from Ivy League American schools, like Béla Vassady (before 1952 spelled Vasady), a graduate of Harvard, with Carl Henry himself seeking a PhD degree from Boston University. Vassady, in his exposure to more prestigious education, had admiration for Karl Barth as well as Neo-Orthodoxy, and was a supporter of the World

---

1. Marsden, *Reforming Fundamentalism*, 80.

Council of Churches.² Eventually a series of unwise faculty and administrative additions would lead to a crescendo with Daniel Fuller, the son of Charles, attending a Continental European school, the University of Basel in Switzerland, with Karl Barth. He had convinced Charles Fuller and some of the seminary that "he must have the highest European credentials if he and the seminary were to make an impact in the scholarly world, and the elder Fullers were confident that he would stand strong in the den of Neo-Orthodoxy."³ History reveals, however, that Neo-Orthodoxy won the day with Daniel and that he became a champion of the hermeneutic of historical criticism that had destroyed the mainline denominations at the turn of the twentieth century.⁴

Eventually, Fuller also rejected inerrancy as a doctrine in an Evangelical Theological Society paper entitled "Benjamin Warfield's View of Faith and History," in which he asserted that "the slight corrective to Warfield that I propose is to understand that plenary verbal inspiration involves accommodation to the thinking of the original readers in non-revelation matters."⁵ The latter position became the point of departure of Fuller from the doctrine of inerrancy in the late 1950s and early 1960s. Thus, at Fuller the desire for recognition from a broader field of academics resulted in an eventual rejection of inerrancy toward that of accommodation to the prevailing philosophies of the mid-twentieth century.

## DO YOU NOT KNOW THAT FRIENDSHIP WITH THE WORLD IS HOSTILITY TOWARD GOD?

Sadly, by the mid-1960s, history was repeating itself. Fuller Theological Seminary is only one example. Prominent voices were scolding fundamentalists for continued isolation and dialogue and interaction once again became the rallying cry. Carl F. H. Henry's criticisms struck deep: "The preoccupation of fundamentalists with the errors of modernism, and neglect of schematic presentations of the evangelical alternative, probably gave Neo-Orthodoxy its great opportunity in the Anglo-Saxon world. . . . If Evangelicals do not overcome their preoccupation with negative criticism of contemporary theological deviations at the expense of the construction of preferable alternatives to these, they will not be much of a doctrinal force in the decade ahead."⁶

Echoing similar statements, George Eldon Ladd (1911–1982) of Fuller Theological Seminary became a zealous champion of modern critical methods, arguing that the two-source hypothesis should be accepted "as a literary fact" and that form criticism "has thrown considerable light on the nature of the Gospels and the traditions

---

2. Ibid., 98.
3. Ibid., 197.
4. See Fuller, "Resurrection of Jesus and the Historical Method."
5. Fuller, "Benjamin B. Warfield's View of Faith and History," 82.
6. Henry, *Jesus of Nazareth*, 9.

they employ," adding, "Evangelical scholars should be willing to accept this light."[7] Indeed, for Ladd, critical methods have derived great benefit for evangelicals: "It has shed great light on the historical side of the Bible; and these historical discoveries are valid for all Bible students even though the presuppositions of the historical-critical method have been often hostile to an evangelical view of the Bible. Contemporary evangelicals often overlook this important fact when they condemn the critical method as such; for even while they condemn historical criticism, they are constantly reaping the benefits of its discoveries and employing critical tools."[8] Ladd asserts, "One must not forget that . . . everyday tools of good Bible study are the product of the historical-critical method."[9] George Ladd catalogued the trend of a "substantial group of scholars" whose background was in the camp of "fundamentalism" who had now been trained "in Europe as well as in our best universities" and were "deeply concerned with serious scholarship."[10] He also chided fundamentalists for their "major preoccupation" with defending "inerrancy of the Bible in its most extreme form," but contributing "little of creative thinking to the current debate."[11]

Although Ladd acknowledged that historical-critical ideology was deeply indebted for its operation in the Enlightenment and the German scholarship that created it openly admitted its intention of "dissolving orthodoxy's identification of the Gospel with Scripture,"[12] Ladd sent many of his students for subsequent study in Britain and Europe in order to enlarge the influence of conservatives, the latter of which influence was greatly responsible for the fundamentalist split at the turn of the twentieth century.[13]

Today, Ladd serves as the recognized paradigm for current attitudes and approaches among evangelical historical-critical scholarship in encouraging evangelical education in British and Continental institutions as well as the adoption and participation in historical criticism to some form or degree, actions which previously were

---

7. Ladd, *New Testament and Criticism*, 141, 168–69.

8. Ibid., 10.

9. Ladd offers two examples: Kittel and Friedrich, *Theological Dictionary of the New Testament*, and Arndt et al., *Greek-English Lexicon of the New Testament* (Ladd, *New Testament and Criticism*, 11).

10. Ladd, "Search for Perspective," 47.

11. Ladd, "Search for Perspective," 47. In a hotly debated book, Harold Lindsell in the mid-1970s detailed the problems facing Fuller, the Southern Baptist Convention, and other Christian institutions due to the encroachment of historical criticism from European influence. See Lindsell, "Strange Case of Fuller Theological Seminary," 106–21.

12. Ladd, "Search for Perspective," 49. Ladd's citing of this admission by Ernst Käsemann may be found in the latter's, *Essays on New Testament Themes*, 54–62.

13. An example of one of Ladd's students is the late Robert Guelich, who wrote *Sermon on the Mount* (1982). Guelich promoted an exegesis "that . . . makes use of the literary critical tools including text, source, form, tradition, redaction, and structural criticism" and goes on to assert "for many to whom the Scriptures are vital the use of these critical tools has historically been more 'destructive' than 'constructive.' But one need not discard the tool because of its abuse." See Guelich, *Sermon on the Mount*, 23.

greatly responsible for the fundamentalist-modernist split.[14] Historical lessons from what caused the last theological meltdown had long been forgotten or carelessly disregarded.[15] Perhaps the young of each generation somehow convince themselves that they can do what others previously have not been able to do, i.e., stay faithful while melding biblical studies with the latest ideologies, philosophies and fads of their own time (Col 2:8; 2 Cor 10:5).

Yet, significantly, Ladd had drawn a line for his scholarly participation that he would not cross. Ladd (d. 1982) lived during the second "search for the 'historical Jesus'" and had correctly perceived, "The historical-critical method places severe limitations upon its methodology before it engages in a quest for the historical Jesus. It has decided in advance the kind of Jesus it must find—or at least the kind of Jesus it may not find, the Jesus portrayed in the Gospels" and "if the Gospel portrait is trustworthy, then 'the historical Jesus' never existed in history, only in the critical reconstructions of the scientific historians. A methodology which prides itself in its objectivity turns out to be in the grip of dogmatic philosophical ideas about the nature of history."[16] Ladd countered, "In sum, the historical-critical method is not an adequate method to interpret the theology of the New Testament because its presuppositions limit its findings to the exclusion of the central biblical message." Instead, Ladd recognized the contribution of a "historical-theological" method of theology based in the *Heilsgeschichte* ("salvation history") approach that takes the New Testament as serious history, and said, "My own understanding of New Testament Theology is distinctly *heilsgeschichtlich*."[17]

In 1976, a book came on the scene that sent massive shockwaves throughout the evangelical movement: *The Battle for the Bible*, by Harold Lindsell.[18] Lindsell catalogued what he perceived was an alarming departure from the doctrine of inerrancy among evangelicals. Around this same time, Francis Schaeffer had argued, "Holding to a strong view of Scripture or not holding to it is the watershed of the

---

14. Mark Noll conducted a personal poll/survey among evangelicals and has, as a result, described Ladd as "the most widely influential figure on the current generation of evangelical Bible scholars." Ladd was "most influential" among scholars in the Institute for Biblical Research and was placed just behind John Calvin as "most influential" among scholars in the Evangelical Theological Society. See Noll, *Between Faith and Criticism*, 97, 101, 112–14 [note esp. 112 for this quote], 116, 121, 159–63, 211–26. Moreover, Marsden described Noll's *Between Faith and Criticism* as making "a major contribution toward understanding twentieth-century evangelical scholarship." See Marsden, *Reforming Fundamentalism*, 250n9. Since Noll marked out Ladd as the outstanding figure influencing the recent paradigm shift in twentieth-century evangelical scholarship toward favoring historical-critical methods and since Marsden promotes Noll's book as making "a major contribution toward understanding twentieth-century evangelical scholarship," this paper uses Ladd as the outstanding paradigm, as well as typical representative, of this drift among evangelicals toward historical-critical ideologies that favor literary dependency hypotheses.

15. For further historical details, see Farnell, "Philosophical and Theological Bent," 85–131.

16. Ladd, "Search for Perspective," 51.

17. Ibid., 47.

18. Lindsell, *Battle for the Bible*.

evangelical world."[19] Lindsell catalogued departures from inerrancy by the Lutheran Missouri Synod, the Southern Baptists, and other groups. He listed what he perceived as deviations that resulted when inerrancy is denied as well as how the infection of denial spreads to other matters within evangelicalism. Because Lindsell was one of the founding members of Fuller Seminary, he especially focused on what he felt were troubling events at Fuller Seminary regarding the watershed issue of inerrancy.[20] Most strategically, Lindsell attributed the "use of historical-critical method" as a foundational cause of the destruction of inerrancy among denominations. He noted, "There are also those who call themselves evangelicals who have embraced this [historical-critical] methodology. The presuppositions of this methodology . . . go far beyond mere denial of biblical infallibility. They tear at the heart of Scripture, and include a denial of the supernatural."[21] In *The Bible in the Balance*, Lindsell dedicated a whole chapter to historical criticism, labeling it "The Bible's Deadly Enemy":

> Anyone who thinks the historical-critical method is neutral is misinformed. . . . It appears to me that modern evangelical scholars (and I may have been guilty of this myself) have played fast and loose with the term because they wanted acceptance by academia. They seem too often to desire to be members of the club which is nothing more than practicing an inclusiveness that undercuts the normativity of the evangelical position. This may be done, and often is, under the illusion that by this method the opponents of biblical inerrancy can be won over to the evangelical viewpoint. But practical experience suggests that rarely does this happen and the cost of such an approach is too expensive, for it gives credence and leads respectability to a method which is the deadly enemy of theological orthodoxy.[22]

As an interpretive ideology, Lindsell noted that both form and redaction criticism are destroying the historical trustworthiness of the Gospels. He noted: "When the conclusion is reached that the Gospels do not reflect true history the consequences are mind-boggling. We simply do not know who the real Jesus was. This undermines Scripture and destroys the Christian faith as a historical vehicle. It opens the door wide to a thousand vagaries and brings us right back to trying to find the canon within a canon."[23]

Reaction to Lindsell's first book was exceedingly swift.[24] Some praised it while others vilified it. In response to the book, many concerned evangelicals began to form

---

19. Schaeffer, *Great Evangelical Disaster*, 51.
20. Lindsell, *Battle for the Bible*, 23.
21. Ibid., 204.
22. Lindsell, *Bible in the Balance*, 283.
23. Ibid., 297.
24. For a more detailed history on this period, see Geisler and Roach, *Defending Inerrancy*, 9–42, which gives an excellent, brief overview detailing the developmental, historical details surrounding the International Council on Biblical Inerrancy.

what would become known as the International Council on Biblical Inerrancy in 1977 that would produce the Chicago Statements on Biblical Inerrancy (1978) and Hermeneutics (1982) as a response.[25] Lindsell himself catalogued the reaction in a second companion volume, *The Bible in the Balance*. Donald Dayton recounted the fear that it produced among evangelicals in the following terms: "Evangelicals are jittery, fearing Lindsell's book might herald a new era of faculty purges and organizational splits—a reply of earlier conflicts, this time rending the evangelical world asunder."[26] Dayton later wrote that "'Evangelical' and 'fundamentalist' controversies over scriptural authority and biblical inerrancy seem endless," citing Lindsell's works as continuing to disturb the evangelical world.[27]

In 1979, Fuller professor Jack B. Rogers and Donald K. McKim responded directly to Lindsell's assertion that plenary, verbal inspiration was the orthodox position of the church in their *The Authority and Interpretation of the Bible* by attempting to argue that Lindsell's position on inerrancy was inaccurate.[28] They argued, "The central Christian tradition included the concept of accommodation"[29] and that modern views of inerrancy did not reflect the church's historic position, but resulted from "extreme positions" taken both from fundamentalism and modernism "regarding the Bible."[30] Lindsell's and many others' views of inerrancy, Rogers and McKim alleged, were from "the old Princeton position of Hodge and Warfield" who had drunk deep from "Scottish common sense realism" rather than reflecting the historic position of the church.[31] They noted, "Our hypothesis is that the peculiar twists of American history have served to distort our view of both the central Christian tradition [concerning inerrancy] and especially of its Reformed Branch."[32] They went on to note:

> The function, or purpose, of the Bible was to bring people into a saving relationship with God through Jesus Christ. The Bible was not used as an encyclopedia of information on all subjects. The principle theological teachers of the church argued that the Bible not be used to judge matters of science, for example, astronomy. Scripture's use was clearly for salvation, not science. The forms of the Bible's language and its cultural context were open to scholarly investigation. The central tradition included the concept of accommodation. . . . God had condescended and adapted himself in Scripture to our ways of thinking and speaking. . . . To erect a standard, modern technical precision in

---

25. "Taking a Stand on Scripture," 25.
26. Dayton, "Battle for the Bible," 976.
27. Dayton, "Church in the World," 79.
28. Rogers and McKim, *Authority and Interpretation*. Rogers and McKim relied heavily upon the work of Sandeen, *Roots of Fundamentalism*.
29. Rogers and McKim, introduction to *Authority and Interpretation*, xxii.
30. Ibid., xxiii.
31. Ibid., 289–98.
32. Ibid., xxii.

language as the hallmark of biblical authority was totally foreign to the foundation shared by the early church.[33]

The Bible was to be viewed as reliable in matters of faith and practice but not in all matters. In 2009, as an apparent result of his approach to Scripture, Rogers released *Jesus, the Bible and Homosexuality*, that calls for evangelical tolerance and acceptance of homosexuality, gay, lesbian, and transgender issues not only for church membership but for ordination in ministry.[34]

As a direct response to Rogers and McKim, John Woodbridge published his *Biblical Authority: A Critique of the Rogers/McKim Proposal* as an effective critique of their proposal.[35] Lindsell's negative historical take on problems has received counterbalancing by Marsden's *Reforming Fundamentalism*, produced in 1987. By 1978, conservative evangelicals who knew the importance of inerrancy as a doctrinal watershed felt the need to produce the Chicago Statement on Biblical Inerrancy and produced another on Hermeneutics in 1982 to reaffirm their historical positions in these areas as a response to Rogers's and McKim's work.[36]

As a direct consequence of these events, Robert Gundry resigned from membership of ETS in 1982 under pressure for his involvement in dehistoricizing Matthew as reflected in his commentary *Matthew: A Commentary on His Literary and Theological Art*.[37] His withdrawal, as will be seen, still raises strong feelings among evangelical scholarship. Gundry contended that Matthew's story of the slaughtering of the babies in Bethlehem should not be seen as historical but as a type of allegorical, midrashic device or illustration.[38] Genre was now being used by evangelicals as a hermeneutical excuse to dehistoricize the plain, normal sense of the Gospels. Using redaction critical hermeneutics centering in genre issues about Jewish midrash interpretation in Matthew 2:7–8, Gundry argued that the theological editor of Matthew redacted or edited the offering of two turtledoves or two young pigeons in the temple (Luke 2:24) and transformed it into Herod's slaughter of the babies in Bethlehem.[39]

As another example, Gundry also asserted that Matthew transformed the Jewish shepherds that appear in Luke 2 into Gentile magi[40] and had also changed the traditional manger into a house. For Gundry, then, the nonexistent house was where the nonexistent magi found Jesus on the occasion of their non-visit to Bethlehem.

---

33. Ibid., xxii.

34. Rogers, *Jesus, the Bible, and Homosexuality*.

35. Woodbridge, *Biblical Authority*.

36. "Chicago Statement on Biblical Inerrancy," 289–96, and "Chicago Statement on Biblical Hermeneutics," 397–401.

37. Gundry, *Matthew: A Commentary on His Literary and Theological Art*. The updated 2nd ed. (1994) is titled *Matthew: A Commentary on His Handbook for a Mixed Church under Persecution*.

38. Ibid., 34–35.

39. Ibid.

40. Ibid., 31.

Gundry's use of genre issues based in historical-critical ideology (redaction criticism) as a means to negate the historicity of events that were always considered genuine historical events by the orthodox community from the beginnings of the church alarmed the vast majority (74 percent) of evangelicals in the Evangelical Theological Society.

Another reaction to Lindsell's works, in addition to the formation of ICBI, was James Barr's response as penned in his two strategic works *Fundamentalism* and *Beyond Fundamentalism*. In 1977, Barr composed his *Fundamentalism* as a direct response against the "fundamentalism" of Lindsell, noting in his foreword: "It is not surprising that, in a time of unusual ferment and fresh openness among evangelicals, there should appear a book like Harold Lindsell's *The Battle for the Bible* . . . insisting on a hard position of total inerrancy of the Bible."[41] Instead, Barr praised Jack Rogers's work, *Confessions of a Conservative Evangelical*,[42] as "a work indicating an openness to new trends among evangelicals" and characterized it as "an interesting expression of a search for an evangelical tradition different from the dominant fundamentalist one."[43]

In *Fundamentalism*, Barr urged evangelicals to separate from and reject fundamentalism's characteristics in three specific areas:

(a) A very strong emphasis on the inerrancy of the Bible, the absence from it of any sort of error.

(b) A strong hostility to modern theology and methods, results and implications of modern critical study of the Bible.

(c) An assurance that those who do not share their religious viewpoint are not really "true Christians" at all.[44]

In his 1984 work, *Beyond Fundamentalism*, Barr again continued to urge evangelicals to continue separation from fundamentalism in these areas: "This [work] seeks to offer help to those who have grown up in the world of fundamentalism or have become committed to it but who have in the end come to feel that it is a prison from which they must escape."[45]

Lindsell's work, as well as ICBI, continued to send shockwaves through evangelical society. In 1982, Alan Johnson, in his presidential address to ETS, asked through analogy whether higher criticism was "Egyptian gold or pagan precipice" and reached the conclusion that "the refinement of critical methodologies under the magisterium of an inerrant scriptural authority can move us gently into a deeper appreciation of sacred Scripture."[46]

41. Barr, foreword to the American edition of *Fundamentalism*, vi.
42. Rogers, *Confessions of a Conservative Evangelical*.
43. Barr, foreword to the American edition of *Fundamentalism*, iv.
44. Ibid., 1.
45. Barr, preface to *Beyond Fundamentalism*, vii.
46. Johnson, "Historical-Critical Method," 15. See also Henry, "Uses and Abuses of Historical Criticism," 385–404.

## Part 2—Inerrancy Defended

Craig Blomberg, in 1984, soon after the ICBI statements, raised questions regarding biblical interpretation in the Gospels, arguing for genre distinctions. Blomberg defended Robert Gundry's midrashic approach to the Gospels wherein Gundry had been dismissive of the historicity of much of Matthew's narrative, especially the infancy narratives in Matthew 1–3, in the following terms:

> Is it possible, even inherently probable, that the NT writers at least in part never intended to have their miracle stories taken as historical or factual and that their original audiences probably recognized this? If this sounds like the identical reasoning that enabled Robert Gundry to adopt his midrashic interpretation of Matthew while still affirming inerrancy, that is because it is the same. The problem will not disappear simply because one author [Gundry] is dealt with *ad hominem* . . . how should evangelicals react? Dismissing the sociological view on the grounds that the NT miracles present themselves as historical gets us nowhere. So do almost all the other miracle stories of antiquity. Are we to believe them all?[47]

Barr's criticisms also stung deep among other evangelicals. At an annual Evangelical Theological Society meeting in Santa Clara, California, in 1997, Moisés Silva, who himself had studied under Barr ("my admiration for Barr knows no bounds"), chided conservative scholarship for their lack of openness to methods of modern criticism in his presidential address entitled "Can Two Walk Together Unless They Be Agreed? Evangelical Theology and Biblical Scholarship."[48] Silva took his mentor, Barr, to task for misrepresenting evangelicals by failing to notice that many evangelicals were open to historical-critical hermeneutics, citing not only recent evangelicals who espoused critical methods but also earlier evangelicals like Machen who took "seriously the liberal teachings of his day."[49] Silva asserted that "there is the more direct approach of many of us who are actually engaged in critical Biblical scholarship."[50] Thus, by 1997, many evangelicals were openly disregarding Lindsell's warning about historical criticism.

The next year, in 1998, Norman Geisler, took quite the opposite approach and warned evangelicals regarding the negative presuppositions of historical-critical ideologies in his "Beware of Philosophy," citing lessons from history as demonstrating their negative consequences.[51] In his address, Geisler featured a 1998 work entitled *The Jesus Crisis* that detailed growing evangelical involvement in historical-critical ideologies like questing for the "historical Jesus." Just like Lindsell's books, *The Jesus Crisis* stirred up a hornet's nest of controversy among evangelicals. To say the least, Geisler's

---

47. Blomberg, "New Testament Miracles," 436.
48. Silva, "Can Two Walk Together," 3–16 (quote from p. 4).
49. Ibid., 8.
50. Ibid., 10.
51. See also Geisler, *Biblical Inerrancy*. The book gives the philosophical background to ideas that lead inevitably to a denial of inerrancy and result in a supposition of errancy regarding Scripture.

address, as well as his praise for *The Jesus Crisis*, revealed a significant cleavage within evangelicalism that had developed since ICBI. While some praised *The Jesus Crisis* as needing to be written,[52] other evangelicals disdained the work as strident, fundamentalist rhetoric that was closed-minded to a judicial use of historical criticism.[53] Darrell Bock reacted to *The Jesus Crisis* with the following: "As a whole, *The Jesus Crisis* displays a lack of discernment about the history of Gospels study. The book should have given a more careful discussion of difficult details in the Gospels and the views tied to them, especially when inerrantists critiqued by the book are portrayed as if they were denying the accuracy of the Gospels, when in fact they are defending it."[54] Bock contended, "Careful consideration also does not support the claim that even attempting to use critical methods judiciously leads automatically and inevitably to denial of the historicity of the Gospels. Unfortunately this work overstates its case at this basic level and so places blame for the bibliological crisis at some wrong evangelical doorsteps."[55]

In a highly irregular move for the Evangelical Theological Society that disallowed book reviews in the form of journal articles, Grant Osborne was given an opportunity in the next issue of *JETS* to counter Geisler's presidential address, wherein Geisler's address, as well as *The Jesus Crisis*, were criticized, saying, "The tone is too harsh and grating, the positions too extreme."[56] In 2003, Geisler, a world-renown Christian apologist and longtime member of ETS, decried the society's acceptance of open theists among its ranks and withdrew his membership, perceiving a drift in the wrong direction for the Evangelical Theological Society, of which he was a founding member. Grant Osborne, however, in his use of redaction-critical hermeneutics, advocated that the Great Commission was not originally spoken by Jesus in the way that Matthew had recorded it, but that "it seems most likely that at some point the tradition or Matthew expanded an original monadic formula."[57] He later reversed his position in the following terms:

> A misunderstanding of my position with respect to this, in fact, has led to widespread dissatisfaction regarding my approach to the triadic baptismal formula of Matt 28:19. There I posited that Matthew had possibly expanded an original monadic formula in order "to interpret the true meaning of Jesus' message for his own day. . . . However, Matthew has faithfully reproduced the intent and meaning of what Jesus said." In my next article mentioned above I clarified this further by stating, "The interpretation must be based on the

---

52. See the back cover page of the work where some called it "a blockbuster" and "the best up-to-date analysis in print of the dangerous drift of evangelical scholarship into negative higher criticism" (Thomas and Farnell, *Jesus Crisis*).

53. Osborne's article constitutes a criticism of not only Geisler but *The Jesus Crisis*; Osborne, "Historical Criticism and the Evangelical," 193–210.

54. Bock, review of *Jesus Crisis*, 232.

55. Ibid., 236.

56. Osborne, "Historical Criticism and the Evangelical," 209.

57. Osborne, "Redaction Criticism and the Great Commission," 80.

original words and meaning imparted by Jesus." Here I would like to clarify it further by applying the implications of my second article to the first. I did not mean that Matthew had freely composed the triadic formula and read it back onto the lips of Jesus. Rather, Jesus had certainly (as in virtually every speech in the NT) spoken for a much longer time and had given a great deal more teaching than reported in the short statement of Matt 28:18–20. In it I believe that he probably elucidated the trinitarian background behind the whole speech. This was compressed by Matthew in the form recorded. Acts and Paul then may have followed the formula itself from the commission speech, namely the monadic form.[58]

In 2001, Craig Blomberg, in his article "Where Should Twenty-First Century Biblical Scholarship Be Heading?" decried *The Jesus Crisis*:

> It is hard to imagine a book such as Thomas and Farnell's *The Jesus Crisis* ever appearing in Britain, much less being commended by evangelical scholars as it has been by a surprising number in this country. Avoiding Thomas's and Farnell's misguided separatism and regular misrepresentation of others' works, a higher percentage of us need to remain committed to engaging the larger, scholarly world in contextually sensitive ways that applaud as much as possible perspectives that we do not adopt while nevertheless preserving evangelical distinctives.[59]

Blomberg went on to praise his own brand of scholarship: "It still distresses me . . . how many religious studies departments in the US (or their libraries) are unaware of the breadth and depth of evangelical biblical scholarship. This situation need not remain this way, as witnessed by the fact that this is an area in which our British counterparts have made considerably more progress in, at times, even less-promising contexts."[60]

Such a response by Blomberg serves as an illustration of the startling erosion of inerrancy among New Testament scholars, especially those who have been schooled in Britain and/or the European continent. Many of these European-trained scholars ignore the lessons of history learned by evangelicals at the turn of the twentieth century and as highlighted in the Chicago Statements of 1978 and 1982. Significantly, Blomberg and those agreeing with him exemplify the substantive shift in hermeneutics that these evangelicals are now engaging in. The Chicago Statement on Inerrancy in 1978 expressly commended the grammatico-historical approach in article XVIII:

---

58. Osborne, "Evangelical and Redaction Criticism," 311; cf. Osborne, "Great Commission," 80, 85; Osborne, "Evangelical and *Traditionsgeschichte*," 128.

59. Blomberg, "Where Should Twenty-First Century Scholarship Be Heading?," 172. This article was also published in "Past, Present and Future of American Evangelical Theological Scholarship," in *Solid Ground*, 314–15.

60. Blomberg, "Where Should Twenty-First Century Scholarship Be Heading?," 172.

We affirm that the text of Scripture is to be interpreted by grammatico-historical exegesis, taking account of its literary forms and devices, and that Scripture is to interpret Scripture. We deny the legitimacy of any treatment of the text or quest for sources lying behind it that leads to relativizing, dehistoricizing, or discounting its teaching, or rejecting its claims to authorship.

Why did they commend the grammatico-historical approach? Because the men who expressed these two watershed statements had experienced the history of interpretive degeneration among mainstream churches and seminaries ("As go the theological seminaries, so goes the church")[61] in terms of dismissing the Gospels as historical records due to historical-critical ideologies. Blomberg, instead, now advocates "The Historical-Critical/Grammatical View"[62] of hermeneutics for evangelicals that constitutes an alarming, and especially unstable, blend of historical-critical ideologies with the grammatico-historical hermeneutic. Blomberg argues for a "both-and-and-and" position of combining grammatico-historical method with that of historical-critical ideologies.[63]

Blomberg chose to ignore *The Jesus Crisis* (1998) that has already extensively catalogued the evangelical disaster that such a blend of grammatico-historical and historical-critical elements precipitates in interpretive approaches.[64] Stemming from this blending of these two elements are the following sampling of hermeneutical dehistoricizing among evangelicals: The author of Matthew, not Jesus, created the Sermon on the Mount; the commissioning of the twelve in Matthew 10 is a compilation of instructions collected and gathered but not spoken on a single occasion; Matthew 13 and Mark 4 are collections or anthologies not spoken by Jesus on a single occasion; Jesus did not preach the Olivet Discourse in its entirety as presented in the Gospels; the scribes and Pharisees were good people whom Matthew portrayed in a bad light; the magi of Matthew 2 are fictional characters; Jesus did not speak all of the parables in Matthew 5:3–12.[65]

*The Jesus Crisis* (as well as the more recent *The Jesus Quest*, edited by Geisler and Farnell) also tellingly reveals Blomberg's "both/and" approach of combining grammatico-historical with historical-critical, a telling admission of the strong impact of British academic training on evangelical hermeneutics, as well as his willingness to create a bridge between Christian orthodoxy and Mormonism. While Blomberg is irenic and embracing with Mormons, coauthoring a book with Brigham Young New Testament professor Stephen E. Robinson, called *How Wide the Divide? A Mormon*

---

61. Machen, *Christian Faith in the Modern World*, 65.
62. Blomberg, "Historical-Critical/Grammatical View," 27–47.
63. Ibid., 28.
64. See Thomas and Farnell, *Jesus Crisis*, noting especially the introduction, "The Jesus Crisis: What Is It?," 13–34.
65. Ibid., 15.

*and an Evangelical in Conversation*,[66] he apparently has great hostility toward those who uphold the "fundamentals" of Scripture.

In his article on "The Historical-Critical/Grammatical" hermeneutic, he asserts that historical criticism can be "shorn" of its "antisupernatural presuppositions that the framers of that method originally employed" and eagerly embraces "source, form, tradition and redaction criticism" as "*all essential* tools for understanding the contents of the original document, its formation and origin, its literary genre and subgenres, the authenticity of the historical material it includes, and its theological or ideological emphases and distinctives."[67] He labels the "Historical-Critical/Grammatical" approach "the necessary foundation on which all other approaches must build."[68] However, history is replete with negative examples of those who attempted this unstable blend, from the Neologians in Griesbach's day[69] to that of Michael Licona's book currently under discussion (see below).[70] Baird, in his *History of New Testament Research*, commented: "The Neologians did not deny the validity of divine revelation but assigned priority to reason and natural theology. While faith in God, morality, and immortality were affirmed, older dogmas such as the Trinity, predestination, and the inspiration of Scripture were seriously compromised. . . . The Neologians . . . appropriated the results of the historical-critical work of Semler and Michaelis."[71]

Interestingly, Craig Blomberg blames books like Harold Lindsell's *Battle for the Bible* (1976) and such books as *The Jesus Crisis* for people leaving the faith because of their strong stance on inerrancy as a presupposition. In an online interview conducted by Justin Taylor in 2008, Blomberg responded this way to books that hold to a firm view of inerrancy. The interviewer asked, "Are there certain mistaken hermeneutical presuppositions made by conservative evangelicals that play into the hands of liberal critics?" Blomberg replied,

> Absolutely. And one of them follows directly from the last part of my answer to your last question. The approach, famously supported back in 1976 by Harold Lindsell in his *Battle for the Bible* (Zondervan), that it is an all-or-nothing approach to Scripture that we must hold, is both profoundly mistaken and deeply dangerous. No historian worth his or her salt functions that way. I

---

66. IVP (1997).
67. Blomberg, "Historical-Critical/Grammatical View," 46–47, italics added.
68. Ibid., 47.
69. Brown comments, "In general, the Neologians sought to transcend both orthodoxy and pietism by restating the Christian faith in the light of modern thought. To them [the Neologians], revelation was a confirmation of the truths of reason. They drew a distinction between religion and theology, and between dogmas and the Bible. In a sense they were pioneers of moderate biblical criticism, maintaining that Jesus deliberately accommodated his teaching to the beliefs and understandings of his hearers." Brown, *Jesus in European Protestant Thought*, 8.
70. For Griesbach and his association with Neologians as well as its impact on his synoptic "solution," see Farnell, "How Views of Inspiration Have Impacted Synoptic Problem Discussion," 33–64.
71. Baird, *History of New Testament Research*, 1:116.

personally believe that if inerrancy means "without error according to what most people in a given culture would have called an error" then the biblical books are inerrant in view of the standards of the cultures in which they were written. But, despite inerrancy being the touchstone of the largely American organization called the Evangelical Theological Society, there are countless evangelicals in the States and especially in other parts of the world who hold that the Scriptures are inspired and authoritative, even if not inerrant, and they are not sliding down any slippery slope of any kind. I can't help but wonder if inerrantist evangelicals making inerrancy the watershed for so much has not, unintentionally, contributed to pilgrimages like Ehrman's. Once someone finds one apparent mistake or contradiction that they cannot resolve, then they believe the Lindsells of the world and figure they have to chuck it all. What a tragedy![72]

To Blomberg, apparently anyone who advocates inerrancy as traditionally advocated by Lindsell is responsible for people leaving the faith.

It is also the hermeneutic of historical criticism through which Blomberg developed his globalization hermeneutical approach. In a very telling article of Blomberg's historical-grammatical hermeneutical approach, he advocates "The Globalization of Biblical Interpretation: A Test Case—John 3–4."[73] This "hermeneutic" clearly has an *a priori* agenda that is imposed on the text when Blomberg summarizes the approach as "asking new questions of the text, particularly in light of the experiences of marginalization of a large percent of the world's population."[74] From Blomberg's perspective "students of scripture . . . have realized that the traditional historical-critical interpretation has been disproportionately Eurocentric and androcentric . . . and various new methodologies have been developed to correct this imbalance."[75] That such a conclusion has any substantial basis in fact, beyond opinion, is not substantiated by the article. Apparently, for Blomberg, the goal of exegesis and interpretation is not to understand the text as was originally intended but to search the biblical text for an already prescribed agenda of "globalization." This is telling, for under this scheme the meaning and significance of the biblical text would be its usefulness in promoting an agenda that is already predetermined, i.e., subjecting Scripture to the shifting sands of interpretation that Blomberg identifies as follows: "issues of liberation theology, feminism, religious pluralism, the disparity between the world's rich and poor, and contextualization of biblical material."[76]

---

72. See http://thegospelcoalition.org/blogs/justintaylor/2008/03/26/interview-with-craig-blomberg.
73. Blomberg, "Globalization of Biblical Interpretation," 1–15.
74. Ibid., 1.
75. Ibid.
76. Ibid., 2; see Blomberg, "Implications of Globalization," 213–28; 241–45.

## Part 2—Inerrancy Defended

In response to Blomberg's assertions regarding such newly developing issues, one cannot help but be reminded of Paul's own warning to the Ephesian church about the purpose of teaching and preaching by God's shepherds over the church:

> And He gave some *as* apostles, and some *as* prophets, and some *as* evangelists, and some *as* pastors and teachers, for the equipping of the saints for the work of service, to the building up of the body of Christ; until we all attain to the unity of the faith, and of the knowledge of the Son of God, to a mature man, to the measure of the stature which belongs to the fullness of Christ. As a result, we are no longer to be children, tossed here and there by waves and carried about by every wind of doctrine, by the trickery of men, by craftiness in deceitful scheming; but speaking the truth in love, we are to grow up in all *aspects* into Him who is the head, *even* Christ. (Eph 4:11–15)

Here Paul clearly warns the church against subjecting the Word of God to "waves" and "winds" of every doctrine and by application, whatever trends may predominate society through the centuries until Jesus' return. A question left unanswered by Blomberg is what happens to the imposition of such interpretation of the text when the next fade or qualitatively different idea or "ism" replaces these emphases. Nor have these emphases necessarily been subjected to Scripture to form any biblical bases whatsoever that they should be imposed on the text of Scripture *a priori* as interpretive principles. Second Corinthians 10:5 warns believers to take every thought captive.

Yet, where he teaches at Denver Seminary, the seminary has such an interpretive approach that it has embraced reflecting "a more central place in its [Denver Seminary's] curriculum . . . focusing on historical Christianity's mandate to worldwide mission" and "goes on to elaborate 'an empathetic understanding of the different genders, races, cultures, and religions to be able to contextualize the gospel more effectively,' 'increased application and promotion of biblical principles to such global issues as economic development, social justice, political systems, human rights, and international conflict,' and related concerns."[77] Blomberg argues, "It is perhaps best to think of the globalization of biblical interpretation as the processes either of asking questions of the biblical passage which are not traditionally asked within a particular interpretive community or of allowing new answers, more supportive of the world's oppressed, to emerge from old questions out of a more careful exegesis of the text itself."[78] He asserts that "these new questions and answers are often suggested as we read the Bible through the eyes of the individuals quite different from ourselves."[79] How one can subjectively view the Bible through the eyes of other individuals is not explained but it does highlight the existentialist basis of the new hermeneutic (Ebeling, Fuchs) where truth rests, not in the text, but in the interpreter's subjective experience.

---

77. "Final Report on the Globalization Project at Denver Seminary," 2.
78. Blomberg, "Globalization of Biblical Interpretation," 3.
79. Ibid.

Here also Blomberg makes a telling admission that his goal in globalization hermeneutics is not necessarily to elucidate original intent of the authors of Scripture but to devise interpretive decisions that are "more supportive of the world's oppressed."[80]

What is even more concerning is his application of these principles to the biblical text. One example must suffice in John 4 with the woman at the well. Here Blomberg's concern for reading feminist issues causes him to see the woman as a "victim rather than a whore" where he dismisses the idea that the woman was sexually promiscuous, which he terms "an unfounded assumption." Instead, Blomberg asserts that "the fault could well have resided more with the men than with the woman; we simply have no way of knowing. That she was currently living with a man to whom she was not legally married might just as easily have stemmed from her fifth husband having abandoned her without a legal divorce and from her need to be joined to a man for legal and social protection."[81] Such an interpretation requires Blomberg to ignore the woman's summoning of the men of the village with the following words: "So the woman left her waterpot, and went into the city and said to the men, 'Come, see a man who told me all the things that I *have* done; this is not the Christ, is it?'" This latter confession is best understood as an admission that Jesus correctly knew the spiritual condition of her immoral lifestyle (cf. 4:18) where Jesus knows how many husbands she had, otherwise it is an empty statement apart from its moral implications.

What is patently obvious is that Blomberg's concern for sociological and political correctness greatly clouds his exegesis of John 3–4. Fortunately, Blomberg realizes that the passage remains "fundamentally Christocentric; Jesus is the principle personage in both passages" and that "the person and work of Christ subordinates all liberationist, feminist, and postmodernist readings, important as they may be."[82] Nevertheless, his assertion that "biblical scholarship which does not yet acknowledge such 'metacriticism' lags behind the social sciences in this respect" is quite disturbing, for it opens up the proverbial Pandora's Box for a host of foreign elements to be imposed on the biblical text, resulting in Scripture being reduced to a tool for the promotion of globalist and/or fleeting agendas that are not anchored to a grammatico-historical understanding of the Scriptures' content or meaning.

## EVANGELICALS JOIN IN THE THIRD QUEST

After decrying Geisler's presidential address as well as the warnings set forth in *The Jesus Crisis*, in 1999 evangelicals who embraced historical-critical ideologies began a significant endeavor by joining in a Third Quest for the "historical Jesus." Most evangelicals up to that time did not participate in the first or second quests, but this evangelical corroboration in searching was a decade-long process of engaging in the

80. Ibid.
81. Ibid., 12.
82. Ibid., 14.

effort. In 2010, Darrell Bock and William Webb produced *Key Events in the Life of the Historical Jesus* that recorded the research of scholars associated with the Institute of Biblical Research (IBR). Operating from the position of postmodernistic historiography, this work asserted that only twelve events in the Gospels had the best chance of probably happening in history. In examining this work, one wonders whether Harold Lindsell's warning regarding historical-critical ideologies was not very prescient: "The use of the historical-critical method . . . leads, as night follows day, to the need for finding the canon within the canon," with Lindsell labeling such a result as a "requirement" of historical criticism.[83] Long ago, Lindsell identified the foundational impact of such questing, when he related that historical criticism results in "the need for finding the canon in the canon" when such a hermeneutic is applied.[84] More than other endeavors, this searching places qualitatively different historical values or trustworthiness on the individual texts of the Gospels, making some pericopae more "probable" relative to the subjective criteria applied to them. The unfortunate result being that large portions of Scripture are neutralized as to their historical value, importance, or relevance for Jesus' life.

Interestingly, in 2010, Scot McKnight withdrew from the Third Search, citing similar reasoning: "A fundamental observation about all genuine historical Jesus studies: *Historical Jesus scholars construct what is in effect a fifth gospel.* The reconstructed Jesus is not identical to the canonical Jesus or the orthodox Jesus. He is the reconstructed Jesus, which means he is a 'new' Jesus."[85]

In a recent IBR article, "Faith and the Historical Jesus," Bock "defends the value of having mediated presentations of Jesus" as exhibited in the third search for the historical Jesus.[86] Bock comments, "For many evangelicals, especially lay evangelicals, the skepticism surrounding much of historical-Jesus work is to be shunned as a rejection of the Bible as the Word of God."[87] Apparently Bock believes that while some Bible students are limited in understanding and ability and, as a result of their educational deficiencies, might not appreciate Jesus research, some New Testament scholars who are as highly trained as he is can engage in the discussion, so long as "one must appreciate the nature of what historical-Jesus work seeks to achieve as well as the limitations such a historically oriented study operates under when it seeks to cross thousands of years to do its work."[88] The problem, for Bock, lies not in the historical-critical approach but in the skill, or lack of skill, of a researcher and realizing that such

---

83. Lindsell, *Bible in the Balance*, 292–93.
84. Ibid.
85. McKnight, "Jesus We'll Never Know," 25.
86. Bock, "Faith and the Historical Jesus," 3.
87. Ibid., 4.
88. Ibid.

studies have limitations "in understanding and ability" in making a case for the New Testament traditions tied to Jesus.[89]

What is, however, even more fascinating is Robert Miller's reply to Bock's article supporting evangelical participation in searching for the "historical Jesus": "When It's Futile to Argue about the Historical Jesus."[90] Miller is an active member of the Society of Biblical Literature and a critic of evangelical participation in historiographical questions that the latter attempt to marginalize or limit in searching for the "historical Jesus." He argues that evangelicals who participate in these studies aren't consistent or critical enough in the historiographical principles needed for answers that academic scholarship is seeking:

> I maintain that the arguments about the historical Jesus can be productive only among those who already agree on a number of contested questions about historiographical method and the nature of the Gospels. Therefore, debates about the historical Jesus that occur between the "evangelical" camp (which sees the canonical Gospels as fully reliable historically) and the "traditional" camp (which sees the Gospel as blends of fact and fiction) are futile.[91]

Furthermore, he argues that the idea that the Gospels are to be compared to ancient *bios* genre is wrong, for he asserts that ancient *bios* genre was more historically accurate than the Gospels, i.e., the comparison is wrong! Miller asserts that no camp is persuaded by the other in their assertions: "Scholarship from one camp is unavoidably unpersuasive to the other camp . . . That's why debates about basic issues in our field never change people's minds in any fundamental way."[92] For evangelicals, the critical scholars go too far in their denigration of the Gospels; for the critical scholars, the evangelicals who have joined the "quest" do not go far enough in allowing dehistoricization of the Gospel material. The end result of such an impasse would appear to be that the Gospels are subject to a scholarly tug-of-war and that, in the process, are denigrated as historically trustworthy, i.e., the Gospels are undermined as reliable historical documents rather than affirmed as is insisted by Bock, Webb, and Keener.

Ironically, evangelical questers are caught in the same criticism that Ladd found himself in that he did not go far enough for some and too far for those who maintained a plenary, verbal inspiration of Scripture. Miller's argument against evangelical questers is similar to Perrin's argument against George Ladd that Ladd refused to allow his acceptance of historical criticism to move him too far. Norman Perrin regarded Ladd's passion for approval among liberals as a motivation that led to Ladd's

---

89. Ibid.
90. Miller, "When It's Futile to Argue," 85–95.
91. Ibid., 85.
92. Ibid., 89–90.

## Part 2—Inerrancy Defended

misconstruing some of the more liberal scholars' positions in order to make them support his own views.[93] Perrin bluntly argued,

> We have already noted Ladd's anxiety to find support for his views on the authenticity of a saying or pericope, and this is but one aspect of what seems to be a ruling passion with him: the search for critical support for his views altogether. To this end he is quite capable of misunderstanding the scholars concerned . . . Ladd's passion for finding support for his views among critical scholars has as its counterpart an equal passion for dismissing contemptuously aspects of their work which do not support him. These dismissals are of a most peremptory nature.[94]

Perrin labeled Ladd's support for the credibility of the Gospels as accurate historical sources for the life of Jesus as "an uncritical view" and that Ladd was guilty of eisegesis of liberals' views to demonstrate any congruity of their assertions with his brand of conservative evangelical. Marsden continues:

> [Ladd] saw Perrin's review as crucial in denying him prestige in the larger academic arena. . . . The problem was the old one of the Neo-Evangelical efforts to reestablish world-class evangelical scholarship. Fundamentalists and conservatives did not trust them . . . and the mainline academic community refused to take them seriously.
>
> Perhaps Perrin had correctly perceived a trait of the new evangelical movement when he described Ladd as torn between his presuppositional critique of modern scholarship and his eagerness to find modern critical scholars on his side. . . . No one quite succeeded philosophically in mapping the way this was to be done, though. The result was confusion, as became apparent with subsequent efforts to relate evangelical theology to the social sciences at the new schools. For . . . Ladd, who had the highest hopes for managing to be in both camps with the full respect of each, the difficulties in maintaining the balance contributed to deep personal anxiety.[95]

As a direct result of Bock's and Webb's *Key Events* and its support for postmodernistic historiography, Geisler and Roach dedicated a whole chapter of their work to analyzing its efforts in their recently released *Defending Inerrancy* (2011).[96] Geisler's and Roach's book arose out of concern for a perceived drift away from the concerns for inerrancy of the ICBI movements in 1978 and 1982. They noted their concern especially in relationship to the Evangelical Theological Society: "Many young evan-

---

93. Perrin commented, "One aspect of Ladd's treatment of sayings and pericopes which the reviewer [Perrin] found annoying is his deliberately one-sided approach to the question of authenticity." Perrin, "Against the Current," 229; cf. Marsden, *Reforming Fundamentalism*, 250.

94. Ibid., 230.

95. Marsden, *Reforming Fundamentalism*, 250.

96. Geisler and Roach, *Defending Inerrancy*.

gelicals trained in contemporary higher criticism have grown increasingly dissatisfied with the traditional view of unlimited inerrancy that was embraced by Warfield, the ETS founders, and the ICBI."[97] They noted that two camps now existed within ETS: those who adhered to the Chicago Statements and their view of unlimited inerrancy and those who did not. They wanted, therefore, evangelicals to remember recent problems surrounding inerrancy in the history of evangelicals that led to the founding of ETS as well as the events that created the Chicago Statements on Inerrancy (1978) and Hermeneutics (1982).

Geisler and Roach counter Bock's claim that historical criticism allows "serious historical engagement" decidedly in the negative: It is *not* serious historical engagement but in postmodernistic historiography the term "history" "bristles with presuppositions" that Bock and Webb choose to ignore.[98] While commending Bock and Webb for their response to the Jesus Seminar, as well as their sincere efforts in seeking to know the actual Jesus of history, Geisler and Roach listed several significant concerns that directly impact the doctrine of inerrancy, among which are: (1) late dating of New Testament books; (2) the use of evangelical redaction criticism that denigrates the role of eyewitnesses involved in the composition of the canonical Gospels; (3) the assumption of methodological naturalism, especially in terms of their assumptions of postmodernistic historiography; (4) failing to account for the fact that the idea of a "quest" for the "historical Jesus" constitutes a de facto denial of inerrancy and impugns the Gospels as historical records; (5) disregarding the Spinozian impact of dealing with alleged sources behind the text rather than the inspired text itself; and (6) neglecting the role of the Holy Spirit in the production of the Gospels (John 14:26; 16:13).[99] Their conclusion was that such participation by Bock, Webb, and other participants in *Key Events* undermine the doctrine of inerrancy as well as the trustworthiness of Scripture. Geisler and Roach argue,

> Bock-Webb wrongly believe that they have cleansed the critical-historical method of its naturalistic biases and purified it for appropriate use by evangelicals to find the historical Jesus . . . this is as naïve as the belief that methodological naturalism as a science, to which they compare their approach (KE, 45) will escape the web of naturalistic conclusions. . . . Many young scholars seem slow to learn that methodology determines theology. And a naturalistic methodology will lead to a naturalistic theology.[100]

---

97. Ibid., 13.
98. Ibid., 209.
99. Ibid., 193–211.
100. Ibid., 201.

As a result, their adoption of "an unorthodox methodology . . . undermines the inerrancy of Scripture,"[101] for an unorthodox methodology results in an unorthodox theology.

## AN EVANGELICAL CRISIS OF ATTITUDE TOWARD INSPIRATION AND INERRANCY

A very recent work reflecting current thinking among evangelicals who received training and/or influence from British and European continental schools, *Do Historical Matters Matter to the Faith?*,[102] highlights changing views regarding inerrancy and historicity issues centering in the Bible. The work relates its purpose as follows:

> We offer this book to help address some of the questions raised about the historicity, accuracy, and inerrancy of the Bible by colleagues within our faith community, as well as those outside it. There will be a special emphasis placed on matters of history and the historicity of biblical narratives, both Old and New Testaments, as this seems presently to be a burning issue for theology and faith. Hence, we begin with a group of essays that deal with theological matters before moving on to topics in the Old Testament, the New Testament, and archaeology.[103]

In reacting against those critical of evangelical scholarship's refusal to embrace historical critical ideologies, such as James Barr and, more recently Kenton Sparks in his *God's Word in Human Words*,[104] the work boasts about the academic degrees of the contributors:

> (The contributors of this book who did their doctoral work in British universities—Aberdeen, Oxford, and Cambridge—would hardly agree with this assessment!) The readers need only to review the list of contributors to see where they completed their PhDs, and it will be abundantly clear that the vast majority worked in secular and critical contexts and had to deal directly with critical issues. In fact, even in the context of Near Eastern studies, the critical approaches of *Altstestamentlers* were a part of the curriculum.[105]

Because the focus of the present chapter is on New Testament issues, not every chapter in this work will be discussed, but only those that focus on inerrancy and New Testament issues that demonstrate this crisis of attitude among evangelicals.

---

101. Ibid., 211.

102. For a more complete review of this work, see Farnell, review of *Do Historical Matters Matter*, 149–57.

103. Preface to *Do Historical Matters Matter*, 23.

104. Sparks, *God's Word in Human Words*.

105. Preface to *Do Historical Matters Matter*, 22 (parenthetical note in original).

In chapter 1, "Religious Epistemology, Theological Interpretation of Scripture, and Critical Biblical Scholarship," Thomas McCall sets forth a philosophy of biblical scholarship for the group. McCall advocates a type of "methodological naturalism" (MN): "MN holds only that the method of CBS [critical biblical scholarship] 'can be followed and may be valuable for historians' but do not give the only or final word on all matters (historical or otherwise)."[106] What McCall fails to consider in his discussion is that often a "methodology" is really an ideology with an underlying agenda in its presuppositional foundations (Col 2:8; 2 Cor 10:5). This chapter suggests a Hegelian/Fichtian dialectic: Fundamentalism (i.e., Reformed Epistemology) is too dismissive or critical of critical biblical scholarship (thesis) and critical biblical scholarship in its historic form is too "binding and obligatory" (antithesis), so the synthesis is expressed by evangelicals who use critical methods to engage in dialogue because "critical biblical scholarship can be 'appropriated' in a way that is both intellectually and spiritually healthy."[107] Acceptance of critical biblical scholarship in various, limited ways is the only way to have influence in the larger marketplace of ideas in biblical criticism.

McCall's idea of influencing, however, is attenuated by 1 Corinthians 1:18—2:14, where Paul sets forth the myth of influence, i.e., the fact that the default response of anyone who does not have the Spirit of God (i.e., unbelievers) is to conclude that the things of God are "foolishness" or "an offense" (1 Cor 1:23) and that God deliberately has planned that wisdom of unsaved men is inherently unable to arrive at a true understanding of the truth of God's Word (1 Cor 2:8–14). This places "critical biblical scholarship" in a tenuous light, for it operates decidedly on a foundation of unbelief. Only those with the Spirit of God can understand the thoughts of God, for no one will boast before God concerning his own wisdom (1 Cor 1:30).

In chapter 3, "The Divine Investment in Truth: Toward a Theological Account of Biblical Inerrancy," Mark Thompson asserts a belief in inerrancy but argues strongly that suspicion regarding inerrancy "stems from the way that some have used assent to this doctrine [inerrancy] as a shibboleth. Individuals and institutions have been black-listed for raising doubts about the way the doctrine has been construed in the past. Only those who are able to affirm biblical inerrancy without qualification are to be trusted."[108] Thompson singles out Harold Lindsell as, "one of the most conspicuous examples" of those who cause this distrust. For Thompson, the greatest suspicion against inerrancy is as follows:

> Most serious of all . . . is the way still others, reared on the strictest form of the doctrine of biblical inerrancy, have abandoned the faith under the intense questioning of biblical criticism. Forced to choose between a perfect, unblemished text and seemingly incontrovertible evidence of error in Scripture, such people begin to lose confidence in the gospel proclaimed throughout

---

106. McCall, "Theological Interpretation and Critical Biblical Scholarship," 52.
107. Ibid., 54.
108. Thompson, "Divine Investment in Truth," 71n2.

Scripture. In light of such cases, the doctrine of biblical inerrancy might even be deemed dangerous.[109]

These evangelicals have apparently forgotten that it was Harold Lindsell who was a great impetus in the ICBI discussion of both 1978 and 1982. History is now being forgotten. He blames people who hold to a strong view of inerrancy for causing people to depart from the faith. Apparently, for Thompson, inerrancy is a cause of defection especially if one holds to it strongly.

Thompson argues instead that "the doctrine should not be judged by the abuse of it or by inadequate explanations."[110] He argues for a solution in the following terms: "Strong convictions about the inerrancy of Scripture need not mean that this aspect of Scripture is elevated above all others in importance. Biblical inerrancy need not entail literalism and a failure to take seriously the various literary forms in which God's words come to us, nor need it repudiate genuine human authorship in a Docetic fashion."[111] Such a statement clearly indicates that Thompson places Scripture on the same level as any other book and is therefore subject to the same assault that historical-critical ideologies, far from neutral, have perpetrated upon it. Thompson concludes that a solution toward resolving any distortions in the doctrine of inerrancy is as follows: "The doctrine of inerrancy almost inevitably becomes distorted when it becomes the most important thing we want to say about Scripture."[112] He affirms Timothy Ward's solution, "Timothy Ward's assessment that inerrancy is 'a true statement to make about the Bible but is not in the top rank of significant things to assert about the Bible' is timely." Thus, Thompson's solution appears to downplay the significance of inerrancy for biblical issues as a way of overcoming difficulties regarding the doctrine as well as recognizing that not all statements in the Bible are to be taken as literal in terms of genre.

In chapter 14, "God's Word in Human Words: Form-Critical Reflections," Robert W. Yarbrough argues for seeing a value to historical critical approaches such as form critical studies by evangelicals even if in a limited way: "Form criticism did call attention to the important point that the Gospels comprise units of expression that may be sorted into discernible categories. Admittedly, form critics approached Gospel sources with premises and convictions that created blind spots in their observations. Limitations to the method as typically practiced amounted to built-in obsolescence that would eventually doom it to irrelevancy in the estimation of most Gospels interpreters today."[113] However, Yarbrough argues that "to study works from the form-critical era is to be reminded that literary sub-units—even sacred sources—can be

---

109. Ibid., 72.
110. Ibid.
111. Ibid.
112. Ibid., 97.
113. Yarbrough, "God's Word in Human Words," 328.

grouped and analyzed according to the type of discourse they enshrine and the clues to the cultural surroundings they may yield."[114] He acknowledges that Eta Linnemann

> renounced her lifelong professional and personal commitment to what she called historical-critical theology . . . she tested the claims of historical-critical views that she had been taught as a student and then as a professor had inflicted on hapless university undergraduates in an attempt to disabuse them of their Christian faith in Jesus and the Bible, the better to equip them for service in enlightened post-Christian German society.[115]

Yet, Yarbrough, delving into his perceived psychoanalysis of Linnemann's perceptions of biblical scholarship, labels her as someone among evangelicals who overreacted to the historical-critical approaches. He noted that "in academic mode, whether lecturing or writing, Linnemann tended toward overstatement and polemics. It is as if a couple of decades of vehement rejection of the Gospels' trustworthiness created a corresponding zeal for their defense once she rejected the 'critical' paradigm she embraced in Bultmann's heyday and under the spell of her identity as one of his students. Her scholarly pro-Bible writings are not a model of balanced scholarship, cautious investigation, and measured, gracious interaction with those she viewed as soft on the question of the Bible's inaccuracy."[116]

However, Yarbrough's psychoanalysis of Linnemann is directly challenged by Linnemann's own story as a former post-Bultmannian who witnessed firsthand the dangerous nature of historical criticism, for she based it on a thorough understanding and analysis of the approach as an ideological one. Eta Linnemann, herself a student of Rudolf Bultmann, the renown *formgeschichtliche* critic, and also of Ernst Fuchs, the outstanding proponent of the New Hermeneutic, notes regarding historical criticism,

> Instead of being based on God's Word . . . it [historical criticism] had its foundations in philosophies which made bold to define truth so that God's Word was excluded as the source of truth. These philosophies simply presupposed that man could have no valid knowledge of the God of the Bible, the Creator of heaven and earth, the Father of our Savior and Lord Jesus Christ.[117]

She stresses that the Enlightenment laid not only the atheistic staring point of the sciences but that of biblical criticism as a whole.[118] One comment is especially insightful that in the practice of the historical-critical methods, "What is concealed from the student is the fact that science itself, including and especially theological science, is by no means unbiased and presuppositionless. The presuppositions which determine the

---

114. Ibid.
115. Ibid., 332.
116. Ibid.
117. Linnemann, *Historical Criticism of the Bible*, 17–18.
118. Ibid., 29.

way work is carried on in each of its disciplines are at work behind the scenes and are not openly set forth."[119] Linnemann notes, "A more intensive investigation [of historical criticism] would show that underlying the historical-critical approach is a series of prejudgments which are not themselves the result of scientific investigation. They are rather dogmatic premises, statements of faith, whose foundation is the absolutizing of human reason as a controlling apparatus."[120] Her rejection stemmed not from psychological motives but years of academic research into the evidence of its dangers.

In chapter 15, "A Constructive Traditional Response to New Testament Criticism," Craig Blomberg sets forth "constructive" solutions to problems in the New Testament text that he believes would be in line with inerrancy and solve difficulties that evangelicals face. In Blomberg's article, he decries the Evangelical Theological Society's dismissal of Robert H. Gundry in 1982 and reaffirms his support for Gundry to be allowed to make a midrashic approach to dehistoricizing (i.e., allegorizing) the story of Herod's killing of babies in Bethlehem in Matthew 2 as consistent with a belief in inerrancy:

> For Gundry, inerrancy would only be called into question if Matthew were making truth claims that were false. But if Matthew were employing a different style, form of genre that was not making truth claims about what happened historically when he added to his sources, then he could not be charged with falsifying the truth. Preachers throughout church history have similarly added speculative detail, local color, possible historical reconstruction, and theological commentary to their retelling of biblical stories. As long as their audiences know the text of Scripture well enough to distinguish between the Bible and the preacher's additions, they typically recognize what the preacher is doing and do not impugn his or her trustworthiness.
>
> A substantial number of voting members of the Evangelical Theological Society present at the annual business meeting of its annual conference in 1983 disagreed that Gundry's views were consistent with inerrancy, at that time the sole tenet in the Society's doctrinal statement, and requested his resignation from the society. I voted with the minority. Following the papers and writings of my own professors from seminary, especially D. A. Carson and Douglas Moo, I believed Gundry had shown how his view could be consistent with inerrancy, even though I did not find his actually approach to Matthew convincing. In other words, the issue was a hermeneutical one, not a theological one. The trustees of Westmont College, where Gundry taught, agreed, and he continued his illustrious teaching and writing career there until his retirement.[121]

---

119. Ibid., 107.
120. Ibid., 111.
121. Blomberg, "Constructive Traditional Response," 349.

In accordance with Gundry, one of Blomberg's solution for difficult problems in New Testament in relationship to inerrancy is to allow for a genre of non-historicity to be considered:

> Though not a panacea for every conceivable debate, much more sensitive reflection over the implications of the various literary and rhetorical genres in the Bible would seem an important first step that is not often taken enough . . . in some contexts it may take some careful hermeneutical discernment to determine just what a text is or is not affirming. Style, figures of speech, species of rhetorical and literary form and genre all go a long way toward disclosing those affirmations.[122]

For Blomberg, difficulties can be resolved at times by realizing the nonhistorical nature of some portions of the New Testament.

In a 1984 article, Blomberg casts doubt on the story of the coin in the fish's mouth, treating it as nonhistorical genre: "It is often not noticed that the so-called miracle of the fish with the coin in its mouth (Matt 17:27) is not even a narrative; it is merely a command from Jesus to go to the lake and catch such a fish. We don't even know if Peter obeyed the command. Here is a good reminder to pay careful attention to the literary form."[123] Unfortunately, this solution would seem to be at odds with the ICBI statement on Hermeneutics when it states in article XIII: "We deny that generic categories which negate historicity may rightly be imposed on biblical narratives which present themselves as factual."

Blomberg offers another solution toward solving problems surrounding pseudonymity in relation to some New Testament books whereby the "critical consensus approach could . . . be consistent with inerrancy, 'benign pseudonymity.'"[124] Blomberg also uses the term "ghost-writer" to describe this activity.[125] Another more common name for this would be pseudepigraphy (as some scholars claim for Ephesians, Colossians, and the Pastoral Epistles) but Blomberg desires to change normally used terminology:

> A *methodology* consistent with evangelical convictions might argue that there was an accepted literary convention that allowed a follower, say, of Paul, in the generation after his martyrdom, to write a letter in Paul's name to one of the churches that had come under his sphere of influence. The church would have recognized that it could not have come from an apostle they knew had died two or three decades earlier, and they would have realized that the true author was writing thoughts indebted to the earlier teaching of Paul. In a world without footnotes or bibliographies, this was one way of giving credit where

---

122. Ibid., 351.
123. Ibid., 354n32.
124. Ibid., 353, 360.
125. Ibid.

credit was due. Modesty prevented the real author from using his own name, so he wrote in ways he could easily have envisioned Paul writing were the apostle still alive today. *Whether or not this is what actually happened*, such a hypothesis is thoroughly consistent with a high view of Scripture and an inerrant Bible. We simply have to recognize what is and is not being claimed by the use of name "Paul" in that given letter.[126]

For Blomberg, the key to pseudonymity would also lie in the motive behind the writing. Blomberg argues that "one's acceptance or rejection of the overall theory of authorship should then depend on the answers to these kinds of questions, not on some *a priori* determination that pseudonymity is in every instance compatible or incompatible with evangelicalism."[127] He argues, "It is not the conclusion one comes to on the issue [of pseudonymity] that determines whether one can still fairly claim to be evangelical, or even inerrantist, how one arrives at that conclusion."[128] Yet, how could one ever know the motive of such ghostwriters? Would not such a false writer go against all moral standards of Christianity? Under Blomberg's logic, Bart Ehrman's *Forged* (2011) only differs in one respect: Blomberg attributes good motives to forgers, while Ehrman is honest enough to admit that these "benign" writings are really what they would be in such circumstances: *Forged: Writing in the Name of God—Why the Bible's Authors Are Not Who We Think They Are.*[129] Is either one of these scholars able to read the proverbial "tea leaves" and divine the motives behind such perpetrations? Not likely!

Blomberg also carries this logic to the idea of "historical reliability more broadly." He relates, "Might some passages in the Gospels and Acts traditionally thought of as historical actually be mythical or legendary? I see no way to exclude the answer *a priori*. The question would be whether any given proposal to that effect demonstrated the existence of an accepted literary form likely known to the Evangelists' audiences, establishes as a legitimate device for communicating theological truth through historical fiction. In each case it is not the proposal itself that should be off limits for the evangelical. The important question is whether any given proposal has actually made its case."[130]

Blomberg evidences the strong leanings of evangelical critical scholarship toward historical-critical ideologies when he applies his historical-critical/grammatical hermeneutic to the Gospel texts. He notes regarding his *Historical Reliability of the Gospels* that "Christians may not be able to prove beyond a shadow of a doubt that the Gospels are historically accurate, but they must attempt to show that there is a strong likelihood of their historicity. Thus the approach of this book is always to argue in

---

126. Ibid., 352.
127. Ibid., 353.
128. Ibid., 352.
129. See Ehrman, *Forged*.
130. Blomberg, "Constructive Traditional Response," 354.

terms of probability rather than certainty, since this is the nature of historical hypotheses, including those that are accepted without question."[131] Again, Blomberg argues, "A good case can be made for accepting the details as well as the main contours of the Gospels as reliable. But . . . even if a few minor contradictions genuinely existed, this would not necessarily jeopardize the reliability of the rest or call into question the entire basis for belief."[132]

The fact, however, is that "probability" logically rests in the "eye of the beholder" and what is probable to one may be improbable to another. For instance, what Blomberg finds "probable" may not be to critics of the Gospels who do not accept his logic. This also places Scripture on an acutely subjective level where the logical impact of this approach is to reduce the Gospels to a shifting sand of "one-upmanship" in scholarly debate as to who accepts whose arguments for what reasons or not. Blomberg argues that "an evenhanded treatment of the data [from analysis of the Gospel material] does not lead to a distrust of the accuracy of the Gospels."[133] But this is actually exceedingly naïve, for who is to dictate to whom what is "evenhanded?" Many liberals would think that Blomberg has imposed his own evangelical presuppositions and is *very far* from being "evenhanded." He convinces only himself with this assertion. Blomberg admits "critical scholarship is often *too* skeptical."[134] The phrase "*too* skeptical" is relative to the critic. Who is to judge whether something is too critical when evangelicals adopt the same ideologies? Yet, since he has chosen to play with the rules of the critical scholars' game concerning the Gospels (however much he modifies their approach—they remain its inventors), they may reply on an equally valid level that Blomberg is too accepting. This is especially demonstrated when Blomberg accepts "criteria of authenticity" that are used to determine whether or not portions of the Gospels are historically reliable. He argues, "Using either the older or the new criteria, even the person who is suspicious of the Gospel tradition may come to accept a large percentage of it as historically accurate."[135] One would immediately ask Blomberg to cite an example, any example, of someone who was previously skeptical but has now come to a less skeptical position, but he does not. Criteria of authenticity are merely *a priori* tools that prove what one has already concluded.[136] If one is skeptical regarding tradition, one can select criteria that enforce the already conceived position. If one is less skeptical, then one can apply criteria that will enforce the already accepted less-skeptical conclusion. Each side will not accept the data of the other. What does suffer, however, is the Gospel record as it is torn apart by philosophical speculation through these criteria. For Blomberg, one may speak only of the "general reliability" of the

131. Blomberg, *Historical Reliability of the Gospels*, 36.
132. Ibid., 37.
133. Ibid., 297.
134. Ibid., 310.
135. Ibid., 312.
136. See Farnell, "Form Criticism and Tradition Criticism," 185–232.

Gospels since he has deliberately confined himself to these philosophically-motivated criteria.

Very telling with Blomberg is that he sees two "extreme positions" on historical reliability: the first being those who affirm the Gospels reliability "simply because they believe their doctrine of the inspiration of Scripture requires them to" and the second being "the other end of the confessional spectrum" consisting of "many radical critics" who "would answer the question [regarding reliability] negatively, thinking that proper historical method requires them to disbelieve any narrative so thoroughly permeated by supernatural events, theological interpretation and minor variation among parallels as are in the four Gospels."[137] Blomberg instead asserts his position as in-between: "The Gospels must be subjected to the same type of historical scrutiny given to any other writings of antiquity but that they can stand up to such scrutiny admirably."[138] The naiveté of this latter position is breathtaking, since historical criticism has been shown to be replete with hostile philosophical underpinnings that apparently Blomberg is either unaware of or choosing to ignore.[139] These presuppositions always control the outcome. Moreover, would those who use such radical ideologies in approaching Scripture be convinced of Blomberg's moderation of them? Most likely, they would interpret his usage as biased. What does suffer, however, is the Gospels' historical credibility in the process.

Blomberg argues that "if it is unfair to begin historical inquiry by superimposing a theological interpretation over it, it is equally unfair to ignore the theological implications that rise from it."[140] A much more pertinent question, however, for Blomberg to answer is, "Is it fair for the Gospel record to be in turn subjected to historical critical ideologies whose purpose was to negate and marginalize the Gospel record?" Blomberg is so willing and ready to remove the former but very welcoming in allowing the latter in his own subjective approach to the Gospels.

Finally, Blomberg, seemingly anticipating objections to many of his ideas, issues a stern warning to those who would oppose the proposals that he has discussed:

> Let those on the "far right" neither anathematize those who do explore and defend new options nor immediately seek to ban them from organizations or institutions to which they belong. If new proposals . . . cannot withstand scholarly rigor, then let their refutations proceed at that level, with convincing scholarship, rather than with the kind of censorship that makes one wonder whether those who object have no persuasive reply and so have to resort simply to demonizing and/or silencing the voices with which they disagree. If evangelical scholarship proceeded in this more measured fashion, neither inherently favoring nor inherently resisting "critical" conclusions, whether or

---

137. Blomberg, *Historical Reliability*, 322–23.
138. Ibid., 323.
139. Farnell, "Philosophical and Theological Bent," 85–131.
140. Blomberg, *Historical Reliability*, 325.

not they form a consensus, then it might fairly be said to be both traditional *and* constructive.[141]

Blomberg had earlier received strong criticism due to his involvement in coauthoring a book with Stephen E. Robinson, a New Testament professor at Brigham Young University, entitled *How Wide the Divide? A Mormon and an Evangelical in Conversation*.[142] As a result, he states, "Many of us who were trained at seminaries that were vigorously engaged in labeling (rightly or wrongly) other historically evangelical seminaries as no longer evangelical and who then came to the UK for doctoral study found the breadth of British definitions of evangelicalism and the comparative lack of a polemical environment like a breath of fresh air."[143] Yet, this desire for lack of criticism and just an irenic spirit in Christian academics hardly finds legitimacy in terms of the biblical model displayed in the Old and New Testaments. Much of the Old Testament castigated God's people for their compromising on belief or behavior (e.g., Num 11–14; Ps 95). Under today's sentiments, the Old Testament might be labeled anti-Semitic due to its criticism of Jewish people. In the New Testament, whole books were composed to criticize false teaching and wrong behavior on the part of God's people, such as Galatians, 1–2 Corinthians, the Pastoral Epistles, the Johannine Epistles, and chapters 2 and 3 of Revelation. Jesus himself fearlessly castigated powerful groups of important people (Matt 21–23). One is reminded of the satirical pieces that have been done on the fact that if Paul wrote Galatians today, he would have been vilified in many popular Christian magazines.[144]

In chapter 16, "Precision and Accuracy," Darrell Bock asserts that the genre of the Gospels is a form of ancient Greco-Roman biography known as *bios*: "When we think about the Gospels, there sometimes is a debate about the genre of this material. There was a time when this material was considered unique in its literary orientation. However, recently a consensus has emerged that the Gospels are a form of ancient *bios*."[145] He echoes the thinking of Charles Talbert and British theologian Richard Burridge who popularized this view.[146] This assertion that the Gospels are a form of ancient *bios* is fraught with dangers regarding historical matters surrounding the Gospels since it can readily lead to de-emphasizing the Gospels as historical documents.

This growing opinion among evangelical scholars that the Gospels are *bios* recently created a storm of controversy when Michael Licona, in his work *The Resurrection of Jesus: A New Historiographical Approach*,[147] used *bios* as a means of de-

141. Ibid., 364.
142. Blomberg and Robinson, *How Wide the Divide?*
143. Trueman et al., *Solid Ground*, 315.
144. For a wonderful satire of this very issue, see Sacred Sandwich (website), "If Paul's Epistle to the Galatians."
145. Bock, "Precision and Accuracy," 368.
146. Talbert, *What Is a Gospel?*; Burridge, *What Are the Gospels?*
147. Licona, *Resurrection of Jesus*.

historicizing parts of the Gospel (i.e., Matthew 27:51–53 with the resurrection of the saints after Jesus crucifixion is nonliteral genre or apocalyptic rather than an actual historical event). Licona argued "*Bioi* offered the ancient biographer great flexibility for rearranging material and inventing speeches . . . and they often included legend. Because *bios* was a flexible genre, it is often difficult to determine where history ends and legend begins."[148]

Licona's work exhibits many commendable items, such as a strong stance on the historical basis for Jesus' bodily resurrection from the dead. One might be encouraged that in light of historical criticism's assault on the miraculous since Spinoza and the Enlightenment, Licona has maintained the historical, orthodox position of the church. However, like Robert Gundry before him in 1983, Licona uses genre issues in historical criticism to negate portions of Scripture that have always been considered historical by orthodox Christianity from the earliest times. He has stirred up much controversy that parallels that of the Gundry/ETS circumstance that resulted in the ICBI documents of 1978 and 1982. Being influenced by historical criticism, Licona has accepted a consensus that has emerged among critically trained historical-critical scholars that the Gospels are a form of ancient "*bios*."

Bock argues,

> In ancient biography actions and sayings are the focus of the portrayal. The timing of the events is of less concern that the fact that they happened. Sometimes figures from distinct periods can be juxtaposed in ways that compare how they acted. The model of the figure that explains his greatness and presents him as one worthy of imitation stands at the core of the presentation. The central figure in a *bios* often is inspiring. The presentation of Jesus in the Gospels fits this general goal . . . This genre background is our starting point.[149]

Operating from this consensus of the Gospels as *bioi*, Bock argues that the Olivet Discourse may have an "updated" saying. Comparing the disciples' question in Mark 13:4 ("Tell us, when will these things be, and what *will be* the sign when all these things are going to be fulfilled?") with Luke 21:7 ("Teacher, when therefore will these things be? And what *will be* the sign when these things are about to take place?") and Matthew 24:3 ("Tell us, when will these things be, and what *will be* the sign of Your coming, and of the end of the age?"), Bock notes that "something is going on between the versions in Mark and Luke in comparison to Matthew." Bock continues,

> Matthew has taken the question as it was in Mark and Luke and has presented what the disciples essentially were asking, even if they did not appreciate all the implications in the question at the time. . . . Whether the disciples say the end is in view or Matthew is drawing that out as inherent in the question asked, the point is that Matthew is drawing that out as inherent in the question

---

148. Ibid., 34.
149. Bock, "Precision and Accuracy," 368.

asked, the point is that Matthew has made the focus of the question clearer than the more ambiguous way it is asked in Mark and Luke.

Bock then asserts that "Matthew may actually be giving us the more precise force and point of the question, now paraphrased in light of a fuller understanding of what Jesus' career was to look like." Apparently, Bock allows for the possibility that the disciples may not have asked the question as is set forth in Matthew 24:3 but that Matthew updated the question by adding this comment to the lips of the disciples regarding the "end of the age": "Matthew has simply updated the force of the question, introducing the idea of the end [of the age] as the topic Jesus implied by his remark about the temple."[150] One is left wondering with Bock's postulation whether the disciples actually asked the question as Matthew presented ("end of the age") or did Matthew add words to their lips that they did not say? Bock's approach here is essentially a subtle form of dehistoricizing the Gospels at this point. Equally plausible, however, is that the disciples did ask the question in the way in which Matthew phrased it and that a harmonization of the passage could be postulated that would not require such creative invention on the part of Matthew.

Echoing the same kind of thinking in this book, Darrell Bock states in a self-review of his own work in *Do Historical Matters Matter?*: "I do not often note books to which I have contributed on this blog, but this work is an exception. *Do Historical Matters Matter to Faith?: A Critical Appraisal of Modern and Postmodern Approaches to Scripture* (Edited by James Hoffmeier and Dennis Magary) explores issues tied to the authority and inspiration of Scripture. This series of essays covers an array of issues from the Old and New Testaments."[151] Yet, this book clearly maintains that inerrancy is not a critical issue in biblical studies.

In Bock's own review of his *Key Events* work as coeditor with Robert Webb, Bock distances himself not only from inerrancy but also from the subject of inspiration as alien to Third Search evangelical critical scholars like himself:

> As a co-editor of this volume, I should explain what this book is and is not. It is a book on historical Jesus discussion. It is not a book that uses theological arguments or categories (as legitimate as those can be) to make its case. This means we chose as a group to play by the rules of that discussion, engage it on those terms, and show even by those limiting standards that certain key events in the life of Jesus have historical credibility. So in this discussion one does not appeal to inspiration and one is asked to corroborate the claims in the sources before one can use the material. This is what we did, with a careful look at the historical context of 12 central events. To be accurate, the article by Webb accepts the resurrection as a real event, but argues for a limitation on what history (at least as normally practiced today) can say about such events.

---

150. Ibid., 372.
151. Bock, "Do Historical Matters Matter."

## Part 2—Inerrancy Defended

The problem here is with what history can show, not with the resurrection as an event. Many working in historical Jesus study take this approach to the resurrection. I prefer to argue that the best explanation for the resurrection is that it was a historical event since other explanations cannot adequately explain the presence of such a belief among the disciples. Webb explains these two options of how to take this in terms of the historical discussion and noted that participants in our group fell into each of these camps. Some people will appreciate the effort to play by these limiting rules and yet make important positive affirmations about Jesus. Others will complain by asking the book to do something it was not seeking to do.[152]

What is most remarkable is that nowhere in such evangelical collaborative works as *Key Events* or *Who Is Jesus?*[153] does Bock (or any other evangelical involved) mention how such principles stand presuppositionally opposed to affirming the Scriptures, especially their inerrancy, nor does Bock issue any warnings in these works that the searchers are conducting their search apart from any consideration of inerrancy. Apparently, critical-evangelical scholars may have personal, subjective beliefs about inerrancy or inspiration, but in Third Search activities that they conduct such ideas are shunned as not a part of this scholarly endeavor. Nowhere in any of Bock's searching books does he mention that this all is an effort to use the arguments of the historical-critics against them. He merely assumes these ideas and it results in a weakening of the Gospels. No apologetic is ever offered in countering such things; no history or presuppositions are mentioned. He treats historical-critical principles such as source, form, redaction, tradition criticism, and postmodernistic historiography as fully valid. Indeed, at the expense of both inspiration and inerrancy, he has succeeded in making the term "historical Jesus" normal when it is truly aberrant from an orthodox understanding. It is founded on a German critical scholarship of *historie* (actual history) versus *geschichte* (faith interpretation of those events); a concept that at its foundation rejects the Jesus of the Bible. He nowhere even hints that these principles are flawed or inconsistent when he writes these works and apparently buys into them substantially. One cannot tell qualitatively where any of these critical evangelical scholars substantively disagrees with any of these "searching" principles. They wrote no caveat about postmodernistic historiography; no counter-chapter or alternative to it was presented. It was treated as normative for these books and not even so much as a footnote was written that would indicate that not all the authors agree with postmodernistic historiography. Bock and those allied with him appear to assume historical-critical validity of the principles as if they completely accept these concepts. He treats searching as normative, standard and as if all evangelical scholars do this kind of thing.

---

152. Bock, "Editor's Thoughts."
153. Bock and Webb, *Key Events*; Bock, *Who Is Jesus?*

In another work, evangelical Daniel Wallace also plays down the importance of inspiration and inerrancy. In a statement from his chapter entitled "Who's Afraid of the Holy Spirit? The Uneasy Conscience of a Non-Charismatic Evangelical," Wallace admits a personal struggle:

> (3) *This emphasis on knowledge over relationship can produce in us bibliolatry.* For me, as a New Testament professor, the text is my task—but I made it my God. The text became my idol. Let me state this bluntly: The Bible is not a member of the Trinity. One lady in my church facetiously told me, "I believe in the Trinity: the Father, Son and Holy Bible." Sadly, too many cessationists operate as though that were so. One of the great legacies Karl Barth left behind was his strong Christocentric focus. It is a shame that too many of us have reacted so strongly to Barth, for in our zeal to show his deficiencies in his doctrine of the Bible, we have become bibliolaters in the process. Barth and Calvin share a warmth, a piety, a devotion, an awe in the presence of God that is lacking in too many theological tomes generated from our circles.[154]

The present writer finds this kind of statement not in accordance with the assertions of Scripture itself. Scripture presents its foundational importance of inspiration and inerrancy with hundreds of verses that present this constant truth. God's Words has exalted status, "I will bow down toward Your holy temple and give thanks to Your name for Your lovingkindness and Your truth; for You have magnified Your word according to all Your name" (Ps 138:2). God's Word is a sanctifying force, "Sanctify them in the truth; Your word is truth" (John 17:17). Jesus affirmed that "the Scripture cannot be broken" (John 10:35) and 2 Timothy 3:16–17 states, "All Scripture is inspired by God and profitable for teaching, for reproof, for correction, for training in righteousness, so that the man of God may be adequate, equipped for every good work." Wallace's logic here is startlingly poor. If the documents cannot be trusted—if they are not inspired and inerrant—then one cannot have a "Christocentric" anything. Apparently, however, good critical scholars are obliged never to bring these verses up in scholarly discussions or risk being labeled unscholarly.

In seeking to counter the damage to the determination of the wording of Scripture by Bart Ehrman's work *Misquoting Jesus*, Wallace is more than willing to surrender inerrancy as an issue:

> Second, what I tell my students every year is that it is imperative that they pursue truth rather than protect their presuppositions. And they need to have a doctrinal taxonomy that distinguishes core beliefs from peripheral beliefs. When they place more peripheral doctrines such as inerrancy and verbal inspiration at the core, then when belief in these doctrines starts to erode, it creates a domino effect: One falls down, they all fall down. It strikes me that something like this may be what happened to Bart Ehrman. His testimony in

154. Wallace, "Who's Afraid of the Holy Spirit?," 8.

## Part 2—Inerrancy Defended

*Misquoting Jesus* discussed inerrancy as the prime mover in his studies. But when a glib comment from one of his conservative professors at Princeton was scribbled on a term paper, to the effect that perhaps the Bible is not inerrant, Ehrman's faith began to crumble. One domino crashed into another until eventually he became "a fairly happy agnostic." I may be wrong about Ehrman's own spiritual journey, but I have known too many students who have gone in that direction. The irony is that those who frontload their critical investigation of the text of the Bible with bibliological presuppositions often speak of a "slippery slope" on which all theological convictions are tied to inerrancy. Their view is that if inerrancy goes, everything else begins to erode. I would say rather that if inerrancy is elevated to the status of a prime doctrine, that's when one gets on a slippery slope. But if a student views doctrines as concentric circles, with the cardinal doctrines occupying the center, then if the more peripheral doctrines are challenged, this does not have a significant impact on the core. In other words, the evangelical community will continue to produce liberal scholars until we learn to nuance our faith commitments a bit more, until we learn to see Christ as the center of our lives and scripture as that which points to him. If our starting point is embracing propositional truths about the nature of scripture rather than personally embracing Jesus Christ as our Lord and King, we'll be on that slippery slope, and we'll take a lot of folks down with us.[155]

Even more startling is Wallace's assertions regarding evangelical theological views like inerrancy or inspiration that apparently reflect a similar view to Rogers and McKim (mentioned earlier in this article): "Our theology is too often rooted in Greek philosophy, rationalism, the Enlightenment, and Scottish Common Sense realism," which he defines as "a philosophical departure from that of the sixteenth-century Reformers, though it was a handmaiden of Princetonian conservative theology in the nineteenth century."[156] For Wallace, evangelicals operate on a "docetic bibliology" regarding Scripture when they insist on the *ipsissima verba* or similar ideas.[157] Thus, Wallace's view encompasses such ideas as Luke altering the meaning of Jesus' words in Luke 5:32 (cf. Mark 2:17; Matt 9:13) so that he asserts, "To sum up: There seems to be evidence in the synoptic gospels that, on occasion, words are deliberately added to the original sayings of Jesus" and "in a few instances, these words seem to alter somewhat the picture that we would otherwise have gotten from the original utterance; in other instances, the meaning seems to be virtually the same, yet even here a certain amount of exegetical spadework is needed to see this. On the other hand, there seem to be examples within the synoptics where the words are similar, but the meaning is

---

155. Wallace, "Gospel according to Bart." Note: this quote is from the full version of Wallace's review of Ehrman.

156. Wallace, "Apologia for a Broad View of *Ipsissima Vox*," 1 (see also 1n2).

157. Ibid., 10.

different."¹⁵⁸ These statements leave one to wonder if Jesus truly said what is recorded in the Gospels or that the substance has been changed redactionally. Wallace concludes, "It seems that our interpretation of inspiration is governing our interpretation of the text. Ironically, such bibliological presuppositions are established in modern terms that just might ignore or suppress the data they are meant to address and which are purportedly derived. And there is an even greater irony here: the fact of the Incarnation—an essential element in orthodox Christology-*invites* (italics in original) rigorous historical investigation. But what if our bibliological presuppositions *reject* (italics in original) that invitation?"¹⁵⁹ What "rigorous historical investigation" entails is not clearly specified, except that it involves at least the utilization of the criteria of authenticity and dissimilarity.¹⁶⁰

In a recent blog entry, Wallace related: "I am unashamedly a Protestant. I believe in *sola scriptura, sola fidei, solus Christus,* and the rest. I am convinced that Luther was on to something when he articulated his view of justification succinctly: *simul iustus et peccator* ('simultaneously justified and a sinner')."¹⁶¹ However, he laments the lack of unification on Protestant theology, and says that three events in his life are having an impact on his thinking: (1) His attendance of Greek Orthodox worship services: "I have spent a lot of time with Greek Orthodox folks. It doesn't matter what Orthodox church or monastery I visit, I get the same message, the same liturgy, the same sense of the 'holy other' in our fellowship with the Triune God. The liturgy is precisely what bothers so many Protestants since their churches often try very hard to mute the voices from the past. 'It's just me and my Bible' is the motto of millions of evangelicals." (2) His own personal experience of seeing a personal friend of his in Protestantism deny Jesus' deity, where he laments the lack of an ecclesiastical hierarchy: "This cancer could have been cut out more swiftly and cleanly if the church was subordinate to a hierarchy that maintained true doctrine in its churches. And the damage would have been less severe and less traumatic for the church." (3) His realization on ecclesiastical hierarchy involved in canon formation: "What is significant is that *for the ancient church, canonicity was intrinsically linked to ecclesiology*. It was the *bishops* rather than the congregations that gave their opinion of a book's credentials. Not just any bishops, but bishops of the major sees of the ancient churches." He relates, "We Protestants can be more sensitive about the deficiencies in our own ecclesiology rather than think that we've got a corner on truth. We need to humbly recognize that the two other branches of Christendom have done a better job in this area. Second, we can be more sensitive to the need for doctrinal and ethical accountability, fellowship beyond our local church, and ministry with others whose essentials but not necessarily particulars don't line up with ours. Third, we can begin to listen again to the voice of the Spirit speak-

---

158. Ibid., 12.
159. Ibid., 19.
160. Ibid., 15.
161. Wallace, "Problem with Protestant Ecclesiology."

ing through church fathers and embrace some of the liturgy that has been used for centuries." Wallace's hinting at a unified ecclesiastical hierarchy superseding the local church appears to reveal his persuading toward seriously contemplating membership in the Anglican Church.[162] In a reply to a comment on the blog entry, Wallace writes:

> Russ, I have thought about the Anglican Church quite a bit actually. I love the liturgy, the symbolism, the centrality of the Eucharist, the strong connection with the church in ages past, and the hierarchy. And yes, I have seriously considered joining their ranks–and still am considering it. There are some superb Anglican churches in the Dallas area. Quite surprising to me has been my choice of academic interns at Dallas Seminary in the last few years. Over half of them have been Anglican, and yet when I picked them for the internship I didn't know what their denominational affiliation was. Exceptional students, devoted to the Lord and his Church, and committed to the highest level of Christian scholarship. And they have respect for tradition and the work of the Spirit in the people of God for the past two millennia.[163]

Sadly, what Wallace fails to discern is that such overwhelming ecclesiastical hierarchy is what caused the need of reformation. The church had rotted from the top down with the rise of Romanism and even later with Anglicanism. Infection spreads much more rapidly in "top-down" hierarchies. Independent local churches such as those exhibited in Protestantism generally preserve a greater safeguard against spreading heresy.

Another contemporary voice worth addressing is William Craig, professor of apologetics at Talbot School of Theology. Interestingly, he uses historical criticism to question the veracity of guards being at Jesus' tomb. In a recent Ankerberg interview, Craig negates the guards in the following manner. In response to Ankerberg's question, "Were there guards at the tomb?" Craig replied:

> Well now this is a question that I think is probably best left out of the program, because the vast, vast majority of New Testament scholars would regard Matthew's tomb story, or guard story as "unhistorical." Um, I can hardly think of anybody who would defend the historicity of the guard at the tomb story and the main reasons for that are two: one is because it's only found in Matthew, and it seems very odd that if there were a Roman guard or even a Jewish guard at the tomb that Mark wouldn't know about it, and there wouldn't be any mention of it. The other reason is that nobody seemed to understand Jesus' resurrection predictions. The disciples who heard them most often had no inkling of what he meant, and yet somehow the Jewish authorities were supposed to

---

162. Wallace cites a work by Dungan that strongly influenced his belief in an ecclesiastical hierarchy. See Dungan, *Constantine's Bible*. Dungan's work highlights Eusebius's record (*Ecclesiastical History*) of the influence of ancient bishops in canon formation. Dungan, however, records the formation of canon prior to the onslaught of Romanism as well as Greek Orthodoxy.

163. Wallace, "Problem with Protestant Ecclesiology."

have heard of these predictions, and understood them so well that they were able to set a guard around the tomb. And again, that doesn't seem to make sense. So, most scholars regard the Guard at the Tomb story as a legend or a Matthean invention that isn't really historical. Fortunately, this is of little significance for the empty tomb of Jesus, because the guard was mainly employed in Christian apologetics to disprove the conspiracy theory that the disciples stole the body—but no modern historian or New Testament scholar would defend a conspiracy theory because it's evident when you read the pages of the New Testament that these people sincerely believed in what they said. So, the conspiracy theory is dead, even in the absence of a guard at the tomb. The true significance of the guard at the tomb story is that it shows that even the opponents of the earliest Christians did not deny the empty tomb, but rather involve themselves in a hopeless series of absurdities trying to explain it away, by saying that the disciples had stolen the body. And that's the real significance of Matthew's "Guard at the Tomb" story.[164]

In reply to this "logic" of Craig, note that *if* evangelicals accepted what the early church always and consistently witnessed—that Matthew was the first Gospel written—instead of accepting historical-critical presuppositions, then Mark actually left out Matthew's guard story. Moreover, if Matthew made up guards around Jesus' tomb, then what stops Craig's reasoning from being extended to the fact that the writers made up the "sincere" response of belief, or for that matter, the whole idea of the resurrection? To start throwing out parts of the Gospels because they aren't recounted in Mark or because "no modern historian or New Testament scholar" thinks they are is not only illogical but dangerous to Christianity.

In another place, Craig seems to give credence to the guards:

> So although there are reasons to doubt the existence of the guard at the tomb, there are also weighty considerations in its favor. It seems best to leave it an open question. Ironically, the value of Matthew's story for the evidence for the resurrection has nothing to do with the guard at all or with his intention of refuting the allegation that the disciples had stolen the body. The conspiracy theory has been universally rejected on moral and psychological grounds, so that the guard story as such is really quite superfluous. Guard or no guard, no critic today believes that the disciples could have robbed the tomb and faked the resurrection. Rather the real value of Matthew's story is the incidental—and for that reason all the more reliable—information that Jewish polemic never denied that the tomb was empty, but instead tried to explain it away. Thus the early opponents of the Christians themselves bear witness to the fact of the empty tomb.[165]

---

164. Craig, interview on Guards at the Tomb.
165. Craig, "Guard at the Tomb," 80.

## Part 2—Inerrancy Defended

The impression one might receive from this is that Craig believes the guards at the tomb story but, at the same time, is not sure of its validity since he leaves it an open question. If Matthew said guards were there, can it be left an "open question" for those who believe in the trustworthiness, let alone, inerrancy of Scripture?

At another point, he echoed a similar statement to Michael Licona regarding the resurrection of the saints in Matthew 27:51–53. In a Youtube video of Craig debating in 2007 at the University of Sheffield, in the United Kingdom, against James Crossley on the bodily resurrection of Jesus, Craig sets forth the idea that admitting to legendary elements in the Gospels (i.e., the resurrection of the saints) "does nothing to undermine the remaining testimony of the gospels to things like the crucifixion of Jesus, the empty tomb, the resurrection appearances" (citing Dale Allison as his authority for this statement). When asked directly by a questioner in the audience if he believed in the story of the resurrection of the saints in Matthew 27:51–53, "I'm not sure what to think." He also says, "It could be part of the apocalyptic imagery of Matthew which isn't meant to be taken in a literal way. That this would be part of the typical sort of apocalyptic symbolism to show the earth shattering nature of the resurrection and need not to be taken historically literally." He goes on to conclude, "This is not attached to a resurrection narrative. This story about the Old Testament saints is attached to the crucifixion narrative. So that if you try to say that because Matthew has this unhistorical element in his crucifixion account, that therefore the whole account is worthless, you would be led to deny the crucifixion of Jesus which is one indisputable fact that everyone recognizes about the historical Jesus. So it really doesn't have any implications for the historicity of the burial story, the empty tomb story or the appearance accounts. It's connected to the crucifixion narrative." Notice that his adoption of historical criticism drives him toward allowing for non-historicity in narrative accounts in the Gospels.[166] The key question for Craig to answer must be that if they made up stories of the saints' resurrection, what would stop them from making up stories about Jesus' resurrection? One cannot have it both ways by saying that one story is historical but the other may be made-up fiction due to apocalyptic imagery.

This view is not uncommon among evangelicals. Craig Evans, an active participant in British-influenced searching for the "historical" Jesus, when commenting on the resurrection of the saints in Matthew 27:51b–53, argues:

> I do not think the tradition in Matthew 27:51b–53, which describes at the time of Jesus's death the resurrection of several saintly persons, has any claim to authenticity. This legendary embellishment, which may actually be a late-first-century or early-second-century gloss, is an attempt to justify the Easter appearances of Jesus as resurrection, in the sense that Jesus and several other saints were the "first fruits" of the general resurrection. This is, of course, exactly how Paul explains the anomaly (1 Cor 15:23).[167]

---

166. Craig, "Dr. Craig Acknowledges."
167. Evans, "In Appreciation of the Dominical and Thomistic Traditions," 195n30.

Similarly, Michael Green, while Senior Research Fellow at Wycliffe Hall, Oxford University, in his *Message of Matthew*, is abruptly dismissive of the resurrection of the saints in Matthew 27:51–53. Green comments,

> Does Matthew mean us to take this literally? Does he mean that the tombs were broken open, and that the bodies were somehow clothed with flesh and brought to life, as in Ezekiel's vision? It is possible, but unlikely that this is how Matthew intended us to read it. After all, he says that these bodies of the saints went into the holy city after Jesus' resurrection. By that phrase he is guarding the primacy of the resurrection of Jesus, "the firstfruits of those who have fallen asleep," yet he presents us with these resuscitated bodies at the cross itself, long before the resurrection. If Matthew meant us to think of these people from a bygone age walking into Jerusalem that Friday evening, how would that accord with his plain insistence throughout this chapter (especially 40–50) that no compelling proofs of Jesus' deity were given at this time of his death any more than they were during his life?
>
> No, Matthew seems to be giving us a profound meditation on what the crucifixion of Jesus means for the destiny of humankind. His death is an eschatological event; it is a foretaste of the end of the world.[168]

Again, citing his agreement with Donald Hagner,[169] Green comments in a footnote on this passage,

> I agree with Donald Hagner that in recording this story [of the saints' resurrection] Matthew wanted, at the very point when Jesus died, to draw out its theological significance. A straightforward historical reading of these verses is hard to contemplate. Who were these people? Were they resurrected or resuscitated? Why did they go into the holy city? What happened to them subsequently? Indeed, what happens to the priority of Jesus's resurrection? And if they *appeared to many people (53)*, why is there no reference to this event elsewhere, either inside or outside the New Testament?[170]

Donald Hagner, after an extensive discussion of the passage, dismisses any substantial historicity to the saints' resurrection, and remarks,

> I side, therefore, with recent commentators . . . in concluding that the rising of the saints from the tombs in this passage is a piece of theology set forth as history. . . . It is obvious that by the inclusion of this material Matthew wanted to draw out the theological significance of the death (and resurrection of Jesus). That significance is found in the establishing of the basis of the future resurrection of the saints. We may thus regard the passage as a piece of realized and

---

168. Green, *Message of Matthew*, 302–3.
169. Hagner, *Matthew 14–28*, 851.
170. Green, 302–3n18.

historicized apocalyptic depending on OT motifs found in such passages as Isa 26:19; Dan 12:2; and especially Ezek 37:12–14.[171]

Interestingly, Hagner wrongly attributes this dehistoricized view to Gundry. While Gundry did dehistoricize, a careful examination of his commentary on *Matthew: A Commentary on His Handbook for a Mixed Church under Persecution* reveals that while Gundry attributed Old Testament motifs to the passage, he believed that the saints' resurrection actually happened.[172]

Finally, Leon Morris, in his *Gospel according to Matthew*, also appears to place significant doubt on the historicity of this section. Morris notes,

> Nobody else mentions this, and we are left to conclude that Matthew is making the point that the resurrection of Jesus brought about the resurrection of his people. Just as the rending of the temple curtain makes it clear that the way to God is open for all, so the raising of the saints shows that death has been conquered. Those so raised went into Jerusalem and *appeared to many*. Since there are no other records of these appearances, it appears to be impossible to say anything about them. But Matthew is surely giving expression to his conviction that *Jesus* is Lord over both the living and the dead.[173]

Instead, Morris prefers to see it as possibly being linked to an idea of general resurrection of God's saints at the end of the age: "It seems that here Matthew has the great death-and-resurrection in mind and links his raising of the saints to the whole happening. Thus he mentions it when he speaks of the death of Jesus but goes on to what he says happened at the time of the resurrection."[174] He concludes that one thing is certain in the passage, "Matthew is surely giving expression to his conviction that Jesus is Lord over both the living and the dead."[175]

## THE HONESTY OF BART EHRMAN

Interestingly, Bart Ehrman directly blames historical criticism as a large reason for his departure from the faith. Ehrman is very honest and open to note that an important, strategic factor in his loss of confidence in his faith was explicitly that of historical-critical ideologies and their impact on seminary students' thoughts:

---

171. Hagner, *Matthew 14–28*, 851–52.

172. Hagner identifies his view of non-historicity as being also Gundry's view; see Hagner, *Matthew 14–28*, 851. However, Gundry nowhere in commenting on this passage negates its historicity. See also Gundry, *Matthew: A Commentary on His Handbook for a Mixed Church Under Persecution*, 576–77.

173. Morris, *Gospel according to Matthew*, 725.

174. Ibid.

175. Ibid.

> The approach taken to the Bible in almost all Protestant (and now Catholic mainline seminaries) is what is called the "historical-critical" method. . . .
>
> The historical-critical approach has a different set of concepts and therefore poses a different set of questions. . . .
>
> A very large percentage of seminaries are completely blind-sided by the historical critical method. They come in with expectations of learning the pious truths of the Bible so that they can pass them along in their sermons, as their own pastors have done for them. Nothing prepares them for historical criticism. To their surprise they learn, instead of material for sermons, all the results of what historical critics have established on the basis of centuries of research. The Bible is filled with discrepancies, many of them irreconcilable contradictions. . . .
>
> But before long, as students see more and more of the evidence [of contradictions], many of them find that their faith in the inerrancy and absolute historical truthfulness of the Bible begins to waver. There simply is too much evidence, and to reconcile all of the hundreds of differences among the biblical sources requires so much speculation and fancy interpretive work that eventually it gets to be too much for them.[176]

He goes on to note that "I came to see the potential value of historical criticism at Princeton Seminary. I started adopting this new (for me) approach, very cautiously at first, as I didn't want to concede too much to scholarship. But eventually I saw the powerful logic behind the historical-critical method and threw myself heart and soul into the study of the Bible from this perspective." He then immediately goes on to note, "It is hard for me to pinpoint the exact moment that I stopped being a fundamentalist who believed in the absolute inerrancy and verbal inspiration of the Bible."[177] The cause of Bart Ehrman's fall from faith came when he embraced historical criticism! Not one of his mentors at the Bible-believing schools he attended had prepared him for historical-criticism's massive assault on Scripture by pointing out the presuppositional biases that anchor historical criticism's assault on Scripture. Bart Ehrman is a tragic figure in that none of his "evangelical" mentors had properly prepared him for the onslaught of historical-critical ideologies.

Judging by Ehrman's comments, perhaps he should not be seen so much as a defector, but as an example of the tragic failure of mentoring in evangelical biblical education. He began his training in a conservative theological school (Moody Bible Institute), but somewhere along his path at Wheaton College someone encouraged him to attend a more prestigious "critical" school (i.e., Princeton) to study. It was at Princeton Seminary, which had abandoned any sense of faithfulness to God's Word long ago, that Ehrman was exposed to historical criticism.[178] Moreover, the evangeli-

---

176. Ehrman, "Historical Assault on Faith," in *Jesus, Interrupted*, 4–6.
177. Ibid., 15.
178. See Ehrman, preface to *Jesus, Interrupted*, x–xii.

cal institutions that had previously trained him apparently did not prepare him for the onslaught of historical criticism that would impact his thinking. Erhman should serve as a salient and very recent example that Hagner is wrong both academically and especially spiritually to encourage students to dabble in historical criticism. When seminaries become degree mills focused on maximizing headcounts and prestigious academia at the expense of quality spiritual formation of the individual students through careful mentoring, disaster always ensues. Notice that while Marshall, Hagner, and other evangelicals call pseudepigraphy by a euphemism and accept it as in line with inspiration, Ehrman recognized this complete inconsistency and was honest enough to call such activity what it truly is: *forged*![179]

While Ehrman is honest, evangelicals who are involved in historical-critical research are not quite as open and frank. Yarborough feels that Linnemann went too far. Ehrman would find commonality in Linnemann's assessment that historical-critical ideologies are an overwhelmingly strategical, negative influence. Harold Lindsell, in his *Battle for the Bible* (1976) as well as his subsequent work, *The Bible in the Balance* (1978), was instrumental in sounding the warning among Bible-believing people of historical criticism's destruction of inerrancy and infallibility. Lindsell warned, "The presuppositions of this methodology . . . go far beyond a mere denial of biblical infallibility. They tear at the heart of Scripture, and include a denial of the supernatural."[180] In *The Bible in the Balance*, Lindsell devoted an entire chapter to the issue, entitled "The Historical Critical Method: The Bible's Deadly Enemy," in which he argued,

> Anyone who thinks that the historical-critical method is neutral is misinformed. Since its presuppositions are unacceptable to the evangelical mind this method cannot be used by evangelicals as it stands. The very use by the evangelical of the term, the historical-critical method, is a mistake when it comes to his own approach to Scripture. . . . It appears to me that modern evangelical scholars (and I may have been guilty of this myself) have played fast and loose with the term perhaps because they wanted acceptance by academia. They seem too often to desire to be members of the club which is nothing more than practicing an inclusiveness that undercuts the normativity of the evangelical theological position. This may be done, and often is, under the illusion that by this method the opponents of biblical inerrancy can be won over to the evangelical viewpoint. But practical experience suggests that rarely does this happen and the cost of such an approach is too expensive, for it gives credence and lends respectability to a method which is the deadly enemy of theological orthodoxy.[181]

Yet, these current critically-trained evangelicals apparently believe that they themselves are somehow immune to its subversive power that Linnemann, Lindsell,

---

179. Ehrman, *Forged and Counterforgery*; Ehrman, *Forged: Writing in the Name of God*.
180. Lindsell, *Battle for the Bible*, 204.
181. Lindsell, *Bible in the Balance*, 283.

and others warned of. Is this the case, or is this hubris on the part of these critically-trained evangelicals? Church history stands as a monumental testimony against any such boldness on their part.

The practical result is genre, as well as historical criticism, can be used to deny anything in the Bible that the interpreter finds offensive in a literal sense. The allegorical school did such a thing, the Gnostics did it to Scripture as well, and now Blomberg applies his updated version of it with genre being applied to hermeneutics. Blomberg's use of genre, to this present writer, smacks of an eerie similarity to Rogers and McKim's deprecation of literal interpretation when they noted Westerner's logic that viewed "statements in the Bible were treated like logical propositions that could be interpreted quite literally according to contemporary standards."[182] In chapter 5 of Blomberg's *Can We Still Believe the Bible?*, "Aren't Several Narrative Genres of the Bible Unhistorical?," his use of hermeneutics continues to be the means by which he can redefine what normal definition of inerrancy would be, and he uses it to deny the plain, normal sense of Genesis 1–3,[183] while advocating that we must understand the author's intent in such passages, with the key question from article XIII of ICBI, "standards of truth and error that are alien to its usage or purpose." Applying a completely wrong understanding of this clause of ICBI as well as the original intent of the founders of ICBI, Blomberg advocates that idea that "the question is simply one about the most likely literary form of the passage."[184] From there, he proceeds to allow for nonliteral interpretation of Genesis 1–3 that are, in his view, fully in line with inerrancy, e.g., Adam and Eve as symbols for every man and woman,[185] evolutionary and progressive creation,[186] a nonhistorical Jonah,[187] the possiblility of three Isaiahs,[188] Daniel as apocalyptic genre rather than prophetic,[189] fully embracing of midrash interpretation of the Gospels as advocated by Robert Gundry as not impacting inerrancy,[190] as well as pseudepigraphy as fully in line with inerrancy in NT epistles under the guide of a "literary device" or "acceptable" form of pseudonymity.[191] He argues that we don't know the opinions of the first-century church well-enough on pseudepigraphy to rule it out: "Barring some future discovery related to first-century opinions, we cannot pontificate on what kinds of claims for authorship would or would not have been considered acceptable in Christian communities, and especially in Jewish-Christian

---

182. Rogers and McKim, *Authority and Interpretation*, xviii.
183. Blomberg, *Can We Still Believe*, 150.
184. Ibid.
185. Ibid., 152.
186. Ibid., 151–53.
187. Ibid., 160.
188. Ibid., 162.
189. Ibid., 163–64.
190. Ibid., 165–68.
191. Ibid., 168–72.

circles when the New Testament Epistles were written. As a result, we must evaluate every proposal based on its own historical and grammatical merits, not on whether it does or does not pass some pre-established criterion of what inerrancy can accept."[192]

Interestingly, the 2013 president of the Evangelical Society, Robert W. Yarborough, praises Blomberg's work *Can We Still Believe?* in the following terms. Although the quote is lengthy, it is necessary to show the degradation of inerrancy among the seminary teachers in America, for he addresses the future of the direction of evangelical academia toward the inerrancy of Scripture:

> This book is refreshing and important not only because of its breadth of coverage of issues, viewpoints, and literature. It is evenhanded in that both enemies of inerrancy and *wrong-headed friends* are called on the carpet. Blomberg revisits incidents like Robert Gundry's dismissal from this society and the kerfluffle over a decade ago surrounding the TNIV and inclusive language. He does not mince words in criticizing those he sees as overzealous for the inerrancy cause. Nor is he bashful in calling out former inerrantists who, Blomberg finds, often make their polemical arguments against what they used to believe with less than compelling warrant. I predict that everyone who reads the book will disagree strongly with the author about something.[193]

Please note that in Blomberg's book, these "wrong-headed" friends are those who hold to an orthodox view of inerrancy as well as the ICBI statements of 1978 and 1982.

Yarborough continues,

> At the same time, the positive arguments for inerrancy are even more substantial. It is clear that Blomberg is not content with poking holes in non-inerrantist arguments. He writes, "I do not think one has to settle for anything short of full-fledged inerrantist Christianity so long as we ensure that we employ all parts of a detailed exposition of inerrancy, such as that found in the Chicago Statement."
>
> Or again: "These Scriptures are trustworthy. We can still believe the Bible. We should still believe the Bible and act accordingly, by following Jesus in discipleship." I am skimming some of his concluding statements, but the real meat of the book is inductive demonstration of inerrancy's plausibility based on primary evidence and scholarship surrounding that evidence. *If only a book of this substance had been available when I was a college or grad school student!*[194]

---

192. Ibid., 172.

193. Yarborough, "Future of Cognitive Reverence for the Bible," 5–18 (quote from p. 9), italics added.

194. Ibid., italics added.

If this is the future of their concept of "inerrancy" in evangelical seminaries, then all hopes of a firm foundation for Scripture are shipwreck.

## HISTORICAL MATTERS DON'T SEEM TO MATTER TO HISTORICAL-CRITICAL EVANGELICALS

In answering the question posed by the book *Do Historical Matters Matter to Faith?*, an alarming trend has been noticed among these evangelicals who pursue such a *modus operandi* based in historical-critical ideologies as delineated above. A subtle and, at times, not so subtle dehistoricizing of the Gospels is taking place. Such an evangelical trend dangerously impacts the ICBI statements crafted in 1978 (Inerrancy) and 1982 (Hermeneutics) for views of the inerrancy and interpretation of the Gospels as well as the entire Old and New Testaments. While the evangelicals involved are to be commended for their assertion that they affirm a belief in inerrancy, their practice seems to be at odds with such an assertion. This question of historical matters mattering would seem to need a negative answer in many instances. Because these evangelicals have a problematic view of the historical basis of the Gospels, many of them have joined together in the pursuit of what is termed "searching for the 'historical Jesus'" which is based on a philosophically driven postmodernistic historiography.

It is now clear that the influence of European training upon American evangelicals has had a very deleterious impact on the trustworthiness of God's Word for a new generation of scholars. Sadly, these evangelicals apparently believe that they themselves are immune to the subversive powers of historical criticism that no one previously ever surmounted. By contrast, the ICBI Statements on Inerrancy (1978) and Hermeneutics (1982) were designed to be a warning and safeguard to future generations of evangelical scholars. History has repeated itself. As at the turn of the twentieth century, a call must go forth today to rally the faithful to expose doctrinal error to preserve a faithful remnant for the glory of our Lord Jesus Christ.

## Chapter 13

# The Resurgence of Neo-Evangelicalism
## Craig Blomberg's Latest Book and the Future of Evangelical Theology

WILLIAM C. ROACH

### INTRODUCTION

Current controversy over the total truthfulness and full integrity of the Scriptures points to a truth many younger evangelicals may not know, i.e., the historic debates that took place over the inerrancy of the Bible in evangelicalism has been a major issue for the last half of the twentieth century.

As in the Reformation of the sixteenth century, participants of the inerrancy battles since the 1950s recognized that to be divided over the formal principle of the authority of Scripture was, inevitably, to be divided over the material principles of doctrine as well. Moderates and conservatives in the overall movement of evangelicalism were divided over controversial issues ranging from abortion rights, the exclusivity of the gospel, and the nature of the atonement. As might be expected, with the compromise of any true commitment to biblical authority, evangelical *consistency* and *authenticity* faced similar division and compromise.

While theological institutions and self-professed evangelicals scattered throughout mainline denominations were tempted to revise their statements of faith in order to meet the demands of the moderate worldview, Francis Schaeffer penned his book *The Great Evangelical Disaster* in 1982. Schaeffer writes:

Within evangelicalism there are a growing number who are modifying their views on the inerrancy of the Bible so that the full authority of Scripture is completely undercut. But it is happening in very subtle ways. . . . What may seem like a minor difference at first [among competing views of Scripture by evangelicals], in the end makes all the difference in the world. It makes all the difference, as we might expect, in things pertaining to theology, doctrine and spiritual matters, but it also makes all the difference in things pertaining to the daily Christian life and how we as Christians are to relate to the world around us. In other words, *compromising the full authority of Scripture eventually affects what it means to be a Christian theologically and how we live in the full spectrum of human life.*[1]

As moderate views spread throughout the United States, some evangelical institutions adopted European models of biblical authority by rejecting an uncompromised commitment to biblical inerrancy and proposing infallibilist views of scriptural authority.[2] Ground zero for this effort was Fuller Theological Seminary. Fuller was by no means a liberal institution during the 1970s, but as Harold Lindsell argues in *The Battle for the Bible*, an inevitable crisis occurred over the inerrancy of Scripture and theological boundaries that once marked evangelicalism.[3] Prominent names favoring the shift were faculty such as Dan Fuller, George Eldon Ladd, Jack Rogers, and Donald McKim. These individuals, along with other moderate evangelicals over the course of the successive generations, influenced a host of institutions and seminarians beyond the Fuller campus. In particular, some of the views are advocated by many present-day evangelicals such as Craig Blomberg, Darrell Bock, and Michael Licona (either intentionally or unintentionally).

## INTERNATIONAL COUNCIL ON BIBLICAL INERRANCY

In order to combat the growing tide of biblical errancy in evangelicalism, individuals such as James Boice, Norman Geisler, Carl F. H. Henry, Kenneth Kantzer, Harold Lindsell, Roger Nicole, J. I Packer, R. C. Sproul, and Francis Schaeffer met in the fall of 1978 producing the historic Chicago Statement on Biblical Inerrancy (CSBI). The

---

1. Schaeffer, "Great Evangelical Disaster," 4:328, emphasis added.
2. The irony about committing oneself to an infallibilist as opposed to an inerrantist view is that etymologically and in theory, infallibility is a stronger term than inerrancy. Infallibility has to do with the fact that Scripture cannot err, where inerrancy claims that Scripture did not err. Infallibility speaks about the potential of Scripture to err, namely, it cannot. Inerrancy means that the final result is without error. For example, there are times when I compose inerrant grocery lists and times when I compose errant grocery lists. The reason for the difference is because I am fallible; hence, I can sometimes not err however I have the ability to err. But, if I were infallible I would always not err. And when it comes to the text of Scripture, since God is the primary author of Scripture, the reason it does not contains errors is because God cannot err.
3. Lindsell, *Battle for the Bible*, 106–21.

## Part 2—Inerrancy Defended

essence of what the International Council on Biblical Inerrancy (ICBI) stood for appears in "A Short Statement," produced at the summit meeting:

1. God, who is himself Truth and speaks truth only, has inspired Holy Scripture in order thereby to reveal himself to lost mankind through Jesus Christ as Creator and Lord, Redeemer and Judge. Holy Scripture is God's witness to himself.

2. Holy Scripture, being God's own Word, written by men prepared and superintended by his Spirit, is of infallible divine authority in all matters upon which it touches: it is to be believed, as God's instruction, in all that it affirms; obeyed, as God's command, in all that it requires; embraced, as God's pledge, in all that it promises.

3. The Holy Spirit, Scripture's divine Author, both authenticates it to us by his inward witness and opens our minds to understand its meaning.

4. Being wholly and verbally God-given, Scripture is without error or fault in all its teaching, no less in what it states about God's acts in creation, about the events of world history, and about its own literary origins under God, than in its witness to God's saving grace in individual lives.

5. The authority of Scripture is inescapably impaired if this total divine inerrancy is in any way limited or disregarded, or made relative to a view of truth contrary to the Bible's own; and such lapses bring serious loss to both the individual and the church.

Looking at the ICBI, now more than a quarter century later, at stake in the formation of the CSBI were indeed real and crucial theological concerns. Methodologically and strategically, the axiom of inerrancy was viewed both as an article of faith and a guideline of biblical interpretation to safeguard the belief that in all the inspired texts, whatever their literary genre and style, God still speaks his mind to humanity through the agency of human writers, culminating in the communication of errorless, cognitive-propositional revelation. In each of these ways then, belief in the inerrancy of Scripture determines the basic attitudes of exegetes and provides a stabilizing influence on the faith of the church and evangelical identity. However, among present-day evangelicals, there seems to be an array of evangelical scholars, in particular Craig Blomberg, who no longer desires to carry on the legacy of the ICBI and the torch of the CSBI.[4] Consequently, their publications indicate there are formal differences between evangelicals pertaining to the doctrine of Scripture and material theological differences over core evangelical beliefs.[5]

---

4. E.g., in the book *Five Views on Biblical Inerrancy*, both Michael Bird and Peter Enns are clear they do not want to carry to torch of inerrancy as defined by the ICBI and CSBI forward. See Gundry, *Five Views on Biblical Inerrancy*. See also Packer, *"Fundamentalism" and the Word of God*.

5. Blomberg and Robinson, *How Wide the Divide?*; Sparks, *God's Word in Human Words*; Enns, *Inspiration and Incarnation*.

## CRAIG BLOMBERG'S CAN WE STILL BELIEVE THE BIBLE?

Craig Blomberg, professor of New Testament at Denver Theological Seminary, recently published a book titled *Can We Still Believe the Bible? An Evangelical Engagement with Contemporary Questions*. The overall purpose of the book is to offer evangelicals reasons to believe the Bible by engaging both liberal and conservative scholarship. Evangelical engagement with liberal academia is nothing new; however for our purposes, what is unique about Blomberg's approach is the *way* he attempts to engage with conservative evangelical scholarship. He writes:

> A handful of very conservative Christian leaders who have not understood the issues adequately have reacted by unnecessarily rejecting the new developments. To the extent that they, too, have often received much more publicity than their small numbers would warrant, they have hindered genuine scholarship among evangelicals and needlessly scared unbelievers away from the Christian faith. As my Christian eighth-grade public school history teacher, Dorothy Dunn, used to love to intone with considerable passion, after having lived through our country's battles against both Nazism and Communism: "The far left and the far right—avoid them both, like the plague!"[6]

Blomberg cites Norman Geisler, Albert Mohler, Danny Akin, Robert Thomas, David Farnell, and myself (William Roach) as examples of these very conservative scholars.[7] He charges Geisler, Farnell, Thomas, and myself with making "attacks" against his writings and those by other evangelical writers such as Darrell Bock, D. A. Carson, and Craig Keener as being too liberal and threatening inerrancy, or denying the historicity of Scripture.[8]

Unsurprisingly, Blomberg continues to discuss my recently coauthored publication with Norman Geisler, titled *Defending Inerrancy*.[9] He claims:

> In his most recent book on inerrancy, Norman Geisler joins William Roach to criticize the work of a variety of scholars ranging all the way from Bart Ehrman, self-confessed agnostic and ex-evangelical who would strongly disavow inerrancy, to Darrell Bock, Dallas Seminary professor and one of the world's leading inerrantist New Testament scholars. Apparently unable to distinguish between genuine contradictions of inerrancy and legitimate in-house

---

6. Blomberg, *Can We Still Believe the Bible?*, 7–8.

7. Ibid., 7–8, 10–11, 120, 142–45, 166–68, 213–14, 222, 249–50, 254–55, 261–64, 272–73.

8. Ibid., 120, 175. I'm still amazed each time I read this comment because I'm left asking myself, "Where did Dr. Geisler and I ever criticize D. A. Carson or Craig Keener?" I can understand the comments about Bock, since we have an entire chapter dedicated to the way his new "quest" undermines the CSBI. However, not once did we even mention Craig Keener's name in our book! D. A. Carson is only mentioned one time in the book on p. 19. Contrary to Blomberg's claim, we cite him favorably. Personally, I have respect and admired Carson's commitment to biblical authority and inerrancy and commend his works to the evangelical world.

9. Geisler and Roach, *Defending Inerrancy*.

inerrantist debates on exegetical, hermeneutical, or methodological questions, Geisler and Roach tar all those they criticize with the same brush. Whether those criticized recognize it or not, Geisler and Roach count them as having denied or threatened inerrancy.[10]

Blomberg believes publications such as *Defending Inerrancy* or *The Jesus Crisis* cause grave problems for evangelicalism. He claims, "If Farnell, Thomas, and Geisler and Roach were to be consistent and chastise every Old and New Testament commentator whose views match those they demonize, they would scarcely find a biblical scholar left in the Evangelical Theological Society who would pass muster in their eyes."[11] Blomberg offers examples of this "demonization" by appealing to the vote to remove Robert Gundry from ETS and the controversy at Trinity Evangelical Divinity School with Murray Harris over the nature of the bodily resurrection.[12] In addition, Blomberg believes our publications stifle scholarship and serve as roadblocks keeping unbelievers from embracing Jesus Christ as their Lord and Savior.

## EVALUATION—CAN WE STILL BELIEVE THE BIBLE?

Blomberg has every right to try and make his case, but his arguments about those he labels as "very conservative" or "extreme" are alarmist and factually inaccurate. Far more than that, his arguments reveal that he and other prominent evangelical scholars and institutions have much more in common with Fuller's Neo-Evangelicalism, and in fact indicate, a resurgence of Neo-Evangelical theology. The ICBI arose to address specifically these types of trends within evangelicalism; however, it seems like individuals such as Blomberg, are now willing to move beyond the vision and legacy of classic evangelicalism and the ICBI.[13] This point will be substantiated by the following three statements.[14]

---

10. Blomberg, *Can We Still Believe the Bible?*, 142.

11. Ibid.

12. Ibid., 166–68; 213–14; 222.

13. For example, the preface to the CSBI states, "The following Statement affirms this inerrancy of Scripture afresh, making clear our understanding of it and warning against its denial. We are persuaded that to deny it is to set aside the witness of Jesus Christ and the Holy Spirit and to refuse that submission to the claims of God's own Word which marks true Christian faith. We see it as our timely duty to make this affirmation in the face of current lapses from the truth of inerrancy among our fellow Christians and misunderstanding of this doctrine in the world at large."

14. The ICBI and CSBI are used as the litmus test for the place inerrancy has to mark out evangelical *identity* and *consistency* because it is the official view of ETS.

## 1. Blomberg Unmistakably Desires to Chart a Version of Evangelicalism without Making Inerrancy a Theological Boundary.

In the articles of affirmation and denial found in the CSBI, the ICBI sought to communicate at least two "essential" truths. First, belief in the inerrancy of Scripture is not a salvific essential of the Christian faith. Hence, one can deny the inerrancy of Scripture and still be considered a Christian. It seems like many advocates of Blomberg's view of Neo-Evangelical theology believe this is the charge being labeled against their views, however, it is not. Instead, what is being claimed is their views are changing theological boundaries that have historically marked evangelicalism (a.k.a., an uncompromised commitment to the inerrancy of Scripture to mark out evangelical *identity* and *consistency*). Second, belief in the inerrancy of Scripture is vital to the health and overall well-being of the Christian faith and the local church. These two truths are made clear in article XIX of the CSBI. It reads:

> *We affirm* that a confession of the full authority, infallibility, and inerrancy of Scripture is vital to a sound understanding of the whole Christian faith. We further affirm that such confession should lead to increasing conformity to the image of Christ.
>
> *We deny* that such confession is necessary for salvation. However, we further deny that inerrancy can be rejected without grave consequences, both to the individual and to the church.

Article XIX speaks to the *functional* authority of inerrancy within the life of the church. It recognizes that belief in the inerrancy of Scripture affects both the totality of the individual believer's life and the corporate life of the church. In addition, the CSBI's official commentary goes on to state, "The framers of the confession are saying unambiguously that confession of belief in the inerrancy of Scripture is not an essential of the Christian faith necessary for salvation. We gladly acknowledge that people who do not hold to this doctrine may be earnest and genuine, zealous and in many ways dedicated Christians. We do not regard acceptance of inerrancy to be a test for salvation."[15] In the following section of the commentary, Sproul writes:

> However, we urge as a committee and as an assembly that people consider the severe consequences that may befall the individual or church which casually and easily rejects inerrancy. We believe that history has demonstrated again and again that there is all too often a close relationship between rejection of inerrancy and subsequent defection from matters of the Christian faith that are essential to salvation. When the church loses its confidence in the authority of sacred Scripture the church inevitably looks to human opinion as its guiding light. When that happens, the purity of the church is directly threatened. Thus, we urge upon our Christian brothers and sisters of all professions and

---

15. Sproul, *Explaining Inerrancy*, 56.

denominations to join with us in a reaffirmation of the full authority, integrity, infallibility and inerrancy of sacred Scripture to the end that our lives may be brought under the authority of God's Word, that we may glorify Christ in our lives, individually and corporately as the church.[16]

The key points from this commentary are: (1) The committee as a whole compiled this article and provide the correct interpretation of it is found in the official commentary. In the foreword to *Explaining Inerrancy*, Sproul offers a list of the following individuals who served on the draft committee of the CSBI: Drs. Edmund P. Clowney, Norman L. Geisler, Harold W. Hoehner, Donald E. Hoke, Roger R. Nicole, James I. Packer, Earl D. Radmacher, and R. C. Sproul.[17] The point being, if someone does not understand the articles of affirmation and denial from the CSBI, consult the official ICBI commentary. If someone still does not understand the articles, there are living framers from the draft committee who can shed light upon the CSBI. (2) The article speaks to the personal and institutional effects of either casually or explicitly denying the inerrancy of Scripture. (3) The article and commentary note that history records incidents from both individuals and institutions who have wavered on the inerrancy of Scripture, to then in turn, waver on one or more essential tenets of the Christian faith.[18] And it is in that sense, the purity of the church and the confessional integrity of institutions are compromised. Moreover, the committee argues that it is not a slippery slope to claim, "If one denies inerrancy, then inevitably, they will start denying other tenets of the Christian faith." The reason is because "history has demonstrated again and again that there is all too often a close relationship between rejection of inerrancy and subsequent defection from matters of the Christian faith that are essential to salvation."[19] Therefore, this claim (that denying the inerrancy of Scripture has negative effects upon the church) is a historically informed observation, not an unjustified or factually unsubstantiated claim.

Consequently, what is in purview in this article is a commitment to the *functional* authority of Scripture in the body of Christ. The CSBI argues that history has demonstrated time and time again, as the inerrancy of Scripture goes, so too, goes the purity of the church.[20] For that reason, many evangelical schools, churches, and organizations such as ETS, have required their constituents to affirm without reservation a

16. Ibid., 56–57.

17. Ibid., 5.

18. A salvific essential is a doctrine that if removed undermines the Christian faith. For example, if someone denies the deity of Christ or sola fide, they have undermined an essential of the Christian faith. In addition, there are appropriate methodological considerations to consider. Namely, most evangelicals recognize that methodologically, the historical-grammatical method of interpretation is the proper method for arriving at the salvific essentials. While some may affirm a salvific essential without affirming the HGM, nonetheless, it is inconsistent with their method. See Geisler and Rhodes, *Convictions Without Compromise*.

19. Sproul, *Explaining Inerrancy*, 56–57.

20. See Lindsell, *Battle For the Bible*.

commitment to biblical inerrancy, in order to preserve institutional integrity and the doctrinal purity of the body of Christ.

Continuing his list of what he considers to be appropriate evangelical engagement with critical issues, Blomberg utilizes some very specific language in order to distinguish himself from "very conservative scholarship" and "watchdog" mentalities. He dedicates his book to the faculty, administration, and trustees of Denver Theological Seminary for creating a "congenial" research environment, while upholding the inerrancy of Scripture without any of the "watchdog mentality that plagues so many evangelical institutions."[21] Blomberg raises the question, "If a person must agree that the Bible is without error in order to hold a position with a school, church, or parachurch organization, doesn't this put a virtual straightjacket on their research?"[22] While he immediately answers this question, one must look throughout the book to find a comprehensive answer. Blomberg believes, "The answer depends almost entirely on whether or not there is good evidence for biblical inerrancy."[23] He believes there is good evidence for inerrancy, however, this is precisely where he starts to show his Neo-Evangelical colors.

According to Blomberg, "institutions or organizations that claim to abide by it [CSBI] must allow their inerrantists scholars the freedom to explore the various literary options without fear of reprisal. Ironically, when individuals draw boundaries of inerrancy more narrowly than this, it is *they* who have unwittingly denied inerrancy, at least as it is defined by the Chicago Statement!"[24] Later in the book, Blomberg illustrates his point by discussing the Licona controversy within the SBC and how the leadership responded to Licona's claim that Matthew 27:51–53 represents a nonhistorical narrative typically featured in Greco-Roman literature *bios*. Blomberg writes:

> Albert Mohler, president of the Southern Baptist Theological Seminary in Louisville, fell into the same trap of censuring Licona, and even a New Testament scholar as sharp as Danny Akin, president of Southeastern Baptist Theological Seminary, at least briefly jumped on the bandwagon, insisting that Licona could never teach full-time for him. All of this would be just plain silly if it were not so tragic and if people's careers and livelihoods didn't hang in the balance.[25]

The point Blomberg tries to make in this quote is clear: The SBC and its leadership *wrongly terminated* and *censured* Licona from teaching at SBC institutions for his views on Matthew 27:51–53. Clearly Blomberg believes the Licona controversy represents best the *way* evangelical institutions should *not* react to disagreements over

21. Blomberg, *Can We Still Believe the Bible?*, v.
22. Ibid., 120–21.
23. Ibid., 121.
24. Ibid., 178, italics in original.
25. Ibid., 175.

literary options and the *way* they should not draw theological boundaries around the doctrine of inerrancy.

Blomberg is not done yet, he goes on to argue that Jesus actually rebukes religious leaders for drawing such theological boundaries and reacting in a confrontational manner.[26] He illustrates his point by drawing his reader's attention to Jesus' interaction with the Pharisee's and the Sadducees and Paul's interactions with the Judaizers. Blomberg writes, "In other words, receiving the most censure are fellow members of the same religious community who *occupy positions of Christian leadership* and have created overly restrictive doctrinal boundaries and should know better."[27] In brief, Blomberg believes organizations such as the SBC and leaders such as Mohler, Geisler, and so forth, ought to know better and quit censuring fellow Christian scholars for crossing the so-called "line of inerrancy."

Blomberg pays attention to the "Battles for the Bible" throughout evangelical organizations and he clearly argues that inerrancy should no longer be considered a theological shibboleth. However, while there is much emotional thrust to his arguments, the weakness of Blomberg's approach is that it offers no actual theological boundaries to map out evangelicalism. While belief in the inerrancy of Scripture is not a salvific essential; historically, it has been essential to understand properly the nature of evangelicalism. Attention to theological boundaries is not a matter of doctrinal policing; instead, it is necessary for the responsibility of any organization to make clear what they do and do not affirm. Without such a clear understanding of evangelicalism, the movement is left without doctrinal formulations or theological trajectories. In fact, the necessity of theological boundaries has been so crucial for evangelicalism that the Doctrinal Basis of ETS requires its members to affirm without reservation: (1) The Bible alone, and the Bible in its entirety, is the Word of God written and therefore inerrant in the autographs (art. III); (2) Every member must subscribe in writing annually to the Doctrinal Basis (art. IV). In addition, ETS also adopted the CSBI as its official guide to understand inerrancy.

My own theological pilgrimage reflects this continual struggle with questions relating to theological boundaries and evangelical identity. For the last several years, I have studied at a Southern Baptist seminary. Throughout our studies, students are reminded of the theological and political battles that mark the Conservative Resurgence. Crucial to the overall success of the Conservative Resurgence was an uncompromised commitment to the total truthfulness and complete accuracy of the Scriptures. There were so-called moderates and conservatives lined up on each side arguing their case for their own theological boundaries and trajectory of the denomination.[28] However, if anything became clear in the SBC, inerrancy provided the necessary foundation to promote a coherent and unified theological vision to recover the denomination and

---

26. Ibid., 216–17.
27. Ibid., 217, italics in original.
28. Dockery, *Christian Scripture*, 177–216.

respective seminaries from theological moderates. Much like the Reformation of the sixteenth century, the principle divisions in the SBC over the nature of the atonement, the factuality of the resurrection, the historicity of events recorded in both the Old and New Testaments, and so forth; represent the underlying disagreement over the formal cause of biblical authority and the nature of Baptist identity.

Despite the fact that Blomberg believes his model of biblical authority is going to allow for so-called "scholarship" to flourish, he must realize that the history of the church and the SBC in particular, indicates that such theological concessions come with a price. The price is typically theological moderates become theological liberals, and unbelievers do not become believers, because as the integrity of the Scriptures goes, so too goes the unvarnished gospel of Jesus Christ.[29]

Returning to Blomberg's use of the Licona controversy and his chiding of individuals such as Mohler and Geisler for drawing theological boundaries around Licona, he is forgetting a few key things. First, Blomberg has never sat in the seat of a seminary president or president of ETS. One of the primary responsibilities of a president is to protect the confessional integrity of their institution or organization. Should a president believe a professor or a view oversteps the theological boundaries of that institution, he has every right and the moral responsibility to enforce his authority and remove that individual. Second, Blomberg forgets that Licona made these concessions within a denomination that has already fought the "Battle for the Bible" and landed on the side of both inerrancy and theological boundaries.[30] Clearly, those in SBC leadership believe Licona's views not only undermine the inerrancy of Scripture, but cross a theological boundary established by the Conservative Resurgence. Last but not least, it is apparent that Blomberg does not approve of hard and

---

29. Blomberg even concedes the point that he would affirm non-evangelical views of Scripture such as Neo-Orthodoxy before moving toward liberalism. He writes, "If I became convinced of a handful of fairly trivial errors in the Bible, I would opt for an infallibilist position (see chap. 4 above) instead. If I felt that some of these errors were more serious, I would fall back on Neo-Orthodoxy. If that became too much of a stretch, I would explore accommodationism or even more liberal Christian epistemologies." Ibid., 222. In addition, if one reads the works of Blomberg, he has even attempted to downplay the true divide between evangelicals and Mormons. However, the point needs to be made that when each community actually reflects the doctrinal convictions of their movements, they differ on the nature of God, Jesus Christ, the Holy Spirit, sin, salvation, the nature of humanity, and almost every other orthodox doctrine of the Christian faith. At stake in the debate over theological boundaries is sometimes the very gospel itself! See Blomberg and Robinson, *How Wide the Divide?*; Blomberg, *Can We Still Believe the Bible?*, 272.

30. Licona knew that the SBC had clear and marked theological boundaries; however, he did not believe his use of genre-criticism overstepped one of those boundaries. Licona clearly knew that denying the bodily resurrection would cost him his job; nonetheless, Licona knew the SBC operated according to theological boundaries and police them accordingly. See Licona, *Resurrection of Jesus*, 132. Licona writes, "I presently enjoy a position of national leadership within the largest Protestant denomination in North America, a position for which I carry influence, am paid fairly and through which I find much satisfaction. I am aware that should my research lead me to the conclusion that Jesus did not rise from the dead I would be dismissed from my position and my employment would be terminated" (ibid.).

fast theological boundaries. But that makes me wonder if Blomberg would oppose the hiring of Norman Geisler, David Farnell, Robert Thomas, Albert Mohler or myself (William Roach) at Denver Theological Seminary. If he has no problems, then he is acting consistent with his "no watchdog" mentality. However, if he excludes any or all of us from the institution based upon our views, then he is guilty of drawing theological boundaries and enacting the same "watchdog" mentality he encourages other evangelical institutions to avoid.

At stake in article XIX of the CSBI is a warning about the effects of denying the inerrancy of Scripture and downplaying the necessity of drawing theological boundaries. In the cases presented above, history indicates that once biblical authority is compromised it has the potential to open Pandora's Box to unorthodox and sometimes heretical theological concessions. In other words, in order for evangelicals to proclaim, "Jesus is Lord" and "Jesus is risen," it requires an uncompromised commitment to, "The Bible says." And central to evangelicals affirming "The Bible says" is a commitment to the total truthfulness and trustworthiness of the Scriptures. This commitment undoubtedly requires evangelical institutions and organizations such as ETS, to set and enforce theological boundaries such as inerrancy.[31] Now is not the time for evangelicalism to compromise on these core commitments![32] However, since Blomberg does not believe inerrancy is a mark of evangelical consistency and identity, it aligns his position much closer to Fuller's Neo-Evangelical theology than the ICBI and classic evangelicalism.

## 2. Some Aspects of Blomberg's Model Undermine the ICBI View of Inerrancy and Hermeneutics.

So as to not claim all of Blomberg's book undermines the CSBI, it should be noted there are many commendable features to *Can We Still Believe the Bible*? His chapters on the transmission and canonicity of the text are phenomenal. The sections interacting with Bart Ehrman will serve the church for years to come because they address some of the most pressing issues raised by Ehrman-like scholarship. Unlike *The Lost World of Scripture* by John H. Walton and D. Brent Sandy, Blomberg still argues for the existence of the inerrant autographs of Scripture.[33] His sections on the canonicity of the text address some of the most pressing questions our culture raises against the Bible, such as: How many books? Was it a political game? What if we found another book? While I disagree with many of his conclusions over the proper philosophy of translation, namely, I believe formal equivalence represents best an inerrantist model

---

31. E.g., Francis Beckwith resigned as the president of ETS because he converted to Roman Catholicism. See Neff, "Q&A: Francis Beckwith"; Hansen, "ETS Resignation"; Cooperman, "Evangelical Leader Returns."

32. See Geisler and Farnell, *Jesus Quest*.

33. Blomberg, *Can We Still Believe the Bible?*, 37. See Walton and Sandy, *Lost World of Scripture*.

for translation rather than the approach taken by the TNIV. Similarly, while I am a cessationist, I do believe Blomberg's final chapter on miracles offers his readers valuable insights for why modernity does not *de jure* rule out the possibility of miracles. Clearly, Blomberg has thought about the issues and there are many areas we can lock arms to fight the battles raised against Christianity. Yet, at the same time, I and many other classic evangelicals cannot fully endorse Blomberg's book because the *way* he understands and frames the inerrancy of Scripture undermines the confessional boundaries spelled out in the CSBI. This point is justified in the following four levels.

### First Level: A Recapitulation of the Rogers/McKim Proposal

At the first level, Blomberg's views raise serious doubts over the true origin of the twentieth-century evangelical view of Scripture. Like many evangelicals today, Blomberg seems to believe the inerrantist view of Scripture finds its basis in philosophical and theological modernity; in particular, the Enlightenment, Thomas Reid's Common Sense Realism, and Scholastic Protestantism. Blomberg claims, "In short, if one tries to demonstrate that every major orthodox Christian thinker before the rise of modern biblical criticism spoke of the Scriptures as inerrant or adopted the four components of Feinberg's definition, one will fail."[34] To be fair to Blomberg, he does go onto say, "But it is difficult to find very many influential Christians throughout the first seventeen centuries of church history—that is, until the Scientific Enlightenment—who did not affirm in a fairly sweeping way the unique truthfulness, reliability, and trustworthiness of the sixty-six books of what came to be the Protestant Bible (debates about the Old Testament Apocrypha notwithstanding)."[35] He also claims that ancient authors were less precise in their writing and standards of precision than modern authors. While Blomberg's assessment might come close to the ICBI view, it nonetheless falls short.

First, the claim that the origin of the technical concept of inerrancy as defined by twentieth-century evangelicals arose from modernist thinking was first proposed by Neo-Evangelical theologians Jack Rogers and Donald McKim in their book titled *The Authority and Interpretation of the Bible*.[36] This proposal was thoroughly critiqued and frankly debunked by John Woodbridge's book *Biblical Authority: A Critique of the Rogers/McKim Proposal*. In addition, the ICBI responded by producing and inspiring a host of books defining and defending the inerrancy of Scripture against the Rogers/McKim proposal. In particular, the book titled *Inerrancy and the Church*, edited by John D. Hannah, who, like Woodbridge, argues that the CSBI view of inerrancy has been the position of the church from its inception. That being said, Blomberg's claim that prior to modern biblical criticism no one spoke of the Scriptures as inerrant or they did not at least utilize the concepts of Feinberg's proposal, is factually inaccurate

---

34. Blomberg, *Can We Still Believe the Bible?*, 131.

35. Ibid.

36. Rogers and McKim, *Authority and Interpretation*.

and reflects no significant interaction with the ICBI responses to the Rogers/McKim proposal.

Second, to claim the doctrine of inerrancy is a recent development arising from modernism fails to take many things into consideration. First of all, just because the creeds or specific writers did not utilize the term "inerrancy," does not entail they were opposed to the concept of inerrancy. Second, the creeds do imply the inspiration (which implies its inerrancy) of the Bible. The inspiration of the Bible was commonly accepted by all of the orthodox fathers and framers of the creeds. Given there were no major challenges to it, the doctrine of inerrancy did not have to be further explained or defended. Third, while it is true that the term "inerrancy" nowhere appears in the Bible or in the writings of many writers, however, neither does the word Trinity. We do not reject the Trinity because there were debates over the use of the term, later clarifications and further explanations of it, or because there is no formal creedal explanation of the doctrine until the fourth century. The issue is not whether a precise theological formulation arose later or it took the church longer to formulate a clearer definition. Instead, what matters is whether the truth of inerrancy is taught in the Bible and affirmed by orthodox theologians throughout church history. In brief, Blomberg seems to overlook the fact that the Rogers/McKim proposal is factually inaccurate and that every orthodox theologian down through the ages has affirmed the total truthfulness or inerrancy of Scripture.

Third, the ICBI explicitly dealt with the claim that inerrancy arose from modernist philosophy. Article XVI states:

> *We affirm* that the doctrine of inerrancy has been integral to the church's faith throughout its history.
>
> *We deny* that inerrancy is a doctrine that was invented by scholastic Protestantism, or is a reactionary position postulated in response to negative higher criticism.

The official commentary indicates that article XVI refers not to the word inerrancy, but the doctrine of inerrancy.[37] The commentary clarifies that the word inerrancy was not used with any degree of frequency and perhaps not even at all before the seventeenth century. Sproul writes:

> But, [the commentary claims when using Luther as an example], Luther argued that the Scriptures never "err." To say that the Scriptures never err is to say nothing more nor less than that the Bible is inerrant. So though the word *inerrancy* is of relatively modern invention, the concept is rooted not only in the biblical witness to Scripture itself but also in the acceptance of the vast majority of God's people throughout the history of the Christian church.[38]

---

37. Sproul, *Explaining Inerrancy*, 51.
38. Ibid., 51–52.

The official commentary on the denial also argues that the doctrine of inerrancy is rooted in the Bible, not modernist philosophy. Sproul writes:

> The denial is simply that inerrancy as a concept is not the product of a rigid, sterile, rationalistic approach to Scripture born of the scholastic movement of seventeenth-century Protestantism. Nor is it proper to understand the doctrine as a twentieth-century reaction to liberal theology or "modernism."[39]

In summary then, it becomes clear that while Blomberg might not claim to the same degree as Roger and McKim that the doctrine of inerrancy was a byproduct of modernism, he nonetheless favors the idea. During the height of the ICBI, scholars from all over the evangelical world arose to debunk the claim that inerrancy is a modern theological convention. As this first level makes clear, Blomberg's views on the origin of inerrancy side with Neo-Evangelicalism and are at odds with article XVI of the CSBI and the official view of inerrancy affirmed by ETS.

## Second Level: Undermining of the CSBI and CSBH

At the second level, many of Blomberg's exegetical conclusions undermine the CSBI understanding of inerrancy. Blomberg includes a chapter titled "Aren't Several Narrative Genres of the Bible Unhistorical?"[40] In this chapter, Blomberg discusses what he believes is the true nature of biblical genres and literary forms. He argues that many portions of Scripture present unhistorical narrative genres. For example, in his survey, Blomberg presents the exegetical studies from scholars who view Genesis 1–3, including the fall of humanity, as unhistorical; deny the historical factuality of Job and Jonah; affirm that multiple authors penned the book of Isaiah; discusses the proper interpretation of Daniel and apocalyptic literature; claim Matthew utilized midrashic approaches; the pseudonymous authorship of New Testament epistles; and the proper interpretation of the book of Revelation. In order to properly assess Blomberg's arguments, he must be quoted at length. Blomberg writes:

> I have deliberately not taken a stand myself on any of the problems as I discussed them in this chapter. Because readers seem invariably curious, I will happily disclose where I come down at the moment, given the varying amounts of study I have devoted to each. I would support an old-earth creationism and opt for a combination of progressive creation and a literary-framework approach to Genesis 1. I lean towards Kidner's approach to Genesis 2–3 but am open to other proposals. I suspect that Jonah really intended to recount a miracle that really did happen, but with Job I gravitate more towards Longman's mediating approach. Despite the overwhelming consensus against it, I still find the arguments for the unity of Isaiah under a single primary author, even

---

39. Ibid., 52.
40. Blomberg, *Can We Still Believe*, 147–78.

if lightly redacted later, more persuasive (or at least problematic) than most do. I remain pretty much baffled by Daniel 11; it is the issue I have researched by far the least. My inherent conservatism inclines me in the direction of taking it as genuine predictive prophecy, but I listen respectfully to those who argue for other interpretations and continue to mull them over. I reject Gundry's approach to Matthew as highly unlikely. I have yet to be persuaded by Licona's initial views of Matthew 27:51–53 but would love to see additional comparative research undertaken. I think good cases can still be mounted for the traditional ascriptions of authorship of the New Testament epistles, allowing for perhaps some posthumous editing of 2 Peter. And I refuse ever to be suckered back into the views of my young adult years, when I actually believed that the end would play out as Hal Lindsey claimed they would![41]

In other words, while Blomberg tries to chart a way forward that is still committed to the ICBI, nonetheless, he is open to a partial evolutionary account of Genesis and the origin of humanity, and leans toward Kidner's Neolithic view of Adam and Eve. While gravitating toward a historical Jonah, he is open to Longman's view of Job. Blomberg claims, "Longman concludes that we dare not be dogmatic, but he notes the view of the book as a *māšāl* (Hebrew for 'parable' and numerous other forms of figurative speech) goes back to the ancient Jewish midrashic and Talmudic literature (*b. Baba Batra* 15a; *y. Sotah* 5.8/20c; *Gen. Rab.* 57.4)."[42] Namely, he is open to a parabolic, nonhistorical Job. Last but not least, Blomberg is open to redaction criticism and posthumous editing of biblical books such as Isaiah, 2 Peter, and denies the historicity of the miracle account in Joshua 10.[43]

While many features of Blomberg's assessment offer exegetical conclusions reconcilable with the CSBI, some of his conclusions undermine the CSBI. First, one of the underlying reasons Blomberg believes he can make these nonhistorical affirmations is because he believes the Bible presents nonhistorical narrative genres. During the Summit II meeting of the ICBI in 1982, the ICBI drafted what is known as the Chicago Statement on Biblical Hermeneutics (CSBH). Much like the CSBI, the CSBH utilizes clear affirmations and denials. Article XIII of the statement claims:

> *We affirm* that awareness of literary categories, formal and stylistic, of the various parts of Scripture is essential for proper exegesis, and hence we value genre criticism as one of the many disciplines of biblical study.
>
> *We deny* that generic categories which negate historicity may rightly be imposed on biblical narratives which present themselves as factual.

---

41. Ibid., 177.
42. Ibid., 156–57.
43. Ibid., 198.

Similar to the CSBI, the CSBH has an official commentary. This time the ICBI chose Norman Geisler to write the commentary. When discussing article XIII of the CSBH, Geisler writes:

> The awareness of what kind of literature one is interpreting is essential to a correct understanding of a text. A correct genre judgment should be made to ensure correct understanding. A parable, for example, should not be treated like a chronicle, nor should poetry be interpreted as though it were a straightforward narrative. Each passage has its own genre, and the interpreter should be cognizant of the specific kind of literature it is as he attempts to interpret it. Without genre recognition the interpreter can be misled in his handling of the passage. For example, when the prophet speaks of "trees clapping their hands" (Isa. 55:21) one could assume a kind of animism unless he recognized that this is poetry and not prose.
>
> The Denial is directed at an illegitimate use of genre criticism by some who deny the truth of passages which are presented as factual. Some, for instance, take Adam to be a myth, whereas in Scripture he is presented as a real person. Others take Jonah to be an allegory when he is presented as a historical person and so referred to by Christ (Matt. 12:40–42). This Denial is an appropriate and timely warning not to use genre criticism as a cloak for rejecting the truth of Scripture.[44]

Blomberg raises the question: Aren't several narrative genres of the Bible unhistorical? He answers with a clear, Yes! However, the ICBI as represented by the CSBH answers with a clear, No! What should be apparent is that Blomberg is moving away from the ICBI definition of inerrancy and approach to hermeneutics. Blomberg's conclusions in chapter five pit him against the denial of article XIII from the CSBH, that states, "*We deny* that generic categories which negative historicity may rightly be imposed on biblical narratives which present themselves as factual." In addition, Blomberg's conclusions also pit him against other articles of the CSBH:[45]

---

44. Sproul and Geisler, *Explaining Inerrancy*, 76.

45. The CSBI also concedes to these points, however, in order to show that Blomberg's views undermine both the CSBI and CSBH, the CSBH has been chosen. In the forward to *Explaining Inerrancy*, on pp. 9–10, Geisler writes: From the beginning, the ICBI spelled out its commitment to the historicity of the biblical narratives. Art. XVIII of the Chicago Statement on Biblical Inerrancy (1978) reads: "*We deny* the legitimacy of any treatment of the text or quest for sources lying behind it that leads to relativizing, dehistoricizing, or counting its teaching, or rejecting its claim to authorship" (emphasis added). The ICBI position became even more explicit in its Chicago Statement of Biblical Hermeneutics (1982). Art.XIII declares: "*We deny* that generic categories which negate historicity may rightly be imposed on biblical narratives which present themselves as factual." Art. XIV goes on to say, "*We deny* that any event, discourse or saying reported in Scripture was invented by the biblical writers or by the traditions they incorporated" (emphasis added). The Chicago Statement on Biblical Inerrancy is clear on this issue. "*We affirm* the propriety of using inerrancy as a theological term with reference to the complete truthfulness of Scripture" (art. XIII). "*We affirm* that inspiration, though not conferring omniscience, guaranteed true and trustworthy utterance on all matters of which the Biblical authors were moved to speak and write" (art. IX). "*We affirm* that Scripture in its entirety is inerrant, being

Part 2—Inerrancy Defended

Article XIV

*We affirm* that the biblical record of events, discourses and sayings, though presented in a variety of appropriate literary forms, correspond to historical fact.

*We deny* that any such event, discourse or saying reported in Scripture was invented by the biblical writers or by the traditions they incorporated.[46]

Article XIX

*We affirm* that any preunderstandings which the interpreter brings to Scripture should be in harmony with scriptural teaching and subject to correction by it.

*We deny* that Scripture should be required to fit alien preunderstandings, inconsistent with itself, such as naturalism, evolutionism, scientism, secular humanism, and relativism.[47]

Article XX

*We affirm* that since God is the author of all truth, all truths, biblical and extra-biblical, are consistent and coherent, and that the Bible speaks truth when it touches on matters pertaining to nature, history, or anything else. We further affirm that in some cases extra-biblical data have value for clarifying what Scripture teaches, and for prompting correction of faulty interpretations.

---

free from all falsehood, fraud, or deceit. *We deny* that Biblical infallibility and inerrancy are limited to spiritual, religious, or redemptive themes, exclusive of assertions in the fields of history and science" (art. XII). "*We affirm* the propriety of using inerrancy as a theological term with reference to the complete truthfulness of Scripture" (art. XII).

The ICBI commentary adds, "Though the Bible is indeed *redemptive* history, it is also redemptive *history*, and this means that the acts of salvation wrought by God actually occurred in the space-time world" (art. XII). With regard to the historicity of the Bible, art. XIII in the commentary points out that we should not "take Adam to be a myth, whereas in Scripture he is presented as a real person." Likewise, it affirms that we should not "take Jonah to be an allegory when he is presented as a historical person and [is] so referred to by Christ." It adds, "We further deny that scientific hypotheses about earth history may properly be used to overturn the teaching of Scripture on creation and he flood" (art. VII of the "Chicago Statement"). In short, the ICBI framers believed that using genre to deny any part of the historicity of the biblical record was a denial of inerrancy.

46. The CSBH commentary notes: "This article combines the emphases of Articles VI and XIII. While acknowledging the legitimacy of literary forms, this article insists that any record of events presented in Scripture must correspond to historical fact. That is, no reported event, discourse, or saying should be considered imaginary. The Denial is even clearer than the Affirmation. It stresses than any discourse, saying, or event reported in Scripture must actually have occurred. This means that any hermeneutic or form of biblical criticism which claims that something was invented by the author must be rejected. This does not mean that a parable must be understood to represent historical facts, since a parable does not (by its very genre) purport to report an event or saying but simply to illustrate a point." Ibid., 75.

47. This article has been chosen because Blomberg has leanings toward figurative approaches to Genesis and the historicity of Adam and Eve. His views are more closely aligned with naturalism and evolutionism than a biblical view of creation.

*We deny* that extra-biblical views ever disprove the teaching of Scripture or hold priority over it.[48]

Article XXII

*We affirm* that Genesis 1–11 is factual, as is the rest of the book.

*We deny* that the teachings of Genesis 1–11 are mythical and that scientific hypotheses about earth history or the origin of humanity may be invoked to overthrow what Scripture teaches about creation.[49]

In summary then, it is apparent that Blomberg's views pertaining to the idea that the Bible contains nonhistorical narratives pits him against both the CSBI and the CSBH. The ICBI and official commentaries are not opposed to understanding the Bible according to its historical or literary context; in fact, that is the very nature of the "historical-grammatical" method of interpretation. However, books such as Blomberg's, while presenting a thorough overview of the current state of scholarship, serve as a reminder that one of the reasons the ICBI was formed was to combat the de-historicizing of the Bible by Neo-Evangelical biblical scholars misappropriating genre criticism (e.g., nonhistorical narrative genres, midrash and so forth).

## *Third Level: Hermeneutics, Authorial Intent, and Inerrancy*

At the third level, Blomberg's book illustrates the use and abuse of authorial intention by present-day evangelical scholars. In the introduction to *Hermeneutics, Inerrancy, & the Bible*, Earl Radmacher raises the questions: "Is 'authorial intention' a poor term to use for expressing the meaning of the author as found in the text? Does it lend itself to the more speculative historical-critical method?"[50] Underlying the answers to these questions raised by scholars are various theories of truth, language, and hermeneutical methods. By way of historical purview, the framers of the CSBI believed in order to remain consistent with the CSBI, one must affirm there is a very specific relationship between inerrancy and hermeneutics. Sproul writes:

> Inspiration without inerrancy is an empty term. Inerrancy without inspiration is unthinkable. The two are inseparably related. They may be distinguished but not separated. So it is with hermeneutics. We can easily distinguish between the inspiration and interpretation of the Bible, but we cannot separate them. Anyone can confess a high view of the nature of Scripture but the ultimate test

---

48. CSBH article XX was chosen because Blomberg is willing to allow extra-biblical views to disprove the teaching of Scripture, in fact, many of the hermeneutical practices hold priority over the clear teaching of narratives and figures deemed historical in the Bible.

49. While Blomberg believes in the factuality of much of Genesis, his views about a Neolithic understanding of Adam and Eve and a literary framework theory of Genesis 1 undermine the historical factuality of Genesis. For that reason, this article was included in this list.

50. Radmacher and Preus, *Hermeneutics, Inerrancy, and the Bible*, xii.

of one's view of Scripture is found in the method of interpreting it. A person's hermeneutic reveals his view of Scripture more clearly than does an exposition of his view.[51]

Much like Sproul, Blomberg notes the distinction between hermeneutics and inerrancy. However, unlike Sproul, Blomberg believes that most of the so-called "inerrancy debates" are really debates over hermeneutics. Blomberg writes:

> Third appears the phrase "properly interpreted" [from Feinberg's definition of inerrancy]. Numerous competing theological and exegetical positions over the centuries have appealed to the inerrancy or trustworthiness of Scripture for their support; in reality they were debates over hermeneutics.... The same is true for many debates that involve the literary form or genre of various biblical passages or even entire books, as chapter 5 will discuss. "Inerrancy" can be wielded as a blunt tool to hammer into submission people whose interpretations of passages differ from ours, when in fact the real issue is not whether a passage is true or not but what kind of truth it teaches.[52]

For Blomberg, the axiom by which one knows whether or not the text is presenting factual history or not is authorial intention. When speaking about the CSBI and authorial intention, Blomberg believes, "If 'dehistoricizing' means regarding as unhistorical something that is intended to be taken as historical, then naturally that would be inconsistent with inerrancy."[53] Later on Blomberg tries to rescue authorial intention by appealing to the framers of the CSBI. He concludes that "if the framers of the Chicago Statement on inerrancy protest that their intention was never to allow for pseudonymity, then they have conceded that the key to interpreting a document (theirs included) is discerning the authors intention, not merely reading the words on a page of text."[54] Blomberg's quotes raise a series of questions about the relationship between authorial intention and the words of text on a page. Is meaning found in the text or is it found in the author's intention? Can meaning be found in both the text and the author's intention? Can the text mean something other than what it says? Can the text say something other than what the author meant? Questions like these and the issues raised by Blomberg will be addressed in the following section.

First, debates over the relationship between hermeneutics and inerrancy are important. There are times when individuals are not denying the inerrancy of Scripture due to difficult exegetical conclusions. For example, someone is not denying the inerrancy of Scripture if they come to a different conclusion whether Jesus is going to return before or after the millennium. That being said, one has to make it clear there are times when so-called "hermeneutics debates" are really debates over the inerrancy

---

51. Sproul, "Biblical Interpretation and the Analogy of Faith," 134.
52. Blomberg, *Can We Still Believe*, 124–75.
53. Ibid., 170.
54. Ibid., 171.

of the Scriptures. For example, there are true differences of opinion over the age of the earth and the length of days in Genesis. While individual's might hold strong, sometimes very strong, opinions over the interpretation of these texts; it would be incorrect to claim that someone is denying inerrancy for believing in an old earth versus a young earth.[55] On the other hand, it would be a denial of inerrancy if someone claimed that creation never occurred. This is clearly outside of the bounds of inerrancy, even though it is the result of a so-called exegetical conclusion. Likewise, the Licona controversy is not merely a debate over a particular interpretation of Mathew 27:51–53 because, unlike the Genesis cases, Licona is not merely questioning the genre of the text and the relevant details surrounding the resurrection of the saints. Instead, he is questioning whether or not the event occurred, even though the historical narrative presents it as a real time-space historical event.[56] For that reason, the Licona controversy is not like debating old and young earth; instead, it is like debating creation and no creation.

Second, underlying Blomberg's assessment over the proper relationship between authorial intention and the text is an underlying view of truth (even though he claims to affirm a correspondence theory of truth). Namely, he seems to deny a correspondence theory favoring an intentionalist theory of truth. Blomberg proceeds to discuss article XIII of the CSBI statement. Throughout his assessment, Blomberg claims, "The standard of truth in a parable is the spiritual point or the point that its author intends to make."[57] One should note by way of historical perspective, the CSBI unquestionably affirms a correspondence theory of truth. In the official commentary, Sproul writes:

> By biblical standards of truth and error is meant the view used both in the Bible and in everyday life, viz., a correspondence view of truth. This part of the article is directed towards those who would redefine truth to relate merely to redemptive intent, the purely personal or the like, rather than to mean that which correspond with reality. For example, when Jesus affirmed that Jonah was in "the belly of the great fish" this statement is true, not simply because of the redemptive significance of the story of Jonah has, but also because it is literally and historically true. The same may be said of the New Testament

---

55. For example, during the time of the ICBI both R. C. Sproul and Walter Kaiser affirmed an old earth view of creation. Now, Sproul affirms a young earth view, whereas Kaiser maintains his old earth position. In addition, Norman Geisler and J. I. Packer affirm an old earth view of creation, whereas John MacArthur and R. Albert Mohler affirm a young earth creationism. In each of these cases, the participants affirm biblical inerrancy but they differ on the age of the earth. In addition, the CSBI and commentaries explicitly did not take a stance on the age of the earth because they noted that individuals such as B. B. Warfield affirmed inerrancy, yet held to an old earth. In addition, issues pertaining to eschatology, in most cases (full-preterism excluded), are not debates over inerrancy but hermeneutics. For example, John MacArthur affirms a pre-tribulation rapture and pre-millennial return of Christ. R. Albert Mohler affirms a post-tribulation rapture and a pre-millennial return of Christ. In each case, both participants affirm biblical inerrancy; however, they differ over the timing of the rapture.

56. See Quarles, review of *Resurrection of Jesus*, 839–44.

57. Blomberg, *Can We Still Believe the Bible?*, 149.

assertions about Adam, Moses, David, and other Old Testament persons as well as about Old Testament events.[58]

That being said, the CSBI view is correspondence view of truth, not an intentionalist theory.

Many present-day evangelicals are falling prey to the argument that claims, "Truth is found in intentions, not necessarily in affirmations." That is, a statement is true if the author intends for it to be true, and a statement is false if he does not intend for it to be true. However, there are some underlying flaws in this approach. First, advocates of an intentionalist theory of truth still believe in a correspondence view of truth, namely, they believe their view of truth actually corresponds with reality. One does not claim "the intentionalist theory of truth is true" because he *intended* for it to be true, but because it corresponds to its actual referent (namely, reality). Second, many statements do not agree with the intention of the author, but they are clearly mistaken. For example, there are slips of the tongue and they are false. But if a statement is true simply because it was intended to be true, even if it was mistaken, then all such errors could be true.

In addition, it is false to claim that the various genres of Scripture present different "kinds" of truth. On the contrary, there is one kind of truth expressed by the various genres of Scripture. The point being, truth must be understood to correspond to *its* kind of reality. For example, no one believes that each parable taught by Jesus includes real referents because the nature of a parable is to use the story to prove a point about a salvific or spiritual truth. However, that truth corresponds to *its* reality. In a similar sense, it is false to claim that the Bible presents "relational" or "personal" truth. There are truths about relationships and about persons in Scripture, but truth itself is not relational or personal. It is propositional, that is, it makes a statement that affirms or denies something about reality.

Third, Blomberg seems to believe that either one incorporates authorial intent or they are left with a bare text, separated from the author's true intention. The problem with this claim is it inherently slips an intentionalist theory of truth into his argument. But, if a correspondence view of truth is correct, then one can rightly affirm that the "text means what it says" and "the author intends what the text says." Unlike normal matters of affair between human beings, God never errs in what he *intends* to communicate and in what he *actually* communicates. For that reason, due to the nature of inspiration there is not a false dichotomy between what the text *says* and what it *means*, because throughout the entire process by the superintendence of God, what the text says, God says; and what God says, the text says.

Fourth, another underlying phenomenon in Blomberg's assessment is a desire to distinguish himself from those who naively assume that literary works exist as autonomous aesthetic entities independent of all minds. If this is what Blomberg is

---

58. Sproul, *Explaining Inerrancy*, 43–44.

challenging, then we are ready to join him! But, we are not willing to join him *if* by authorial intent he claims that the text can mean something different than what the affirmation claims by using the supposed author's intention to change either the meaning or the historical factuality of the event and/or text. Clearly one recognizes with Hirsch, that once a person abandons the author's meaning of a text, then the meaning of a text can be altered. If authorial intention no longer stabilizes the text *then anyone can reread that text according to the emotional, psychological, historical conditions, presuppositions, and biases.* However, if the meaning of a text is not the creative invention of a reader, but the purposeful product of an author, then the meaning of a text cannot be readily altered. The author and the text hang or fall together; to abandon the authors intention is to abandon the possibility of an objective meaning for any text.

But this stress on the importance of the author's intention can be misapplied. For example, it is now often assumed, in the interest of hermeneutics, the scriptural writers did not intend to communicate history in their revelatory writings. The issue, however, is the exegete is bound to the text that expresses the mind of God and the writer's purpose. He has no other access to this purpose except by way of the text taken in its literary and historical context.

During the Summit II meeting of the ICBI on hermeneutics, Carl F. H. Henry addresses an evangelical "use and abuse" of authorial intention. In order to capture the force of his argument, Henry must be quoted at length.[59] He writes:

> Little did I realize that I was not the first to steal the Bible. The medieval church had kept the Book from the masses for whom it was intended and we evangelicals kept it from nurturing our own lives. But in recent years a different type of theft has emerged as some fellow evangelicals, along with non-evangelicals, wrest from the Bible segments they derogate as no longer the Word of God. *Some now even introduce authorial intention or cultural context of language as specious rationalizations for this crime against the Bible, much as some rapist might assure me that he is assaulting my wife for my own or for her good.* They misuse Scripture in order to champion as biblically true what in fact does violence to Scripture. It is one of the ironies of church history that even some professed evangelicals now speak concessively of divine revelation itself as culture-conditioned, and do so at the precise moment in Western history when the secular dogma of the cultural relativity of all truth and morality and religious beliefs need fervent challenging.[60]

---

59. One should also note that Radmacher and Preus claim, "This paper [Henry's] was the message delivered at the closing session of the Summit II: Hermeneutics Conference. It is included here because it summarizes the issues of the conference and affirms the role of the Bible in today's world." Radmacher and Preus, *Hermeneutics, Inerrancy, and the Bible*, 915.

60. Ibid., 917, emphasis added.

## Part 2—Inerrancy Defended

Abuses of authorial intention are not a new challenge. In the 1980s Henry cautioned the ICBI to not use authorial intention in such a way so as to dismiss the clear propositional statements of Scripture. However, many individuals such as Blomberg and other Neo-Evangelical scholars have failed to heed to Henry's warning.

One can find many contemporary examples to illustrate Henry's concern of an abuse of authorial intention in present-day scholarship. The first is an example from Licona's dehistoricizing of the raising of the saints in Matthew's Gospel.[61] Licona responds to his critics in a paper delivered to the Evangelical Philosophical Society, claiming, "I hope that it has become clear in this paper that my intent was not to dehistoricize a text Matthew intended as historical. If I had, that would be to deny the inerrancy of the text. Instead, what I have done is to question whether Matthew *intended* for the raised saints to be understood historically."[62] This is precisely what Henry cautioned the ICBI to avoid as an abuse of authorial intention. For in doing so, interpreters such as Licona invalidate the clear meaning of Scripture and use "authorial intention" to assault the clear propositions of the Bible.

The second illustration is the *way* Kevin Vanhoozer argues for authorial intention. In Gregory Alan Thornbury's book *Recovering Classic Evangelicalism*, he discusses the influence Henry might have in this debate on authorial intention. In the section titled "Henry Versus Vanhoozer," Thornbury remarks that one of Vanhoozer's primary complaints against Henry is that he puts "authorial intent vis á vis inerrancy, implying that Henry had little appreciation of genre and discourse. Vanhoozer refers to Henry's discussion in volume 4 of *GRA* in which Henry openly worries that a narrow focus on authorial-intent interpretation can tempt commentators to sidestep the matter of the reliability and historicity of texts."[63] Thornbury openly chastises Vanhoozer's reading of Henry, claiming he is reading Henry in the "worst possible light."[64] Thornbury claims, "If one makes the author's intent supreme, and if one says the authors intention was a genre other than historical and scientific accuracy, we have opened Pandora's Box. Once you make this move, Henry warns, you can take any problematic or disputed text as a matter of genre confusion."[65] Thornbury continues to say:

61. Geisler and Roach, "Defending Inerrancy," 61–87; Quarles, review of *Resurrection of Jesus*, 839–44; Mohler, "Devil Is in the Details."

62. Licona, "When the Saints Go Marching In."

63. Thornbury, *Recovering Classic Evangelicalism*, 106.

64. The comment by Thornbury is: "As is the case with other figures in the critical reception of Henry, Vanhoozer reads Henry in the worst possible light, namely, that Henry claims no more than one way to read a text of Scripture. Vanhoozer's conclusion, aimed at Henry, states: 'It is Scripture that reveals God, not a set of detached propositions. Revealed truths are not abstract but canonically concrete. This is our evangelical birthright—truth in all of its canonical radiance, not a diluted mess of propositionalist pottage.' If you put the choices like that, who would settle for an allusion to Esau's ill-fated stew?" Ibid., 106–7. Thornbury does not criticize Vanhoozer for raising questions against Henry's view; yet, he believes that Vanhoozer is reading Henry out of context.

65. Ibid., 107.

As we will discuss later in this volume, this is precisely the interpretive move behind crucial abandonments of inerrancy in contemporary evangelicalism. So, for example, if you are uncomfortable saying that Genesis 1 literally reveals the way God created the universe, don't worry. Simply say that the author's purpose was literary, poetic, or allegorical, and your problem is solved. This was Carl Henry's fear, and he was right to be concerned—if not with Vanhoozer, then with others who do not possess the better angels of Kevin's theological nature.[66]

Thornbury does not shy away from naming the names of those who use authorial intention to deny the inerrancy of the Bible. In the chapter of his book titled "Inerrancy Matters," Thornbury lists Peter Enns, John Schneider, Daniel Harlow, and Michael Licona as examples of individuals who have utilized this "authorial intention" argument, and have been fired from their posts over charges of violating the inerrancy of Scripture.[67] In any event, the point is that in his address at the ICBI, Henry almost prophetically foresaw many of the evangelical uses and abuses of authorial intention and the negative effects a poor use of authorial intention could have upon the doctrine of inerrancy and evangelicalism.

At this point, it is instructive to note, contrary to Blomberg's views, *how* Henry affirms that reason is operant for establishing the truth value of any text, ensuring the authors intention corresponds with the grammatical meaning of the sentence. Henry's theological method and hermeneutic opposes views such as Blomberg and Licona's, that attempt to use a supposed "author's intent" to alter, deny or contradict the grammatical meaning of the Bible (specifically in cases pertaining to the historical-factuality of the text).[68] Henry also insists that an interpreter can know the author's intent only by using the grammatical-historical method of interpretation, and that the author's intention corresponds with the grammatical meaning of the text. He rejects all theories that bifurcate authorial intent and the grammatical meaning of the Bible (e.g., theories that look for meaning behind, in front of, or beneath the text). In other words, Henry (like classic evangelicalism and the CSBI) believes interpreters must uphold the motto made famous by Walter Kaiser: "Keep your finger *on* the text!"

66. Ibid.

67. Ibid., 122.

68. Henry would oppose the notion that in order to properly understand a text, one must "read it the way they would have read it." For, according to Henry, either the original readers would have read it according to its historical, logical, grammatical meaning, or they would have not. If they do not read it according to its historical, logical, and grammatical meaning; Henry would claim they are abusing authorial intent. For Henry, there are two types of reader response. Either the present day reader can change the meaning of the text or the present day reader can change the meaning of the text by claiming the original author did not "intend" his audience to read it that way. However, according to Henry, there is only one type of logic, and due to the image of God in humanity, there is only one kind of mind. In brief, as was seen in the quote by Henry at the ICBI, any attempt by interpreters of Scripture to use "authorial intention" to override the grammatical aspects of the text, is considered a misguided approach and abusive to the Bible as the Word of God.

Part 2—Inerrancy Defended

*Fourth Level: Models of Biblical Authority and Inerrancy*

At a fourth level, Blomberg rightly notes there are two methods of affirming the inerrancy of Scripture, one being an inductive method and the other deductive. He claims:

> The *inductive approach* begins with the phenomena of the Bible itself, defines what would count as an error, analyzes Scripture carefully from beginning to end, and determines that nothing has been discovered that would qualify as errant. The *deductive approach* begins with the conviction that God is the author of Scripture, proceeds to the premise that by definition God cannot err, and therefore concludes that God's Word must be without error.... Whether following evidentialism or presuppositionalism, this deductive approach ultimately views inerrancy as a corollary of inspiration, not as something to be demonstrated from the texts of Scripture itself. If the Bible is God-breathed (2 Tim 3:16), and God cannot err, then the Bible must be inerrant.[69]

While Blomberg does not come right out and say, "I hold to the inductive approach." One can gather from the tone and overall trajectory of his writings, he follows an inductive approach to inerrancy. In our book *Defending Inerrancy*, Geisler and I respond to the claim, "Inerrancy is derived purely deductively from other teachings and is not based in an inductive study of Scripture."[70] The reason we include this objection is because many Old and New Testament scholars and those following the Biblical Theology movement, claim that we must keep our view of inerrancy accountable to the text of Scripture. I adamantly agree! Evangelicalism has always been marked by a clear commitment to the sufficiency of Scripture to address all matters pertaining to faith and practice; including the way someone approaches the very text of Scripture itself.[71]

Like Geisler and I present in *Defending Inerrancy*, Blomberg's claim hinges upon two key premises: First, the doctrine of inerrancy is not explicitly taught in the Bible. Second, deduction is not an appropriate method to understand the inerrancy of Scripture. Investigating the first point, it is apparent that neither is the doctrine of the Trinity explicitly taught in the Bible. But it is taught implicitly and logically, as is the inerrancy of the Bible. Both premises from which inerrancy is derived are necessary and logical conclusions taught in the Bible. For example, the Bible teaches that (1) it is the Word of God (John 10:35; 2 Tim 3:16), and (2) the Word of God cannot err (John 17:17; Heb 6:18). Hence, it follows logically that (3) the Bible cannot err.

The same is true with other key doctrines of the Christian faith, including: (1) The Trinity; (2) Jesus is one person; (3) Jesus is fully God; (3) Jesus is fully human.

---

69. Blomberg, *Can We Still Believe*, 121, 123.

70. Geisler and Roach, *Defending Inerrancy*, 322–23.

71. Note that Blomberg does not agree with classic evangelicalism at this point. In his book, Blomberg argues against the sufficiency of Scripture. In particular, as it pertains to secular versus biblical counseling. Blomberg, *Can We Still Believe*, 77–78.

Scripture contains all of the pieces in order to affirm each of these doctrines, however, the Bible nowhere explicitly teaches the hypostatic union or the Trinity. Nonetheless, both doctrines are biblically based doctrines, being contained implicitly in the Scriptures. For example, the Bible teaches (1) there is one God (Deut 6:4; 1 Cor 8:4), and (2) there are three distinct persons who are God: the Father, the Son, and the Holy Spirit (Matt 3:16; 28:18–20; 2 Cor 13:14). Hence, the only logical conclusion is that (3) there are three distinct persons in one and only one God (namely, the Trinity). The point being, a doctrine should not be rejected because it is taught in the Bible only implicitly and logically, not explicitly.

As it pertains to claims made by Blomberg concerning the relationship between induction and deduction, several points can be made. First of all, no one operates according to an either purely inductive or deductive method. Throughout one's daily life each individual uses induction and deduction in order to function in the space-time world. Second, it is false to claim inerrancy does not have a strong inductive basis in Scripture. For both premises from which the conclusion is derived, are the result of a complete (perfect) induction from Scripture: (1) God cannot err; (2) The Bible is the Word of God. Both of these truths result from a complete study of all the Scriptures. This is called a "perfect induction" in logic since it involves an exhaustive study of the data in limited areas. And perfect induction can come to knowledge that is certain. For example, one can be certain about the truth of the statement, "All the coins in my pocket are pennies." Likewise, the Bible is a larger but also finite (limited) area, which one can study exhaustively any given doctrine and come to a certain conclusion. That being the case, both premises on which inerrancy is based are completely inductive, and we can be certain about them.

Third, if Blomberg and others are willing to object to the deductive approach, then they must deny the laws of thought, which is both self-defeating, or they must affirm the laws of logic and agree with the only logical conclusion that can be drawn from premises 1 and 2 above is (3) the Bible cannot err. So the conclusion is a logically necessary inference from two certain premises. In order to deny this conclusion, someone must deny one or more of the premises. But it is simply untrue to argue that the only two premises from which we derive inerrancy are completely inductively based.

Fourth, a growing concern with the Biblical Theology movement is its repudiation of systematic theology. Many of these theologians believe exegesis is the begin-all and end-all of theological study. They think that what cannot be derived from "pure exegesis" is not a proper conclusion derived from Scripture. Besides being philosophically naïve, this view is badly mistaken and self-defeating. If applied to nature, it would involve the repudiation of all science, which attempts to systematically categorize and draw logical inferences from the data of nature. This is also what systematic theology tries to do with the data derived from the exegesis of Scripture. It is also self-defeating because exegesis requires the use of logical thinking and necessary inferences. These sometimes include both inductive and deductive reasoning.

Fifth, to deny that logically necessary conclusions are derived exegetically (inductively) from Scripture and their appropriate relationship to deductive reasoning, will lead to the denial of other orthodox doctrines. As has already been shown, the orthodox doctrines of the Trinity and the hypostatic union of the two natures of Christ are derived from logically necessary deductions. So too is much of orthodox Christian theology. Thus, to deny the procedure by which evangelicals derive the inerrancy of Scripture is to deny the basis for many other orthodox doctrines.

Sixth, there is a strong use of logic and deductive reasoning in the Protestant and Evangelical traditions. For example, the *Westminster Confession of Faith* speaks in chapter 1, section 6 of the "whole counsel of God . . . [is] either expressly set down in Scripture, or *by good and necessary consequence may be deduced from Scripture.*" Hence, it is clear that the use of logic and deduction is not contrary to the Protestant principles of interpretation. In fact, since the *Westminster Confession* is typically considered the pinnacle of Protestant confessions, one could make the case that the use and acceptance of deduction is one of the key marks of Protestant biblical interpretation and systematic theology. Thus, in keeping with the laws of logic, namely the law of non-contradiction, the repudiation of deduction and logical thinking excludes individuals such as Blomberg from *fully* adhering to this great interpretive tradition (even though much of his work is in complete agreement with the Protestant principles of biblical interpretation).

## 3. Blomberg's Book Serves as a Catalyst to Promote the Resurgence of Neo-Evangelical Theology (a.k.a., Limited Inerrancy).

Given what has already been noted in this article we are faced with some important questions: Where have we seen theological views of biblical authority and evangelical identity similar to Blomberg's presented in the history of evangelicalism? Do the individuals who endorsed the book (Scot McKnight at Northern Seminary; Darrell Bock at Dallas Theological Seminary; Paul Copan at Palm Beach Atlantic University; Craig Keener at Asbury Theological Seminary; and Leith Anderson, current president of the National Association of Evangelicals) each agree with Blomberg's conclusions regarding the nature of biblical inerrancy and evangelical identity? Last but not least, is there a division taking place in the broader evangelical community over biblical inerrancy and evangelical identity?

One does not have to look back very far in evangelical history to find views of biblical authority and evangelical identity similar to Blomberg's; namely, Fuller Theological Seminary. According to Harold Lindsell, Charles Fuller founded Fuller

Seminary requiring that inerrancy be in their doctrinal statement.[72] Lindsell was the first dean and with Wilbur Smith, Everett F. Harrison, and Carl Henry, they formed the first faculty. The doctrinal statement of Scripture read: "The books which form the canon of the Old and New Testament as originally given are plenary inspired and free from all error in the whole and in the part. These books constitute the written Word of God, the only infallible rule of faith and practice." Such a statement meant that the Bible is free from errors in matters of fact, science, history, and chronology, as well as in matters having to do with salvation.

In *Reforming Fundamentalism*, George M. Marsden tracks the "Crisis and Turning" at Fuller.[73] In a letter to Billy Graham, Wilbur Smith wrote, "So you see, as everyone realizes, our Seminary is split straight down the middle on the most important single question [inerrancy], apart from the Deity of Christ, that can be considered."[74] Marsden goes on to demonstrate Fuller Seminary split over the issue of biblical inerrancy and the influence of Dan Fuller, Charles Fuller's son. Dan Fuller, after being trained in some of the finest European schools, returned to Fuller Seminary. In a letter to his father, Marsden records that Dan conceded to the following points claiming evangelicals are merely playing lip service to their openness to the latest archaeological findings if they affirm that the Bible is without error in the whole and in part.[75] Marsden then goes on to note:

> Some of the chronologies in Scripture, Fuller [Dan] explained to his parents were simply wrong, and, although the errors were innocent bookkeeping errors, it was an apologetic disaster to act as though such errors in details did not exist. It made a sham of evangelical claims to take history seriously on vitally important matters as the fact of the Resurrection. *So the Fuller creed should be revised to say that the infallibility had to do with its statements on faith and practice, not its precise historical detail.* "How tragic," he observed, "that we went overboard so on this in order to make it too hot for Vassady." He also knew, as a matter of fact, that the current creed made it too hot for Jewett as well, who had resorted to letting Carnell teach the parts of his systematics courses that deal with the doctrine of Scripture. As for Dan, he was anticipating trying out his views on his seminary colleagues to "see whether the faculty can blow holes in it."[76]

As time progressed, individuals at Fuller started to deny the historicity of Adam and Eve, the historical factuality of numerous Old Testament events, and called for a revision of their doctrinal statement to reflect their new theological concessions.

---

72. Lindsell, *Battle for the Bible*, 106–21.
73. Marsden, *Reforming Fundamentalism*, 197–219.
74. Ibid., 197.
75. Ibid., 201.
76. Ibid., emphasis added.

## Part 2—Inerrancy Defended

Faculty such as George Ladd knew that questioning inerrancy could cost him his job.[77] The faculty also started to question the various methods of inerrancy: deductive vs. inductive. Many were conceding to the argument that inerrancy is a modernist convention arising from Scottish Common Sense Realism. Eventually, these concessions lead up to what was known as "Black Saturday," where the seminary faculty split over the issue of biblical inerrancy and evangelical identity.

As is probably already apparent, Blomberg's book and his vision of evangelicalism is much closer to Dan Fuller's moderate and Neo-Evangelical wing at Fuller Theological Seminary than that of ICBI. Like the faculty at Fuller, Blomberg is committed to a version of inerrancy (limited inerrancy). Blomberg's model of biblical authority tries to take the phenomena of Scripture seriously, yet it does not want to claim too much. He does not believe that historical inaccuracies about the historicity of Job and the creation of Adam matter to the overall storyline and metanarrative of Scripture. In addition, like the Neo-Evangelical faculty at Fuller, he believes that much of the modern inerrancy movement springs from Common Sense Realism. Much like Dan Fuller, Blomberg does not want to see his fellow evangelicals dismissed or fired over their views of biblical inerrancy. Last but not least, like Fuller, Blomberg does not believe that an affirmation of the total truthfulness and inerrancy (unlimited) of Scripture is required for evangelical *consistency* or *identity*. He believes that evangelicals can give up nonessential historical details, just so long as the essential historical details are true.[78]

Blomberg's views have much more in common with Fuller Seminary's Neo-Evangelicalism (limited inerrancy) than the classic evangelical views represented by the ICBI (unlimited inerrancy). The differences between classic evangelicalism (unlimited inerrancy) and Neo-Evangelicalism (limited inerrancy) can be seen in the following chart.

---

77. Ibid., 213.

78. Blomberg writes, "I may be convinced that there are good reasons for seeing a certain segment as historical, but I must distinguish between the more essential and more peripheral parts when I assess how significant someone's doubts about the segments are. As we have seen, almost nothing is at stake if Job never existed, whereas everything is at stake if Jesus never lived." Blomberg, *Can We Still Believe*, 223. Also see the list of historical details Blomberg is willing to give up or hold mediating views (177).

| Classic Evangelical<br>View of Unlimited Inerrancy | Neo-Evangelical<br>View of Limited Inerrancy |
|---|---|
| True in both whole and parts | Truth in the whole but not in the parts |
| True spiritually and scientifically | True spiritually but not always scientifically or historically |
| True in what it intends and affirms | True in what it intends, not in all it affirms |
| Truth is found in correspondence | Truth is found in intention |
| Consistent use of correspondence | Inconsistent use of correspondence |
| Divine adaptation to finitude | Divine accommodation to error—especially when they utilize pagan literature and genre criticism |
| No errors of any kind in the Bible | No major or redemptive errors in the Bible |
| All mistakes are errors | Only intentional mistakes are errors |

In response to the growing limited inerrancy and inerrancy of intention movements, a conglomeration of three hundred evangelical scholars met to form the International Council on Biblical Inerrancy. One of the primary reasons the ICBI met was to set theological boundaries and to proclaim that inerrancy matters and it provides axioms for doctrinal integrity necessary for the health of the church. Roger Nicole, in his introduction to the ICBI commentary, writes:

> It [ICBI] has as its purpose the defense and application of the doctrine of biblical inerrancy as an essential element for the authority of Scripture and a necessity for the health of the church. It was created to counter the drift from this important doctrinal foundation by significant segments of evangelicalism and the outright denial of it by other church movements.[79]

In the midst of the current controversy over the inerrancy of Scripture, present-day evangelicals must remember that the ICBI was formed in order to counter the drift away from unlimited inerrancy by Neo-Evangelicalism. It is becoming ever apparent that the conclusions reached by Blomberg in his book *Can We Still Believe The Bible?* are nothing new to the scene of evangelical theology. In fact, at the most important points his arguments resemble the same ones advocated by the Neo-Evangelicalism of Fuller Seminary. While individuals such as Bock, Copan, Keener, and so forth claim to be committed to the ICBI unlimited inerrancy, they are clearly endorsing a book committed to limited inerrancy. Moreover, especially in the publications of Bock and Keener, it is apparent they are committed to the same methodology and conclusions of Neo-Evangelical theologians and limited inerrancy.[80]

Much like the faculty of Fuller, it seems like there are a growing number of scholars willing to forego classic evangelicalism and the doctrine of unlimited inerrancy, in order to promote a version of evangelicalism compatible with so-called new

---

79. Nicole, foreword to *Explaining Biblical Inerrancy*, 22.
80. See Geisler and Farnell, *Jesus Quest*; Geisler and Roach, *Defending Inerrancy*, 193–214.

discoveries in scholarship. This trend clearly represents a split in the midst of evangelicalism over the nature of biblical *authority* and evangelical *identity*. Much like the nation of Israel, evangelical scholars and institutions quickly forget their history and for that reason, each generation is faced with their own *Battle for the Bible*. Let us hope and pray that this current debate over the nature of biblical inerrancy will not lead evangelicalism into its own "Babylonian captivity of the church"; where evangelicals bend their knee to "scholarship," and desire passionately a "seat at the table."

## CONCLUSION

In the final analysis, the last question to be answered is: Why is an evaluation of this nature and tone of Blomberg's book necessary? On the one hand, it is necessary because the issue of inerrancy is never a settled issue and it is never going to go away. Modernity presents the watching world a spectrum of issues pertaining to epistemology, authority, and controlling axioms. Evangelicals will either present a coherent affirmation of divine inerrancy or they will not. Unless evangelicals mandate that inerrancy provide a sure and stable ontological and epistemological place to stand, evangelicalism as a movement will inevitably suffer the consequences that are part-and-parcel with the modern world—namely, the breakdown of revelation and the crisis of truth. The inevitable result will be the compromise of any sure Word from God.

On the other hand, the inerrancy debate is about truth and confessional identity. Should present-day evangelicals fail to heed the warnings about the necessity of affirming the total truthfulness and integrity of Scripture, then evangelicalism as a unified theological movement will inevitably face theological compromise, if not complete apostasy and sociological concession to philosophies adverse to the nature of God and anti-Logos dogmas. Sadly, much of what qualifies as "scholarship" within ETS reflects this trend.

Last but not least, the battle for the Bible is a debate on the nature of religious authority. Is Scripture both an authoritative and totally true source of religious knowledge revealing the mind of God in matters pertaining to history, salvation, doctrine, practice, and able to bind the conscience? In many respects, present-day evangelicals answer this question claiming, either: "No, Scripture does not contain that type of truthfulness or authority," or they undermine sacred Writ as a controlling axiom by relegating and relativizing it to pagan mythology and mitigating forms of hermeneutical nihilism. In effect, Jewish and/or Pagan mythology and hermeneutical practices become the authoritative axioms for knowledge and biblical exposition. In other words, while these so called "evangelicals" repudiate inerrancy as a modernist paradigm, they too, by their own hermeneutical practices and theological concessions, reveal they are unable to escape the consequences of modernity. This is seen best in the way they synthesize the Scriptures with critical theories of knowledge and precarious forms of biblical interpretation.

Yet at the end of the day and with eternity in view, just like the faithful forefathers in the faith, let classic evangelicals always remember that just as death was unable to keep the Word of God made flesh in the grave, the crisis of revelation and truth presented by modernity and Neo-Evangelicalism cannot keep the Word of God made propositional bound to mediating epistemological and hermeneutical axioms or so-called "evangelical" synthesizes. May the Word of God stand forever!

# Chapter 14

# The Battle for the Bible Begins Anew

## PHIL FERNANDES

### INTRODUCTION

This chapter is not meant to divide brothers in Christ. Rather, it is a call to honesty. Those who call themselves evangelicals must truly be evangelicals. Now is not the time to redefine terms like inerrancy. Now is the time for evangelicals to hold each other accountable. If we sign a doctrinal statement, we must actually believe what we affirmed in that statement. We should not have the liberty to redefine the doctrines addressed in that statement. If we are permitted to do so then evangelicalism will become an empty term signifying nothing. Hence, this chapter should not be understood as an attack on Christian brothers. Rather, it is an indictment on the present state of evangelical scholarship itself.

### BATTLE FOR THE BIBLE—PART 1 (1970S)

In the 1970s, some "evangelical" scholars believed that the Bible was only true in spiritual and moral issues. They argued that the Bible contained errors in historical and scientific areas. Many other evangelicals disagreed, believing this to be a rejection of the biblical doctrine of inerrancy—the idea that the Bible is totally without error and is totally true in all that it teaches. Among these evangelicals who took a stand for inerrancy were: R. C. Sproul, J. I. Packer, Norman Geisler, Francis Schaeffer, Harold Lindsell, James Boice, Carl Henry, Earl Radmacher, and John Wenham. These evangelicals formed the 1978 International Council on Biblical Inerrancy (ICBI). At this council, the ICBI Statement was formulated and signed by 240 evangelical scholars. The ICBI Statement, article XII states:

> *We affirm* that Scripture in its entirety is inerrant, being free from all falsehood, fraud, or deceit.
>
> *We deny* that Biblical infallibility and inerrancy are limited to spiritual, religious, or redemptive themes, exclusive of assertions in the fields of history and science.[1]

Article XVIII reads:

> *We affirm* that the text of Scripture is to be interpreted by grammatico-historical exegesis.
>
> *We deny* the legitimacy of any treatment of the text or quest for sources lying behind it that leads to relativizing, dehistoricizing, or discounting its teaching.[2]

Article XIX reads:

> *We deny* that such confession is necessary for salvation. However, we further deny that inerrancy can be rejected without grave consequences, both to the individual and to the church.[3]

## THE EVANGELICAL THEOLOGICAL SOCIETY

The Evangelical Theological Society was founded in 1949. Originally, the doctrinal statement read, "The Bible alone, and the Bible in its entirety, is the Word of God written and is therefore inerrant in the autographs."[4] A second statement was later added to the doctrinal basis of ETS: "God is a Trinity, Father, Son, and Holy Spirit, each an uncreated person, one in essence, equal in power and glory."[5] To be a member of ETS, a person "must subscribe in writing annually to the Doctrinal Basis"[6] (the two doctrinal affirmations listed above: inspiration plus inerrancy, and the Trinity). In 2003, the Evangelical Theological Society embraced the ICBI Statement as the authoritative definition of the evangelical view of inerrancy.[7]

At this point, several problems should be noted. If the Evangelical Theological Society is supposed to define what an evangelical actually is, then why are inspiration,

---

1. Geisler and Roach, *Defending Inerrancy*, 29.
2. Ibid., 30.
3. Ibid.
4. Geisler and Farnell, *Jesus Quest*, 349.
5. ETS Constitution, art. III, http://www.etsjets.org/about/constitution#A3.
6. Evangelical Theological Society website.
7. Geisler and Roach, *Defending Inerrancy*, 32.

inerrancy, and the Trinity the only doctrines mentioned in the doctrinal statement? Why is there no mention of salvation by grace alone through faith alone in Jesus alone? Why is there no mention of the sinfulness of man and his inability to save himself? The virgin birth, substitutionary death, bodily resurrection, and future return of the Lord Jesus are nowhere to be found in the ETS doctrinal statement. Creation by God is also absent. (However, the deity of Christ is contained in the doctrine of the Trinity—hence it is found in the ETS doctrinal statement.)

It is assumed that evangelicals hold to these other doctrines. But, how can adherence to these other doctrines be enforced since no one is required to sign a statement with these other doctrines listed? And, to make matters worse, many so-called evangelicals actually deny or re-define inerrancy even though they have signed the ETS doctrinal statement which clearly espouses the doctrine of inerrancy.

## PROBLEMS AT ETS WITH INERRANCY

Problems with inerrancy at the Evangelical Society are not new. In 1983, Robert Gundry was removed from ETS for his midrashic (allegorical) view of the Gospels. Gundry's midrashic approach to interpreting the Gospels enabled him to explain away certain biblical miracles as metaphors, while still claiming to affirm inerrancy. In essence, Gundry was dehistoricizing the biblical text, something forbidden by article XVIII of the ICBI Statement. Since the 1978 ICBI statement is viewed as a guide to explaining what ETS means by inerrancy, Gundry was removed from the society.[8]

In 2003, 63 percent of ETS members voted to remove Open Theist Clark Pinnock from ETS membership. But, this vote failed to reach the required 67 percent for Pinnock to be removed. Besides Pinnock's Open Theist views, he also dehistoricized numerous passages from the Gospels.[9]

## BATTLE FOR THE BIBLE—PART TWO: MIKE LICONA'S NEW HISTORIOGRAPHICAL APPROACH

Mike Licona is a brother in Christ who loves the Lord. He is a great scholar and one of the leading defenders of Jesus' bodily resurrection. Evangelicals benefit greatly from reading his works. However, his views have strayed from the doctrine of inerrancy as spelled out in the ICBI Statement. In his seven-hundred-page defense of Jesus' resurrection (*The Resurrection of Jesus: A New Historiographical Approach*), he classifies the Gospels as Greco-Roman biography. Mike Licona states:

---

8. E.g., Gundry denied the historicity of the wise men visiting Jesus. See Geisler and Roach, *Defending Inerrancy*, 296.

9. Pinnock denied the historicity of the saints being raised when Jesus was crucified and the coin being found in the mouth of a fish. He also doubted the historicity of the creation, fall, flood, and tower of Babel accounts. See Pinnock, *Scripture Principle*, 119–25.

> Given the presence of phenomenological language used in symbolic manner in both Jewish and Roman literature related to a major event such as a death of an emperor or the end of a reigning king. . . . It seems to me that an understanding of the language in Matthew 27:52–53 as "special effects" with eschatological Jewish texts and thought in mind is most plausible.[10]

Hence, Licona is saying that, using his new historical approach, he believes it is plausible that the saints who rose when Jesus was crucified did not really rise. Matthew was using figurative language—it was not a literal, actual, historical miracle.[11]

Licona also believes the soldiers falling to the ground when Jesus identified himself as "I Am" is a possible embellishment.[12] In addition, Licona admitted, in a debate with Bart Ehrman at Southern Evangelical Seminary, that he believes that John probably altered the date of Jesus' crucifixion—Jesus did not actually die on the Passover.[13] Licona states concerning the Gospels:

> There is somewhat of a consensus among contemporary scholars that the Gospels belong to the genre of Greco-Roman biography (*bios*). *Bioi* offered the ancient biographer great flexibility for rearranging material and inventing speeches in order to communicate the teachings, philosophy, and political beliefs of the subject, and they often included legend. Because *bios* was a flexible genre, it is often difficult to determine where history ends and legend begins.[14]

Licona verbally (and in writing) affirms the doctrine of inerrancy. But, is his hermeneutic consistent with the evangelical doctrine of inerrancy? Former ICBI president R. C. Sproul stated:

"As the former & only President of ICBI during its tenure and as the original framer of the Affirmations and Denials of the Chicago Statement on Inerrancy, I can say categorically that Dr. Michael Licona's views are not even remotely compatible with the unified Statement of ICBI."[15]

Norman Geisler, one of the three living framers of the Chicago Statement on Biblical Inerrancy, stated that "Licona claims to be an inerrantist of the ETS and ICBI variety, but ICBI framers have flatly rejected his views."[16] J. I. Packer, another framer of the Chicago Statement, wrote: "As a framer of the ICBI Statement on biblical inerrancy who studied Greco-Roman literature at an advanced level, I judge Mike Licona's view that, because the Gospels are semi-biographical, details of the narratives

---

10. Licona, *Resurrection of Jesus*, 552.
11. Ibid., 548–53.
12. Ibid., 306.
13. Geisler and Farnell, *Jesus Quest*, 353.
14. Licona, *Resurrection of Jesus*, 34.
15. Letter to Norman Geisler, May 22, 2012.
16. Geisler and Farnell, *Jesus Quest*, 354.

may be regarded as legendary and factually erroneous, to be both academically and theologically unsound."[17]

Despite Licona's claim to believe in inerrancy, he stated, "I mean I believe in biblical inerrancy but I also realized that biblical inerrancy is not one of the fundamental doctrines of Christianity."[18] If Licona means by "fundamental doctrine" a doctrine essential to salvation, then he is correct. For, the Bible nowhere says that someone has to believe in biblical inerrancy to be saved. But, if he means that inerrancy is not essential to conservative, biblical Christianity or evangelicalism, then he is mistaken. If someone trusts in the true Jesus of the Bible alone for salvation, I do not question their salvation. However, if someone claims to be an evangelical while either implicitly or explicitly denying inerrancy, then he is in no way a true evangelical. While inerrancy is not essential to a person's salvation, it is essential to being an evangelical.

It should also be noted that, even though inerrancy is not essential to salvation, it is inconsistent with robust Christian belief. If someone believes the Bible contains errors, how is one to know whether or not the passages that deal with salvation through Christ contain some of those errors?

## ASSESSMENT OF THE SITUATION: REMARKS, QUESTIONS & SUGGESTIONS

First, evangelicals must be required to do more than merely say we believe in inerrancy—we must have a hermeneutic consistent with inerrancy. A conservative view of inerrancy is inconsistent with a very loose, liberal hermeneutic. Someone could claim that he holds to inerrancy but believes every miracle in the Bible is a metaphor. With the "any-hermeneutic-allowed" approach to inerrancy, the doctrine of inerrancy becomes totally void of meaning.

Second, why would the Gospel authors write Greco-Roman literature when they had and respected 1,500 years of Jewish religious literature? I see no good reason for the Gospel authors to include figurative or poetic miracles in their writings. Why would the Gospel authors complicate issues by reporting metaphorical miracles, side by side, with historical miracles while trying to convince their readers to believe in the historical miracles? This would be very counterproductive.

Third, we should allow Scripture to interpret Scripture rather than allowing supposed human wisdom concerning genre to interpret Scripture. Evangelicals should allow the biblical text to speak for itself. We must use proper exegesis (taking from the text what is actually in the text) rather than eisegesis (putting into the text some foreign meaning based on something outside the text). The rising of the saints when Jesus was crucified (Matt 27:52–53) sounds like historical reporting, as the entire context shows. The context of the entire passage in question is not figurative at all—the

17. Letter dated May 8, 2014.
18. Licona, "Michael Licona Discusses What Makes a Biblical Contradiction."

saints rising is historical narrative in the midst of a larger historical narrative (Matt 27:45–56, for instance).[19] Could not someone using Licona's "New Historiography" say that they accept inerrancy but believe the virgin birth and bodily resurrection are merely metaphors? Obviously, Licona's approach can lead to further deviations from evangelicalism.

Fourth, we should determine genre by finding the meaning of the text, not the meaning of the text by the supposed genre. If Licona is correct and the proper way to interpret the passion accounts is by referring to Greco-Roman literature, then are we to believe the church has been mistaken about these Gospel miracles until Mike Licona discovered his "new historiographical approach?" This seems highly unlikely. Dr. Tom Howe of Southern Evangelical Seminary states: "But how can an interpreter attempt to classify a piece of writing into its appropriate genre unless he is able to read and understand what the text is saying prior to deciding its genre?"[20]

Fifth, a minimal facts case for the resurrection, based on the consensus of the vast majority of leading New Testament scholars, is a great way to defend the resurrection. But, we must never allow the minimal facts case to evolve into a minimal facts evangelicalism or a minimal facts New Testament scholarship. Evangelical scholars should not have to appeal to the vast majority of New Testament scholars before deciding if a Gospel miracle is figurative or literal. We can appeal to the consensus of leading New Testament scholars to build a case for the resurrection. But, our interpreting of the biblical text must be consistent with our belief in the doctrine of inerrancy. In debate, we can take what our opponents give us and argue from there. But, we must not begin to agree with our opponents when this takes us outside of evangelical beliefs.

Please note there is nothing wrong if an evangelical apologist feels led to only defend God's existence, Jesus' resurrection, and/or Christ's deity. There is nothing wrong with an evangelical apologist deciding not to argue for biblical inerrancy with non-believers. We cannot defend everything, so we must be selective—time is of the essence. If the evangelical apologist chooses to defend only "mere Christianity" or "essential Christianity," that is fine. But, if this apologist claims to be an evangelical, he must, at the very least, acknowledge inerrancy in all its fullness regardless of whether or not he decides to devote his ministry to a defense of this doctrine. The evangelical apologist can say, "Even *if* you are right [i.e., playing 'the devil's advocate' by dealing with a hypothetical] and the saints did not rise, the evidence for Christ's resurrection still stands." On the other hand, the so-called evangelical ceases to be a true evangelical

---

19. Other historical events in this passage include: darkness falling on the land, a question from Jesus on the cross, discussion about what Jesus meant, someone putting a sponge with sour wine on a reed and offering it to Jesus, Jesus cries out and dies, the veil in the temple is torn, an earthquake, the centurion's confession that Jesus is the Son of God, and the identification of three women watching the crucifixion from a distance. There is no hint in the context of the passage that anything is to be taken in any other sense than historical.

20. Howe, "Does Genre Determine Meaning?"

when he says, "I think you are right that the saints did not rise. I am only arguing that Jesus rose. The resurrection of these saints is merely a metaphor."

Sixth, one of the reasons why Licona is willing to remove from the pages of history the saints rising during Christ's crucifixion seems to be that it lacks multiple attestation—it is only mentioned in Matthew's Gospel.[21] Two things should be noted here. First, much of accepted ancient history lacks multiple attestation. And, second, this could create a license to remove any Gospel miracles that lack multiple attestation. For instance, the man born blind who was healed by Jesus is only mentioned in chapter nine of John's Gospel. It lacks multiple attestation. What would stop Bible readers from removing this miracle from history? Since the passage talks about the blind spiritually seeing and those who think they spiritually see remaining blind, why not turn this miracle into a mere parable or some type of poetic device? Where does it stop? How many Gospel miracles can be removed if we allow some principle like multiple attestation to influence our decisions concerning the historicity of Gospel miracles?

Could it be that Matthew is the only Gospel author to record the saints rising during Jesus' death because, as the early church fathers told us (in direct opposition to theories proposed by many New Testament scholars today), he may have written the first Gospel while the church was still based in Jerusalem? Many of his readers may have been in Jerusalem for the Passover Feast during which Jesus was crucified. They may have already have known that people were raised while Jesus died on the cross. Hence, Matthew's inclusion of this event in his Gospel could be viewed as extra, corroborating evidence for the uniqueness of Christ and his death. The other three Gospels were written later than Matthew's Gospel (according to the early church fathers—contrary to the views of most contemporary New Testament scholars) and the authors may have chosen to leave this event out of their narratives since it did not fit with their purposes for the writing of their Gospels.

Seventh, I believe we need to enlarge the ETS doctrinal statement—it needs to contain more than just the Trinity, inspiration, and inerrancy. Other doctrines such as the virgin birth, substitutionary death, bodily resurrection, and visible return need to be added—the deity of Christ is already contained in the doctrine of the Trinity (which is already found in the ETS statement). Should creation by God be added to the ETS doctrinal statement? Or, should the Evangelical Theological Society be open to allowing membership to theistic evolutionists?

Should ETS require, in writing, the belief that man is fallen and sinful, and that he cannot save himself? Should evangelical theologians be required to sign a statement acknowledging salvation by grace alone, through faith alone, in Jesus alone?

What about the doctrine of eternal conscious torment? Today, many "evangelicals" now believe in annihilation of the wicked and deny eternal conscious torment. Are those who hold to annihilation of the wicked really evangelicals? What about

---

21. Licona, *Resurrection of Jesus*, 548.

God's infallible foreknowledge of future free choices? Are Open Theists (those who deny that God infallibly foreknows future free choices) true evangelicals? Do we really even know anymore what evangelicalism is? We assume scholars believe certain doctrines, but if these doctrines are not in the doctrinal statement, can we be confident that professing evangelicals actually embrace these beliefs?

I do not claim to have the authority or the knowledge to answer every one of the above questions. Still, that does not dismiss the fact that these questions need to be answered. If they are not answered then evangelicalism will be an incoherent movement with adherents that share little in common.

If it is difficult to hold evangelicals accountable to a written statement, how can they be held accountable to those essential or important doctrines that are not clearly annunciated in that statement? It seems that more emphasis on christological and soteriological doctrines in the ETS doctrinal statement is needed. It is rather difficult to take a stand for evangelical convictions when no one knows exactly what these convictions are.

## CONCLUDING REMARKS

If the majority of evangelical scholars choose to change the definition and implications of the ICBI doctrine of inerrancy, then evangelicalism itself will have changed. If this is the case, then I am no longer an evangelical; I will have to call myself a "conservative evangelical." By this I mean that I still hold to the ICBI statement on inerrancy.

However, if the majority of evangelical scholars choose to retain the ICBI definition of inerrancy and its hermeneutical implications, then I am still an evangelical. In that case, then those who embrace Licona's new hermeneutic would be "Neo-Evangelicals," not evangelicals. I believe Mike Licona's new hermeneutic, if widely embraced, will build a wedge between evangelical scholarship and intelligent lay evangelicals who are less impressed with the "findings" of current New Testament scholarship. The intelligent lay evangelicals that I know do not tolerate the practice of interpreting Gospel miracles in a figurative way. If the Evangelical Theological Society and evangelical seminaries accept the new hermeneutic, many lay evangelicals will look for a new "back to the Bible" movement. Intelligent lay evangelicals will lose trust in any "evangelical" seminary which does not take a firm stand in favor of the doctrine of inerrancy as spelled out by the ICBI statement.

At the very least, there is an urgent need to clearly define exactly what evangelicals must believe to be evangelical. We may have to differentiate between "conservative evangelicals," "evangelicals," and "Neo-Evangelicals." Distinctions must be made, or "evangelical" will be a meaningless term, assuming that this is not already the case.

Chapter 15

# Inerrancy as a Litmus Test of Evangelical Orthodoxy?
## Clarifications on Carl F. H. Henry's View

CHRISTOPHER T. HAUN

Daniel Wallace was correct when he pointed out that Carl F. H. Henry remained averse to setting biblical inerrancy as the litmus test of orthodoxy. But any attempt to enlist Henry in the cause of diminishing the importance of inerrancy among evangelicals would be grossly unwarranted. Yet that seems like direction Wallace may have been attempting to lead his readers when he wrote:

> And it is this very problem that one of the architects of modern evangelicalism, Carl Henry (who could hardly be condemned as being soft on inerrancy!), addressed in his book, *Evangelicals in Search of Identity*. It seems that many evangelicals are still not listening. And yet Henry saw, forty years ago, that the evangelical church was making inerrancy *the* litmus test of orthodoxy to its discredit.[1]

There is no actual contention here on this point. The notion that a believer can legitimately lay claim on being a bona fide, orthodox, evangelical Christian while also holding that the Bible may contain errors is not in question. The authors and signers of the Chicago Statement on Biblical Inerrancy, for example, said essentially the same thing in article XIX.[2] There seems to be a misrepresentation of "many evangelicals"

---

1. Wallace, review of *Defining Inerrancy*.
2. Sproul, *Explaining Biblical Inerrancy*, 61. While Carl Henry did not participate directly in

here. There is also a misrepresentation of Henry's view based on omission. The flip side of Henry's view needs to be heard. For while Henry held that while inerrancy is not a test of evangelical *authenticity*, he did maintain that it still remains a test of evangelical *consistency*. That is, one could be saved and orthodox on all other essential evangelical beliefs and not believe in inerrancy. Nonetheless, a staunch commitment to biblical inerrancy remains vital to the life and endurance of the Christian church.

In *Evangelicals in America*, Ronald Nash praised Henry as representing "the very best of evangelical scholarship over a period of some forty years."[3] In the preface, Nash noted that Carl Henry himself had been "kind enough to offer suggestions and corrections as this book neared completion."[4] This is surely enough to make it rank highly as an authoritative source for Henry's views on the evangelical movement and inerrancy. The first of several helpful clarifications about Henry's view Nash provided is:

> Carl Henry, himself a firm advocate of inerrancy, agreed with Lindsell that the doctrine of biblical inerrancy was in fact being denied in a number of institutions that were supposed to be evangelical. But *Henry disagreed with Lindsell's insistence that the doctrine of inerrancy was the litmus test of being a true evangelical. However much Henry regretted the fact that some evangelicals*

---

the Chicago Council on Biblical Inerrancy or sign the statement produced there he was extremely interested in it and did affirm its articles later. Henry also played important roles in the subsequent ICBI summits and statements.

3. Nash, *Evangelicals in America*, 89–90. Nash's tribute to Henry may be helpful for those who are not familiar with him:

> While Carl F. H. Henry's name is not nearly so familiar to the general public as that of Billy Graham or Jerry Falwell, he has probably had more influence on the development of contemporary Evangelicalism than anyone, save Graham. Without question, Carl Henry is the foremost evangelical theologian of the twentieth century. . . . He was undoubtedly the intellectual leader of the evangelical movement that began in the late 1940s. When Fuller Seminary was started in the late 1940s, Henry was a member of the founding faculty. . . . In 1956, Henry left Fuller to become the founding editor of *Christianity Today*. After leaving the journal in 1968, Henry taught at such schools as Eastern Baptist Seminary, Trinity Evangelical Divinity School, Calvin Theological Seminary, and Hillsdale College. . . . Henry is the author or editor of more than thirty books. The culmination of his publishing activity is his massive six-volume work *God, Revelation and Authority*. According to Henry, the time has come to be done with nebulous views of the Christian God and with skepticism about either humankind's ability to attain knowledge about God or God's ability to communicate truth. In Henry's view, the entire enterprise of Christian theology must be grounded on God's self-revelation. . . . Revealed religion is possible because God has made humankind in his image and has given him ability to perceive the trust that God has revealed. Carl Henry represents the very best of evangelical scholarship over a period of some forty years.

4. Ibid., preface.

*were wavering on the doctrine of inerrancy*, he was not quite ready—on that count alone—to dismiss them from the evangelical camp.⁵

Second, Nash also provided insight into why Henry wasn't willing to make inerrancy *the* litmus test:

> There are several aspects to Henry's stand on this issue: (1) Some religious cults (for example, the Jehovah's Witnesses) that are decidedly non-evangelical accept biblical inerrancy. Therefore, an acceptance of inerrancy cannot be the only test of true Evangelicalism; (2) nonetheless, *Henry maintains, inerrancy is normative for evangelicals; it is a position that evangelicals should accept*; (3) but Henry believes it is too extreme to say that someone is not really an evangelical if he or she rejects inerrancy while still subscribing to all the great historical creeds; (4) *it would be more accurate, Henry thinks, to say such a person is an inconsistent evangelical.*⁶

Third, Nash also portrays Henry's attitude about the critical importance of evangelical scholars holding firmly to the doctrine of inerrancy:

> Have the defenders of inerrancy answered all the challenges? Have they resolved all the problems? Carl Henry admits that they have not. But, Henry counters, while the list of alleged errors in the Bible has grown shorter over the years, the list of the errors made by critics of Scripture grows longer. While the inerrancy case is not helped by simply ignoring the problems, Henry declares, the history of the attack on inerrancy provides grounds for optimism that future discoveries will resolve the remaining difficulties. *The critically important question is whether evangelical scholars approach the Bible with the conviction that it is wholly trustworthy and reliable and that all of its teaching is the word of God, who cannot lie.*⁷

These same positions are clear in the words Henry himself penned:

(1) Inerrancy is the evangelical heritage, the historic commitment of the Christian church.⁸

(2) Evangelical scholars are fully aware that the doctrine of the Bible controls all other doctrines of the Christian faith.⁹

(3) Evangelicals do not dispute the fact that for a time at least Christianity may function with an impaired doctrine of Scripture. But it does so at its own peril and inevitably must then lose much of its essential message.¹⁰

---

5. Ibid., 98, emphasis added.

6. Ibid., 117, emphasis added. Nash also wrote, "For Henry's own views on inerrancy, see Henry, *God, Revelation and Authority*, vol. 4, 129–242."

7. Ibid., 101–2, emphasis added.

8. Henry, *Carl Henry at His Best*, 29.

9. Ibid., 61.

10. Ibid. Excerpted from *Frontiers in Modern Theology*, 139.

(4) If the strength of American evangelicalism rests in its high view of Scripture, its weakness lies in a tendency to neglect the frontiers of formative discussion in contemporary theology[11]

(5) It is no accident that those who deplore the concept of biblical inerrancy are increasingly uncomfortable with the doctrine of biblical inspiration as well, and prefer to speak instead, sometimes quite amorphously at that, only of the authority of Scripture.[12]

(6) The first thing the Bible says about itself is not its inerrancy or its inspiration, but its authority. . . . Just as in the Gospels the most important thing is the incarnation, death and resurrection, while the how of the incarnation, the virgin birth, lies in the hinterland; so also in respect to the doctrine of Scripture, while inspiration is as clearly taught as the virgin birth, it lies rather in the hinterland. The Bible teaches is authority and inspiration explicitly, while inerrancy, it seems to me, is an inference from this.[13]

(7) Those who reject inerrancy have never adduced any objective principle, either biblical, philosophical, or theological, that enables them to distinguish between those elements which are supposedly errant in Scripture and those that are not.[14]

(8) An unregenerate inerrantist is spiritually worse off than a regenerate errantist. But an unstable view of religious knowledge and authority jeopardizes not only an adequate definition of regeneration but one's insistence on its absolute necessity. The alternatives therefore seem much like choosing whether to have one's right or left leg amputated.[15]

(9) If one asks what, in a word, eclipsed the biblical doctrine of the inspiration of Scripture, what theological redefinition of inspiration in nonconceptual categories, and what encouraged neo-Protestant denial of inspiration as a decisive New Testament concept, the answer is modern biblical criticism.[16]

In summary, the parts of Henry's view that Wallace neglected to mention are:

(1) Biblical inerrancy is the evangelical heritage.

(2) Inerrancy is the historic commitment of the Christian church.

(3) Inerrancy is normative for evangelicals.

(4) Inerrancy is the position evangelicals should accept.

---

11. Ibid., 62.

12. Ibid., 28–29.

13. Ibid., 28. Note that Henry does not say it is a "mere inference" as if a logical inference of implications of one doctrine stem into another doctrine were a bad thing. Henry was a champion of the validity and importance of logic. He seems to be saying that those who believe that the Bible is divinely inspired should also see that it follows logically that the divinely inspired scriptures cannot possibly contain error.

14. Ibid., 29.

15. Ibid.

16. Ibid.

(5) Henry regretted the fact that some evangelicals were wavering on the doctrine of inerrancy. (6) One cannot be a consistent evangelical while denying inerrancy.

(7) A denial of inerrancy is an impaired view of Scripture.

(8) It is "critically important" for evangelical scholars to hold to an uncompromising view of biblical inerrancy.

(9) Those who hold an impaired view of inerrancy probably hold an impaired view of biblical inspiration as well.

(10) Those who deny inerrancy have no objective principle by which to distinguish truth from error in the Bible.

(11) The doctrine of the Bible controls all other doctrines of the Christian faith.

(12) Evangelicalism denies inerrancy at its own peril and inevitably loses much of its essential message.

(13) The strength of American evangelicalism rests in its high view of Scripture (which involved the belief in inerrancy).

When Henry was asked about the possibility of reliving his life and redoing whatever he could, he responded:

> From the outset of my Christian walk I have treasured the Book that speaks of the God of ultimate beginnings and ends, and illumines all that falls between. . . . An evangelical Christian believes incomparable good news: that Christ died in the stead of sinners and arose the third day as living head of the church of the twice-born, the people of God, whose mission is mandated by the scripturally given Word of God. The term evangelical—whose core is the "evangel"—therefore embraces the best of all good tidings. . . . That good news as the Apostle Paul makes clear, is validated and verified by the sacred Scriptures. Those who contrast the authority of Christ with the authority of Scripture do so at high risk. Scripture gives us the authentic teaching of Jesus and Jesus exhorted his apostles to approach Scripture as divinely authoritative. There is no confident road into the future for any theological cause that provides a fragmented Scriptural authority and—in consequence—an unstable Christology. Founded by the true and living Lord, and armed with the truthfulness of Scripture, the church of God is invincible. Whatever I might want to change in this pilgrim life, it would surely not be any of these high and holy commitments.[17]

What does all this add up to? Clearly Henry held firmly that belief that inerrancy is critical if not crucial to the orthodoxy of the evangelical church—at least in any vital and enduring sense. In view of all these statements, it is difficult see how it does not add up to the belief that inerrancy is ultimately (if not immediately) a kind of litmus test for orthodoxy. The paradox may be stated this way:

---

17. Carson and Woodbridge, *God and Culture*, 392–93.

*An evangelical can remain orthodox and evangelical without being an inerrantist; but evangelicalism cannot remain orthodox when evangelicals are not inerrantists.*

Chapter 16

# Can We Still Believe Critical Evangelical Scholars?
## The Danger from Within

F. DAVID FARNELL

### INTRODUCTION: A CALL TO ALARM

My ancestors hail from England. My great grandparents came from Staffordshire County, England, and emigrated to America at the end of the nineteenth century. My name David reflects my great grandfather David Farnell. My great grandmother was Rhoda Griffiths Farnell, whose life exhibited a strong commitment to the Word of God. She constantly prayed for the safety of my father, her grandson, who fought, in the American Army, alongside the British Eighth Army, in World War II in North Africa and Italy. According to my father, his grandmother always had her afternoon tea with biscuits, as well as her mincemeat pies at Christmas that reflected her ancestry. My father always was thankful for his British grandmother's constant prayers. Her prayers brought him back safe from that horrific global conflict. Once he was home safe, she soon passed into glory speaking of seeing "God's shining light." He became a Christian because his grandmother never ceased praying. I believe that I am in ministry due also to her prayers.

When my great-grandparents left England, England had experienced many centuries of a global influence for Christianity, for it was responsible for evangelizing most of the known world. Wherever the British Empire went, British missionaries followed. Indeed, the Great Awakening in America was stirred by such a great British preacher as George Whitfield in 1730–1740. No other country in the nineteenth century, not even the United States, could claim such a heritage when my ancestors came to the United States.

Today, many Christian churches and cathedrals in England are boarded up or now serve as museums or bars. British newspapers declare Christianity dead in England.[1] Indeed, even the Archbishop of England declared that she is a "post-Christian nation."[2] The British and Scottish universities are spiritually dead, yet the irony is that American evangelicals send their students to be trained at these prestigious institutions. Iain Murray, in his excellent book *A Scottish Christian Heritage*,[3] catalogued "The Tragedy of the Free Church of Scotland," wherein the University of Aberdeen, once a lighthouse for the inerrancy of God's Word, fell by the wayside and now is a center of virulently anti-biblical thinking that influences many young scholars who now attend its hallowed halls and whose hearts so rapidly turn away from childlike faith in the glorious gospel of Jesus Christ.

What caused Christianity in England and Scotland to fail so decisively? What turned Aberdeen and other once great Christian universities away from a vital belief in God's Word and trust in the Savior, the Lord Jesus Christ? Neither threats from twentieth-century communism nor the might of the Nazis were able to defeat the Christian heritage of England and Scotland. Christianity fell from within, from the carelessness of her clergy and her people who did not recognize the danger (Acts 20:28–31) inside her own gates; from self-professing academics who claimed "discipleship" of Jesus but were not genuinely or firmly committed to his Word (Matt 10:37–38; 16:24–27) but instead with evangelistic zeal championed radical theories of German critics who assaulted God's Word and had long ago lost their way spiritually. These theories destroyed the faith of the preachers that they were training in these schools, who, in turn, weakened or destroyed the faith of those who attended the sermons of these luke-warm clergy ("I wish that you were either hot or cold but you are lukewarm"—Rev 3:15–17). The British and Scottish Christian heritage was destroyed internally by its own membership.

America now is facing the same crisis that destroyed Christianity *from within* in the United Kingdom. Soon "Ichabod" or "the glory has departed" will be written about America's Christian heritage as was with England and Scotland. American evangelicals now send their best and brightest to radical schools in Germany, but especially England and Scotland, where long ago God's Word was weakened, rejected, and is now mocked. These Continental- and British-trained evangelical American scholars hold vast influential sway in seminaries founded in the United States at the turn of the twentieth century; schools and seminaries that once fought firmly for God's Word in the modernist-fundamentalist struggle that destroyed mainline denominations in

1. Ross, "Ageing Church of England."
2. Ross et al., "Former Archbishop of Canterubry."
3. Murray, *Scottish Christian Heritage*.

the United States in the first decades of that century. America evangelicalism is being threatened, not from without, but from within its own ranks. Scholarship now reigns over Lordship; radicalism over spiritual renewal and revival. The light of God's Word becomes enveloped in a growing darkness and skepticism rather than a vibrancy of trust.

As a professor of New Testament, I train seminary students in New Testament language and literature who come to The Master's Seminary from literally around the world (e.g., former Soviet Union countries, Russia, China, North Korea). These students are a monumental testimony that communism and atheistic dictatorships are not able to weaken God's people or their trust in his Word. These students, their families, indeed, their ancestors faced the onslaught from without. The faithful in Russia, China, and Korea withstood the danger from without. But today, *the influx of radical scholarship from within now threatens God's people in these nations as the outward evil could not*. Indeed, Russian, Chinese, and Korean Christians were safer when facing the KGB, Chinese secret police, and Korean tyranny than they are with evangelicals now trained in Continental and British Universities. This series will demonstrate the foundational truth of this latter assessment of the grave danger from within. These countries are now being weakened by the influx of cults and heretics, as well as radicalized, doubting Christian academics within evangelicalism.

Every Christian generation must be willing to take a stand for the Word against those whose goal is to destroy God's people from within, whether these do so deliberately, carelessly, or unwittingly. Always must the faithful be vigilant. A book I have written, along with apologist Norman Geisler, entitled *The Jesus Quest: The Danger from Within*, has traced this danger being faced now by Christian evangelicals. The book details the shocking degeneration of the spiritual vitality of evangelical seminaries and churches that have been infected by scholarship that reigns over the Lordship of Jesus and his Word. The next article will briefly trace how America at the turn of the twentieth century fought off the last conflict from within, but now is rapidly losing the spiritual battle once again from within. As England and Scotland had suffered in the loss of their Christian heritage, so also American evangelicalism is traveling rapidly down the same path toward an irreversible destruction of trust in the inerrancy of God's Word.

## THOSE WHO DO NOT LEARN THE LESSONS OF CHURCH HISTORY

At the beginning of the twentieth century, in World War I the fires of destruction engulfed Europe. In the United Kingdom, the privilege of being a torch light for the gospel had been extinguished, the embers growing cold and dark. The shameful irony of that period was that while Charles Darwin, the man who singlehandedly did more damage to the church than any other in recent times with his preposterous hypothesis of evolution that had no true scientific foundation, was honored by being enshrined in Westminster Abbey. Meanwhile John Knox, the great Presbyterian reformer who was one of the greatest champions of the gospel in modern times, lies buried under a parking lot with a small plate marking the spot. Oddly, a cryptic remark by German physician Albert Schweitzer in his book written at that time, spoke of the infiltration of the German universities long ago by a group doing great damage to the church in Germany known by the name of the "illuminati."[4]

In America during this period, a similar shadow of darkness was attempting to extinguish the glorious light of the gospel. The Great Awakening of the eighteenth century had long lost its influence. America's churches grew spiritually cold and dead, yet a small remnant remained within them. Bible colleges that were originally founded for the proclamation of the gospel in the "Colonies" had grown intellectually but decayed spiritually. Harvard, Yale, Princeton, all originally designed to train preachers, were fountainheads of virulent atheism and rampant unbelief. This period in America was marked by several characteristics:

## AS IN THE UNITED KINGDOM WHO HAD TREAD A SIMILAR PATH PREVIOUSLY . . .

(1) Evolution had gained hold in Christian institutions with Genesis 1–11 being regarded as symbolic fiction or worse, a fairy-tale, instead of genuine history of the Divine creation of man in God's image. Adam and Eve were regarded as symbolic rather than mankind's first parents. The catastrophism of a worldwide flood, so evidenced in the geologic columns, was dismissed as either a mere local flood or so much literary fiction.

(2) Higher criticism, what is known today as "historical criticism," assaulted not only the Old Testament but also the New Testament. Virulent doubt and unbelief pervaded the interpretation of every book of the Bible.

(3) The Gospel records—Matthew, Mark, Luke, and John—were dismissed as untrue, fictional or at best, symbolic rather than historical documents of Jesus' life.

(4) American denominations were training their clergy with scholarship for their religious schools and churches from German and British institutions that had long ago turned hostile to the Word of God. Future American preachers sat under prestigious professors from Oxford, Cambridge, Aberdeen, Tübingen, Göttingen, Harvard, Yale, etc., whose ears were filled with anti-biblical theories that denied the foundational historicity and factuality of the biblical text. The "fire in the bellies" for preaching God's Word was diminished by influencing the next generation of preachers. One could characterize the period with Jesus' words in Matthew 23:15, "Woe to you, scribes and Pharisees, hypocrites, because you travel around on sea and land to

---

4. Schweitzer wrote an enigmatic statement in this work, that many theologians in German "wrote under the impression of the immense influence exercised by the order of the Illuminati at the end of the eighteenth century." Schweitzer, *Quest of the Historical Jesus*, 4.

make one proselyte; and when he becomes one, you make him twice as much a son of hell as yourselves."

(5) The American Christian atmosphere filled with a desire for new thinking, i.e., "novelty" in its colleges and schools. Faithfulness to God's Word, echoing Paul's command in 2 Timothy 2:2 "The things which you have heard from me in the presence of many witnesses, entrust these to faithful men who will be able to teach others also," was dismissed as old-fashioned, not in keeping with the modern world.

(6) Churches dismissed inerrancy. Errancy pervaded every part of Christian churches and schools. Infallibility, the term for inerrancy of the time, was redefined to include errors.

(7) As a result, Jesus was lost. The first search for the "historical Jesus" was being conducted because the Gospels had lost credibility in mainline denominations. The Jesus of the Gospels was considered fictitious, so scholars searched for him in unbelieving ways.

In this dark time for America, a faithful remnant began praying. The precious Spirit of God sovereignly demonstrated his mercy to those who were praying for revival. As chapters 11 and 12 have noted, in 1909, God moved two Christian laymen, wealthy California oil magnates who were brothers named Lyman and Milton Stewart, to set aside a large sum of money for issuing twelve volumes that would set forth the fundamentals of the Christian faith and which were to be sent free of charge to ministers of the gospel, missionaries, Sunday School superintendents, and others engaged in aggressive Christian work through the English-speaking world. A committee of twelve men who were known to be sound in the faith was chosen to have the oversight of the publication of these volumes. Entitled *The Fundamentals*, they were a twelve-volume set published between 1910 and 1917 that presented the fundamentals of the Christian faith. Three million individual volumes were distributed. R. A. Torrey related his own personal knowledge and experience with these volumes in the following terms:

> Rev. Dr. A. C. Dixon was the first Executive Secretary of the Committee, and upon his departure for England Rev. Dr. Louis Meyer was appointed to take his place. Upon the death of Dr. Meyer the work of the Executive Secretary developed upon me. We were able to bring out these twelve volumes according to the original plan. Some of the volumes were sent to 300,000 ministers and missionaries and other workers in different parts of the world. On the completion of the twelve volumes as originally planned the work was continued through The King's Business, published at 536 South Hope St., Los Angeles, California. Although a larger number of volumes were issued than there were names on our mailing list, at last the stock became exhausted, but appeals for them kept coming in from different parts of the world.[5]

---

5. Torrey, preface to *Fundamentals*.

An immediate impact of *The Fundamentals* was the alerting of God's people regarding the worsening spiritual condition that the church was experiencing. God's people issued a call to assemble throughout America, rallying in defense of God's inerrant Word. Warren Wiersbe related, "At that time in history, Fundamentalism was become a force to reckon with, thanks to effective preachers, popular Bible conferences and the publications that taught 'the fundamentals' and also exposed the growing apostasy of that day . . . It was a time of growth and challenge."[6] From May 25 to June 1, 1919, six thousand Christians met in Philadelphia at the "World Conference on Christian Fundamentals." W. H. Griffith Thomas chaired the Resolutions Committee, while popular well-known fundamentalist preachers spoke for those days, such as W. B. Riley, R. A. Torrey, Lewis Sperry Chafer, James M. Gray, and William L. Pettingill. Delegates came from forty-two states in America, most of the Canadian provinces, as well as seven foreign countries to rally against the infiltration of destructive higher criticism and liberalism of the day in the church. The conference issued *God Hath Spoken* that consisted of twenty-five addresses that were delivered at the conference and stenographically recorded for posterity.[7] Unfortunately, at the turn of the twenty-first century, American churches once again are facing the *very same challenges* that they already had experienced at the beginning of the twentieth century. The hour grows dark again for the glorious light of the gospel in the United States.

## SPIRITUAL LESSONS OF CHURCH HISTORY IN THE TWENTIETH CENTURY NOW FORGOTTEN IN THE TWENTY-FIRST CENTURY

The early twentieth-century church in America faced a sobering assessment of the spiritual decay of Bible understanding and interpretation, especially in terms of the inspiration and inerrancy of Scripture. At best, a partial inspiration of Scripture was promulgated among churches, with scholars arbitrarily picking and choosing portions of the Old and New Testament to either spiritualize or allegorize away any form of literal, plain interpretation, or outrightly reject the text of Scripture completely. In light of this very serious decay of sound Bible teaching, the early twentieth-century Bible-believing community began to rally support for the Scriptures in a determined effort to counter the spiraling downward effects that mainstream denominations in America were experiencing.

Since mainline denominations were so sorely infected, large numbers withdrew from denominations deemed now spiritually beyond repair. The faithful formed a host of Bible colleges, Christian colleges, and seminaries in the first fifty-or-so years of the twentieth century that would promote the inspiration, inerrancy, and plain, normal interpretation. Moody Bible Institute was founded in 1886 by evangelist Dwight L. Moody. In 1909 Lyman Stewart funded the production of *The Fundamentals*

6. Wiersbe, foreword to *The Fundamentals*.
7. Bible Conference Committee, *God Hath Spoken*.

(mentioned above) which heralded the founding of the Bible Institute of Los Angeles. By 1912, Torrey, coming from Moody Bible Institute, became dean of the Bible Institute of Los Angeles and assumed editorial leadership in publishing *The Fundamentals* as a four-volume work in 1917. The warning of J. Gresham Machen that "as go the theological seminaries, so goes the church" struck deep at the heart of Bible-believing scholars everywhere: "Many seminaries today *are* nurseries of unbelief; and because they are nurseries of unbelief the churches that they serve have become unbelieving churches too. As go the theological seminaries, so goes the church."[8] In 1929, Machen was influential in founding Westminster Theological Seminary as a result of Princeton's direction.[9] Dallas Theological Seminary was founded in 1924[10] and Fuller Theological Seminary was founded in 1947 by Biola graduate Charles E. Fuller along with Harold Ockenga. These are just a select few of the many schools founded by faithful men in this period. The hope was that these new schools would preserve a faithful, orthodox view of Scripture.

After this strategic withdrawal by fundamentalists of the first generation who fought the battle to preserve Scripture from the onslaught of historical criticism as well as its subsequent searching for the historical Jesus, subsequent generations from fundamentalist groups became discontent with their isolation from liberal-dominated mainstream biblical scholarship. The lessons of history from the battle fought at the turn of the twentieth century were forgotten by subsequent American generations. By the mid-1960s, prominent voices were scolding fundamentalists for continued isolation, and dialogue and interaction once again became the rallying cry. Carl F. H. Henry's criticisms struck deep, "The preoccupation of fundamentalists with the errors of modernism, and neglect of schematic presentations of the evangelical alternative, probably gave Neo-Orthodoxy its great opportunity in the Anglo-Saxon world. . . . If Evangelicals do not overcome their preoccupation with negative criticism of contemporary theological deviations at the expense of the construction of preferable alternatives to these, they will not be much of a doctrinal force in the decade ahead."[11]

George Eldon Ladd (1911–1982) of Fuller Theological Seminary became a zealous champion of modern historical-critical methods, arguing that the two-source hypothesis should be accepted "as a literary fact" and that form criticism "has thrown considerable light on the nature of the Gospels and the traditions they employ," adding, "Evangelical scholars should be willing to accept this light."[12] Indeed, for Ladd, critical methods have derived great benefit for evangelicals, "it has shed great light

---

8. Machen, *Christian Faith in the Modern World*, 65.

9. For a revealing look at Machen's struggle, see Machen, *Christianity and Liberalism*; Machen, *Virgin Birth of Christ*; Machen, *What Is Faith?*

10. For a recent recounting of the history of Dallas Theological Seminary, see Hannah, *Uncommon Union*.

11. Henry, *Jesus of Nazareth*, 9.

12. Ladd, *New Testament and Criticism*, 141, 168–69.

on the historical side of the Bible; and these historical discoveries are valid for all Bible students even though the presuppositions of the historical-critical method have been often hostile to an evangelical view of the Bible. Contemporary evangelicals often overlook this important fact when they condemn the critical method as such; for even while they condemn historical criticism, they are constantly reaping the benefits of its discoveries and employing critical tools."[13] Ladd asserts, "One must not forget that . . . everyday tools of good Bible study are the product of the historical-critical method."[14] George Ladd catalogued the trend of a "substantial group of scholars" whose background was in the camp of "fundamentalism" who had now been trained "in Europe as well as in our best universities" and were "deeply concerned with serious scholarship."[15] He also chided fundamentalists for their "major preoccupation" with defending "inerrancy of the Bible in its most extreme form," but contributing "little of creative thinking to the current debate."[16] Although Ladd acknowledged that historical-critical ideology was deeply indebted for its operation in the Enlightenment and the German scholarship that created it openly admitted its intention of "dissolving orthodoxy's identification of the Gospel with Scripture,"[17] Ladd sent many of his students for subsequent study in Britain and Europe in order to enlarge the influence of conservatives, the latter of which influence was greatly responsible for the fundamentalist split at the turn of the twentieth century.[18]

The end result of these calls for acceptance of historical-critical ideologies is that Bible colleges, Christian universities, and seminaries, once founded to guard faithfulness to Scripture in the early and mid-twentieth century, are now once again becoming the hotbed of the latest teachings of the theological left of the United Kingdom and European schools; the very same errors that crept in at the beginning of the twentieth century. History now repeats itself.

---

13. Ibid., 10.

14. Ladd offers two examples: Kittel and Friedrich, *Theological Dictionary of the New Testament*, and Arndt et al., *Greek-English Lexicon of the New Testament*; Ladd, *New Testament and Criticism*, 11.

15. Ladd, "Search for Perspective," 47.

16. Ibid. In a hotly debated book, Harold Lindsell in the mid-1970s detailed the problems facing Fuller, the Southern Baptist Convention and other Christian institutions due to the encroachment of historical criticism from European influence. See Lindsell, "Strange Case of Fuller Theological Seminary," 106–21. Marsden's book also covers this period in *Reforming Fundamentalism*.

17. Ladd, "Search for Perspective," 49; Ladd's citing of this admission by Ernst Käsemann may be found in the latter's *Essays on New Testament Themes*, 54–62.

18. An example of one of Ladd's students is the late Robert Guelich who wrote *The Sermon on the Mount: A Foundation for Understanding*. Guelich promoted an exegesis "that . . . makes use of the literary critical tools including text, source, form, tradition, redaction, and structural criticism" and goes on to assert "for many to whom the Scriptures are vital the use of these critical tools has historically been more 'destructive' than 'constructive.' But one need not discard the tool because of its abuse."

Part 2—Inerrancy Defended

# HISTORY DÉJÀ VU ("ALREADY SEEN") AMONG AMERICAN EVANGELICALISM

The following chart illustrates the problems that occurred in the American Churches in the early twentieth century and now in the early twenty-first gaining vast strength among evangelicals whose spiritual ancestors so fervently fought against these trends:

| Early Twentieth Century American Churches | Early Twenty-First Century Evangelicals in America |
|---|---|
| Inerrancy was disregarded or rejected; "partial" forms of inerrancy or really "errancy" predominated. Churches dismissed inerrancy. Errancy pervaded every part of Christian churches and schools. | Inerrancy is now rejected, disregarded, or re-defined to "partial" forms of inerrancy or really "errancy" predominated. Churches dismissed inerrancy. Errancy pervades every part of Christian churches and schools. |
| Higher criticism destructive of Scripture predominated. Grammatico-historical or plain, normal interpretation was rejected. | Historical criticism (the new name for "higher criticism") prevails to interpret Scripture. Grammatico-historical or plain, normal interpretation is rejected. |
| First "search" for "historical Jesus" conducted. Jesus is lost; Gospels rejected. The Jesus of the Gospels was considered a fiction, so scholars searched for him in unbelieving ways. | Third Search for "historical Jesus" conducted. Gospels deprecated within evangelical camp. Evangelicals dismissive of foundational Gospel events and join in "The Quest." |
| Evolution had gained hold in Christian institutions with Genesis 1–11 being regarded as symbolic, fiction or worse, a fairy-tale, instead of genuine history of the Divine creation of man in God's image. Adam and Eve were regarded as symbolic rather than mankind's first parents. The catastrophism of a world-wide flood, so evidenced in the geologic columns, was dismissed as either a mere local flood or so much literary fiction. | Evolution has gained hold in Christian institutions with Genesis 1–11 being regarded as symbolic, fiction or worse, a fairy-tale, instead of genuine history of the Divine creation of man in God's image. Adam and Eve were regarded as symbolic rather than mankind's first parents. The catastrophism of a world-wide flood, so evidenced in the geologic columns, was dismissed as either a mere local flood or so much literary fiction. |
| Higher criticism, what is known today as "historical criticism," assaulted not only the Old Testament but also the New Testament. Virulent doubt, unbelief pervaded the interpretation of every book of the Bible. | "Historical criticism," assaults not only the Old Testament but also the New Testament. Virulent doubt, unbelief pervades the interpretation of every book of the Bible. |
| The Gospel records, Matthew, Mark, Luke, and John were dismissed as untrue, fictional or, at best, symbolic rather than historical documents of Jesus' life. | Significant portions of the Gospel records, Matthew, Mark, Luke, and John are dismissed as untrue, fictional or, at best, symbolic rather than historical documents of Jesus' life. |

| | |
|---|---|
| American mainline denominations trained its clergy and scholarship for its religious schools and churches from German and British institutions that long ago had turned hostile to the Word of God. Future American preachers sat under prestigious professors from Oxford, Cambridge, Abeerdeen, Tübingen, Göttingen, Harvard, Yale, etc., whose ears were filled with anti-biblical theories that denied the foundational historicity and factuality of the biblical text. The "fire in the bellies" for preaching God's Word was diminished by influencing the next generation of preachers. One could characterize the period with Jesus' words in Matthew 23:15, "Woe to you, scribes and Pharisees, hypocrites, because you travel around on sea and land to make one proselyte; and when he becomes one, you make him twice as much a son of hell as yourselves." | Evangelical denominations now training large portions of its clergy and scholarship for its religious schools and churches from German and British institutions that long ago had turned hostile to the Word of God. Future American preachers sat under prestigious professors from Oxford, Cambridge, Abeerdeen, Tübingen, Göttingen, Harvard, Yale, etc., whose ears were filled with anti-biblical theories that denied the foundational historicity and factuality of the biblical text. The "fire in the bellies" for preaching God's Word was diminished by influencing the next generation of preachers. One could characterize the period with Jesus' words in Matthew 23:15, "Woe to you, scribes and Pharisees, hypocrites, because you travel around on sea and land to make one proselyte; and when he becomes one, you make him twice as much a son of hell as yourselves." |
| The American Christian atmosphere filled with a desire for new thinking, i.e., "novelty" in its colleges and schools. Faithfulness to God's Word, echoing Paul's command in 2 Timothy 2:2 "The things which you have heard from me in the presence of many witnesses, entrust these to faithful men who will be able to teach others also," was dismissed as old fashioned, not in keeping with the modern world. | The American Christian atmosphere filled with a desire for new thinking, i.e., "novelty" in its colleges and schools. Faithfulness to God's Word, echoing Paul's command in 2 Timothy 2:2 "The things which you have heard from me in the presence of many witnesses, entrust these to faithful men who will be able to teach others also," was dismissed as old fashioned, not in keeping with the modern world. |

Recently, the writer of this chapter was involved in the coediting and writing of a book called *The Jesus Quest: The Danger from Within*.[19] This work catalogues the dangerous, alarming drift away from inerrancy that has been held by the orthodox Christian church from its nascent beginnings that has been occurring among evangelicals, especially from what many in a group that identify themselves often as critical evangelical scholarship. The reader is encouraged to read this work as a follow-up to this chapter. The book reveals that a horrific, as well as historic, event is now occurring among evangelicals regarding inerrancy. John MacArthur, noting the hour of the time that evangelicals now face in regard to belief and integrity of God's Word, wrote the following regarding the work,

> The hard-fought victory of ICBI proved to be short-lived and of precious little lasting consequence. . . . Now a new surge of old-style academic skepticism is rolling in again. . . . The men who have written the essays in this volume see the heaving swells on the horizon and are braced for the onslaught. . . . My hope is that these essays will help rally a new generation of young evangelicals

---

19. Geisler and Farnell, *Jesus Quest*.

to stand together in a sober-minded, steadfast, earnest defense of biblical inerrancy and true biblical scholarship . . . *Tolle lege*."[20]

Please note that Dr. MacArthur (1) realized through reading this work and others like it[21] the danger that now confronts evangelicalism; (2) that the ICBI documents are now being dismissed or disregarded by elements within evangelicalism; and (3) a clarion call for God's faithful to come together in support of the trustworthiness of Scripture needed to sound forth. Four other seminary presidents (Dr. Albert Mohler of The Southern Baptist Seminary, Dr. Paige Patterson of Southwestern Baptist Theological Seminary, Dr. Richard Land of Southern Evangelical Seminary, and Dr. Joseph Holden of Veritas Evangelical Seminary) also whole-heartily endorsed the work, sounding their alarm as to the dangerous drift in Bible colleges and seminaries from inerrancy that is now occurring throughout the United States and the world.

Albert Mohler related in his foreword to *The Jesus Quest*,

> The inerrancy of Scripture has not been universally accepted by all who would call themselves evangelical and who would function within the evangelical movement. In fact, the doctrine has seen many challenges in recent years. Embodied in the "quest for the historical Jesus" movement, a skepticism has returned that attempts to redefine and rethink Jesus in a way that denies the biblical record by placing primary importance upon extra-biblical documents and legends. Most recently, some have warned that an affirmation of Scripture's inerrancy would lead to intellectual disaster for the evangelical movement. Still others complain that the concept is bothersome at best and inherently divisive at worst.
>
> If we do not confess that the whole Bible is totally true and trustworthy, then we have set ourselves upon a project of determining which texts of the Bible reflect God's perfection, if any. We will use human criteria of judgment to decide which texts bear divine authority and which texts can be trusted. We will decide, one way or another, which texts we believe to be God speaking to us.[22]

Mohler correctly notes that today's critical evangelical scholars, in their hubris, now have decided to pick and choose what texts they arbitrarily deem trustworthy and what they consider untrustworthy. Today, more than ever before, evangelicals face a crisis being directed at orthodox concepts of inerrancy as has never before been experienced within evangelicalism. That a crisis is now brewing among evangelicals that threatens the very foundations of the inspiration and inerrancy of God's Word is no exaggeration.

---

20. MacArthur, foreword to *Jesus Quest*, xv–xvii.
21. E.g., see Geisler and Roach, *Defending Inerrancy*.
22. Mohler, foreword to *Jesus Quest*, xviii–xix.

As of 2014, this danger to inerrancy is no longer from without but from within. This occurrence, though quite shocking, should not take Bible-believing people by surprise since Jesus warned that when he returns sound doctrine ("the faith") would be absent from the church ("I tell you that He will bring about justice for them quickly. However, when the Son of Man comes, will He find faith on the earth?"—Luke 18:8); Paul also warned that internal infiltration of God's people by grievous "wolves" would cause doctrinal deviation ("I know that after my departure savage wolves will come in among you, not sparing the flock; and from among your own selves men will arise, speaking perverse things, to draw away the disciples after them"—Acts 20:29–30). Paul continued in 2 Timothy 4:2–4 that God's faithful must "preach the word; be ready in season *and* out of season; reprove, rebuke, exhort, with great patience and instruction. For the time will come when they will not endure sound doctrine; but *wanting* to have their ears tickled, they will accumulate for themselves teachers in accordance to their own desires, and will turn away their ears from the truth and will turn aside to myths." Both 2 Peter and Jude warned of false teachers. The problem is that God's people have a tendency to wander and forget these warnings. Not deliberately, but carelessly they think that maybe these warnings apply to other Christian generations but not themselves. This tendency to disregard these warnings has caused much grief for God's people in church history, especially in the last one hundred years or so.

## HISTORY DEJA VIEW

This crisis that now occurs is historically very significant, since as this article has noted, almost exactly one hundred years ago, Lyman Stewart and his brother, Milton, were instrumental in funding *The Fundamentals*. The essays were written by sixty-four different authors, representing most of the major Christian denominations. These essays were designed to affirm, among other things, conservative Protestant beliefs, especially those of the Reformed tradition, and defend against ideas deemed inimical to them. They are widely considered to be the foundation of modern Christian fundamentalism. The essays were to set out what they believed to be the fundamentals of the Christian faith. These were sent free to ministers, missionaries, Sunday school superintendents and others active ministry throughout the world. The volumes defended orthodox Protestant beliefs and attacked higher criticism (a.k.a. "historical criticism"), liberal theology, Romanism, socialism, Modernism, atheism, Christian Science, Mormonism, Millennial Dawn, spiritualism, and evolutionism.

For a while the tide was stemmed against the onslaught of God's Word. Soon, however, evangelical drift began again with some calling for education of Bible-believing students in Ivy League and European schools to gain prestige for the institutions that taught the Bible.[23] Having forgotten the lessons of history that evangelicalism

---

23. Farnell, "Searching for the Historical Jesus," 423–24.

experienced for the very same reasons, many Bible colleges and seminaries sent their men to the Continent and England. The result was disastrous for inspiration and inerrancy among schools. The warning of J. Gresham Machen in 1936, who fought the first battle in the twentieth century, was disregarded by evangelicals as unnecessary that "as go the theological seminaries, so goes the church" struck deep at the heart of Bible-believing scholars everywhere: "Many seminaries today *are* nurseries of unbelief; and because they are nurseries of unbelief the churches that they serve have become unbelieving churches too. As go the theological seminaries, so goes the church."[24]

As a result of careless or inadvertent evangelical drift from Machen's warning during the 1940s to the 1960s, some thirty-five years ago the drift away from inerrancy and inspiration of God's Word began again. Harold Lindsell's works *The Battle for the Bible* (1976) and *The Bible in the Balance* (1979) had just previously been written that catalogued the dangerous drift from inerrancy among Lutherans, Southern Baptists, Fuller Theological Seminary, as well as many parachurch organizations. Lindsell wrote in chapter 10 of *The Battle for the Bible*, "How Infection Spreads,"

> History affords us notable examples of institutions and denominations that have gone astray. As times it is not easy to perceive *how* this happened. The trend away from orthodoxy may be slow in movement, gradual in scope, and almost invisible to the naked eye. When people awaken to what has happened, it is too late.... Theological aberrations, like cancer, begin as a small and seemingly insignificant blemish, but when it is left to itself it grows and spreads.[25]

Why did Lindsell write these two books? Because he personally experienced what happened to Fuller Theological Seminary in its drift away from the inerrancy of the Bible. Rogers and McKim had also started a firestorm at Fuller Seminary at the same time with their book, *The Authority and Interpretation of the Bible*, and its dismissal of the full inerrancy and authority of God's Word by asserting, "In this century both fundamentalism and modernism sometimes take extreme positions regarding the Bible" and "God has accommodated his ways and thoughts to our limited, human ways of thinking and speaking" so that "statements in the Bible" cannot be treated "quite literally according to contemporary standards" and "to erect a standard of modern technical precision in language as a hallmark of biblical authority was totally foreign to the foundation shared by the early church."[26] With one broad brush stroke, the entire plain normal sense of Scripture was flippantly tossed away again by many evangelicals.

---

24. Machen, *Christian Faith in the Modern World*, 65.

25. Lindsell, *Battle for the Bible*, 185.

26. Rogers and McKim, *Authority and Interpretation*, xvii–xxiii. See also Rogers, *Biblical Authority*.

Once again, faithful evangelicalism gathered together because of a threat from outside regarding God's Word and formulated the International Council on Biblical Inerrancy (1978) and Hermeneutics (1982). These two documents were historic in that they defended the grammatico-historical sense of the Scripture, its plain, normal sense and declared that inerrancy was a watershed issue that cannot be surrendered.

## LESSONS FORGOTTEN AGAIN . . . AND AGAIN . . . AND AGAIN

Once again, in the interim from ICBI to today, evangelicals forgot these warnings and lessons. Dangerous troubling signs now appear again since the ICBI documents were expressed. The following Scripture events are now disregarded as non-historic or immaterial to evangelical belief. For evidence, proof of this alarming state, the reader is once again asked to read *The Jesus Crisis*; *The Jesus Quest: The Danger from Within*; and *Defending Inerrancy* as basic introductions that will provide substantiation for the following list of events or items in the Gospels or other places in the New Testament that are dismissed by many critical evangelical scholars as either unhistorical, symbolic, or untrue.

According to many critically-trained evangelicals, the following Gospel events did not happen or happen as the Gospels record according to evangelicals, many of which say they support inerrancy. These are merely examples. Much more could be found but these will serve the purpose of this chapter. A reading of this chart demonstrates that the very same assaults on God's Word in both the OT and NT are now occurring again, but not within mainline denominations in America; mainline denominations long ago lost spiritual vitality in the early twentieth century. The following compilation is only a very small sample or partial list of Gospel events that are now suspected by American evangelicals as not being historically true or somehow being nonliteral or nonhistorical in genre:

1. The Sermon on the Mount. Jesus did not preach the Sermon on the Mount as is recorded in Matthew. It is perhaps a collection of Jesus' sayings placed into the genre of a sermon on a mountain by the writer of Matthew (see below). Jesus did not say all of the beatitudes in Matthew 5:3–12. He may have said three or four of the eight or nine total.

2. The commissioning of the twelve in Matthew 10 is a group of instructions compiled on different occasions and organized by the author of Matthew. It was not spoken of by Jesus on a single occasion as presented.

3. The parables of Matthew 13 and Mark 4 are collections (i.e., anthologies) that Jesus uttered on different occasions rather than on a single occasion as the author of Matthew presented.

4. The Olivet Discourse in Matthew 24 did not happen in its entirety as is presented in Matthew. The writers artificially created this sermon and changed elements of it.

5. The negative portrayal of the Pharisees in the Gospels is not accurate. They were in reality decent people whom Matthew (or the other Gospel writers) portrayed in a negative light because of bias against them.

6. The genealogies of Matthew and Luke are not accurate records.

7. The visit of the magi is fictional and the magi are not real characters.

8. Jesus did not say the Great Commission as is recorded in Matthew 28.[27]

9. "Clearly, Matthew treats us to history mixed with elements that cannot be called historical in a modern sense. All history writing entails more or less editing of materials. But Matthew's editing often goes beyond acceptable bounds. . . . Matthew's subtractions, additions, and revisions of order and phraseology often show changes in substance; i.e., they represent developments of the dominical tradition that result in different meanings and departures from the actuality of events" (623).[28]

10. "Comparison with the other Gospels, especially with Mark and Luke, and examination of Matthew's style and theology show that he materially altered and embellished historical traditions and that he did so deliberately and often" (639).

11. "We have also seen that at numerous points these features exhibit such a high degree of editorial liberty that the adjectives 'midrashic' and 'haggadic' become appropriate" (628). Midrash means it did not happen in history as it was presented in the Gospels.

12. "We are not dealing with a few scattered difficulties. We are dealing with a vast network of tendentious changes" (625). This means it did not happen in history as it was presented in the Gospels.

13. "Hence, 'Jesus said' or 'Jesus did' need not always mean that in history Jesus said or did what follows, but sometimes may mean that in the account at least partly constructed by Matthew himself Jesus said or did what follows" (630). This means it did not happen in history as it was presented in the Gospels.

14. "Semantics aside, it is enough to note that the liberty Matthew takes with his sources is often comparable with the liberty taken with the OT in Jubilees, the Genesis Apocryphon, the Targums, and the Midrashim and Haggadoth in rabbinic literature" (628). This means it did not happen in history as it was presented in the Gospels.

15. "These patterns attain greatest visibility in, but are by no means limited to, a number of outright discrepancies with the other synoptics. At least they are discrepancies so long as we presume biblical writers were always intending to write history when they used the narrative mode" (624).

---

27. The list of 1–8 are catalogued in Thomas's introduction to *Jesus Crisis*, 13–34. See also Geisler and Farnell, *Jesus Quest*, for the worsening of these conditions among evangelicals today.

28. The list of 9–18 as well as page numbers cited are from Gundry, *Matthew: A Commentary on His Literary and Theological Art*.

16. "Matthew selects them [the magi] as his substitute for the shepherds in order to lead up to the star, which replaces the angel and heavenly host in the tradition" (27). The magi, the star and the heavenly hosts did not happen as is presented in the Gospels.

17. "That Herod's statement consists almost entirely of Mattheanisms supports our understanding Matthew himself to be forming this episode out of the shepherd's visit, with use of collateral materials. The description of the star derives from v. 2. The shepherds' coming at night lies behind the starry journey of the magi" (31).

18. "He [Matthew] changes the sacrificial slaying of 'a pair of turtledoves or two young pigeons,' which took place at the presentation of the baby Jesus in the Temple (Luke 2:24; cf. Lev 12:6–8), into Herod's slaughtering the babies in Bethlehem (cf. As. Mos. 6:2–6)" (34, 35). This means these did not happen in history as it was presented in the Gospels.

19. Jesus' command to Peter of the coin in the fishes mouth is not historical, it did not happen (Matt 17:24–27). Craig Blomberg asserts in reference to the story of the coin in the fish's mouth in Matthew 17:24–27, "It is often not noticed that the so-called miracle of the fish with the coin in its mouth (Matt 17:27) is not even a narrative; it is merely a command from Jesus to go to the lake and catch such a fish. We don't even know if Peter obeyed the command. Here is a good reminder to pay careful attention to the literary form."[29]

20. Craig Blomberg, Denver Seminary, defended Robert Gundry's nonliteral or "midrashic" approach to the Gospels in the following terms:

> Is it possible, even inherently probable, that the NT writers at least in part never intended to have their miracle stories taken as historical or factual and that their original audiences probably recognized this? If this sounds like the identical reasoning that enabled Robert Gundry to adopt his midrashic interpretation of Matthew while still affirming inerrancy, that is because it is the same. The problem will not disappear simply because one author [Gundry] is dealt with *ad hominem* . . . how should evangelicals react? Dismissing the sociological view on the grounds that the NT miracles present themselves as historical gets us nowhere. So do almost all the other miracle stories of antiquity. Are we to believe them all?[30]

21. Resurrection of saints in Matthew 27:51–53 did not happen. It is special effects. Michael Licona, in his work *The Resurrection of Jesus: A New Historiographical Approach*,[31] used *bios* as a means of dehistoricizing parts of the Gospel (i.e., Matt 27:51–53 with the resurrection of the saints after Jesus crucifixion is nonliteral genre or apocalyptic rather than an actual historical event).[32] Licona argued, "*Bioi*

---

29. Blomberg, "Constructive Traditional Response," 354n32
30. Blomberg, "New Testament Miracles," 436.
31. Licona, *Resurrection of Jesus*.
32. Ibid.

offered the ancient biographer great flexibility for rearranging material and inventing speeches . . . and they often included legend. Because *bios* was a flexible genre, it is often difficult to determine where history ends and legend begins."[33] Licona labels it a "strange little text,"[34] and terms it "special effects" that has no historical basis[35] His apparent concern also rests with only Matthew as mentioning the event. He concludes that "Jewish eschatological texts and thought in mind" as "most plausible" in explaining it.[36] He concludes that "it seems best to regard this difficult text in Matthew a poetic device added to communicate that the Son of God had died and that impending judgment awaited Israel."[37]

22. Jesus' resurrection "probably" happened is the best we can say about this event historically.

23. The Gospels only give us the "footprints" of Jesus or the "surviving traces."

24. The Jesus of the Bible and the Jesus of history are not necessarily the same. This category is fully legitimate for evangelicals to assert.

25. We must search for the historical Jesus to find out how Jesus was actually in history and what he really said and did.

26. All history is interpretation. The Gospels are historical interpretations. The Gospels containing surviving traces of Jesus' life but they have been placed into historical narratives that have been interpreted according to the writers' perspectives. In order to discover the "surviving traces" of Jesus' life, we must apply criteria of authenticity based in critical methods to determine if the events actually happened as they are portrayed.

27. A scale of probability, possibility or not historically verifiable must be used to describe Gospel sections.

28. Very few events in the Gospels are capable of "probability" assessment since the Gospel writers placed their own interpretation on it.[38]

## FALSE ASCRIPTION OR PSEUDEPIGRAPHY NOW BEING NORMALIZED FOR EVAGNELICALISM

Evangelicals contend that the following books of the New Testament were not written by the New Testament Writers whose names are attached to them, i.e., false ascription. Blomberg asserts,

33. Ibid., 34.
34. Ibid., 548.
35. Ibid., 552.
36. Ibid.
37. Ibid., 553.
38. Items from 16–22 are cited and discussed in chapters 9–12 of *Jesus Quest*, 361–520. Consult also Bock and Webb, *Key Events in the Life of the Historical Jesus*, esp. 9–94; and Bock, *Who Is Jesus?* The latter are involved in the third search for the "historical Jesus."

> A *methodology* consistent with evangelical convictions might argue that there was an accepted literary convention that allowed a follower, say, of Paul, in the generation after his martyrdom, to write a letter in Paul's name to one of the churches that had come under his sphere of influence. The church would have recognized that it could not have come from an apostle they knew had died two or three decades earlier, and they would have realized that the true author was writing thoughts indebted to the earlier teaching of Paul. In a world without footnotes or bibliographies, this was one way of giving credit where credit was due. Modesty prevented the real author from using his own name, so he wrote in ways he could easily have envisioned Paul writing were the apostle still alive today. *Whether or not this is what actually happened*, such a hypothesis is thoroughly consistent with a high view of Scripture and an inerrant Bible. We simply have to recognize what is and is not being claimed by the use of name "Paul" in that given letter.[39]

Apparently, to Blomberg, pseudepigraphy is fully consistent with inspiration and inerrancy.

Donald Hagner indeed argues that "we have very little to lose in allowing the category of Deutero-Pauline letters. If it happens that some other persons have written these four, or even six, documents in the name of Paul, we are not talking about forgery or deception."[40] Again, Hagner asserts, "The ancient world on the whole did not have the same kind of sensitivity to pseudenymity that is typical of the modern world" and he prefers the term "allonymity" in deference to his teacher, I. Howard Marshall, who adopted the term.[41]

The following chart gives a general summary of many evangelical critical scholars' approach to authorship of New Testament books, although great variance exists among them. Each evangelical critical scholar should be carefully examined for their individual approach to each book. Sometimes the word "evangelist" in commentaries also serves as a code term for doubts about traditional views of authorship:

| Book of New Testament | Authorship—Evangelical Position of Many |
|---|---|
| Matthew | Unknown Evangelist, possibly associated with Matthew |
| Mark | Unknown Evangelist, but might be Mark. Mark was first Gospel even if church history never even stated it was the first. The early church always said Matthew was first Gospel. |
| Luke | Enknown Evangelist |
| John | Unknown Evangelist—probably by an unknown school of St. John that wrote it |

---

39. Ibid., 352.

40. For an example of an evangelical who hold such views on pseudepigraphy, see Hagner, *New Testament Introduction*, 194, 236, 426–35, 563, 586, 615, 672, 689, 714, 728, and 761 (quote from 428).

41. Ibid., 429, 431.

Part 2—Inerrancy Defended

| Acts | Unknown evangelist. The "we" sections of Acts are a literary device. |
|---|---|
| Romans | Paul |
| 1–2 Corinthians | Paul |
| Galatians | Paul |
| Ephesians | Pseudepigrapher wrote in Paul's name |
| Colossians | Pseudepigrapher wrote in Paul's name |
| Ephesians | Pseudepigrapher wrote in Paul's name |
| Philippians | Paul |
| 2 Thessalonians | Unknown pseudepigrapher wrote in Paul's name |
| Pastorals | Unknown Pseudepigrapher wrote in Paul's name |
| 2 Peter | Unknown Pseudepigrapher wrote in Paul's name |
| Revelation | Some other John or unknown pseudepigrapher |

## WHAT CAN WE BELIEVE FROM CRITICAL EVANGELICAL SCHOLARS?

Perhaps one of the most recent crescendos in critical evangelical scholarship's attack on orthodox views of inerrancy comes from Craig Blomberg's *Can We Still Believe The Bible? An Evangelical Engagement with Contemporary Questions*. Baker hails the book in the following terms,

> Challenges to the reliability of Scripture are perennial and have frequently been addressed. However, some of these challenges are noticeably more common today, and the topic is currently of particular interest among evangelicals. In this volume . . . Craig Blomberg offers an accessible and nuanced argument for the Bible's reliability in response to the extreme views about Scripture and its authority articulated by both sides of the debate. He believes that a careful analysis of the relevant evidence shows we have reason to be more confident in the Bible than ever before. As he traces his own academic and spiritual journey, Blomberg sketches out the case for confidence in the Bible in spite of various challenges to the trustworthiness of Scripture, offering a positive, informed, and defensible approach.[42]

He dialogues in questions of textual criticism, canon issues, translations, inerrancy, genre interpretation, and miracles, offering various solutions to various problems that center in these topics. This book is highly commended by Scot McKnight (Northern Seminary), Darrell Bock (Dallas Theological Seminary), Paul Copan (Palm Beach Atlantic University), Craig S. Keener (Asbury Theological Seminary) and Leith

---

42. See the "About" section of the Baker Publishing Group's web page for *Can We Still Believe the Bible?*, http://bakerpublishinggroup.com/books/can-we-still-believe-the-bible/343100.

Anderson (National Association of Evangelicals).[43] Bock himself encourages the reader to "read and consider anew how to think about Scripture" on the back cover.[44]

Blomberg immediately tips his hand regarding the true nature of this work when the dedication page says, "To the faculty, administration, and trustees of Denver Seminary who from 1986 to the present have created as congenial a research environment as a professor could hope for, upholding the inerrancy of Scripture without any of the watchdog mentality that plagues so many evangelical institutions."[45] This statement reveals the dual nature of this work in that it not only reveals Blomberg's unusual take on inerrancy but is intended to deride those who would question Blomberg's positions that he sets forth in the work.

In evaluating this book, several thoughts immediately come to mind: Perhaps the term most summarizing the book is "angry rant" against anyone who would dare disagree with a critical British-trained scholar. The hubris and overestimation of the writer is so stunning that it constitutes a basic warning of Paul to believers ("For through the grace given to me I say to everyone among you not to think more highly of himself than he ought to think; but to think so as to have sound judgment, as God has allotted to each a measure of faith"—Rom 12:3). Does not the Scripture warn against pride? Very little humility is displayed in this work, but an attack mode is maintained throughout. He relates that "a handful of very conservative Christian leaders who have not understood the issues adequately" as having "reacted by unnecessarily rejecting new developments."[46] Rogers and McKim took a similar position in 1979 when they wrote about the twentieth century, "In this century both fundamentalism and modernism sometimes took extreme positions regarding the Bible."[47]

In terms of Blomberg's take on inerrancy, he attacks "extremely conservative Christians" who continue to insist on following their modern understandings of what should or should not constitute errors in the Bible and censure fellow inerrantists whose views are less "anachronistic."[48] Blomberg's proverbial "loophole" in the concept of inerrancy, however, is the issue of "genre."[49] He argues: "Most important, simply because a work appears in narrative form does not automatically make it historical or biographical in genre. History and biography themselves appear in many different forms, and fiction can appear identical to history in form."[50] He contends that "the way in which the ancients wrote history is clearer now than ever before. Once again

---

43. See the Brazos Press blog, http://www.thebrazosblog.com/2014/03/blog-tour-for-can-we-still-believe.

44. A blog tour was conducted at www.canwestillbelieve.com, but the site is no longer active.

45. Blomberg, *Can We Still Believe*, v.

46. Ibid., 7–8.

47. Rogers and McKim, *Authority and Interpretation*, xxiii.

48. Blomberg, *Can We Still Believe*, 10.

49. Ibid., 10–11.

50. Ibid., 11.

the result is that we know much better what we should be meaning when we say we 'believe the Bible,' and therefore such belief is more defensible than ever."[51] He denigrates "ultraconservatives" who do not abide by his assessment in the following terms, "once again, unfortunately, a handful of ultraconservatives criticize all such scholarship, thinking that they are doing a service to the gospel instead of the disservice that they actually render."

The first three chapters of the book present nothing really controversial, but chapter 4, "Don't These Issues Rule Out Biblical Inerrancy,"[52] and chapter 5, "Aren't Several Narrative Genres of the Bible Unhistorical"[53] warrant special scrutiny for anyone who would affirm belief in, and especially inerrancy of, the Bible.

In chapter 4, Blomberg addresses the "fundamentalist-modernist controversy." He claims that the idea of inerrancy as understood by American efforts is largely an American phenomena: "Other branches of evangelicalism, especially in other parts of the world not heavily influenced by American missionary efforts, tend to speak of *biblical authority, inspiration*, and even *infallibility*, but not inerrancy."[54] He contends that some have "consciously rejected inerrancy as too narrow a term to apply to Scripture,"[55] and that these misunderstandings about inerrancy emerge especially "among those who are noticeably more conservative or those who are noticeably more liberal in their views of Scripture than mainstream evangelicalism."[56] He mentions the following who, in his belief, have misunderstood inerrancy because they are too conservative: "From the far right of the evangelical spectrum, Norman Geisler, William Roach, Robert Thomas, and David Farnell attack my writings along with similar ones by such evangelical stalwarts as Darrell Bock, D. A. Carson, and Craig Keener as too liberal, threatening inerrancy, or denying the historicity of Scripture."[57] In response to his contentions here, readers are urged to examine the latest book from Geisler and Farnell, *The Jesus Quest: The Danger From Within*, to evaluate properly the interpretative approaches of Blomberg and these scholars especially in terms of inerrancy.

Importantly, Blomberg believes that the real debate on inerrancy is one of "hermeneutics."[58] As a result, "Genesis 1 can be and has been interpreted by inerrantists as referring to a young earth, and old earth, progressive creation, theistic evolution, a literary framework for asserting God as the creator of all things irrespective of his methods, and a series of days when God took up residence in his cosmic temple for the sake of newly created humanity in his image. Once again, this is a matter

---

51. Ibid.
52. Ibid., 119–46.
53. Ibid., 147–78.
54. Ibid., 119.
55. Ibid.
56. Ibid.
57. Ibid., 120.
58. Ibid., 125.

for hermeneutical and exegetical debate, not one that is solved by the shibboleth of inerrancy."[59] One must note, however, that Blomberg reveals his startling differences with inerrancy as defined by ICBI in 1978: "*We affirm* that the text of Scripture is to be interpreted by grammatico-historical exegesis, taking account of its literary forms and devices, and that Scripture is to interpret Scripture. *We deny* the legitimacy of any treatment of the text or quest for sources lying behind it that leads to relativizing, dehistoricizing, or discounting its teaching, or rejecting its claims to authorship. Blomberg's position here is neither grammatical, historical, or literal, for Blomberg argues, "Defenders of inerrancy do not reflect often enough on what it means to say that non-historical genres are wholly truthful."[60] Blomberg also reflects Rogers's and McKim's position when he argues, "But often without realizing it, we impose on ancient documents twenty-first-century standards that are equally inapproapriate," for Rogers and McKim, contended that "to erect a standard of modern, technical precision in language as the hallmark of biblical authority was totally foreign to the foundation shared by the early church."[61] Blomberg also supports elements of speech-act theory and maintains that "Vanhoozer's work is indeed very attractive, but it is scarcely at odds with the Chicago Statement."[62] One wonders at this statement of Blomberg, since Vanhoozer denies the grammatico-historical approach, and as Geisler/Roach conclude, "[Vanhoozer] also claims to affirm much of the ICBI statement as he understands it. But that is precisely the problem since the way he understands it is not the way the framers meant it, as is demonstrated from the official commentaries on the ICBI statements."[63]

The practical result is genre can be used to deny anything in the bible that the interpreter finds offensive as a literal sense. The allegorical school did such a thing, the Gnostics did it to Scripture, and now Blomberg applies his updated version of it with genre being applied to hermeneutics. Blomberg's use of genre has much similarity to Rogers's and McKim's deprecation of literal interpretation when they cast a decided negativity on the idea that "all persons in all places thought alike and that Western logic was the clue to reality" and "statements in the Bible were treated like logical propositions that could be interpreted quite literally according to contemporary standards."[64]

In chapter 5, "Aren't Several Narrative Genres of the Bible Unhistorical," Blomberg's use of hermeneutics continues to be the substantive means by which he redefines

---

59. Ibid., 126.
60. Ibid., 128.
61. Rogers and McKim, *Authority and Interpretation of the Bible*, xxii.
62. Ibid., 126. The reader is referred here to Geisler/Roach evaluation of Vanhoozer for a very different perspective about Vanhoozer's position in relationship to ICBI, "Kevin Vanhoozer on Inerrancy," in *Defending Inerrancy*, 132–59.
63. Geisler and Roach, *Defending Inerrancy*, 159.
64. Rogers and McKim, *Authority and Interpretation*, xviii.

what an orthodox definition of inerrancy would indicate regarding historicity of biblical narratives as reflected in the ICBI statements. Blomberg advocates that idea that "the question is simply one about the most likely literary form of the passage."[65] From this position, he allows for nonliteral interpretation of Genesis 1–3 that are, in his view, fully in line with inerrancy, e.g., Adam and Eve as symbols for every man and woman,[66] evolutionary and/or progressive creation,[67] a nonhistorical, allegorical Jonah,[68] the possibility of two or three Isaiahs,[69] Daniel as apocalyptic genre rather than prophetic genre,[70] fully embracing of midrash interpretation of the Gospels as advocated by Robert Gundry as not impacting inerrancy,[71] as well as pseudepigraphy as fully in line with inerrancy in NT epistles under the guide of a "literary device" or "acceptable form of pseudonymity."[72]

What is absolutely fascinating is that while advocating a nonliteral approach to these passages, Blomberg quotes in support for doing so with the book of Jonah by quoting ICBI article XVIII, "or to repeat the words of the Chicago Statement, we must not 'evaluate Scripture according to standards of truth and error that are alien to its purpose or usage.'"[73] This quoting is so completely out of context that it is almost laughable. Article XIII went on to declare: "*We deny* that generic categories which negate historicity may rightly be imposed on biblical narratives which present." Article XIV goes on to say, "*We deny* that any event, discourse or saying reported in Scripture was invented by the biblical writers or by the traditions they incorporated," while article XVIII went on expressly to warned against the denial historicity, "*We deny* the legitimacy of any treatment of the text or quest for sources lying behind it that leads to relativizing, dehistoricizing, or counting its teaching, or rejecting its claim to authorship."

Blomberg also allows for the possibility of pseudepigraphy (as mentioned previously). He argues that one doesn't know the opinions of the first-century church well-enough on pseudepigraphy to rule it out: "Barring some future discovery related to first-century opinions, we cannot pontificate on what kinds of claims for authorship would or would not have been considered acceptable in Christian communities, and especially in Jewish-Christian circles when the New Testament Epistles were written. As a result, we must evaluate every proposal based on its own historical and

---

65. Blomberg, *Can We Still Believe*, 150.
66. Ibid., 152.
67. Ibid., 151–53.
68. Ibid., 157–59.
69. Ibid., 162.
70. Ibid., 163–64.
71. Ibid., 165–68.
72. Ibid., 168–72.
73. Ibid., 160.

grammatical merits, not on whether it does or does not pass some pre-established criterion of what inerrancy can accept."[74]

In sum, under the logic of Blomberg's negative reaction against those who stand firm on the issue of an orthodox view of inerrancy of Scripture as reflected in ICBI, one would wonder if critical evangelical scholars today would allow the following to stay in Scripture:

1. Galatians might not have be accepted by critical evangelical scholars today since in it Paul has quite a few charged statements against the Judaizers that today's evangelicals might seem unfair or even-handed, such as "If I or an angel from heaven preach to you a different gospel than that which you heard, let them be anathema": "I am amazed that you are so quickly deserting Him who called you by the grace of Christ, for a different gospel; which is *really* not another; only there are some who are disturbing you and want to distort the gospel of Christ. But even if we, or an angel from heaven, should preach to you a gospel contrary to what we have preached to you, he is to be accursed! As we have said before, so I say again now, if any man is preaching to you a gospel contrary to what you received, he is to be accursed! For am I now seeking the favor of men, or of God? Or am I striving to please men? If I were still trying to please men, I would not be a bond-servant of Christ" (Gal 1:6–10).

2. In Galatians, Paul says in that those false teachers who advocate circumcision, "I wish that those who are troubling you would even *mutilate* themselves" where Paul advocates that the false teachers who proclaimed works in salvation through circumcision should slip with their knife and cut off some important part of the body (Gal 5:12).

3. In the Philippians, Paul calls out two ladies who are bickering with each other by name, "I urge Euodia and I urge Syntyche to live in harmony in the Lord" (Phil 4:2).

4. In the Pastorals, Paul calls heretics by name and delivers them over to Satan, "among these are Hymenaeus and Alexander, whom I have handed over to Satan, so that they will be taught not to blaspheme" (1 Tim 1:20), and "Alexander the coppersmith did me much harm; the Lord will repay him according to his deeds" (2 Tim 4:14).

5. Jude's stiff warning about false teaching that "crept in unnoticed" might be considered too strong (Jude 4).

6. Second Peter's language might be offensive since he says in no uncertain terms, "But false prophets also arose among the people, just as there will also be false teachers among you, who will secretly introduce destructive heresies, even denying the Master who bought them, bringing swift destruction upon themselves. Many will follow their sensuality, and because of them the way of the truth will be maligned; and in their greed they will exploit you with false words; their judgment from long ago is not idle, and their destruction is not asleep" (2 Pet 2:3–4).

---

74. Ibid., 172.

7. Surely Jesus' severe condemnation of the Pharisees in Matthew 23 was within the bounds of evangelicalism today, one would hope at least.

Would not Paul's warning not to be taken captive by philosophy and traditions of men (Col 2:8); to take every thought captive (2 Cor 10:5) call for rigorous examination of all evangelical positions so that evangelicals might be faithful to God's Word (1 Cor 4:4)?

Second, Blomberg shows a remarkable lack of understanding the ICBI 1978 and 1982 statements, and, at times, clearly is in opposition to them. He clearly does not accept them as originally intended or as a guideline that he will abide.

## CONCLUSION TO THE MATTER

The assault is now occurring among evangelicals who founded new churches, schools, and ministries to guard God's people against such an attack on Scripture. Want proof? The condition of evangelicalism in America is much worse than can demonstrated in the few words of these articles. The reader is directed to the following resources to start: Norman L. Geisler and F. David Farnell, *The Jesus Quest: The Danger from Within*; Robert L. Thomas and F. David Farnell, *The Jesus Crisis: The Inroads of Historical Criticism into Evangelical Scholarship*; Norman L. Geisler and William C. Roach, *Defending Inerrancy*; and the many articles that can be found at www.defendinginerrancy.com

While not every evangelical who studies in elite academic schools in America or Europe would necessarily be influenced against the inerrancy of Scripture, vast stretches of evangelical history stand as monumental testimony that the vast majority are negatively influenced. Spiritual lessons from the past are being disregarded. Academic prestige is not what is necessary for God's people, but faithfulness to his Word. As Paul warned long ago,

> Preach the word; be ready in season and out of season; reprove, rebuke, exhort, with great patience and instruction. For the time will come when they will not endure sound doctrine; but wanting to have their ears tickled, they will accumulate for themselves teachers in accordance to their own desires, and will turn away their ears from the truth and will turn aside to myths (2 Tim 4:2–4).

What God's heart desires above all is faithfulness, not novelty:

> The things which you have heard from me in the presence of many witnesses, entrust these to faithful men who will be able to teach others also (2 Tim 2:2).

Chapter 17

# The "Magic" of Historical Criticism

## F. DAVID FARNELL

### INTRODUCTION

What is the true nature of the historical-critical method of liberal biblical scholars that has been so wholeheartedly adopted by critical evangelical scholars? How can one place its true nature on a practical level of understanding for the average reader of the Scriptures? How should the layperson or serious Bible student understand the impact of historical criticism on their understanding of Scripture? These questions go to the very heart of understanding historical criticism in its impact, both ideological and psychological, on the Bible interpreter when it is applied to the exegesis of the biblical text. Indeed, few exegetes understand this very important principle that is involved in historical criticism.

In its essential nature, historical criticism is a psychological operation that is conducted on the mind to control thinking and/or behavior. A psychological operation may be defined as planned operation to convey selected information and indicators to audiences in order to influence their emotions, motives, objective reasoning, and ultimately the behavior of groups and individuals. Its aim is to control people's thinking in a desired way for a desired outcome. Integral to perception management, psychological operations are designed to induce or reinforce attitudes and behavior favorable to the originator's objectives.

The British were one of the first major military powers to use psychological warfare in both World Wars in a very scientific manner, although many of the principles used go back to ancient times. The British Tavistock Institute of Human Relations

(TIHR) may be considered the most prominent of such endeavors.[1] Indeed, this institute may be considered the leading center for manipulating belief and behavior. They have perfected the science of manipulating minds.

A central concept of any psychological operation is *to use accepted terms but to change their meaning to one that is desired by those conducting the operation. The essence of a psychological operation is to confuse the meanings of words and infiltrate the mind with conflicting concepts* to change one's thinking toward the desired goal of those who are conducting the operation. It uses misleading language to manipulate any person to produce in them a desired outcome. Each word claims to be something that it is not in reality or at least not to be understood in its original, traditional sense. It creates confusion in the person regarding the original intent of the term so as to establish a desired, changed definition or understanding, i.e., to infiltrate the mind with conflicting concepts so as to produce the desired change in thinking.

A prominent example of this change in definitions is found in the book *1984*, written in 1949 by famed British writer George Orwell (whose real name was Eric Arthur Blair). In it the author warned of the manipulation of words and their meanings as an important key to controlling what people think about someone or something. He called it "newspeak," defined by *Merriam-Webster* as a noun, often capitalized, for propagandistic language marked by euphemism, circumlocution, and the inversion of customary meanings. Newspeak was a language "designed to diminish the range of thought," in the novel *1984*. Words were imbued with meaning in "newspeak" that were totally emptied of their original meaning to serve the purposes of those in control. Also involved is "doublethink," another term that Orwell popularized through his work, although he did not use the term itself. Doublethink employed terms that could be used in conflicting ways to produce language that deliberately disguises, distorts, or reverses the meaning of words from their normative, original sense. Its goal is confuse the meaning of words for a desired outcome.[2]

Why bring up such a subject? Because one can only truly understand the nature of historical criticism by viewing it in this manner. At its heart, historical criticism is neither "historical" nor "critical" in the traditional sense of the term. It is doublespeak and newspeak. It does not genuinely believe biblical revelation contains history in the sense of what actually happened in a time-space continuum. Instead, historical criticism is postmodernistic in that it asserts that all history is by nature a subjective interpretation of surviving traces of events. Hence, Scripture does not convey what actually happened. Even when the Bible presents itself in its plain, normal sense as conveying historical information, historical criticism *a priori* rejects its history outright. It is already biased against history in any traditional sense of the term.

---

1. http://www.tavinstitute.org.

2. See Orwell, "Principles of Newspeak," appendix to *Nineteen Eighty-Four*, available online at http://orwell.ru/library/novels/1984/english/en_app.

Moreover, it is not true criticism, for criticism in its traditional, normative sense refers to applying criteria to any of various methods of studying texts or documents for the purpose of dating or reconstructing them, evaluating their authenticity, analyzing their content or style. In other words, for criticism to be truly criticism it must seek an objective outcome of true understanding of any literature. Historical criticism does not seek an objective, honest outcome of the biblical text. The goal of its criticism is to change the plain, normal sense of the text to an already predetermined outcome that is acceptable to the critic's whims and desires. Seeking what is acceptable to him or her is the goal, rather than evaluating any text for what it truly is. The historical critic's goal is to interpret the biblical text according to the current fads of the time. Traditional meaning or understanding is not the goal of this method. The goal is conformity of the text to the subjective "sensibility" of the critic.

Therein lies the "magic" of historical criticism. When the text of Scripture offends current sensibilities or perceptions, i.e., the fads and popular ideas of the critics of the day, the biblical critic can apply historical criticism to the text in any way desired to guarantee the interpretive outcome. For instance, Genesis 1–3 presents itself as historic events in a time-space continuum, a historical recounting of the creation of the universe as well as the earth. Yet, modern historical critics, having been conditioned by current scientism, override the plain, normal sense of Scripture and dismiss the account as nonhistorical, figurative, or altogether false. Such an action is hardly objective or seeking to understand the literature as the original author intended. Another instance can be found in Matthew 23 where Jesus excoriated the Pharisees of his day in what are now considered "politically incorrect" and shocking terms. In light of holocaustic hermeneutics, i.e., the post-World War II prevalent thinking of our day, even evangelical critics dismiss this chapter as being historically inaccurate. Jesus' words are dismissed as not being spoken by him since one might face the accusation of being anti-Semitic for accepting the chapter as genuine. Instead, the cause of these tensions between Jesus and the Pharisees is attributed to an alleged conflict in the synagogue between Matthew's assumed community and the Jews of Matthew's day. Indeed, Westerholm attributes these sayings in the following terms: "The Gospels' depiction of Pharisees reflect both memories from the career of Jesus and subsequent development in the Christian communities."[3] Historical criticism magically makes the politically incorrect problem disappear by dismissing the historical accuracy of the Gospels in recording the actual words and deeds of Jesus. Hence, it is neither historical nor critical in the traditional sense of the terms. Historical critics of both liberal and evangelical camps constantly use this magic of historical criticism to remove anything in the biblical record that affronts their biases and subjective sensibilities.

---

3. E.g., see Westerholm, "Pharisees," 613.

Part 2—Inerrancy Defended

# THE GOAL OF THE ICBI STATEMENTS ON INERRANCY AND HERMENEUTICS

The ICBI Statements on Inerrancy (1978) and Hermeneutics (1982) arose as hard-won documents from previous decades of attacks on the trustworthiness of the Bible. Significantly, these documents affirm "grammatical-historical" rather than "historical-critical" hermeneutics as employed by these critically-trained evangelicals. Why? Because the authors and those who signed their affirmation to these documents knew the ruinous impact that historical-critical ideologies had upon God's Word in church history. However, these British and European critically-trained evangelicals who now advocate the adoption of some form of historical criticism have effectively annulled these two hard-won documents because they have forgotten history, especially the reasons why these articles were formulated.

First, the ICBI developers knew that historical criticism dehistoricizes the plain, normal reading of the text. Article XVIII reads:

> We affirm that the text of Scripture is to be interpreted by grammatico-historical exegesis, taking account of its literary forms and devices, and that Scripture is to interpret Scripture. We deny the legitimacy of any treatment of the text or quest for sources lying behind it that leads to relativizing, dehistoricizing, or discounting its teaching, or rejecting its claims to authorship.

What is the true essence of the term "historical criticism" which arose from the days of Spinoza? It is the ingredient that is used to make the Bible say whatever the researcher wants it to say. It is the dissolvent that destroys the plain, normal sense of Scripture and, in turn, can make the Bible reflect any prejudice of the interpreter that is imposed upon it. When Bible "scholars" want to make the Bible say something that it does not naturally say, they apply judicious and generous portions of historical criticism to accomplish that magic! When Bible "scholars" are offended by something in Scripture, i.e., something unacceptable to them for a variety of their own prejudices, it allows the scholar to remake anything in Scripture to their own liking—either by negating it entirely or manufacturing an entirely different sense or meaning for a particular portion of Scripture. It allows the Bible to be *remolded* into something acceptable to the critical scholar's whims. The philosophical pedigree of historical criticism guarantees that magic of transforming the Bible into something more acceptable to the modern, critical mind. This has been most prominent in "historical Jesus" research in which historical-critical criteria are the tools that German- and British-trained critical scholars use (borrowed from Spinoza) to find a Jesus that they have already decided on in order to determine how they think he must really, truly be—a Jesus they find acceptable to them. These authenticity criteria tools are the solvent that allows critical scholars to dissolve the canonical Gospels and the information therein in order to find a Jesus that they prefer through the genius of historical criticism. *However, no two critical scholars agree on the same list of criteria or their exact definition and nature—proof positive that great evangelical confusion exists over terminology and the practice of interpretation.*

By contrast, the goal of the grammatical-historical method is to find the meaning which the authors of Scripture intended to convey and the meaning comprehended by the recipients. Special allowance is made for (1) inspiration, (2) the Holy Spirit, and (3) inerrancy. It may be understood as *the study of inspired Scripture designed to discover under the guidance of the Holy Spirit the meaning of a text dictated by the principles of grammar and the facts of history.*

Grammatical-historical criticism, advocated by the both the Reformers as well as the signers of the ICBI statements of 1978 and 1982, allows the Bible to say what it naturally says plainly and normally without an *a priori* agenda as with historical-critical ideologies. As more recent evangelicals receive their education from schools that advocate some form of historical criticism, an unstable blending of these two approaches is occurring. Much confusion exists in current evangelical circles regarding grammatical-historical and historical-critical approaches to exegesis.[4] These two hermeneutical disciplines are distinct and must not be confused by evangelicals. In contrast to the Reformation roots of the grammatical-historical method, the historical-critical hermeneutic has its roots in deism, rationalism, and the Enlightenment. Edgar Krentz, favorable to the practice, readily admits in his *Historical-Critical Method* that "historical method is the child of the Enlightenment."[5] Maier, opposed to historical criticism, argued, "Historical criticism over against a possible divine revelation presents an inconclusive and false counterpart which basically maintains human arbitrariness and its standards in opposition to the demands of revelation."[6]

Another way that historical criticism, used especially by critical evangelical scholars, is assaulting the Scripture is through genre and speech-act theory. Evangelicals often use a term that signals their desire to dehistoricize the Gospels as "midrash" or "apocalyptic Judaism" genre. Robert Gundry employs such methods in his commentary on Matthew.

Perhaps the most pernicious way that historical criticism assaults the Bible is by redefining inerrancy to mean something other than its traditional, orthodox meaning as was understood throughout the centuries of the church age.

## HOW "ERRANCY" MASQUERADES AS "INERRANCY"

One cannot overstress that psychological operations are a central force in the historical-critical method, i.e., ideology. It is neither "historical" since its assumption of postmodernistic historiography (i.e., postmodernism) does not believe that real knowledge of history is possible, or even desirable, since only surviving traces of

---

4. See Thomas, "Current Hermeneutical Trends," 241–56.
5. Krentz, *Historical-Critical Method*, 55.
6. Maier, *End of the Historical-Critical Method*, 25.

events remain, nor is it critical since it seeks a preconceived, *a priori* outcome and its focus is not upon "truth" but upon preconceived conclusions that it desires to reach. The essence of any psychological operation is to change definitions and affect the mind of those who would be the object of that operation. Such an operation has occurred especially in the area of the orthodox definition of inerrancy as defined by the Chicago Statements on Inerrancy (1978) and Hermeneutics (1982) by critically-trained Neo-Evangelicals who now hold sway in academia.

Such operations are vastly more effective than outright assaults on ideas and concepts. Outright assaults often, if not almost exclusively, receive immediate opposition and rejection of any opposing idea that attempts replacement. Psychological operations against current thinking are much more effective because they are (1) more subtle and careful, indirect rather than direct. To replace an idea effectively time must be taken to replace concepts without awareness of that process being realized. This is the "magic" of historical-critical ideologies. (2) Another reason is that historical-criticism, at heart, is parasitic, adaptive, and pliable in its approach. That is, historical criticism's indirect assault on the biblical text is adoptive of standard, even orthodox terminology but changes those meanings subtly over time, i.e., it is in no hurry, for the goal or ends justifies the means of changing normative terminology into that which is acceptable to the preconceived notions of the interpreter.

Importantly, a subtle and gradual movement away from orthodox concepts of the integrity of the Scripture in terms of its historical accuracy and meaning is occurring among evangelicals, especially by what is now known as evangelical critical scholars.[7] A significant portion of evangelicalism no longer adheres to the nascent beliefs of the Christian church of the plenary (complete), verbal (word for word) inspiration (God-breathed) of Scripture and its resultant concomitant inerrancy. This is not the first time that the church has drifted away from these foundations. This writer has catalogued such a drift that historically occurred in chapters 11 and 12. These chapters catalogue the eerily similar drifts among Christian denominations in the early part of the twentieth century when one examines current events among critical evangelical scholars in the twenty-first century. Similar historical events that caused the former drift away from the inerrancy and inspiration of the biblical texts now are shaking the foundations of orthodox belief once again.

## HOW THE TERM "INERRANCY" NO LONGER SIGNIFIES ITS NORMAL DEFINITION

In order to understand this monumental shift that is now recurring in the church, especially in terms of orthodox views of inerrancy, we must revisit history, for God's people so quickly forget. In 1978 and 1982, evangelicals met under the auspices of

---

7. For examples of this dangerous drift among evangelicals, see Farnell, "Part Four: Beware of 'Critical' Post-Modern History," in Geisler and Farnell *Jesus Quest*, 359–520.

the International Council on Biblical Inerrancy. Its purpose was "the defense and application of the doctrine of biblical inerrancy as an essential element for the authority of Scripture and a necessity for the health of the church. It was created to counter the drift from the important doctrinal foundation by significant segments of evangelicalism and the outright denial of it by other church movements."[8] ICBI reflects a long history, stretching back to *The Fundamentals* written in 1915 and reflects the thinking of the vast majority of conservative, orthodox theologians well back into the twentieth century that saw so much denial toward the dehistoricizing of the plain, normal sense of Scripture. This article is strategic for this discussion of the "magic" of historical criticism, since historical criticism's aim is not to understand the text in its plain, normal sense but to make it pliable to contemporary trends of scholarship, no matter what the era or time. In contrast, grammatico-historical criticism seeks to discover the meaning of the text that the text conveys, plainly, normally, i.e., letting the text and its context convey the meaning rather than imposing foreign philosophical concepts upon the text.

## INERRANCY AFFIRMS THE PLAIN, NORMAL SENSE OF SCRIPTURE: WHEN THE PLAIN SENSE OF SCRIPTURE MAKES SENSE SEEK NO OTHER SENSE

Article XVIII becomes very pertinent to this discussion of the "magic" of historical criticism that is now being advocated by evangelical critical scholars. History is being forgotten. Article XVIII states:

> *We affirm* that the text of Scripture is to be interpreted by grammatico-historical exegesis, taking account of its literary form and devices, and that Scripture is to interpret Scripture.
>
> *We deny* the legitimacy of any treatment of the text or quest for sources lying behind it that leads to relativizing, dehistoricizing, or discounting its teaching, or rejecting its claims to authorship.

In commenting on this article, R. C. Sproul, one of the founding and principle members of ICBI, made the following comments in his *Explaining Inerrancy: A Commentary* that explained the committee's reasoning what grammatico-historical exegesis's goal is ("*We affirm*" and what it also was trying to prevent ("*We deny*"):

> Article XVIII touches on some of the most basic principles of biblical interpretation. Though this article does not spell out in detail a vast comprehensive system of hermeneutics, it nevertheless gives basic guidelines on which the framers of the confession were able to agree. *The first is that the text of Scripture is to be interpreted by grammatico-historical exegesis*. Grammatico-historical is

---

8. From the ICBI Catalogue, International Council on Biblical Inerrancy, 1983; Nicole, foreword to *Explaining Inerrancy*, 7–8.

a technical term that refers to the process by which we take the structures and time periods of the written texts seriously as we interpret them. Biblical interpreters *are not given the license to spiritualize or allegorize texts against the grammatical structure and form of the text itself.*[9]

The ICBI Statements, including the ICBI Statement on Hermeneutics, and its heritage reflected in *The Fundamentals* going back into history of the twentieth-century attacks on the biblical text (see ch. 11), rejected historical critical hermeneutics for the very reason that it disregarded the plain, normal sense of the text as well as the fundamental historicity of what the text was communicating. ICBI rejected historical-criticism's attempt to dehistoricize the plain, normal reading of the text. Sproul continued,

> The Bible is not to be reinterpreted to be brought into conformity with contemporary philosophies but is to be understood in its intended meaning and word usage as it was written at the time it was composed. To hold to grammatico-historical exegesis is to disallow the turning of the Bible into a wax nose that can be shaped and reshaped according to modern conventions of thought. The Bible is to be interpreted as it was written, not reinterpreted as we would like it to have been written according to the prejudices of our own era.[10]

Here both ICBI documents emphasized the (1) grammatico-historical exegesis in direct contrast to the historical critical method, either combined with grammatico-historical or modified in its more radical form, now maintained by Neo-Evangelicals.[11] Why did they commend the grammatico-historical approach? Because the men who expressed these two watershed statements had experienced the history of interpretive degeneration among mainstream churches and seminaries ("As go the theological seminaries, so goes the church")[12] in terms of dismissing the Gospels as historical records due to historical-critical ideologies. Any attempt at dismissing the grammatico-historical, plain sense of Scripture is contrary to the orthodox inerrancy view.

## EVANGELICAL HISTORICAL CRITICS EMBRACE HISTORICAL CRITICISM TO REMOVE THE PLAIN, NORMAL SENSE INVOLVED IN ORTHODOX INERRANCY

Many critical-evangelical scholars, especially the large number of those trained in British and Continental European Schools, believe that historical criticism (HC) can

---

9. Sproul, *Explaining Inerrancy*, 54, italics added.

10. Ibid.

11. For instance, Craig Blomberg advocates a combining of historical-criticism and the grammatico-historical in while other evangelicals like Bock, see Blomberg, "Historical-Critical/Grammatical View," 27–47.

12. Machen, *Christian Faith in the Modern World*, 65.

be *modified* in some way to produce positive results for understanding Scripture, both in the OT and NT, i.e., the negative presuppositions can be removed to allow for the miraculous. Evangelicals modify or call for modifying the "definition" of HC to make it compatible to evangelical sensibilities as follows. I. Howard Marshall, mentor to many evangelical critical scholars today that are achieving such prominence, in his "Historical Criticism" article, introduced evangelicals to his take on the discipline in 1977: "The study of any narrative which purports to convey historical information in order to determine what actually happened and is described or alluded to in the passage in question."[13] Marshall goes on to note, "Because the Bible is a divine-human book, it must be treated as both equal to and yet more than an ordinary book. To deny that the Bible should be studied through the use of literary and critical methodologies is to treat the Bible as less than human, less than historical, and less than literature."[14] This stands in direct contrast to ICBI 1978 that warned against dehistoricizing the plain, normal sense of Scripture due to human authorship as noted in article IX: "*We deny* that the finitude or fallenness of these writers, by necessity or otherwise, introduced distortion or falsehood in God's Word."

Furthermore, Marshall's view of authorship of New Testament books allowed false attribution, i.e., pseudepigraphy or the alleged use of well-known apostolic names for some New Testament books that were supposedly not really written by the apostles whose names these unknown imitators attached to the canonical books. In order to avoid carefully any idea of deceit, however, by his own acceptance of the concept of pseudepigraphy, Marshall coined a new term as a euphemism for such *false attribution*. He used the words "allonymity" and "allepigraphy" in which the prefix *pseudos* ("false") is replaced with *allos* ("other") which gives a more positive concept to the writing of a work in the name of another person. Marshall argued,

> It is not too great a step to a situation in which somebody close to a dead person continued to write as (they thought that) he would have done. An incomplete work can be completed by someone else . . .
>
> In none of these cases does the element of intentional deceit raise. . . . It is free from the moral stigma that early Christians attached to the practice of pseudonymity. Since the nuance of deceit seems to be inseparable from the use of the terms "pseudonymity" and "pseudepigraphy" and gives them a pejorative sense, we need another term that will refer more positively to the activity of writing in another person's name without intent to deceive: perhaps "allonymity" and "allepigraphy" may be suggested as suitable alternatives.[15]

Hence, in Marshall's logic, Paul did not write the Pastoral Epistles, for "although the objections vary in strength [to Pauline authorship of the Pastorals], their

---

13. Marshall, "Historical Criticism," 126.
14. Ibid.
15. Marshall, *Critical and Exegetical Commentary*, 84.

cumulative effect is to cast doubts on the traditional defence of direct Pauline authorship" although he allows that perhaps the books were written by "an unknown compiler" who based the letters perhaps on "some Pauline material" being used.[16] He sums up by arguing, "The probability that some Pauline material was used and the impossibility of identifying a named author should not obscure the fact that we are dealing with a person of considerable theological skill who was capable of putting his own stamp on his material and producing a set of documents marked by a unified and fresh expression of Pauline theology."[17] Blomberg, in another work, *Do Historical Matters Matter to Faith?*, advocates this idea of Marshall as fully in line with inerrancy and inspiration, arguing,

> A *methodology* consistent with evangelical convictions might argue that there was an accepted literary convention that allowed a follower, say, of Paul, in the generation after his martyrdom, to write a letter in Paul's name to one of the churches that had come under his sphere of influence. The church would have recognized that it could not have come from an apostle they knew had died two or three decades earlier, and they would have realized that the true author was writing thoughts indebted to the earlier teaching of Paul. In a world without footnotes or bibliographies, this was one way of giving credit where credit was due. Modesty prevented the real author from using his own name, so he wrote in ways he could easily have envisioned Paul writing were the apostle still alive today. *Whether or not this is what actually happened*, such a hypothesis is thoroughly consistent with a high view of Scripture and an inerrant Bible. We simply have to recognize what is and is not being claimed by the use of name "Paul" in that given letter.[18]

Blomberg, in his article on "The Historical-Critical/Grammatical" hermeneutic, asserts that historical criticism can be "shorn" of its "anti-supernatural presuppositions that the framers of that method originally employed" and eagerly embraces "source, form, tradition and redaction criticism" as "*all essential* tools for understanding the contents of the original document, its formation and origin, its literary genre and subgenres, the authenticity of the historical material it includes, and its theological or ideological emphases and distinctives."[19] Blomberg advocates "the Historical-Critical/Grammatical View" of hermeneutics for evangelicals that constitutes an alarming, and especially unstable, blend of historical-critical ideologies with the grammatico-historical hermeneutic. Blomberg argues for a "both-and-and-and" position of combining grammatico-historical method with that of historical-critical ideologies.[20] As will be seen, Blomberg's utilization of historical criticism causes him to start chang-

16. Ibid., 86, 89.
17. Ibid., 89.
18. Ibid., 352.
19. Blomberg, "Historical-Critical/Grammatical View," 46–47, italics added.
20. Ibid., 28.

ing traditional understanding of the term "inerrancy" especially as the idea of false attribution is now fully in line, in his thinking, with inspiration, i.e., a book alleged to have been written Paul does not necessarily mean that it actually was written by Paul.

He labels the "Historical-Critical/Grammatical" approach "the necessary foundation on which all other approaches must build."[21] However, history is replete with negative examples of those who attempted this unstable blend, from the neologians in Griesbach's day to that of Michael Licona's book currently under discussion (see below).[22] Baird, in his *History of New Testament Research*, commented:

> The neologians did not deny the validity of divine revelation but assigned priority to reason and natural theology. While faith in God, morality, and immortality were affirmed, older dogmas such as the Trinity, predestination, and the inspiration of Scripture were seriously compromised. . . . The neologians, however, appropriated the results of the historical-critical work of Semler and Michaelis.[23]

Significant similarities exist between today's evangelical historical critics and the neologians of Griesbach's day in terms of intent to combine popular methods of their day with faith.

Darrell Bock, another student of Marshall at Aberdeen, concurs with Marshall's definition of historical criticism, "I need to introduce these methods because of their importance to the contemporary discussion about Jesus, as well as the *potential merit their judicious use* brings to an understanding of the Gospels. Any approach that helps us to understand better the nature of the Gospels and how they might work is worth considering."[24] Bock fails to define or explain what he means by "a judicious use," so one is left wondering what such use may involve. He hints at the use of form criticism for evangelicals, however, with his statement, "In the hands of a skilled exegete who uses the tools of interpretation in a way that fits what they are capable of, Form Criticism can be a fruitful aid to understanding and to exposition."[25] The *Jesus Crisis* has already catalogued the bankruptcy of this hubris in that no evangelical scholar who practices historical criticism has been able to separate the skeptical nature of the discipline in exegetical decisions.[26]

Graham N. Stanton writes about the unifying factor historical criticism has been as a rapprochement between Protestants and Roman Catholics in hermeneutical approaches: "There is now considerable agreement among Protestants and Roman Catholic scholars about the appropriate tools and methods to be used in exegesis."

---

21. Ibid., 47.
22. For Griesbach and his association with neologians as well as its impact on his synoptic "solution," see Farnell, "How Views of Inspiration," 33–64.
23. Baird, *History of New Testament Research*, 116.
24. See Bock, *Studying the Historical Jesus*, 139, italics added.
25. Bock, "Form Criticism," 192.
26. Farnell, "Form and Tradition Criticism," 185–232.

Stanton continues, "Presuppositions adopted either consciously or unconsciously by the interpreter are far more influential in New Testament scholarship than disagreements over method."[27] Here Stanton reveals that the thin-line between Romanism and Protestantism holds merely at the line of presupposition. If those presuppositions disappear, then so will the hermeneutical and exegetical differences.

Peter H. Davids also extols the virtue of historical criticism practiced by evangelicals, "The sum of this discussion is that critical study of Scripture can clarify the message that the authors were trying to communicate either by showing how the author came to produce his or her work (through examining sources) or by clarifying the content in which the message was communicated. And while critical methodologies have undoubtedly led to a doubting of biblical authority by some, that is not their necessary conclusion, but one resulting from assumptions connected to them or perhaps even a misuse of them."[28]

Donald Hagner, like his evangelical counterparts, admits the danger inherent in historical criticism when it is practiced,

> The way out of the quandary [concerning critical method] is neither to continue to use the historical-critical method as classically conceived nor to abandon it outright because of its destructive past, but rather to modify it so as to make it more appropriate to the material being questioned . . .
>
> The historical-critical method is indispensable to any adequate and accurate understanding of the Bible, but only where it is tempered by an openness to the possibility of supernatural causation in the historical process. Without this tampering of method it is clearly inappropriate and ineffective, given the fact that the Bible is after all the story of God acting in history. In short, without this tampering the method can only be destructive. One of the great challenges facing evangelical scholarship is precisely that of modifying the historical-critical method so that it becomes productive and constructive.[29]

Hagner does not indicate whether biblical critics as a whole, such as those in the Society of Biblical Literature, would accept this evangelical "tampering" or whose tampered version of historical criticism would be adopted among evangelicals as a whole.

Hagner applies historical criticism in his recent work, *The New Testament: A Historical and Theological Introduction* (2012). The work is praised as follows on the Amazon website, reflecting similar wording on its jacket cover:

> This capstone work from widely respected senior evangelical scholar Donald Hagner offers a substantial introduction to the New Testament. Hagner deals with the New Testament both historically and theologically, employing the

---

27. Stanton, "Presuppositions in New Testament Criticism," 60.
28. Davids, "Authority, Hermeneutics and Criticism," 31–32.
29. Donald Hagner, "New Testament, History, and the Historical Critical Method," 86, 88.

framework of salvation history. He treats the New Testament as a coherent body of texts and stresses the unity of the New Testament without neglecting its variety. Although the volume covers typical questions of introduction, such as author, date, background, and sources, it focuses primarily on understanding the theological content and meaning of the texts, putting students in a position to understand the origins of Christianity and its canonical writings.

The book includes summary tables, diagrams, maps, and extensive bibliographies. It is praised in reviews by such scholars as James D. G. Dunn, I. Howard Marshall, Craig Keener, and Thomas Schreiner.

One may note two strategic factors regarding Hagner's New Testament *Introduction*. First, his work represents the cutting edge of evangelical, British-influenced and trained critical scholarship who are currently teaching the next generation of preachers and scholars in the United States, both on a college and seminary level. Second, Hagner's work will most likely replace the late Donald Guthrie's *New Testament Introduction* that was last revised in 1990. If one wants to know where evangelical critical scholarship is moving, Hagner's work provides that trajectory. These two strategic factors are also the works gravest weaknesses. The work attributes the word "inspired" to the New Testament Scripture.[30] Yet, Hagner maintains, "the inspired word of God comes to us through the medium of history, through the agency of writers who lived in history and were a part of history" which "*necessitate the historical and critical study of Scripture.*"[31] He says that the use of the word "critical" does not mean "tearing it down or demeaning it—but rather to exercising judgment or discernment concerning every aspect of it."[32] Therefore, Hagner asserts that "we must engage in historical criticism, in the sense of thoughtful interpretation of the Bible" and "the historical method is indispensable precisely because the Bible is the story of God's act in history."[33] What Hagner means by this is the need for historical critical ideologies rather than grammatico-historical criticism. This is the first signal that British-influenced evangelical scholars are shifting markedly away from the Reformation tradition of grammatico-historical criticism and training the next generation of preacher's in historical criticism that markedly differs in approach both presuppositionally, historically, and in the qualitative kind of conclusions such an ideology reaches. Like many British-influenced evangelical critical scholars, he believes that he can use historical criticism and be immune from its more negative elements: "The critical method therefore needs to be tempered so that rather than being used against the Bible, it is open to the possibility of the transcendent or miraculous within the historical process and thus is used to provide better understanding of the Bible."[34] This latter admission

---

30. Hagner, *New Testament*, 4.
31. Ibid.
32. Ibid., 5.
33. Ibid.
34. Ibid., 7.

is telling, since it is an admission, no matter how indirect, of the dangers of historical criticism. Hagner argues that "keeping an open mind concerning the possibility of the transcendent in history does not entail the suspension of critical judgment. There is no need for a naïve credulity and acceptance of anything and everything simply because one's worldview is amenable to the supernatural."[35] Hagner apparently believes that he has discovered the proper balance of presuppositions and practice in the historical-critical method displayed in this work: "It must be stressed once again that the critical method is indispensable to the study of Scripture. It is the sine qua non of responsible interpretation of God's word. The believer need have no fear of the method itself, but need only be on guard against the employment of improper presuppositions."[36] An old pithy saying, however, is that the "devil is in the details." Hagner's argument here ignores the marked evidence or proof from history of the presuppositions and damage that historical criticism has caused by even well-intentioned scholars who have eviscerated the Scripture through such an ideology. History constitutes a monumental testimony against Hagner's embracing of the ideologies of historical criticism as well as the damage that it has caused the church.

Hagner excoriates "very conservative scholars" and "obscurantist fundamentalism" that refused to embrace some form of moderated historical-critical ideology. Hagner commends Hengel's belief that "fundamentalism" and its accepting belief in the full trustworthiness in Scripture is actually a form of atheism,[37] quoting and affirming Hengel's position that "Fundamentalism is a form of 'unbelief' that closes itself to the—God intended—historical reality."[38] Hagner insists that "repudiation of the critical Study of Scripture amounts to a gnostic-like denial of the historical character of the Christian faith."[39] Apparently, Hagner (and Hengel) believes that since the Scriptures were mediated through history and human agency, this opens the documents up to the documents being fallible human products. Because of the Scripture being based in historical knowledge, one cannot use the word "certain" but only "probable," for Hagner in regards to New Testament. He insists that the "word 'prove,' although perhaps appropriate in mathematics and science, is out of place when it comes to historical knowledge."[40] He approvingly quotes Hengel's observation that "the demand to 'compellingly prove' something appears all too often in New Testament literature and indicates a lack of historical consciousness."[41] Thus, in studying Scripture, compelling proof will always be lacking regading the New Testament, "we

---

35. Ibid.
36. Ibid., 11.
37. Hengel, "Eye-Witness Memory," 70–96.
38. Ibid., 94n100.
39. Hagner, *New Testament*, 10.
40. Ibid., 9.
41. Hengel, "Eye-witness Memory," 88n77.

function quite well in life with knowledge that usually amounts to probability and not certainty."[42]

With this operating assumption about understanding Scripture, some sampling highlights of Hagner's "balanced" approach to historical-critical ideologies: First, "we have no reliable chronology of Jesus ministry" in the Gospels.[43] Since the Gospels are "historical narratives" they involve "interpretation" by the evangelists and that "level of interpretation can be high."[44] Since the Gospel writers largely (but not completely) reflect ancient Roman *bioi* as the "closest analogy from antiquity" and since *bioi* were not necessarily always without interpretation,[45] "the Evangelists compare well with the secular historians of their own day, and their narratives remain basically trustworthy."[46]

Second, like other critically trained European scholars, Hagner accepts Lessing's "ugly ditch" and the German/British concept of *historie* (actual verifiable events) vs. *geschichte*—(faith interpretations of events) of a dichotomy between the Jesus of the Gospels and the "historical Jesus."[47] Although critical of some historical Jesus research, Hagner concedes that "the Jesus of history was to some extent different from the Gospels' portrayal of him" and "if we cannot look for a one-to-one correspondence between the Jesus of history and the Jesus of the early church's faith, we can at least establish a degree of continuity between the two."[48] Furthermore, "we are in no position to write a biography of Jesus" based in the information from the New Testament since the Gospels are "kerygmatic portrayals of the story of Jesus."[49]

Third, Hagner embraces the idea that "pseudonymity" is acceptable in the New Testament canon. Hagner argues, "We have very little to lose in allowing the category of Deutero-Pauline letters. If it happens that some other person have written these four, or even six documents [e.g., Ephesians, Pastorals] in the name of Paul, we are not talking about forgery or deception."[50] "The ancient world on the whole did not have the same kind of sensitivity to pseudonymity that is typical in the modern world, with its concern for careful attribution and copyright."[51] "The authority and canonicity of the material is in no way affected" by books put into final shape by disciples of the prophets.[52] "The fact is that the Pauline corpus, with deutero-letters as well as without

42. Ibid.
43. Hagner, *New Testament*, 63.
44. Ibid.
45. Ibid., 61.
46. Ibid., 65.
47. Ibid., 83–104.
48. Ibid., 97.
49. Ibid., 98.
50. Ibid., 429.
51. Ibid.
52. Ibid.

them, stands under the banner of the authoritative Paul."[53] Hagner supports British scholar, I. Howard Marshall's view on "pseudonymous" writings in the New Testament: "In order to avoid the idea of deceit, Howard Marshall has coined the words 'allonymity' and 'allepigraphy' in which the prefix *pseudos* ('false') is replaced with *allos* ('other') which gives a more positive concept to the writing of a work in the name of another person."[54] Hagner says, "We do not know beyond a shadow of a doubt that there are Deutero-Pauline letters in the Pauline corpus, but if in the weighing of historical probabilities it seems to us that there are, we can freely admit that this too is a way in which God has mediated Scripture to us."[55] Apparently, to Hagner and others, God uses false attribution to accomplish his purpose of communication of his Word that encourages the highest ethical standards upon men! Thus, for Hagner, most likely did not write Ephesians as well as the Pastoral Epistles (1–2 Tim and Titus).[56] They should be viewed in the category of Deutero-Pauline letters.[57] Hagner even devotes a whole section of his *Introduction* to this category of Deutero-Pauline letters.[58] He regards the book of James as possibly not written by James: "We cannot completely exclude the alternative possibility that the book is pseudonymous. Already in the time of Jerome it was regarded as such. . . . Least likely of all, but again not impossible, the letter could have been written by another, little known or unknown, person named 'James.'"[59] Second Peter is "almost certainly not by Peter. Very probably written by a disciple of Peter or a member of the Petrine circle."[60] The author of Revelation is "almost certainly not by the Apostle John. Possibly by John 'The Elder" but more probably by another John, otherwise unknown to us, who may have been a member of the Johannine circle."[61]

In sum, Hagner's work represents what may well replace Guthrie's *New Testament Introduction*. One can only imagine the impact will be that British and European evangelical critical scholarship represented by Hagner's assertions regarding his "balanced" use of historical-critical presuppositions will have on the next generation of God's preachers and teachers! As Machen said long ago, "as go the theological seminaries, so go the churches."[62]

---

53. Ibid.
54. Ibid., 431; Marshall, *Critical and Exegetical Commentary*, 84.
55. Hagner, *New Testament*, 432.
56. Ibid., 428.
57. Ibid., 429.
58. Ibid., 585–642.
59. Ibid., 675.
60. Ibid., 714.
61. Ibid., 761.
62. Machen, *Christian Faith in the Modern World*, 65.

## ERRANCY NOW MASQUERADES AS INERRANCY AMONG CRITICAL EVANGELICAL SCHOLARS

These evangelical quotes about their adoption and definition, or perhaps better, redefinition of historical criticism to accommodate evangelical beliefs, bring to focus the destructive skepticism that this ideology contains. Because critical evangelical scholars seek to adopt some form of historical criticism, the inevitable result is skepticism regarding biblical revelation. This is the unavoidable fruit of such recombination or hybridization of the grammatico-historical and historical-critical methods. The skepticism of historical criticism will always manifest itself in their exegetical decisions that drive their modified hermeneutic that encompasses some form of historical criticism. The core of the critical evangelical scholars' attempts to redefine inerrancy is the driving reason why new heterodox versions of "inerrancy" are now emerging. In other words, historical criticism cannot encompass any orthodox view of inerrancy. Inerrancy views must be shifted to accommodate the skepticism of historical criticism, with the resulting heterodox views of errancy among evangelical critical scholars that masquerade as under the false rubric of "inerrancy." That is, they have changed the definition of inerrancy to errancy to accommodate the skepticism of historical criticism. The following are merely a few examples of the critical evangelical scholars who now stand in prominence in the Evangelical Theological Society, a society which has "inerrancy" as its sole core statement.

## THE HISTORICAL-CRITICAL MAGIC OF THE DISAPPEARING CREATION ACCOUNT OF GENESIS 1–3

The present writer has reviewed John D. Walton's and D. Brent Sandy's *Lost World of Scripture* previously.[63] The good news is that Walton and Sandy say that they believe in the "inerrancy" of Scripture. The writers state that their "specific objective is to understand better how both the Old and New Testaments were spoken, written, and passed on, especially with an eye to possible implications for the Bible's inspiration and authority."[64] They add, "Part of the purpose of this book is to bring students back from the brink of turning away from the authority of Scripture in reaction to the misappropriation of the term *inerrancy*."[65]

They assert that as Wheaton College professors, they work "at an institution and with a faculty that take a strong stand on inerrancy but that are open to dialogue" and that this openness "provided a safe context in which to explore the authority of Scripture from the ground up."[66] Walton wrote the chapters on the Old Testament, while

---

63. Farnell, review of *Lost World of Scripture*, 121–29.
64. Walton and Sandy, *Lost World of Scripture*, 9.
65. Ibid.
66. Ibid., 10.

Sandy wrote the chapters on the New Testament. Walton and Sandy have written this book especially for "Christian students in colleges, seminaries and universities" with the hopes that they will find their work "useful," as well as writing for "colleagues who have a high view of Scripture, especially for those who hold to inerrancy."[67] The book is also "not intended for outsiders; that is, it's not an apologetic defense of biblical authority. Rather, we're writing for insiders, seeking to clarify how best to understand the Bible."[68] The writers also assure the readers that they have a "very high view of Scripture"; "we affirm inerrancy" and "are in agreement with the definition suggested by David Dockery that the 'Bible properly interpreted in light of [the] culture and communication developed by the time of its composition will be shown to be completely true (and therefore not false) in all that it affirms, to the degree of precision intended by the author, in all matters relating to God and his creation."[69]

The central thrust of the book is that the world of the Bible (both Old and New Testament) is quite different from modern times:

> Most of us are probably unprepared . . . for how different the ancient world is from our own. . . . We're thousands of years and thousands of miles removed. It means we frequently need to put the brakes on and ask whether we're reading the Bible in light of the original culture or in light of contemporary culture. While the Bible's values were very different from ancient cultures,' it obviously communicated in the existing languages and within cultural customs of the day.[70]

Such recognition includes that the "evidence assembled in this book inevitably leads to the question of inerrancy."[71] "The truth of the matter is, no term, or even combination of terms, can completely represent the fullness of Scripture's authority."[72] They then quote the Short Statement of the Chicago Statement on Biblical Inerrancy of 1978.[73] This creates the impression that they are in agreement with the whole ICBI statement. However, this is deceptive because this book constitutes an essential challenge to the entire substance of what the Chicago Statements expressed. This uneasiness with the Chicago Statement can also be seen in those who are listed as endorsers of the work, Tremper Longman III who is the Robert H. Gundry Professor of Biblical Studies, as well as Michael R. Licona who recently, in his *Resurrection of Jesus*, used genre criticism to negate the resurrection of the saints in Jerusalem in Matthew 27:51–53 at Jesus' crucifixion as apocalyptic genre rather than indicating a literal resurrec-

---

67. Ibid.
68. Ibid.
69. Dockery, *Christian Scripture*, 64.
70. Walton and Sandy, *Lost World of Scripture*, 13.
71. Ibid.
72. Ibid.
73. Ibid., 14.

tion, and Craig Evans, Acadia Divinity College, who is not known for his support of the Chicago Statements.

The book consists of twenty-one propositions that seek to nuance biblical authority, interpretation, and an understanding of inerrancy, with the essential thought of these propositions flowing basically from two areas: (1) their first proposition, "Ancient Near Eastern Societies were *hearing dominant* and had nothing comparable to authors and books as we know them" (in modern times since the printing press) while modern societies today are "*text dominant*"[74] and (2) speech-act theory that they frequently refer to in their work.[75] They qualify their latter acceptance of speech-act theory: "We do not agree with many of the conclusions with speech act theory, but we find its foundational premise and terminology helpful and have adopted its three basic categories. The communicator uses *locutions* (words, sentences, rhetorical structures, genres) to embody an *illocution* (the intention to do something with those locutions—bless, promise, instruct, assert) with a *perlocution* that anticipates a certain response from the audience (obedience trust, belief)."[76]

They go on to assert that God accommodated his communication in the Scripture: "Accommodation on the part of the divine communicator resides primarily in the locution, in which the genre and rhetorical devices are included."[77] And,

> Genre is largely a part of the locution, not the illocution. Like grammar, syntax and lexemes, genre is a mechanism to convey an illocution. Accommodation takes place primarily at the locutionary level. Inerrancy and authority related to the illocution; accommodation and genre attach at the locution. Therefore inerrancy and authority cannot be undermined, compromised or jeopardized by genre or accommodation. While genre labels may be misleading, genre itself cannot be true or false, errant or inerrant, authoritative or non-authoritative. Certain genres lend themselves to more factual detail and others more toward fictional imagination.[78]

While admittedly the book's propositions entail many other ideas, from these two ideas, an oral dominated society in the ancient times of the OT and NT vs. a written/text dominant society of modern times and the implications of speech-act theory cited above, flow all that they develop in their assertions to nuance their take on what a proper view of inerrancy and biblical authority should be. The obvious implication of these assertions is that Robert Gundry, who was removed from ETS due to his dehistoricizing in 1983, was wronged because value judgments about genre do not impact the doctrine of inerrancy. Gundry was perfectly in the confines of inerrancy to

---

74. Ibid., 19, italics added; see also 17–28.
75. Ibid., 41–46, 48, 51, 200, 213–18, 229, 288.
76. Ibid., 41.
77. Ibid., 42.
78. Ibid., 45.

dehistoricize because, according to Walton and Sandy, it was ETS that misunderstood the concept of inerrancy as not genre driven. It is the illocution (purpose or intent) not the wording that drives inerrancy. Gundry's theorizing of a midrashic genre, according to this idea, had nothing at all to do with inerrancy. Gundry believed sincerely in inerrancy but realized the midrashic, not historical, nature of Matthew 2.

Walton's and Sandy's work is reminiscent of Rogers and McKim, in their now famous *Authority and Interpretation of the Bible: An Historical Approach* (1979), who made a similar error in their approach to Scripture. They also spoke of "the central Christian tradition included the concept of accommodation"; that today witnesses a "scholastic overreaction to biblical criticism"; "the function and purpose of the Bible was to bring people into a saving relationship with God through Jesus Christ"; "the Bible was not used as an encyclopedia of information on all subjects"; and "to erect a standard of modern, technical precision in language as the hallmark of biblical authority was totally foreign to the foundation shared by the early church."[79] Walton and Sandy similarly assert in their implications of an oral society that "the Bible contains no new revelation about the material workings and understanding of the Material World,"[80] so that

> [the Bible's] explicit statements about the material world are part of the locution and would naturally accommodate the beliefs of the ancient world. As such they are not vested with authority. We cannot encumber with scriptural authority any scientific conclusions we might deduce from the biblical text about the material world, its history or its regular processes. This means that we cannot draw any scientific conclusions about such areas as physiology, meteorology, astronomy, cosmic geography, genetics, or geology from the Bible. For example, we should believe that God created the universe, but we should not expect to be able to derive from the biblical texts the methods that he used or the time that it took. We should believe that God created humans in his image and that through the choices they made sin and death came into the world. Scientific conclusions, however, relating to the material processes of human origins (whether from biology in general or genetics in particular) may be outside the purview of the Bible. We need to ask whether the Bible is making those sort of claims in its illocutions.[81]

They continue, "The Bible's claims regarding origins, mechanics, or shape of the world are, by definition of the focus of its revelation in the theological realm."[82]

According to Walton and Sandy, what the Bible says plainly in the words of Genesis 1 may not be what it intends. Immediate special creation cannot be read into the text; rather the door is open for evolution and the acceptance of modern

---

79. Rogers and McKim, *Authority and Interpretation of the Bible*, xxii.
80. Walton and Sandy, *Lost World*, 49–59.
81. Ibid., 55.
82. Ibid.

understandings of science. Thus, Genesis 1 and 2 may well indicate God's creation but not the means of how he created, even when the locutions say "evening and morning," "first day," etc. Much of what is in Genesis 1 reflects "Old World Science": "One could easily infer from the statements in the biblical text that the sun and moon share space with the birds (Gen 1). But this is simply a reflection of Old World Science, and we attach no authority to that conclusion. Rather we consider it a matter of deduction on the part of the ancients who made no reason to know better."[83] For them, "the Bible's authority is bound into theological claims and entailments about the material world." For them, since the Bible is not a science textbook, its "authority is not found in the locution but has to come through illocution."[84] Genesis 1–2, under their system, does not rule out evolution; nor does it signify creation literally in six "days." Such conclusions press the text far beyond its purpose to indicate God's creation of the world but not the how of the processes involved. They conclude, "We have proposed that reticence to identify scientific claims or entailments is the logical conclusion from the first two points (not a science textbook; no new scientific revelation) and that a proper understanding of biblical authority is dependent on recognizing this to be true."[85] They assert that "it is safe to believe that Old World Science permeates the Old Testament" and "Old World Science is simply part of the locution [words, etc.] and as such is not vested with authority."[86]

Apparently, Walton and Sandy believe that modern science has a better track record at origins. This assumption is rather laughable. Many "laws" of science for one generation are overturned in other generations. Scientific understanding is in constant flux. Both of these authors have failed to understand that modern science is predominated overwhelmingly by materialistic philosophies rather than presenting any evidence of objectivity in the area of origins. Since true science is based on observation, testing, measurement and repeatability, ideas of origins are beyond the purview of modern science, too. For instance, the fossil record indicates the death of animals, but how that death occurred and what the implications of that fossil record are delves more into philosophy and agendas rather than good science. Since no transitional forms exist between species in the fossil record, evolution should be rendered tenuous as an explanation, but science refuses to rule it out due to a dogmatic *a priori*.

While Walton and Sandy quote the ICBI Short Statement, their work actually is an assault on the articles of affirmation and denial of the 1978 Chicago Statement on Inerrancy. Article IX noted, "*We affirm* that inspiration, though not conferring omniscience, guaranteed true and trustworthy utterance on all matters of which the biblical authors were moved to speak and write," and article XII, "*We deny* that biblical infallibility and inerrancy are limited to spiritual, religious, or redemptive themes,

---

83. Ibid., 57.
84. Ibid., 54.
85. Ibid., 59.
86. Ibid., 300.

exclusive of the fields of history and science. We further deny that scientific hypotheses about earth history may properly be used to overturn the teaching of Scripture on creation and the flood." Article XI related, "Far from misleading us, it is true and reliable in all matters in addresses."

Another area that is troubling is in their theorizing of text-canonical updating. Walton's and Sandy's adoption of multiple unknown redactor/editors who updated the text over long periods of time in terms of geography, history, names, etc., actually constitutes an argument, not for inerrancy, but for deficiency in the text of Scripture and hence an argument for errancy, not inerrancy. Due to the OT being an oral- or ear-dominated society, Walton and Sandy also propose a text-canonical updating hypothesis: "The model we propose agrees with traditional criticism in that it understands the final literary form of the biblical books to be relatively late and generally not the literary product of the authority figure whose words the book preserves."[87] Thus, while Moses, Isaiah, and other prominent figures were behind the book, perhaps multiple, unknown editors were involved in any updating and final form of the books in the OT/NT that we have. For them, in the whole process of Scripture, "the Holy Spirit is behind the whole process from beginning to end in spite of the involvement of unknown hands in their final development."[88] Walton and Sandy negate the central idea of inerrancy that would center around original autographs that were inerrant, or that such autographs even existed: "Within evangelical circles discussing inerrancy and authority, the common affirmation is that the text is inerrant in the original autographs . . . since all copies were pristine, inerrancy could only be connected with the putative originals."[89] Modern discovery of the Dead Sea Scrolls has made it "clear that there was not only one original form of the final literary piece" of such books as Samuel and Jeremiah.[90] Which version is original cannot be determined. Under their view, it does not make any difference because "in the model that we have proposed here, it does not matter. The authority is associated with Jeremiah, no matter which compilation is used. We cannot be dependent on the 'original autographs,' not only because we do not have them, but also because the very concept is anachronistic for most of the Old Testament."[91] For Walton and Sandy, "inerrancy and authority are connected initially to the figure or the authoritative traditions. We further accept the authority represented in the form of the book adopted by faith communities and given canonical status."[92] "Inerrancy and authority attach to the final canonical form of the book rather than to putative original autographs."[93] Later on in their work, Walton

87. Ibid., 66.
88. Ibid., 66.
89. Ibid.
90. Ibid., 67.
91. Ibid.
92. Ibid.
93. Ibid., 68.

and Sandy assert that "inerrancy would then pertain to the role of the authorities (i.e., the role of Moses or Isaiah as dominant, determinative, and principle voice), not to so-called authors writing so-called books—but the literature in its entirety would be considered authoritative."[94] For them, "authority is not dependent on the original autographs or an author writing a book. Recognition of authority is identifiable in the beliefs of a community of faith (of whom we are heirs) that God's communications through authoritative figures and traditions have been captured and preserved through a long process of transmission and composition."[95] To them, Mosaic authorship of the Pentateuch "does not decide the matter" regarding its authority, for many may have been involved in the final form of the first five books of Moses.[96] The final form involved perhaps many unknown editors and updaters: "Our interest is in the identity of the prophet as the authority figure behind the oracles, regardless of the composition history of the book."[97] Accordingly, while Moses, Jeremiah, for instance were the originators of the tradition or document and names are associated with the books, this approach of many involved in the product/final form of the book and variations, "allows us to adopt some of the more important advances that critical scholarship has offered."[98] For them, unknown editors over long periods of time would have updated the text in many ways as time passed. They argue, "It is safe to believe that some later material could be added and later editors could have a role in the compositional history of a canonical book."[99] Their positing of such a scheme, however, is suggestive that the text had been corrected, updated, revised all which smacks of a case for errancy more than inerrancy in the process.

Again, orthodox views of inerrancy, like the 1978 Chicago Statement, were not so negative about determining the autographs as article X related, "*We affirm* that inspiration, strictly speaking, applies only to the autographs of Scripture, which in the providence of God can be ascertained from available manuscripts with great accuracy."

Walton and Sandy also assert that "exacting detail and precise wording were not necessary to preserve and transmit the truths of Scripture"[100] because they were an ear-related culture rather than a print-related culture ("Proposition 13").

In reply to Walton and Sandy, while this may be true that the New Testament was oral, such a statement needs qualification in their propositions throughout. No matter what the extent of orality in the Old and New Testaments, as posed by Walton and Sandy, the reportage in these passages is accurate though it may not be, at times precise. While they are correct that "exacting detail and precise wording were not

94. Ibid., 281.
95. Ibid., 68.
96. Ibid., 69.
97. Ibid., 72.
98. Ibid., 74.
99. Ibid., 299.
100. Ibid., 181.

necessary to preserve and transmit the truths of Scripture," two competing views need to be contrasted in that reportage that was written down in the text of Scripture: an orthodox view and an unorthodox view of that reportage. This important distinction is lost in Walton and Sandy's discussion:[101]

| Orthodox View | Unorthodox View |
|---|---|
| Reporting them | Creating them |
| Selecting them | Constructing them |
| Arranging them | Misarranging them |
| Paraphrasing them | Expanding them |
| Change their form (grammatical change) | Changer their content (theological change) |
| Changer their wording | Changer their meaning |
| Translate them | Mistranslate them |
| Interpret them | Misinterpret them |
| Editing | Redacting |

Article XIII of the 1978 Chicago Statement was careful to note that inerrancy does not demand precision at all times in reportage. Any criticism of the Chicago Statements in this area is ill-advised. "We further deny that inerrancy is negated by biblical phenomena such as a lack of modern technical precision, irregularities of grammar or spelling, observational descriptions of nature, the reportage of falsehoods, the use of hyperbole and round numbers, the topical arrangement of material, variant selections of material in parallel accounts, or the use of free citations." Walton and Sandy, however, argue: "It is not necessary to explain away the differences by some means of harmonization in order to it fit modern standards of accuracy."[102]

While anyone may note many examples of trite harmonization, this does not negate the legitimacy or need for harmonization. Tatian's *Diatessaron* (ca. 160–175) is a testimony to the ancient church believing that the Gospels could be harmonized since they were a product of the Holy Spirit. From the ancient Christian church through to the time of the Reformation, the church always believed in the legitimacy and usefulness of harmonization. It was not until the modern philosophical presuppositions (e.g., Rationalism, Deism, Romanticism, etc.) that created the historical-critical ideology arose that discredited harmonization. The orthodox position of the church was that the Gospels were without error and could be harmonized into a unified whole. The rise of modern critical method (i.e., historical criticism) with its accompanying low or no views of inspiration discredited harmonization, not bad examples of harmonization.[103]

Walton and Sandy contend that they wrote their book with the following in mind: "Our intention is to strengthen the doctrine of biblical authority through a realistic

---

101. See Geisler and Farnell, *Jesus Quest*, 681–83, for a full discussion.
102. Walton and Sandy, *Lost World*, 151.
103. See McArthur, *Quest through the Centuries*, 85–101.

application of knowledge of the ancient world, and to understand what inerrancy can do and what it can't do."[104] They believe that the term inerrancy is a term that "is reaching its limits" and also that "the convictions it sought to express and preserve remain important."[105] "Inerrancy" is no longer the clear, defining term it once was and that "has become diminished in rhetorical power and specificity, it no longer serves as adequately to define our convictions about the robust authority of Scripture."[106]

They cite several errors of inerrancy advocates in the past. Most notably are the following two: (1) Inerrancy advocates "have at times misunderstood 'historical' texts by applying modern genre criteria to ancient literature, thus treating it as having claims that it never intended."[107] Apparently, this position allows Walton and Sandy to read magically the findings of modern "scientism" (i.e., evolution, day-age hypothesis) into the plain, normal sense of the biblical text (creation in six literal days, creationism) that conflicts with today's popular hypotheses of origins. (2) Inerrancy advocates "have at times confused locution [words, sentences, rhetorical structures, genres] and illocution [the intention to do something with those locutions—bless, promise, instruct, assert]." They argue that "inerrancy technically applies only to the latter, though of course, without locutions, there would be no illocution."[108] Walton and Sandy here confuse inerrancy of the words of the text with interpretation of a text. In reply to them, no one's "interpretation" of the words in the text is inspired, but each and every word is inspired (i.e., plenary, verbal inspiration), but the understanding or interpretation of those words should not be considered "inerrant." Interpretations will vary but the inerrancy of the words does not. Moreover, if Genesis 1 says in its plain, normal sense of the words "evening and morning" and "first," "second" day, it is tenuous to imply that these terms are so flexible in interpretation to allow for long periods of time to accommodate evolutionary hypotheses. Otherwise, words have no real meaning. They can mean whatever the interpreter wants them to mean, so in essence they have no true meaning. Yet, Walton and Sandy assert that traditional inerrantists "have been too anxious to declare sections of the Old Testament to be historical in a modern sense, where it may not be making those claims for itself."[109] Here, Walton and Sandy use this idea to negate any part of the Old Testament that does not accord with modern sensibilities. It creates a large opening to read into the text rather than allow the text to speak for itself. They assert that positions such as "young earth or premillenialism may be defensible interpretations, but they cannot invoke inerrancy as a claim to truth."[110] For Walton and Sandy, "the Israelites shared

104. Walton and Sandy, *Lost World*, 274.
105. Ibid.
106. Ibid., 275.
107. Ibid., 279.
108. Ibid.
109. Ibid.
110. Ibid., 282.

the general cognitive environment of the ancient world. . . . At the illocutionary level we may say that traditions in the early chapters of Genesis, for example served the Israelites by offering an account of God and his ways and conveying their deepest beliefs about how the world works, who they are and how it all began. These are the same questions addressed by the mythological traditions of the ancient world, but the answers given are very different."[111] Sadly, Walton and Sandy must remove the plain, normal historical sense in order to impose their novel interpretation of the passage, i.e., the novel interpretation that currently reigns among the academic elites due to prevalent evolutionary philosophies of the day. Magically, through these historical-critical principles the plain, normal grammatico-historical sense of the text does not have to be a roadblock but is readily removed. Historical criticism becomes the dissolvent to make the text pliable to current sensibilities.

One other area where the elasticity of Walton's and Sandy's concept of history centers in that they allow for hyperbolic use of numbers in the Old Testament: "It is safe to believe that the Bible can use numbers rhetorically with the range of the conventions of the ancient world."[112] They argue,

> We may conclude that they are exaggerated or even that contradictory amounts are given in sources that report the same event. These may well be inaccuracies or contradictions according to our conventions, but that doesn't meant that they jeopardize inerrancy. Again, numerical quantity is locution [words]. Authority ties to the illocution [interpretation] and what the narrator is *doing* with those numbers. Whatever he is doing, he is doing with the accepted conventions of their world.[113]

Magically, Walton and Sandy encompass false statements (cf. "you shall not lie") as perfectly in line with inerrancy. If traditional inerrantists object to such logic, they would reply that the latter misunderstands the culture of the time, which ancient culture thought nothing of exaggerated or contradictory amounts. Apparently, doing such things was considered perfectly normal. Such objective falsities are subjectively true and part of inerrancy; perfectly normal for the times in which the Bible was written.

Finally, Walton and Sandy argue that "our doctrine of authority of Scripture has become too enmeshed in apologetics. . . . If we tie apologetics and theology too tightly together, the result could be that we end up trying to defend as theology what are really just apologetic claims we have made."[114]

In summing up, they contend: "Ill-formed versions of inerrancy have misled many people into false understandings of the nature of Scripture, which has led to

---

111. Ibid., 303–4.
112. Ibid., 302.
113. Ibid.
114. Ibid., 306.

poor hermeneutics for interpreting Scripture and to misunderstandings of Bible translations. Even more serious, certain views of inerrancy have led people away from the Christian faith. Such views can also keep people from considering more important matters in Scripture. If there is a stumbling block to people coming to the faith, should it not be Christ alone rather than a wall that we inadvertently place in the way of spiritual pilgrimages?"[115] In reply to all of their logic, one must ask the following: if the documents cannot be trusted in their plain, normal sense (e.g., creation), then how can their testimony about Christ be trusted? If the documents have as much flexibility as hypothesized by Walton and Sandy, how can they be trusted to give a reliable, accurate and faithful witness to him? While Walton and Sandy have wrapped their work in an alleged improvement of current concepts of inerrancy and its implications, they have actually presented a system that is (1) quite inferior to that of the ICBI statements of 1978 and 1982 and (2) one that really is designed to undermine the years of evangelical history that went into the formulation of those documents against the onslaught of historical-critical ideologies that Walton and Sandy now embrace. They treat the history and reasons for the formulation of ICBI statements in a dismissive fashion that is perilous, for those who do not remember the events of the past are doomed to repeat its mistakes as evidenced in this work of Walton and Sandy. A better title for this book would have been *Lost World of Inerrancy* since their system undermines the very concept. One is left wondering what form of "inerrancy" is really advocated by Walton and Sandy. It is not any stretch to say that their view really masquerades "errancy" in the form of "inerrancy."

## THE MAGIC OF THE DISAPPEARING JESUS IN HISTORICAL CRITICISM

One other area regarding the magical nature of historical criticism must be noted. With historical criticism, the Jesus of the Gospels has now magically disappeared and the "real" Jesus must be rediscovered through searching for him. Sadly, evangelical critical scholars have now joined in the third search for what is known as the "historical Jesus."[116]

For the past several hundred years, scholars have conducted what is known as "the search for the historical Jesus" or also today as "historical Jesus research." Such a search operates under the *a priori* assumption that the four canonical Gospels, the only documents written about the life of Jesus, are in some significant ways deficient, incorrect, or inadequate in their presentation of Jesus' life and work in actual history. This search posits a sharp cleavage between the Gospel portraits of Jesus and his

---

115. Ibid., 308.

116. For a more thorough analysis of this questing for Jesus, see Farnell, "Searching for the 'Historical Jesus': The Rise of the Three Searches," 361–420, and "Searching for the Historical Jesus: Evangelical Participation in the Third Search," 467–502.

actual existence in first-century Palestine and seeks to establish a scholarly consensus view of Jesus that would be considered a more accurate representation of his life than what is contained in the Gospels. The overarching purpose of which is to deliberately destroy the influence of the Gospels and the church upon society. While this purpose is openly and honestly admitted by theological liberals, evangelicals who participate now in the "third quest" are far less candid as to its design. These searches started with the rise in dominance of the ideology of historical criticism over two hundred years ago and are a natural consequence of the innate historical skepticism replete in them. The first two searches ended as declared failures by those who engaged in them. Now some of the same scholars who have inspired the New Perspective on Paul have also been largely influential in stimulating the "third search for 'the historical Jesus'" (e.g., Sanders, Wright, Dunn). When the evidence is examined, only one overall "search for the 'historical Jesus'" has actually existed. All three are unified by sharing, to some degree, the unifying characteristics of significant degrees of suspicion regarding the Gospels, similar ideological approaches in utilizing historical criticism, a refusal to accept the biblical accounts as truly depicting Jesus as he actually was in history, and a marked preference for developing a view of Jesus that is acceptable to scholarship.

## THE CONSISTENT TESTIMONY OF THE ORTHODOX CHURCH FOR 1,700 YEARS

From the nascent beginnings of the church until the seventeenth century, orthodox Christians held that the four canonical Gospels (Matthew, Luke, Mark and John) were historical, biographical, albeit selective (cf. John 20:30–31) eyewitness accounts of Jesus' life[117] written by the men whose names were attached to them from the beginning.[118] These Gospels are virtually the only source for our knowledge of the acts and teachings of Jesus. The Gospels were considered by the church as the product of Spirit-energized minds (John 14:26; 16:13; 1 John 4:4) to give the true presentation of Jesus' life and work for the thirty-plus years that he lived on the earth. The consistent, as well as persistent, testimony expressed in early church history was that the Apostle Matthew, also known as Levi, wrote the book of Matthew as the first account of Jesus' life; the physician, Luke, companion of the Apostle Paul, wrote his Gospel based on careful interviews of those who interacted with Jesus (Luke 1:1–4); Mark, the interpreter for Peter, wrote his Gospel based on the preaching of Peter; while the Apostle John, the

---

117. In a disputed passage, Josephus has a brief reference to Jesus' ministry, see Josephus *Antiquities* 18.3.3 §63–64; Acts 20:35 has a record of a saying of Jesus quoted by Paul but not found in the canonical Gospels ("it is more blessed to give than receive").

118. These views of the early church regarding the four Gospels as coming from the eyewitness apostles whose names were attached to them are ancient and persistent. E.g., Eusebius *Ecclesiastical History* 3.39.1–6, 14–16; 5.11.1–4; 5.20.4–8; 6.14.5–7; Clement *Hypotyposeis* 6; Irenaeus *Against Heresies* 5.33.3–4; Clement *Stromateis* 1.1.1.11 For greater delineation of these references, see Farnell, "Synoptic Gospels in the Ancient Church," *MSJ* 10.1 (1999) 53–86.

disciple whom Jesus loved as well as a specially intimate disciple of Jesus, wrote the last canonical Gospel that bears his name. Since these men had either accompanied Jesus' ministry from its inception (Matthew, John) or been in direct contact with those who had (Mark, Luke), the accounts were considered absolutely trustworthy witnesses to Jesus' life and ministry as it actually occurred in history.

One cannot overstress that the rise of modern *philosophical* ideologies inherent in historical criticism generates any such distinctions between the Jesus as he is presented in the canonical Gospels and any conceptualizations of how he is alleged to have been actually in history. Hostile philosophical underpinnings of the ideology in terms of a virulent *anti-supernaturalism* create these hypothetical distinctions.[119] *The overarching intent in these searches is the destruction of the influence of the Gospels, as well as the church, over society.*

## THE "HISTORICAL JESUS" RESEARCH IS SEARCHING FOR A DEFINITION OF THE TERM

The term "historical Jesus" cannot truly be defined with any degree of satisfaction or consensus among those who advocate such research. These researchers search for a concept of Jesus that cannot be defined. The irony of this state of affairs in its definition has resulted from the fact that no consensus has occurred as to what the "historical Jesus" is or was. Hagner incisively comments,

> It deserves to be emphasized that in both the nineteenth-century writing on Jesus and that of today, what seems to be wanting is not so much *a truer* view of Jesus as an *alternative* view. The traditional view of Jesus, the view held by the early church, is old-fashioned, uninteresting, and thought to be unconvincing. What the world craves is a debunking of the traditional Jesus, a Jesus rescued from the dogma of the church for twenty-first-century human beings. What will sell books and bring fame or notoriety are new explanations of Jesus—explanations acceptable to the proclivities and sensitivities of the modern world.[120]

After two hundred-plus years of questing for whatever the "historical Jesus" might be, involving possibly three perceived "quests," no general agreement exists among biblical scholars who pursue this discipline as to what the term means. Renowned British theologian N. T. Wright, himself a strategic impetus for a "third quest" for the "historical Jesus" now known officially as the "Life of Jesus Research," laments, "The current wave of books about Jesus offers a bewildering range of competing hypotheses. There is no unifying theological agenda; no final agreement about method;

---

119. For a much more detailed discussion, see Farnell, "Philosophical and Theological Bent," 85–131.
120. Hagner, "Analysis of Recent 'Historical Jesus' Studies," 82.

certainly no common set of results."[121] All quests, however, have in common the refusal to allow the possibility of the truly supernatural in history and thus take away any adequate or Gospel-based understanding of Jesus. An acute subjectivity reigns in every presentation of whatever the "historical Jesus" is/was. William Hamilton, reflecting somewhat of a Bultmannian or Tillichian mode that assumes *a priori* negative historiography involved in historical criticism, rejects the whole process as "beyond belief," concluding, "Jesus is inaccessible by historical means," preferring instead a "Quest for the Post-Historical Jesus." According to Hamilton, Jesus in history can never be defined or known. Thus, not only is the Gospel portrait rejected but no certainty can exist or be known about Jesus even in an alleged post-Easter circumstance.[122] Perhaps the crescendo of this type of thought is found with Jewish theologian Neusner when he stated that the questing for the historical Jesus is "disingenuous" and "irrelevant," since modern standards of historiography "cannot comprise supernatural events," and "religious writings such as the Gospels cannot, and should not, attempt to meet [such standards]."[123] Since the heart of the Gospels entails the supposition that God entered human history with Jesus, anything supernatural is *a priori* ruled out from being investigated historically.

## WHATEVER THE "HISTORICAL JESUS" IS, IT MUST NOT BE THE CHRIST OF THE GOSPELS

In 1959, James M. Robinson, a leader of what is now known as the "second quest" period, did, however, stress what the term could *not* mean:

> The term "historical Jesus" is not simply identical with "Jesus" or "Jesus of Nazareth," as if the adjective "historical" were a meaningless addition. Rather the adjective is used in a technical sense, and makes a specific contribution to the total meaning of the expression. "Historical" is used in the sense of "things in the past which have been established by objective scholarship." Consequently the expression "historical Jesus" comes to mean: "What can be known of Jesus of Nazareth by means of scientific methods of the historian." Thus we have to do with a technical expression which must be recognized as such, and not automatically identified with the simple term "Jesus."[124]

Robinson continues regarding the first alleged quest that "this was in fact the assumption of the nineteenth-century quest of the historical Jesus. For this quest was

---

121. Wright, "Jesus, Quest for the Historical," 800.

122. Hamilton, *Quest for the Post-Historical Jesus*, 8–9, 19. See also Georgi, "Interest in Life of Jesus Theology," 51–83.

123. Neusner, "Who Needs 'The Historical Jesus'?," 113–26. For how Jewish theologians have used historical-critical ideologies to find a Jesus compatible to them, see Hagner, *Jewish Reclamation of Jesus*.

124. Robinson, *New Quest of the Historical Jesus*, 26–27.

initiated by the enlightenment in its effort to escape the limitations of dogma . . . unrestricted by the doctrinal presentations of him in the Bible, creed and church."[125] Because no perceived agreement or consensus exists as to who or what the "historical Jesus" is or even if such a definition can even be determined, the consequence appears to be that it is to be defined negatively since a general agreement exists among questers that whatever the "historical Jesus" is or was, He is not, and indeed cannot be, equated fully with the Jesus who is presented in the Gospels. Since historiography, i.e., hypotheses of what can take place in a time-space continuum in reference to historical-critical ideology, cannot encompass the supernatural, and indeed, rules it out from the very beginning, whatever the "historical Jesus" is, he cannot be equated with the Jesus presented in the Gospels.[126]

## THE EXISTENTIAL JESUS OR "WHAT THE 'HISTORICAL JESUS' MEANS TO YOU"

As a result, the term "historical Jesus" is best perhaps termed the "existential Jesus," for, as will be seen, a close examination of the questing reveals that the "historical Jesus" is whatever the quester *a priori* determines Jesus to be or wants him to be as somehow significantly distinct from the biblical documents. This subjectivity is highlighted in reviewing terms used today in the "third search" to define the "historical Jesus": an eschatological prophet, a Galilean holy man, an occult magician, an innovative rabbi, a trance-inducing psychotherapist, a Jewish sage, a political revolutionary, an Essene conspirator, an itinerant exorcist, an historicized myth, a proto-liberation theologian, a peasant artisan, a Torah-observant Pharisee, a Cynic-like philosopher, a self-conscious eschatological agent, and the list could go on and on.[127] No one embraces all of these images, but they are presented by their advocates as the most reasonable reconstruction of the "historical Jesus." After an arbitrary *a priori* decision has been made on a preconceived concept of Jesus, criteria of authenticity stemming from tradition criticism can be applied to the Gospels in order to affirm that same preconceived concept of Jesus. Since the criteria are subjective and conflicting, other criteria can be invented and applied to ensure the outcome desired. The critical weakness, as well as subjectivity, of these criteria lies in the fact that the same criteria can be applied or countered with different criteria to ensure whatever view has already been assumed.[128] It is in essence a game in which all the participants make up their own

---

125. Ibid., 27–28.

126. For further discussion of the operating agenda of historical criticism, see Farnell, "Philosophical and Theological Bent," 85–131; Krentz, *Historical-Critical Method*; Troeltsch, "Historical and Dogmatic Method," 11–32.

127. For these various portraits of what or whom the "historical Jesus" has been in the search since its beginnings to the present day, see Schweitzer, *Quest of the Historical Jesus*; Weaver, *Historical Jesus*; Riches, *Century of New Testament*; Beilby and Eddy, *Historical Jesus*.

128. For discussion of these criteria of authenticity as conflicting, see Farnell, "Form Criticism and

rules in order to make sure that they win. The current situation of widely conflicting views on whom the "historical Jesus" was has prompted Jesus Seminar participant John Dominic Crossan to comment that "*Historical Jesus research* today is becoming something of a scholarly bad joke" and "an academic embarrassment" as well as giving the "impression of acute scholarly subjectivity in historical research." He goes on to note, however, something he deems positive: "the number of competent and even eminent scholars producing pictures of Jesus at wide variance with one another."[129] As a consequence, he deems necessary a reexamination of methodologies involved in the search.[130]

## THE SEARCHING DEFINED

Importantly, therefore, the "questing" or "searching" for the "historical Jesus" may be defined as *a philosophically-motivated historical-critical* construct that the Jesus as presented in the Gospels is not the same or not to be identified fully with the Jesus who actually lived in history. Underlying the questing is the assumption that "scientific" research has shown that the Jesus of history was different from the Christ of Scripture, the creeds, orthodox theology, and Christian piety.[131] To one degree or another, such an activity has as its underlying operating assumption the premise that the Gospels cannot be taken as wholly trustworthy in their presentation of Jesus' life since belief or faith has mediated their presentation. In other words, faith and history are perceived as in opposition in reference to proper or legitimate historical methods due to its standard pronouncement of a closed-continuum of cause and effect. This idea of historiography means that the phrase "historical Jesus" is oxymoronic. If Jesus is to be understood historically, according to the standards of accepted historiography replete in the ideology of historical criticism, then he cannot be the Jesus presented in the Gospels. If one accepts the Jesus in the Gospels, then such a Jesus is not historical. One must default to a departure from the New Testament presentation of Jesus out of perceived necessity so that the "historical Jesus" *must be* something other than exactly the Jesus of the Gospels.[132]

One cannot overstress that *presuppositional philosophical underpinnings* of historical criticism have driven a qualitative, as well as quantitative, wedge between how Jesus is presented in the Gospels and current hypothesizing as to how Jesus actually was alleged to be in history in *all* quests for the "historical Jesus." This philosophical, presuppositional basis for the "historical Jesus" or the "Jesus of history" results in a Jesus removed from the supernatural as well as much of the uniqueness of Jesus as he

---

Tradition Criticism," 199–207.

129. Crossan, *Historical Jesus*, xxvii–xxviii.
130. Ibid., xviii.
131. See Brown, "Quest of the Historical Jesus," 718–756 (note esp. p. 718).
132. Hagner, "Analysis of Recent 'Historical Jesus' Studies," 83.

is presented in the Gospels. The degree of separation is, admittedly, somewhat one of degree depending upon the philosophical underpinnings arbitrarily accepted by the individual "searcher," but usually, it is a very sharp separation, especially in terms of any violation of a closed-continuum of cause and effect. As a result, biblical scholars who follow this mode of thought are forced *a priori* to "search" for the "historical Jesus" to find how he actually was in reality. Thus, "questing" for who Jesus actually was has been done since the 1700s.

Importantly, the idea of a "historical Jesus" distinct from the Gospel presentations as well as the practice of "questing" or "searching" for this presumed historical Jesus is an axiomatic consequence foundational to the tenets of historical criticism. The more one is consistent with the application of historical-critical ideology, the further the concept of a "historical Jesus" is removed from the Gospels' presentation of him. To put it bluntly, the "historical Jesus" is a *chimera* of historical criticism that has philosophical motivations at its foundation. For evangelicals who hold to an orthodox view of inspiration and inerrancy as maintained in church history, the great irony is that the true "myth" of historical criticism is its idea of the "historical Jesus."

## TWELVE KEY EVENTS BASED ON PROBABILITY OF OCCURRENCE ACCORDING TO AN EVANGELICAL ADOPTION OF POSTMODERNIST HISTORIOGRAPHY

At the end of the twentieth century (ca. 1999), the Institute for Biblical Research began a series of meetings "that spanned more than a decade from start to finish," resulting in the publication of *Key Events in the Life of the Historical Jesus: A Collaborative Exploration of Context and Coherence* (2009).[133] At the time of the writing, this work constitutes one of the latest, and most significant, evangelical attempts at the third quest. The editors discussed this decade-long meeting in the following terms as they dialogued on historical Jesus research among a diverse group of evangelicals:

> The meetings of the IBR Jesus Group have been a pleasure from start to finish. Our participants came from three continents, and though separated by geographical distance, close relationships have been built, and friendships have been deepened as a result of our annual meetings. Our meetings were marked by lively conversations about Jesus, Second Temple Judaism, and historical method. But these times also included wonderful snacks as we worked (M&Ms, cake, cookies, and chips) as well as marvelous evening meals out to close our meetings. The closing meal each year became a traditional adjournment of our time together. Nothing quite equals a Brazilian steak house to a bunch of hungry scholars![134]

---

133. Bock and Webb, preface to *Key Events*, v. This book is now in simplified form to influence a larger audience. See Bock, *Who Is Jesus?*

134. Bock and Webb, preface to *Key Events*, v.

One is immediately impressed by this statement as an oddly casual comment since these evangelical scholars met to decide the future of evangelical conceptions of the Gospels as well as Jesus in history.

Bock's and Webb's IBR group chose twelve events that they considered strategic in this work, relating that the group made the decision "to focus our attention on exploring key events and activities in the life of Jesus which met two criteria: a strong case could be made for a judgment of high probability that the core event was historical, and that it was likely significant for understanding Jesus."[135] They continue,

> The goal was to see the extent to which a study of key events might provide an overall framework for understanding Jesus. Once these key events had been selected, each essay was to do three things: first, it was to set forth a case for the probable historicity of the event using the criteria of authenticity. The focus was to, first, establish the probable historicity of the event's core rather than concerning itself with all of the details. Second, explore the socio-cultural contextual information that contributes to understanding the event in its first-century context. Third, in light of this context, to consider the significance of the event for understanding Jesus. Thus, each study would have both macro and micro concerns, being both analytic and synthetic.[136]

The term "probability" or even "high probability" as a label to apply to the historicity of these events also strikes one as an odd term for evangelicals to apply to Gospel events, for it immediately implies a relative degree of doubt as to the event or at least the possibility that the event. That is, it casts a pale of uncertainty over the Gospel materials. To assert that an event probably happened or even had a high probability also allows the possibility for the event not to have taken place at all or at least not to have taken place as described. To assert that the "core" of the Gospels is reliable in probability opens up the issue that other elements apart from the core may not be reliable.

Bock and Webb go on to issue a caveat, "In a very real sense this work reflects the input of the group. The collaborative learning experience was very stimulating. Each author, however, remains alone responsible for the views expressed in their particular essay. In other words, the author of each essay had the final call on its contents" but they also assert that "among the team there are differences in particulars, but *in general the synthesis set forth is one the team* embraces as providing the most coherent understanding of what Jesus did as a historic figure."[137]

Bock and Webb note, significantly, that Robert Webb's article on history, historiography, and historical method ("The Historical Enterprise and Historical Jesus Research") is important because it "opens the book *to set the direction of what we sought to do and the issues we consistently faced throughout our* meetings. It reflects

---

135. Ibid., 4.
136. Ibid., 5.
137. Ibid., 5, italics added.

discussions that regularly came up as individual events were considered and assessed. In other words, this essay was written at the end of our process; it was not written as a guideline at the beginning of it."[138] They continue,

> We write for an audience interested in historical Jesus study. . . . Such a study concentrates on what it thinks can be demonstrated in a corroborative manner about Jesus. All sources are available for consideration and each is sifted critically. By working with the criteria, our goal was to work with a method that is generally used in such study. We are quite aware that such methods have been subject to important critiques from all sides of the debate, but in many ways these are the best means we have to engage in such a sifting process. *Webb's essay summarizes the criteria we used and how we intended to see their importance after we completed our study. It also places the criteria within a larger framework of broad historical method.*[139]

The introduction concludes by acknowledging "the importance of recognizing, taking into account, and making one's horizon, including one's biases and pre-understanding," noting that this IBR Jesus Group has as its vision "to foster excellence in biblical studies, doing so within a faith commitment. Thus each of us has a commitment to the Christian faith. While some of us would call ourselves 'Evangelical Christian,' others might prefer 'biblically orthodox Christian.'"[140] The often-repeated use of the term "probable" or "probability" of Gospel events in this introduction also struck the present writer of this chapter with unease as to the possible widespread implications of the term for evangelicals today.

## QUESTING EVANGELICALS EMBRACE A POSTMODERNISTIC VIEW OF BIBLICAL HISTORY: CERTAINTY IS OUT, PROBABILITY IS IN

What must be also pointed out is that what these evangelicals have embraced in the "historical" part of the historical-critical method is postmodernism. Postmodernism is a result of philosophical concepts that are based in the extreme skepticism of existentialism. In tracing its roots, it can be directly traced to atheistic existentialism of the nineteenth century with Frederic Nietzche (1844) and in the twentieth century to Martin Heidegger (1889–1976) who were profound critics of the modern ideas of certainty. Their skeptical view of history was also popularized by the French philosopher Jacques Derrida (1930–2004) in the 1960s, spread to British schools in the 1970s with Quetin Skinner (b. 1940); with the ideology spreading to America and now throughout the academic world.[141]

---

138. Ibid., 5–6, italics added.
139. Ibid., 6, italics added.
140. Ibid., 7.
141. For an excellent discussion on postmodernism, see Windschuttle, *Killing of History*, 1–37.

## Part 2—Inerrancy Defended

In essence, postmodernistic historiography may be described as posing "no fundamental distinction anymore between history and myth" and "it is impossible to tell the truth about the past or to use history to produce knowledge in any objective sense."[142] Thus, one cannot tell the difference between fiction and non-fiction in writing of past events. While for most of the last 2,400 years, the essence of history was to tell the truth about the past, at least as best as possible, postmodernism has rejected this tradition view of history and replaced it with profound skepticism. For postmodernists, Western historical tradition has been wrong in several areas: (1) knowledge, i.e., inductive reasoning cannot provide a basis for knowledge; (2) truth is subjective and relative, not absolute; (3) science is not value free; and (4) traditional sciences, especially the humanities and social sciences, are inappropriate.[143] Thus, because of bias, or "rose-colored glasses," each culture cannot be objective since they interpret events through their own subjective experience. No "facts" in an objective sense exist. This kind of thinking has not confined itself to secular history but is now infiltrating the thinking of critical evangelical scholars in how they approach the Gospels and the history that is contained in them. It is a basic reason why Jesus has become lost and now evangelicals are searching for the "historical Jesus." Its adoption among these evangelicals is evident in that they must now talk in probabilities about the Gospels but not any certainties.[144]

Since Webb's article plays such an important role in fostering their approach to Jesus studies in *Key Events*, one must examine its assertions. The article is complex but an examination of it reveals how history is now being theorized and approached by many evangelicals. Webb's article follows immediately after the introduction to the work and constitutes chapter 2, "The Historical Enterprise and Historical Jesus Research."[145] One notices immediately that Webb attempts to issue a counter in Bock's and Webb's introduction that focused on the importance of his essay, asserting that his discussions "represent my [Webb's] view on the subject, and they do not necessarily represent all members of the project. . . . I remain solely responsible for its contents . . . this chapter was written at the conclusion of this project . . . but it never functioned as the guide that preceded the project."[146] Webb's statement, however, is immediately reduced in its attempt to distance his assertions from others participating in the work when one observes that the volume presents no substantial counter to his view of the philosophy of history and historiography. His essay also received prominence as setting the stage after the Introduction and prior to any discussion or evaluation of the

---

142. Windschuttle, x.

143. Ibid.

144. For further information on postmodernism, consult Appleby et al., *Telling the Truth about History*, ch. 6, "Postmodernism and the Crisis of Modernity," 198–240; Tosh, "Impact of Postmodernism," in *Historians on History*, 287–88.

145. Webb, "Historical Enterprise and Historical Jesus Research," 9–93.

146. Ibid., 11.

"historicity" of the key events chosen by the participants. The very nature of choosing twelve key events that the group as a whole felt could be demonstrated as historically "probable" also affirms this chapter as the underlying thinking of the project. It also subtly reveals that the editors of the work should realize the implications of its impact on the Gospel material.

For Webb, the distinctions between concepts of the "Jesus of history" and the "Christ of faith" are "not to be preferred over the other" for both "are equally legitimate subjects of inquiry" that use "different means to provide answers to different questions."[147] The logical result of his assertion here is to legitimize fully possible distinctions of a sharp cleavage between Jesus as he is presented in the Gospel accounts and scholarly speculations of how he might have actually existed in history. This distinction of Webb also smacks of the German theological distinction between *historie* (actual history) and *geschichte* (faith interpretation).

He next provides "the foundation for the historical enterprise" in questing by defining history, historiography, and historical method. In Webb's view, history is not what happened in the past, since "we do not have *direct* access to these past events. . . . What survives might be a written document or some form of inscription alluding to the event." Instead, what remains, according to Webb, are "traces" that have survived.[148] He adopts Elton's view of postmodernistic history that "historical study is not the study of the past but the study of present traces of the past."[149] The term "traces" is used because "in most cases (if not all) these are only partial and fragmentary, but they are all we have to provide access to the past event. Thus, rather than having direct access to past events, all we really can access today is the surviving traces from the past."[150] The practical impact is "in actuality what one really 'knows' [about what happened] is based on the surviving traces. . . . Thus, while in popular parlance the term 'history' may be used to refer to past events, this usage is problematic and may ultimately be misleading."[151] He continues:

> Surviving traces (i.e., ST) are the material used by the historian. Usually this material consists of written records of past events as reported and recorded by those closely (or not so closely) involved in the events. These written accounts may be based upon oral traditions that have been collected later or an account derived from eyewitnesses of the events. It may even be written by an eyewitness or, to the other extreme, it may be written by someone who has no real knowledge of the events but has an idea what could have, or should have, happened. Whatever is the case, surviving traces involve the perspectives and interests of the eyewitnesses, the perspectives and traces of those who passed

147. Ibid., 10.
148. Ibid., 11, 13.
149. Elton, *Practice of History*, 8. See Webb, "Historical Enterprise," 13n8 and n11.
150. Webb, "Historical Enterprise," 13–14.
151. Ibid., 14.

on the traditions, and the perspectives and interests of the person who wrote the account.... Surviving traces (ST) are hardly "raw" or "objective" data. The nature of those surviving traces is such that they require the later historian to develop a historical method . . . to properly handle these surviving traces. So these surviving traces are not "history" either, for they are only the "stuff" that has survived from the past—fragmentary, incomplete, and quite possibly biased, and perhaps even contradictory and incorrect.[152]

What the modern historian must do, in Webb's reasoning, is to "sift through and interpret these surviving traces using the tools and processes of the historical method to come to their understanding of the past event being studied."[153] After completing all the research and analysis, "the historian procures an account of his/her understanding of the past event which narrates a description and explanation of it."[154] Thus, according to this view, all events are mediated through the subjective understanding of the interpreter of the events (i.e., the historian) as he/she understood them through the surviving traces.

For Webb, "the term 'history' should be reserved for a later historian's narrative account (i.e., NA) of a past event (i.e., PE) that is his/her understanding of that event based upon *the interpretation* of surviving traces (i.e., ST)."[155] Thus "history" is a narrative account that involves *intepretation* or, in other words, the potential biases of the historian, conscious or otherwise, that interplay with the surviving traces. History is mainly indirect knowledge rather than direct. Webb directly applies these principles to the Gospels and historical Jesus studies with some observations: "With reference to Jesus, the surviving traces . . . consist of two basic types: the discrete narrative episodes in the Gospels (i.e., the individual pericopae) and other sources (e.g., Josephus), as well as the overall portraits created by these early authors . . . these earliest portraits are . . . the earliest surviving attempts" to give "a coherent picture" about Jesus.[156] This term "surviving traces" seems to correspond closely to Bock's "footprints" of Jesus in the Gospels.[157]

Importantly, the writing of history involves one's philosophy of history or what is known as "historiography." Webb contends that under the Enlightenment's influence, history has been wrongly understood as "scientific history," or a scientific endeavor that can be pursued with neutrality, objectivity, and value-free observations. Webb rejects the possibility of these factors in the writing of history or historiography, and instead argues, "The rise of postmodern historiography has contributed significant insights into the historical enterprise. . . . All historians interpret and write from their

152. Ibid.
153. Ibid.
154. Ibid.
155. Ibid., 15, italics added.
156. Ibid., 16n13.
157. Bock, "Abandon Studying the Historical Jesus?"

own perspective." As a result, "the historian's explanation and interpretation of the facts and providing causal and explanatory links between them is a contribution made by the historian and thus is 'invention.'"[158] For Webb, such an invention "*does not mean* that which is fictional and purely imaginary" and "it is possible to embrace the strengths of what postmodern historiography can teach us, without slipping into total relativism."[159]

To avoid extremes of postmodernistic historiography, he adopts twin principles: understanding of history as representation (a "representation of the past" and "not a description referring to something in the past; rather, it is a representation portraying something about the past") and adopting the philosophical stance of the principle of critical realism (exemplified by the hermeneutical circle or spiral as expressed by existentialist Gadamer).[160] Practically, this involves allowing one's own experience, initial understanding, and continuing critical judgment (the subject) to affect understanding of what one is studying (the object). The resulting understanding is only provisional and subject to expansion and development as the process continues and these two elements interact and fuse with each other. Although Webb may not admit the practical impact of this approach, the *practical impact, nonetheless, is that understanding of history is always changing and temporary and is greatly impacted by the changing bias(es) of the interpreter as he "dialogues" or examines the object studied. Any such information gained in the process would be fleeting and temporary as views changed through time and interaction.* Biblical understanding has no objective basis, because the moorings are always subject to change and even contradiction.

Yet, such complexity is dubious in understanding God's Word. Objectivity in interpretation is possible and must be defined in understanding God's thoughts as a Spirit-guided process of thinking God's thoughts in his Word as he intended. This latter position is a firm biblical position for those who are truly born again. Jesus promised the disciples that the Spirit of truth (John 14:26; 16:13; cf. 1 John 4:6) would guide them into truth. Such is the result of the New Covenant process whereby the genuine believer is provided with the teaching ministry of the Holy Spirit (1 John 2:26–27; cf. Ezek 36:25–27; Jer 31:31–33). To today's evangelicals, this explanation might appear simplistic compared to the perceived sophistication of historical criticism that is rooted in the wisdom of men (1 Cor 1:18—2:14). The ground for understanding the Gospels as God intended is fully provided by the Holy Spirit, who indwells the believer, providing a check against false teaching as well as an affirmation of the truth of God's Word. As a result of postmodernism, evangelicals reject any such certainty and replace it with, at best, probability, i.e., these events probably happened. The latter leaves the door wide open for the significant possibility that the events did not occur as asserted in the Gospels or cannot be affirmed. Moreover, because some believers

---

158. Webb, "Historical Enterprise," 23.

159. Ibid., 23–24.

160. Ibid., 24, 26–29 cf. Gadamer, *Truth and Method*, 172–267.

are not entirely filled with God's Spirit (or controlled by him), as well as due to differing mental capacities of exegetes, some variance in interpretation is to be expected.

In terms of historical criticism, evaluation of the Gospel material or, for that matter any historical record, for Webb (and others in *Key Events*) involves: (1) the preliminary phase where the interpreter must be self-aware of his/her horizon or biases/predispositions that are brought to the study; (2) the first main phase then involves the historian gathering and interpreting/evaluating the surviving traces or "raw data"; (3) the second main phase is the historian interpreting and explaining the relevant data with hypotheses; and (4) the concluding phase is to gather the evidence (i.e., surviving traces), arguments and hypotheses into a coherent and complete historical narrative that the historian considers to be the most plausible representation (i.e., "narrative account" or NA) of that chunk of past reality being considered (i.e., the "past event" or PE).[161] Again, although Webb may not directly admit the impact of such assertions, *the practical impact here in interpreting the Gospels would again depend upon the a priori biases and prejudices of the interpreter and be anchored firmly in the relativity and subjectivity of the resulting interpretation.*

Applying his study to the Bible accounts like the Gospels, Webb allows for possible distinctions between the biblical event itself (the event that is being described by the biblical author) and the biblical author's interpretive explanation of divine causality for that event. He also asserts that "the possible history of an event itself is a distinct matter from discussing the causal explanation provided in the ancient text."[162]

The net result of this "magic" of historical criticism, especially the skepticism of postmodernistic historiography, is that Jesus has "disappeared" and now evangelicals are on a quest, with their liberal counterparts in theology, to find him. The biblical text must be examined through the judicious application of "criteria of authenticity," developed by tradition criticism, a subcategory of historical criticism, to determine if the events in the Gospels had probability, possibility, or cannot be confirmed according to postmodernistic historiography. The following chart contrasts liberal historical criticism with evangelical critical scholars as to their approach in dealing with Gospel material:

---

161. Webb, "Historical Enterprise," 32–36.
162. Ibid., 39.

## Overview of Methodology: The Jesus Seminar (Westar Institute) Vs. British-Influenced Evangelical Critical Scholarship

| Ideological & Methodological Approaches Used to Determine Veracity of Gospels ||
|---|---|
| Jesus Seminar<br>Westar Institute | British-Influenced Evangelical<br>Critical Scholars |
| 2/4 Source Hypothesis | 2/4 Source Hypothesis |
| form criticism | form criticism |
| redaction criticism | redaction criticism |
| criteria of authenticity<br>tradition criticism | criteria of authenticity<br>tradition criticism |
| postmodernistic historiography | postmodernistic historiography |
| Atomistic approach (part):<br>Centers on Jesus' sayings,<br>i.e., *what did Jesus really say?*<br><br>*Important—Also Wholistic: focuses on what Jesus did Robert Funk: *Acts of Jesus* (1998) | Holistic approach (whole):<br>Centers on Jesus' deeds & events,<br>i.e., *what did Jesus really do?*<br><br>Investigates predetermined key events in Jesus' life to see if the event is postmodernistically verifiable in terms of history.<br><br>Important: Considers many events not verifiable historically using postmodernistic historiography. |
| Burden of Proof:<br>Shifted to the Jesus Seminar scholars to demonstrate reliability:<br><br>"The Seminar has accordingly assumed the burden of proof: the Seminar is investigating in minute detail the data preserved by the gospels and is also identifying those that have some claim to historical veracity" (*Five Gospels*, 5)<br><br>and<br><br>"What do we know about the deeds of Jesus? About the shadowy figure depicted in snapshots in more than twenty gospels and gospel fragments that have survived from antiquity? The short answer is that we don't know a great deal. But there are some stories that probably preserve distant historical memories, and we can infer some deeds from his parables and aphorisms" (*What Did Jesus Really Do?*, 527) | Burden of Proof:<br>Shifted to the evangelical-critical scholars' historical skills in applying criteria of authenticity:<br><br>"burden of proof should lie with historian who is making the case, whether for authenticity or against it" (*Key Events*, 74) |
| The "whisper of his voice"<br>contained in the Gospels<br><br>Posits Christ of faith<br>vs.<br>historical Jesus | The "footprints" of Jesus<br>contained in the Gospels<br><br>Posits Christ of faith<br>vs.<br>historical Jesus |

## Part 2—Inerrancy Defended

| Color-coding of Jesus-sayings in terms of red, black, gray, white that indicates probability of whether the real Jesus actually spoke the saying or performed a deed. | Probability scaling of Jesus' events "probability," "possibility" or historically non-verifiable scale for pericopes as to whether Jesus; deeds or events surrounding Jesus happened or did not happen. |
|---|---|
| Result:<br><br>15 sayings and a few distant historical memories (events)<br>*deemed "probably" authentic*<br>out hundreds of sayings in the Gospels<br><br>Result: *Completely rejects* any assertions of "probability" from evangelical critical scholarship!<br>score = 0<br><br>i.e., neither convinces the other | RESULT:<br><br>12 events<br>*deemed historically "probable"*<br>out of hundreds of acts/deeds in the Gospels<br><br>Result: *Rejects* many assertions from the Westar Institute!<br>score = 0<br><br>i.e., neither convinces the other |

## CONCLUSION TO THE "MAGIC" OF HISTORICAL CRITICISM

The present writer could multiply the examples of critical evangelical scholars who "say" that they believe in "inerrancy." However, their practice and assertions in biblical interpretation really support unorthodox errantist views. The present writer has reviewed several additional works and invites the reader to examine his reviews of these works, for all their authors assert a belief in inerrancy, but their works actually affirm errancy.

Evangelicals are in very deep difficulty at the beginning of the twenty-first century. Many critical evangelical scholars say that they believe in "inerrancy," while their views assault tradition views of inerrancy. Importantly, from this point in evangelical history, when someone says that they believe in inerrancy, one must now ask, "What do you mean by the term 'inerrancy'?" since the orthodox definition of inerrancy has now been hijacked and changed.

# Chapter 18

## Part One: A Critical Evaluation of Robert H. Gundry's Westmont College Lecture, "Peter: False Disciple and Apostate according to Saint Matthew"[1]

### F. DAVID FARNELL

#### INTRODUCTION

In 2013, the Evangelical Theological Society (ETS) had as its theme "Evangelicalism, Inerrancy, and ETS." The present writer had learned from direct eyewitnesses who were present that there was a strong call for Robert Gundry's reinstatement as a member of ETS. Strong verbal cries as well as applause broke out in one particular session. This is not surprising, for troubling events have been occurring at ETS as it pertains to the degeneration of the orthodox meaning of inerrancy for many years now. Even in the present writer's days as a doctoral student from 1986 to 1990, ominous developments among its members regarding changes in evangelical definitions of inerrancy were becoming increasingly frequent. These developments manifested themselves in many of the classes attended, which are now conducted by prominent ETS members who have risen to take on influential roles at the society.

Another troubling event at the 2013 gathering was the presidential address delivered by Robert Yarborough, professor of New Testament at Covenant Theological

---

1. Westmont College, "Gundry to Unveil Peter as False Prophet," and Gundry, "Peter: False Disciple." Gundry has expanded and published this lecture as a book, *Peter: False Disciple and Apostate according to Saint Matthew* (Eerdmans, 2015).

## Part 2—Inerrancy Defended

Seminary, wherein Yarborough praised another ETS scholar, Craig Blomberg, for his latest book, *Can We Still Believe the Bible?*[2] Yarborough's high praises for Blomberg are as follows:

> Excellent recent books demonstrate the cogency and vitality of a reverent and indeed an inerrantist stance. Two such books were made available to me in pre-publication form for this address.
>
> 1. Craig Blomberg, *Can We Still Believe the Bible?* The first is by Craig Blomberg, *Can We Still Believe the Bible? An Evangelical Engagement with Contemporary Questions*. Blomberg takes up six issues that he finds foundational to an affirmation of the Bible's comprehensive credibility like that affirmed by this society. In each of these categories, Blomberg cites the literature of those who reject a high view of the Bible's veracity or authenticity. As he points out, those critical of the Bible's truth often do not return the favor, stonewalling evangelical arguments and publications as if that class of scholarship did not even exist. Blomberg calls attention to the best studies he can find that reject his viewpoint. He then argues for the position from his inerrantist standpoint. He notes, "Not a single supposed contradiction" in Scripture "has gone without someone proposing a reasonably plausible resolution." He also notes the irony that some are abandoning inerrancy today when "inerrantists have the ability to define and nuance their understanding of the doctrine better than ever before."
>
> This book is refreshing and important not only because of its breadth of coverage of issues, viewpoints, and literature. It is evenhanded in that both enemies of inerrancy and wrong-headed friends are called on the carpet. Blomberg revisits incidents like Robert Gundry's dismissal from this society and the kerfuffle over a decade ago surrounding the TNIV and inclusive language. He does not mince words in criticizing those he sees as overzealous for the inerrancy cause. Nor is he bashful in calling out former inerrantists who, Blomberg finds, often make their polemical arguments against what they used to believe with less than compelling warrant. I predict that everyone who reads the book will disagree strongly with the author about something. At the same time, the positive arguments for inerrancy are even more substantial. It is clear that Blomberg is not content with poking holes in non-inerrantist arguments. He writes, "I do not think one has to settle for anything short of full-fledged inerrantist Christianity so long as we ensure that we employ all parts of a detailed exposition of inerrancy, such as that found in the Chicago Statement." Or again: "These Scriptures are trustworthy. We can still believe the Bible. We should still believe the Bible and act accordingly, by following Jesus in discipleship." I am skimming some of his concluding statements, but the real meat of the book is inductive demonstration of inerrancy's plausibility based on primary evidence and scholarship surrounding that evidence. If only

---

2. Yarborough, "Future of Cognitive Reverence for the Bible," 5–18.

a book of this substance had been available when I was a college or grad school student!³

Why does the present writer mention these troubling statements and events together? Because support for Gundry (as will be seen in this discussion), the current trends at ETS, and Blomberg's book share in common a massive assault on orthodox views of inerrancy as expressed by the ICBI documents of 1978 and 1982. The present writer doubts strongly that one can both affirm honest belief or genuine support of the ICBI view of inerrancy and hermeneutics while simultaneously endorsing and praising Blomberg's book (esp. his chs. 4–5).⁴ Yarborough's title constitutes an irony in that if his article indicates a future trend at ETS (the largest evangelical scholarly society in the world), the society is in grave difficulty since many of its members now embrace aberrant concepts of inerrancy in contradiction to the ETS doctrinal statement that has adopted ICBI as its definition of inerrancy.

Not only did Yarborough praise Blomberg's work,⁵ but so also did evangelical critical scholar Darrell Bock in the following terms,

> Craig Blomberg's fourth chapter in *Can We Still Believe the Bible*, examines some objections to inerrancy from both the right and the left. Yes, there is a position to the right of holding to inerrancy. It is holding it in a way that is slow to recognize solutions that fit within the view by undervaluing the complexities of interpretation. People are far more familiar with those who challenge inspiration and doubt what Scripture declares on the left, but others attempt to build a fence around the Bible by being slow to see where legitimate discussion exists about how inerrancy is affirmed. To make the Bible do too much can be a problem, just as making it do too little.⁶

History is now being forgotten, definitions of inerrancy either disregarded or changed at ETS, or something else quite unsettling is afoot for the future of evangelicalism as represented by this Society that happens to be home to several thousand evangelical scholars. Robert Gundry's recent lecture⁷ serves as a very timely, strategic reminder as well as a call to vigilance by those who would affirm faith in the trustworthiness of God's Word. This paper will analyze the reappearance of Gundry and his hermeneutical approach.

---

3. Ibid., 8–9.

4. For a more extensive review of Blomberg's work, see Farnell, review of *Can We Still Believe the Bible*, 99–104.

5. See Geisler and Farnell, *Jesus Quest*; note esp. 361–520 for this discussion.

6. From http://canwestillbelieve.com (site no longer active). See also "Craig Blomberg's Can We Believe the Bible," at Bock's blog.

7. See Gundry, "Peter: False Disciple," lecture given October 6, 2014, Westmont College.

Part 2—Inerrancy Defended

## A BRIEF REVIEW OF HISTORY

In 1982, ETS was rocked by a crisis that was, at that time, considered a major storm on the subject of inerrancy.[8] ETS had been founded in 1949 by evangelical scholars who had witnessed the assault on the inspiration and authority of Scripture in the fundamentalist/modernist controversy of the early twentieth century. The theme of the Society was simple, "The Bible alone, and the Bible in its entirety, is the Word of God and is therefore inerrant in the autographs." Since God was considered the author of both the Old and New Testament by members of ETS at the time, neither God nor his Word could err. However, in 1982, a blatant example of signing the inerrancy statement by Gundry and yet contradicting such an affirmation came to the forefront through his *Matthew: A Commentary on His Literary and Theological Art*, with the second edition entitled *Matthew: A Commentary on His Handbook for a Mixed Church under Persecution* (1994).[9] Gundry applied "midrash," i.e., a Jewish hermeneutic approach popular in Second Temple Judaism during the Intertestimental and New Testament periods that essentially dehistoricized and/or allegorized much of the historical content of Scripture, in his commentary on Matthew. Offering no demonstrable proof that much of Matthew was to be understood as nonhistorical in nature but merely *a priori* forcefully applying rabbinical midrash on the sheer weight of his scholarship. As a result, Gundry denied the historical nature of the Gospel of Matthew, especially, but not limited to the infancy narratives.[10]

A firestorm at ETS resulted, for many found shocking that Gundry fully asserted his belief in inerrancy and yet dehistoricized large portions of Matthew as literary allegory or fiction rather than as historical, the latter being what the orthodox church had maintained throughout the centuries. The question of literary genre used to dehistoricize large portions of the Gospels had come to prominence at ETS. Gundry was asked to resign from ETS by a 74-percent vote. To his credit, Gundry resigned rather than cause further disturbance to the society.

The resignation was not without supporters for Gundry. For instance, Craig Blomberg defended Robert Gundry's midrashic approach to the Gospels in the following terms:

> Is it possible, even inherently probable, that the NT writers at least in part never intended to have their miracle stories taken as historical or factual and that their original audiences probably recognized this? If this sounds like the identical reasoning that enabled Robert Gundry to adopt his midrashic interpretation of Matthew while still affirming inerrancy, that is because it is the

---

8. For an excellent historical review of the crisis surrounding Robert Gundry, see Geisler, "Brief History of the Evangelical Theological Society," 349–57.

9. Gundry, *Matthew: A Commentary on His Literary and Theological Art*, and the 2nd ed., entitled *Matthew: A Commentary on His Handbook for a Mixed Church under Persecution*.

10. See ch. 12 for greater details of Gundry's dehistoricization of Matthew's content.

same. The problem will not disappear simply because one author [Gundry] is dealt with *ad hominem* . . . how should evangelicals react? Dismissing the sociological view on the grounds that the NT miracles present themselves as historical gets us nowhere. So do almost all the other miracle stories of antiquity. Are we to believe them all?[11]

Yet, Blomberg continues as a member of ETS signing the sole doctrinal statement of "inerrancy" as defined by ICBI. He also takes historically understood sections of the Gospel as nonhistorical. According to Blomberg, Jesus' command for Peter to get the coin in the fish's mouth is not historical, it did not happen (Matt 17:24–27). Blomberg asserts in reference to the story of the coin in the fish's mouth in Matthew 17:24–27, "It is often not noticed that the so-called miracle of the fish with the coin in its mouth (Matt 17:27) is not even a narrative; it is merely a command from Jesus to go to the lake and catch such a fish. We don't even know if Peter obeyed the command. Here is a good reminder to pay careful attention to the literary form."[12]

Another recent example is Michael Licona, who pursues a tactic similar to Gundry and Blomberg. For example, according to Licona, the resurrection of saints in Matthew 27:51–53 did not happen. It is special effects. In his work *The Resurrection of Jesus: A New Historiographical Approach*,[13] used Greco-Roman *bios* literature, a tactic similar to Gundry's allegorical midrashic approach, as a means of dehistoricizing parts of the Gospel (i.e., Matt 27:51–53 with the resurrection of the saints after Jesus crucifixion is nonliteral genre or apocalyptic rather than an actual historical event). Licona argued "*bioi* offered the ancient biographer great flexibility for rearranging material and inventing speeches . . . and they often included legend. Because *bios* was a flexible genre, it is often difficult to determine where history ends and legend begins."[14] Licona labels it a "strange little text"[15] and terms it "special effects"[16] that have no historical basis. His apparent concern also rests with only Matthew as mentioning the event. He concludes that "Jewish eschatological texts and thought in mind" as "most plausible" in explaining it.[17] He concludes that "it seems best to regard this difficult text in Matthew a poetic device added to communicate that the Son of God had died and that impending judgment awaited Israel."[18]

All of these, Gundry as well as the others cited, sign the ETS doctrinal statement, but one is left wondering what they mean by the term "inerrancy," especially

---

11. Blomberg, "New Testament Miracles," 436.
12. Blomberg, "Constructive Traditional Response," 354n32.
13. Licona, *Resurrection of Jesus*.
14. Ibid., 34.
15. Ibid., 548.
16. Ibid., 552.
17. Ibid.
18. Ibid., 553.

since ICBI of 1978 warned against such dehistoricizing of the plain, normal sense of Scripture. Article XVIII states:

> *We affirm* that the text of Scripture is to be interpreted by grammatico-historical exegesis, taking account of its literary form and devices, and that Scripture is to interpret Scripture.
>
> *We deny* the legitimacy of any treatment of the text or quest for sources lying behind it that leads to relativizing, dehistoricizing, or discounting its teaching, or rejecting its claims to authorship.

History is being forgotten. Gundry's upcoming Festschrift that prompted his appearance at Westmont College on October 6, 2014, as well as current developments in ETS among its members, serve at this strategic time in history to stir memory of past events to prevent future tragedies for evangelicalism that are now rearing up again.

## GUNDRY'S POSITION ON THE APOSTLE PETER: "PETER THE APOSTATE AND FALSE DISCIPLE ACCORDING TO ST. MATTHEW"[19]

How does Gundry make such a startling claim that Matthew regarded Peter as an apostate, especially since no one in the twenty-seven New Testament books or in church history regarded Peter as such? Gundry's position here, however, is not new, for his 1994 (2nd ed.) commentary, *Matthew: A Commentary on His Handbook for a Mixed Church Under Persecution*, as well as his 1982 (1st ed.) commentary, *Matthew: A Commentary on His Literary and Theological Art*, maintained a similar position to this lecture.[20] So this position goes back to his days at ETS when he signed the inerrancy statement for membership.

Never in the history of the church has Peter ever been regarded in the sense in which Gundry says Matthew portrays him. When confronted with the issue of novelty, Gundry has no problem with his novelty. Gundry responds to novelty suggestions as follows:

> But there's another question that may be running through your heads it's this: "in the history of interpretation, why hasn't it been recognized 'til now that Matthew portrays Peter as a false disciple and apostate?" My former colleague here at Westmont, Moisés Silva, thinks this question may be the "Achilles heel" of what I've presented to you. I'll divide my answer into three parts. First, from the earliest times Christians were bothered by differences between the Gospels

---

19. All quotes from Gundry's lecture come from a transcript of the video posted on the Westmont College website.

20. See, e.g., both of Gundry's editions of *Matthew: A Commentary*, 548–49, 589–90, for this position (same pages in both editions).

so they tried to harmonize them. Already in the second century, the early church father Tatian produced a harmony of the gospels called "The Diatessaron" by weaving together the various texts of Matthew, Mark, Luke, and John. The highly influential St. Augustine produced another such harmony. The protestant reformer, Andreas Osiander, produced yet another one, in which to avoid discrepancies between the various accounts of Peter's denials of Jesus, Osiander posited eight denials of Jesus by Peter, a number of denials even exceeding the six that were posited much later by Harold Lindsell, a former trustee of Westmont, in his book *Battle for the Bible*. When in a telephone conversation I objected that the Bible said three denials not three times, an answer I consider more harmful than helpful to a high view of biblical inspiration. Regrettably, the college course that I took in New Testament Survey had as a required textbook *A Harmony of the Gospels*, compiled by the great Southern Baptist Greek scholar A. T. Robertson. But why should I complain? I myself used and required Robertson's harmony for some years when first teaching Life in Literature in the New Testament right here at Westmont. Until I woke up to how unscriptural it was. The New Testament gives us four different gospels, not one harmonious gospel. My point is that the apologetic impulse toward harmonization, to make everything agree, joined forces with the accounts of Peter's rehabilitation in Luke, Acts, and John 21, and by implication the rest of the New Testament, the apologetic influence and impulse joined forces also with the tradition of Peter's martyrdom to ameliorate, to soften the harshness of Matthew's portrayal in the minds of those who read and heard the first Gospel. In view of what we know about Peter elsewhere, surely Matthew's portrayal can't be taken at face value. Or so it seemed to Christians who fear any disagreements among the Gospels. Second, the softening of Matthew's harsh portrayal of Peter, the airbrushing of it, has proved irresistibly attractive because it offers comfort to Christians who see in themselves a Peter like mixture of good and bad behavior, of success and failure, and at the same time a promise of ultimate salvation. How often do you hear people say Peter is their favorite apostle? Just last summer somebody told me that very thing and gave me that very reason, "I see myself in Peter." Well if you don't want to see yourself as a false disciple and apostate, neither do you want to see your favorite apostle, Peter, as a false disciple and apostate no matter what Matthew says. The attractiveness of Peter, a Peter who offers us a mirror image of our flawed selves, remains a hindrance to evenhanded, clear-eyed exegesis. Third, the somewhat tardy, but growing weight of Roman Catholicism's appeal to the purported authority of Peter, left a largely favorable impression of him not only in the minds of people inside the Roman Catholic communion, but also as a carryover from pre-Reformation days even on the minds of Protestants and Orthodox Christians. The current ecumenical movement and friendly Protestant, Roman Catholic dialogue, plus the larger cultural emphasis on tolerance and God's supposedly unconditional love, create further obstacles to an unblinking recognition that Matthew does indeed like it or not portray Peter as a false disciple and apostate.[21]

In sum, how can Gundry reach such a novel approach, being the only one in church history who has ever seen Peter in such a light? First, by deprecating, or really, eliminating harmonization. Second, by a subjective, imaginative assertion of psychology that somehow the church found comfort in Peter's "good and bad behavior." Third, the influence of Romanism on the church, as well as the current ecumenical movement toward dialogue with Roman Catholicism.

Gundry's second and third assertions carry no weight for support to his argument. Psychological assertions like his have no real substance. He offers no proof, just his subjective bias. Might such subjective bias as Gundry displays reflect his own personal subjective, internal disposition regarding his own behavior? One cannot know except that the second argument bears no weight whosoever to substantiate his claim.

As with the second argument, the third argument proffered has no weight either. The Reformers, who were no friend of the Papacy, never reflected such a bias toward Peter as Gundry's hypothesis sustains. Such a bias might naturally have arisen among them since the papacy and Romanism, constituted for them a virulent enemy that had to be defeated decisively.

Gundry's first argument, however, regarding his rejection of the principle of harmonization, is quite telling, for Gundry's hypothesis could not really proceed unless he is dismissive of such a decisive hermeneutical procedure. Indeed, it is only by rejecting harmonization outright that Gundry's thesis can be sustained. A close look at the other Gospel writers as well as other books of the New Testament reveals quite a different picture of Peter.

For instance, Mark 16:7 specifically lists Peter as being told by Jesus to meet him in Galilee. Papias is very clear that Mark's Gospel reflects the apostolic preaching of Peter. For example, in Eusebius' *Ecclesiastical History*, 3.39.15–16,[22] Papias commented that in composing his Gospel, Mark, being Peter's interpreter, "wrote accurately all that he remembered . . . of the things said *or done* by the Lord" and immediately after this spoke of Peter as "not making, as it were, an arrangement of the Lord's oracles so that Mark did nothing wrong in thus writing down single points as he remembered them."[23] Papias's testimony answers the question as to whether Mark was in any sense dependent on Matthew as the Two-Gospel Theory would require, for Mark wrote on the basis of Peter's preaching, not on the basis of literary dependence on Matthew. If

---

21. Transcript of Gundry's lecture on October 6, 2014.
22. This quote is taken from Eusebius, *Ecclesiastical History*, 297.
23. Eusebius, *Hist. eccl.*, 3.39.15–16, emphasis added.

Papias's ancient and very early testimony is to be accepted, and no substantive reason really exists for discounting it, then even Peter himself did not view his denial in the terms that Gundry takes it. While Matthew excludes Peter specifically in Matthew 28:7, this constitutes an argument from silence rather than any other substantive proof for Gundry. Indeed, if Matthew is the first Gospel,[24] and not the product of Mark, Matthew may merely have generalized the command of Jesus, while Mark especially singled out his mentor, Peter, based on Peter's remembering of Jesus' command to meet him in Galilee. Moreover, the likelihood that Jesus mentioned Peter is strengthened when one remembers that Mark reflects Peter's preaching and who would better remember his own personal invitation to meet Jesus than Peter himself!

Second, a look at other portions of the New Testament also reveal a contradictory position to that of Gundry's novel view on Peter in Matthew's Gospel. The Gospel of Luke foreshadows not only Peter's denial but Peter's restoration in the following terms, "but I have prayed for you, that your faith may not fail; and you, when once you have turned again, strengthen your brothers" (Luke 22:32). Luke 22:55–62 also records Peter's denial and bitter weeping because of it. Luke 24:12 has Peter at the Jesus' tomb upon hearing of his resurrection, an indication of a change of mind in sharp contrast to his denial. The Gospel of John 21:15–19 has Jesus seeking Peter out specifically, ministering to Peter and restoring him to full ministry with the commands to "feed my sheep" and "follow Me." The Gospel of John also has John and Peter competing in a footrace to the empty tomb (John 20:4–5). Acts 1–13 gives a very prominent role to Peter in the early days of the church. Far from being presented in Gundry's terms, Peter is leading the disciples on the day of Pentecost (Acts 2); boldly proclaiming Jesus with the Apostle John before the Sanhedrin after the healing of the lame man at the temple (Acts 3–4), taking prominence in the church discipline of Ananias and Sapphira (Acts 5), and prominence in reaching the Gentiles, as typified with Cornelius (Acts 10). Indeed, two books were accepted as canonical by the early church with Peter's name (1–2 Peter), so that it is dubious that the early church, and Matthew the tax collector, ever thought of Peter in Gundry's terms.[25]

All of this is acknowledged by Gundry in his presentation. One could pursue further harmonization throughout the NT with regard to Peter, but Gundry remains undisturbed by these efforts. Why? He outright rejects such harmonization with other portions of the New Testament. To Gundry, these harmonizations fail to reveal Matthew's position of Peter's false discipleship and apostasy. Gundry will not have any external evidence brought into Matthew. In his recent lecture, Gundry contends,

> Well, in the first place, Matthew isn't Mark, Luke, John, or Paul, so Matthew's take on Peter doesn't have to agree with theirs, unless you hold to a certain

---

24. See Farnell, "Synoptic Gospels in the Ancient Church," 53–86.

25. For an excellent history of the canon of the early church and its integrity from the very nascent beginnings of Christianity, consult Dungan, *Constantine's Bible*, noting especially ch. 5, "Against Pagans and Heretics," 54–93.

view of scriptural inspiration. More about that issue later. In the second place, look at the evidence in Matthew's passages that deal with Peter. And, at least for the time being, keep out of your mind the portrayals of Peter elsewhere in the New Testament. If you had only the Gospel of Matthew, what would you think of Peter?[26]

To Gundry, Matthew alone "exacerbates the denial by having Peter deny before all" who are referenced in Matthew 26:69–75 (cf. Matt 10:33). Thus, Matthew (really in Gundry's take on Matthew's portrayal of Mark) takes a uniquely contrary position on Peter in contrast to the rest of the portrayals offered in the New Testament. For Matthew, Peter is a false disciple based on Gundry's internal examination of Matthew's Gospel.

Notice also that Gundry ties his position as against "a certain view of scriptural inspiration." Therein is a very strategic key to understanding Gundry's thinking for this assertions.

## THE THOUGHTS BEHIND GUNDRY'S THOUGHTS REGARDING PETER

Why does Gundry so vigorously reject harmonization? Gundry urges his listeners, "And, at least for the time being, keep out of your mind the portrayals of Peter elsewhere in the New Testament." However, if even slight harmonization be allowed, Gundry's position stands defeated before he has begun. Gundry cites Harold Lindsell's attempt at harmonizing the crowing of the rooster at Peter's denial in the Gospels as evidence for the lack of credibility of harmonization in dealing with Scripture. In other words, Gundry is dismissive of the practice because he cites a few aberrant examples in church history. One should not make a principle of rejection by citing only extremely bad examples of its practice. Such exceptions or bad practice of harmonization do not make a rule to reject its validity. At the same time Gundry tries to defeat the logic of harmonization, he also reveals his own illogic. Of course, bad examples of harmonization can always be cited, but this does not mean that harmonization is wrong or not effective in dealing with problems from eyewitness accounts as evidenced in the Gospels.

Gundry goes another step further, not only does he reject harmonization, but reveals a reason for his bias against it:

> So what about the doctrine of biblical Inspiration, let's admit Matthew's portrayal of Peter disagrees with the portrayals elsewhere in the New Testament. What gives? *Well, there are many similar disagreements in the Bible.* According to Revelation 22:17 for example, a human being who wills to drink the water of life will be saved, but Romans 9:16 says that salvation does not depend

---

26. Taken from a transcript of Gundry's lecture of October 6, 2014.

on the human being who wills it. According to Matthew, Mark, and Luke, Jesus kept his Messiahship secret from the public 'til his trial before the Jewish Supreme Court on the very eve of his crucifixion, but in John's Gospel, Jesus broadcasts his Messiahship, his Divine Sonship, his being the I Am before Abraham's lifetime, the Bread of Life, the Light of the World, the Way the Truth and the Life and so on. In public as well as in private and from the very beginning of his ministry. *Other examples of disagreement, both historical and theological, could be multiplied indefinitely.* What we have to say is that pastoral, ecclesiastical, evangelistic, and other authorial purposes often trumped theological and historical consistency in the writing of Scripture. In his work called "Poetics" the ancient Greek philosopher, Aristotle, defended the rights of poets to engage factual inconsistencies if those inconsistencies were necessary to make a desired point. *In other words, truth is sometimes, not always, but sometimes, to be found on a different plane from the factual, so too in the Bible, if you want to maintain both a high view of its inspiration and an honest appraisal of its verbal phenomenon.*[27]

Here Gundry reveals his real beliefs about the inspirational nature of Scripture, i.e., the Bible contains contradictions "both historical and theological." Indeed, because it is contradictory, it cannot be harmonized. For Gundry, only by recognizing these contradictions, both factual and theological, can a "high view of inspiration and an honest appraisal of its verbal phenomenon" be achieved.[28]

Clearly, Robert Gundry's view of inspiration allows for errors and contradictions, both factual and theological. So Gundry's defense of a high view of Scripture's inspiration is to agree that it internally has "factual inconsistencies" in itself! Such a defense is no real defense of Scripture but a subtle, and yet not-so-subtle, undermining of its inspiration and inerrancy, all under the guise of defending it. If this was Gundry's position when he was a member of ETS, one wonders not only what his definition of inerrancy is, but his intellectual honesty in signing the ETS statement of faith. Intellectual honesty would seem to preclude such a signing.

Ironically, Gundry sees his presentation/understanding of Peter in Matthew as somehow warning and guarding against apostasy by those in the church. Gundry states, "Finally, because the persecution of Christians is now on the upsurge throughout the world, and therefore the danger of apostasy too, we should take Matthew's portrayal of Peter as a dire warning against apostasy."

In Gundry's logic, all Christians must be willing to die for the testimony of Jesus Christ, remembering Peter who apostatized in Matthew. Yet, his logic escapes us. Why would anyone be willing to affirm a testimony for Jesus Christ under persecution that is based on documents like the Gospels, which, according to Gundry contain such contradictions that "could be multiplied indefinitely"? Someone would be dying for a

27. Ibid.
28. Ibid.

witness to Jesus' life and message that was hardly trustworthy in its presentation. Such logic is not only unsatisfying, but truly self-defeating.

Furthermore, Gundry is clearly guilty of selective presentation of evidence to maintain his hypothesis. For example, even Matthew demonstrates that Peter, after his denial, went and "wept bitterly"—"And Peter remembered the word which Jesus had said, 'Before a rooster crows, you will deny Me three times.' And he went out and wept bitterly" (Matt 26:75; cf. Luke 22:62). While the weeping may clearly be interpreted as a sign of remorse and repentance on Peter's part, Gundry will have none of it. Instead, he links Peter's weeping to "weeping and gnashing of teeth" in Matthew 8:12; 13:42, 50; 22:13; 24:51; 25:30. Yet, not only is Matthew 26:75 not similar since it only mentions weeping while the others mention "gnashing of teeth," judgment is clearly in the context in other places in Matthew but not in Matthew 26:75!

Another example is Matthew's mention of Judas. Judas's apostasy is frequently connected to betrayal (e.g., Matt 10:4; 26:14, 25, 47, 49; 27:3), so why does he spare Peter who also blatantly, and publicly, denied Jesus according to Gundry's hypothesis? Still another example is Matthew 28:16 where Matthew mentions the disciples as "the eleven." Clearly only Judas has been subtracted due to his apostasy and betrayal, not Peter. In 10:2, Peter is given prominence in the list of disciples, mentioned first (Matt 10:2), so why would an apostate have such prominent mention? Well, of course, Gundry's imagination always supplies an answer. For Gundry, perhaps Matthew wanted to show how great Peter's apostasy was. Similar is the logic in Peter's confession. Here Matthew includes high praise for Peter in his answer, regardless of whether Peter is the "rock." Why such great praise for an apostate and false disciple? Judas is never praised in any way like that in Matthew, but Peter is. This hardly indicates that Peter was always negative in Matthew's eyes. Matthew gives an honest appraisal of Peter, good and bad, without necessarily at all suggesting apostasy. Supporting this latter statement is Jesus' rebuke of Peter in Matthew 16:22 for saying that Jesus should not suffer the cross. Peter, in Matthew's eyes both fails and succeeds. Instead of viewing him only in a cycloptic, one-eyed view maintained by Gundry, Matthew presents Peter in all his human frailty, good points and bad. Gundry deliberately excludes legitimate evidence internally that *contradicts* his hypothesis, i.e., selective use of evidence to fulfill his prejudice.

## BIBLICAL THEOLOGY AND REDACTION CRITICISM ARE CENTRAL IN GUNDRY'S THINKING

Finally, where does Gundry's logic stem from in rejecting harmonization? This emerges from two areas, his affirmation of his view of biblical theology as well as redaction criticism, all of which demonstrate that Gundry, in reality, has a low or no view of inspiration. The church throughout its early history, until the seventeenth century, believed that the Bible could be harmonized. Even the heretic Tatian, in his

*Diatessaron*, believed so. The traditional view of harmonization centering in a high view of inspiration continued through the Reformation and beyond. McArthur comments, "A striking phenomenon of the study of the Bible in the sixteenth century was the sudden flowering of Gospel harmonies."[29] Those producing these works had two reasons for composing their harmonies: (1) to edify the faithful by the presentation of a total picture of Jesus life and ministry and/or (2) to refute the critics of the Gospels "by demonstrating the essential and astonishing agreement of the Gospels."[30] Dungan adds to this, "These sixteenth- and seventeenth-century harmonies share one significant characteristic: they are without exception strikingly literal in their understanding of the Gospel narratives," and "these traditional Gospel harmonies proceeded on the basis of Augustine's assumption that all four Gospels were uniformly true and without admixture of the slightest degree of error. The traditional way of stating this assumption was to claim that each had been written with the aid of the Holy Spirit, or the Spirit of Christ, so that all four were evenly true in all parts and passages."[31] Importantly, the independence approach identifies itself with this traditional approach to harmonization.

Yet, with the onslaught of historical-critical ideologies, traditional harmonization waned under modern philosophical influences that were inimical to the grammatico-historical understanding of Scripture. During the height of rationalism, deism and the Enlightenment, the traditional high standard of inspiration associated with Gospel harmonies began to fade. Ephraim Gotthold Lessing, a Spinozist (rationalist and anti-supernaturalist; see the section under rationalism), published the work *Fragmente eines Ungenannten* ("Fragments by an Unknown Person") between 1774 and 1778.[32] It was written anonymously by rationalist and deist Hermann Samuel Reimarus (1694–1768), a personal friend of Lessing. In this work, Reimarus's purpose was to discredit the origins of Christianity. In the fragments, he presented Jesus as an unsuccessful messianic pretender and that the disciples were disappointed charlatans who stole Jesus' body and invented the story of the resurrection in order to start a new religious movement and avoid working for a living.[33]

In the half century or so that followed the publication of Reimarus's *Fragments*, wildly contradictory hypotheses that deprecated the gospels as to composition and

29. McArthur, *Quest through the Centuries*, 85.

30. Ibid., 87.

31. Dungan, *History of the Synoptic Problem*, 304–5.

32. The work consisted of seven anonymous pieces written by Reimarus, but these seven pieces were a part of a much larger work of Reimarus's *Apologie oder Schutzschrift für die vernünftigen Verehrer Gottes*. A critical edition of this work was published in 1972; see Reimarus, *Apologie oder Schutzschrift für die vernünftigen Verehrer Gottes*. See also Brown, *Jesus in European Thought*, 1–6.

33. This reference has special note to the sixth "Ueber die Auferstehungsgeschichte" ("Concerning the Resurrection Story") and seventh fragment, *Von dem Zwecke Jesu und seiner Jünger* ("On the Purpose of Jesus and that of his Disciples"). An English translation of the sixth and seventh fragments may be found in *Reimarus: Fragments*.

authorship came into print. One of the first scholars to attempt a historical-critical approach to the Scripture was Johann David Michaelis (1717–1791). Michaelis came strongly under the influence of Deism. In 1750 he published his *Einleitung in die göttlichen Schriften des Neuen Bundes* which constituted a comprehensive presentation of alleged historical problems in the New Testament. Michaelis's work inaugurated the modern "science" of New Testament introduction. Neill and Wright comment, "The orthodoxy of the time [Michaelis's day] took it for granted that, because the NT is divinely inspired in every part, it is *a priori* impossible that there should be any contradictions between the Gospels; any apparent contradiction must be due only to the imperfection of our understanding, and must be susceptible of resolution into harmony. Michaelis was prepared to face the possibility that there really might be contradictions."[34] Interestingly, Michealis rejected the idea of literary dependence among the Gospel writers, tracing their shared characteristics to their common use of apocryphal gospels that he hypothesized from Luke 1:1.

Eventually, Greisbach came under "the decisive influence"[35] of the skepticism of Michaelis at the University of Halle where Griesbach was his student. From his student days with Semler and Michaelis, Griesbach "had been exposed to Europe's skeptical historicist interpretation of the New Testament and Church history."[36] Griesbach's skeptical attitude toward the Gospels caused him to reject traditional harmonization of them. Instead, as noted above, he belied that it was not possible to harmonize the Gospels in the way that the church had done throughout its history. Such skepticism caused him to develop a different approach, the synopsis, which placed the Gospels not into a harmonious whole but into parallel columns so that minute differences and/or alleged contradictions could stand out sharply and be magnified. In its historical development, therefore, the synopsis is based in historical skepticism regarding the Gospels. Also under the influence of Romanticism and its concept of development, Griesbach developed his synoptic approach.[37] Indeed, at the heart of all modern discussion of modern synoptic dependency hypotheses is a "skepticism regarding the chronological value of the Gospels."[38]

Also important is the fact that Gospel synopses played a decisive role in the development of modern synoptic dependency hypotheses that arose from modern skepticism regarding the Gospels. Both the Two-Source (also, Four-Source) and Two-Gospel hypotheses were greatly facilitated to prominence through this vehicle.[39] More significantly, grave suspicion is cast upon any neutrality of synopses in dealing with the synoptic question. They are circular at core, being constructed to prove depen-

---

34. Neill and Wright, *Interpretation of the New Testament*, 6.
35. Dungan uses this precise term. See Dungan, *History of the Synoptic Problem*, 310.
36. Ibid., 311–12.
37. Ibid., 302–26.
38. Ibid., 307.
39. Ibid., 332–41.

dency hypotheses already chosen on an *a priori* basis. Dungan comments that most modern synopses are highly biased toward the Two- and Four-Source hypothesis: "The same circular process of argument emerged in Germany that later appeared in England. A source theory was invented and a synopsis created to illustrate it. Charts were then created based on that synopsis which were held to 'prove' the theory. This *circulus in probando* was camouflaged in Germany by Huck's claim that his synoptic arrangement was 'neutral' with respect to all source theories."[40]

In contrast, harmonization of the Gospel texts was based on a traditional view of inspiration. Instead of skepticism, there is a prevailing optimism regarding the ability of the Gospels to be harmonized historically. While synopses are not necessarily to be rejected, they should be recognized as highly prejudiced instruments rooted in skepticism and deliberately designed to promote dependency hypotheses. A high view of Scripture should reject redactional hermeneutics because it naturally seeks theological motivation rather than harmonization, and, in doing so, has a marked tendency toward dehistoricizing the Gospels as historical documents.[41] This is clearly evidenced in Gundry's commentary on Matthew.

Admittedly, at times traditional harmonization has been done superficially by its practitioners, producing less than viable solutions to problem passages.[42] Such a problem, however, centers in the exegete's skill at harmonizing the text, not in the legitimacy or primacy of harmonization itself. Proper harmonization takes time, patience, and diligent work on the part of the exegete. Suspension of judgment may be necessary until further data is forthcoming on a particular problem. At no time, however, if no data resolves the difficulty, is redactional hermeneutics a legitimate pursuit as Gundry practices since its natural tendency is to pit one Gospel against another or isolate one Gospel's affirmations from another.

One final note should be made on the biblical theology so prominently advocated by Gundry in his presentation. Gerhard Hasel, in his excellent work *New Testament Theology: Basic Issues in the Current Debate*, presents a sober assessment of the historical roots of biblical theology, now practiced by many evangelicals, especially Gundry. Biblical theology was developed through the influence of Neologian and rationalist Johann Philipp Gabler (1753–1826). Gabler, as noted by Hasel,

---

40. Ibid., 336.

41. See Thomas, "Redaction Criticism," 233–67.

42. An example of this would be Lindsell who attempted to harmonize the text by assuming six denials; see Lindsell, *Battle for the Bible*, 174–76. In spite of Lindsell's solution, his perception of the problem provokes a correct assessment: "It is plain they were not coached in that testimony, as is also the fact that they testified independently of each other" (176). Lindsell correctly recognized that the existence of this "problem" of harmonization actually constitutes an argument for the accounts being independent rather than stemming from literary dependency. For if the accounts stemmed from one Gospel as a source, why did not the Gospel writer who used another Gospel as the "source" attempt to harmonize his account with his source?

Marks the beginning of Biblical theology's role as a purely historical discipline, completely independent from dogmatics . . . (1) Inspiration is to be left out of consideration . . . (2) Biblical theology has the task of gathering carefully the concepts and ideas of the individual writers, because the Bible does not contain the ideas of a single man . . . (3) Biblical theology as a historical discipline is by definition obliged to distinguish between the several periods of the old and new religion.[43]

In other words, the practice of biblical theology originates from a low view of Scripture that suggests competing, often contradictory viewpoints, among the writers. The true goal of biblical theology is to contrast and highlight alleged contradictions between writers, not any harmonization. Gundry's assertions match this goal well. Whenever evangelicals practice biblical theology, there is a danger of returning to its historical roots of hypothesizing alleged contradictions between the writers of the NT, especially the Gospels.

One final note deserves mention. Gundry argued,

> In his work called "Poetics" the ancient Greek philosopher, Aristotle, defended the rights of poets to engage factual inconsistencies if those inconsistencies were necessary to make a desired point. In other words, truth is sometimes, not always, but sometimes, to be found on a different plane from the factual, so to in the Bible, if you want to maintain both a high view of its inspiration and an honest appraisal of its verbal phenomenon.[44]

The present writer finds it very telling that Gundry compares the Gospel literature to "poetics." Such a comparison reveals Gundry's true take on the Gospels as not historical documents but fictionalized material of a poetic nature. This latter point also reveals why he dehistoricized so much of Matthew's infancy narratives in Matthew 1–3. His "midrashic" hypothesis also corresponds to his take on the "poetic" nature of these accounts. In contrast, the present writer believes that, as supported by the whole history of the orthodox church, the Gospels are historical narratives of the actual life and ministry of Jesus and correspond to historical reality. It is not Peter who has apostatized, nor Matthew who has portrayed him as such.

## ONE FINAL, DELICIOUS IRONY TO GUNDRY'S HYPOTHESIS

In Gundry's lecture, one final proverbial "elephan in the room" that goes unmentioned in his hypothesis. In Gundry's commentary, he heavily relies upon the hypothesis of Markan priority, arguing, "The peculiarities of Matthew derive almost wholly from his own revisions of and additions to Mark and the materials shared only

---

43. Hasel, *New Testament Theology*, 22–23.
44. Taken from transcript of Gundry's lecture of October 6, 2014.

with Luke (i.e., the materials usually designated Q)."[45] He further argues, "In examining the way Matthew uses Mark and the materials shared only with Luke, we discover the outstanding features of his style."[46] And again Gundry notes, "But if Mark wrote first and Matthew and Luke used Mark and shared another tradition, such words signal Matthew's editorial work. As already implied, this commentary rests on the latter hypothesis [i.e., Two-/Four-Source hypothesis], mainly because it provides the framework for what seems to be the most cogent explanations of the similarities and differences of detail among the synoptics."[47]

One learns however, from Papias that Mark based his Gospel on the preaching of Peter. In Eusebius's *Ecclesiastical History* 3.39.15–16, Papias commented that in composing his Gospel, Mark based it on Peter's preaching: "Mark became Peter's interpreter and wrote accurately all that he remembered . . . of the things said *or done* by the Lord."[48] Papias's testimony continues, "For he [i.e, Mark] had not heard the Lord, nor had he followed him, but later on, as I [i.e., Papias] said, followed Peter, who used to give teaching as necessity demanded but not making, as it were, an arrangement of the Lord's oracles, so that Mark did nothing wrong in thus writing down single points as he remembered them. For to one thing he gave attention, to leave out nothing of what he had heard and to make no false statements in them. This is related by Papias about Mark."[49]

The delicious irony here of course is that the early church, i.e., Papias, affirms that Mark based his Gospel on the allegedly "apostate false disciple" Peter's preaching, thus Gundry's own view of synoptic interrelationships brings Matthew's Gospel into complete suspicion as a text, for Matthew ironically would be using Mark who wrote down Peter's preaching! Of course, Gundry will have none of this since his hypothesis would be blatantly contradicted by accepting the early testimony of Papias regarding Peter's contribution to Mark's Gospel. Perhaps Gundry might want to adopt an entirely different synoptic hypothesis and rewrite his commentary to support his thesis of Peter as an apostate since Peter supplied Mark's information and, under Gundry's view, Matthew used Mark as the foundation to his Gospel!

## CONCLUSION TO THE MATTER OF GUNDRY

While listening to Gundry's lecture, one is reminded of Luke's characterization of those who assembled at Areopagus to hear him in Acts 17:21—"Now all the Athenians and the strangers visiting there used to spend their time in nothing other than telling or hearing something new." Truly, Gundry has obtained the Athenian ideal in

45. Gundry, *Matthew*, 2.
46. Ibid.
47. Ibid., 3.
48. Emphasis added. *Hist. Eccl.* 3.39.15.
49. Ibid., 3.39.15–16.

his assertions regarding Peter utilizing biblical theology and redaction criticism for his novelty not seen throughout the history of the orthodox church until now.

One final note must be stressed. Mentoring is important. A privilege exists in teaching future generations of Christian scholars. James reminds us that "teachers have the greater judgment" because they use their tongues to train (James 3:1–5). What we teach students about God's Word has a weighty judgment for teachers. Tremper Longman III, who now holds Gundry's chair at Westmont and is also Gundry's former student, introduces him in the following terms, "Bob is a wonderful defender of our Christian faith but also willing to explore what some people think are controversial issues" and,

> I mean I remember in my very early career one of the first evangelical theological societies I went to where his new Matthew commentary was an item of some controversy and discussion and I just am so thankful to be associated with Bob in this Chair because of his honest biblical scholarship as well as his affirmation robust affirmation of Christianity. And Bob taught here at Westmont College for thirty-eight years and he has influenced many, many students who have gone on in different careers. This Festschrift that was just published by his students and I was privileged to write the preface to it is called *Reconsidering the Relationship between Biblical and Systematic Theology in the New Testament*. And this is an incredibly important topic because often systematic professors and biblical professors kind of war with each other. But Bob has trained his students to think well about the interrelationship between the two.[50]

Longman considers Gundry as someone who "robustly" defends the faith. One finds that odd since over 70 percent of ETS members requested him to resign for a lack of intellectual integrity in signing the ETS doctrinal statement and then publishing a commentary that dehistoricized the infancy narratives of Matthew, narratives which form a strategic foundation for who Jesus was and what he did. What legacy does someone leave to his students who sows doubt into their minds about the trustworthiness of the Gospels as historical records of Jesus? I am reminded of Jesus' words in Matthew 23:15, "Woe to you, scribes and Pharisees, hypocrites, because you travel around on sea and land to make one proselyte; and when he becomes one, you make him twice as much a son of hell as yourselves." I am also reminded of Paul's Words to Timothy in 2 Timothy 2:2, "The things which you have heard from me in the presence of many witnesses, entrust these to faithful men who will be able to teach others also." Novelty is not what we should teach future generations of Christians, but faithfulness to the Gospel texts.

---

50. Taken from transcript of Gundry's lecture of October 6, 2014.

# Chapter 19

# Part Two: A Critical Evaluation of Robert H. Gundry's Westmont College Lecture, "Peter: False Disciple and Apostate According to Saint Matthew" (and Now Recently Released Book)

F. DAVID FARNELL

## INTRODUCTION

This article is part 2 in response to evangelical critical scholar Robert H. Gundry's newly released book entitled *Peter: False Disciple and Apostate according to Saint Matthew*. The first article that I wrote against his hypothesis was published on www.DefendingInerrancy.com on October 14, 2014, and was based on a transcript of his lecture at Westmont College on October 6, 2014, that celebrated Gundry's fiftieth year of teaching.[1] Gundry's presentation is now in book form by the same title, *Peter False Disciple Apostate according to Saint Matthew* (Eerdmans, 2015). The book presents his thesis in 119 pages, with 108 pages representing Gundry's discussion, with the remaining section being indexes. In his lecture and his now-published book, Gundry utilized historical-critical ideologies to formulate his central thesis that the author of the Gospel of Matthew presented Peter as a false disciple and apostate from the faith in contrast to elsewhere in the New Testament where Peter is presented in a favorable light (e.g., Acts 1–13; 1–2 Pet). This contention of Gundry is not really a new position for him, for in his *Matthew: A Commentary on His Handbook for a Mixed Church Under Persecution*, and 1982 (1st ed.) commentary, *Matthew: A Commentary*

---

1. See http://defendinginerrancy.com/robert-gundry-declares-peter-apostate.

*on His Literary and Theological Art*, maintained a similar position to this lecture.[2] In essence, his position goes back to his days at ETS when he signed the inerrancy statement for membership.

Gundry's accomplished this startling and novel declaration based on his understanding of the function of bibliology. Bibliology, in its origin and history, seeks to understand writers of the New Testament as presenting their own unique, distinctive contributions to theology, positing that each individual writer was not necessarily in agreement with other written portions of the New Testament, i.e., manifest contradictions and disagreements existed in the unique theological content of the books of the New Testament. Indeed, Gundry uses bibliology in its true historical-critical sense, since the discipline arose to prominence as a reaction and rejection of dogmatic or systematic theology. Gerhard Hasel, in his excellent work *New Testament Theology: Basic Issues in the Current Debate*, presents a sober assessment of the historical roots of biblical theology, now practiced by many evangelicals and especially Gundry. One must stress that biblical theology was developed through the influence of Neologian and rationalist Johann Philipp Gabler (1753–1826). Gabler, as noted by Hasel,

> marks the beginning of Biblical theology's role as a purely historical discipline, completely independent from dogmatics . . . (1) Inspiration is to be left out of consideration . . . (2) Biblical theology has the task of gathering carefully the concepts and ideas of the individual writers, because the Bible does not contain the ideas of a single man . . . (3) Biblical theology as a historical discipline is by definition obliged to distinguish between the several periods of the old and new religion.[3]

Harvey K. McArthur has demonstrated that as orthodox views of inspiration were rejected by the growing discipline of historical criticism, bibliology arose to predominance. The church from its early history until the seventeenth century believed that the Bible could be harmonized. Even the heretic Tatian, in his *Diatessaron*, believed so. The traditional view of harmonization centering in a high view of inspiration continued through the Reformation and beyond. McArthur comments, "A striking phenomenon of the study of the Bible in the sixteenth century was the sudden flowering of Gospel harmonies."[4] Those producing these works had two reasons for composing their harmonies: (1) to edify the faithful by the presentation of a total picture of Jesus' life and ministry and/or (2) to refute the critics of the Gospels "by demonstrating the essential and astonishing agreement of the Gospels."[5] David Laird Dungan adds to this characteristic of bibliology its rejection of harmonization,

---

2. For example, both Gundry's *Matthew: A Commentary on His Literary and Theological Art* and *Matthew: A Commentary on His Handbook for a Mixed Church Under Persecution* (Eerdmans, 1994) contended for this same position. See pp. 548–49, 589–90 (same pages for both editions).

3. Hasel, *New Testament Theology*, 22–23.

4. McArthur, *Quest through the Centuries*, 85.

5. Ibid., 87.

remarking the following about the falling away from traditional harmonization as historical-critical ideologies predominated: "These sixteenth- and seventeenth-century harmonies share one significant characteristic: they are without exception strikingly literal in their understanding of the Gospel narratives" and "these traditional Gospel harmonies proceeded on the basis of Augustine's assumption that all four Gospels were uniformly true and without admixture of the slightest degree of error. The traditional way of stating this assumption was to claim that each had been written with the aid of the Holy Spirit, or the Spirit of Christ, so that all four were evenly true in all parts and passages."[6] Hence, bibliology, by its very nature and historical antecedents, rejects harmonization. In contrast, dogmatic or systematic theology is the much older discipline, going back to the nascent beginnings of the church that believed harmonization of the texts, due to the assumption of the inspiration of the Holy Spirit upon the New Testament writers, could be placed into a unified expression without any real contradictions between the varied writers. In utilizing the traditional nature of bibliology, Gundry presents, in reality, a low or no view of inspiration and inerrancy in spite of assurances that he would sign the inerrancy statement of the Evangelical Theological Society.[7]

In light of this, Gundry accomplishes the goal of his thesis by (1) rejecting traditional harmonization as noted above, arguing "the old method of harmonizing what we can and holding the rest in suspension has seen its day, like worn-out scientific theories that no longer explain newly discovered phenomena well enough";[8] and (2) arbitrary, selective use of evidence. This latter charge can be demonstrated in an examination of Matthew 26. In Matthew 26 the focus is upon the last supper of the twelve with Jesus (26:17–36). In the context, Matthew relates that Jesus identified Judas as the betrayer (26:21, 25). In 26:21, Jesus then says to the remaining disciples, "You will all fall way because of this night," with the emphasis in the sentence on the "you all." Thus, all eleven are involved in falling away, not just Peter. Matthew uses the term "fall away" several times in his Gospel regarding defection in discipleship with Christ (13:21; 24:10). Evidently, Peter was not the exception for Matthew includes them all in "falling away" and reports that Jesus bases their action in fulfillment of Zechariah 13:7 about striking down the shepherd and scattering the flock. Matthew presents this as fulfillment of prophecy, not something unnatural to Peter or the other disciples, i.e., it was predicted to happen. Peter is not the sole disciple who falls away, but all of them do so as evidenced in Matthew 26:56, with the statement by Matthew "then all the disciples left him and fled." While Peter remained a little while longer, he nonetheless, joined the others in defection quickly, i.e., they all "fell away." Herein all denied him before men (Matt 10:33) since none stood with him but fled from the scene. Indeed, Peter's defection might be viewed as less problematic than the rest since

---

6. Dungan, *History of the Synoptic Problem*, 304–5.
7. Gundry, "Theological Postscript," in *Matthew*, 623–47.
8. Ibid., 639.

Matthew portrays Peter as vainly attempting to remain with Jesus longer than the others who went into hiding.

Sandwiched directly between this pronouncement of falling away of all the disciples (26:31) and Jesus' focus on Peter in 26:33–35a is Jesus' command to meet them in Galilee in 26:32: "But after I have been raised I will go before you to Galilee." Whatever "falling away" Jesus had in mind, as well as in Matthew's presentation of these events, Jesus [and Matthew] clearly does not view this defection of "all" as permanent, for he promises to meet these defectors in Galilee after his resurrection. Indeed, later he commands the women at the tomb to tell "his disciples" (Matt 28:7) after his resurrection to meet him in Galilee and "take word to my brethren [Matt 28:10] to leave for Galilee, and there they shall see me." One finds it odd, that Matthew would have utilized the designation "his disciples" in the angelic command to go to Galilee (Matt 28:7) as well as Jesus' direct attribution of them as "my brethren" (Matt 26:31) in reference to the disciples who "all" "fell away" as predicted in Matthew 26:31. Adding further weight against Gundry is that Matthew 28:16 says, "the eleven disciples preceded to Galilee, to the mountain which Jesus had designated." Since Judas is the betrayer and removed by Matthew from the narrative, the number eleven, by simple mathematics, naturally would include Peter, in spite of Gundry's attempts to dismiss this verse since it constitutes an obvious problem for his hypothesis.

Furthermore, in Matthew 26:35b, immediately after Peter's boast, "Even if I have to die with you, I will not deny you," Matthew includes all of the disciples as boasting the same thing: "All the disciples said the same thing too." If Gundry's idea of defection upon Peter's part has substance in Matthew, then "all" the disciples are guilty from Matthew's recording of this universal boast by the disciples, i.e., all of the disciples would be "false disciples and apostates," not merely Peter. The point, of course, here is that only by selective cherry-picking of the evidence can Gundry sustain his hypothesis, for a close examination of the evidence in the bibliology of Matthew dissipates Gundry's contentions quite forcefully.

## GUNDRY'S SYNOPTIC THEORY DIRECTLY CONTRADICTS HIS THESIS REGARDING PETER AS AN APOSTATE AND FALSE DISCIPLE

Standing in direct contradiction to Gundry's contentions in bibliology regarding Peter as an apostate and false disciple is his synoptic approach. Throughout Gundry's commentary on Matthew, he fervently maintains Markan priority or the 2- or 4-source hypothesis. He contends for his first edition commentary that "the comparisons undertaken here will show that the peculiarities of Matthew derive almost wholly from his own revisions of and additions to Mark and the materials shared only with Luke (i.e., the materials usually designated as Q)" and "Matthew uses Mark and the materials shared only with Luke."[9] In the 1994 revision, he continued to maintain the 2/4 source hypothesis: "[My assumptions] have included Matthew's use of Mark and Q and a Q larger than ordinarily conceived."[10] And, "I started doctoral work on the quotations in Matthew with the purpose of helping prove the priority of Matthew over Mark and the nonexistence of Q. Studying the data in detail convinced me to the contrary that Markan priority, and the existence of Q, and Matthew's use of Mark and Q offer a much better explanation. Renewed study for the writing of the present commentary strengthened this conviction."[11] Indeed, Gundry seems to view Matthew as, at times, slavishly following Mark, with, for example, even small changes in conjunctions, tense form and other minute points of rewording from Mark throughout his treatment of Matthew, i.e., "Matthew changes" the phraseology and working of Mark's Gospel, etc.[12] Indeed, one would not exaggerate to contend that Gundry's commentary creates the firm impression that Matthew had Mark before him and painstakingly observed and minutely changed even the micro-wording of Mark as his guide in formulating his own Gospel. The point here being that Matthew is viewed by Gundry as a product of Mark, even slavishly so.

The delicious irony is that Gundry's synoptic approach manifests a blatant contradiction to his contentions in his lecture and book on the alleged apostasy and false discipleship of Peter. This can be observed especially in the testimony of the early church regarding both Matthew and Mark.[13]

## The Testimony of the Church to the Priority of Matthew's Gospel

The Gospel of Matthew was the church's most popular Gospel in the decades up to the time of Irenaeus (ca. AD 180). After an extensive analysis of Matthew's influence on early Christianity, Massaux relates,

> Of all the New Testament Writings, the Gospel of Matthew was the one whose literary influence was the most widespread and the most profound in Christian literature that extended into the last decades of the second century.... Until the end of the second century, the first gospel remained the gospel par excellence.... The Gospel was, therefore, the normative fact of Christian life. It created the background for ordinary Christianity.[14]

---

9. Ibid., 2.
10. Ibid. (1994), xiv.
11. Ibid.
12. Hundreds of examples might be given, but one must suffice for this article. For example, "Matthew changes the verb 'comes' (so Mark and Luke) to 'he who ... comes'; Matthew "drops out" Mark's adversative" (Matt 3:11–12); ibid., 48.
13. For much greater detail, see Farnell, "Synoptic Gospels in the Ancient Church," 53–86.
14. Massaux, *Influence of the Gospel of Saint Matthew*, 3:186–87.

Moreover, the unanimous and unquestioned consensus of the church fathers was that Matthew was the first Gospel written, and almost without exception, the early church placed the Gospel of Matthew first in the canon of the New Testament. Petrie observes, "Until the latter half of the eighteenth century, the apostolic authorship of 'the Gospel according to Matthew' seems to have been generally accepted."[15] The present writer is not out to prove Matthean priority but merely to demonstrate that the consistent testimony of the nascent church was that Matthew was written first. At no time was Mark ever said to be the first Gospel written.

However, the Enlightenment and its spawning of historical-critical methodologies—particularly that aspect of the system called "Source Criticism"—marked the beginning of the end of that viewpoint.[16] Most New Testament scholars at the turn of the twenty-first century resoundingly reject the unanimous testimony of the early church regarding Matthean priority in favor of the Two- or Four-Source Theory[17] of how the Synoptic Gospels came into existence.[18] That rejection characterizes not only those of a liberal-theological perspective. It extends also to include many who probably would classify themselves as conservative, yet historical-critical evangelicals.[19] Few historical-critical evangelicals today dare to challenge the "findings" of Source Criticism.

Furthermore, concepts of literary dependency as maintained by Gundry were non-existent in the nascent church. A work, *Mark*, vol. 2 from the Ancient Christian Commentary on Scripture, buttresses these contentions. This work, by appealing to the ancients, circumnavigates such sacrosanct, as well as highly erroneous, historical-critically cherished icons originating out of source, form, tradition and redaction criticism, revealing some interesting contradictions with post-Enlightenment assertions. For instance, the volume on Mark reveals that the early church fathers overwhelmingly neglected Mark and rarely produced a sustained commentary on Mark. Instead, Matthew and John received the most attention. While one could argue that they held

---

15. Petrie, "Authorship of 'The Gospel According to Matthew,'" 15. Stonehouse, a leading advocate of Markan priority, admitted, "The tradition concerning the apostolic authorship of Matthew is as strong, clear, and consistent and . . . the arguments advanced against its reliability are by no means decisive . . . the apostolic authorship of Matthew is as strongly attested as any fact of ancient church history"; see Stonehouse, *Origins of the Synoptic Gospels*, 46–47, cf. 76–77.

16. Orchard and Riley, *Order of the Synoptics*, 111; see also ch. 2 of Thomas and Farnell, *Jesus Crisis*.

17. The Two-Source Theory contends that Mark was written first, then Matthew and Luke wrote in dependence on Mark and a document called "Q" which contained material common to Matthew and Luke but not found in Mark. The Four-Source Theory adds documents called "M"—used by Matthew in addition to the others—and "L"—used by Luke in addition to the others.

18. See Orchard and Longstaff, *J. J. Griesbach*, 134; Farmer, *Synoptic Problem*, 48–49; Streeter, *Four Gospels*, 151–98. Orchard and Longstaff cite Griesbach as an example of one who criticized the early fathers. Farmer cites the lack of evidence supporting the Two- (or Four-) Source Theory.

19. Hill, *Gospel of Matthew*, 28; Carson, Moo, and Morris, *Introduction to the New Testament*, 70–71; France, *Matthew*, 34–38; Martin, *New Testament Foundations*, vol. 1 of *The Four Gospels*, 139–60, 225.

Matthew and John in high esteem because they were apostolic, one still wonders why, if Mark was really the first written Gospel as so ardently maintained by source criticism (contra the Two-Document Hypothesis), did the fathers so persistently neglect it. Moreover, the volume also reveals that the Fathers consistently maintained that Mark actually wrote Mark (not some unknown "evangelist" as maintained by historical criticism) and that it reflected Peter's preaching rather than being a condensation of Matthew and Luke (contra the Two-Gospel Hypothesis). The conclusion the work reaches is astoundingly refreshing: "It had always been evident that Mark presented a shorter version of the Gospel than Matthew, but the premise of literary dependency was not generally recognized. The view that Matthew and Luke directly relied on Mark did not develop in full form until the nineteenth century."[20] Such a perspective also indicates that the Fathers regarded Matthew, not Mark, as the first Gospel to be written. From this reviewer's perspective, only by *a priori* reading into the church fathers of these two recent synoptic hypotheses move from acute speculation to enslaving dogma.

The most important point rendering Gundry's hypothesis about Peter null is what the early church fathers consistently witnessed regarding Mark's origins: Mark based his Gospel on Peter's preaching! In Eusebius's *Ecclesiastical History* 3.39.15–16, Papias commented that in composing his Gospel, Mark, being Peter's interpreter, "wrote accurately all that he remembered . . . of the things said *or* done by the Lord" and immediately after this spoke of Peter as "not making, as it were, an arrangement of the Lord's oracles, so that Mark did nothing wrong in thus writing down single points as he remembered them." What must be remembered about Papias that makes him very credible in the information that he imparts (along with his friend and contemporary, Polycarp) was that he was a disciple and personal acquaintance of the Apostle John, because Irenaeus wrote that Papias was "the hearer of John."[21] Unfortunately, Papias's writings are no longer extant. Only fragments of his works remain and are largely known through quotations by later Fathers, especially Eusebius. Papias wrote a series of five treatises entitled *Interpretation of the Oracles of the Lord* in which he draws information from the remaining, living-eyewitness sources, i.e., the Apostle John himself and another original disciple of Jesus named Ariston, concerning what

---

20. Oden and Hall, *Mark*, xxix.

21. See Irenaeus *Adversus haereses* 5.33.4; also quoted by Eusebius *Hist. eccl.* 3.39.1. Regarding Eusebius' skeptical attitude about whether Papias ever heard the Apostle John (*Ecclesiastical History* 3.39.1–2) see Schoedel, *Polycarp, Martyrdom of Polycarp, Fragments of Papias*, 89–92; Helm, *Eusebius Werke*, 193–94; 412–13. For persuasive evidence that Papias *did* have direct contact with the apostle, see Gundry, *Matthew: A Commentary on His Handbook for a Mixed Church under Persecution*, 611–13. Eusebius's skepticism may have stemmed from his anti-chiliastic view as opposed to that of Papias (and Irenaeus) who strongly affirmed a physical reality of the millennium; see Eusebius, *Ecclesiastical History* 3.39.12–13. Or, it may have resulted from Papias's alleged preference for oral tradition rather than authorized books as his sources; see Eusebius, *Hist. eccl* 3.39.4; cf. also Grant, introduction to *Apostolic Fathers*, 86.

the apostles had said or done.[22] In essence, Papias's assertions had their foundation in direct "eyewitness" (i.e., firsthand) reports.[23] If Papias wrote ca. AD 95–110, then the information that he imparts reaches well back into the first century and is an invaluable source of information regarding the Gospels.

Assuming, for the sake of argument, Gundry's synoptic approach of the priority of Mark, then Matthew would have based his account of Peter being an apostate and false disciple directly from Mark who, from Papias's testimony, based his composition in his own Gospel of Mark largely in the teaching and preaching of Peter. Why would Matthew use Mark's account if Matthew really believed that Peter was truly a false disciple? The very existence of Mark's account witnesses to Mark's consideration of Peter as faithful. Gundry's very assertion that Matthew used Mark in terms of a literary source stands in manifest contradiction to Gundry's bibliology hypothesis. He attempts to have it both ways by selective use of evidence either way. The great irony is that early church fathers' testimonies render Gundry's hypothesis quite ludicrous.

Furthermore, in Gundry's own commentary, he gives much credence to Papias in regard to Papias's testimony regarding Matthew's composition that bears his name, arguing that "even with the concession that Papias and other Fathers of the church made historical mistakes, the persistent and unrivalled character of this particular tradition calls for a higher estimate of its worth."[24] He further argues that "Papias stands only once removed from these original and closest disciples of Jesus, including Matthew, whom he names along with six others of the twelve (Eusebius, *H. E.* 3.39.3–4). We have, then, only three links, not four, in the chain of tradition: (1) the apostles; (2) those who heard the apostles; and (3) Papias."[25] Gundry also takes Irenaeus's testimony (*Eccl. Hist.* 3:39.7; ca. AD 180) that Papias was "the hearer of John" [the Apostle]. He remarks, "Ireneaus's designation and Eusebius's agreement with it suggests that Eusebius found in parts of Papias's 'Exposition of the Lord's Oracles' no longer available to us indications that Papias did hear John. His hearing John could

---

22. Eusebius denied that Papias was a direct hearer of the Apostle John by inferring that another John, John the Elder who was different from John the Apostle, lived in Ephesus at the time (*Ecclesiastical History* 3.39.5–6). A close reading of Papias's words, however, reveals that he neither affirmed nor denied that he was hearer or eyewitness of the apostles. He does not mention it in the passage. Petrie argues, "There is nothing to justify the careless confidence with which Eusebius contradicts Irenaeus"; see Petrie, "Authorship," 15–32 (esp. 17–18). Furthermore, even if Papias was not a personal disciple of John, as Lightfoot contended, "still his age and country place him in more or less close connection with the traditions of the Apostles; and it is this fact which gives importance to his position and teaching"; see Lightfoot, *Essays on the Work Entitled Supernatural Religion*, 142.

23. Eusebius *Hist. eccl.* 3.39.15–16. Papias's statement regarding John the disciple and the Elder John probably referred to one and the same person, i.e., John the Apostle; see Petrie, "Authorship," 18–24; Gundry, *Matthew*, 611–13.

24. Gundry, *Matthew* (1994), 610.

25. Ibid., 611.

only strengthen the case for taking his quotation of the elder's statements about Mark and Matthew very seriously."[26] Gundry even takes seriously Papias's statement,

> But how can we believe that Matthew, an apostle, used the gospel of a non-apostle, Mark? The elder quoted by Papias as saying that Matthew wrote our Gospel also indicates that Mark wrote down the reminiscences of Peter concerning the ministry of Jesus (Eusebius, *H.E.* 3.39.15). According to extremely early tradition then, the Gospel of Mark is essentially apostolic. Therefore we should put the question as follows: Is it too hard to think that one apostle took material that came from a fellow apostle? Of course not—especially since the apostle borrowed from was none else than the foremost of the twelve [i.e., Peter]. Furthermore, Matthew did not merely copy the Petrine tradition set forth in Mark. He used it in ways we are just now beginning to appreciate for their originality.[27]

By Gundry's own admission, Peter stands behind Mark and Matthew used Mark to compose his own Gospel, so it is very, very unlikely that Matthew would have regarded Peter as a false disciple and apostate when he utilized that apostate's information for his own Gospel! Once again, Gundry is selective, as well as inconsistent, in the use of evidence for his hypothesis.

## CONCLUSION TO THE MATTER OF PETER AS A FALSE DISCIPLE AND APOSTATE

As noted in the previous article, the guild is pressing for Gundry's acceptance back into the Evangelical Theological Society. Why? I would think they share his low or no view of inerrancy, since "birds of a feather, flock together." Orthodox concepts of inerrancy are now dismissed in the guild. Gundry's approach to bibliology reflects their approach to bibliology; Gundry's approach to redefining inerrancy reflects their redefinition of the term. They would like to welcome him back and Eerdmans prints the "Welcome Home!" celebration of that fact in 2015. I hear that the rumor or speculation is that Gundry would prefer, however, to stay away. He is a wise man.

26. Ibid.
27. Ibid., 621.

Chapter 20

# A Critical Review of Donald Hagner's "Ten Guidelines for Evangelical Scholarship"

## F. DAVID FARNELL AND NORMAN L. GEISLER[1]

### INTRODUCTION

Baker Books blog published on March 12, 2013, Donald Hagner's "Ten Guidelines for Evangelical Scholarship."[2] These guidelines were praised by Craig Blomberg[3] in the first comment on the blog where Craig Blomberg noted, "Excellent, Don, excellent. And I'm so enjoying reading your book. I hope you still have several more good ones to come!" immediately below Hagner's listing of ten guidelines. Here are Hagner's guidelines (and we suspect many more critical evangelical scholars would concur with his list). We cut and paste verbatim from Hagner's blog entry:

"Ten Guidelines for Evangelical Scholarship," by Donald A. Hagner:

Proposals for an evangelical criticism that affirms the indispensability of the critical method, i.e., being "reasonably" critical: We must:

1. See *what is there* (avoiding maximal conservatism, anachronistic approaches, harmonizing and homogenizing, partial appeals to historical evidence).

---

[1]. This chapter originally appeared in the *Journal of the International Society of Christian Apologetics*, 6.1 (2013) 179–205.

[2]. http://blog.bakeracademic.com/don-hagners-ten-guidelines-for-evangelical-scholarship.

[3]. Please also read Geisler and Farnell, "Erosion of Inerrancy among New Testament Scholars," at http://normangeisler.net/articles/Bible/Inspiration-Inerrancy/Blomberg/DenialOfMiracleStory.htm.

2. Affirm the full humanity of the scriptures (the word of God in the words of men).

3. Define the nature of inspiration inductively (not deductively), i.e., in light of the phenomena of scripture (doing justice to it as it is).

4. Acknowledge that no presuppositionless position is possible and that the best we can do is attempt to step outside of our presuppositions and imagine "what if." (Only a relative degree of objectivity is attainable.)

5. Modify the classical historical-critical method so far as its presuppositions are concerned, i.e., so as to allow openness to the transcendent, the action of God in the historical process, the possibility of miracles, etc. Develop a method not alien but rather appropriate to what is being studied.

6. Maintain a unified worldview, avoiding a schizophrenic attitude toward truth and criteria for the validation of truth. That is, all truth is God's truth, including that arrived at through our rationality.

7. Acknowledge that in the realm of historical knowledge, we are not dealing with matters that can be proven (or disproven, for that matter!), but with probability. Historical knowledge remains dependent on inferences from the evidence. Good historical criticism is what makes best sense, i.e., the most coherent explanation of the evidence.

8. Avoid the extremes of a pure fideism and a pure rationality-based apologetics. Blind faith is as inappropriate as rationalism. Faith and reason, however, both have their proper place. What is needed is a creative synthesis.

9. Develop humility, in contrast to the strange (and unwarranted!) confidence and arrogance of critical orthodoxy (concerning constructs that depend on presuppositions alien to the documents themselves).

10. Approach criticism by developing a creative tension between intellectual honestly and faithfulness to the tradition (each side needs constant reexamination), with the trust that criticism rightly engaged will ultimately vindicate rather than destroy Christian truth.

Note: The Holy Spirit cannot be appealed to in order to solve historical-critical issues or in the issue of truth-claims. Nevertheless, it is true that *for the believer* the inner witness of the Spirit confirms the truth of the faith existentially or in the heart.

> Concede: Our knowledge is fragmentary and partial, and all our wisdom is but stammering. Full understanding can only come after our perfection, and then it will no longer be understanding alone but also worship.[4]

---

4. Italics in original.

Part 2—Inerrancy Defended

## ANALYSIS OF PROPOSED GUIDELINES

Now let us respond to each of Hagner's ten evangelical scholarship "guidelines," even though the "proof in the pudding" is readily seen in what has been written already. The bottom line is that critical evangelical scholars are becoming so much like their left-wing counterparts that little differences remain on the whole. Ability to distinguish between these two groups in terms of presuppositions and conclusions is blurring rapidly and disappearing.

## Proposed Guideline 1:

"See *what is there* (avoiding maximal conservatism, anachronistic approaches, harmonizing and homogenizing, partial appeals to historical evidence)."

*Response*:

1. Historical criticism is really the anachronistic approach, spawned by Spinoza in the seventeenth century and aided by alien negative presuppositions.[5]

2. Historical criticism does not accept "what is there" but wants to see what they *a priori* have chosen *not* to be there (i.e., slaughtering of the babies in Bethlehem [Gundry], resurrection of saints in Matthew 27:51–52 [Licona]).

3. Historical criticism, no matter how "modified," assaults the integrity of God's Word. This is the inevitable "fruit" of historical criticism. It attacks rather than affirms; casts doubt, rather than confirms. Many evangelical critical scholars seem to be blind to such effects.

4. No matter how much Hagner would attempt to modify historical criticism, most true historical critics (i.e., non-evangelicals) probably would not accept that modification.

5. Plenary, verbal inspiration allows for harmonization, while historical criticism divides God's word into what is acceptable and what is *not* acceptable to the individual historical critic.

## Proposed Guideline 2:

"Affirm the full humanity of the Scriptures (the word of God in the words of men)."
*Response*:

1. Although the full-humanity of Scripture is true, since God is the author of Scripture and God cannot lie or err, the Scripture cannot err (John 14:26; 16:13; 17:17).

2. The Bible is fully human without error; it is God's Word as well as man's words (2 Sam 23:2; 2 Tim 3:16). It is a theanthropic book, as Christ is a theanthropic person.

3. By Hagner's same logic, Jesus must have erred (and sinned).

---

5. Please read, Geisler, "Philosophical Roots of Modern Biblical Criticism," 65–85.

## Proposed Guideline 3:

"Define the nature of inspiration inductively (not deductively), i.e., in light of the phenomena of scripture (doing justice to it as it is)."

*Response*:

1. This is a false disjunction since both induction and deduction are involved in determining the doctrine of Scripture, as they are in other doctrines as well.

2. The doctrine of inspiration is based on a complete inductive study of all Scripture which yields two basic truths: (a) the Bible is the written Word of God; (b) God cannot error. From which we rightly deduce that (c) the Bible cannot err. As the *Westminster Confession of Faith* put it, the basis for our faith is "the whole counsel of God . . . [which] is either expressly set down in Scripture, *or by good and necessary consequence may be deduced from Scripture.*"[6]

3. Of course, the doctrine of Scripture should be understood in the light of the data of Scripture. However, as the International Council on Biblical Inerrancy put it, "We further deny that inerrancy is negated by the Biblical phenomena" (art. XIII). The data of Scripture do not contradict the doctrine of Scripture; they merely nuance and enhance our understanding of it.[7]

## Proposed Guideline 4:

"Acknowledge that no presuppositionless position is possible and that the best we can do is attempt to step outside of our presuppositions and imagine 'what if.' (Only a relative degree of objectivity is attainable.)"

*Response*:

1. While this is true in a very important sense, Hagner apparently ignores the history and presuppositions of historical criticism to his own detriment.

2. The question is not *whether* one approaches Scripture with presuppositions, but *which* presuppositions he uses.

3. As evangelical scholars, we approach the Bible as the inerrant written Word of God by way of the historical-grammatical method of interpretation. Current critical scholarship denies both of these in the historic evangelical sense.

4. As ICBI stated, "We affirm that the text of Scripture is to be interpreted by grammatico-historical exegesis, taking in account of its literary forms and devices, and that Scripture is to interpret Scripture"[8] (art. XVIII).

5. ICBI adds importantly, "We deny the legitimacy of any treatment of the text of quest for sources lying behind it that leads to relativizing, dehistoricizing, or discounting

---

6. Westminster Confession of Faith, ch. 1, art. V (emphasis added).
7. See Geisler, *Systematic Theology*, 1:205–26.
8. CSBI, art. XVIII.

its teaching, or rejecting its claims to authorship."[9] But this is exactly what Hagner and his British-trained New Testament cohorts do.

6. Hagner comes dangerously close to denying that one can truly obtain an "objective" interpretation of Scripture. Besides being a self-defeating claim to objectivity in denying objectivity, he apparently has not read and interacted with the excellent work by Thomas Howe titled *Objectivity in Biblical Interpretation*.

## Proposed Guideline 5:

"Modify the classical historical-critical method so far as its presuppositions are concerned, i.e., so as to allow openness to the transcendent, the action of God in the historical process, the possibility of miracles, etc. Develop a method not alien but rather appropriate to what is being studied."

*Response*:

1. If the "historical-critical method" needs to be "modified" before it can be safely used, then this is an admission that it is a dangerous method.

2. Further, if is it modified of its anti-supernaturalism, then why accept the method to begin with?

3. What value does this critical methodology have that could not have been gained by the traditional historical-grammatical method?

4. If it is not radically modified, then it does not help evangelicals. But if it is radically modified to suit evangelicalism, then why accept it to begin with? If you have to radically modify a Ford to make a Cadillac, they why not start with a Cadillac?

5. Methodology determines theology, and an unorthodox methodology will yield unorthodox theology.

## Proposed Guideline 6:

"Maintain a unified worldview, avoiding a schizophrenic attitude toward truth and criteria for the validation of truth. That is, all truth is God's truth, including that arrived at through our rationality."

*Response*:

1. As the ICBI framers put, "Truth is what corresponds to the facts."[10] Whether God revealed it in Scripture (John 17:17; 2 Tim 3:16) or in nature (Ps 19:1; Rom 1:1–20), and God does not contradict himself.[11]

2. We deny that truth is "*arrived at through our rationality*," as Hagner meant it, since God is the source of all truth, whether in general or special revelation. The ICBI

---

9. Ibid.
10. CSBI, art. XIII, official commentary.
11. CSBI, arts. V and XIV.

framers declared emphatically, "We affirm that the written Word in its entirely is a relation given by God . . . [and] we deny that the Bible . . . depends on the responses of men for its validity."[12] As for other alleged sources of truth, "We further deny that scientific hypotheses about earth's history may properly be used to overturn the teaching of Scripture."[13]

3. However, good reason must always be in accord with and enlightened by revelation and God's Holy Spirit. As article XVII declares: "We affirm that the Holy Spirit bears witness to the Scriptures, assuring believers of the truthfulness of God's written Word. We deny that this witness of the Holy Spirit operated in isolation from or against Scripture."

## Proposed Guideline 7:

"Acknowledge that in the realm of historical knowledge, we are not dealing with matters that can be proven (or disproven, for that matter!), but with probability. Historical knowledge remains dependent on inferences from the evidence. Good historical criticism is what makes best sense, i.e., the most coherent explanation of the evidence."

*Response*:

1. Historical knowledge can rise above mere "probabilities." One can have moral certainty about many historical events things. Luke spoke of "*convincing proofs*" of the resurrection of Christ (Acts 1:3).

2. Luke begins his Gospel with the assurance to the reader that he "may know the *exact truth* about the things you have been taught" (Luke 1:4).

3. In determining the truth of a historical presentation one certainly wants the interpretation that "makes best sense, i.e., the most coherent explanation of the evidence." However, it begs the question whether what Hagner means by "good historical criticism" is the best way to achieve this. As a matter of fact, as manifest in the writings of many contemporary scholars who have adopted this method, it clearly did not lead to the best conclusion. Certainly, it did not lead to the most evangelical conclusion.

## Proposed Guideline 8:

"Avoid the extremes of a pure fideism and a pure rationality-based apologetics. Blind faith is as inappropriate as rationalism. Faith and reason, however, both have their proper place. What is needed is a creative synthesis."

*Response*:

1. To speak of "blind faith" as one of the poles is a straw man since one can be a Fideist (e.g., like Alvin Plantinga) without having blind faith.

---

12. CSBI, art. III.
13. CSBI, art. XII.

Part 2—Inerrancy Defended

2. True Christian scholarship involves "faith seeking understanding," as the Bible exhorts when it asks us to "give a reason for the hope that is in us" (1 Pet 3:15). Indeed, God said through Isaiah, "Come let us reason together" (Isa 1:18). And Jesus commanded that we love the Lord our God with our "mind," as well as with our heart and soul (Mark 12:30).

3. There are other apologetics alternatives to Fideism and a rationally-based approach. Aquinas spoke of faith *based in* God's Word but *supported by* evidence.[14] And Cornelius Van Til's transcendental reduction to the necessity of accepting the Triune God revealed in Scripture was certainly not a form of pure Fideism or pure rationalism in apologetics.

4. Faith and reason do both have a proper place and need a "creative synthesis," but they do not find it in critical method proposed by Donald Hagner's "Ten Guidelines for Evangelical Scholarship."

## Proposed Guideline 9:

"Develop humility, in contrast to the strange (and unwarranted!) confidence and arrogance of critical orthodoxy (concerning constructs that depend on presuppositions alien to the documents themselves)."

*Response*:

1. This guideline is an ironic example of the very orthodox view it is criticizing. It is hardly an example of humility to exalt one's own methodology and stereotype one's opponent as having a "strange (and unwarranted!) confidence and arrogance." Humble statements do not condemn others as having unwarranted confidence and arrogance!

2. The humble thing to do would have been to show some respect of the orthodox view of Scripture.[15]

## Proposed Guideline 10:

"Approach criticism by developing a creative tension between intellectual honesty and faithfulness to the tradition (each side needs constant reexamination), with the trust that criticism rightly engaged will ultimately vindicate rather than destroy Christian truth."

*Response*:

1. Certainly Hagner does not mean what he says, since he says "intellectual honesty" needs "constant reexamination," too!

---

14. See Geisler, *Thomas Aquinas*, ch. 5.

15. Hannah, *Inerrancy and the Church*; Geisler, *Biblical Inerrancy*, and the venerable historical-grammatical way of interpreting it; see ICBI Hermeneutics Articles and Commentary.

2. Further, "faithfulness to the tradition" one has should not be a goal. Rather, it should be faithfulness to the Word of God.

3. Further, the phrase "rightly engaged" is bristling with presuppositions that Hagner leaves unstated and unspecified.

4. Judging by these ten guidelines, Hagner is "engaging" in a form of biblical criticism that is ill-founded and destined to disaster. For *bad methodology leads to bad theology, and he has adopted a bad methodology.*

## Hagner Note:

"Note: The Holy Spirit cannot be appealed to in order to solve historical-critical issues or in the issue of truth-claims. Nevertheless, it is true that for the believer the inner witness of the Spirit confirms the truth of the faith existentially or in the heart.

Concede: Our knowledge is fragmentary and partial, and all our wisdom is but stammering. Full understanding can only come after our perfection, and then it will no longer be understanding alone but also worship."

*Response*:

1. This is an odd comment coming from an evangelical since Scripture affirms the role of the Holy Spirit in the production of his Word: John 6:63—"the words that I have spoken to you are spirit and are life"—and 2 Peter 1:19—"So we have the prophetic word made more sure, to which you do well to pay attention as to a lamp shining in a dark place, until the day dawns and the morning star arises in your hearts."

2. The Spirit of God never affirms anything contrary to the Word of God. Further, the Holy Spirit is essential in a proper interpretation and application of the Word of God.[16] As the Holy Spirit lead the apostles in writing the Word of God (John 14:26; 16:13), even so he leads the believers in understanding the Word of God (1 John 2:26–27).

3. Just because *perfect* understanding of Scripture does not come until heaven (1 Cor 13:10–13) does not mean we cannot have an *adequate* understanding of it here. Nor does it relieve us of our obligation, to "test the spirits" to discover the "false prophets" and to know "the Spirit of truth" from "the spirit of error" (1 John 4:1, 6). After all, we have in Scripture "a prophetic word made more sure" (2 Pet 1:19), and we are exhorted to use it to "contend earnestly for the faith which was once for all handed down to the saints" (Jude 3).

16. See CSBH, arts. 4, 5, 6.

Part 2—Inerrancy Defended

## THE RESULTS OF FOLLOWING THESE GUIDELINES IN HAGNER'S WRITINGS

Now let us look at the consequences of these principles from which Hagner's own recently published New Testament introduction operates, i.e., his *The New Testament: A Historical and Theological Introduction*.

The work is praised as follows on the Amazon website, reflecting similar wording on its jacket cover:

> This capstone work from widely respected senior evangelical scholar Donald Hagner offers a substantial introduction to the New Testament. Hagner deals with the New Testament both historically and theologically, employing the framework of salvation history. He treats the New Testament as a coherent body of texts and stresses the unity of the New Testament without neglecting its variety. Although the volume covers typical questions of introduction, such as author, date, background, and sources, it focuses primarily on understanding the theological content and meaning of the texts, putting students in a position to understand the origins of Christianity and its canonical writings.

The book includes summary tables, diagrams, maps, and extensive bibliographies. It is praised by such scholars as James D. G. Dunn, I. Howard Marshall, Craig Keener, and Thomas Schreiner.

One may note two strategic factors regarding Hagner's New Testament *Introduction*: First, his work represents the cutting edge of evangelical, British-influenced and trained critical scholarship who are currently teaching the next generation of preachers and scholars in the United States both on a college and seminary level. Second, Hagner's work will most likely replace the late Donald Guthrie's *New Testament Introduction* that was last revised in 1990. If one wants to know where evangelical critical scholarship is moving, Hagner's work provides that trajectory.

These two strategic factors are also the work's gravest weaknesses. Hagner attributes the word "inspired" to the New Testament Scriptures,[17] yet also maintains, "The inspired word of God comes to us through the medium of history, through the agency of writers who lived in history and were a part of history," which "*necessitate the historical and critical study of Scripture.*"[18] He says that the use of the word "critical" does not refer to "tearing it down or demeaning it—but rather to exercising judgment or discernment concerning every aspect of it."[19] Therefore, Hagner asserts that "we must engage in historical criticism, in the sense of thoughtful interpretation of the Bible" and "the historical method is indispensable precisely because the Bible is the story of God's act in history."[20] What Hagner means by this is the need

---

17. Hagner, *New Testament*, 4.
18. Ibid.
19. Ibid., 5.
20. Ibid.

for historical-critical ideologies rather than grammatico-historical criticism. This is the first signal that British-influenced evangelical scholars are shifting markedly away from the Reformation tradition of a grammatico-historical approach and training the next generation of preachers in historical criticism that markedly differs in approach presuppositionally, historically, and in the qualitative kind of conclusions such an ideology reaches. Like many British-influenced evangelical critical scholars, he believes that he can use historical criticism and be immune from its more negative elements: "The critical method therefore needs to be tempered so that rather than being used against the Bible, it is open to the possibility of the transcendent or miraculous within the historical process and thus is used to provide better understanding of the Bible."[21] This latter admission is telling, since it is an admission, no matter how indirect, of the dangers of historical criticism. Hagner argues that "keeping an open mind concerning the possibility of the transcendent in history does not entail the suspension of critical judgment. There is no need for a naïve credulity and acceptance of anything and everything simply because one's worldview is amenable to the supernatural."[22] Hagner apparently believes that he has discovered the proper balance of presuppositions and practice in the historical-critical method displayed in this work: "It must be stressed once again that the critical method is indispensable to the study of Scripture. It is the *sine qua non* of responsible interpretation of God's word. The believer need have no fear of the method itself, but need only be on guard against the employment of improper presuppositions."[23] An old pithy saying, however, is that the "devil is in the details." Hagner's argument here ignores the marked evidence or proof from history of the presuppositions and damage that historical criticism has caused by even well-intentioned scholars who have eviscerated the Scripture through such an ideology. History constitutes a monumental testimony against Hagner's embracing of the ideologies of historical criticism that displays the damage it has caused the church.

Hagner excoriates "very conservative scholars" and "obscurantist fundamentalism" that refused to embrace some form of moderated historical-critical ideology. Hagner commends Hengel's belief that "fundamentalism" and its accepting belief in the full trustworthiness of Scripture is actually a form of atheism,[24] quoting and affirming Hengel's position that "Fundamentalism is a form of 'unbelief' that closes itself to the—God intended—historical reality."[25] Hagner insists that "repudiation of the critical study of Scripture amounts to a gnostic-like denial of the historical character of the Christian faith."[26] Apparently, Hagner agrees with Hengel that "Fundamentalist polemic against the 'historical-critical method' does not understand his-

21. Ibid., 7.
22. Ibid.
23. Ibid., 11.
24. Cf. Hengel, "Eye-Witness Memory," 70–96.
25. Hengel, "Eye-Witness Memory," 94n100.
26. Hagner, *New Testament*, 10.

torical perception" and believes (with Hengel) that since the Scriptures were mediated through history and human agency, this opens the documents up to being fallible human products. Because of the Scripture being based in historical knowledge, one cannot use the word "certain" but only "probable," for Hagner insists that the "word 'prove,' although perhaps appropriate in mathematics and science, is out of place when it comes to historical knowledge."[27] In studying Scripture, compelling proof will always be lacking.[28]

In response, Hagner (and Hengel) apparently do not understand the issue, for what he calls "Fundamentalism" (e.g., *The Jesus Crisis*) never argued against criticism but only the kind of criticism utilized and the philosophical principle involved in such criticism that closed off the study of Scripture *a priori* before any analysis could be done, i.e., historical-critical ideologies. Historical criticism is a purposeful, psychological operation designed to silence Scripture and deflect away from its plain, normal sense implications, i.e., to dethrone it from influence in church and society. While liberal critical scholarship will openly admit this, "moderate" evangelicals like Hagner choose to ignore the intent of historical criticism.

Considering this operating assumption about understanding Scripture, here is a sampling of Hagner's "balanced" approach to historical-critical ideologies: First, he says, "we have no reliable chronology of Jesus ministry" in the Gospels.[29] Since the Gospels are "historical narratives" they involve "interpretation" by the evangelists and that "level of interpretation can be high."[30] Since the Gospel writers largely (but not completely) reflect ancient Roman *bioi* as the "closest analogy" from antiquity" and since *bioi* were not necessarily always without interpretation,[31] "the Evangelists compare well with the secular historians of their own day, and their narratives remain basically trustworthy."[32]

Second, like other critically trained European scholars, Hagner accepts Lessing's "ugly ditch" and the German/British concept of a *historie* (actual verifiable events) vs. *geschichte* (faith interpretations of events) dichotomy between the Jesus of the Gospels and the "historical Jesus."[33] Although critical of some historical Jesus research, Hagner concedes that "the Jesus of history was to some extent different from the Gospels' portrayal of him" and "if we cannot look for a one-to-one correspondence between the Jesus of history and the Jesus of the early church's faith, we can at least establish a degree of continuity between the two."[34] Furthermore, "we are in no position to

27. Ibid., 9.
28. Ibid.
29. Ibid., 63.
30. Ibid.
31. Ibid., 61.
32. Ibid., 65.
33. Ibid., 83–104.
34. Ibid., 97.

write a biography of Jesus" based on the information from the New Testament since the Gospels are "kerygmatic portrayals of the story of Jesus."[35]

Third, Hagner embraces the idea that "pseudonymity" is acceptable in the New Testament canon. Hagner argues, "We have very little to lose in allowing the category of Deutero-Pauline letters. If it happens that some other persons have written these four, or even six documents [e.g., Ephesians, the Pastoral Epistles] in the name of Paul, we are not talking about forgery or deception."[36] He continues, "The ancient world on the whole did not have the same kind of sensitivity to pseudonymity that is typical in the modern world, with its concern for careful attribution and copyright."[37] And "the authority and canonicity of the material is in no way affected by books put into final shape by disciples of the prophets."[38] "The fact is that the Pauline corpus, with deutero-letters as well as without them, stands under the banner of the authoritative Paul."[39] Hagner supports British scholar I. Howard Marshall's view on "pseudonymous" writings in the New Testament: "In order to avoid the idea of deceit, Howard Marshall has coined the words 'allonymity' and 'allepigraphy' in which the prefix *pseudos* ('false') is replaced with *allos* ('other') which gives a more positive concept to the writing of a work in the name of another person."[40] Hagner notes that another British scholar James Dunn has come to a similar conclusion. Hagner says, "We do not know beyond a shadow of a doubt that there are Deutero-Pauline letters in the Pauline corpus, but if in the weighing of historical probabilities it seems to us that there are, we can freely admit that this too is a way in which God has mediated Scripture to us."[41] Apparently, to Hagner and others, God uses false attribution to accomplish his purpose of communicating his Word that encourages the highest ethical standards upon men! Thus, for Hagner, Paul most likely did not write Ephesians as well as the Pastoral Epistles (1–2 Timothy and Titus),[42] but believes they should be viewed in the category of Deutero-Pauline letters.[43] Hagner even devotes a whole section of his introduction to this category of Deutero-Pauline letters.[44] He also regards the book of James as possibly not written by James: "We cannot completely exclude the alternative possibility that the book is pseudonymous. Already in the time of Jerome it was regarded as such. . . . Least likely of all, but again not impossible, the letter could have

---

35. Ibid., 98.
36. Ibid., 429.
37. Ibid.
38. Ibid.
39. Ibid.
40. Ibid., 431. See Marshall, *Critical and Exegetical Commentary*, 84.
41. Hagner, *New Testament*, 432.
42. Ibid., 428.
43. Ibid., 429.
44. Ibid., 585–642.

been written by another, little known or unknown, person named 'James.'"[45] Second Peter is "almost certainly not by Peter. Very probably written by a disciple of Peter or a member of the Petrine circle."[46] Revelation is "almost certainly not by the Apostle John. Possibly by John 'The Elder' but more probably by another John, otherwise unknown to us, who may have been a member of the Johannine circle."[47]

Due to space limitations, a final concatenation surrounding Hagner's view of the composition and authorship of the NT must satisfy for various assertions of Hagner's *Introduction*: The Gospels involve "interpretation"; that "level of interpretation can be high" at times, and display "basic reliability," "basically trustworthy" in their presentation;[48] "it is a great pity that the word 'Pharisee,' which ought to be a complementary term, has become in the English language synonymous with 'hypocrite,' to be a Pharisee was to wear a badge of honor," "to a considerable extent, Jesus himself, in his call to righteousness, actually resembled the Pharisees, as has been rightly pointed out by many Jewish scholars. And, of course, one tends to be most harshly critical of those who are closest to the truth";[49] "that the Jesus of history was to some extent different from the Gospels' portrayal of him can hardly be doubted"; in the Gospels "details were added or altered to make narratives clearer or more applicable to the church. An example, in Peter's confession, is Matthew's alteration of Mark's simple 'You are the Christ' to 'You are the Christ, the Son of the Living God'" (i.e., meaning that Peter did not originally say the whole statement, but Matthew added to it for further meaning); "if we cannot look for a one-to-one correspondence between the Jesus of history and the Jesus of the early church's faith, we can at least establish a degree of continuity between the two";[50] the oral transmission of the Gospel material has "basic reliability"; "to a certain degree, even a number of his [Jesus'] sayings are reworked by the early church, but the primary goal in all of this has been to understand them better."[51] Hagner assumes modern historical-critical approaches such as form and redaction criticism: "that the tradition of Jesus's words and deeds experience some degree of transformation in the different between the first [i.e., the *Sitz im Leben* of Jesus] and the third time frames [i.e., the *Sitz im Leben* of the Evangelist] seems inevitable. Nevertheless, such a view is not incompatible with the conclusion that the tradition has been handed down in a substantially accurate and trustworthy form. We are not talking about the kind of modifications of the tradition that end up in a gross distortion wherein Jesus of the church bears little relationship to the Jesus of history";[52]

45. Ibid., 675.
46. Ibid., 714.
47. Ibid., 761.
48. Hagner, *New Testament*, 64–65.
49. Ibid., 35.
50. Ibid., 97.
51. Ibid., 115.
52. Ibid., 119.

"Mark serves as a model followed by the Evangelists Matthew and Luke"; "the content of Mark is of fundamental importance and provides the basic building blocks of Jesus";[53] "[although] the disciple Levi-Matthew possibly is the collector and editor of the five Matthean discourses, the Gospel as it stands likely is the work of an unknown disciple or disciples of the Matthean circle—that is, associated with Matthew";[54] "the fact is that the Pauline corpus, with deutero-letters as well as without them, stands under the banner of the authoritative Paul"; "from a canonical perspective, the corpus as it stands represents Paul, even if the Deutero-Pauline letters require special awareness and care when they are used to speak of Paul himself. It is not unfair to say that the deutero-Pauline letters represent Paul in their own way as much as the authentic letters. But it is indeed Paul whom they represent, and therefore to that extent they involve no deception";[55] "there is nothing crucial at stake here for those who, like, myself, treasure the NT as Scripture. The acceptance of this kind of pseudonymity, based on actual association with and dependence upon Paul or other apostles, should in no way threaten the canonical authority of these documents."[56] Hagner lists the following four books as deutero-Pauline (i.e., not written by Paul): Ephesians ("probably by a disciple of Paul")[57] and the Pastoral Epistles of 1–2 Timothy and Titus ("a slight probability favors a disciple or disciples of Paul, possibly making use of fragments of Paul");[58] "we do not know beyond a shadow of a doubt that there are Deutero-Pauline Letters in the Pauline corpus, but if in the weighing of historical probabilities it seems to us that there are, we can admit freely that this too is a way in which God has mediated Scripture to us";[59] the book of James is "very possibly by James, the brother of Jesus. But it is equally possible that the prescript is pseudonymous (or 'allonymous'), so that the real author is unknown to us. A third possibility is that he material of the epistle traces back to James but was put into its present shape by a later redactor,"[60] the book of 1 Peter "very possibly Peter, through Silvanus, but if not, possibly by a disciple or associate of the Apostle";[61] the authorship of Jude has "no certainty possible, but probably Judas, the brother of Jesus and James";[62] 2 Peter "almost certainly not by Peter. Very probably written by a disciple of Peter or a member of the Petrine circle";[63] although he says he favors the authorship of the Johannine Epistles to that

---

53. Ibid., 163.
54. Ibid., 194.
55. Ibid., 429.
56. Ibid., 431.
57. Ibid., 586.
58. Ibid., 615.
59. Ibid., 432.
60. Ibid., 672.
61. Ibid., 689.
62. Ibid., 708.
63. Ibid., 714.

of the Apostle John, he also argues that "authorship of the letters by a member of the Johannine circle remains a possibility";[64] and as for Revelation, Hagner argues "almost certainly not by the Apostle John. Possibly by John 'the Elder,' but more probably another John, otherwise unknown to us, who may have been a member of the Johannine circle."[65]

In sum, Hagner's work represents what may well replace Guthrie's *New Testament Introduction*. One can only imagine the impact that British and European evangelical critical scholarship as represented by Hagner's assertions regarding his so-called "balanced" use of historical-critical presuppositions will have on the next generation of God's preachers and teachers! As Machen said long ago, "As go the theological seminaries, so go the churches."[66]

## CONCLUSION TO HAGNER'S PRINCIPLES

Church history testifies against Hagner's principles as being profitable for orthodox Christianity as well as evangelicals as a whole. Such principles are not "excellent" but disastrous for the inerrancy and inspiration of the Scriptures. When adopted by evangelical scholarship, such principles lead to a denigration of God's Word. No compelling reason exists for their adoption. Rather, they seem to be driven largely by a desire motivated to gain some form of acceptance by critical scholarship.

In 2007, Andreas Köstenberger edited a work entitled *Quo Vadis Evangelicalism?* The work consisted of a highly selected choice of presidential addresses of Evangelical Theological Society scholars who, in the history of the society, favored the move in the society toward historical-critical ideologies. No presidential addresses that warned against historical-critical ideologies were allowed. The work related that ETS has been "polarized" into two camps, one represented by Eta Linnemann and Norman Geisler who warned against historical-critical ideologies and that of Darrell Bock and others who heartily embrace "the judicious use of a historical-critical approach."[67] The book was extremely prejudicial toward one side and hardly objective at all. Köstenberger never stated what a "judicious" use of historical criticism was or whose version would be accepted. He did note, however, that "the pendulum [at ETS] seems to have swung toward the side of the latter ['judicious use'] group."[68] It actually constituted a personal vanity toward praising a direction that the editor apparently embraced. He concluded his preface by noting, "Speaking personally, reading and digesting these presidential addresses—spanning a half-century and delivered by some of evangelicalism's most distinguished leaders—has given me, a third-generation scholar in the

---

64. Ibid., 728.
65. Ibid., 761.
66. Machen, *Christian Faith in the Modern World*, 65.
67. Köstenberger, *Quo Vadis Evangelicalism?*, 18.
68. Ibid., 18.

ETS, a much fuller and deeper appreciation for the history of the evangelical movement and my place within it."[69] He concluded, "In my judgment the present volume offers great hope for the future of a movement whose best days, by God's grace and abundant mercy, may yet lie ahead."[70]

One writer of this present chapter had a rather aged church history professor during his days at Talbot Seminary who issued a warning that he has not forgotten to this day. He would say that church history teaches consistently that by the third generation of any Christian group, the original intent of the organization was lost (Harvard, Yale, Princeton, etc.) and the loss in these organizations is always away from a steadfast trust in the Word of God. What is noticed here is that Köstenberger admits that ETS is now in its third generation and is now open to many of Hagner's principles in historical criticism. The new third generation is in charge.

Long ago, Harold Lindsell, the scorn of much of these younger scholars today, said this about his own day:

> Anyone who thinks the historical-critical method is neutral is misinformed. Since its presuppositions are unacceptable to the evangelical mind this method cannot be used by the evangelical as it stands. The very use by the evangelical of this term, historical-critical method, is a mistake when it comes to describing its own approach to Scripture. The only way he can use it is to invest it with a different meaning. But this can only confuse the uninformed. Moreover, it is not fair to those scholars who use it in the correct way with presuppositions which are different from those of the evangelical. It appears to me that modern evangelical scholars (and I may be guilty of this myself) have played fast and loose with the term because the wanted acceptance by academia. They seem too often to desire to be members of the club which is nothing more than practicing an inclusiveness that undercuts the normativity of the evangelical theological position. This may be done, and often is, under the illusion that by this method the opponents of biblical inerrancy can be one over to the evangelical viewpoint. But practical experience suggest that rarely does this happen and the cost of such an approach is too expensive, for it gives credence and lends respectability to a method which is the deadly enemy of theological orthodoxy.[71]

Church history stands as a monumental testimony against this third generation of ETS evangelicals who have thought that they are somehow special, endowed with exceptional abilities, and able to overcome historical criticism's negative bias against Scripture which no one else in church history has been able to accomplish. Later chapters in this work cite recent, salient examples from both past and current evangelical history that demonstrate the disastrous consequences of adopting these type of

---

69. Ibid., 26.
70. Ibid.
71. Lindsell, *Bible in the Balance*, 283.

guidelines set forth by Hagner. Let the reader be warned, whenever historical-critical principles are applied to the study of God's Word—regardless of who applies them—the inerrancy of God's Word and, ultimately, the whole body of Christ suffers.

… Chapter 21

# On Licona Muddying the Waters of the Chicago Statements of Biblical Inerrancy and Hermeneutics

## NORMAN L. GEISLER

### COOL, CLEAR WATERS

Before Mike Licona wrote his recent article (June 2, 2014) "On Chicago's Muddy Waters,"[1] the waters were clear. That is, the Chicago Statement on Biblical Inerrancy was clear on the meaning of inerrancy. It affirmed that "dehistoricizing" sections of the Gospels, such as Licona has done, was contrary to inerrancy. It declared in article XVIII:

> We deny the legitimacy of any treatment of the text or quest for sources lying behind it that leads to relativizing, *dehistoricizing*, or discounting its teaching, or rejecting its claim to authorship.[2]

Article XIII declares emphatically:

> *We deny that generic categories which negate historicity may rightly be imposed on biblical narratives* which present themselves as factual.

ICBI Hermeneutics article XIV adds,

---

1. See Licona's personal website, http://www.risenjesus.com/chicagos-muddy-waters.
2. Emphasis added to the following ICBI Inerrancy and Heremeneutics affirmations and denials.

Part 2—Inerrancy Defended

*We deny that any event, discourse or saying reported in Scripture was invented by the biblical writers or by the traditions they incorporated.*

Further, ICBI Statement on Hermeneutics (1982), article XX declared,

*We deny that extra-biblical views ever disprove the teaching of Scripture or hold priority over it.*

The official ICBI commentary on article XII adds,

> Though the Bible is indeed *redemptive* history, it is also redemptive *history*, and this means that the acts of salvation wrought by God actually occurred in the space-time world.[3]

## COOL, CLEAR FRAMERS AGREE

All living framers (R. C. Sproul, J. I. Packer, and N. L. Geisler) agree that ICBI excludes a view like Licona embraced in his book.[4]

*R. C. Sproul* declared clearly and emphatically:

> As the former and only president of ICBI during its tenure and as the original framer of the Affirmations and Denials of the Chicago Statement on Inerrancy, *I can say categorically that Mr. Michael Licona's views are not even remotely compatible with the unified Statement of ICBI.*[5]

He added, "You can use this comment by me however you wish."[6]

*J. I. Packer* added plainly:

> *As a framer of the ICBI statement on biblical inerrancy* who once studied Greco-Roman literature at advanced level, *I judge Mike Licona's view* that, because the Gospels are semi-biographical, details of their narratives may be regarded as legendary and factually erroneous, *to be both academically and theologically unsound.*[7]

*Norman L. Geisler*:

> I have spoken repeatedly of the similarity of Licona's views with those of Robert Gundry who was asked to resign (in 1983) from the Evangelical Theological Society (ETS) by an overwhelming 74-percent vote. No attempt to minimize this vote can negate its legitimacy, clarity, or finality, no matter how much some may wish to do so. What could be clearer than the ICBI statements on

---

3. Sproul, *Explaining Biblical Inerrancy*, 45.
4. Licona, *Resurrection of Jesus*, 185–87; 530, 548, 552, 553.
5. Letter to Geisler, May 22, 2012, emphasis added.
6. Ibid.
7. Letter, May 8, 2014, emphasis added.

this matter and the clear and emphatic words of the only living framers of the ICBI statements?

## CASTING MUD AT DEFENDERS OF THE ICBI STATEMENT

If any waters have been muddied, it is from the mud cast at the defenders of the Chicago Statement on inerrancy. They call the ICBI defenders "New Fundamentalist" eight times in Licona's short article.[8] They insist we are "rigid" and engage in "ferocious fratricide." They are designated inerrancy "police" or "police officers" who have a "most wanted" list. They consider an inerrancy defender a "tar baby." They "politicize" this issue. He even goes so far as to question our "motives," rather than be content with evaluating our statements.

Licona and his supporters believe we engaged in a personal "crusade" against Licona. In what seemed like a kind of doctrinal paranoia, Licona falsely claims Geisler is "criticizing *me*" or a "crusade against *me*" (emphasis mine). He said, "I've been in the crosshairs of Norman Geisler," as though he was a special target I wanted to kill. The truth is we have never attacked him as a *person*, but only his *views*. I have said many times that I like Mike as a person and love him as a brother in Christ. However, we try never to put fraternity over orthodoxy or cloud our love for God's truth by how nice a guy is or how good a friend the person is. This cannot be said of Licona or his friends for their writings are toxic with personal attacks. One can look to Craig Blomberg's recent book to illustrate the point.

Craig Blomberg, engaged without substantiation in a tirade in print against defenders of ICBI inerrancy (see his *Can We Still Believe the Bible?*). He insists that we are "very conservative";[9] "overly conservative";[10] "ultra conservative";[11] "hyperconservative";[12] "extremely conservative."[13] Of course, this tends to make his views look more moderate by comparison, when, as we shall see, they are in direct opposition to the mainstream evangelical view as reflected in the ICBI statements. Blomberg even likens ICBI defenders of inerrancy to the extreme views of Nazism and Communism![14] He quotes with approval the statement, "The far left and the far right—avoid them both, like the plague."[15] He claims that we "simplistically" distorted the evidence in order to oust Robert Gundry from the Evangelical Theological

---

8. Quotes throughout this section are from Licona, "On Chicago's Muddy Waters."
9. Blomberg, *Can We Still Believe*, 7.
10. Ibid., 217.
11. Ibid., 11, 214.
12. Ibid., 13.
13. Ibid., 7.
14. Ibid., 8.
15. Ibid., 8.

Society.[16] He charges that we engaged in a "political campaign" against Gundry.[17] Elsewhere, he alleges that we have utilized a "standard ploy throughout his [Geisler's] career" when "trying to get someone removed from an organization."[18] He adds the allegation that inerrancy is used as "a blunt tool to hammer into submission people whose interpretation of passages differs from ours."[19] These charges of an alleged sinister and continuous career of unjustified activity on my part are untrue, unjustified, and unethical. Someone has rightly asked why it is that those who defend inerrancy are attacked and those who attack inerrancy are defended.

When mud-slinging occurs one can be reasonably sure that the attackers have run out of reasons and evidence to use in a rational argument and, thus, have resorted to attacking the person instead of the argument.

## MUDDYING THE CHICAGO WATERS

Licona and his colleagues have insisted on muddying the Chicago ICBI waters by claiming the ICBI position is not clear. They have made the following charges:

*There are other interpretations of the ICBI Statements on Inerrancy.* Of course there are, no one disputes this. However, that is not the question. The question is: Are there better ones? Do they correspond with the meaning expressed by the framers of the ICBI statements? The answer is an emphatic "No." The framers have spoken in commentaries and letters (see above).

Further, the "other" interpretations are not supported by the historical evidence.[20] Church history is virtually unanimous on the orthodox view of inerrancy. It is unlimited inerrancy as expressed by the ICBI statements.[21]

What is more, I know of no other inerrancy statement ever made that was the work of some three hundred interdenominational and international scholars that is more extensive and more complete and has been more widely accepted than that of the ICBI. Even the membership of the largest body of evangelical scholars who believe in inerrancy, the Evangelical Theological Society (ETS), consisting of over three thousand members, adopted the ICBI statement as the definition of their brief inerrancy statement by an overwhelming 80-percent vote in 2006. If Dr. Licona and his New Testament critical friends think they can improve upon it, let them try.

*The Chicago Statement is not a creed.* Of course it isn't, and it does not claim to be. That does not keep it from being a very good statement, or even the best one produced by a broad group of scholars to date. Nor does it hinder it from being right when it

---

16. Ibid., 167.
17. Ibid.
18. Ibid., 262n111.
19. Ibid., 125.
20. See Hannah, *Inerrancy and the Church*.
21. See Woodbridge, *Biblical Authority*.

condemns "dehistoricizing" the Gospels as many critical scholars are doing today (see citations above).

*The Chicago Statement is too "Conservative."* It all depends where one is standing. This is a relative term. If one is already standing left of Scripture, then no doubt ICBI will seem too conservative. However, when judged by the views of the church fathers from the earliest times down to and through the Reformation to modern times,[22] the Chicago Statement is on target. In fact, it is the Licona Neo-evangelical view of Scripture that is too "liberal."

*The Lausanne Covenant Statement on Inerrancy is more widely accepted.* There is no comparison between Lausanne and Chicago statements on inerrancy. Lausanne has only a brief statement on inerrancy as follows: "We affirm the divine inspiration, truthfulness and authority of both Old and New Testament Scriptures in their entirety as the only written word of God, without error in all that it affirms, and the only infallible rule of faith and practice" (1974). The Chicago statement is a more comprehensive statement containing numerous affirmations and denials. Indeed, there are two major statements with accompanying commentaries. The ICBI conference, unlike Lausanne, focused only on inerrancy and consisted of scholars trained on the topic. So, for a detailed statement on inerrancy, the ICBI statement has been the most widely disseminated, embracing the three thousand members of the ETS and influencing numerous denominations, including the largest Protestant denomination in the world—the Southern Baptist Convention.

It is noteworthy that Billy Graham signed the Lausanne statement on inerrancy. However, he also gave money to help start the International Council on Biblical Inerrancy which produced the Chicago Statements on inerrancy. And more recently, both Billy and his son Franklin Graham made statements in support of inerrancy on the www.DefendingInerrancy.com website. In fact, the worldwide circulation of Billy Graham's magazine *Decision* (May 2014) on "the dangers of compromise" featured an article defending ICBI inerrancy by the former president of the Evangelical Theological Society.

*Many books defending ICBI inerrancy were not published by standard publishers.* This is an irrelevant and misleading charge for several reasons. First, numerous books defending ICBI inerrancy have been published through standard publishers. To name only a few: *The Erosion of Inerrancy in Evangelicalism*, by G. K. Beale; *Defending Inerrancy*, by myself and William Roach; *A Critique of the Roger/McKim Proposal*, by John Woodbridge; indeed, the ICBI itself produced many volumes defending inerrancy all of which were published by standard publishers (like Zondervan, Baker, and Moody). These include: *Inerrancy*; *Biblical Errancy: Its Philosophical Roots*; *The Church and Inerrancy*; *Hermeneutics, Inerrancy, and the Bible*.

Second, this charge is amazing since Licona was able to divine the reason for ICBI inerrantists using a non-standard publisher (like Xulon Press) as that we "could

---

22. See Hannah, *Inerrancy and the Church*.

not find an interested publisher." As most writers know, there are other reasons for using non-standard publishers as well, including time, money, control of the content, and owning the rights. And there are also reasons to reject some "standard" publishers who would have published it.

Third, this objection assumes that truth is conveyed best, if not exclusively, by what they view as "standard" publishers. This supports a kind of professional elitism and academic snobbery. Truth is what corresponds to reality no matter who publishes it.

Fourth, this charge is amusing and ironic since the recent book attacking ICBI inerrancy which was blessed by Licona and many of his New Testament critic friends was self-published by Licona's son-in-law and his friend!

## MANY MUDDY STATEMENTS BY LICONA

Licona and friends have made many statements that are clearly not traditional orthodox views on Scripture. They include the following:

(1) *Licona charges that we believe the Gospels speak with "legal precision" or "photographic accuracy."* The Chicago Statement spoke directly to this point, saying, "We further deny that inerrancy is negated by biblical phenomena such as lack of modern technical precision . . . and round numbers, the topical arrangement of material . . . or the use of free citations" (art. XIII).

(2) *He believes there are or may be errors in the Gospels, for example:* (a) on the report about when Jarius's daughter died; (2) on whether the centurion made his request in person to Jesus; (c) whether the woman anointed Jesus two days before the Passover.

(3) *Licona even goes so far as to affirm there is an error in the Gospels regarding on which day Jesus was crucified.* He said, "Jesus may have changed the day and time of Jesus's crucifixion in order to make a theological point." Earlier in a debate with Bart Ehrman at Southern Evangelical Seminary (Spring 2009) he said, "I think that John probably altered the day [of Jesus' crucifixion] in order for a theological—to make a theological point there."

But this is clearly contrary to the ICBI view of inerrancy which demands "the unity and internal consistency of Scripture" (art. XIV). Also, "We deny that later revelations . . . ever contradict it" (art. V). "We affirm the unity, harmony, and consistency of Scripture. . . . We deny that Scripture may be interpreted in such a way as to suggest that one passage corrects or militates against another" (CSBH, art. XVII). "We affirm that since God is the author of all truth, all truths, biblical and extra-biblical, are consistent and cohere" (CSBH, art. XX).

(4) *Licona affirmed that Joseph Holden, president of Veritas Evangelical Seminary dismissed Gary Habermas and Paul Copan as adjunct faculty members* because "they denied the inerrancy of the Bible on account of their failure to condemn the

interpretation of Matthew's raised saints."²³ President Holden affirmed in a letter (June 2, 2014) that this is false. Holden wrote, "In the footnotes, it says I dismissed Habermas and Copan for their support of Licona and failure to condemn his interpretation of Matthew's raised saints. When in fact, they were dismissed because of *their own expressed view of inerrancy* that became apparent in their defense of Licona."

(5) *Licona also wrongly affirmed that I was the founder of Veritas Evangelical Seminary*. I was not. It was Joe Holden's idea and he asked me to join with him and be a cofounder of the seminary.

(6) *Licona affirmed that I refused to attend a particular panel discussion*. In any event, one cannot help but be impressed with the quasi-omniscient powers of critics who can read another's mind. This leads to arrogant charges like the following: Licona asserted that "in Geisler's mind, there is no need for discussion in an academic forum because he apparently thinks he already knows the correct answers; all of them." I have participated in untold academic discussions and debates over the last fifty years, so I have learned to pick carefully the ones in which I participate.

(7) *He alleged that we never offered a solution to the alleged contradictions he raised in the Gospels*. This too is false. I have presented it many times in official presentations on alleged contradictions in the Bible. Further, it is in one of the "20 articles" Licona said I wrote on the issue, titled "Mike Licona Admits Contradiction in the Gospels" (January 2013) which he apparently did not read.

(8) He claims that "many of the original signers [of the ICBI Statement on Inerrancy] do not agree with how Geisler and others interpret it." In response, two brief comments are in order. First, even according to Licona, the true meaning of a text is in the "intention" of the framers, not the signers. Second, all living framers (see above) agree on its meaning, especially as it applies to Licona's view. So, it is not just my view on the matter.

(9) *ICBI view of inerrancy actually undermines inerrancy*. By a strange twist of logic Licona argues that the ICBI view of inerrancy actually undermines the authority of the Bible because showing one error overthrows the faith.

First, by this same logic people should not believe Christ rose from the dead since a sophisticated naturalist might convince them that miracles are not credible. Or, people should not believe God exists since a sharp atheist might convince them that he does not exist.

Second, this objection confuses reliability and inerrancy. If a critic could prove (and none have) one real error in the Bible, it would overthrow the ICBI *view* of inerrancy, but it would not overthrow the faith.

Inerrancy is to be distinguished from the reliability of the Bible. My CPA is a very accurate bookkeeper, but if he made one mistake in math that would not overthrow his reliability. On the other hand, if he claimed divine authority and inerrancy, then

---

23. http://www.risenjesus.com/chicagos-muddy-waters, n6.

one error would overthrow *his claim to divine authority* because God cannot make even one mistake (Heb 6:18; Titus 1:2; John 17:17).

This is what B. B.Warfield meant, and Licona misunderstands. For Warfield too believed that the Bible was divinely authoritative and inerrant and, as such, one error would destroy that *divine authority/inerrancy*. However, it would not overthrow the faith since the faith could be true apart from inerrancy. Inerrancy is not a test of evangelical *authenticity* but of evangelical *consistency*. Licona confuses Warfield's apologetics and his theology. Warfield used apologetics (based on the evidence to show the *reliability* of the Bible). But once he knew from good reason that the Bible was more than reliable; it was the inerrant Word of God, then Warfield believed that only an inspired and inerrant Word of God is an adequate basis for our belief in the *divine authority* of the doctrines of the Bible.

So, likewise, Licona misinterprets our statement about inerrancy being a "fundamental" of the faith. We said clearly that it is not a *doctrinal* or theological fundamental; it was an *epistemological* fundamental. For without an inerrant Bible we have no *divinely authoritative* basis for our Faith.

(10) *Licona also makes other statements that are seriously mistakes.* One is that (a) "the doctrines of the divine inspiration and inerrancy of the Gospels are faith doctrines that cannot be proven." (b) Another is that a historian should be "making no theological assumptions pertaining to whether they [the Gospels] are divinely inspired or inerrant." These are both based on Licona's admission that he (c) "unashamedly confess[es] the historical-critical method." Given that Licona sees Genre criticism as part of this endeavor, no wonder he can believe in contradictions in the Gospels (see above) and say, "*Bioi* offered the ancient biographers great flexibility for rearranging material and *inventing speeches . . . and they often included legend. Because* bios *was a flexible genre, it is often difficult to determine where history ends and legend begins.*"[24]

(11) *Licona contends that "biblical inerrancy is a secondary or tertiary doctrine."* Statements like this show a serious lack of understanding and appreciation for the doctrine of divine inspiration which entails inerrancy as a necessary concomitant. For a divinely inspired error is nonsense. If the Bible is the Word of God, and that is what divine inspiration means, then it is inerrant. For God cannot error. So, to attribute error to God's Word is to attribute error to God himself. As John Calvin affirmed, "Our faith in doctrine is not established until we have a perfect conviction that God is its author. Hence, the highest proof of Scripture is uniformly taken from the character of him whose word it is."[25]

(12) *Licona criticized me for twisting the arms of other seminary presidents.* This reckless charge misrepresents the facts. At the same time, he has attempted unsuccessfully to convince some of the orthodoxy of his view. He even made a yet unadmitted trip of some distance to try to convince one influential Christian leader of the

---

24. Licona, *Resurrection of Jesus*, 34.
25. Calvin, *Institutes* 1.7.4.

orthodoxy of his unorthodox view—only to be unsuccessful. Another one even set up a forum for him to express his view, after which the seminary president said he would not hire him on his faculty. Licona tried to convince a third seminary to accept his view, after which they dropped him from their Adjunct Faculty. One faculty member who attended the meeting said, "It was worse than I thought." Yet I did not contact a single seminary and ask them to reject Licona from their faculty. Nor did I "turn" to seminary presidents "to come out publicly" against him when I could no longer get enough high-caliber scholars to speak against his view.

Furthermore, this accusation is an insult to the integrity and autonomy of these different seminary leaders. As for asking others to support the inerrancy cause, of course we do, as do those who oppose it. In fact, we have a website dedicated to it defending inerrancy (www.DefendingInerrancy.com). Licona's son-in-law has a website dedicated to attacking me regularly by name and even made an insulting YouTube video with Licona's blessing. Anyone who examines the two approaches can see the difference.

(13) *He rejected (without giving any evidence) the strong case we made for all the main orthodox church fathers* between the apostles and the Reformers of holding that the story of the resurrected saints in Matthew 27:51–53 as being history not poetry or legend.[26]

Just to cite a couple examples:

(a) *Irenaeus* (AD 120–200), who knew Polycarp, a disciple of the Apostle John, wrote:

> He [Christ] suffered who can lead those souls aloft that followed His ascension. This event was also an indication of the fact that when the holy hour of Christ descended [to Hades], *many souls ascended and were seen in their bodies.*

(b) *Even Origen* (AD 185–254), who had the Neoplatonic tendency to spiritualize literal events, believed Matthew 27 was literal history, declaring:

> "But," continues Celsus, "what great deeds did Jesus perform as being a God? . . . Now to this question, *although we are able to show the striking and miraculous character of the events which befell Him*, yet from what other source can we furnish an answer than the Gospel narratives, which state that 'there was an earth quake, and that *the rock were split asunder, and the tombs were opened*, and the veil of the temple was rent in twain from top to bottom, and the darkness prevailed in the day-time, the sun failing to give light.'"[27]

(c) *Augustine* (AD 356–430), the greatest biblical theologian of his time, wrote:

> As if Moses's body could not have been hid somewhere . . . and be raised up therefrom by divine power at the time when Elias and he were seen with

---

26. See Geisler, "Early Fathers and the Resurrection," ch. 30, at http://normangeisler.net.
27. Origen, *Against Celsus*, bk. 2, ch. 33, 444–45.

Christ: *Just as at the time of Christ's passion many bodies of the saints arose, and after his resurrection appeared, according to the Scriptures, to many in the holy city.*[28]

(d) *John Calvin (1509–1564)* added,

Yet we may doubt whether this opening of the tombs happened before the resurrection, *for the resurrection of the saints which is shortly after added followed in my opinion the resurrection of Christ.* It is absurd for some interpreters to image that they spent three days alive and breathing, hidden in tombs." For "It seems likely to me that *at Christ's death the tombs at once opened; at His resurrection some of the godly men received breath and came out and were seen in the city.* Christ is called the Firstborn from the dead (1 Cor 15:20; Col 1:18)."[29]

These kinds of statements are found to and through the Reformation to modern times. So, those who deny the historicity of this Matthew 27 passage on the saint's resurrection have virtually the whole of the history of the Christian church against them.

## CONCLUSION

Mike Licona wrote his recent article (June 2, 2014) on "Chicago's Muddy Waters," but it was not the Chicago Statement or the interpretation of it by the living framers that muddied the waters. This represents the crystal clear evangelical view down through the centuries of full inerrancy and complete historicity of the Bible. To be sure, the waters have been muddied, but they were muddied by Neo-evangelical scholars like Licona who have adopted the new historical-critical method and have become New Evangelicals or Neo-evangelical on their view of Scripture, creating a new "battle for the Bible."

This leaves us with the conclusion that the ICBI statement represents the biblical view of inerrancy which we call the evangelical view. Hence, Licona and his supporters, whom he lists as Darrel Bock, Dan Wallace, Craig Blomberg, Michael Bird, William Lane Craig, Jeremy Evans, Craig Keener, Lee McDonald, Kevin Vanhoozer, Robert Yarborough, and Gary Habermas, embrace a new kind of evangelicalism—Neo-evangelicalism—with regard to Scripture, which has been its label now for a generation. It is definitely not the biblical or traditional view; hence, its view of Scripture has no rights to the use the unqualified term "Evangelical." It is more properly described as Neo-evangelical. While Licona and Bird would have us believe that they are fighting the barbarians at the gates of the city, in actuality they are escorting the Trojan horse of the barbarians through the gates and deep into the city.

---

28. Augustine, *On the Gospel of St. John*, tractate cxxiv, 3.
29. Calvin, *New Testament Commentaries*, 3:211–12.

# Chapter 22

# The Early Church Fathers and the Resurrection of the Saints in Matthew 27:51–54

## NORMAN L. GEISLER

### THE BIBLICAL PASSAGE IN QUESTION

Matthew wrote: "And behold, the veil of the temple was torn in two from top to bottom; and the earth shook and the rocks were split. The tombs were opened, and many bodies of the saints who had fallen asleep were raised; and coming out of the tombs after his resurrection they entered the holy city and appeared to many. Now the centurion, and those who were with him keeping guard over Jesus, when they saw the earthquake and the things that were happening, became very frightened and said, 'Truly this was the Son of God!'"

### THE CURRENT CHALLENGE TO ITS HISTORICITY

In his book on *The Resurrection of Jesus*, Mike Licona speaks of the resurrection of the saints narrative in Matthew 27:51–54 as "*a weird residual fragment*";[1] and a "*strange report*."[2] He called it "*poetical*," a "*legend*," an "*embellishment*," and literary "*special effects*."[3] He claims that Matthew is using a Greco-Roman literary genre which is a

---

1. Licona, *Resurrection of Jesus*, 527. Licona has subsequent questions about the certitude of his view on Matthew 27, but he has not retracted the view or the critical historical basis that led to the view.

2. Ibid., 530, 548, 556, emphasis added in these citations.

3. Ibid., 306.

"flexible genre" in which "it is often difficult to determine where history ends and legend begins."[4] Licona also believes that other New Testament texts may be legends, such as, the mob falling backward at Jesus claim "I am he" in John 18:4–6[5] and the presence of angels at the tomb recorded in all four Gospels (Matt 28:2–7; Mark 16:5–7; Luke 24:4–7; John 20:11–14).[6]

Licona cites some contemporary evangelical scholars in favor of his view, such as, Craig Blomberg who doubted historical authenticity of the miracle of the coin in the fish's mouth in Matthew (Matt 17:27).[7] Blomberg also said, "All kinds of historical questions remain unanswered about both events [the splitting of the temple curtain and the resurrection of the saints]."[8] He also cites W. L. Craig, siding with a Jesus Seminar fellow Dr. Robert Miller, that Matthew added this story to Mark's account and did not take it literally. Although he claims to believe it, Craig concluded that there are "probably only a few [contemporary] conservative scholars who would treat the story as historical."[9] On the contrary, in terms of the broad spectrum of orthodox scholars down through the centuries, there are relatively "few" contemporary scholars who deny its authenticity, and they are overshadowed by the "many" (vast majority of) historic orthodox scholars who held to the historicity of this Matthew 27 resurrection of the saints.

## THE EVIDENCE FOR ITS HISTORICITY

In spite of these contemporary doubts and denials,[10] other scholars have pointed out the numerous indications of historicity in the Matthew 27:51–54 text itself, such as: (1) It occurs in a book that presents itself as historical (cf. Matt 1:1, 18); (2) Numerous events in this book have been confirmed as historical (e.g., the birth, life, deeds, teachings, death, and resurrection of Christ); (3) It is presented in the immediate context of other historical events, namely, the death and resurrection of Christ; (4) The resurrection of these saints is also presented as an event occurring as a result of the literal death and resurrection of Christ (cf. Matt 27:52–53); (5) Its lineage with the preceding historical events is indicated by a series of conjunctions (and . . . and . . . and, etc.); (6) It is introduced by the attention getting "Behold" (v. 51) which focuses on its reality;[11] (7) It has all the same essential earmarks of the literal resurrection of Christ,

---

4. Ibid., 34.
5. Ibid., 306n114.
6. Ibid., 185–86.
7. Blomberg, "Constructive Traditional Response," 354n32.
8. Blomberg, *Matthew*, 421.
9. From Craig's comments in Paul Copan, *Will the Real Jesus Please Stand Up?*
10. See Licona, "When the Saints Go Marching In."
11. Henry noted that "calling attention to the new and unexpected, the introductory Greek *ide*—See! Behold!—stands out of sentence construction to rivet attention upon God's awesome

including: (a) empty tombs, (b) dead bodies coming to life, and (c) these resurrected bodies appearing to many witnesses; (8) It lacks any literary embellishment common to myths, being a short, simple, and straightforward account; (9) It contains elements that are confirmed as historical by other Gospels, such as (a) the veil of the temple being split (Mark 15:38; Luke 23:45), and (b) the reaction of the centurion (Mark 15:39; Luke 23:47). If these events are historical, then there is no reason to reject the other events, such as, the earthquake and the resurrection of the saints.

Further, it is highly unlikely that a resurrection story would be influenced by a Greco-Roman genre source (which Licona embraces) since the Greeks did not believe in the resurrection of the body (cf. Acts 17:32). In fact, bodily resurrection was contrary to their dominant belief that deliverance is *from* the body, not a resurrection *in* the body, and was of the essence of salvation. Homer said death is final and resurrection does not occur.[12] Hans-Josef Klauck declared, "There is nowhere anything like the idea of Christian resurrection in the Greco-Roman world."[13] D. A. Carson makes an interesting observation about those who deny the historicity of this text, saying, "One wonders why the evangelist, if he had nothing historically to go on, did not invent a midrash [legend] with fewer problems."[14]

## A SURVEY OF THE GREAT TEACHERS OF THE CHURCH ON THE PASSAGE

Despite his general respect for the early Fathers, Mike Licona refers to the Fathers' statements on this passage as "vague," "unclear," "ambiguous," "problematic," and "confusing."4 However, this is clearly not the case, as the readers can see for themselves in the following quotations. For even though they differ on details, *the Fathers surveyed are unanimous as to the historical nature of this event*. Indeed, no one has given and clear and unambiguous evidence that any orthodox Father held that this passage was not historical. In the following passage we have highlighted their important words which affirm the literal and historical nature of the event.

### Ignatius (AD 70–115)

The apostolic father Ignatius was the earliest one to cite this passage, and Licona acknowledges that his writings "are widely accepted as authentic and are dated ca. AD 100–138 and more commonly to ca. AD 110."[15] He adds that these writings provide

---

intervention." Henry, *God Revelation and Authority*, 2:17–18.

12. *Iliad*, 24.549–51.
13. Klauck, *Religious Context of Early Christianity*, 151.
14. Carson, "Matthew," 581.
15. Licona, *Resurrection of Jesus*, 248.

"valuable insights for knowledge of the early second-century church."[16] If so, they are the earliest and most authentic verification of the historicity of the resurrection of the saints in Matthew 27 on record—one coming from a contemporary of the Apostle John!

*Ignatius to the Trallians.* Ignatius affirmed clearly the literal historical nature of the resurrection of these saints, declaring, "*For Says the Scripture, 'Many bodies of the saints that slept arose,' their graves being opened. He descended, indeed, into Hades alone, but he arose accompanied by a multitude.*"[17]

*Ignatius to the Magnesians.* "Therefore endure, that we may be found the disciples of Jesus Christ, our only Master—how shall we be able to live apart from him, whose disciples the prophets themselves in the Spirit did wait for him as their Teacher? And *therefore he who they rightly waited for, being come, raised them from the dead.*"[18]

## Irenaeus (AD 120–200)

Irenaeus was also closely linked to the New Testament writers. He knew Polycarp who was a disciple of the Apostle John. Irenaeus wrote: "*He* [Christ] *suffered who can lead those souls aloft that followed his ascension. This event was also an indication of the fact that when the holy hour of Christ descended* [to Hades], *many souls ascended and were seen in their bodies.*"[19] This is followed (in XXIX) by this statement: "The Gospel according to Matthew was written to the Jews. For they had particular stress upon the fact that Christ [should be] of the seed of David. *Matthew also, who had a still greater desire [to establish this point], took particular pains to afford them convincing proof that Christ is the seed of David.*"[20]

## Clement of Alexandria (AD 155–200)

Another second-century Father verified the historicity of the resurrection of the saints in Matthew 27, writing, "'But those who had fallen asleep descended dead, but ascended alive.' Further, the Gospel says, 'that many bodies of those that slept arose,'—plainly as having been translated to a better state."[21]

---

16. Ibid.

17. Ignatius, *Trallians*, IX. Some scholars dispute the authenticity of this longer form of the text. Nevertheless, it is found in some manuscripts and undoubtedly represents an early view. No contrary view is found in the early Fathers.

18. Ignatius, *Magnesians*, IX, emphasis added. This is from the shorter form of the text.

19. Fragments from the Lost Writings of Irenaeus, XXVIII.

20. Ibid.

21. Clement, *Stromata*, VI.

## Tertullian (AD 160–222)

The Father of Latin Christianity wrote: "'And the sun grew dark at mid-day;' (and when did it 'shudder exceedingly' except at the passion of Christ, when the earth trembled to her centre, and the veil of the temple was rent, and *the tombs burst asunder*) 'because these two evils hath my people done.'"[22]

## Hippolytus (AD 170–235)

"And again he exclaims, 'The dead shall start forth from the graves,' that is, from the earthly bodies, being born again spiritual, not carnal. For this he says, is the Resurrection that takes place through the gate of heaven, through which, he says, all those that do not enter remain dead."[23] The editor of the *Ante-Nicene Fathers* footnotes this as a reference to the resurrection of the saints in Matthew 27:52, 53, as indeed it is (see 54n6).

## Origen (AD 185–254)

Despite the fact that Origen was known for his Neoplatonic spiritualizing of some biblical texts, Origen declared that Matthew 27 spoke of a literal historical resurrection of these saints. He wrote: "Now to this question, *although we are able to show the striking and miraculous character of the events which befell him*, yet from what other source can we furnish an answer than the Gospel narratives, which state that 'there was an earth quake, and that *the rock were split asunder, and the tombs were opened*, and the veil of the temple was rent in twain from top to bottom, and the darkness prevailed in the day-time, the sun failing to give light.'"[24] "But if this Celsus, who, in order to find matter of accusation against Jesus and the Christians, extracts from the Gospel even passages which are incorrectly interpreted, *but passes over in silence the evidences of the divinity of Jesus, would listen to divine portents, let him read the Gospel, and see that even the centurion, and they who with him kept watch over Jesus, on seeing the earthquake, and the events that occurred* [viz., the resurrection of the saints], were greatly afraid, saying, 'This man was the Son of God.'"[25]

## Cyril of Jerusalem (ca. AD 315–ca. 386)

Early Fathers in the East also verified the historicity of the Matthew text. Cyril of Jerusalem wrote: "But it is impossible, someone will say, that the dead should rise; and

22. Tertullian, *Answer to the Jews*, XIII.14.
23. Hippolytus, *Refutation of All Heresy*, V.
24. Origin, *Against Celsus*, bk. II, XXXIII.
25. Ibid., XXVI.

yet Eliseus [Elisha] twice raised the dead,—when he was live and also when dead . . . and is Christ not risen? . . . But in this case both the Dead of whom we speak himself arose, and *many dead were raised* without having even touched him. For *many bodies of the Saints which slept arose, and they came out of the graves after his Resurrection, and went into the Holy City,* (evidently this city in which we now are) *and appeared to many*."[26] "Further, *'I believe that Christ was also raised from the dead,* both from the Divine Scriptures, and from the operative power even at this day of him who arose;— *'who descended into hell alone, but ascended thence with a great company for he went down to death, and many bodies of the saints which slept arose through him.*"[27]

## Gregory of Nazianzus (ca. AD 330–ca. 389)

"He [Christ] lays down his life, but he has the power to take it again; and the veil rent, for the mysterious doors of Heaven are opened;[28] *the rocks are cleft, the dead arise.* He dies but he gives life, and by his death destroys death. He is buried, but he rises again. *He goes down to Hell, but he brings up the souls; he ascends to Heaven,* and shall come again to judge the quick and the dead, and to put to the test such words are yours."[29]

## Jerome (AD 342–420)

Speaking of the Matthew 27 text, he wrote: "*It is not doubtful to any what these great signs signify according to the letter, namely, that heaven and earth and all things should bear witness to their crucified Lord.*"[30] "As Lazarus rose from the dead, so also did many bodies of the Saints rise again to shew forth the Lord's resurrection; yet notwithstanding that the graves were opened, they did not rise again before the Lord rose, that he might be the first-born of the resurrection from the dead."[31]

---

26. Cyril, *Catechetical Lectures*, XIV.16.

27. Ibid., XIV.18.

28. Despite the curious phrase about the "mysterious doors of Heaven are opened" when the veil was split, everything in this passage speaks of literal death and literal resurrection of Christ and the saints after his death. The book of Hebrews makes the same claim that after the veil was split that Christ entered "once for all" into the most holy place (heaven) to achieve "eternal salvation" for us (Heb 9:12).

29. Schaff, ibid., vol. VII, sect. XX, 309.

30. Cited in Aquinas, *St. Matthew*, 964.

31. Cited ibid., 963.

## Hilary of Poitiers (ca. AD 315–ca. 357)

"*The graves were opened, for the bands of death were loosed. And many bodies of the saints which slept arose*, for illuminating the darkness of death, and shedding light upon the gloom of Hades, *he robbed the spirits of death*."[32]

## Chrysostom (AD 347–407)

"When he [Christ] remained on the cross they had said tauntingly, *he saved others, himself he cannot save. But what he should not do for himself, that he did and more than that for the bodies of the saints. For if it was a great thing to raise Lazarus after four days, much more was it that they who had long slept should not shew themselves above; this is indeed a proof of the resurrection to come. But that it might not be thought that that which was done was an appearance merely*, the Evangelist adds, *and come out of the graves after his resurrection, and went into the holy city, and appeared unto many*."[33]

## St. Augustine (AD 354–430)

The greatest scholar at the beginning of the Middle Ages, St. Augustine, wrote: "As if Moses's body could not have been hid somewhere . . . and be raised up therefrom by divine power at the time when Elias and he were seen with Christ: *Just as at the time of Christ's passion many bodies of the saints arose, and after his resurrection appeared, according to the Scriptures, to many in the holy city*."[34]

Augustine says further,

> Matthew proceeds thus: "And the earth did quake, and the rocks rent; *and the graves were opened; and many bodies of the saints which slept arise, and come out of the graves after the resurrection*, and went into the holy city, and appeared unto many." There is no reason to fear that these *facts*, which have been related only by Matthew, may appear to be inconsistent with the narrative present by any one of the rest [of the Gospel writers]. . . . For as the said Matthew not only tells how the centurion "saw the earthquake," but also appends the words [in v. 54], "and those *things that were done*." . . . Although Matthew has not added any such statement, it would still have been perfectly legitimate to suppose, that *as many astonishing things did place at that time* . . . the *historians were at liberty to select for narration any particular incident which they were severally disposed to instance as the subject of the wonder. And it would not be fair to impeach them with inconsistency, simply because one of them may have*

---

32. Ibid.
33. Cited by Aquinas, ibid., 963–64, emphasis added.
34. Augustine, *On the Gospel of St. John*, tractate cxxiv, 3, emphasis added.

*specified one occurrence as the immediate cause of the centurion's amazement, while another introduces a different incident.*[35]

## St. Remigius (ca. 438–ca. 533) "Apostle of the Franks"

St. Remigius related the following,

> But someone will ask, what became of those who rose again when the Lord rose. We must believe that they rose again to be witnesses of the Lord's resurrection. Some have said that they died again, and were turned to dust, as Lazarus and the rest whom the Lord raised. But we must by no means give credit to these men's sayings, since if they were to die again, it would be greater torment to them, than if they had not risen again. We ought therefore to believe without hesitation that they who rose from the dead at the Lord's resurrection, ascended also into heaven together with Him.[36]

## Thomas Aquinas (1224–1274)

As Augustine was the greatest Christian thinker at the beginning of the Middle Ages, Aquinas was the greatest teacher at the end. *And too he held to the historicity of the resurrection of the saints in Matthew 27*, as is evident from his citations from the Fathers (with approval) in his great commentary on the Gospels (*The Golden Chain*), as all the above Aquinas references indicate, including Jerome, Hilary of Poitiers, Chrysostom, and Remigius.[37]

## John Calvin (1509–1564)

The chain of great Christian teachers holding to the historicity of this text continued into the Reformation and beyond. John Calvin wrote:

> Matt. 27.52. *And the tombs were opened.* This was a particular portent in which God testified that His Son had entered death's prison, not to stay there shut up, but to lead all free who were there held captive . . . That is the reason why he, who was soon to be shut in a tomb opened the tombs elsewhere. Yet we may doubt whether this opening of the tombs happened before the resurrection, *for the resurrection of the saints which is shortly after added followed in my opinion the resurrection of Christ. It is absurd for some interpreters to image that they spent three days alive and breathing, hidden in tombs. It seems likely*

---

35. Augustine, *Harmony of the Gospels*, bk. 3, chap. 21, emphasis added.
36. Cited in Aquinas, ibid., 964, emphasis added.
37. Ibid., 963–64, emphasis added.

to me that at Christ's death the tombs at once opened; at his resurrection some of the godly men received breath and came out and were seen in the city. Christ is called the Firstborn from the dead (1 Cor 15:20; Col 1:18). . . . This reasoning agrees very well, seeing that the breaking of the tombs was the presage of new life, and the fruit itself, the effect, appeared three days later, as Christ rising again led other companions from the graves with himself. And in this sign it was shown that neither his dying nor his resurrection were private to himself, but breathe the odour of life into all the faithful.[38]

## CONCLUDING COMMENTS

Of course, there are some aspects of this Matthew 27 text of the saints on which the Fathers were uncertain. For example, there is the question as to whether the saints were resurrected before or after Jesus was and whether it was a resuscitation to a mortal body or a permanent resurrection to an immortal body. *However, there is no reason for serious doubt that all the Fathers surveyed accepted the historicity of this account.* Their testimony is very convincing for many reasons:

First, the earliest possible confirmation as to the historical nature of the resurrection of the saints in the Matthew 27 passage goes all the way back to Ignatius, a contemporary of the Apostle John (d. ca. AD 90). One could not ask for an earlier verification that the resurrection of these saints than that of Ignatius (AD 70–115). He wrote: *"He who they rightly waited for, being come, raised them from the dead."*[39] And in the Epistle to the Trallians he added, *"For Says the Scripture, 'Many bodies of the saints that slept arose,' their graves being opened. He descended, indeed, into Hades alone, but he arose accompanied by a multitude."*[40] The author who is a contemporary of the last apostle (John) is speaking unmistakably of the saints in Matthew 27 who were literally resurrected after Jesus was. Although the authenticity of the Ignatius quote has been challenged, they no doubt represent an early tradition. And no evidence to the contrary has been found in this early period.

Second, the next testimony to the historicity of this passage is found in Irenaeus who knew Polycarp, a disciple of the Apostle John. Other than the apostolic fathers, Irenaeus is as good as any witness to the earliest post-apostolic understanding of the Matthew 27 text. And he made it clear that *"many"* persons *"ascended and were seen in their bodies."*[41]

Third, there is a virtually unbroken chain of great fathers of the church after Irenaeus (second century) who took this passage as historical (see above).[42] Much of the

38. Calvin, *New Testament Commentaries*, 3:211–12.
39. Ignatius, ch. IX.
40. Ignatius, *Trallians*, IX.
41. Irenaeus, *Fragments of the Lost Writings of Irenaeus*, XXVIII.
42. See an excellent article clearing up this matter by Wenham, titled "When Were the Saints

alleged "confusion" and "conflict" about the text is cleared up when one understands that, while the tombs were opened at the time of the death of Christ, nonetheless, the resurrection of these saints did not occur until "*after* his resurrection" (Matt 27:53, emphasis added) since Jesus is the "firstfruits" (1 Cor 15:23) of the resurrection.

Fourth, the great church father St. Augustine stressed the historicity of the Matthew 27 text about the resurrection of the saints, speaking of them as *"facts"* and *"things that were done"* as recorded by the Gospel *"historians."*[43]

Fifth, many of the Fathers used this passage in an apologetic sense as evidence of the resurrection of Christ. This reveals their conviction that it was a historical event resulting from the historical event of the resurrection of Christ. Irenaeus was explicit on this point, declaring, "Matthew also, who had a still greater desire [to establish this point], took particular pains to afford them *convincing proof that Christ is the seed of David."*[44]

Some, like Chrysostom, took it as evidence for the resurrection to come. "For if it was a great thing to raise Lazarus after four days, much more was it that they who had long slept should not shew themselves above; this is indeed a proof of the resurrection to come."[45]

Origen understood it as *"evidences of the divinity of Jesus."*[46] None of these Fathers would have given it such apologetic weight had they not been convinced of the historicity of the resurrection of these saints after Jesus' resurrection in Matthew 27.

Sixth, even the church father Origen, who was the most prone to allegorizing away literal events in the Bible, took this text to refer to a literal historical resurrection of saints. He wrote of the events in Matthew 27 that they are *"the evidences of the divinity of Jesus."*[47]

Seventh, some of the great teachers of the church were careful to mention that the saints rose as a result of Jesus' resurrection which is a further verification of the historical nature of the resurrection of the saints in Mathew 27. Jerome wrote: *"As Lazarus rose from the dead, so also did many bodies of the Saints rise again to shew forth the Lord's resurrection*; yet notwithstanding that the graves were opened, they did

---

Raised?," 150–52. He argues convincingly for repunctuating the Greek to read: "And the tombs were opened. The bodies of the sleeping saints were raised, and they went out from their tombs after the resurrection." While this affects the alleged poetic flavor of the passage, it is bizarre to hold that the saints were raised at Christ's death and sat around opened tombs for three days before they left. It also contradicts 1 Cor 15:20 which declares that Christ is the "firstfruits" of the resurrection and Matt 27:53 which says they did not come out of the tombs until "after" Christ's resurrection.

43. Augustine, *Harmony of the Gospels*, bk. 3, ch. 21, emphasis added.
44. Irenaeus, ibid., 573.
45. Cited by Aquinas, ibid., 963–64.
46. Origin, ibid., bk. 2, ch. 36.
47. Origen, ibid.

not rise again before the Lord rose, that he might be the first-born of the resurrection from the dead."[48]

John Calvin added, "Yet we may doubt whether this opening of the tombs happened before the resurrection, *for the resurrection of the saints which is shortly after added followed in my opinion the resurrection of Christ*. It is absurd for some interpreters to image that they spent three days alive and breathing, hidden in tombs." For "it seems likely to me that *at Christ's death the tombs at once opened; at his resurrection some of the godly men received breath and came out and were seen in the city*. Christ is called the Firstborn from the dead (1 Cor 15:20; Col 1:18."[49]

Eighth, St. Augustine provides an answer to the false premise of contemporary critics that there must be another reference to a New Testament event like this in order to confirm that it is historical. He wrote, *"It would not be fair to impeach them with inconsistency, simply because one of them may have specified one occurrence as the immediate cause of the centurion's amazement, while another introduces a different incident."*[50]

So, *contrary to the claims of many current New Testament critics, the Matthew 27 account of the resurrection of the saints is a clear and unambiguous affirmation of the historicity of the resurrection of the saints. This is supported by a virtually unbroken line of the great commentators of the Early Church and through the Middle Ages and into the Reformation period* (John Calvin). Not a single example was found of any Father surveyed who believed this was a legend. Such a belief is due to the acceptance of modern critical methodology, not to either a historical-grammatical exposition of the text or to the supporting testimony of the main orthodox teachers of the church up to and through the Reformation.

Ninth, the impetus for rejecting the story of the resurrection of the saints in Matthew 27 is not based on good exegesis of the text or on the early support of the Fathers but is based on fallacious premises:

(1) First of all, there is an anti-supernatural bias beginning in the seventeenth century and lying beneath much of contemporary scholarship. But there is no philosophical basis for the rejection of miracles,[51] and there is no exegetical basis for rejecting it in this text. Indeed on the same ground one could reject the resurrection of Christ since it supernatural and is found in the same text.

(2) Further, there is also the fallacious premise of double reference which affirms that if an event is not mentioned at least twice in the Gospels, then its historicity is questioned. But on this grounds many other events must be rejected as well, such as, the story of Nicodemus (John 3), the Samaritan woman at the well (John 4), the story of Zacchaeus (Luke 19), the resurrection of Lazarus (John 11), and even the birth of

---

48. Cited by Aquinas, ibid., 963.
49. Calvin, *New Testament Commentaries*, 3:211–12.
50. Augustine, *Harmony of the Gospels*, bk. 3, ch. 21, emphasis added.
51. See Geisler, *Miracles and the Modern Mind*.

Christ in the stable and the angel chorus (Luke 2), as well as many other events in the Gospels. How many times does an event have to be mentioned in a first-century piece of literature based on reliable witnesses in order to be true?

(3) There is another argument that seems to infect much of contemporary New Testament scholarship on this matter. It is theorized that an event like this, if literal, would have involved enough people and graves to have drawn significant evidence of it in a small place like Jerusalem. Raymond Brown alludes to this, noting that "many interpreters balk at the thought of many known risen dead being seen in Jerusalem—such a large scale phenomenon should have left some traces in Jewish and/or secular history!"[52] However, at best this is simply the fallacious argument from silence. What is more, "many" can mean only a small group, not hundreds of thousands. Further, the story drew enough attention to make it into one of the canonical Gospels, right alongside the resurrection of Christ and with other miraculous events. In brief, it is in a historical book; it is said to result from the resurrection of Christ; it was cited apologetically by the early Fathers as evidence of the resurrection of Christ and proof of the resurrection to come. No other evidence is needed for its authenticity.

## A DENIAL OF INERRANCY

According to the official statements by the International Council on Biblical Inerrancy, the denial of the historicity of the Matthew 27 resurrection of the saints is a denial of the inerrancy of the Bible. This is clear from several official ICBI statements.

(1) The Chicago Statement on Inerrancy speaks against this kind of "dehistoricizing" of the Gospels, saying, "We deny the legitimacy of any treatment of the text or quest for sources lying behind it that leads to relativizing, *dehistoricizing*, or discounting its teaching, or rejecting its claims to authorship."[53]

(2) The statement adds: "*All the claims of the Bible must correspond with reality, whether that reality is historical, factual or spiritual.*"[54]

(3) ICBI framers said, "Though the Bible is indeed *redemptive* history, it is also redemptive *history*, and this means that the acts of salvation wrought by God *actually occurred in the space-time world.*"[55]

(4) Again, "When the quest for sources produces a *dehistoricizing* of the Bible, a rejection of its teaching or a rejection of the Bible's own claims of authorship [then] it has trespassed beyond its proper limits."[56]

Subsequently, Sproul wrote: "As the former and only President of ICBI during its tenure and as the original framer of the Affirmations and Denials of the Chicago

---

52. Brown, "Eschatological Events," 64.
53. CSBI, art. XVIII, emphasis added.
54. Sproul, *Explaining Inerrancy*, 43–44.
55. Ibid., 37.
56. Ibid., 57.

Statement on Inerrancy, I can say categorically that *Mr. Michael Licona's views are not even remotely compatible with the unified Statement of ICBI.*"[57]

Another ICBI founder, J. I. Packer, wrote: "As a framer of the ICBI statement on biblical inerrancy who once studied Greco-Roman literature at advanced level, *I judge Mike Licona's view* that, because the Gospels are semi-biographical, details of their narratives may be regarded a legendary and factually erroneous, *to be both academically and theologically unsound.*"[58]

(5) Also, "*We deny that generic categories which negate historicity may rightly be imposed on biblical narratives which present themselves as factual.*"[59] "*We deny that any event, discourse or saying reported in Scripture was invented by the biblical writers or by the traditions they incorporated.*"[60]

(6) Finally, as a framer of the ICBI statements I can testify that Robert Gundry's similar views of dehistoricizing Matthew were an object of these ICBI statements. And they lead to his being asked to resign from the Evangelical Theological Society (by a 74-percent majority vote). Since Licona's views do the same basic thing, then they should be excluded on the same basis. Gundry used Jewish midrash genre to dehistoricized parts of Gospel history, and Licona used Greco-Roman genre and legends, but the principle is the same.

---

57. Letter to Norman L. Geisler, May 22, 2012, emphasis added.
58. Letter to Norman L. Geisler, May 8, 2014, emphasis added.
59. CSBH, art. XIII.
60. CSBH, art. XIV.

Chapter 23

# Can We Still Believe in the Bible?

## NORMAN L. GEISLER

### INTRODUCTION

Can We Still Believe in the Bible? The real answer to the question posed by Craig Blomberg's book title is: yes, we can believe in the general reliability of the Bible, but no, we do not believe in its inerrancy, at least not in the sense meant by the framers of the International Council on Biblical Inerrancy (ICBI), even though some, like Blomberg, claim to believe in their own version of inerrancy which they mistakenly attribute to the ICBI.

In general there are many helpful things said by Blomberg in the first three chapters in defense of the reliability, canonicity, and transmission of the Bible. Indeed, we have often positively cited his book on *The Historical Reliability of the Gospel*. However, our focus here is on Blomberg's strong attack on inerrancy as we presented it in our recent book, *Defending Inerrancy: Affirming the Accuracy of Scripture for a New Generation* (Baker, 2011), and in particular his personal attack on the authors of the book and some other supporters of ICBI inerrancy.

However, our response here is not with persons but with principles. So, our critique is not against any person but only the ideas expressed. Our evaluation is focused on what they teach, not on their character or motives. We respect the individuals as scholars who disagree with inerrancy and love them as brothers in Christ. Our concern is with one thing and one thing only: is their teaching in accord with the doctrine of inerrancy as defined by the International Council on Biblical Inerrancy? So, when we use of the word "inerrancy" in this article we mean the ICBI view of inerrancy as expressed in the following documents.

## The ICBI Documents on Inerrancy

There were four official documents produced by ICBI related to defining inerrancy as follows:

(1) *The Chicago Statement on Biblical Inerrancy* (1978)—CSBI

(2) *The official ICBI Commentary on the Chicago Statement*—CSBI Commentary

(3) *The Chicago Statement on Biblical Hermeneutics* (1982)—CSBH

(4) The official ICBI commentary titled *Explaining Hermeneutics: A Commentary on the Chicago Statement on Biblical Hermeneutics*—CSBH Commentary

These four documents are found in one unit at http://bastionbooks.com/shop/explainingicbi. Together they express the official ICBI view on the meaning of inerrancy, although other related books were published under the ICBI label such as, *Inerrancy* (Geisler, ed.), *Hermeneutics, Inerrancy and the Bible* (Earl Radmacher and Robert Preus, eds.), *Inerrancy and the Church* (John Hannah, ed.), and *Biblical Errancy: Its Philosophical Roots* (Geisler, ed.).

## Blomberg's View on the ICBI Statements

Blomberg is aware of all these ICBI statements on inerrancy and even cites some of them.[1] He even goes so far as to claim agreement with everything in the "Chicago Statement" (CSBI) on inerrancy except one implied word, the word "always" in the last line.[2] He believes that ICBI is claiming that a denial of inerrancy *always* has grave consequences. Otherwise, Blomberg even calls the "Chicago Statement" on Biblical inerrancy (CSBI) "a carefully crafted document."[3] Further, he praises article XVIII of CSBI, saying, "This affirmation reinforces everything we have been discussing."[4] In addition, he commends the "reasonably well highlighted" statement on genre criticism in CSBI.[5] Strangely, Blomberg even commends one Chicago statement more than the other, declaring: "The Chicago Statement on Biblical Hermeneutics has not had nearly the lasting effect that the Chicago Statement on Biblical Inerrancy did, which is a shame, because in many ways it is the superior of the two documents."[6]

---

1. Blomberg, *Can We Still Believe*, 136, 149, 170, 178, 222, 262.

2. Ibid., 273. Blomberg alleges that he disagrees with CSBI, art. XIV, "The one affirmation in the Chicago Statement with which I would disagree is not part of its description of the meaning of inerrancy but a closing reflection. . . . 'We further deny that inerrancy can be rejected without grave consequences.' . . . I agree that the consequences can be detrimental and that sometimes they can be grave, but to imply that they are *always* grave is too strong a statement, not borne out by actual experience."

3. Ibid., 149.

4. Ibid., 170.

5. Ibid., 178.

6. Ibid., 261n98.

Part 2—Inerrancy Defended

# BLOMBERG'S VIEWS ON INERRANCY CONTRADICT ICBI

## A Statement of His View

Although Blomberg claims he does not personally hold many of the views which he describes below,[7] nonetheless, he believes that none of them are inconsistent with belief in inerrancy. *In other words, according to Blomberg, one can hold any of the following views without denying the inerrancy of Holy Scripture*:

1. He denied the historicity of Jesus' command about getting the coin from the mouth of the fish in Matthew 17:27, saying, "Yet even the most superficial application of form criticism reveals that this is not a miracle story, because it is not even a *story*."[8] But this is a futile attempt to defend his disbelief by diverting attention from his denial of the historicity of this text on the grounds that it was not a story but a command.[9] By focusing on these factors, attention is deflected from a crucial point, namely, that Blomberg does not believe this event ever happened as the Bible says it did. Blomberg added, "Further problems increase the likelihood of Jesus's command being metaphorical."[10]

2. According to Blomberg, "The author's intention [in Genesis] is almost entirely to narrate the 'who' rather than the 'how' of creation."[11] So, almost nothing informs us about how origins occurred, whether by creation or by evolution.

3. Blomberg claims that "some [inerrantists] opt for forms of theistic evolution in which God creates the universe with all the mechanisms built in to give rise ... to each new development in the creative 'week.'"[12] This too is deemed compatible with inerrancy according to Blomberg.

4. He adds, "Must there have been a historical Adam and Eve? ... Many scholars, including a few evangelicals, think not."[13] Blomberg adds, "Nothing in principle should prevent the persons who uphold inerrancy from adopting a view that sees *adam* ('man' or Adam) and *hawwa* ('life' or Eve) as symbols for every man and woman."[14]

5. Further, Blomberg believes that "none of this theology [about Job's view on suffering] requires Job to have ever existed any more than the teaching of the parable of the Good Samaritan requires the Samaritan to have been a real person."[15] He added,

---

7. Ibid., 177.
8. Blomberg, "New Testament Miracles and Higher Criticism," 433.
9. Blomberg, *Can We Still Believe*, 263n113.
10. Blomberg, "New Testament Miracles," 433.
11. Blomberg, *Can We Still Believe*, 151.
12. Ibid.
13. Ibid., 152.
14. Ibid.
15. Ibid., 156.

"Almost nothing is at stake if Job never existed, whereas everything is at stake if Jesus never lived."

6. Likewise, he asserts that "surely, however, someone might argue, Jonah must be completely historical, because Jesus himself likens his death and resurrection to Jonah's experience with the great fish (Matt 12:40; Luke 11:30). Actually, this does not follow at all."[16]

7. Further, "Ultimately, what one decides about its [the book of Isaiah's] composition or formation need not have anything to do with biblical inerrancy at all,"[17] even though he admits Jesus mentioned "the prophet Isaiah" as being author of texts in both sections of Isaiah.[18]

8. Isaiah may not have predicted "Cyrus" by name 150 years in advance (Isa 45:1) of his reign because "Cyrus could in fact be a dynasty name (like 'Pharaoh' in Egypt) rather than a personal name."[19] This too is deemed compatible with inerrancy.

9. According to Blomberg, the prophet Daniel may not have predicted all the things his book indicates because "perhaps two works associated with the prophet Daniel and is successor, written at two different times, were combined."[20]

10. Blomberg, argues that treating sections of "Matthew as Midrash" and not as history would have been taken by his audience "who would have understood exactly what he was doing, not imagining his embellishment to be making the same kinds of truth claims as his core material from Mark and Q."[21]

11. Likewise, Blomberg believes that the story of "Lazarus" (Luke 16) is a "parabolic fiction."[22]

12. Although Blomberg attempts to downplay it,[23] he has shown an openness to aberrant views in his book coauthored with a Morman titled *How Wide the Divide* in that they agree on twelve affirmations, the first of which is: "The Father, the Son, and the Holy Spirit are one eternal God."[24] But anyone who has studied Mormonism knows that Mormons do not believe in the Trinity but in the heresy of tritheism. Further, they believe in polytheism of which the prophet Joseph Smith said: "God himself was once as we are now, and is an exalted man for I am going to tell you how God came to be. We have imagined and supposed that God was God from all eternity. . . . I will refute that idea, and take away the veil, so that you may see" (April 6, 1844). Since Mormons have not repudiated the prophetic office of Smith

---

16. Ibid., 157.
17. Ibid., 162–63.
18. Ibid., 161.
19. Ibid., 162.
20. Ibid., 164.
21. Ibid., 166.
22. Ibid., 150.
23. Ibid., 272.
24. See Blomberg and Robinson, *How Wide the Divide?*

or any of official Mormonism's many denials of essential Christian doctrines, cozying up to Mormonism is not the most doctrinally discerning thing one can do.[25]

In short, according to Blomberg, it is consistent with inerrancy to deny the historicity of Adam, Eve, Job, and Jonah, as well as the historicity of early Genesis and the doctrine of creation. Likewise, he holds that an inerrantist need not believe that there was only one Isaiah or that he and Daniel made the supernatural predictions traditionally attributed to them. He claims that even the Mormon cult has significant commonalities with evangelical Christianity so that the divide is not so wide as evangelicals have traditionally thought, even though Mormons deny the deity of Christ, the Trinity, and salvation (to the highest heaven) by grace alone through faith in Christ alone, and many other evangelical beliefs.[26]

## BLOMBERG'S VIEWS CONTRADICT THE ICBI VIEW ON INERRANCY

Blomberg's claims to the contrary, one thing is certain: his views are contrary to the clear statements of the ICBI. Consider the following ICBI declarations against Blomberg's view on some of these very issues:

1. *Genesis 1–11 is historical.* The Chicago Statement on Biblical Hermeneutics (CSBH), article XXII "affirms that Genesis 1–11 is factual, as is the rest of the book." CSBI article XIII reads: "We deny that generic categories which negate historicity may rightly be imposed on biblical narratives which present themselves as factual. Some for instance, take Adam to be a myth, whereas in Scripture he is presented as a real person."

2. *Historicity of the flood.* CSBH, article XIX affirms "the factual nature of the account of the creation of the universe, all living things, the special creation of man, the Fall, and the Flood. These accounts are all factual, that is, they are about space-time events which actually happened as reported in the book of Genesis (see art. XIV)."

3. *Theistic evolution and Genesis.* CSBH, article XIX: "We deny that Scripture should be required to fit alien preunderstandings, inconsistent with itself, such as naturalism, *evolutionism*, scientism, secular humanism, and relativism." Further, "it is important to apply the 'literal' hermeneutic espoused (art. XV) to this question. The result was a recognition of the factual nature of the account of the creation of the universe, all living things, the special creation of man, the Fall, and the Flood. These accounts are all factual, that is, they are about space-time events which actually happened as re-ported in the book of Genesis (see art. XIV)."[27] Further, "There was . . . complete agreement on denying that Genesis is mythological or unhistorical. Likewise, the

---

25. See Ron Rhodes, *Reasoning from the Scriptures with Mormons*.
26. See Geisler and Rhodes, *Conviction without Compromise*.
27. Geisler and Sproul, *Explaining Hermeneutics*, 83.

use of the term 'creation' was meant to *exclude the belief in macroevolution, whether of the atheistic or theistic varieties.*"[28]

4. *Historicity of Jonah*. CSBI, article XIII reads: "We deny that generic categories which negate historicity may rightly be imposed on biblical narratives which present themselves as factual. . . . Others take Jonah to be an allegory when he is presented as a historical person and [is] so referred to by Christ."

5. *Historicity of the Gospels*. CSBI, article XVIII reads: "We affirm that the text of Scripture is to be interpreted by the grammatico-historical exegesis, taking account of its literary forms and devices, and Scripture is to interpret Scripture. We deny the legitimacy of any treatment of the text or quest for sources lying behind it that leads to relativizing, *dehistoricizing*, or discounting its teaching, or rejecting its claim to authorship." CSBH, article XIV says: "We affirm that the biblical record of events, discourses and sayings, though presented in a variety of appropriate literary forms, corresponds to historical fact. We deny that any event, discourse of saying reported in Scripture was invented by the biblical writers or by the traditions they incorporated." Further, CSBH, article XIII asserts that "we deny that generic categories which negate historicity may rightly be imposed on biblical narratives which present themselves as factual." Blomberg tries in vain to avoid the impact of this statement by presupposing that the Gospel narratives do not all "present" themselves as historical. However, this is clearly contrary to (1) what the Gospel of Luke claims (Luke 1:1–4); (2) the literal historical-grammatical method ICBI adopts; and (3) the correspondence view of truth employed by ICBI which presumes narratives are literal unless shown to be otherwise.

6. *The use of extra-biblical genre*. Traditionally, many have considered the Gospels to be a genre of their own (*sui generis*) because of their unique nature as a revelation of God. However, Blomberg buys into the currently popular notion that the Gospels should be interpreted by extra-biblical genre. He wrote: "Once we determine, as best we can, what a passage affirms, according to the conventions of its style, and genre, a commitment to inerrancy implies acceptance of the truth of those affirmations. But a commitment to inerrancy does not exclude *a priori* any given literary style, form, or genre that is not inherently deceptive."[29] In short, we must determine first what a passage means *according to its genre*. We cannot know in advance that it is going to be historical just because it is a narrative or is in a historical book. Further, the genre can be an extra-biblical like the Greco-Roman genre. Hence, an extra-biblical genre can determine the meaning of a biblical text. This is, of course, contrary to the ICBI statements on genre for several reasons.

First, ICBI article XIII forbids the use of extra-biblical genre to determine the meaning of a biblical text. It reads, "*We deny that generic categories which negate historicity may rightly be imposed on biblical narratives which present themselves as factual*" (emphasis added). Further, CSBH, article XIV says: "*We affirm thatthe biblical record*

---

28. Ibid., emphasis added.
29. Blomberg, *Can We Still Believe*, 164.

*of events, discourses and sayings, though presented in a variety of appropriate literary forms, corresponds to historical facts"* (emphasis added).

Second, ICBI demands interpreting "Scripture by Scripture" (CSBI, art. XVIII), not the Bible by extra-biblical genre. That is, nothing external to the New Testament text should be hermeneutically determinative of the meaning in the text. In some cases, one can derive the meaning (use) of a term from contemporary use of the word. But the meaning of a text is discovered from studying the text in its grammatical and historical setting, as compared to related Scripture on that text.

Third, the alleged "purpose of the author" of which Blomberg speaks is not the determinative factor in understanding a text, for there is no way to know what the author had in his mind behind the text except by what he affirmed in the text. Hence, the appeal to the linguistic philosophy of John Austin to determine the illocutionary (purpose) act or the perlocutionarly act (results) is futile. Usually, all we have in Scripture is the locutionary act (i.e., what is affirmed). So, the locus of meaning has to be in *what* is affirmed, not *why* it is affirmed because often we are just guessing about that. Thus, the genre critic Blomberg is using extra-biblical ideas to determine the meaning of the biblical text.

## BLOMBERG'S ATTACK ON DEFENDERS OF THE ICBI STATEMENTS

Not only do the ICBI statements repeatedly contradict Blomberg's view on inerrancy, but he repeatedly distorts the ICBI statements and demeans the character of those who defend the inerrancy of Scripture. We note first of all his unscholarly and unprofessional characterizations of those who defend the historical biblical view of inerrancy as represented in the ICBI statements.

### His Excessively Negative Language about the Defenders of Inerrancy

Blomberg often employs *condemnation* and *exaggeration* instead of *refutation* related to inerrantists claims. He labels inerrantists, for example, as "very conservative,"[30] "overly conservative,"[31] "ultra conservative,"[32] "hyperconservative,"[33] "extremely conservative."[34] Of course, this tends to make his views look more moderate by comparison, when, as we shall see, they are in direct opposition to those the mainstream evangelical view as reflected in the ICBI statements. He even likens ICBI defenders of inerrancy to Nazis and Communists.[35] He quotes with approval the statement, "The

30. Ibid., 7.
31. Ibid., 217.
32. Ibid., 11, 214.
33. Ibid., 13.
34. Ibid., 7.
35. Ibid., 8.

far left and the far right—avoid them both, like the plague."[36] At one point he stops just short of questioning the Christianity of ICBI supporters.[37] What is more, he sometimes makes it very clear about whom he is speaking by name (Robert Thomas, David Farnell, William Roach, and myself)–all PhDs in biblical-related studies who have written critical reviews of Blomberg's positions. He also addresses Dr. Al Mohler and The Master's Seminary in negative terms.

Such exaggerated language is not only unprofessional and unscholarly, it borders on being morally libelous, as the following statements reveal. Strangely and inconsistently, Blomberg responds strongly when other scholars use a negative term about his views.[38]

## His Unjustified Condemnation of Alleged Motives and Character of Inerrancy Defenders

Blomberg goes further than extremist labeling of inerrancy defenders. He claims that we "simplistically" distorted the evidence in order to oust Robert Gundry from the Evangelical Theological Society (ETS) over his midrash denial of the historicity of certain sections of Matthew.[39] He charges that we engaged in a "political campaign" against Gundry.[40] Elsewhere, he alleges that we have utilized a "standard ploy throughout his [my] career" when "trying to get someone removed from an organization."[41] He adds the allegation that inerrancy is used as "a blunt tool to hammer into submission people whose interpretation of passages differs from ours."[42] These charges of an alleged sinister and continuous career of unjustified activity on my part are untrue, unjustified, and unethical. Indeed, they are serious moral judgments of motives for which Blomberg should apologize. Someone has rightly asked why it is that those who defend inerrancy are attacked and those who attack inerrancy are defended.

Without attributing motives, one thing seems clear: Blomberg is dead-set on broadening the acceptable borders of orthodoxy on inerrancy, the result of which would be a more inclusive statement that would embrace scholars (like Blomberg himself) who have moved well beyond inerrancy as traditionally understood and as expressed by the ICBI. This may explain the use of such passionate and uncalled for language in describing those who wish to retain a more traditional stand on inerrancy.

36. Ibid.
37. Ibid., 254.
38. Ibid., 254.
39. Ibid., 167.
40. Ibid.
41. Ibid., 262n111.
42. Ibid., 125.

Part 2—Inerrancy Defended

Perhaps a lot of their passion and zeal arises from the fact that those who hold a more liberal view on inerrancy may fear their view may be deemed unorthodox too.

## His Many Errors and Mischaracterizations of the Defenders of Inerrancy

Ironically, Blomberg's attack on those who defend an inerrant Bible is filled with errant statements. Here is a list of some that come to mind. Contrary to Blomberg's charge, it is not true that:

1. *No one offered an "intelligent response" to Gundry.*[43] Even Blomgberg acknowledged that D. A. Carson wrote a critique of it, as did Doug Moo, not to mention the scholarly response given at ETS and articles published in the *Journal of The Evangelical Theological Society* (JETS, 2003).

2. *A majority of speakers at ETS were in favor of retaining Gundry in its membership.*[44] This is a misleading statement since, when given a chance to vote almost three-quarters of the membership voted to ask Gundry to resign.

3. *The proceeding of the ETS which resulted in Gundry's removal from membership was not fair or representative.*[45] On the contrary, it was the result of a long (two-year) process, during which papers and articles were presented pro and con. The meeting at which the vote took place was deliberate and orderly and the vote was taken properly. Even Gundry accepted its conclusion.

4. *The vote for Gundry's removal was not a bare minimum "just over" what was necessary.*[46] The vote was 116 in favor of his removal and 41 opposed (as reported by *Christianity Today*, Feb 3, 1984) which is almost 74 percent in favor of his removal. This is nearly three-quarters of the membership present and well over the two-thirds (67 percent) necessary.

5. *ETS did not "expel" Gundry from membership.*[47] The vote was to ask Gundry to *resign*, not to expel him. If he had refused to resign, then there could have been another vote to expel which was unnecessary because Gundry voluntarily resigned.

6. *The process of Gundry's removal was a "political campaign" in which "circulating advertisements" occurred.*[48] This too is false. No "campaign" was held and no "advertisements" were circulated. Each ETS member was given a paper with quotations from Gundry's book so that they could make an intelligent decision on how to vote.

---

43. Ibid., 167.
44. Ibid., 166.
45. Ibid., 166–67.
46. Ibid., 167.
47. Ibid.
48. Ibid.

7. *"Gundry's views were simplistically presented" at the ETS meeting.*[49] This too is false. Exact and complete quotations were given of Gundry's views to each member. There was nothing simplistic about it.

8. *Geisler utilized a "standard ploy throughout his career . . . when he is trying to get someone removed from an organization," namely, getting all the living framers to agree with him in order to oust a member.*[50] I never did and such thing. In the Pinnock issue, Roger Nicole contacted all the founders of ETS, but I was not a founder of ETS and was not part of any such effort. I have argued Licona's views are contrary to the ICBI framers, but I was never part of a "ploy" or effort to get him ousted from the ETS organization, nor any other group. Neither, have I done it "throughout my career" (which is now almost sixty years long) because there was never another occasion in all those years where a group of framers were involved in getting someone removed from an organization in which I participated. These are serious, sinister, and slanderous charges that impugn the character of another brother in Christ and call for an apology from the one who made them.

9. *Geisler resigned from ETS because they exonerated Clark Pinnock of the charges against him.* This is partly true. After all, Pinnock claimed to believe in inerrancy, yet he has said in print that there were false predictions in the Bible and he denied the Bible is the written Word of God.[51] I was also disappointed with the process by which Pinnock was retained because it was not completely fair and open. However, the main and underlying reason I left ETS was because I believed it has lost its integrity by allowing a scholar to join who did not have to believe the doctrinal statement on inerrancy as the founders meant it.[52]

10. *Geisler has become increasingly more conservative over the years as indicted by the successive schools at which he has taught.*[53] This is false. In each case my move to an established school was because I was offered what appeared to be a better opportunity for service. In the case of the two seminaries I helped start, they were after I retired and was asked by others to help them start two seminaries (where I still teach) which stress apologetics which has been a passion of mine from the beginning. It had nothing to do with the degree of conservativeness of the seminaries. They all have sound doctrinal statements. None of them was significantly more conservative than the others.

11. *Only a "tiny minority" throughout history held that inerrancy is the only legitimate form of Christianity.*[54] This is a purely straw man argument since almost no one holds this view. ICBI, the view we are representing, states clearly that "we deny that

---

49. Ibid.
50. Ibid., 262n111.
51. Pinnock, *Scripture Principle*, 128.
52. See my article "Why I Resigned."
53. Blomberg, *Can We Still Believe*, 143–44.
54. Ibid., 221.

such a confession is necessary for salvation."[55] It adds, "We affirm that the doctrine of inerrancy has been integral to the Church's faith throughout its history."[56] ICBI also held that there are "grave consequences"[57] for denying inerrancy, but it never affirmed that it is the only legitimate form of Christianity. So, this criticism is an empty charge, applying to almost no one.

## BLOMBERG'S MISINTERPRETATION OF THE ICBI STATEMENTS

Not only did Blomberg attack those who defend ICBI inerrancy but he distorts the meaning of the ICBI statements. As noted earlier, Blomberg affirms the ICBI statements and even acknowledges the official commentaries. Nonetheless, he often distorts the meaning of these statements to support his own unorthodox views which are, in fact, contrary to the ICBI statements. Consider the following examples.

### ICBI View of Truth as Correspondence

One of the reasons Blomberg can claim he agrees with the ICBI statements (and yet hold views opposed to them) is that he misinterprets the ICBI statements. CSBI, article XIII affirms: "We deny that it is proper to evaluate Scripture according to standards of truth and error that are alien to its usage or purpose." But after acknowledging this, Blomberg proceeded to read his own purpose into certain texts of Scripture so as to doubt or deny their historicity (see midrash discussion below). This he does in direct contradiction to the ICBI official commentary (that he acknowledges) which declares a correspondence view of truth, as opposed to an intentionalist view which stresses (like Blomberg) the alleged purpose of the author, not the propositional affirmation of the author in the text. This is directly contrary to the CSBI commentary which declares: "*By biblical standards of truth and error is meant the view used both in the Bible and in everyday life, viz., a correspondence view of truth.* This part of the article is directed toward those who would redefine truth to relate to merely redemptive intent, the purely personal, or the life, rather than to mean that which corresponds with reality."[58] When truth is defined as correspondence with the fact, one cannot easily escape the fact that that the sections of the Gospels doubted or denied by Blomberg, Robert Gundry, or by Mike Licona are a denial of inerrancy (see next).

---

55. CSBI, art. XIX.
56. Ibid., art. XVI.
57. Ibid., art. XIX.
58. Geisler and Sproul, *Explaining Hermeneutics*, 50.

## ICBI View of Genre

It is difficult to understand how Blomberg can praise the ICBI statements as a whole and yet hold a genre view which is directly contrary to the ICBI view. A hint as to how he does this is when he praises one half of an ICBI statement on genre (which he takes out of context) and questions the other half which speaks directly against his view. For example, he agrees with CSBI, article XVIII when it affirms that "Scripture is to be interpreted by grammatico-historical exegesis, *taking account of its literary forms and devices*," and that "Scripture is to interpret Scripture," especially to the part we highlighted. However, he is not sure how this is consistent with the very next line which asserts: "We *deny the legitimacy of any treatment of the text of quest for sources behind it that leads to relativizing, dehisorticizing, or discounting its teaching, or rejecting its claim to authorship*" (emphasis added). And well he should disagree with this part because it is precisely what he approves of in the cases of Gundry, Licona, and himself. He approves of relativizing, dehistoricizing, and rejecting the claim to authorship as consistent with inerrancy.

*Relativizing*. Once the correspondence view of truth is not fully accepted, then truth becomes relativized because there is not objective reality to which it must correspond. Blomberg asserts, "What it means to say the Bible is wholly true varies widely from one genre to the next."[59] So, the "truth" is relative to the genre, and the genre choices are not absolute by any stretch of the imagination.

*Dehistoricizing*. For example, the choice of a midrash genre (Gundry) or a Greco-Roman genre (Licona) will determine whether or not the narrative is historically true or is just a legendary embellishment (see below). So, for New Testament critics' truth is relative to genre which in turn is relative to the interpreter.

*Pseudonymity*. Blomberg even allows for the use of an author's name to be used when in part or in whole he did not write the biblical book with his name on it. He himself believed that part of 2 Peter was not written by the Apostle Peter, and he allows (as consistent with inerrancy) for whole books to be such.[60]

## BLOMBERG'S DEFENSE OF ROBERT GUNDRY

According to Robert Gundry, whose view is defended by Blomberg as consistent with orthodoxy, whole sections of Matthew (like the Visit of the Magi—Matthew 2) are not historical because the author's purpose was not to affirm what corresponded with reality (as in a correspondence view of truth), but to use a midrashic embellishment understood as such by his Jewish audience.[61] So viewing "Matthew as Midrash" and not historical "would have understood exactly what he was doing, not imagining

---

59. Blomberg, *Can We Still Believe*, 131.
60. Ibid., 171,
61. Ibid., 165–68.

his embellishment to be making the same kinds of truth claims as his core material from Mark and Q."[62]

Of course, Blomberg laments that an overwhelming majority (nearly 74 percent) of the ETS voted to ask Gundry to resign from ETS because of his denial of the historicity of certain passages in Matthew. Blomberg remains proud that his is one of the small minority who voted to retain Gundry in ETS. Indeed, as even Blomberg admits,[63] the framers of the statement (of which I was one) "had Gundry in mind" when the CSBH statements were made which we certainly did. We wrote: "We deny that generic categories which negate historicity may rightly be imposed on biblical narratives which present themselves as factual" (CSBH Commentary on art. XIII). No amount of reinterpretation can override the clarity of this statement or the testimony of living framers as to its meaning. And when the framers die, the written words of the framers (as here) will remain to vouch for the meaning of their words.

## BLOMBERG'S DEFENSE OF MURRAY HARRIS

There seems to be a camaraderie among many biblical scholars that blinds them to some serious errors and prompts them to put fraternity over orthodoxy. Professor Murray Harris had claimed the resurrection body was "essential immaterial,"[64] even though the Bible (Luke 24:39; Acts 2:31) and the early creeds affirmed the resurrection in the "flesh." Further, Harris affirmed the ascension of Christ was a "parable."[65] Further, he held that believers receive a spiritual resurrection body at death[66] while their physical bodies remain rotting in the grave. In spite of all this, Blomberg, in an act that seeming puts fraternity above orthodoxy, defends his fellow New Testament scholar's view as orthodox.

Further, Blomberg was unaware of what the real issues were,[67] namely, that we had written a whole book responding to Harris's objection.[68] Neither did Blomberg show awareness of the fact that some ninety counter-cult groups pronounced Harris's views as "false doctrine," "unorthodox," or even "cultic."[69] Nor was Blomberg cognizant of the fact that Harris had been warned by Trinity that he would lose his position, if he did not change his view on the resurrection of believers. Harris did change his view over the weekend when Trinity appointed (not ETS related) a committee of three

---

62. Ibid., 166.
63. Ibid., 168.
64. Harris, *Raised Immortal*, 53–54.
65. Ibid., 92.
66. Ibid., 44, 100.
67. See Geisler, *Battle for the Resurrection*.
68. See esp. ch. 5 of Geisler, *In Defense of the Resurrection*.
69. Blomberg, *Can We Still Believe*, 189.

scholars to meet with him. One would have expected that a scholar of Blomberg's reputation would have looked into this issue more carefully before pontificating on it.

## BLOMBERG'S DEFENSE OF MIKE LICONA

It is incredible that anyone, let alone a biblical scholar, would defend the orthodoxy (i.e., compatibility with inerrancy) of Mike Licona's Greco-Roman genre views. Licona has yet to retract his view that the resurrection of the saints in Matthew 27 is a legendary, poetic embellishment,[70] even though he is now not as sure of it as he once was. Further, Licona embraces the Greco-Roman *Bios* which admits that it is "a flexible genre [wherein] it is often difficult to determine when history ends and legend begins."[71] This is ironic in view of Blomberg and Licona's criticism that the defenders of inerrancy are imposing their modern view of what an error is on the Bible when in fact it is they who are imposing their modern view of genre criticism on the Bible.

*More importantly, Licona believes there is a contradiction in the Gospels about the day on which Jesus was crucified*, yet he insists this is consistent with a belief in inerrancy! In a debate with Bart Ehrman in the spring of 2009, Licona said, "I think that John probably altered the day [on which Jesus was crucified] in order for a theological—to make a thelogical point there. But that does not mean that Jesus wasn't crucified."

The ICBI framers condemned Licona's kind of view in clear and unequivocal language when they spoke against "dehistoricizing" the Gospels (CSBI, art. XVIII). Likewise, they affirmed: "We deny that generic categories which negate historicity may rightly be imposed on biblical narratives which present themselves as factual" (CSBH Commentary on art. XIII). Licona's view is so far from measuring up to ICBI standard for orthodoxy that R.C. Sproul wrote: "As the former and only President of ICBI during its tenure and as the original framer of the Affirmations and Denials of the Chicago Statement on Inerrancy, *I can say categorically that Mr. Michael Licona's views are not even remotely compatible with the unified Statement of ICBI*."[72]

## CONCLUSION

*One fact emerges from Blomberg's recent book, namely, whatever its merits may be, the view which he defends is contrary to the ICBI view of inerrancy*. And since the ETS has accepted the ICBI definition of inerrancy (in 2003), it is also contrary to the statement of largest group of inerrantist scholars in the world! So much for Blomberg's charge that the defenders of the ICBI statements on inerrancy, including living framers like J. I. Packer, R. C. Sproul, and myself, are a tiny extremist minority. And to debunk the

70. See Licona, *Resurrection of Jesus*, 552, 548.
71. Ibid., 34.
72. Letter to Norman Geisler, May 22, 2012, emphasis added.

living framers, as Blomberg did,[73] because they will someday be dead, misses the point, namely, they are the best testimony to the meaning of their own words while they are alive. And their written words will still live on even after they die.

Finally, we do agree with Blomberg's words when he wrote: we should embrace a "full-fledged inerrantist Christianity so long as we ensure that we employ all parts of a detailed exposition of inerrancy, such as that found in the Chicago Statement on Biblical Inerrancy . . . and not just those sections that are most amenable to our personal philosophies or theologies. This also means that we interpret the Chicago Statement, like the Bible, in terms of what is actually written, and not merely what one of its authors might have wanted to write or might have wanted it to mean."[74] Unfortunately, however, as has been shown above, such a view is not the view that Blomberg *promotes*, but it is the view he *attacks*.

---

73. Blomberg, *Can We Still Believe*, 262n111.
74. Ibid., 222.

# Chapter 24

# ICBI Inerrancy Is Not for the Birds

## JOSEPH M. HOLDEN

The current trend among evangelical New Testament scholars to utilize or approve of genre criticism (e.g., Craig Blomberg, Michael Licona, Darrell Bock, Michael Bird, Carlos Bovell, Kevin Vanhoozer, et al.) to dehistoricize the biblical text appears to stem from an aversion to the correspondence view of truth. To achieve their criticism, correspondence is replaced with the preferred intentionalist view of truth that seeks after unexpressed intentions and purposes of the biblical author as they correspond with extra-biblical literature of similar genre to determine meaning. For Bird, the Gospels give us a reliable "big picture" about Jesus, but the details do not matter. Regarding his approach and view of historical reliability, Bird affirms:

> My own approach is what I would term "believing criticism." This approach treats Scripture as the inspired and veracious Word of God, but contends that we do Scripture the greatest service when we commit ourselves to *studying it in light of the context and processes through which God gave it to us.* Scripture is trustworthy because of God's faithfulness to his own Word and Scripture is authoritative because the Holy Spirit speaks to us through it. Nonetheless, God has seen fit to use human language, human authors, and even human processes as the means by which he has given his inscripturated revelation to humanity. *To understand the substance of Scripture means wrestling with its humanity, the human face of God's speech to us in his Word.*[1] *After due allowances are made for the artistic license, theological embellishment, and inherent biases of the tradents of the tradition,* our witnesses to Jesus remain steadfast in their conviction that the Jesus whom they

---

1. Bird, "Evangelical and Critical Approach," emphasis added.

narrate is historically authentic as much as he is personally confronting.² *This means that we are actually liberated to read the Gospels as they were intended to be read: as historically referential theological testimonies to Jesus as the exalted Lord. It does not matter then whether there was one demoniac (Mark 5:2; Luke 8:27) or two demoniacs (Matt 8:28) that Jesus healed on the eastern shore of the Sea of Galilee.* Jesus healed a demon possessed man in the vicinity and Matthew just likes couplets, making everything two's where he can! Similarly, trying to prove that mustard seeds really are the smallest plants of the earth (Mark 4:31) or that Peter denied Jesus three times before the cock first crowed and then three times again afterwards (Matt 26:69–74; Luke 22:56–60; John 18:16–27; Mark 14:66–68) is like trying to understand the Magna Carta by arguing about whether the commas are in the right position. John Calvin himself said: "We know that the Evangelists were not very exact as to the order of dates, or even in detailing minutely everything that Christ did or said" [Calvin, *Commentary on a Harmony of the Evangelists* (Grand Rapids, MI: Eerdmans, 1989), 216]. *The Evangelists give us the big picture about Jesus, the gist of his words, the major outlines of his career,* they position him in relation to the prophetic promises, and they declare the all important significance as to who he was and why he died. The details should not be treated with indifferences, but they are not the focus of the stories we call "Gospels." While I think the overall historical reliability of the Gospels is vitally important less we treat Gospels as religiously laden fiction, we should not import anachronistic and modernist criteria of historical reality into our treatment of the Gospels and make it a condition for theological validity.³

Again, Bird remarks:

So then, how do we as a believing and confessing community approach the critical questions that the texts of the Gospels present to us? . . . It entails we go through the Gospels unit by unit and ask what exactly did Jesus *intend* and how would his hearers have understood him. It equally entails asking *why* the Evangelists have told the story this way and *why* do they have the peculiarities that they do. Third, we have to explore the impact that the Gospels *intended* to make upon their implied readers and how the Four Gospels as a whole *intend* to shape the believing communities who read them now.⁴

## ICBI REJECTION OF BIRD'S VIEW OF TRUTH

ICBI rejected this intentionalist view of truth and affirmed a correspondence view of truth that every affirmation must correspond to the facts in order to be true: It

2. Ibid.
3. Ibid.
4. Ibid.

declared: "We affirm that the Bible expresses God's truth in propositional statements, and we declare that biblical truth is both objective and absolute. We further affirm that a statement is true if it represents matters as they actually are, but is an error if it misrepresents the facts."[5] What is more, the commentary on Chicago Statement on Hermeneutics states, "By 'biblical standards of truth and error' is meant the view used both in the Bible and in everyday life, viz., a correspondence view of truth. This part of the article is direct toward those who would redefine truth to relate merely to redemptive intent, the purely personal, or the like, rather than that which corresponds with reality."[6]

So, clearly, Michael Bird, Craig Blomberg, and Michael Licona and all who agree with their approach are in denial of the ICBI view of biblical inerrancy which the Evangelical Theological Society has embraced as a guide for understanding inerrancy.[7]

---

5. CSBH, art. VI.

6. Geisler and Sproul, *Explaining Hermeneutics*, 50.

7. See Blomberg, *Can We Still Believe*, 136, 170–71; Licona, *Resurrection of Jesus*, 185–86, 552–53, 555–56; Bovell, *Rehabilitating Inerrancy in a Culture of Fear*, 55–58; Vanhoozer, *Is Their Meaning in the Text?*; see Bock's blog statement approving Blomberg's *Can We Still Believe* and approving genre criticism as consistent with ICBI inerrancy (Bock, "Craig Blomberg's Can We Believe the Bible"). Bock asserts, "Craig Blomberg's fourth chapter in *Can We Still Believe the Bible*, examines some objections to inerrancy from both the right and the left. Yes, there is a position to the right of holding to inerrancy. It is holding it in a way that is slow to recognize solutions that fit within the view by undervaluing the complexities of interpretation."

# Chapter 25

# Contemporary Evangelical NT Genre Criticism
## Opening Pandora's Box?

## JOSEPH M. HOLDEN

Perhaps I should have titled the last chapter, "ICBI Is Not for the Birds," addressing Michael Bird et al.'s critical approach to Scripture, as "ICBI Is Not for the Mocking Birds." After reading Bird's response, one wonders what article he actually read and whether Neo-Evangelical critics take seriously challenges to their views (also see Blomberg's satirical and mocking rant below). Whatever the case may be, those within the critically-trained evangelical NT scholarly guild, I would assume, consider their ability to handle, teach, write, research, and discuss Scripture, a blessing given to them by God. Most, if not all, would agree they are also responsible to God and to those they interact with to imitate the character of Christ in love, especially to our own Christian brothers and sisters no matter what disagreements they have. One does not have to be a scholar to be aware of the susceptibility within the academy to be puffed up with pride and forget that the Word of God must guide our reason and interactions with others. To fall short of these standards is both unscholarly, unnecessary, and reveals little respect for the crucial issues pertaining to God's Word. There is no place for a lack of respect, mockery, or the cavalier handling of various topics discussed within inerrancy despite what we think about views we deem as unpersuasive.[1] The Scriptures deserve our best. But what should we expect from critical evangelicals that deny historical affirmations presented in Scripture and/or view historical narrative in the Gospels as candidates for fiction? Perhaps I should adjust my expectations and

---

1. See Bird, "Beware the Dangerous Heresy."

not expect critics to handle issues pertaining to the Scriptures in a manner likened to those who actually believe the biblical author's expressed intentions. Though this adjustment may be necessary when dealing with unbelieving critics, it should not dominate the landscape in this case since believers are involved. There is no reason that critical NT interpreters cannot be cordial in fostering an atmosphere of discovery rather than elevating fraternity above orthodoxy.

Yet despite identifying with evangelical traditions, stereotypes, impugning motives, demeaning comments, and personal attacks are offered without hesitation. For example, see Blomberg's descriptions of ICBI Inerrantists as "Nazism," "Communism," "far right," "extreme," "avoid them like the plague," "hindered genuine scholarship among evangelicals," "overly," "hyper," "ultra," and do "disservice" to the gospel in *Can We Still Believe the Bible?*,[2] which may be an attempt to standardize his own views as "mainstream" by polarizing the opposition. In addition, Blomberg makes a bizarre comment, asserting Geisler, a former ICBI framer and staunch defender of inerrancy, "Denies . . . ICBI Inerrancy!"[3] This is like saying the pope has denied Catholicism. Bird is not exempt from these personal attacks either, he says Geisler is the "villain," and his views are "extreme" and "to the right of Atilla the Hun," "not a . . . pleasant chap," and remarks Geisler "has never found an institution worthy of him."[4] Bird's latest response was also filled with inaccuracies and mockery such as "Joseph Holden, the president of something called Veritas Evangelical Seminary" which is "a subsidiary of Geisler industries." Bird claims, without explanation, that the post was a "really weird ultra conservative critique."[5] Licona has his share of doozies as well (e.g., Geisler and company are theological bullies, satirical mockeries of Geisler in cartoon form, etc). Though *ad hominem* can be an effective way to make an orthodox view look "radical," it is actually Bird, Blomberg, and Licona's view of Scripture that are alien to the church's view of Scripture from its beginning and to the ICBI definition.[6]

By contrast, Geisler's view (and my view) of inerrancy spelled out in CSBI is substantially the same as the Christian church's historic position that the Scriptures are without error in all they affirm.[7] Moreover, there is no example of the orthodox Christian church adopting a view that dismisses historical narrative as fiction, error, or legend based on genre criticism.

Despite deep disagreements between ICBI inerrantists and the conclusions and methodology offered by critically-trained evangelical NT interpreters, we are hopeful

---

2. Blomberg, *Can We Still Believe*, 7–8, 11, 120, 125, 141–45, 214, 217.
3. See Peters, "It Finally Happened," Scholarship and Inerrancy (blog), April 29, 2014.
4. See Bird's review of *Can We Still Believe*
5. Ibid.
6. Gospel texts presented as historical narrative in the Gospels may be fiction/legend. The view is considered consistent with ICBI inerrancy by critical evangelical interpreters such as Blomberg and Licona et al.; see Bird's *Five Views*, 145–73, and Albert Mohler's response, 174–79.
7. See Hannah, *Inerrancy and the Church*, and Woodbridge, *Biblical Authority and Interpretation*.

there can be cordial interaction on inerrancy. Otherwise, critical evangelical interpreters not only risk loosing their Christian witness in the eyes of those they seeks to serve, but also their credibility among already critic-wary pastors and laity who may question whether the critics have the ability to communicate objective research that is not blindly tied to the scholarly fraternity or self-preservation. It would seem easy enough for Blomberg and Licona, and those interpreters who approve of their brand of using extra-biblical genre sources to determine the *unexpressed* intentions of biblical authors and turn their *expressed* historical affirmations to fiction, to simply identify themselves with some other brand of "inerrancy." The distinction between views is explained in unambiguous terms in the ICBI documents. Though ICBI allows for responsible genre criticism to ensure proper exegesis of the various genres found in Scripture, ICBI explicitly rejects this dehistoricizing approach in article XIII which states, "We deny that generic categories which negate historicity may rightly be imposed on biblical narratives which present themselves as factual." What is more, article XVIII rejects "the legitimacy of any treatment of the text or quest for sources lying behind it that leads to relativizing, dehistoricizing, or discounting its teaching." Genres do not change facts or the expressed authorial intent (i.e., affirmations in the text).

If the Bible affirms an event, and it really didn't happen then the Bible is in error. That is to say, the biblical affirmation either corresponds to reality or it does not. Any attempt to arrive at the biblical author's *unexpressed* intentions to dehistoricize his expressed intentions through extra-biblical literature is guess work. The biblical author's unexpressed intentions are lost to us at his death, so nothing short of a séance will suffice in securing unexpressed intent! Similarity in genre does not secure our knowledge of unexpressed authorial intent no matter how "similar" it is to the Gospels, since we would still be left without knowing whether the biblical author's intent was the same as the pagan author's intent. Anything else is pure speculation. This method elevates what the author *intended* to say over and above what he did *actually* say. Truth-value is contained in propositions/affirmations, not hidden intentions. Not recognizing this opens a Pandora's Box of speculation as to which historical narratives are historical and which are fiction and can only lead to unorthodox conclusions.[8] This leads him to question the historical nature of all biblical miracles since extra-biblical miracle stories from antiquity are also presented as historical. Therefore, he asks, "Are we to believe all of them [are historical]?"[9] Evidently, for Blomberg, claiming miracle representations in Scripture are historical in form get us nowhere, which unfortunately leads one to reverse the traditional burden of proof. That is, it mistakenly assumes the Gospel narratives could be fiction unless proven historical (cf. Luke 1:1–4; 2 Pet 1:16;

---

8. See Blomberg, "New Testament Miracles and Higher Criticism," 433, 436, where he says Jesus' statement to Peter about the coin in the fish's mouth is most likely a "metaphor" (Matt 17:27).

9. Ibid.

1 John 1:1). Here again we see the narrative affirmations in the biblical text bowing to extra-biblical sources for their confirmation.

## CONCLUSION

The consequences of this flaw are further reinforced by Blomberg and Licona when they remind us that history and fiction can be identical in form, and that it becomes difficult for the interpreter to determine where history ends and legend begins.[10] According to Blomberg, Gerd Theissen's sociological view of New Testament miracles and H. C. Kee's analysis of extra-biblical miracle stories should lead us to ask the question, "Is it possible, even inherently probable, that the NT writers at least in part never intended to have their miracle stories taken as historical or factual and that their original audiences probably recognized this?"[11] This he says is the identical reasoning that led Robert Gundry to his unorthodox midrashic interpretation of Matthew,[12] and who was later asked to resign from the Evangelical Theological Society by a 74-percent vote. Three living framer's of ICBI (N. L. Geisler, R. C. Sproul, and J. I. Packer) have attested to the fact that ICBI documents were drafted with Gundry's midrashic approach in mind, and was endorsed by nearly three hundred evangelical scholars from various backgrounds (Presbyterian, Methodist, Baptist, Pentecostal, etc). When asked to comment on Licona's genre-critical approach to the Gospels, R. C. Sproul responded, "As the former and only President of ICBI during its tenure and as the original framer of the Affirmations and Denials of the Chicago Statement on Inerrancy, I can say categorically that Dr. Michael Licona's views are not even remotely compatible with the unified Statement of ICBI."[13]

---

10. See Blomberg, *Can We Still Believe*, 11; Licona, *Resurrection of Jesus*, 34.
11. Blomberg, "New Testament Miracles and Higher Criticism," 436.
12. Ibid.
13. Letter to Norman Geisler, May 22, 2012.

Chapter 26

# Book Review
Craig Blomberg's *Can We Still Believe the Bible?*

JOSEPH M. HOLDEN

## INTRODUCTION

The following reflections offer comments on some ideas put forth by *Can We Still Believe the Bible?* (*CWSBB*), authored by Dr. Craig Blomberg, Distinguished Professor of New Testament at Denver Seminary. Because our central aim is to discuss the various points presented in the work relating to inerrancy, these reflections do not offer an exhaustive evaluation of all points of theological and methodological agreement or disagreement. In addition, we intend to critically review Blomberg's ideas, not assail his motives or personal character as a brother in Christ. Thus, the comments will center on various statements, points, logic, and approaches offered in *CWSBB* as they relate to the doctrine of inerrancy and to the documents of the International Council on Biblical Inerrancy (ICBI). Indeed, the ICBI documents are cited with approval throughout the book,[1] and have been adopted by the Evangelical Theological Society in 2006 as a guide to understanding the meaning of inerrancy; ironically, however, this definition seems to be at odds with some of the content of *CWSBB*.

I enjoyed reading the many relevant topics discussed in the book, finding myself in agreement with most of its contents, including the section on Bart Ehrman and variants, its strong stand on crucial bibliological topics such as the canon and textual

---

1. E.g., *Can We Still Believe*, 273n20.

transmission, as well as Blomberg's general support for the historical reliability of the Old and New Testaments. However, my comments are offered to those who value the traditional understanding of the inerrancy of Scriptures as well as to those interested in maintaining the authoritative nature of the doctrines that flow from them. They are also offered to a broader audience: namely, any Christian who is interested in the effects that a change in this traditional understanding of inerrancy and its undergirding of authoritative doctrines may have upon the evangelical church at large and on its future.

Blomberg is no stranger to controversial views. These include, but are not limited to his ardent support of the use of genre criticism to dehistoricize portions of the Gospels by Michael Licona (using Greco-Roman *bios*) and by Robert Gundry (using midrash), as well as his own expressed doubts of the historicity of Jesus' command about retrieving the coin from the fish's mouth;[2] he considers the passage a metaphorical statement without a basis for its historical fulfillment.[3] In addition, Blomberg has drawn criticism for his alleged doctrinal compromises with his Mormon coauthor, Stephen Robinson, in *How Wide the Divide? A Mormon and Evangelical in Conversation*.

Blomberg's latest work is no exception. Evangelicals ought to be concerned that *Can We Still Believe the Bible?* identifies his acceptance and application of what some have called the "new historiography" or Licona's brand of genre criticism.[4] Licona describes the "new historiography" thus: "The Gospels belong to the genre of Greco-Roman Biography (*bios*).... *Bioi* [pl.] offered the ancient biographer great flexibility for rearranging material and inventing speeches ... and often include legend."[5]

In addition, Licona writes, "Because *bios* was a flexible genre, it is often difficult to determine where history ends and legend begins."[6] Genre criticism has brought grave consequences: Licona has denied a host of historical passages in the Gospels, including but not limited to the resurrection of the saints in Matthew 27:51–54 and the appearance of the angels at Jesus' tomb because they may reflect "poetic" elements or even "legend."[7]

Even though Licona has had to leave several evangelical institutions as a result of his genre-critical assertions, Blomberg's open and vocal support for this alien approach to the biblical text has aligned him with those who either deny or cannot affirm the historical veracity of straightforward narrative passages in the Gospels. Blomberg asserts,

---

2. Ibid., 263n113; Matt 17:27.
3. Blomberg, "New Testament and Historical Criticism," 433–38.
4. Licona, *Resurrection of Jesus*.
5. Ibid., 34.
6. Ibid.
7. Ibid., 185–56, 527–28, 548; 552–53.

> Simply because a work appears in narrative form does not automatically make it historical or biographical in genre. History and biography themselves appear in many different forms, and fiction can appear identical to history in form. Other contextual and extratextual indicators must be consulted as well, including comparisons with noncanonical literature of similar form, in order to determine the kinds of narratives we are reading. Occasionally, what has seemed to many throughout the centuries to reflect straightforward history can now be seen to represent a different genre. . . . Yet once again, unfortunately, a handful of ultraconservatives criticize all such scholarship, thinking they are doing a service to the gospel instead of the disservice they actually render.[8]

This new trend among many NT evangelical scholars seeks to use extra-biblical genre (e.g., as we have seen from Licona and supported by Blomberg,[9] the Greco-Roman *bios* in the tradition of Virgil, Plutarch et al.) to determine the meaning of the biblical text. In particular, the trend promotes the use and application of extra-biblical literature that is discovered to be of similar genre as the Gospels to dehistoricize certain narrative biblical passages that present themselves as straightforward historical fact.

According to Blomberg et al., because of these extra-biblical genres' similarity with the gospel genre, the customary license (i.e., flexibility to include legend, fiction, and invent speeches) and form associated with these extra-biblical authors were most likely employed to write certain portions of the biblical text. It is argued that these extra-biblical texts help inform us which biblical narrative passages are genuine history and which are merely literary effects (i.e., fiction, apocalyptic, poetic, legend, embellishment, etc.) in the "form" of history. Among many other problems, this approach offers the interpreter a confusing dilemma to sort out since, as Blomberg says, "Fiction may appear identical to history in form."[10]

Apparently, Blomberg seeks to free himself, and by extension free modern evangelicalism, from the tenets of an "extreme" view of inerrancy as traditionally defined.[11] He seeks to "nuance" and "[re-]define" inerrancy because of the "unprecedented" understanding of biblical cultures NT scholars possess today.[12] Why is this nuancing and redefining necessary? According to Blomberg, it is because modern evangelicals are now questioning the doctrine of inerrancy (e.g., Kenton Sparks, Peter Enns, Carlos Bovell, Christian Smith). For Blomberg, the traditional position of full inerrancy (that does not recognize that biblical authors employ fiction and error) is no longer defensible. Sadly, according to Blomberg, these "extremely conservative

---

8. Ibid., 11.
9. Ibid., 11, 164.
10. Ibid., 11.
11. Ibid., 10.
12. Ibid.

Christians" who insist on holding to their more "anachronistic" concept of inerrancy and censuring those who seek to introduce their new understandings of the doctrine hinder his genre-critical efforts.[13]

Whatever the motivations may be to redefine and nuance the doctrine of inerrancy, a fair question would be, to what degree? If I proposed to nuance and offer a new definition to the doctrine of the Trinity or the incarnation of Christ, how much latitude would there truly be for such "nuancing"? I'm afraid Blomberg and company are slow to recognize and understand that the inerrancy of Scripture is the fundamental of the fundamentals of Christian doctrine and that the nature of truth is a narrow road; propositions are either true or false by their correspondence to reality, which is not among the tertiary issues that invite intramural debate (e.g., the gifts of the Spirit or the length of the "days" of creation in Genesis 1). Admittedly, inerrancy is not a salvific doctrine that emerges from Scripture, though it is deduced logically from an inductive survey of the whole of Scripture attesting to the facts that (1) God cannot err (John 16:13; Titus 1:2; Heb 6:18) and (2) the Bible is the Word of God (John 17:17; 2 Tim 3:16). Only one conclusion (deduction) emerges from this logic: the Bible cannot err (*inerrancy*).

To avoid this conclusion, one must show one of the two foregoing premises to be false. To which of these premises does Blomberg object? The same kinds of deductions are gathered from Scripture to form conclusions about the doctrine of the Trinity. The inerrant Scriptures are the sole fundamental and essential source from which all our knowledge of these crucial and essential doctrines emerge, and these doctrines are no more authoritative than the God-breathed (*theopneustos*) text from which they emerge (2 Tim 3:16; John 10:35). What is more, since biblical doctrines often emerge directly from historical events, as stated in Scripture (Rom 4:25; 10:9–10), it follows that these doctrines are no more authoritatively secure than the historical truth from which they flow (John 3:12).

One thing is clear: there is a shift in paradigm occurring among evangelical NT scholars who seek to introduce critical methodologies into the inerrancy discussion—and sadly, this shift has resulted in nothing less than the denial of several historical narratives in Scripture. *There can be no doubt that the traditional concept of biblical inerrancy of the Scriptures (i.e., the Bible is without error) is at stake*. In a word:

(1) If the biblical authors use legend, fiction, and speeches that never took place in reality to convey and support the Bible's message, how can we, and the historic church that came before us (as Blomberg's title asks) "still believe the Bible" in all it reports and affirms is free from error or legend?

(2) If truth is that (i.e., propositions) which corresponds to reality, and the Bible says God's Word is truth (John 17:17), how then is the Bible inerrant—without error—if narrative passages includes legend or statements that do not correspond to reality?

13. Ibid.

Part 2—Inerrancy Defended

In a startling admission, according to Blomberg, instead of presuming that the narrative biblical text offers the reader true history, the way to discover whether a passage is really historical is not because the Bible affirms it to be, but rather "extratextual indicators *must* be consulted . . . including comparisons with noncanonical literature of similar form"[14] in order to answer the historical question. On the face of it, this approach mistakenly elevates extra-biblical sources to a status far above the biblical authors' straightforward presentation of historical truth, and makes the truth-value of historical passages relative to non-inspired extra-biblical literature.

## MARGINALIZING FULL INERRANCY AND STANDARDIZING GENRE CRITICISM

The approach promulgated in *CWSBB* is a radical departure from full inerrancy as envisoned by ICBI. Nonetheless, the reader may be left with the false impression that since Blomberg appears to distance himself from the critical theories on the left, and since he asserts many times he is a "mainstream" evangelical (having enjoyed a balanced graduate and postgraduate education), the book's contents are entirely benign and should be considered generally accepted by evangelicals.

However, *CWSBB* is the next installment in a campaign to create space on the evangelical inerrancy spectrum, so to speak, for Blomberg's unorthodox views. In an attempt to gain the book more exposure as well as standardize his genre method on a popular level, a cadre of individuals were enlisted for the book's "blog tour." All contributors offer uncritical applause to various aspects of Blomberg's work without criticism of his genre method or its dubious conclusions. These include Michael Bird, Darrell Bock, Daniel Wallace, David Capes, Nijya Gupta, Craig Keener, Phillip Long, Lee McDonald, Matthew Montonini, Ken Schenck, and Joel Watts. The controversial Michael Licona is conspicuously absent, though I assume he would be one of Blomberg's strongest supporters.

When beginning my journey through the book, I immediately noticed in the preface Blomberg's attempt to legitimize and standardize the book's contents by claiming no "new breakthrough," and that the views are "widely held" in "mainstream evangelical circles."[15] The unwary reader may mistakenly conclude that all the views are time-tested and occupy a well-established part of historical Christianity. Then he wisely qualifies these statements so as to "not claim more consensus than exists." However, note the implication in what follows. Why does he "not claim more consensus than exists"? Because evangelicalism is "fragmented into numerous subgroups."

Thus, if Blomberg's views are held "widely" by "mainstream evangelicalism" as he claims, the "numerous subgroups" where there is no consensus, by his implication, refer to the fringes of evangelicalism (i.e., the far left and far right of mainstream). For

14. Ibid., 11.
15. Ibid.

the left would consider him too conservative and the right would consider him too liberal.

To discover where Blomberg is going with these initial claims, one must realize that to him it is the evangelicals he identifies as on the "far right" of mainstream evangelicalism who pose the greatest threat, since they are openly critical to his view. These are the same evangelicals—and scholars–who hold to a strong view of inerrancy as defined by the ICBI statements and reject his unorthodox genre methodology. He is not referring simply to "conservative" evangelical scholars, but those he characterizes as being to the "far right." How does Blomberg further describe these evangelical scholars? Throughout the book they are called "very conservative,"[16] "overly conservative,"[17] "ultraconservative,"[18] "hyperconservative,"[19] "extremely conservative,"[20] and on "the far right spectrum";[21] they hold "extreme" views on inerrancy and often use the doctrine as a "blunt tool designed to bludgeon" others.[22] Without justification, these scholars are said to be ignorant of the issues and slow to recognize the complexities involved in biblical interpretation (Darrell Bock also affirms this on his blog), which according to Blomberg has led to the "rejection of new developments" in the area of literary genres.[23]

I noticed that Blomberg was careful not to attribute the designation of "scholar(s)" to the so-called far-right extremist evangelicals. Instead they are labeled "leaders" and described as "small in numbers" and "hindrances" to his "genuine scholarship."[24] He says they are deceived in their service to the gospel and actually are doing "disservice" to the gospel.[25] While discussing these "very conservative" extremist leaders who hinder his scholarly progress, the book took a sharp turn for the worse, taking on a dark and disrespectful tone. Blomberg goes so far as to approvingly quote his eighth-grade schoolteacher, who construed a crucial principle she learned through observing our country's battles against Nazism and Communism as saying, "The far left and the far right—avoid them both, like the plague!"[26]

Blomberg has unmistakenly painted those who are critical of his views as representative of these radical, extreme, horrific, and genocidal regimes; he says such extreme critics should thus be avoided like the plague. I was alarmed at the frequency

16. Ibid., 7.
17. Ibid., 217.
18. Ibid., 214.
19. Ibid., 13.
20. Ibid., 7.
21. Ibid., 120.
22. Ibid., 125, 141–42.
23. Ibid., 8.
24. Ibid.
25. Ibid., 11.
26. Ibid., 8.

and nature of the personal attacks directed against those who have criticized his dehistoricizing of the biblical text. And who are these "extremist" evangelicals to whom he refers? You may be thinking he is referring to the "King James only" crowd, who sees that translation as lowered from heaven on a string. No; rather, he is describing scholars such as Norman Geisler (chancellor and Distinguished Professor of Theology and Apologetics at Veritas Evangelical Seminary and a living framer of the Chicago Statement on Biblical Inerrancy); F. David Farnell (professor of New Testament at The Master's Seminary); Robert Thomas (professor of New Testament at The Master's Seminary); William Roach (PhD, coauthor of *Defending Inerrancy*, 2011); and others.[27] All of these have been openly critical of Blomberg's (and Michael Licona's) endorsement of genre criticism.

If the aforementioned scholars are considered far-right extremists, then why not include other living framers of the ICBI documents such as R. C. Sproul and J. I. Packer—or the nearly three hundred scholars who signed the Chicago statement, or for that matter anyone who rejects using extra-biblical genre to dehistoricize the plain meaning of narrative passages in the biblical text? As a matter of fact, R. C. Sproul is on record declaring that "Michael Licona's views are not even remotely compatible with the unified Statements of ICBI. You may use this comment by me however you wish."[28] In addition, J. I. Packer commented on Licona's unorthodox methodology when he writes, "As a framer of the ICBI statement on biblical inerrancy who once studied Greco-Roman literature at advanced level, I judge Mike Licona's view that, because the Gospels are semi-biographical, details of their narratives may be regarded as legendary and factually erroneous, to be both *academically and theologically unsound*."[29]

Perhaps Blomberg would include the thousands of scholars who are members of ETS who also signed a doctrinal statement adopting the "far-right" and "extreme" position (ICBI) as the society's view of inerrancy, not to mention all those who participated in formulating and editing the ICBI documents and the ensuing publications.

Blomberg's attempt to characterize proponents of the traditional position on inerrancy as far-right extremists is unscholarly, unprofessional, and simply false. It is true, without question, that proponents of full ICBI inerrancy are to the right of Blomberg's critical notions—but not because full inerrancy is "extreme," but because Blomberg's genre-critical methodology *can only move one's view of inerrancy to the left*. Why? By nature his methodology assumes the biblical text could be in error unless proven historical and strips away historical truth from historical narrative, which tends in the direction of liberal scholarship and the demythologizing of Bultmann. (I'm looking forward to seeing where Blomberg's evangelical "mainstream" genre methodology *historicizes* passages that previously were considered nonhistorical.) Nevertheless, one

27. Ibid., 120.
28. Letter to Norman L. Geisler, May 22, 2012.
29. Letter to Norman L. Geisler, May 8, 2014, emphasis added.

thing is certain: the "extremist" rhetoric is not helpful to the discussion; it will most definitely hinder any discovery of truth by all involved.

At this point, even before I had completed my reading of the preface and introduction, I wondered what had led the Baker/Brazos editorial board to allow such character-bashing of other Baker authors—Geisler and Roach-Geisler in particular, who has some twenty books published with the group. *CWSBB* was quickly beginning to seem like a venue for Blomberg to grind an axe, not a productive interaction (or "Engagement" as the book's subtitle claims) with ideas critical to his view. It appeared to me that his unscholarly characterizations of and *ad hominem* insinuations against these outspoken scholars was a tactic to make Blomberg's own views appear mainstream rather than foster the discovery of truth through substantive discussion with Geisler, Farnell, Thomas, Roach, et al. A campaign to radicalize counterpoints to his unorthodox methodology (i.e., genre criticism) will almost always attempt to make such a methodology (e.g., dehistoricizing) appear "mainstream" in the eyes of others.

Instead, I was hoping *CWSBB* would respond to, or at least interact with, the problems with genre hermeneutics raised by the orthodox scholars in previously published works such as *The Jesus Crisis* (Farnell and Thomas, 1998), *Defending Inerrancy* (Geisler and Roach, 2013) and the dozen responses offered to Licona over the last three years regarding these same methodological issues. As of 2014, there is even more opportunity to interact with these scholars' ideas, as well as with the ideas presented by a host of contributing scholars, in the recently published *The Jesus Quest: The Danger from Within* (Geisler and Farnell, eds.), which documents the problems and false assumptions associated with questing for the historical Jesus.

I was also hoping Blomberg would have used academically respectable and measured words to his Christian brothers—words in the tenor he used in his conversations with his Mormon coauthor in *How Wide the Divide*.[30] Unfortunately, Blomberg's negative focus on the personal character of scholars critical of his views continues deep into the book, especially on pp. 141–42 (also see 166–68). Here no substantive interaction with Geisler, Farnell, Thomas, or Roach occurred; rather, only stories of alleged personal motives and intentions were offered, stories that contained several factual errors. Some of the more obvious errors include but are not limited to the following:

(1) Dr. Geisler did not "found" Southern Evangelical Seminary; he "*co*founded" Southern Evangelical Seminary.

(2) Geisler did not transition from SES to Veritas Evangelical Seminary (VES); rather, he *currently* teaches at and is involved with both graduate schools. These seminaries were founded after Geisler's retirement at the request of others and not as a result of political and doctrinal differences as Blomberg claims. Moreover, one should not assume to know Dr. Geisler's motives in changing schools, though ironically, this is the same type of "motive" guesswork employed in his genre criticism of biblical

30. Blomberg and Robinson, *How Wide the Divide?*

authors; and it is false logic to identify his (or anyone's) theological and political positions simply based on the leanings of an institution.

(3) Geisler did not lead a "political campaign" to "oust" or "expel" Robert Gundry from ETS as Blomberg claims. Rather, ETS voted to ask him to *resign*.

(4) Gundry's views were not "simplistically presented," but three years of discussion and papers were presented by the ETS membership before a vote (see *JETS*, 2003).

(5) The vote taken by ETS on Gundry was not, as Blomberg claims, "just over the necessary two-thirds majority to expel Gundry." The actual vote, according to the *Christianity Today* reporter who attended, was nearly three-quarters (74 percent) in favor of asking Gundry to resign.[31]

A more thorough response to Blomberg's factual errors presented in *CWSBB* regarding Geisler can be found in Geisler's "Response to Blomberg's *Can We Still Believe in the Bible?*" at www.DefendingInerrancy.com. It truly saddened me, as it should any Christian who believes in Christian brotherly love, to see the disrespectful, condemning, and accusatory tone Blomberg took toward Geisler, a man who is a former president of the Evangelical Theological Society, who has authored or coauthored nearly ninety books, and is recognized as one of the greatest evangelical scholars of our time.

## BLOMBERG'S VIEW OF INERRANCY ALLOWS FOR FICTION AND DEHISTORICIZING BIBLICAL TEXTS

Apparently, the view of inerrancy articulated in *CWSBB* allows for straightforward biblical narrative passages in the Bible to be considered fiction. Here are some twenty unorthodox characteristics of Blomberg's view of inerrancy which also contradict the ICBI view. Blomberg affirms that:

(1) *Inerrancy is consistent in principle with the view that sees named historical persons in the Bible as "symbols."* Blomberg asks, "Must there have been a historical Adam and Eve?"[32] He responds that "nothing in principle should prevent the person who upholds inerrancy from adopting a view that sees *adam* ('man' or Adam) or *hawwa* ('life' or Eve) as symbols for every man and woman."[33]

Article XXII of CSBI (the Chicago Statement on Biblical Inerrancy) affirms, "Genesis 1–11 is *factual* . . ."

(2) *Inerrancy is consistent with some forms of theistic evolution.*[34] Blomberg writes, "Some opt for forms of theistic evolution in which God creates the universe with all the mechanisms built in to give rise, in his perfect timing, to each new development

---

31. Keylock, "Evangelical Scholars Remove Robert Gundry."
32. Blomberg, *Can We Still Believe*, 152.
33. Ibid.
34. Ibid., 151.

of the creative 'week.'"[35] In the next paragraph, he says that "belief in inerrancy, at least as defined by the Chicago Statement, does not preclude any of the interpretive options presented here [including theistic evolution]."[36] But the ICBI framers affirmed that "Genesis 1–11 is factual, as is the rest of the book."[37] CSBI, article XIX affirms, "We deny that Scripture should be required to fit alien preunderstandings, inconsistent with itself, such as naturalism, *evolutionism*, scientism, secular humanism, and relativism." This includes forms of atheistic and *theistic* evolution.

(3) *Inerrancy is consistent with the belief that Job need not be a historical person.*[38] Nothing is at stake if Job never existed.[39] Blomberg says, "*None of this theology [of suffering] requires Job to have ever existed* any more than the teaching of the parable of the Good Samaritan requires the Samaritan to have ever been a real person."[40] He adds, "Many interpreters chart a plausible middle ground [for the book of Job] between the two alternatives of literal history and complete fiction. . . . There is little precedent for the latter [complete fiction] in the ancient Near East. Epic and legend are usually built around historical characters."[41]

Article XIV states "that the biblical record of events, discourses and sayings, though presented in a variety of literary forms, corresponds to *historical fact.*"

(4) *Inerrancy is consistent with using fiction in the Bible as an adequate basis and illustration of historical reality.*[42] According to Blomberg, "It does not follow at all" that Jesus' statement concerning his own burial and resurrection—"For as Jonah was three days and three nights in the belly of a huge fish, so the Son of Man will be three days and three nights in the heart of the earth" (Matt 12:40; cf. Luke 11:30)—implies that the fish story is historical.[43] According to Blomberg, there is no more reason to assume Jesus' words are referring to a real historical event than J. R. R. Tolkein's *The Lord of the Rings* films when he asserts, "A contemporary preacher could predict that Christians may have to face spiritual warfare of great magnitude, 'just as Frodo and his companions faced life-threatening opposition and dark powers throughout their journey to Mordor.'"[44] In essence, the statement of our Lord of Life concerning the three days he would spend in the grave could be equivalent in truth-value as *The Lord of the Rings* trilogy!

35. Ibid.
36. Ibid.
37. CSBH, art. XXII.
38. Blomberg, *Can We Still Believe*, 155–56.
39. Ibid., 223.
40. Ibid., 156 cf. 170, emphasis added.
41. Ibid.
42. Ibid., 157.
43. Ibid.
44. Ibid.

## Part 2—Inerrancy Defended

CSBI, article XIV affirms, "We deny that any such event, discourse or saying reported in Scripture was *invented* by the biblical writers or by the traditions they incorporated." In addition, article XIII's commentary on truth states, "When Jesus affirmed that Jonah was in 'the belly of the great fish' *this statement is true*, not simply because of the redemptive significance the story of Jonah has, but also because it is *literally and historically true*."

(5) *Ernst Wendland presents a "sane middle ground"* between viewing the book of Jonah somewhere between pure history and pure fiction, according to Blomberg.[45]

In response, the reader is directed to article XIV as quoted in point 3 above.

(6) *James Bruckner's comment* that "it is even possible to hold to the doctrine of inerrancy of the original manuscripts of Scripture and regard Jonah as a *unique parable* about a real prophet" is approvingly cited by Blomberg.[46]

In response, the reader is directed to article XIV as quoted in point 3.

(7) *Inerrancy has "nothing to do at all" with what one decides about Isaiah's composition and formation.*[47] According to Blomberg, NT attestation to the first section of Isaiah is "suggestive" but "inconclusive."

Yet, the reader is directed to read Jesus' quotation of both sections of Isaiah in John. 12:38–41 and his attribution of the quotations to "the prophet Isaiah."

(8) *Inerrancy is consistent with the view that the story of the Rich Man and Lazarus (Luke 16) is "overwhelmingly likely" a "parabolic fiction,"*[48] despite Jesus' affirming that "there was a rich man . . ." (Luke 16:19) and a man named "Lazarus."[49]

(9) *Inerrancy is consistent with Michael Licona's view that the resurrection of the saints after Christ's resurrection as reported in Matthew 27:51–54 may not be historical,* but as "one of the strangest New Testament texts of all"[50] could instead be legend, embellishment, apocalyptic, or poetic.[51] Even though Licona's certainty of this has moderated, yet he has not denied it or his assertion that it is consistent with inerrancy to hold this.

(10) *Inerrancy is consistent with the view that says Isaiah may not have prophesied about "Cyrus" (Isa 45) as the name of a specific individual;* rather, the reference may be a dynastic title.[52]

---

45. Ibid., 159–60.
46. Ibid., 160, emphasis added.
47. Ibid., 161–3.
48. Ibid., 150.
49. See also discussion on parables in the section entitled "Blomberg's 'Fatal Flaws.'"
50. Ibid., 174.
51. Ibid., 174–75; see also Licona, *Resurrection of Jesus*, 185–86, 552–53.
52. Ibid., 162.

(11) *Inerrancy is consistent with the view that says the book of Daniel may have been written by Daniel and his successors at two different times* and combined into one book.[53]

(12) *Inerrancy is consistent with the approach to discovering meaning that says we cannot be assured that narrative passages found in a historical book in the Bible are recording actual history.* Blomberg says, "Once we determine, as best we can, what a passage affirms, *according to the conventions of style, form, and genre,* a commitment to inerrancy implies acceptance of the truth of those affirmations. But *a commitment to inerrancy does not exclude a priori any given literary style, form, or genre* that is not *inherently deceptive.*"[54] Blomberg seems unaware that not only is it problematic to foist style, form, and genre onto the biblical text to determine its meaning, but that style, form, and genre emerge *from* the text's words and sentences. According to Blomberg, "inherently deceptive" means the biblical writers cannot use fiction dressed up in the garb of history in an attempt to lie or deceive. However, he believes, biblical writers have license, like any other writer of extra-biblical Greco-Roman *bios* genre, to offer historical statements *as if* they are true, but in reality they could be fiction, legend, poetic, apocalyptic, inventions, or something else. This is a subtle attempt to redefine error as that which "misleads" (through deceptive intent) and not that which "misrepresents" (regardless of intent). Understood in this way, Blomberg can easily say the Bible never *misleads* but it may have mistakes, fiction, legend, or error in it. The more obviously troubling idea in this approach is that error is defined by its *function* or simply the author's intent to deceive, rather than by its lack of correspondence to reality regardless of the author's intent.

CSBH, article VI says, "We deny that . . . error should be defined as that which willfully deceives." Error is that (i.e., propositions/affirmations) which does not correspond to reality. In addition, how Blomberg plans to discover the writer's *unexpressed intentions* ("illocution")[55] to either deceive or tell the truth is left unexplained.

Article XIII asserts, "We deny that *generic categories* which *negate historicity* may rightly be imposed on biblical narratives which present themselves as factual" (emphasis added).

(13) *Inerrancy is consistent with the view that approaches biblical narratives as not necessarily presenting themselves as factual.*[56] For Blomberg, extra-biblical genre research is *necessary* to determine the historical/factual content of a biblical narrative[57] that presents itself as factual. Unfortunately, we believe this makes the Bible relative to extra-biblical literature and wrongly assumes the Bible could be in error unless proven historical, which favors historical skepticism.

53. Ibid., 164.
54. Ibid., emphasis added.
55. Ibid., 136.
56. Ibid., 168.
57. Ibid., 164.

## Part 2—Inerrancy Defended

(14) *Inerrancy is consistent with the view that "fiction may appear identical to history in form" within biblical passages.*[58] This wrongly assumes the critical notion that the Bible could be in error unless proven historical; again, consider the disastrous consequences of applying this mistaken methodology in Licona's treatment of Matthew 27:52–53.[59]

(15) *Inerrancy is consistent with the view that narrative parables do not require descriptions to correspond to reality.*[60] As noted in point 3, Blomberg says, "None of this theology [of suffering] requires Job to have ever existed *any more than the teaching of the parable of the Good Samaritan requires the Samaritan to have ever been a real person.*"[61]

(16) *Inerrancy is consistent with the view that believes the reader of the biblical narrative can know the author's unexpressed "intentions" and unexpressed "purpose" for writing the text.*[62] In other words, the biblical text's historicity is understood by what the author *intends* to say and is determined by the *purpose* for which it is said—not by what the author *actually* does say in the text. According to Blomberg, the biblical author's intention is often ascertained by a comparison of the biblical text with uninspired extra-biblical literature. How he proposes to know what a biblical author "intended" based on another's intention and literature is left unexplained.

(17) *Inerrancy is consistent with the view that allows fiction into the biblical text without contradicting the belief that narrative Scripture is without error and entirely true (inerrant).* In his section titled "Pseudonymous Epistles?"[63] Blomberg denies that a portion of 2 Peter was written by Peter. Moreover, he asserts that it is acceptable to allow the possibility that other biblical books are similarly pseudonymous, since false ascription of authorship was routine among contemporary writers when one did not want to take credit for another's work.[64] According to Blomberg, there is no *intention* to deceive by employing pseudonymity in biblical works; in fact it was common among Greco-Roman authors.

Unfortunately, with this logic we would also have to consider truthful any sincere well-intentioned cultist offering false doctrine at our front door. Moreover, it defines truth in terms of function and not its correspondence to reality. Further, besides the problem associated with discovering the "intentions" and sincerity of an ancient writer, if Peter and Paul really did not author the books that bear their names, then the Bible is in error for claiming they did. This is tantamount to saying that God (who cannot lie or err) inspired error! Even if extra-biblical writers did this in their day and

---

58. Ibid., 11.
59. See Licona, *Resurrection of Jesus*, 185–86, 552–53, as discussed in point 9.
60. Ibid., 156.
61. Ibid. Cf. also 170. See also "Fatal Flaws" section of this article.
62. Ibid., 170.
63. Ibid., 168.
64. Ibid., 170–72.

according to their custom and convention, this does not necessarily make it acceptable for writers of divinely inspired Scriptures who claim to record revealed truth. How does Blomberg know if God sanctioned and approved this "flexibility" for the biblical authors?

(18) *Inerrancy is consistent with the view that truth need not correspond to reality*; rather, truth is found in intentions, purpose, literary forms, and genre.[65]

(19) *Inerrancy is consistent with the view that biblical authors of narrative portions of Scripture don't always* intend *to record history*,[66] but rather can use fiction. How does Blomberg know these unexpressed intentions? How does he propose to legitimately transfer one extra-biblical author's *expressed* intention to form the meaning of a biblical author's *unexpressed* intention?

(20) *Inerrancy is consistent with viewing as "plausible" and "sane" that some biblical narratives stand somewhere between literal (or pure) history and complete (or pure) fiction.*[67] This implies that biblical narratives could be in error. How is this consistent with full inerrancy as defined by ICBI?

(21) *Inerrancy is consistent with denying the miracle of the sun standing still and the moon stopping in Joshua 10.*[68]

## FATAL FLAWS OF CAN WE STILL BELIEVE THE BIBLE?

Blomberg's methods and conclusions are inconsistent with inerrancy as defined by the ICBI as shown above. This, ultimately, is *CWSBB*'s fatal flaw. However, several comments can be made to elucidate and expand upon this observation and expose other serious flaws—but, in the end, point the way to constructive engagement. This should be the goal of any scholar.

(1) *Room to Improve*. Blomberg could greatly enhance the readability of the *CWSBB* and avoid reader alienation if a few adjustments were made. Most of these could have been avoided by going through the publishing process with an editor who is sensitive to the needs of the reader and to the reputation of the author. It seems these factors may have been jettisoned to accommodate the author's personal goals.

First, eliminate the personal attacks on those critical to the author's views. It makes the reader think the author is angry and personally affected by legitimate criticism. Rather, interact with their ideas.

Second, eliminate the scorn for institutions that have confessions and doctrinal statements, for everyone researches from within some kind of framework. This is necessary to preserve evangelical orthodoxy and identity. This is true for Blomberg as well as Denver Seminary. Besides, Blomberg's comments smack of elitism and ivory-tower

65. Ibid., 125, 170–72.
66. Ibid., 176.
67. Ibid., 156, 159–60.
68. Ibid., 198.

academic snobbery, especially in the eyes of lay readers who may be already suspicious of higher education.

Third, convey ideas with humility and willingness to learn instead of characterizing those who disagree as ignorant, slow, small, extreme, far-right, and anachronistic; as Nazi/Communist, as hindrances, and those who do disservice to the gospel. The reader may think these *ad hominem* expressions carry over to the author's genre research and perhaps blind his objectivity. Moreover, such characterizations send the wrong message to the reader: that the author believes that those he has marginalized have nothing to contribute to the discussion; and that the author himself may be too narrow to consider alternatives. By achieving this, the reader will gain the impression that the author is not so much preoccupied with fraternity and acceptance among scholars, but that this will take a backseat to orthodoxy among believers.

Fourth, be more familiar with the ICBI documents and their application to the inerrancy issues; and be willing to adjust when made aware of the *expressed* intent of the ICBI framers concerning their affirmations and denials and not so much interested in discovering (or speculating upon) the unexpressed intent and purposes of the biblical authors. To disregard or ignore the repeated statements by ICBI framers Sproul, Packer, and Geisler, regarding the academically and theologically unsound nature of Licona's brand of genre criticism (which Blomberg supports as consistent with biblical inerrancy) suggests that Blomberg may not be after authorial intentions. Despite these statements, Blomberg continues to build his new brand of inerrancy constructed in a way that he thinks is defensible in the eyes of everyone. Whatever the case may be, his (and Licona's) new brand of inerrancy is not that which was agreed upon by the ICBI statements or their framers.

(2) *Foreign Bird with a Local Walk?* Evangelical scholars are not immune to alien methodologies and current fads like the "new historiography," which can have devastating effects. The introduction of liberalism and negative higher criticism into North American universities at the turn of the twentieth century and the more recent history of Fuller Seminary's drift, as well as the disastrous effects on Michael Licona's career and reputation among evangelicals, are glaring cases in point.

Blomberg's notions of a sound method of interpretation that incorporates extra-biblical genre as determinative of the meaning of the biblical text were soundly rejected decades prior in the ICBI documents, which have been shown to explicitly contradict his view of inerrancy. It may also reveal that Blomberg has forgotten the lessons of recent history. Utilizing genre criticism in this manner has never, despite Blomberg's claim to the contrary, been considered "mainstream" in the history of the church or within conservative evangelicalism.[69] Dehistoricizing the Gospel narratives through genre criticism is alien to evangelicalism; it is more akin to liberal and

---

69. See Hannah, *Inerrancy in the Church*; Radmacher and Preus, *Hermeneutics, Inerrancy and the Bible*; Geisler, *Inerrancy*; *Biblical Errancy: Its Philosophical Roots*; Geisler and Farnell, *Jesus Quest*; Farnell and Thomas, *Jesus Crisis*.

Neo-Orthodox scholars of the twentieth century. We have no historical evidence that these ideas have ever been in whole or part accepted within classical Christianity's approach to Scripture, let alone been representative of "mainstream" evangelicalism. On the contrary, through an induction of Scripture evangelicals have understood the Gospels to be written as straightforward historical narrative conveying truth (John 3:12; 17:17—if Jesus said, "Your word is truth" how then can it be fiction/legend?), recording the way events actually occurred. Luke's Prologue in 1:1–4 clearly states:

> Inasmuch as many have undertaken to compile an account of the things accomplished among us, just as they were handed down to us by those who from the beginning were eyewitnesses and servants of the word, it seemed fitting for me as well, having investigated everything carefully from the beginning, to write it out for you in consecutive order, most excellent Theophilus; so that you may know the exact truth about the things you have been taught.

The implication is clear: our view of the Gospels recording historical fact emerges from an assessment of the text and is the basis from which the heavenly doctrines and their divine authority flow (John 3:12; Rom 4:25). To approach the biblical text without this presupposition of straightforward history shifts the burden of proof upon those who allow the biblical passages to affirm their own historicity. Frankly, the "old historiography" has served the church well for the last two thousand years.

(3) *Living Dangerously*. It is strange logic to appeal to *non*-divinely inspired literature and its genre (which have no divinely inspired guarantee of truth) to guide the genre critic's determination of what the biblical authors *intended* to say. In fact, there is no way to access the author's *illocutions* (authorial intention)—as Kevin Vanhoozer would say—or for that matter his *perlocutions* (results/purposes) since they are often unexpressed in the text. Any attempt to know these would appear to be guesswork at best. And therein lie the fatal flaws of Blomberg's and Licona's brand of genre criticism.

First, the critic reaches his conclusions not by what the biblical author *does say* but by what he *does not say*. In reality, the critic reaches his conclusions about what the *biblical author* intends to say by what the *extra-biblical author* does *say* (and how he says it). However, truth is not known by what one *does not* say, but by what one *does* say.

Second, the genre critic assumes to know too much: namely, whether or not, and where and when, the biblical author intends to use the same license (i.e., to introduce fiction in narrative form) as the extra-biblical author may have used it. Even if you compare uninspired extra-biblical literature to the Bible, the genre critic would have no way of knowing know whether God or the biblical author's "intended" or "sanctioned" the inclusion of error in the Bible as the pagans did. Nothing short of a séance would even come close to discovering unexpressed intentions in dead authors. The end of such an approach is pure speculation, which in turn overrides the plain meaning of the biblical text in favor of historical skepticism. By what process is the genre-critics assured of God's sanction and intention to include error/legend from another's extra-biblical text into inspired Scripture which claims to be (and must be) wholly true?

Third, since the genre critic does not really know the author's unexpressed intentions, his conclusions can at best be hedged about with terms such as "maybe," "plausible," "probable," "could be," "might be," "seems likely," "middle way," "candidate for inclusion," etc. This does not result in the kind of certainty that inspires confidence in the biblical text nor the critic's method and conclusions.

Fourth, postulations about what the biblical author's unexpressed *intention* or *purpose* can be used by the critic to change the *expressed* affirmation in the text. CSBI, article XVI states, "We deny the legitimacy of allowing any method of biblical criticism to question the truth or integrity of the writer's expressed meaning." Moreover, what assurance does the genre critic have that extra-biblical authors employ literary characteristics such as legend, invented speeches, fiction, and embellished statements couched in historical form *in a God-ordained or God-approved manner*? That is to say, what if God does not approve of the way these extra-biblical authors used their literary "license" to convey their message? God forbid that we use these alien texts to bring the biblical text into conformity with them.

Perhaps here is where the genre critic, who affirms that the Bible is divinely inspired and therefore inerrant, should use the inspired biblical text to gain a more accurate understanding of the *differences* from non-inspired extra-biblical literature and its form. Moreover, many consider the inspired biblical literature to be a unique genre (*sui generis*). If this is the case, perhaps using genre from an uninspired class of literature to determine what is actually historical in the biblical text is unwise and even a category mistake.

(4) *First Things First*. Scholars have consistently argued that allowing the text to speak for itself through the grammatical-historical method *is* the very method genre critics must employ in identifying which genre classification a biblical text must correspond. CSBI article XVIII affirms that "the text of Scripture is to be interpreted by grammatico-historical exegesis, taking account of its literary forms and devices, and that Scripture is to interpret Scripture."

Genre methodology cannot be employed at this *primary* level since that is the very question being sought. In other words, genre identification emerges from the text itself, not the other way around. If this is true, how then can genre determine meaning? Thomas Howe's excellent article "Does Genre Determine Meaning?" in *The Jesus Quest* explores the relationship between genre and meaning, insightfully describing the dilemma confronting the genre critic:

> But, what is the interpreter doing when he reads a text in order to discover its patterns? Is he engaging in interpretation at this stage? It certainly cannot be the case that the interpreter is interpreting the text by employing a certain type of genre classification, for that is the very thing that is being sought. An

> interpreter cannot know the genre of a text before he knows how the text is structured or before he finds the characteristics in the text that suggest its genre. An interpreter cannot discover how a text is structured until he reads the text, grasps the meanings of the words and sentences, and thereby uncovers the structure of the piece. In other words, the genre must be discerned and discovered in the text as one reads it.[70]

There is no doubt that genre classification can enhance our understanding of the meaning of a passage or even qualify our initial understanding of meaning—but genre does not determine meaning.[71] This flows from the idea that genre expectations should not be foisted onto the text, but that genre emerges from the text itself.[72] And if the grammatical-historical interpretation of Scripture is good enough to offer the interpreter an accurate method by which to understand the text's words and sentences in order to discover genre classification, it should also serve the interpreter well in his discovery of the meaning of the biblical text—without imposing *secondary genre literary form* onto the text's *primary material meaning*, which is comprised solely of words and sentences (and not unexpressed authorial *purpose, intentions*, or both).

(5) *Parables Are No Excuse.* Parables are no excuse to dehistoricize narrative or claim the Bible can rightly employ error or fiction to convey its message as Blomberg claims. We cannot deny that Jesus used parables within the context of narrative. According to Blomberg, the Gospel narratives contain "parabolic fiction" (e.g., Luke 16), thus opening the door for biblical authors to use narrative fiction as employed by extra-biblical authors.

To the contrary, though parables are designed to illustrate a particular principle or truth or lesson by use of story, the case can be made they are nevertheless illustrations that correspond to reality in a *general* sense. That is to say, parables most often lack *particular* correspondence to a *specific* person, place, thing, event, or time. However, they do possess *general* correspondence to the way the world actually is. Article XIV of the CSBI describes the relationship between literary forms and factual history when it states "that the biblical record of events, discourses and sayings, though presented in a variety of literary forms, corresponds to historical fact."

The point is that parables are grounded in reality and real historical events that occur in everyday life or are characteristic of the human condition, with all of which the hearers would readily identify. Jesus never offers whimsical, bizarre, magical, mythic, erroneous, fictional, or legendary illustrations, such as unicorns flying over the sea, or necks stretching into the clouds, or rocks debating points of theology with the Pharisees. Rather, Jesus uses *real* illustrations that correspond to reality: farmers sowing seed, prodigal sons returning home, wages being paid to laborers, a man buying a field, building homes on rock vs. on sand, lamps, lights on a hill, salt, labor,

---

70. Howe, "Does Genre Determining Meaning?," 525.
71. Ibid., 528.
72. Ibid., 529.

etc. There is no reason why the interpreter cannot responsibly navigate the parables and account for figures of speech, metaphor, simile, analogy, hyperbole, and the like without classifying the parables as myth, legend, error, or fiction. CSBI, article XIV says, "We deny that any such event, discourse or saying in Scripture was invented by the biblical writers or the tradition they incorporated." Parables would be classified as examples of literary devices that often elevate words above their literal sense without attempting to fabricate a storyline; whereas myth, legend, or fiction belong to a literary genre whose storyline is without historical correspondence to reality.

Further, parables within the Scriptures are usually identified as such, e.g., "He told them many things in parables" (Matt 13:2). At other times, they are identified by nature; namely, they are general and illustrative, not using specific names, places, and events.

What is more, ICBI affirms clearly that "Scripture is to interpret Scripture" (art. XVIII), not extra-biblical pagan literature to interpret scriptural meaning. The Bible's propositional truth-value is not to be determined by uninspired extra-biblical text or the authors' unexpressed purposes or intentions.

(6) *Opening Pandora's Box. Can We Still Believe the Bible?* opens up a Pandora's Box of issues that cut to the very foundation of Christian doctrine. One of the most crucial addresses the notion of Scripture's doctrinal claims. Blomberg does not account for how one could justify the Bible's untestable doctrinal claims such as Christ's position at the right hand of the Father, heaven, hell, etc (cf. John 3:12). If fiction could populate historical claims, what prevents fiction from populating untestable doctrinal claims? What is more, many doctrines flow out of historical events (e.g., atonement, justification, cf. Rom 4:25) and/or are embedded in these events, and if the historical narrative could be fiction, these doctrines would appear to be no more true than the fiction from which they come. Of course, one could simply "believe" these doctrines, but justified true belief would not seem possible under this critical model. We must ask: On what basis and hermeneutical principle are we assured these doctrines are true? Are these doctrines true because extra-biblical pagan literature says they are true? Or, are they true because God (who cannot err or lie) says they are true?

## CONCLUSION

Whatever redeeming value *Can We Still Believe the Bible?* contains—and there is some, as noted in the introduction to these reflections—it takes away at least as much as it gives. In a word, Blomberg's views concerning inerrancy are contrary to the ICBI definition, as seen above. His view appears to be a hybrid that on the one hand has adopted alien historical-critical assumptions and on the other hand is trying desperately to remain evangelical in regard to Scripture (see, for instance, Blomberg's praise for

Donald Hagner's "Ten Guidelines for Evangelical Scholarship" on the blog of Baker Books; Blomberg says the guidelines are "excellent").[73]

In sum, if we cannot trust the biblical authors to convey inspired historical truth instead of Tolkein's "Frodo and his companions," how then can we trust the doctrinal formulations that flow out of redemptive history? Since according to Scripture God or his Word cannot err, still believing the Bible is the easy part. Yes, we can still believe the Bible, but not for all the reasons Blomberg offers. In my estimation, Blomberg offers many reasons why evangelicals *should not* still believe the Bible and *should not* have justified true belief in the doctrines of the Bible. Perhaps the more important question we should be asking is, "Can we still believe the ideas offered by New Testament evangelical scholars?

---

73. Also see Farnell's and Geisler's critical review of Hagner's principles elsewhere in this volume.

# Chapter 27

# Book Review
## *The Lost World of Adam and Eve*

### NORMAN L. GEISLER

THE LOST WORLD OF *Adam and Eve: Genesis 2–3 and the Human Origins Debate* is by John Walton (InterVarsity, 2015), 255 pages. John Walton is professor of Old Testament at Wheaton College and Graduate School. Walton also functions on the Advisory Council of BioLogos.org whose mission is inviting "the church and the world to see the harmony between science and biblical faith as we present an evolutionary understanding of God's creation."[1] The organization affirms "*evolutionary creation*, recognizing God as Creator of all life over billions of years."[2]

Being a graduate of both Wheaton schools (BA, MA), I was especially interested in Professor Walton's book. And having been a founding member of the International Council on Biblical Inerrancy and a co-framer of its statements, I was further intrigued with one of the recommendations of the book by Skye Jethal which said, "We who are committed to the authority of Scripture believe it is inerrant in all that it affirms. Determining what it's affirming is the tricky part, and that is precisely what John Walton helps us discern" (inside front cover).

---

1. http://biologos.org/about.
2. Ibid., emphasis in the original.

## THE AUTHOR'S SUMMARY OF HIS BOOK

The author did his readers a service by summarizing his own thoughts near the end of the book: "Throughout this book, I have offered biblical support for the possibility that humanity was created *en masse* in Genesis 1, that the presence of other people is assumed in Genesis 4 and that Genesis 2 does not intend to offer an account of fully *de novo* material origins. If the evidence should prove persuasive that (1) no theology is dependent on or derived from the traditional assertions of the *de novo* creation of Adam and Eve as the first two humans, who were alone in the world and the direct progenitors of the entire human race, and if (2) sound, faithful exegesis offers plausible alternative interpretations, then we would have no reason to be committed to those traditional beliefs as the only acceptable interpretation. In such a case, inerrancy and the text would not demand them from us, and we would hold them by our preference."[3]

Walton continues, "If it turns out (as I believe it does) that science offers evidence to the contrary, we are free to consider its claims. In other words, if neither exegesis nor theology intractably demands those conclusions that argue against the modern scientific consensus premised on common descent, we have no compelling reason to contest the science."[4]

His consolation prize is that "we can contend that Adam and Eve are theologically and historically significant even if they were not the first humans. We can contend that Adam and Eve are appropriately positioned as fountainheads of humanity even if we are not all their direct descendants. We can contend that humanity has a distinct place in the created order, unique among species, even if Adam and Eve are not *de novo* creations."[5]

## WALTON OFFERS FOUR PRACTICAL REASONS FOR HIS POSITION

(1) *Creation Care*: God has appointed us to be vice-regents to care for this world. "We have the responsibility to maintain the space that is ultimately sacred and ultimately his."[6]

(2) *Ministry*: We need to encourage those in scientific fields in the church "not by making them choose (Bible or science) but by charting a path of convergence and compatibility."[7]

(3) *Evangelism*: "They [unbelievers] have heard that to accept Christianity means to abandon their brains" or "to accept Christ means to reject certain scientific

---

3. Walton, *Lost World of Adam and Eve*, 204.
4. Ibid.
5. Ibid., 206.
6. Ibid., 207.
7. Ibid., 208.

conclusions—a step they cannot take" or "no evolution model is acceptable by a Christian."[8]

(4) *Considering the Future*: "They [our young people] have heard that their revered pastors tell them that people who believe in evolution cannot be Christians."[9] This is why many young people leave the church.

## A SUMMARY OF THE CRUCIAL POINTS OF WALTON'S BOOK

A summary of the critical points in Walton's thesis is necessary to evaluate his book properly. There are many subsidiary issues, but the main pillars of his view are:

(1) The Bible does not teach that a literal historical Adam and Eve are progenitors of the human race.

(2) The scientific evidence supports the belief in macroevolution.

(3) Holding both 1 and 2 is not contrary to the doctrine of inerrancy.

(4) An acceptance of 1–3 is crucial to fulfilling the mission and proper growth of the church.

It is noteworthy that the first two of these points must be true to validate Walton's conclusion in the third point. If either is false, then his overall thesis fails, even if the other one is true.

## ANALYSIS OF THE CRUCIAL POINTS OF WALTON'S BOOK

First we will state each point in Walton's own words, and then we will evaluate it from a biblical and evidential point of view.

(1) *The Bible does not teach that a literal historical Adam and Eve are progenitors of the human race.* This point is dependent on a previous one which Walton grants, namely, that there was a literal historical Adam and Eve. However, he has two significant caveats.

First, he confessed, "I do affirm the historicity of Adam. But I do not consider interpreters who are trying to be faithful to Scripture to be denying inerrancy if they arrive at a different conclusion."[10] Apparently, then, any sincere exegete could deny the historicity of Adam and still be consistent with inerrancy? How about those who deny the historicity of Christ's resurrection?

Second, "perhaps what Genesis is telling us is that *God chose one pair from the rest of early hominids for a special, strange, demanding vocation.* This pair (call them Adam and Eve if you like) were to be the representatives of the whole human race, the ones in whom God's purposes to make the whole world a place of delight and joy

---

8. Ibid., 208–9.

9. Ibid., 209.

10. Ibid., 202.

and order."[11] So, to establish this first point we must show that (a) the Bible teaches us that there was a literal couple, commonly called Adam and Eve, (b) who were the progenitors of the entire human race. Let's take them in order:

(a) There was a literal first man called Adam (who had a wife called Eve). Walton claims that "current scientific understanding maintains that there was no first human being because humanity is the result of an evolving population. The evidence of genetics also points to the idea that the genetic diversity that exists in humanity today cannot be traced back to two individuals—a single pair—but that such diversity requires a genetic source population of thousands."[12] He sees that as no problem since "Genesis 1 and 2 raised the possibility that the Adam and Eve account in Genesis 2 could have come after an *en masse* creation of humanity in Genesis 1, though Adam and Eve should be considered as having been included in that group."[13]

However, strong evidence for the fact that Adam was literally the first human, being made in God's image (Gen 1:27), is found both in the Old and New Testaments, as well as in the history of Judaism and the Christian church. Consider first the biblical evidence.

The cumulative biblical evidence for a literal Adam and Eve is very strong. (1) First of all, Genesis presents Adam and Eve as actual persons and even narrates events in their lives (their creation, naming animals, marriage, fall, and their expulsion from the garden). (2) Adam is presented as a literal being who came "from dust" (Gen 2:7) and will return "to dust" (Gen 3:19). (3) Further, Adam and Eve gave birth to real children who also had real children (Gen 4–5) and had "other sons and daughters" (Gen 5:4). (4) There existed real rivers still known (Euphrates and Tigris, Gen 2:14). (5) Eve is the name of the first woman, and it notes her temptation by the devil (1 Tim 2:14; 2 Cor 11:3). (6) Furthermore, their sons Cain and Abel are listed with other historical persons in Hebrews 11:4. (7) Also, the phrase "This is the history of" (Gen 2:4) is used of Adam (5:1) and later historical persons, such as Ishmael (25:12), Isaac (25:19), Esau (36:1), and Jacob (37:2). (8) Also, Paul affirmed that "Adam was first formed, and then Eve" (in 1 Tim 2:13–14). (9) In addition, the OT puts Adam at the beginning of the genealogy of real people (1 Chron 1:1). (Even Walton acknowledges this as an evidence of Adam's historicity, saying, "It would not be surprising if Israelites in the Old Testament and New Testament times believed that Adam was the first human being."[14] He adds, "Consequently there would be no precedent for thinking of the biblical genealogies differently from others in the ancient world.) By putting Adam in ancestor lists, the authors of Scripture are treating him as a historical person."[15] (10) Also, Hosea 6:7 names "Adam" as the first person who broke God's covenant. (11)

11. Ibid., 177–78.
12. Ibid., 183.
13. Ibid.
14. Ibid., 188.
15. Ibid., 102.

And the NT places Adam at the beginning of Jesus' genealogy of real people (Luke 3:38). (12) Indeed, Jesus referred to Adam and Eve as the first literal male and female united by God as the basis for a literal marriage (Matt 19:4–5). (13) Adam is called "the first man Adam [who] became a living being" (1 Cor 15:45). (14) Paul affirms that "Adam was formed first; then Eve" (1 Tim 2:13; cf. Gen 2:7, 22). (15) Adam, who is compared to another literal human being, Christ who is called "the last Adam."[16] (16) And the Apostle Paul declared that literal death came upon all men because of Adam's sin (Rom 5:12–14). (17) Adam is compared with the literal person of Christ (in 1 Cor 15:22).

## EVE WAS A CO-PROGENITOR OF THE HUMAN RACE WITH ADAM

(1) Eve was also a literal person who, with Adam, were physical progenitors of the human race. For "the man called his wife's name Eve, because she was the mother of all *the* living" (Gen 3:20). Even translated in the present as "the mother of all *the* living," her name (*hawwa*, living or life-giver) "signifies that the woman became a pledge in the continuation of the race, in spite of the curse."[17] Her name also reflects the earlier prediction that the "seed of the woman" (Gen 3:15) would bring life and salvation into the world through her "seed" (offspring). Contrary to Walton,[18] whatever else it may imply it does not exclude being the genetic progenitor. Likewise, a similar phrase "father of all" used of Jubal (Gen 4:21) implies a genetic progenitor since he was the genetic father of all "those [humans] who played" the harp; he was not the father of the organ.

(2) Further, God made them "male *and female*" (Gen 1:27). The woman along with the man were created in God's image. Both were physical beings.

(3) God made Eve from "one of his [Adam's] ribs" (Gen 2:21). This implies a genetic similarity with Adam.

(4) As Paul put it, "For Adam was first formed, then Eve" (1 Tim 2:11–14). Both were made by God, and each was a physical match for the other. And Paul based a theological teaching upon this God-ordained order.

(5) The apostle adds, "woman was made from man" (1 Cor 11:12). Here again these are not, as Walton contends, incidental references on which the apostle bases no teaching.

## WAS A HISTORICAL ADAM CREATED DE NOVO?

President Philip Ryken of Wheaton College presented six significant arguments for a historical Adam: (1) It explains humanity's sinfulness; (2) It accounts for the

16. Ibid.
17. See Ross, *Creation and Blessing*, 148.
18. Walton, *Lost World of Adam and Eve*, 187.

presence of evil in the world; (3) It clarifies the biblical position on sexual identity and family relationships; (4) It assures us that we are justified before God; (5) It advances the missionary work of the church; (6) It secures our hope in the resurrection of the body and life everlasting.[19] He added, "We cannot understand the world of our faith without a real, historical Adam."[20] But Wheaton Professor Walton summarily dismisses his arguments, claiming that "some of these are a matter of interpretation" and "even if we accept without question all these points, we could still maintain that no theology is built on the scientific implications commonly associated with Adam and Eve: that they must (theologically speaking!) be created *de novo*, as the only people at the beginning of humanity and those from whom we are all descended."[21]

Since we have already given the evidence that Adam and Eve were the primal parents of the human race, let me speak briefly of *de novo* creation. Walton defines "*de novo*" as "direct material act of God distinct from any predecessor, and using no biological process."[22]

In response, the literal historical-grammatical interpretation endorsed by ICBI (CSBI, art. XVIII) demands a *de novo* creation of God because: (1) Adam was created from "dust" [not from lower animals], and he will return to dust (Gen 2:7; 3:19; Job 34:15; Eccl 3:20); (2) Eve was made from Adam's "rib" (Gen 2:21); (3) God "created" (not developed through evolution) every living things (Gen 1:21); (4) All acts of "creation" (*bara*) in Genesis 1 (1:1; 1:21; 1:27) resulted from God "speaking" and it occurred. Paul describes the creation of light as *ex nihilo* (out of nothing), "Let light shine out of darkness" (2 Cor 4:6). Darkness does not evolve into light; rather, lightning strikes it from the outside; (5) Every form of life "produced its own kind" (it did not evolve into another kind); (6) Humans were made in God's image, "male and female" which involves bodies (Gen 1:27); (7) Humans could speak and name things from the beginning (Gen 2:19–20; 3:3, 10); (8) Humans had moral capacity and responsibility from the beginning (Gen 2:16–17); (9) Humans had God-consciousness from the start (Gen 3:1–13). (9) Jesus affirmed this was all "from the beginning" (Matt 19:4) and from the "beginning of world" (Matt 24:21). The only normal, literal interpretation of these verses is that the creation of Adam was *de novo*.

## FALSE DISTINCTION BETWEEN AUTHORITATIVE AFFIRMATION AND INCIDENTAL REFERENCE

In order to justify his claim that certain biblical references to Adam have no authority,[23] Walton makes a false distinction between what the Bible teaches *authori-*

---

19. Ibid., 203.
20. Ibid.
21. Ibid., 203–4.
22. Ibid., 204.
23. Ibid., 181, 183.

*tatively* and what it merely refers to *incidentally*.[24] For example, references to Adam in a genealogy are merely incidental,[25] as is the mention of a person believing in his heart. Also, the references to human origins fall into this category.[26]

However, this distinction involves a denial of inerrancy for several reasons. First, the Bible is inspired on whatever topic it *touches*, as well as those it *teaches*. Second, Whatever the Bible affirms (on any topic) is inspired. For whatever, the human author of Scripture affirms, God affirms. The Bible is a coauthored book. So, whatever the Bible says is so, God says is true too. So, if the Bible affirms Adam is the genealogical progenitor of the human race, then it is true that Adam is the genetic progenitor of the race. To deny this is to deny the full inerrancy of the Bible for a form of limited inerrancy.

The ICBI doctrinal statements make this point clear in the following references: "We affirm that the whole of Scripture and all its parts, down to the very words of the original, were given by divine inspiration. We deny that the inspiration of Scripture can rightly be affirmed of the whole without the parts, or of some parts but not the whole."[27] Further, "We affirm that inspiration . . . guaranteed true and trustworthy utterances on all matters of which the biblical authors were move to speak and write."[28] What is more, "We deny that biblical infallibility and inerrancy are limited to spiritual, religious or redemptive themes, exclusive of assertions in the fields of history and science."[29] The official ICBI Commentary on this point declares clearly that "the Bible does have something to say about the origin of the earth, about the advent of man, about creation, and about such matters that have scientific import."[30]

## ADAPTATION VERSUS ACCOMMODATION

In so-called "incidental" references, Walton wrongly assumes an *accommodation* view of revelation wherein God accommodates to the incidental beliefs of the author which are not true.[31] But he never affirms anything that is false. This view compromises the inerrancy of Scripture by claiming that human authors of the Bible sometimes accommodate to error when they are writing. Actually, they adapt to human finitude so that the common reader can understand them, but they never accommodate to error. For example, a parent may adapt to the finitude of a small child by saying "babies come

---

24. Ibid., 201, 206, 208.
25. Ibid., 188–89.
26. Ibid., 186.
27. CSBI, art. VI.
28. Ibid., art. IX.
29. Ibid., art. XII.
30. Ibid.
31. Walton, *Lost World of Adam and Eve*, 201.

from their mother's tummy." But they should not accommodate to error by claiming that "storks bring the babies."

Walton's illustration is the biblical reference to the "heart." He wrote, "To return to the example of thinking with the heart, one could not necessarily claim that inerrancy demands that we believe that the heart is physically the center of the intellect. Inerrancy pertains to that which the text affirms, and we have concluded that physiology is not affirmed by the text: instead ancient views of physiology were accommodated."[32] The error here is childlike. The word "heart" (Gk: *kardia*) as used of the inner human being is not a reference to a physical organ. It refers to the whole inner man or person. As every interpreter should know, the meaning of a term is discovered by its context. And when the Bible speaks of the heart thinking, believing, or living (Matt 22:37; Rom 10:9) it is not referring to the blood pump in the middle of our chest. In short, what the heart (as the whole inner person) should believe is not an incidental accommodated truth; it is a divinely authoritative one.

Professor Walton misconstrues John Calvin on this very point, citing him as though he believed in accommodation to error, when all Calvin was approving was the Bible adapting to our finitude and speaking in common language.[33] What Calvin said was, "Moses wrote in a popular style things which, without instruction, all ordinary persons, endued with common sense, are able to understand."[34]

## WALTON'S REINTERPRETATION OF BIBLICAL TEXT TO SUPPORT HIS EVOLUTIONARY VIEW

Acts 17:26 says explicitly that God "made from one man every nation of mankind to live on all the face of the earth." In addition, not only was Adam the first human being (with Eve his wife), but they became the progenitors of the whole human race. He believes that this echoes Genesis 10:32 which declares that "these are the sons of Noah who descended from Adam, and from these the nations spread abroad on the earth after the flood" (Gen 5:2, 32).

Further, Walton argues that Acts 17:26 is referring to Noah, not Adam, saying of Genesis 10:32 that "this is the only verse in the Old Testament that talks about the origin of the nations as a group and is therefore arguably the verse to which Paul refers [in Acts 17:26]. If that is so, the 'one' that he refers to is Noah, not Adam."[35] He further insists that Paul is referring to origin of "nations" as an ethnic group and not to individual genetically.

---

32. Ibid.
33. Ibid., 202.
34. Ibid.
35. Ibid., 187.

Part 2—Inerrancy Defended

## A RESPONSE TO WALTON'S VIEW ON HUMAN ORIGINS

However, there is multiple evidence that Paul is including all individuals (of which nations are made). First, the word "made" (*epoie[set macron over e]sen*) is used in this same context (*poie[set macron over e]sas*, Acts 17:24) of God making the world (*cosmos*). Second, it is used elsewhere in Acts 4:24 of "the Sovereign Lord, who made heaven and earth and the sea and everything in them" (cf. Acts 7:49–50). Third, it urges all men to seek him (v. 27) and claims that all humans exist only "in Him we live and move and have our being" (v. 28) and, therefore should seek him (v. 29). All this implies a genetic view of human beings who are connected to each other and to this one God by creation. Fourth, Paul elsewhere speaks of "the condemnation of all men" in Adam (Rom 5:12, 13, 17), showing their unity and origin in him. In view of the context, to reduce this text to God forming or organizing nations is to reveal more of a Platonic influence (where the Demiurgos orders the eternal chaos into a cosmos but does not bring it into being). As St. Augustine put it, we are born "with a propensity to sin and a necessity to die."[36]

So, all men spring from Adam genetically. We were "in Adam" (1 Cor 15:22; cf. Rom 5:12). Contrary to Walton, at birth we inherit the "propensity to sin." Since we all come from Adam by a natural process, we share in his fall and inherit his fallen nature. Walton's first point is without scriptural support. Considering the lack of evidence for his denial that there was a literal physical Adam from whom the whole human race sprang, one wonders why Walton has pursued this issue so strongly. The motivation could lie in his second point. If macroevolution is correct and there was no one first parent from which we all sprang, then he either has to (a) discard his belief in the Bible or (b) reinterpret the Bible in view of the modern "scientific consensus" called macroevolution. Walton has chosen the later.

## THE HISTORICAL EVIDENCE FOR A LITERAL FIRST MAN ADAM

There is abundant historical evidence for the belief in a literal first man Adam. It begins in the Old Testament itself. Without space for elaboration, consider the outline of the cumulative case. (1) The Old Testament speaks of a literal from beginning to end (Gen 1–3; 4–5; 1 Chron 1:1; Hos 6:7); (2) The New Testament affirms the same (Rom 5:12–14; 1 Cor 15: 20–21; 15:45; Matt 19:4–5; 1 Tim 2:13–14); (3) Jesus (Matt 19:4–5; Mark 10:6–8); (4) The early church Fathers believed in a literal Adam; (5) So did orthodox Jews (ancient and modern); (6) The Catholic Church and all popes also held the traditional view of Adam; (7) The Protestant Church (Luther, Calvin, et. al.) followed suit; (8) Most Evangelicals have held the same position.

While historical arguments are not infallible, nonetheless, some are very convincing and supplement the biblical arguments (see above). This is especially true

---

36. Augustine, *City of God*, 14.1.

of the cumulative argument which proves to be very strong. And considering the magnitude of the evidence for a literal view of Adam as the first human being, it is little wonder that Walton takes time to offer his counter argument which call for brief comment. He claims that:

1. "The Church Fathers often disagree deeply with one another."[37] *Response*: So do many scientists disagree about the origin of life, but we do not discard scientific evidence because of it. Nor do we disregard good cumulative evidence because of such disagreement.

2. The early Fathers regularly held positions that no one holds today. *Response*: So did early scientists hold views that virtually no one accepts today. For example, current evolutionists disown early evolutionary views of inheritance of acquired characteristics.

3. Their writings were driven by the needs (heresies) of their time, not by what the Bible intended to say. *Response*: Heresies are often the *occasion* for the Fathers clarifying and defending the truth, but they were not the *cause* of it. The basis for truth was the inspired Scripture.

4. They were primarily driven by Christology, not by a text in its ancient context. *Response*: The great creeds were *occasioned by heresy*, nonetheless were usually *based on* sound biblical teaching. There is not necessary disconnection between Christology and their view of Scripture.

5. Most of the time they were not familiar with Hebrew and Greek. *Response*: As helpful as studying the original languages is in understanding the nuances and technicalities of exegesis and theology, their value is sometimes overestimated, especially by the teachers of the languages. All the major doctrines in Scripture can be discerned by the common languages. In fact, some of the great theologians of the church past and present were not proficient in Hebrew and Greek—St. Augustine and Thomas Aquinas among them.

6. They had no access to the ancient world as we do through archaeology. *Response*: As helpful and insightful as archaeology can be,[38] no essential of the faith is impossible to discover from Scripture itself. Further, unfortunately some scholars who are most trained in the surrounding culture are the most tempted to misuse it in misinterpreting the Bible. Even Walton himself warns that "we should note, however, that the Israelites often show marked dissimilarities from the surrounding world. Proper interpretation will recognize both."[39]

7. Walton claimed that the early Fathers did know and expressed some of the ideas he had in his book.[40] *Response*: Contrary to Walton, this would indicate that all of our new ideas are not dependent on studying these new cultures. However, many of

---

37. Walton, *Lost World of Adam and Eve*, 205.
38. See Holden and Geisler, *Popular Handbook on Archaeology and the Bible*.
39. Walton, *Lost World of Adam and Eve*, 199.
40. Ibid., 205.

these new studies are the source of unorthodox teachings entering the bloodstream of evangelicalism.

In brief, the historical argument for the traditional literal view of a first Adam and Eve as progenitors of the whole human race is a helpful supplement to the sound biblical arguments (given above). Combined, they render Walton's speculations about theistic evolution highly implausible.

If the biblical evidence is so strong for a literal first man Adam, one has to wonder why a biblical scholar like Walton has adopted an opposing view. The answer seems to lie in the second main point of his argument—the influence of macroevolution.

## THE SCIENTIFIC EVIDENCE SUPPORTS THE BELIEF IN MACROEVOLUTION?

### Walton's Claim for Macroevolution

While Walton disavows expertise in science, nonetheless, he claims a high degree of certainty about certain scientific issues. For example, he is firmly convinced of macroevolution, including the genetic evolution of the first human beings. Consider the following: "The current *scientific consensus* is that humans share a common ancestor with other species based on the evidence of material (phylogenetic) continuity."[41] "*The modern scientific consensus* affirms that there is material continuity between all species of life (technically designated phylogenetic continuity)." "All species have a common ancestor . . . [This] idea is *almost universally affirmed among scientists*."[42] He adds, "It ['evolution'] is not inherently atheistic or deist. It has plenty of room for the providence of God as well as the intimate involvement of God."[43] He adds, the evidence for macroevolution "is *compelling*."[44]

Walton concludes that there are atheistic evolutionists, but "other scientists, however, accept the concept of common descent, and even some evolutionary models, but view God as one who is creating through a process that features change over time from a common ancestor. This approach is known as 'evolutionary creation.'"[45]

As for evidence for his belief in macroevolution, Walton declares: "With the [human] genome . . . the history is passed on from generation to generation and can be compared to other species. In such a comparison, remarkable similarities become evident that have indicated a material continuity between species, suggesting relatedness of similar histories. Thus the understanding of common descent where genetic analysis

---

41. Ibid., 206, emphasis added.
42. Ibid., 190, emphasis added.
43. Ibid., 191, emphasis added.
44. Ibid., 182, emphasis added.
45. Ibid., 191.

provided evidence of a gradual development that would explain genetic diversity."[46] "The evidence for this shared history uncovered by comparative genomics is *compelling* and would be readily accepted were it not for the belief of some that, if such a history actually happened, it would contradict claims that are made in the Bible."[47]

The added emphases in the above citations indicate Walton's belief in the relative certainty of macroevolution—a field in which he admits no expertise. Yet he feels enough pressure from the scientific culture of the day to yield the long-held evangelical views to this supposed "consensus" and "conform" (cf. Rom. 12:2) to the culture of the times.

## An Evaluation of Walton's Claim for Macroevolution

Several observations are in order. First, evidentially macroevolution is a significant over claim. Its evidence is not only not compelling, it is virtually non-existent. Similarity, so often used as proof of evolution, can be used for a common Creator, not a common ancestor. What is more, recent studies reveal how the similarities are vanishing. The alleged 98 percent similarity between chimps and humans has been reduced to 70 percent. This is about the same as the similarities between a bird and a human. This means there are about one billion genetic letter differences between humans and chimps.[48] This is more than enough to make possible the unique rational, moral, and spiritual qualities unique to human beings. Dr. Sanford adds, "The collapse of the 98 percent identity paradigm demolishes the evolutionary explanation for human origins."[49]

Further, the so-called "junk" genes used to establish evolution has vanished with the discovery of very important functions of these genes. Just as the once alleged 180 vestigial organs that were used to argue for evolution have diminished to zero, the so-called "junk" genes seem doomed to the same failure. Likewise, the evolutionary so-called "junk" genes argument collapses since scientists have now found functions for what were previously thought to be hangovers from evolution like the vestigial organs were once considered to be. Indeed, most "junk" genes are now known to have highly complex functions that are "essential for life."[50] So, rather than opposing the unique creation of human beings, the genetic evidence strongly supports it.[51]

The importance of this point is sometimes lost. Even the noted theistic evolutionist, Francis Collins, claimed that "the evidence for macroevolution that has emerged in the past few years is now overwhelming. Virtually all geneticists consider

---

46. Ibid., 182.
47. Ibid, emphasis added.
48. Sanford, "In the Light of Genetics," 57–58.
49. Ibid.
50. Ibid., 67–70.
51. See Meyer, *Signature in the Cell*.

that the evidence proves common ancestry with a level of certainty comparable to the evidence that the earth goes around the sun."[52] However, the discovery that "junk" genes are not junk but serve highly complex and purposeful roles in bodily functions shows how overzealous and overstated even the "best" evidence for macroevolution is. Nathan Jeanson, Harvard PhD, stated it succinctly: "The collapse of the 98 percent identity paradigm demolishes the evolutionary explanation for human origins."[53]

Further, Walton admits there is absolutely no evidence for the evolution of the distinctive element in human beings known as "the image of God" or in what is commonly known as the human "soul." He wrote: "Human distinctiveness is spiritual. . . . First . . . we can see that Adam and Eve are distinguished from any other humans that may have existed in their time by having been designated as priests serving representatively in sacred space. . . . Second, it is the Christian belief that humans have a spiritual nature. . . . We believe that there is some part of us, in fact, the most important part of us, that survives the death of the body."[54] And "the image of God would be given to humans at a particular time in that history. It would not be detectable in the fossil record or in the genome."[55] The image of God has four aspects: function, identity, substitution, and divine-human relationship.[56] This distinguishes humans from other creatures.[57]

In short, the evolutionary process itself does not account for a human being like the biblical Adam who is created in the image of God. And, as for the rest of the alleged process of leading up to the biblical man, there is no certainty but only conflicting theories. As Walton admits, it is "still under vigorous debate."[58] So much for the serious lack of solidity in Walton's second premise. We turn then to the third premise:

## HOLDING TO A NON-LITERAL ADAM AND EVE AND MACROEVOLUTION IS NOT CONTRARY TO THE DOCTRINE OF INERRANCY

Walton sees no contradiction between his first and second premise—and he is right. The problem is, as we have seen, that the evidence does not support either premise. And, of course, if both are false, then they can be complimentary to each other. But no true conclusion follows from false premises.

However, since Walton brought up the subject of inerrancy, he must have it on his mind. Indeed, both of the schools where he teaches (Wheaton College and Graduate

---

52. Collins, *Language of God*, 49.
53. Jeanson, "Did Adam and Eve Exist?," 58.
54. Walton, *Lost World of Adam and Eve*, 193.
55. Ibid., 194.
56. Ibid., 195–96.
57. Ibid.
58. Ibid., 190.

School) and the organization to which he belongs (the Evangelical Theological Society) require their members to believe in inerrancy. And the latter (ETS) has adopted the famous International Council on Biblical Inerrancy (ICBI) for a guide in understanding the meaning of the term inerrancy. But, as we will see, the ICBI framers are on record as condemning both of Walton's first two premises.

## ICBI INERRANTISTS CONDEMN WALTON'S VIEW OF THEISTIC EVOLUTION

For example, "when Jesus affirmed that Jonah was in 'the belly of the great fish' this statement is true, not simply because of the redemptive significance the story of Jonah has, but also because it is literally and *historically true*. The same may be said of the New Testament assertions about *Adam*, Moses, David and other Old Testament persons as well as about Old Testament events."[59] It adds, "*We deny* that generic categories which negate historicity may rightly be imposed on biblical narratives which present themselves as factual."[60] Further, "*We affirm* that the biblical record of events, discourses and sayings, though presented in a variety of appropriate literary forms, corresponds to *historical fact. We deny* that any such event, discourse or saying reported in Scripture was invented by the biblical writers or by the traditions they incorporated."[61] Again, "*we affirm* that since God is the author of all truth, *all truths, biblical and extra-biblical, are consistent and cohere, and that the Bible speaks truth when it touches on matters pertaining to nature, history, or anything else. . . . We deny* that extra-biblical views ever disprove the teaching of Scripture or hold priority over it."[62]

Further, "*we affirm that Genesis 1–11 is factual, as is the rest of the book. We deny that the teachings of Genesis 1–11 are mythical and that scientific hypotheses about earth history or the origin of humanity may be invoked to overthrow what Scripture teaches about creation.*"[63] The denial is directed at an illegitimate use of genre criticism by some who deny the truth of passages which are presented as factual. *Some, for instance, take Adam to be a myth, whereas in Scripture he is presented as a real person.* Others take Jonah to be an allegory when he is presented as a historical person and so referred to by Christ (Matt 12:40–42). This denial is an appropriate and timely warning not to use genre criticism as a cloak for rejecting the truth of Scripture.

"*We affirm* that any preunderstandings which the interpreter brings to Scripture should be in harmony with scriptural teaching and subject to correction by it. We deny that Scripture should be required to fit alien preunderstandings, inconsistent with

---

59. CSBH, art. VIII, emphasis added in all these citations.
60. Ibid., art. VIII.
61. Ibid., art. XIV.
62. Ibid., art. XX.
63. Ibid., art. XXII.

itself, such as naturalism, *evolutionism*, scientism, secular humanism, and relativism."[64] On the other hand, this does not give one license arbitrarily to reinterpret Scripture to force it into *conformity to secular theories of origins* or the like. For example, if the secular community asserts that the origin of humanity is the result of a cosmic accident or the product of blind, impersonal forces, such a view cannot possibly be reconciled with the biblical view of the purposive act of God's creation of mankind without doing radical violence to the Bible itself.[65]

Finally, "There was . . . complete agreement on denying that Genesis is mythological or unhistorical. Likewise *the use of the term 'creation' was meant to exclude the belief in macroevolution, whether of the atheistic or theistic varieties.*"[66]

In short, the official ICBI view on inerrancy in its written documents by its framers supports a historical Adam, supports the biblical view of creation, and opposes evolutionism and theistic evolution (which Walton embraces).

## A RESPONSE TO WALTON'S PRACTICAL ARGUMENTS

Contrary to his claim, adopting the historic biblical view on inerrancy does not undermine the church; in actuality, it undergirds the church. As the psalmist put it, "If the foundation is destroyed, then what can the righteous do." And by any serious analysis inerrancy is a fundamental of the faith. After all, the divine authority for every other biblical doctrine is the infallible/inerrant Word of God.[67] Let's evaluate his arguments one by one.

First, one fails to see how denying the direct (*de novo*) creation of Adam helps motivate one to care more for God's creation.[68] In fact, one could make a strong argument to the contrary. For knowing "this is my Father's world" should motivate me to care for it with great concern.

Second, it is difficult to see how denying inerrancy and the biblical teaching about a first literal Adam is a path of "convergence and compatibility."[69] Compromise on crucial beliefs does not lead to real compatibility. It leads to chaos. Try compromising on the quality of steel in a sky scrapper.

Third, one fails to see how unless a person accepts theistic evolution and denies inerrancy, they must "abandon their brains."[70] The intelligent design movement has

---

64. Ibid., art. XIX.
65. Ibid., art. XII.
66. CSBH, art. XXII; see Geisler and Sproul, *Explaining Hermeneutics*, 83.
67. The Bible is both infallible (incapable of error) and inerrant (without error). Of course, a book could be without error (a perfect math book) but not infallible, but a book cannot be infallible without it being inerrant.
68. Walton, *Lost World of Adam and Eve*, 207.
69. Ibid., 208.
70. Ibid., 208–9.

attracted some very smart scientists like Charles Thaxton, Philip Johnson, Hugh Ross, Fuz Rana, and Stephen Meyer, to mention only a few.

Fourth, Walton contents that "they [our young people] have heard their revered pastors tell them that people who believe in evolution cannot be Christians,"[71] thus leading them to leave the church. However, this is largely a straw man argument since few actually say "they cannot be a Christian," if they accept evolution. The most conservative usually only say that evolution is contrary to Christian teaching—which is something else. Further, the real question is not whether some may leave the church if the doctrine is taught (whatever it is) but whether or not it is an *important truth* of the Christian faith. And, as for the doctrine of creation, it is certainly an important truth of the Christian faith since both the apostles and Jesus connected it with many significant Christian teachings. For instance, the Bible offers the doctrine of creation as the basis of (or connected to) the doctrines of: (1) human dignity (Jas 3:9–10); (2) governmental authority (Gen 9:6; cf. Rom 13:1, 4); (3) marital fidelity (Matt 19:4–6); (4) ecological responsibility (Pss 14:1; 8:4); (5) ecclesiastical authority (1 Tim 2:13–14; cf. Heb 13:17); (6) family identity (1 Cor 11:3–8); (7) human mortality (Rom 5:12); (8) redemptive activity (1Cor 15:45–49); (9) resurrection reality (1 Cor 15:22); and (10) human mortality (2 Pet 3:3–4).

## SUMMARY AND CONCLUSION

The biblical evidence for one man Adam being the progenitor of the entire human race is strong biblically and historically. But, motivated by a "consensus" of contemporary science, some (like Walton) have attempted to reinterpret the biblical data to fit into a theistic evolutionary scheme. However, a strong group of intelligent design scientists have eroded the genetic basis for macroevolution. And an examination of the strained biblical exegesis of Wheaton's professor Walton has left the whole Biologos evolutionary dreams (to convert evangelical Christianity to theistic evolution) without biblical, historical, or scientific grounds.

The Bible is clear, Adam was the "first man" (1 Cor 15:45) and God "made from one man every nation of mankind to live on all face of the earth" (Acts 17:26). Further, "Therefore, just as through one man sin entered into the world, and death through sin, and so death spread to all men, because all sinned . . . death reigned from Adam until Moses, even over those who had not sinned in the likeness of the offense of Adam, who is a type of Him who was to come" (Rom 5:12–14). This is what I was taught at Wheaton a generation ago and have been teaching it ever since.

However, a new generation has arisen that knows not Kantzer, Culver, and Kaiser. They have convinced themselves from extra-biblical sources, in whose light they reinterpret the Bible, that Adam was not the first man; that his body is genetically

---

71. Ibid., 209.

the same as other early hominids, that all humans are not Adam's descendants; that human death is not the result of Adam's sin, and that Darwin was basically right about common ancestry! All I can say is that this is not the Wheaton I knew, nor is it the one to which I can recommend my grandchildren.

Chapter 28

# An Exposition and Refutation of the Key Presuppositions of Contemporary Jesus Research

## PHIL FERNANDES

Before the late eighteenth century, leading thinkers of Western Civilization usually assumed the reliability of the New Testament. Hence, these thinkers considered "the Jesus of the Bible" (also known as "the Jesus of Faith") to be identical with "the Jesus of history." No distinction was drawn between the biblical portrait of Jesus and the Jesus of history. But as the nineteenth century approached, the intellectual climate in Western culture had changed due to a major shift in Western philosophical thought. Human reason was elevated and miracles were discounted as mere superstitions of the uneducated masses of past centuries. When this thinking was applied to the Scriptures, a great divide was erected separating "the Jesus of Faith" from "the Jesus of history."

### RENE DESCARTES AND THE ELEVATION OF HUMAN REASON

Although a professing Christian, Rene Descartes (1590–1650) is considered by many to be the thinker responsible for the elevation and exaltation of human reason above God's revelation in Scripture. This high view of human reason ultimately led to Modernism—the attempt to find all truth and solve all problems through unaided human reason.[1] Though he was a rationalist, Descartes used skepticism as a method to find truth. He decided to doubt everything until he could find something that could not be doubted. This would be a point of certainty from which he could deduce all other knowledge. The more Descartes doubted, the more he became aware of the existence

---

1. Grenz, *Primer on Postmodernism*, 63.

of the doubter—himself. Since doubting is a form of thinking, Descartes proclaimed his famous phrase "cogito ergo sum"—"I think therefore, I am."

Thus began the modern project and the "Age of Reason" (i.e., the Enlightenment). Modernism was characterized by the attempt to find all truth with certainty through unaided human reason. But, if man through unaided human reason could find all truth, then what need is there for revelation from God? This led to deism (the belief in a God who does not perform miracles) and atheism (the belief that no God exists). The supernatural realm was eventually rejected, and the dominant perspective of Western culture became characterized by an atheistic or deistic mindset as well as a bold confidence in the power of unaided human reason to find truth and solve the problems which mankind faced.[2] Hence, Descartes's attempt to defend Christianity failed, for Modernism is no friend of Christianity.

## SPINOZA AND HUME'S REJECTION OF MIRACLES

Descartes's glorification of human reason paved the way for other thinkers who followed him. Future thinkers used human reason to sit in judgment on the Bible and decide what should be accepted as historically authentic from the Bible as opposed to what the rational person should reject from the Bible. The strongest philosophical argumentation against miracles came from the pens of Benedict Spinoza (1632–1677) and David Hume (1711–1776).

Spinoza was a pantheist.[3] He believed in an impersonal god that was identical to the universe. He reasoned that an impersonal god could not choose to perform miracles, for only personal beings make choices. Whatever an impersonal god does, it must do by necessity. Spinoza believed that nature necessarily operates in a uniform manner. Therefore, he argued that the laws of nature cannot be violated. Since miracles would be violations of the laws of nature, they are impossible.[4]

David Hume was a deist. He believed that after God created the universe, he no longer involved himself with his creation. Hume reasoned that miracles, if they occur, are very rare events. On the other hand, the laws of nature describe repeatable, everyday occurrences. Hume argued that the wise man will always base his beliefs on the highest degree of probability. Since the laws of nature have a high degree of probability while miracles are improbable, Hume considered the evidence against miracles always greater than the evidence for miracles. Therefore, according to Hume, the wise man will always reject the proposed miracle.[5]

Thus the thought of Spinoza and Hume dealt a damaging blow to the biblical account of a supernatural Jesus, for the supernatural was rejected *a priori* (before an

---

2. Ibid., 64.
3. Geisler, *Miracles and the Modern Mind*, 18.
4. Ibid., 15.
5. Hume, *Inquiry concerning Human Understanding*, 117–41.

examination of the evidence). All liberal New Testament studies and liberal quests for the true Jesus of history have begun with this presupposition—miracles are impossible. If one wishes to defend the biblical portrait of a miracle-working, divine Jesus, one must first refute the arguments against miracles proposed by Spinoza and Hume.

## LESSING'S CONTRIBUTION TO JESUS STUDIES

The application of the philosophical rejection of miracles to biblical studies can be traced back to Gotthold Ephraim Lessing (1729–1781). Lessing was a critic of the Bible who denied biblical inerrancy. He taught that religious beliefs could not be proven through reason or historical evidences.[6] He was a fideist—he held that faith rested on subjective experience rather than on objective evidence. He believed that religions should be judged by their effect on the moral conduct of their followers. Evidence for or against religious truth claims were irrelevant.

Lessing imagined an "ugly ditch" between faith and historical facts.[7] This ditch could not be crossed. No one could know for sure if the Jesus of the Gospels is in fact the true Jesus of history. Religious beliefs could not be defended by appealing to objective facts. Only practical results could be used to determine the worth of a religious system. Testing religious truths is a subjective, inward task. Any appeal to objective evidence is futile.

Christian theologian Gregory Boyd states that "from 1774–1778, Gotthold Lessing published a number of 'fragments' of a text that was clearly written from a deist perspective."[8] Though Lessing claimed he did not know the identity of the anonymous author, Boyd relates that "these fragments were eventually confirmed to have come from the pen of Hermann Samuel Reimarus (1694–1768), a German professor of Semitic languages."[9] Apparently, Reimarus's daughter gave the fragments to Lessing shortly after her father's death. The seventh fragment was called *On the Intention of Jesus and His Disciples*. In this fragment, Reimarus argued for a sharp distinction between the true Jesus of history and the Jesus found in the Gospels. Thus began the first quest for the historical Jesus.

## THE FIRST QUEST FOR THE HISTORICAL JESUS

Hermann Samuel Reimarus (1694–1768) was the first scholar to clearly differentiate between the Jesus of history and the Jesus of the New Testament.[10] As a deist, he could not accept the miraculous, divine Jesus of the Scriptures as a real historical per-

6. Copleston, *History of Philosophy*, bk. 2, vol. 6, 126–31.
7. Erickson, *Word Became Flesh*, 115.
8. Boyd, *Cynic Sage or Son of God?*, 20–21.
9. Ibid.
10. Strimple, *Modern Search for the Real Jesus*, 16–19.

son. Reimarus proclaimed a natural religion of reason, a religion devoid of miracles. He proposed his theory that Jesus conceived of his kingdom in purely political terms, but he utterly failed to usher in God's kingdom by failing to defeat the Romans. In short, Jesus was an unsuccessful revolutionary who was executed by the Romans. Reimarus attempted to explain away the New Testament accounts of Jesus' resurrection by speculating that the apostles stole the body of Jesus and fabricated the stories of the post-death appearances of Christ.[11] In essence, the Jesus of Faith (i.e., the biblical Jesus) was nothing more than the lies proclaimed by the apostles. Reimarus never explained why the apostles would be willing to die for their lies; still, his influence on the future of Jesus research was enormous.

H. E. G. Paulus (1761–1851) tried to defend Christianity from the deistic attacks it had suffered at the hands of Reimarus. Unfortunately, Paulus viewed true religion as having nothing to do with miracles; instead, true Christianity is the highest level of moral teaching. He emphasized the ethical aspects of Christianity while ignoring the eschatological focus Jesus had on God's coming kingdom. Paulus believed the Bible was written during prescientific, superstitious times. He did not deny the historical events recorded in the New Testament; he reinterpreted these events in a non-miraculous way. In the case of the resurrection accounts, Paulus argued that the apostles did not lie—they were mistaken. Jesus did not actually die on the cross; he merely "swooned" or passed out on the cross and was mistaken for dead by those who placed him in the tomb. Jesus later revived and the apostles mistook him for having been raised from the dead.[12] Hence, Paulus portrayed Jesus as a non-miraculous, moral teacher. He rejected Jesus as the miraculous God-man who died for our sins and rose from the dead. Again, a wall was erected dividing the Jesus of faith from the Jesus of history.

David Friedrich Strauss (1808–1874) published his work *The Life of Jesus Critically Examined* in 1835 when he was only twenty-seven years old.[13] Strauss, like the scholars who preceded him, rejected the possibility of miracles. Still he disagreed with Reimarus's view (the miracles of Jesus were lies) and Paulus's view (the apostles were naïve and deceived into believing Jesus rose and performed miracles). Rather, Strauss concluded that the apostles were recording myths—they were teaching spiritual truth by telling stories. In this interpretation of the Gospels, the apostles were not guilty of being naïve, nor were they deceivers. They were merely using myths as a means to convey spiritual truth.[14] According to the theory of Strauss, "myth is not to be viewed as a distortion of the essential gospel message but rather as the communicative medium of that message."[15] For Strauss, religion portrays the truth in symbolic and

---

11. Boyd, *Cynic Sage or Son of God?*, 20–23.
12. Strimple, *Modern Search for the Real Jesus*, 20–24.
13. Ibid., 27.
14. Moore, "Quest for the Historical Jesus," 174–75.
15. Strimple, *Modern Search for the Real Jesus*, 30.

earthly terms. He believed that when we search for historical truth, we must begin by eliminating the supernatural, for the laws that govern nature are universal—they allow no exceptions.[16]

Adolph von Harnack (1851–1930) realized that, up to his day, the search for the historical Jesus "had produced many divergent and contradictory pictures of the 'historical Jesus.'"[17] Von Harnack decided to take a different approach by ignoring any attempt to discover the events of the life of Jesus; instead he chose to simply focus on the teachings of Jesus.[18] In 1900 von Harnack wrote *What Is Christianity*, a work which eliminated any reference to eschatology (i.e., issues such as the end time judgment, return of Christ, etc.) and molded the teachings of Jesus so that they were compatible with nineteenth-century liberal theology (denial of miracles, inherent goodness of man, no need for salvation from sin, etc). Von Harnack accommodated the message of Jesus to the dominant philosophies of his day by removing any "offensive" material from the teachings of Christ.[19] Therefore, von Harnack removed any reference to miracles, the end time judgment, and eternal damnation.[20]

Albert Schweitzer (1875–1965) is credited for putting an end to the first quest for the historical Jesus.[21] In his work *The Quest for the Historical Jesus*, Schweitzer argued that if one rejects the overwhelming presence of Jesus' eschatological teachings, the end result will be a Jesus created in the image of the scholar doing the investigation.[22] Schweitzer brought to the forefront Jesus' teachings about the end of days. Unfortunately, however, Schweitzer also created a Jesus in his own image. Schweitzer taught that though Jesus predicted he would usher in the kingdom of God during his lifetime, he failed to do so.[23] Schweitzer's thesis (i.e., the historical Jesus cannot be separated from his teachings about the end times) was so unpopular in scholarly circles that when he submitted his dissertation at the university he attended, it was rejected.[24]

## THE PERIOD OF "NO QUEST"

The period from the printing of Schweitzer's work *The Quest for the Historical Jesus* in 1906 until the end of World War II is now known as the period of "no quest."[25] In the 1930s Rudolph Bultmann (1884–1976) proclaimed that almost nothing can be known

16. Ibid., 33.
17. Moore, "Quest for the Historical Jesus," 175.
18. Ibid., 175–76. See also Kee, *Jesus in History*, 24.
19. Moore, "Quest for the Historical Jesus," 176.
20. Ibid., 177.
21. Ibid.
22. Ibid., 176, 178. See also Schweitzer, *Quest for the Historical Jesus*, 396.
23. Strimple, *Modern Search for the Real Jesus*, 82.
24. Moore, "Quest for the Historical Jesus," 178.
25. Ibid.

about the Jesus of history.[26] He believed that the Gospels were so filled with legendary material that it was no longer possible to find the historical Jesus on their pages. This expressed the general climate of this period. The quest for the historical Jesus had been dismissed as a failure. As an alternative to the Jesus quest, Bultmann proposed that the real Jesus was to be found in the preaching of the church, not in the Jesus who lived in history. What Jesus did or said was no longer considered important. All that mattered was what was believed and proclaimed about him in the church.

During this period, following Bultmann's lead, New Testament scholars gave up searching for the true Jesus of history—they believed he could not be found. All that mattered was the Christ of faith—the Jesus proclaimed by the church. However, these scholars, due to their bias against miracles, believed that the Christ of faith was different from the Jesus of history. Their view concerning the historical Jesus was one of total skepticism.

## THE SECOND QUEST FOR THE HISTORICAL JESUS

The "new quest" is also known as the "second quest." This search for Jesus was started just after World War II by former students of Bultmann. These scholars came to disagree with their mentor's assertion that nothing could be known about the historical Jesus. Thus began the "second quest" for the Jesus of history. Unfortunately, this group of scholars, like Bultmann and the scholars associated with the first quest before him, continued to reject anything miraculous found in the Scriptures. Their bias against miracles dictated that they repudiate much of the New Testament portrait of Jesus.[27]

Norman Perrin from the University of Chicago was a famous representative of the second quest for the historical Jesus. In 1974 he listed what he and his colleagues considered well-established facts about the life of Jesus. According to New Testament scholar Craig Blomberg, in his article titled "Where Do We Start Studying Jesus?," Perrin's list included: Jesus' baptism by John, his proclamation of the present and future kingdom of God, his teaching in parable, his gathering of disciples, his Last Supper, opposition from the Jewish religious leaders of Jesus' day, his arrest and trials, his being charged with blasphemy by the Jewish religious leaders and sedition by the Romans, and his death by crucifixion.[28] Though this list admitted we could know much about the Jesus of history, a large portion of the Gospel material concerning Jesus was rejected. The growing dissatisfaction with this led numerous scholars to embark on the "third quest" for the historical Jesus.

---

26. Bultmann, *Kerygma and Myth*, 1–44.
27. Moore, "Quest for the Historical Jesus," 183–85.
28. Blomberg, "Where Do We Start," 25–26.

## THE THIRD QUEST FOR THE HISTORICAL JESUS

The third quest began in the early 1980s. The defining aspect of the third quest for the historical Jesus is the emphasis on placing Jesus in his first-century, Jewish cultural context. Any description of Jesus that does not account for this is usually rejected by the scholars of this quest.[29] Both liberal and conservative New Testament scholars in this quest attempt to place Jesus in his Jewish culture. Blomberg states that "the most significant observation about the third quest is that none of its major contributors are evangelical Christians."[30] Blomberg lists some of the world's leading New Testament scholars who are at the forefront of the third quest for the historical Jesus. This list includes: Ben Meyer of McMaster University, E. P. Sanders of Duke University, James Charlesworth of Princeton University, Geza Vermes of Oxford, Richard Horsley of the University of Massachusetts, Gerd Theissen of Heidelberg, and A. E. Harvey of Oxford.[31] All of these scholars, as well as many others, paint a believable portrait of Jesus by viewing him through the lenses of first-century Judaism. And, contrary to the scholars of the former quests, many of the details of the New Testament Jesus are recovered. The skepticism of Rudolph Bultmann concerning the historical Jesus has been replaced by a confidence that, through serious historical research, we can uncover much about the true Jesus of history.

The only exception among current New Testament scholarship today is that of the Jesus Seminar. This group of scholars and their disciples (not all members of the Jesus Seminar have established their scholarship in the area of New Testament studies) are a throwback to an earlier time when skepticism reigned concerning the historical Jesus. Contrary to the American media's portrayal of the Jesus Seminar as mainstream, the views and the conclusions of the Jesus Seminar are considered radical by the majority of New Testament scholars belonging to the third quest.

## IDENTIFYING THE PRIMARY LIBERAL PRESUPPOSITIONS FOR JESUS RESEARCH

When one examines the history of Jesus research and the conclusions drawn by the researchers, several of their presuppositions become evident. It should be noted that these scholars were theologically liberal—they rejected traditional Christian beliefs such as the deity of Christ, the doctrine of the Trinity, and the divine inspiration of the Bible. Although these critics claim to have proven much, their conclusions are contradictory (they lead to several totally different and irreconcilable descriptions of Jesus' life) and are based upon assumptions that have no evidential basis in history. They go where their biases lead them, not where the evidences point. After examining

---

29. Habermas, *Historical Jesus*, 24.
30. Blomberg, "Where Do We Start," 27.
31. Ibid., 26.

a list of liberal presuppositions, we will attempt to identify the primary assumptions that form the foundation for the other presuppositions.

First, the liberal New Testament scholars believed they needed to search for the "real" Jesus of history because they assumed that miracles are impossible. Since they deny miracles, they cannot acknowledge the existence of a miracle-working, divine Jesus who bodily rose from the dead. Hence, they assume that the "real" Jesus of history must be a non-miraculous first-century Jew. The important issue is this: they never disprove the miraculous, divine Jesus of the Bible; they merely assume his nonexistence and then speculate to try to produce an alternative, non-supernatural Jesus. This anti-supernaturalistic bias of liberal Jesus scholars leads them to make several other unreasonable assumptions and dictates their unorthodox conclusions. Christian scholar Gregory Boyd, in his thoroughly researched book *Cynic Sage or Son of God*, commented on this foundational liberal bias that jump-started the search for the so-called "historical Jesus." Boyd states:

> It is this deistic Enlightenment mind-set that supplied both the historical-critical method and the quest for the historical Jesus with their original philosophical and religious presuppositions. Chief among these presuppositions was the rejection of the ideas of the supernatural and divine revelation, presuppositions that were, a priori, at odds with the biblical worldview and its claims. . . . These presuppositions entail that the search for the "historical" Jesus is, almost by definition, a search for an alternative, "de-supernaturalized" Jesus.[32]

Second, liberal New Testament scholars believe the New Testament books should be viewed as false until proven true. This contradicts the approach scholars take when studying non-biblical, ancient documents: they consider all other documents true until evidence can be produced calling their reliability into question. There is no reason for someone to be biased against the New Testament books before examining and researching their historical background.

Third, liberal scholars tend to assume the latest date possible for each book. Since liberal scholars reject the miracle-working, divine Jesus, they do not want to acknowledge that the New Testament books were written by eyewitnesses or people who knew eyewitnesses. The later the date for the composition of each book, the easier it is for scholars to doubt that it reports historically accurate information.

Fourth, the writers of the New Testament books, especially the four Gospels, are biased accounts (i.e., propaganda) because they were written by believers—followers of Jesus. There is no good reason to assume that the followers of Jesus were not capable of recording accurate information about their rabbi. Liberal critics assume the Gospels are biased accounts in order to prove they are biased accounts. In short, they are guilty of circular reasoning.

---

32. Boyd, *Cynic Sage or Son of God?*, 23.

Fifth, liberal scholars assume that the apparent contradictions in the Gospel accounts cannot be resolved, and that these contradictions prove that the accounts, as a whole, cannot be trusted. First, even if there are contradictions in the Gospels, a point contested by conservative scholars, if these contradictions deal only with peripheral issues, then there would still be good reason to accept the reliability of the main events being recorded since the Gospels agree on these points. For instance, all four Gospels agree that Jesus was a miracle-worker who claimed to be the Savior and was tried by Pontius Pilate, sentenced to death by crucifixion, but rose from the dead on the third day after his death. There is no reason to reject these accounts of Christ's miracles, teachings, death, and resurrection merely because the minor details of the accounts may be difficult to harmonize. Law enforcement investigators encounter this phenomenon on a regular basis—eyewitnesses often report the same events from different perspectives and may even seem to contradict each other until further questioning explains the differences. Second, New Testament scholar N. T. Wright states that the harmonizing of distinct accounts of the same event is a normal part of historical studies when dealing with more than one source. Wright states:

> I am, after all, suggesting no more than that Jesus be studied like any other figure of the ancient past. Nobody grumbles at a book on Alexander the Great if, in telling the story, the author "harmonizes" two or three sources; that is his or her job, to advance hypotheses which draw together the data into a coherent framework rather than leaving it scattered.[33]

Sixth, liberal scholars (and now many conservative scholars who follow their lead) assume that Mark's Gospel was written first, and that Matthew and Luke borrowed much of their material from Mark. It is also assumed that John's Gospel was written much later than the other three. According to liberal scholars, none of the four Gospels was written by an eyewitness. This contradicts the unanimous testimony of the early church. In an interview with Strobel, Blomberg states:

> The uniform testimony of the early church was that Matthew, also known as Levi, the tax collector and one of the twelve disciples, was the author of the first Gospel in the New Testament; that John Mark, a companion of Peter, was the author of the Gospel we call Mark; and that Luke, known as Paul's "beloved physician," wrote both the Gospel of Luke and the Acts of the Apostles. . . . There are no known competitors for these three Gospels. . . . Apparently, it was just not in dispute.[34]

Strobel points out that the case for the traditional authors of Matthew, Mark, and Luke is strengthened by the fact that they were unlikely candidates. Mark and Luke were not even of the original twelve apostles, while Matthew was known as a former

---

33. Wright, *Contemporary Quest for Jesus*, 36–37.
34. Blomberg interviewed by Strobel, *Case for Christ*, 22–23.

tax collector, a profession that aroused hatred in many first-century Jews.[35] If the early church invented the names of the authors of the first three Gospels, they would have most certainly chosen names from among the twelve apostles, but not one who was a former tax collector, considered a traitor by many Jews.

Strobel admits that there is some difficulty in identifying the author of the Gospel of John.[36] This is due to the fact that an early church father named Papias, writing about AD 125, speaks of John the Apostle and John the elder.[37] It is unclear if Papias considered them two separate people or two different ways to refer to the Apostle John. Whatever the case, Blomberg, in his interview with Strobel, states that apart from the ambiguous passage from Papias, "the rest of the early testimony is unanimous that it was John the Apostle—the son of Zebedee—who wrote the Gospel."[38]

Seventh, liberal New Testament critics presuppose that Paul did not accurately represent the original beliefs of Christianity; supposedly, he was an innovator whose beliefs differed from the original Jerusalem church. Though liberal scholars agree that Paul wrote his letters between AD 49 and 67, they claim he invented doctrines such as Jesus' resurrection, his deity, his claim to be Messiah, and his death for the sins of the world. Liberal scholars acknowledge that Paul is the author of Galatians; yet, in this letter, Paul claims that he and Barnabas received the right hand of fellowship from the leaders of the Jerusalem church (i.e., Peter, James, and John) in the late AD 40s (Gal 2:1–10). Most scholars, even of the most liberal sort, would admit that Paul was an honest man. Hence, it is hard to believe that the gospel Paul preached was any different in important aspects to the gospel preached by the first-generation Jerusalem church.

Eighth, liberal New Testament scholars assume that there had to be an original non-supernatural collection of the original sayings of Jesus. They call this imaginary document "Q" from the German word *quelle* which means source. "Q" consists of the sayings of Jesus found in both Matthew's Gospel and Luke's Gospel, but are absent in Mark's Gospel. The belief in "Q" is now so widespread that even many conservative scholars accept the existence of "Q." Liberal critics assume the existence of this ancient sayings document merely because they assume that Jesus was primarily a teacher and a speaker who did not really perform miracles. These critics believe that the gospel was originally the sayings of Jesus, and that, years later, fictional events were added to these sayings. However, this is circular reasoning. These scholars assume that the miraculous works of Christ are not in the original manuscripts in their attempt to prove that Jesus was not a miracle-worker.

Ninth, many liberal scholars believe that the early church was not concerned with recording accurate history. It is assumed that the authors of the New Testament

---

35. Ibid., 23.
36. Ibid.
37. Lightfoot and Harmer, *Apostolic Fathers*, 528.
38. Blomberg, interviewed by Strobel, *Case for Christ*, 23.

books were superstitious and prescientific, and therefore unable to separate fact from fiction. Supposedly, the apostles did not have any real interest in reporting accurate history. However, we have much recorded history from this period, showing that ancient Jews were concerned with history. The writings of the Jewish historian Josephus (AD 37–97) are an example of a first-century Jew who attempted to record accurate history.

Tenth, New Testament critics believe that the similarities found in the Gospels of Matthew, Mark, and Luke prove that the authors borrowed material from each other's writings. However, there are other possible ways to explain these similarities. First, the apostles may have taken notes or memorized many of Jesus' teachings. Second, the apostles may have kept copies of these notes. Third, if the Gospel authors were eyewitnesses of Jesus' ministry or knew eyewitnesses of Jesus' ministry, this would explain much of the similarities found in the four Gospels, especially the first three (Matthew, Mark, and Luke).

Eleventh, these critics, at the start of their investigation, assume that the Jesus of the Gospels is not the true Jesus of history. Since they reject the possibility of miracles, they cannot accept the miracle-working Jesus portrayed in the pages of the New Testament. Hence, they are forced to try to discover a non-miraculous Jesus in history. This is a crucial point: they have not proven that the true Jesus of history is not the Jesus of the Gospels—they assume this to be the case before they began their investigation.

Twelfth, they assume that Matthew, Mark, and Luke are closer to the historical Jesus than the Jesus of the Gospel of John. Because it appears that John emphasizes Jesus' deity more than the other Gospels, liberal critics dismiss it as a historically unreliable document. However, a strong case can be made for the Apostle John as the author of the fourth Gospel, thus making him an eyewitness of the events he records.[39] Even if one denies the traditional view that the Apostle John was the author, a robust case can still be made that the author of the fourth Gospel was an eyewitness who knew Jesus.[40]

Thirteenth, these scholars presuppose that the authors of the New Testament were superstitious people with a false (supernatural) world view due to the fact they lived in the ancient, prescientific world. They treat the New Testament authors as somewhat gullible at times, and thus unable to adequately test miracle claims. In reality, first-century Jews were not gullible; they tested the religious views of their day by their Jewish beliefs. It is actually a case of chronological snobbery when contemporary scholars assume they are much more stable-minded than first-century traditional Jews.

Fourteenth, these critics assume that they themselves are not biased and that they live in an intellectually superior age than that of the New Testament authors. These liberal New Testament critics fail to see that their own biases (i.e., anti-supernaturalism,

---

39. Thiessen, *Introduction to the New Testament*, 162–70.
40. Bauckham, *Testimony of the Beloved Disciple*, 12–16, 25–29, 238.

etc.) are based upon their own questionable philosophies (i.e., deism, atheism, etc). New Testament scholar N. T. Wright states that the motivation for critical studies of the Gospels "came from the presupposition that this or that piece of synoptic material about Jesus could not be historical.[41]

Fifteenth, liberal New Testament scholars believe they have a better grasp of who Jesus really was than the New Testament authors had, despite the fact that the liberal critics are living almost two-thousand years after the events supposedly occurred and that the New Testament authors were contemporaries of Jesus. Once again, this is a case of chronological snobbery. It is an arrogance that should have no place in honest historical research. The documents should be studied based on their own merits and not based on the alleged intellectual superiority of the modern researchers.

The sixteenth liberal assumption is what is referred to as the principle of double dissimilarity. Strobel explains that this principle assumes that we must reject as a true saying of Jesus anything that Jesus is pictured as saying in the Gospels that either is consistent with first-century Jewish rabbinical teachings or the teachings of the first-century church.[42] It is hard to imagine anyone considering this principle reasonable. Are we to believe that Jesus was a first-century, traditional Jew who was not influenced one bit by first-century rabbinical Judaism? Are we also to assume that Jesus is the only founder of a religion whose teachings did not resonate in the teachings of his first generation of disciples? Boyd expresses this dilemma well: "The obvious problem is that Jesus was Jewish and he founded the Christian church, so it shouldn't be surprising if he sounds Jewish and Christian!"[43] The liberal critic's bias against the Jesus of the Bible forces him to believe that the first-century church put their own words and teachings in the mouth of Jesus in order to promote their own biased agenda. It seems to me that if anyone is biased here it is not the early church—it is the modern-day, liberal New Testament critics.

The seventeenth liberal presupposition is called the principle of multiple attestation. This principle would be reasonable, when used of ancient literature, if it merely meant that we can be more confident of the truth of an account if we find multiple reports of it. However, extreme liberal critics go much further with this principle. They dogmatically assert that we cannot accept as true anything found in the Gospels unless we find more than one source attesting to it. This principle is even more biased then it originally appears, for the liberal scholar assumes that Matthew, Mark, and Luke "borrowed" from each other. Therefore, the same account or saying of Jesus found in more than one Gospel is not considered reliable because it is, according to the liberal critic, derived from the same source! Boyd states, "In fact, most of ancient history is based on single sources" and that "an increasing number of scholars are

---

41. Wright, *Contemporary Quest for Jesus*, 35.
42. Boyd interviewed by Strobel, *Case for Christ*, 117.
43. Ibid.

expressing serious reservations about the theory that Matthew and Luke used Mark."[44] Since most of ancient history is based on single sources and the dependency of Matthew and Luke on Mark's Gospel is assumed and not proven, the principle of multiple attestation is at best overused and at its worst should be rejected.

After examining these seventeen presuppositions of liberal scholars, it becomes apparent that four of these assumptions are foundational: they force the critics to accept the other thirteen presuppositions. Therefore, we will take a closer look at these four assumptions. If they can be shown to be unreasonable, then the entire edifice of liberal critical New Testament Jesus research can be called into question.

## REFUTING THE PRIMARY LIBERAL PRESUPPOSITIONS FOR JESUS RESEARCH

We will now take a closer look at the four primary/foundational presuppositions that dictate not only the other thirteen presuppositions, but also the conclusions of liberal New Testament studies concerning Jesus. These four presuppositions are: (1) a bias against the possibility of miracles; (2) the New Testament books should be considered false until proven true; (3) only the latest possible date of composition for each of the New Testament books should be accepted; and (4) the true Jesus of history could not possibly be the Jesus of the Bible (for this would entail the possibility of miracles).

Liberal New Testament scholars reject the possibility of miracles based upon the arguments against miracles found in the works of Benedict Spinoza and David Hume. However, if these arguments against the possibility of miracles can be shown to be weak, then scholars should be open to the possibility of miracles rather than biased against them.

Spinoza believed miracles were impossible because he believed in the existence of a non-personal, pantheistic God. This type of God, reasoned Spinoza, does not choose to do anything and, therefore, cannot choose to do a miracle. A non-personal God can make no choices—whatever it does, it does by necessity. Hence, Spinoza concluded that the laws of nature are necessarily set in motion by God—they could not have been different. Hence, the laws of nature cannot be violated, interrupted, or superseded by miracles.

Spinoza's argument against miracles has serious problems. First, there are strong arguments against the existence of a pantheistic God—a non-personal God that is identical to the universe.[45] The existence of the physical universe (as acknowledged by common sense and experience), the beginning of the universe (proven by modern science—energy deterioration and the big bang model of the universe), the reality of moral absolutes (pointing to an absolute moral Lawgiver—i.e., a personal God), and

---

44. Ibid., 117–18.
45. Fernandes, *God Who Sits Enthroned*, 66–68; Geisler, *Christian Apologetics*, 173–92.

the existence of other minds all show the pantheistic world view to be implausible.[46] Second, there is strong evidence that a theistic God (i.e., a God who is personal; a God who transcends the universe, but is also immanent in it—a God who can perform miracles) exists.[47] The beginning of the universe, the continuing existence of the universe, the intelligent design found in the universe, the existence of absolute moral laws, and the existence of absolute truths are just some of the indicators that a personal God exists and that he is capable of performing miracles.[48] Since there is strong evidence against the existence of a pantheistic God (a God who cannot perform miracles) and a strong case for the existence of a theistic God (a God who can choose to perform miracles), then we have good reason to believe miracles are possible. Hence, miracles should not be rejected a priori—before examining the evidence concerning a particular miracle claim.[49]

The second problem with Spinoza's argument against the possibility of miracles is his insistence that the laws of nature cannot be interrupted, violated, or superseded. Modern science now rejects the view Spinoza held that the laws of nature are prescriptive. Modern science now views the laws of nature as descriptive of the way things generally occur rather than prescriptive of how things must occur.[50] Simply because there are general laws of nature does not make miraculous events impossible.

Third, Spinoza's definition of a miracle as a violation of the laws of nature can be questioned. It is possible that miracles do not violate the laws of nature, and that they merely supersede the laws of nature. The great Christian apologist C. S. Lewis argued along these lines.[51]

The fourth problem with Spinoza's rejection of the possibility of miracles is this: if God created the universe, then the laws of nature are subject to him. God can choose to suspend the laws of nature anytime he chooses.[52] Hence, Spinoza failed to show that miracles are impossible.

Hume, unlike Spinoza did not argue for the impossibility of miracles. Instead, he argued that miracles were so unlikely that the evidence against them will always be greater than the evidence for them. Hume argued that miracles are improbable, and that the wise man will only believe that which is probable. Hence, the wise man will never accept any evidence for a miracle.[53]

The traditional Christian can respond to Hume's faulty reasoning in the following manner. Just because usual events (i.e., the laws of nature) occur more often does

46. Fernandes, *God Who Sits Enthroned*, 66–68.
47. Ibid., 87–119; Geisler, *Christian Apologetics*, 237–58.
48. Fernandes, *No Other Gods*, 71–87.
49. Ibid., 134.
50. Ibid., 135.
51. Lewis, *Miracles*, 59–60.
52. Fernandes, *God Who Sits Enthroned*, 135.
53. Ibid.

not mean the wise man will never believe that an unusual event (i.e., a miracle) has occurred.[54] The wise man should not *a priori* rule out the possibility of miracles. The wise man will examine the evidence for or against a miracle claim, and base his judgment on the evidence. Since the Apostle Paul stated that he knew of over five hundred witnesses who claimed to have seen Jesus risen from the dead, a wise man would not reject the miracle of the resurrection merely because all other men he knew of remained dead. It seems that a wise man should examine a miracle claim if there are reliable eyewitnesses. Without good reasons for rejecting the testimony of the witnesses, it seems that a wise man would accept their testimony that a miracle has occurred.[55]

In summary, it is apparent that the arguments of Spinoza and Hume against miracles are clearly circular—they assume miracles are impossible or unbelievable in an attempt to prove miracles are impossible or unbelievable. Spinoza and Hume assumed what they were claiming to have proved. Therefore, the New Testament critic should not assume miracles are impossible before examining the data of the New Testament. Instead, the New Testament critic should examine the New Testament with an open mind and allow the historical evidence to guide his conclusions.

We must now consider the second foundational presupposition of the liberal New Testament critic: his belief that the New Testament books are false until proven true. This is a totally unfair approach to take since, except for the Bible, all other ancient literature that portrays itself as being historically accurate is considered to be true until proven false. This bias against the Bible flows directly from the liberal New Testament critic's bias against miracles. The critic's anti-supernaturalistic bias forces him to view Scripture with suspicion.

The third foundational assumption of the liberal New Testament critic is his prejudicial dating of the New Testament books—the idea that we should accept the latest possible dates for the composition of each book. Common sense dictates that the New Testament books be treated like all other literature in this regard: when one is trying to date the composition of a written work, one should attempt to establish both the earliest and the latest possible dates of composition, and then work within those parameters to narrow down the approximate date.

The fourth foundational assumption of liberal New Testament scholarship is that the true Jesus of history cannot possibly be the Jesus portrayed on the pages of the New Testament. This is a viscous example of arguing in a circle, for the liberal starting point (a non-miraculous, non-divine Jesus) dictates the liberal conclusion (a non-miraculous, non-divine Jesus).

---

54. Geisler, *Miracles and the Modern Mind*, 23–31.
55. Fernandes, *God Who Sits Enthroned*, 135–36.

Part 2—Inerrancy Defended

## PROPOSING NEUTRAL PRESUPPOSITIONS FOR JESUS RESEARCH

We have seen that the four foundational biases of liberal New Testament scholarship are unreasonable principles to use when searching for the true Jesus of history. These biases do not promote an honest examination of the historical evidence. Rather, they encourage the creation of a false Jesus made in the image and likeness of the researcher himself. Instead of examining the evidence in an unbiased manner and trying to determine if the Jesus of the Bible is the true Jesus of history, these liberal critics assume that the Jesus of the Bible cannot possibly be the true Jesus of history, since they reject any possibility of a miracle-working, divine, risen Jesus. The faulty presuppositions of these critics lead inevitably to contradictory views of Jesus or a total skepticism about his life and work, despite so much first-century data about his life.

Current research (ironically, even liberal research) on New Testament studies and Jesus studies has provided much evidence for the evangelical belief that the Jesus of the Bible is the true Jesus of history. A growing number of New Testament scholars acknowledge so much in the New Testament as historically reliable that the case for Christ's resurrection and deity is stronger today than at any other time during the last two centuries. Still, many liberal scholars (especially those affiliated with the Jesus Seminar) refuse to go where the evidence leads them and continue to create contradictory lives of Jesus, each liberal scholar creating a Jesus in his own image. The liberal presuppositions for Jesus studies are biased, unreasonable, and lead to either contradictory lives of Christ or skepticism about the Jesus of history. Hence, these liberal presuppositions should be replaced by alternative presuppositions which are more conducive to a fair treatment of the historical data in question.

Unfortunately, many conservative evangelical scholars use the same liberal presuppositions in their Jesus studies. Therefore, I propose a reformation in Jesus studies. I propose that we abandon the biased foundation of liberal New Testament scholarship and propose four alternative presuppositions for future Jesus research. These four presuppositions are much more in line with the honest examination of other ancient works, and the results they produce are not contradictory. The four alternative presuppositions are neutral presuppositions—they are neither liberal nor conservative.

If we were to use conservative/evangelical presuppositions in our Jesus research, they would be as follows: (1) the true Jesus of history is the miracle-working, divine Jesus; (2) the Jesus of the Bible is identical to the true Jesus of history; (3) the New Testament books are inspired by God and totally without errors; and (4) we should accept the traditional dates of composition and the traditional authorship of each of the New Testament books. Though conservative/evangelical scholars believe these four presuppositions, they can, for the sake of unbiased historical research, lay aside these assumptions and utilize four neutral presuppositions in their research. My thesis is that both liberal and conservative scholars, like any good historian, should lay aside their philosophical or religious beliefs and use four neutral presuppositions before embarking on their search for the historical Jesus. The historian should not allow his preconceived ideas to dictate his conclusions; rather, he should examine the evidence before drawing his conclusions, and his conclusions should be based on the evidence.

The neutral presuppositions I propose are: (1) we should not rule out the possibility of miracles at the outset of our research—miracles may be possible; historical evidence will help us determine if they in fact occurred in history; (2) we must be open to the possibility that the Jesus of the Bible is an accurate depiction of the true Jesus of history; (3) we must consider the New Testament books (like all other ancient writings which purport to be historical) as true until proven false—the New Testament books should be given the benefit of the doubt (as is the case with the study of all literature); and (4) we should not be forced to accept the latest date of composition for each of the New Testament books; instead we should establish the parameters by identifying the earliest possible date, as well as the latest possible date, for each New Testament book. As we utilize these neutral presuppositions, the historical evidence we uncover may favor the liberal or conservative/evangelical position. The honest historian must go wherever the evidence leads.

The third quest for the historical Jesus surprisingly has shown that even research tainted with biased, liberal presuppositions can lead us extremely close to the Jesus of the Bible (assuming the liberal critic will go where the evidence leads him). Neutral presuppositions—presuppositions that are more balanced—may lead us all the way to the Jesus of the Bible. We must not allow liberal critics to dictate the presuppositions for Jesus research, for that will always corrupt the conclusion to one degree or another.

If liberal scholars refuse to use neutral presuppositions in their search for the historical Jesus, then their quest is a pseudo-historical search that is actually a philosophical bias (i.e., anti-supernaturalism) masquerading as an unbiased historical investigation. The researchers are not really conducting a historical investigation; instead, they are forcing their philosophical world view on the data in question.

I believe that an unbiased examination of the historical data, using neutral presuppositions, will lead us directly to the Jesus of the Bible. In short, once set free from the bondage of liberal, biased presuppositions, honest New Testament research will provide a strong case that the true Jesus of history is in fact the Jesus of the Bible.

## DIFFERENT STARTING POINTS FOR JESUS RESEARCH

| Liberal Presuppositions | Neutral Presuppositions | Conservative Presuppositions |
|---|---|---|
| (1) miracles are impossible | (1) miracles may be possible | (1) Jesus is God and he actually performed miracles |
| (2) the Jesus of the Bible is not the true Jesus of history | (2) the Jesus of the Bible might be the true Jesus of history | (2) the Jesus of the Bible is the true Jesus of history |

| (3) New Testament books are false until proven true | (3) New Testament books should be considered true until proven false | (3) New Testament books are totally true |
| --- | --- | --- |
| (4) accept only the latest possible dates of New Testament books | (4) find earliest possible dates as well as oldest possible dates and then research within these parameters | (4) accept the traditional dates and authors of the New Testament books |

## POSTSCRIPT: A WORD OF CAUTION FOR EVANGELICAL SCHOLARS

Though I believe evangelical apologists have had great success in using the core historical data accepted by the vast majority of the world's leading New Testament critics to build a strong case for Jesus' bodily resurrection, a word of caution is needed. We must never allow a minimal facts case for the resurrection to evolve into a minimal facts evangelicalism or an erosion of the evangelical doctrine of biblical inerrancy. For instance, we must not be open to discarding some of the biblical miracles, clearly reported in the Bible as historical events, merely because they lack multiple attestation (or some other liberal critical principle) or because they seem "similar" to metaphorical reports found in ancient Greek or Roman literature[56]

Some evangelical apologists are so focused on only that data which liberal New Testament critics will give us that they often discourage apologists from arguing for New Testament reliability.[57] This approach could backfire in two ways. First, it could lead to a lack of confidence in the historical reliability of the New Testament in the minds of some evangelicals. And second, some anti-Christian secularists (i.e., those who believe Jesus never existed) do not care about the current consensus of the vast majority of New Testament critics. If the Christian apologist is to answer these secularists, arguments for the historical reliability of the New Testament would be a good place to start.

In the past, due to Enlightenment rationalism, liberal critics allowed "human reason" to determine which biblical accounts could or could not have actually occurred in history. Today, some evangelicals allow their own historical methodology to do the same thing. But, this should not be the case. If we are truly evangelicals, we must allow the Bible to be the final authority—not human reason or historical methodology.

As evangelical apologists, we must diligently guard our biblical hermeneutical method. We must not allow our hermeneutics to fall prey to liberal presuppositions. In our debates, we can go behind enemy lines and use what our opponents give us to build our case for the biblical Jesus. But, in the process, we must not allow the

---

56. Licona, *Resurrection of Jesus*, 48–553; Craig, "Resurrection and the Real Jesus," 164–65.
57. Craig, *Reasonable Faith*, 11–12.

assumptions of liberal Jesus research to become our assumptions, thus doing great damage to our own evangelical views and "the faith once for all delivered to the saints."

# Chapter 29

# Redating the Gospels

## PHIL FERNANDES

Evangelical apologists often accept the earliest dates for New Testament books allowed by liberal New Testament critics. But, this should not be the case. There are solid arguments for even earlier dates for several New Testament books. This is true of the Gospels as well. Using the data accepted by one's opponent is an excellent debate tactic. Still, evangelical New Testament scholarship should not blindly accept the theories promoted by liberal New Testament critics. Accepting minimal data for purposes of building a case for the resurrection is a worthy endeavor.[1] However, refusing to question the assumptions and conclusions of liberal New Testament criticism can be and has been detrimental to the cause of evangelicalism.[2]

This paper is a call for evangelical apologists to ask a question seldom asked: "What are the earliest possible dates for the four Gospels?" Evangelical apologists need the courage to risk academic respectability by questioning liberal presuppositions and conclusions.

### DO PAUL'S LETTERS NECESSARILY PREDATE THE GOSPELS?

Liberal scholars, due to their biases against miracles and traditional Christianity, assume that Paul's letters were written before any of the Gospels were written. Liberal

---

1. The works of Habermas and Licona, *Case for the Resurrection of Jesus*, and Craig, *Reasonable Faith*, are excellent examples of taking the data accepted by the vast majority of New Testament scholars and using this data to build a case for Christ's bodily resurrection.

2. Geisler and Roach point to Gundry and Pinnock as two examples of "evangelicals" who have allowed liberal higher critical assumptions to damage their doctrine of inerrancy. See Geisler and Roach, *Defending Inerrancy*, 45–60.

critics assume that decades passed before any Gospel was recorded in writing. They also assume that no eyewitnesses wrote any of the Gospels. Evangelicals should question these liberal assumptions. Evangelicals should take a second look at the dating of the four Gospels.

In Paul's letters, Paul would first teach Bible doctrines (i.e., theology) and then he would move on to practical application. This was due to the fact that Paul believed that our behavior should be based on true beliefs. But, Paul was a Jew, and the Jewish faith was based on history (i.e., the Old Testament Jewish history). In Paul's writings he alludes to historical events from the life of Jesus. Hence, early Christianity more likely progressed in this order: (1) history, (2) doctrine, and (3) practice. Therefore, it makes more sense that the early church would have been motivated to record in writing the historical data of the life of Christ before dealing with doctrinal issues in print. The historical data (i.e., the Gospels) would establish the basis for Christian doctrines (i.e., Jesus' deity and messiahship, salvation through his death and resurrection, etc). The liberal assumption that the early church would initially be interested in recording doctrine and practice, and only later be concerned about recording historical events, seems unlikely. The early church would have been greatly concerned with the historical aspects of Jesus' ministry—his life and teachings. Then after these matters are recorded and proclaimed, theological and practical implications would be drawn from this historical data. Therefore, it is possible that at least some of the Gospels were in print before the Apostle Paul began to write his doctrinal and practical letters.

## NEW TESTAMENT SCHOLARS WHO ACCEPTED EARLY DATES FOR THE GOSPELS

There have been scholars in the past and present who have speculated that the Gospels (as well as other New Testament books) may have been written much earlier than liberal critics will allow. A few examples will suffice. New Testament scholar John A. T. Robinson, in his book *Redating the New Testament*, dated the composition of the entire New Testament to before the destruction of the Jewish temple in AD 70.[3] This was because no New Testament book mentions the destruction of the temple, though the temple plays a very significant role in the New Testament.[4]

William F. Albright, one of the world's leading archaeologists, stated that there is absolutely no good reason to date any New Testament book after about AD 80. He even went so far to say, "In my opinion, every book of the New Testament was written by a baptized Jew between the forties and the eighties of the first century AD."[5]

New Testament scholar John Wenham rejects the later dates for the synpotic Gospels (i.e., Matthew, Mark, and Luke) given by liberal New Testament critics. In

---

3. Robinson, *Redating the New Testament*, 352.
4. Ibid., 10.
5. McDowell, *Evidence That Demands a Verdict*, 62–63.

Wenham's work entitled *Redating Matthew, Mark, and Luke*, he dates Matthew's Gospel at around the AD forties, Mark's Gospel at about AD 45, and Luke's Gospel at around the early AD fifties.[6] New Testament scholar Henry Thiessen also gives early dates for the Synoptic Gospels.[7]

Roman Catholic scholars Claude Tresmontant and Jean Carmignac date the synoptic Gospels (i.e., Matthew, Mark, and Luke) as early as the AD forties or fifties.[8] There is no reason for evangelicals to accept, without question, the late dates for the Gospels promoted by liberal New Testament critics. If we are not biased against the possibility of miracles, we should be open to early dates of the Gospels. This is especially true when we consider what the early church fathers wrote about the composition of the Gospels.

If scholars are to be unbiased in their studies of the New Testament, then they must be open to the earliest possible dates of the composition of each Gospel, rather than merely accept the latest possible date. In this paper, we will look at evidence for the earliest possible dates of the Gospels. Though we must be tentative in dating ancient works, since the early church fathers generally accepted the earlier dates, honest scholarship should at least be open to the possibility of these early dates.

John Wenham, in his work *Redating Matthew, Mark, and Luke*, gives an interesting quote from the Yale scholar and expert on Semitic languages C. C. Torrey: "I challenged my New Testament colleagues [in 1934] to designate even *one* passage from any of the four Gospels giving clear evidence of a date later than AD 50.... The challenge was not met, nor will it be, for there is no such passage."[9] The truth of the matter is this: only liberal, anti-Christian assumptions prevent evangelicals from dating the four Gospels earlier than we normally date them. We must not be content with accepting only the earliest dates that far left, critical New Testament scholars will allow. We must be willing to think "outsdie the box." Conservative evangelical scholars must be willing to ask the question: "How early could the Gospels have been written?"

Before we discuss the four Gospels themselves, we must look at the literary relationship (if one exists) between the four Gospels, the writings of the apostolic fathers, as well as possible ancient fragments of the Gospels. This will help us to more accurately date the Gospels.

## THE INDEPENDENCE THEORY OF MATTHEW, MARK, AND LUKE

Matthew, Mark, and Luke are commonly refered to as the "Synoptic Gospels" because the material they contain has much more in common with each other than with the fourth Gospel—the Gospel of John. The Christian church throughout the ages held

---

6. Wenham, *Redating Matthew, Mark, and Luke*, 243.
7. Thiessen, *Introduction to the New Testament*, 101–61.
8. Keating, *What Catholics Really Believe*, 40–44.
9. Wenham, *Redating Matthew, Mark, and Luke*, 299.

that Matthew, Mark, and Luke, though very similar in content, were written independently of each other. However, with the advent of the Enlightenment, biblical scholars began to attempt to explain the similarities found in the Synoptic Gospels as due to dependence between them (i.e., the authors borrowed material from one another—their Gospels were not written independently of each other).

The different dependence theories of the origin of the Synoptic Gospels were formulated by scholars who did not believe the Bible was inspired by God and inerrant. These scholars viewed the Bible as merely a human book and they attempted to explain the similarities found in Matthew, Mark, and Luke. It is rather sad that today many evangelical (i.e., Bible-believing) New Testament scholars accept one of the dependence theories for the origin of the Synoptic Gospels.

There are three main views concerning the origin of the Synoptic Gospels: the Markan Priority Hypothesis, the Two-Gospel Hypothesis (which views Matthew as the first Gospel written but accepts a literary dependence between the Synoptic Gospels), and the Literary Independence Theory.[10] The Literary Independence theory is by far the oldest theory of the origin of the Gospels of Matthew, Mark, and Luke. In my view, the Literary Independence Theory should not have been abandoned by many contemporary evangelical New Testament scholars.

The Literary Independence Theory accepts the unanimous testimony of the early church fathers that the Synoptic Gospels were written independently of each other. The main reason for the origin of the various dependence theories of the Synoptic Gospels is to discredit the historical reliability of the Gospel accounts. It is therefore suprising that so many evangelical New Testament scholars would embrace these dependence theories. I agree with Robert L. Thomas and F. David Farnell (two New Testament scholars from The Master's Seminary in Sun Valley, California) in their

---

10. Adherents of the Markan Priority Hypothesis believe that Mark was the first to write his Gospel based upon Peter's preaching. Mark himself was not one of the original apostles. There are two subcategories within the Markan Priority Hypothesis: the Two-Source View and the Four-Source View. The Two-Source View declares that Mark's Gospel and a no longer extant document called "Q" formed the foundation for the Gospels of Matthew and Luke. The Two-Source adherents believe that Matthew and Luke received much of their material from Mark, but the material common to Matthew and Luke but not found in Mark came from a hypothetical document called "Q." No one has ever found a copy of the supposed ancient document called "Q." In fact, many New Testament scholars doubt it ever existed.

The Four-Source View within the Markan Priority Hypothesis posists the existence of two additional hypothetical documents called "M" and "L." According to this speculative theory, "M" was an ancient source used by Matthew in addition to Mark and "Q." And "L" was supposedly an ancient source used by Luke in addition to Mark and "Q." Like "Q," no copy of "M" or "L" have ever been found. Again, many New Testament scholars doubt that these hypothetical documents ever existed.

The Two-Gospel View of Synoptic Dependence claims that Matthew was written first, followed by Luke and Mark. Supposedly, Luke utilized Matthew as a source, whereas Mark "borrowed" from both Matthew and Luke. What the two Markan Priority views and the Two-Gospel View have in common is that Matthew, Mark, and Luke were not written independently of each other. The Gospels of Matthew, Mark, and Luke were dependent upon each other.

assessment that evangelical scholars should never have forsaken the Literary Independence Theory.

Farnell points out that throughout the history of the church until the rise of enlightenment Deism, the independence theory of the Synoptic Gospels reigned supreme as the dominant view of scholars. Only with the rise of antisupernaturalism (the philsophical assumption that miracles are impossible) did the independence theory fall out of favor among scholars.[11] The demise of the independence theory was not due to evidence found within the pages of the Gospels; rather, it was caused by a philosophical bias against the possibility of miracles. Hence, it is rather strange that evangelical (Bible-believing) New Testament scholars of the twentieth century would so quickly abandon the independence theory. For evangelical scholars believe in miracles and accept the traditional doctrines of inspiration and inerrancy.

Farnell notes that some twentieth-century evangelical New Testament scholars refused to compromise. Like Farnell and Thomas, they continued to hold to the independence theory of the Synoptic Gospels. Some of these scholars noted by Farnell are: Louis Berkhof, Henry C. Thiessen, Eta Linnemann (a former historical-critical scholar), Robert Gromacki, Merrill C. Tenney, Jacob Van Bruggen, and John M. Rist. Farnell also informs us that John Wenham and Bo Reicke hold to modified independence theories of the origin of the Synoptic Gospels.[12] There is no reason why contemporary evangelical New Testament scholars should continue to promote dependence theories.

Farnell gives an overview of the early church's view of the origin of the Synoptic Gospels. Speaking about the view of the early church fathers, Farnell states that "the Fathers' writings verify a unanimous consensus that Matthew, not Mark, was the first Gospel written and that the Gospel writers wrote independently of each other." Farnell adds that "the Fathers' writings also reveal that Luke probably wrote second and Mark third, although at times Mark is placed second."[13]

Farnell shows that the apostolic father named Papias, writing about AD 110, wrote that Mark based his Gospel on Peter's preaching, not on Matthew's Gospel.[14] Farnell notes that Eusebius, the great historian of the early church, quotes Clement of Alexandria (AD 150–215) as giving the chronological order of the composition of the Gospels as: Matthew, Luke, Mark, and John.[15] Farnell adds that Clement of Alexandria is in general agreement on these issues with other early church fathers such as Papias, Ireneaeus, and Tertullian, and that there is no hint of any literary dependence between the Gospel authors whatsoever.[16]

11. Farnell, "Case for the Independence View," 235.
12. Ibid., 242–49.
13. Ibid., 237.
14. Ibid., 237.
15. Ibid., 238.
16. Ibid., 239–41.

Farnell offers his own defense of the independence theory of the Synoptic Gospels. While acknowledging that the differences in the Gospels are due to the fact that the authors did not borrow from one another (the Gospel writers were not dependent upon one another for their information), Farnell lists five factors that explain the common aspects found in the Synoptic Gospels.[17] First, the authors had direct, eyewitness knowledge of the events they recorded. Farnell points out that the early church fathers unanimously considered the Gospels written by the apostles or their close associates. Therefore, they had access to eyewitness information.

Second, the authors had access to oral tradition based upon the teachings of the apostles. The early church inherited their respect for oral tradition and their memorization skills from the first-century AD Jewish culture. Rabbis expected their disciples to memorize and pass on their key teachings to others. There is no reason to believe that oral tradition had any less of an important role in the early church.[18]

Third, Farnell states that, besides the first-century AD Jewish emphasis on oral tradition, the authors of the Synoptic Gospels probably had access to short written accounts. Several New Testament scholars (even some dependence theory advocates) suspect that Matthew may have been the "note-taker" for the apostles.[19] In fact, Jesus refers to his disciples as "scribes" in Matthew 13:51–52 (see also Matt 23:34), implying that they took notes of his sermons.

Fourth, Farnell notes that the authors of the Synoptic Gospels (Matthew, Mark, and Luke) probably had personal contacts with each other.[20] A careful study of the book of Acts and Paul's letters reveal that the apostles met in John Mark's home (Acts 12:12; the full name of the author of the Gospel of Mark was John Mark) and that John Mark and Luke were close associates of each other and of the Apostle Paul (Col 4:10, 14; Phlm 24). Luke accompanied Paul on several of his journies, which would have given him numerous occassions to meet with some of the original apostles.

And fifth, Farnell reminds evangelical New Testament scholars that, as evangelicals, they are supposed to believe in the inspiration of the Holy Spirit. That is, the Holy Spirit guided the Gospel authors to record his Word without error.[21] Since they were protected from introducing errors into the biblical texts, it is no surprise that we would find so many similarities in the three Synoptic Gospels.

Farnell's Case for the Independence Theory of the Origin of the Synoptic Gospels can be summarized as follows. (1) The early church fathers taught that the authors of the Synoptic Gospels worked independently of each other. (2) This view was held by the Christian church throughout the centuries until the advent of the Enlightenment. (3) The dependence theory of the origin of the Synoptic Gospels was produced

---

17. Ibid., 273–94.
18. Ibid., 279–81.
19. Ibid., 283.
20. Ibid., 291.
21. Ibid., 292.

by enlightenment thinkers who rejected the possibility of miracles. (4) Evangelical New Testament scholars believe that God performed miracles such as the inspiration of Scripture. Therefore, they should not have abandoned the traditional view of the Christian church because of the anti-supernaturalistic bias of enlightenment thinkers. (5) Numerous evangelical scholars, though in the minority, were able to prove their scholarship without abandoning their adherence to the independency theory. And (6) evangelical scholars can explain the similarities found in the Synoptic Gospels without accomodating to the dependency theories.

Farnell's defense of the Independence Theory of the origin of the Synoptic Gospels is sound. Therefore, I join with scholars like Farnell and Thomas as they call evangelical scholars to reject dependency theories and return to the position that the Christian church had held for the first seventeen centuries of her history. Now is not the time to compromise. The same presupposition (i.e., bias against miracles) that led to the dependency theories of the origin of the Synoptic Gospels has also led to the denial of the Christian doctrines of inspiration and inerrancy. Evangelicals should not cave in to pressure from the world to compromise. There is no reason to reject the early church's view on the Synoptic Gospels—there is no reason to reject the independence theory of the Gospels.

## THE APOSTOLIC FATHERS: EVIDENCE FOR EARLY DATES OF THE GOSPELS

The apostolic fathers were selected by the apostles and their colleagues for positions of leadership in the church. In short, the apostles passed the baton of leadership to the apostolic fathers. Since the apostolic fathers quoted from or alluded to many of the New Testament books, the New Testament books they quote must be dated before the writings of the apostolic fathers. For this reason, liberal critics, who do not want to date the New Testament books early, will often date some of the works of the apostolic fathers later than they should be dated. We will now examine some of these writings and attempt to determine the approximate dates of their composition. This will help us to more accurately date the Gospels.

*The Didache* is also called *The Teaching of the Twelve Apostles*.[22] This document has many hints of an extremely early date of composition.[23] First, it speaks of "the two ways," one way leading to life and the other leading to death. This was a similar theme among pre-Christian Jewish writings such as the *Qumran Manual of Discipline* found in the Dead Sea Scrolls. Second, *The Didache* is a very practical writing; it is concerned with practice, not doctrine. Yet, the church organization found in this document is very primitive—it is not the advanced stage of church organization found in second-century documents. In *The Didache*, the bishops are merely the elders, the leaders of

---

22. Lightfoot and Harmer, *Apostolic Fathers*, 213–35.
23. Robinson, *Redating the New Testament*, 322–27.

the local congregations. The bishop is not part of a hierarchy; he is not the head of a collection of churches in a city or region. The church organization is rather like that of Paul's epistles and the book of Acts (i.e., elders and deacons). It is clearly primitive, first-century church organization (which implies a first-century document).

Third, the offices of "apostles and prophets" are still functioning—this indicates a very early stage in church history. Fourth, set days for fasting are prescribed and dietary instructions are given. This implies that the church is functioning as if it is still a branch of Judaism. In fact, Friday is still called the day of preparation—the day set aside to prepare for the Sabbath Day—this also implies close ties to Judaism. Still, Sunday corporate worship (i.e., the Lord's Day) is practiced as well as baptism in the name of the Triune God. In fact, instructions on how to baptize in water are given. All these factors imply a very early time in the history of the church—Christianity is still in its infancy.

For reasons such as these, John A. T. Robinson dates *The Didache* from AD 40 to 60.[24] At the least, it appears that *The Didache* paints a picture of Christian corporate worship that predates AD 70. Yet, this work references numerous passages from Matthew and Luke. It is possible that *The Didache* also alludes to Mark. At a minimum, *The Didache* indicates the antiquity of Matthew and Luke.

Many scholars date the *The Epistle of Barnabas* to around AD 135. However, Robinson argues persuasively for a AD 75 date for this writing.[25] The unknown author—he is probably not Paul's colleague Barnabas—speaks of the temple having been recently torn down by the enemies of the Jews (16:4). Lightfoot and Harmer also date this epistle to the AD seventies, shortly after the temple was destroyed.[26] This epistle references several passages from Matthew's Gospel. It may also refer to the Gospel of John. If the earlier date of *The Epistle of Barnabas* is accepted, then Matthew and John must be dated earlier as well.

*Clement of Rome* wrote a letter to the church of Corinth. Since Clement was the bishop of Rome toward the close of the first century, many scholars date this letter to AD 95–96. However, in this epistle, the position of elder seems closer to what Paul described in his letters thirty years earlier (1 Tim 3 and Titus 1). Hence, the church government resembles the pre-AD 70 model, not the early second-century model which elevated the role of the bishop. It should also be noted that, in his letter, Clement never appeals to his authority as the bishop of Rome. Due to this, Robinson believes that Clement wrote this letter while a representative of the Roman church, but long before he was bishop. This is confirmed by Clement's statement that the Jerusalem temple was still standing at the time of this writing (1 Clem 41:2). Since Clement does mention the martyrdoms of Peter and Paul (1 Clem 5:1–7), which occurred around AD 67, but says the temple had yet to be destroyed, Robinson concludes that Clement

24. Ibid., 327, 352.
25. Ibid., 313–19.
26. Lightfoot and Harmer, *Apostolic Fathers*, 241.

wrote his letter to the Corinthians in early AD 70, before the temple was destroyed by the Romans.[27] In Clement's letter, he alludes to or quotes from Matthew, Mark, and Luke.

Scholars often date *The Shepherd of Hermas* to the mid-second century due to the fact that the Muratorian Fragment identifies Hermas with the brother of Pius who was the bishop of Rome from AD 141 to 155.[28] But, Robinson believes the Muratorian Fragment is incorrect on this point, for church fathers like Ireneaus, Tertullian, and Origen all treated *The Shepherd of Hermas* as if it were an ancient document, not a second-century document which had been recently authored. This would not have been the case if it was a recent composition. Though *The Shepherd of Hermas* mentions Clement of Rome as a comtemporary, Robinson believes this letter was written before Clement was the bishop of Rome. This work speaks of the apostles, bishops, teachers, and deacons—this reflects the earliest stages of Christianity. Hence, Robinson dates *The Sheherd of Hermas* to around AD 85.[29] This work mentions passages from several of the Gospels: Matthew, Mark, John.

The seven letters of *Ignatius* were written in AD 107 as Ignatius was enroute to be martyred for the faith. Ignatius was martyred about AD 107; hence, Lightfoot and Harmer, as well as most scholars, date Ignatius's seven letters to about AD 107.[30] Ignatius was the bishop of Antioch of Syria. In his seven letters he referenced Matthew and John (and possibly Luke).

*Polycarp* was a disciple of the Apostle John. He eventually became the bishop of Smyrna. At age eighty-six, he experienced martyrdom when he was burned at the stake in AD 156.[31] Around the time of Ignatius's martyrdom (AD 107), Polycarp wrote his *Epistle to the Philippians*. In this letter, Polycarp quotes or paraphrases from the Gospels of Matthew, Mark, and Luke.

The writings of *Papias* are mostly lost to mankind. Only a few fragments of his works remain, and these are found quoted by other ancient writers like Eusebius. Papias was born between AD 60 and 70, and he died between AD 130 and 140. He was a disicple of the Apostle John. Papias wrote his *Exposition of Oracles of the Lord*; however, as mentioned above, only fragments remain. In those fragments, Papias tells us that Matthew wrote his Gospel first, Mark's Gospel is based on Peter's preaching, and the Apostle John wrote the Gospel of John.[32]

Many liberal critics date Clement's letter, the *Shepherd of Hermas*, the *Epistle of Barnabas*, and the *Didache* much later than the dates given above. But, the primitive church polity seems much closer to the church polity of Paul's epistles (AD fifties

---

27. Robinson, *Redating the New Testament*, 327–35.
28. Ibid., 319.
29. Ibid., 319–22, 352.
30. Lightfoot and Harmer, *Apostolic Fathers*, 97.
31. Cairns, *Christianity through the Centuries*, 76–77.
32. Lightfoot and Harmer, *Apostolic Fathers*, 527–35.

and sixties) than the later church polity of the second century AD. By the second century AD, the authority of the bishop was greatly elevated—this is not the case in the writings of the apostolic fathers mentioned above. It is possible that the desire of the liberal critics to date the New Testament books late forces them to date some of the writings of the apostolic fathers late as well. However, a strong case can be made for dating the Gospels much earlier than the earliest dates allowed by liberal critics (due to their anti-supernaturalistic bias).

## POSSIBLE EARLY FRAGMENTS OF THE NEW TESTAMENT?

Few Christians are aware of the fact that possible fragments of the New Testament exist that might date all the way back to the first century AD. Liberal critics are not open to identifying these fragments with portions of the New Testament. This is because some of these fragments were written before the critics believe the original New Testament manuscripts were written. Some of these fragments are acknowledged as New Testament copies by liberal critics, but they are dated late so as to not conflict with critical theories of the late dates for the Gospels and other New Testament books.

The famous John Ryland's fragment of John 18:31–33 is dated by the majority of scholars to about AD 125 to 130. However, the late papyrologist (i.e., an expert on identifying ancient fragments) Carsten P. Thiede reminds his readers that when Colin Roberts originally dated this fragment, though he settled on AD 125, he did acknowledge numerous parallels with several first-century documents. Hence, it is possible that the John Ryland's fragment of John 18 could date back to the nineties.[33] Since this copy was found in Egypt, the original Gospel of John had to have been written much earlier.[34]

The Chester Beatty Papyri contain portions of all four Gospels (as well as major portions of the entire New Testament). Thiede points out that though these papyri are usually dated to about AD 200, papyrologist Young-Kyu Kim argued in 1988 that the Chester Beatty Papyri should be dated to the late first century.[35] The idea of first-century copies of any New Testament book is too radical for most New Testament critics to accept. However, New Testament scholars should pay more attention to the results of recent research conducted by papyrologists, rather than merely dismiss any empirical evidence that contradicts liberal speculation.

The late Carsten B. Thiede, toward the end of his life, built upon the work and research of the great Spanish papyrologist Jose O'Callaghan. O'Callaghan identified several ancient fragments in cave seven of Qumran with portions of New Testament books. Though most scholars resist the notion of New Testament copies in the Dead Sea Scrolls, it is possible that the Jewish community in Qumran collected as much

---

33. Thiede, *Rekindling the Word*, 10–11, 26–27.
34. Ibid., 122.
35. Ibid., 178.

Jewish literature as they could, including Greek copies of New Testament writings. It must be remembered that the early church was originally considered to be a branch of Judaism, though a unique branch at that. Cave seven is the only known collection of Greek fragments in the Dead Sea Scrolls. It is possible that the research of O'Callaghan and Thiede is on target, and that fragments of copies of the New Testament existed between AD 50 and 70—the latest possible date for any of these Dead Sea Scrolls. In cave seven of Qumran, the following fragments of Mark's Gospel were found: 7Q6 (4:28), 7Q15 (6:48), 7Q5 (6:52–53), 7Q7 (12:17). Though these fragments are tiny and identification can be disputed, the acknowledgement that they are copies from the New Testament should not be dismissed merely for *a priori* reasons.[36]

Thiede also argued that the oldest existing fragments of Matthew's Gospel should be dated to the first century AD, possibly even prior to AD 70.[37] The oldest copies of Matthew's Gospel consist of five small scraps, three which are kept at Magdalene College, Oxford, with the other two fragments in Barcelona, Spain.[38] Obviously, if these fragments are actually this old, then Matthew's Gospel must have been authored very early in the history of the church. Since most New Testament critics reject such an early date for Matthew's Gospel, Thiede's conclusions are considered very controversial. However, if one places more confidence in the views of the early church fathers and less confidence in the speculation of contemporary liberal critics, then Thiede's work deserves consideration. Also, it should be noted that Thiede's work is not based on speculative theories like that of New Testament critics. Rather, Thiede's research was based on empirical research—comparing the ancient fragments with other ancient fragments of known date.[39]

Due to a reexamination of the dates of the writings of the apostolic fathers, and the possible identification of ancient first-century fragments as copies of the Gospels, the dating of the four Gospels deserves a second look.

## THE GOSPEL OF MATTHEW

Most New Testament scholars assume that the Gospels were not written until after Paul's letters. This would mean that the Gospels were written, at the earliest, thirty to seventy years after Jesus' death and resurrection. But, this is not necessarily the case. Jesus referred to the apostles as "scribes" (Matt 13:51–52; 23:34). This implies that the apostles took notes when Jesus taught them. Matthew had been a tax collector before Jesus selected him to be one of his disciples. His profession necessitated good writing skills. It is very possible that Matthew was the stenographer for the twelve apostles—he may have been the lead scribe. Since the Old Testament is in written form, it makes

36. Geisler, *Baker Encyclopedia of Christian Apologetics*, 530, 547–48.
37. Thiede, *Rekindling*, 26–27.
38. Ibid., 20.
39. Ibid., 33.

sense that the New Testament would be in written form as well. The apostles would have had the incentive to record in writing Jesus' sayings (and maybe his miracles as well) almost immediately. He was their rabbi (their teacher), and his miracles would have convinced them that he might be the Messiah. It is very likely that the apostles would record in writing the most important teachings and acts of Jesus' ministry.

It is possible that the original edition of Matthew's Gospel consisted of Matthew's notes on Jesus' sermons. These notes would date back to between AD 27 and 30 or between AD 30 and 33 (depending on the dates of Jesus' public ministry). This may explain why the apostolic father Papias refers to the original edition of Matthew's Gospel as "the words" (*ta logia* in Greek) of the Lord.[40]

Papias, writing about AD 107, also says that Matthew was the first to write his Gospel (contrary to the popular theory among New Testament scholars that Mark wrote first), and that he originally wrote his Gospel in Hebrew.[41] It makes sense that Matthew would be the first to write a Gospel since the original preaching of the Gospel would emphasize proving that Jesus is the Jewish Messiah. It is no coincidence that Matthew's Gospel contains many more Old Testament prophecies fufilled by Jesus than any of the other three Gospels.[42]

In fact, it might be correct to consider Matthew's Gospel the "Jerusalem Gospel" since he includes in his Gospel several events that would have greater relevance for the Jerusalem church than for churches located elsewhere. These events would include: the rising of recently departed saints who entered Jerusalem after Jesus' resurrection to show others they were alive (Matt 27:52–53), the earthquake that occurred in Jerusalem as Jesus died (Matt 27:51), the name of the field (i.e., Potter's Field) purchased with the money Judas received to betray Jesus (Matt 27:7), and the stolen body rumor started by the chief priests (Matt 28:11–15). The first preaching of the Gospel took place in Jerusalem. It emphasized the teaching that Jesus is the Jewish Messiah. It only makes sense that Matthew's Gospel, with its many Old Testament prophecies fulfilled by Christ and its unique Jerusalem details, would be the first Gospel written.

Thiessen correctly states that "the early church unanimously ascribed this Gospel to the Apostle Matthew."[43] First-century works (such as *The Didache*, *The Epistle of Barnabas*, and *The Shepherd of Hermas*), Ignatius's early second-century writings, and the work of mid-second-century AD apologist Justin Martyr all quote from or allude to passages from Mathew's Gospel. Papias (AD 110), Irenaeus (AD 180), and Origen (AD 230) all name Matthew as the author of the first Gospel.[44]

It should also be noted that it is unlikely that the leaders of the early church would lie by claiming that Matthew was the author of the first Gospel (or any Gospel

---

40. Wenham, *Redating Matthew, Mark, and Luke*, 124.
41. Ibid., 121–35.
42. Thiessen, *Introduction to the New Testament*, 132, 138.
43. Thiessen, *Introduction to the New Testament*, 131.
44. Ibid., 130–39; see also Wenham, *Redating Matthew, Mark, and Luke*, 116–21.

for that matter). Since Matthew had been a tax collector, most Jews would not have held him in high esteem. Some would have considered him a traitor to the Jewish cause. Certainly, if the early church decided to pretend an apostle wrote the first Gospel, Matthew would not have been their first choice. Therefore, it is unlikely that the early church lied about Matthew as the author of the first Gospel. Hence, there is excellent evidence to support Matthew as the author of the first Gospel (despite current speculation of New Testament scholars that Mark wrote first).

For the above reasons, John Wenham dates Matthew's Gospel to about AD 40, while Henry Thiessen dates it to between AD 45 and 50.[45] Robinson dates Matthew's Gospel to AD 40 to 60.[46] If we do not ignore the unanimous consent of the early church fathers, these early dates for the composition of Matthew's Gospel seem far more probable than the later dates given by the liberal New Testament critics of the twenty-first century.[47]

John Wenham reports that a sixth-century Alexandrian author named Cosmas dated Matthew's Gospel as early as AD 33, while the late third-century church historian Eusebius dated Matthew's Gospel to the third year of Caligula's reign—approximately AD 41.[48] It is possible that Matthew may have written the first edition of his Gospel in Hebrew (this is consistent with what the apostolic father Papias wrote) for the Jerusalem church in the AD mid-thirties, and then translated his Gospel into Greek before leaving Jerusalem in the early AD forties due to the persecution of the apostles during the reign of Herod Agrippa I (Acts 12:1–19). Whatever the case, Wenham notes that conservative scholars continued to date Matthew's Gospel to the AD thirties and forties into the nineteenth century.[49]

A strong case can be made that James's epistle was written around AD 45, and that it was one of the earliest New Testament books written. James was the undisputed leader of the Jerusalem church, at least since the AD mid-forties when the original apostles had to flee during persecution from Herod Agrippa I (see Acts 12).

---

45. Wenham, *Redating Matthew, Mark, and Luke*, 243; Thiessen, *Introduction to the New Testament*, 137.

46. Robinson, *Redating the New Testament*, 352.

47. Archaeological corroboration for the early date of Matthew's Gospel may also exist. The late Carsten P. Thiede was an expert on fragments of ancient writings. He argued that the oldest existing fragments of copies from Matthew's Gospel should be dated to the first century AD and not the second century as previously assumed. He concluded that these fragments may even date to before AD 70. Three of these fragments are kept at Magdalene College, Oxford, while the other two fragments reside in Barcelona, Spain. These fragments contain portions of Matthew 26; see Thiede, *Rekindling the Word*, 3, 15, 20, 26–27. Obviously, if the earliest known copies of Matthew's Gospel are first-century copies (and not second-century copies), then the probability of an earlier date for Matthew's Gospel increases. Thiede argued that the writing style of middle first-century fragments found in the Dead Sea Scrolls match the Magdalene fragments of Matthew's Gospel. If Thiede is correct, we may have fragments from Matthew's Gospel that go back to the mid-first century; Matthew's Gospel would have to have been written very early (possibly as early as the mid-thirties to the early forties AD).

48. Wenham, *Redating Matthew, Mark, and Luke*, 239.

49. Ibid.

Yet, James's epistle shows a knowledge of Matthew's Gospel, especially Jesus' Sermon on the Mount (Matt 5–7). Most modern translations of the Bible list over thirty-five parallel passages in James with Matthew's Gospel. Hence, if James was written around AD 45, then Matthew's Gospel had to be written earlier. Enough time had to pass for Matthew's Gospel to be recognized as an authoritative account of Jesus' life, ministry, death, and resurrection. This link between Matthew's Gospel and the letter of James is further confirmed by the fact that Matthew is the most Jewish of all the Gospels (i.e., it contains far more Old Testament Messianic prophecies fulfilled by Jesus than the other three Gospels), and James was the leader of the Jerusalem church. Therefore, an AD 35 to 42 date for Matthew's Gospel is not unrealistic—it could have been written that early.

The common objection to such an early date for Matthew's Gospel is Matthew's use of the phrase "to this day." Matthew wrote that the field purchased with the betrayal money "has been called the Field of Blood to this day" (Matt 27:8). He also wrote that the chief priests' rumor that the disciples stole the body while the soldiers slept was "widely spread among the Jews, and is to this day" (Matt 28:15). In response, it should be noted that the phrase "to this day" does not necessitate that decades had passed since Christ's death and resurrection; one or two years would be sufficient.[50] There is no reason why Matthew's Gospel should not be dated as early as AD 35 to 42.

In fact, a close study of the first two chapters of Matthew may indicate that Matthew was able to interview Joseph, the step-father of Jesus, before Joseph's death. The events recorded in these chapters seem to be from Joseph's perspective. It is possible that Joseph was still alive early in Jesus' ministry. In John 6:42, Joseph is spoken of as if he is still alive. Hence, it is possible that Matthew was already taking notes of Jesus' life and teachings during Jesus' public ministry. However, it is obvious that Matthew's Gospel, in the form we have it today, was not completed until after Jesus' ascension. We do not know exactly how long it took Matthew to complete his Gospel. But, it may have been only a few years after Jesus ascended to heaven, rather than several decades.

## GOSPEL OF MARK

Since there is no mention of the destruction of the temple in the Gospel of Mark, this book was probably written before AD 70 (the year the temple was destroyed). The early church fathers Papias (AD 110), Justin Martyr (AD 150), and Irenaeus (AD 180) tell us that Mark received the material for his Gospel from the Apostle Peter's sermons.[51] Clement of Alexandria, Tertullian, Origen, and Eusebius also acknowledge that Mark was the author of this Gospel.[52] Since Mark (also known in the Bible as John Mark) was not one of the original apostles (although he was a co-laborer of

50. Wenham, *Redating Matthew, Mark, and Luke*, 242.
51. Thiessen, *Introduction to the New Testament*, 140–46.
52. Ibid., 141.

the Apostle Peter), it is highly unlikely that the early church lied about him being the author—there would be no reason to fabricate a lie making a non-apostle the author of a Gospel.

The unanimous consent of the early church was that Mark wrote this Gospel and got his information from the Apostle Peter. In fact, most New Testament critics acknolwedge John Mark as the author and agree he received the content of his Gospel from Peter's preaching. Still, most contemporary critics date the composition of Mark's Gospel from AD 67 to 69. However, the real date of the writing of this Gospel may be earlier than this. Eusebius records a report that Papias claimed he received from the Apostle John:

> And the Elder said this also: Mark, having become the interpreter of Peter, wrote down accurately everything that he remembered, without however recording in order what was either said or done by Christ. For neither did he hear the Lord, nor did he follow Him; but afterwards, as I said, (attended) Peter, who adapted his instructions to the needs (of his hearers) but had no design of giving a connected account of the Lord's oracles. So then Mark made no mistake, while he thus wrote down some things as he remembered them; for he made it his one care not to omit anything that he heard, or to set down any false statements therein.[53]

In AD 180, Irenaeus wrote, in his work *Against Heresies* (3.1.2), that Mark was the disciple and interpreter (possibly the stenographer?) of Peter, and that when Peter departed, Mark wrote his Gospel based on Peter's sermons about Jesus' life and ministry. There is much debate concerning Irenaeus's use of the Greek word "exodus" for departure. Most scholars have translated it to mean "death." Hence, they believe that Irenaeus meant that Mark wrote his Gospel after Peter's death in AD 67. However, the more common meaning of the word exodus is "departure." Wenham and Thiede understand Irenaeus to be saying that after Peter departed Rome, Mark wrote his Gospel based on what he learned from Peter's preaching. Since Peter may have been in Rome from AD 42 to 44, Mark may have written his Gospel as early as AD 45.[54]

The hypothesis that Mark wrote his Gospel while Peter was still alive is consistent with what the church fathers Papias and Clement of Alexandria reported on the matter. For, Eusebius, commenting on the writings of these church fathers from the second century AD, relates a tradition that after Peter preached the gospel in Rome, he departed the region. The Christians in Rome then pleaded with Mark to put into writing Peter's gospel. Mark did so; he authored the Gospel that bears his name. When Peter learned of Mark's Gospel, he gave it his approval and allowed it to be read in the churches.[55] This means that it is possible that Mark's Gospel was written as early

---

53. Lightfoot and Harmer, *Apostolic Fathers*, 529.
54. Wenham, *Redating Matthew, Mark, and Luke*, 169–72, 243.
55. Eusebius, *Hist. eccl.*, 2.15.

as AD 45. This early date is corroborated by the apostolic fathers: Clement of Rome quotes from or alludes to Mark's Gospel in AD 70, the *Didache* alludes to it in the AD sixties, while the *Shepherd of Hermas* does so about AD 85.[56]

Carsten B. Thiede ageed with papyrologist Jose O'Callahan that there exists archaeological evidence supporting the earlier dating of Mark's Gospel in the Dead Sea Scrolls. A growing number of papyrologists have identified a small fragment called 7Q5 as Mark 6:52–53. The latest the fragment can be dated is AD 68 (when the Qumran community was dispersed). But, some papyrologists believe the fragment should be dated as early as AD 50. This would be a very early copy of Mark's Gospel and confirmation that the Gospel was originally written in the AD mid-forties.[57]

## GOSPEL OF LUKE AND THE BOOK OF ACTS

Both the Gospel of Luke and the book of Acts were written to the same recipient—a man named Theophilus (Luke 1:1–4; Acts 1:1–3). The prologues of these books show us that Acts is the sequel of Luke; therefore, Luke was written before Acts. Acts focuses on the key characters Peter, Paul, and James (the half-brother of Jesus), yet it does not record their deaths. Peter and Paul died between AD 64 and 67, while James died in AD 62. Since Acts records the deaths of people less significant to the purposes of the book (i.e., Ananias, Sapphira, Stephen, James son of Zebedee, and Herod Agrippa I), it appears that Acts must have been written before Peter, Paul, and James were executed. Also, though Jerusalem is one of the major cities of the book of Acts and the temple plays a key role in Acts, no mention is made of the war with the Romans (which started AD 66) and the destruction of the temple (AD 70). This is further confirmation that Acts was written early. Acts is a book filled with adventure, yet it ends anticlimactically with Paul in Rome in chains in AD 61. This makes no sense unless Acts was completed in AD 61 and then sent to Theophilus. This early date for Acts is confirmed by the fact that the *Didache*, which was probably written in the AD sixties, alludes to Acts 4:32.

Since Acts is the sequel to Luke's Gospel, the Gospel of Luke had to be written at an even earlier date. This is also confirmed by the fact that Paul quotes from Luke's Gospel as Scripture in the AD mid-sixties (1 Tim 5:18). Therefore, both Luke and Acts were written before AD 62.

It is also unlikely that the early church would have made up the idea that Luke was the person who wrote this Gospel and the book of Acts. Luke was not one of the original apostles. In fact, he probably never even met Jesus during Jesus' earthly ministry. If the apostles merely fabricated the identity of the author of Luke and Acts, they would have probably chosen one of the original apostles to be the author.

---

56. Lightfoot and Harmer, *Apostolic Fathers*, 12, 30, 223, 316.
57. Thiede, *Rekindling*, 48–51.

## Part 2—Inerrancy Defended

Is it possible that the reason why Paul did not discuss, in detail, the life and ministry of Jesus in his letters was because his readers already had access to a written account of Jesus' life and ministry? Is it possible that Luke's Gospel was written even before Paul wrote his first letter (in my opinion, Paul's Letter to the Galatians)? Is it possible, as John Wenham argues, that Luke is the brother famous for his "Gospel" spoken of by Paul in 2 Corinthians 8:18? John Wenham believes that Luke's Gospel was well-known by the AD mid-fifties.[58] In fact, Paul quotes Luke's Gospel as Scripture in the early AD sixties (1 Tim 5:18). It is possible that Luke's Gospel could have been written as early as the AD mid-forties. Luke's Gospel was also referenced very early (the AD sixties) in the *Didache*.[59]

Also, much of the first two chapters of Luke's Gospel seems to represent the perpective of Mary, the mother of Jesus (see Luke 1:26–56; 2:19, 51). Luke may have interviewed her for this information. This would also indicate that Luke's Gospel was written early—during the life of Mary.

When Paul discusses the Lord's Supper with his Corinthian readers, he seems to be giving Luke's account of the Lord's Supper (1 Cor 11:23–26; Luke 22:19–20). This is another clue that Luke was written before AD 55, since 1 Corinthians was written about AD 55.

In 2 Corinthians 8:16–18, Paul tells the Corinthians that he is sending to them Titus and two other Christian brothers who have been entrusted to carry the donations for the Judean Christians. Paul refers to one of Titus's colleagues as "the brother whose fame in the gospel has spread through all the churches." John Wenham points out that many of the church fathers (i.e., Origen, Eusebius, Ephraem, Chrysostom, and Jerome) identified the brother famous in all the churches for the gospel as Luke. They believed the gospel (*euaggelion* in the Greek) referred to the Gospel written by Luke.[60]

Modern critics disagree for two reasons. First, they do not believe the Gospels were called "Gospels" in the first century AD. Second, these critics also do not believe that Luke's Gospel was written early enough to be referred to in 2 Corinthians, which was written in AD 56.

In response to the first argument, Mark starts his Gospel with these words: "The beginning of the gospel of Jesus Christ, the Son of God" (Mark 1:1). Though it is doubtful that Mark was actually calling his book "the gospel," he was saying that his book contained the "good news" of Jesus Christ. For, gospel literally means "good news." But, it was probably not long before the early church began to call the four Gospels by the name "Gospel" due to Mark 1:1. The four recognized books that proclaim the good news of Jesus were eventually called "Gospels." But, how early did this occur? The apostolic father Ignatius referred to the Gospels as "the Gospel" in AD 107, while

---

58. Wenham, *Redating Matthew, Mark, and Luke*, 243.
59. Lightfoot and Harmer, *Apostolic Fathers*, 217, 221–24.
60. Wenham, *Redating Matthew, Mark, and Luke*, 230–37.

the *Didache* in the AD sixties refers to allusions to the Gospels as "the Gospel."[61] Hence, it is not unrealistic to acknowledge that the mid-first-century church already referred to Matthew, Mark, Luke, and John as "Gospels."

In response to the second argument, it should be noted that the critics assume what they are supposed to prove—they are guilty of arguing in a circle. They assume that Luke's Gospel could not possibly have been written before 2 Corinthians (AD 56) in order to "prove" that 2 Corinthians could not possibly refer to Luke's Gospel. But, if we are correct in arguing for an early date of Luke's Gospel, then there is no reason to rule out the possibility that Paul was speaking of Luke, who was famous in all the churches of that region for his Gospel. The early church fathers had no problem interpreting this 2 Corinthians 8:18 in this light.

If Mark could refer to his written work about Jesus as "the good news" (i.e., the gospel), then there is no reason why Paul could not refer to Luke's written work about Jesus as "the good news" (i.e., the gospel). It should be noted that if Paul merely means "the brother who is famous for his *preaching* of the gospel," then it is unlikely that his readers would know about whom he was writing. There were many disciples famous for preaching the gospel to the churches, but, throughout the Corinthian region of the world—Macedonia and Achaia (i.e., the area of ancient Greece)—there was probably only one written Gospel known to all the churches at that time—the Gospel of Luke.

If this reasoning is correct, then Luke's Gospel was already famous throughout ancient Greece in AD 56 (when 2 Corinthians was written). How long would it take (in the first century AD) to write a book, have copies of it made, have it distributed throughout Greece, and read in the churches throughout the region? And, how long would it take before the author of the book would become famous throughout all the churches of that region? It seems that if Luke was famous for his Gospel throughout the churches of the region by AD 56, he had to write his Gospel at a significantly earlier time. Hence, a date for Luke's Gospel of between AD 45 and 50 seems appropriate.

## GOSPEL OF JOHN

The Gospel of John had, in the past, been dismissed as a second-century document because the Christology (i.e., doctrine of Christ) appeared to be far too developed for the first century. But, this is not the case, for the Christology found in Philippians (or other Pauline letters) is no more primitive. In fact, Paul already taught that Jesus is fully divine in his earliest letters (i.e., Gal and 1 Thess). In these letters, Paul referred to Jesus as "the Lord Jesus Christ." In Philippians, Paul stated that Jesus continues to exist in nature as God and that every knee will someday bow to Jesus (Phil 2:6–11). In other words, the fact that the Gospel of John teaches the full deity of Christ and his preexistence is not a sufficient reason for rejecting a first-century date for its composition.

---

61. Ibid., 234–35.

## Part 2—Inerrancy Defended

There is ample evidence for John's Gospel being a first-century AD document.[62] It is quoted or paraphrased frequently by the apostolic fathers (i.e., *Epistle of Barnabas*, Ignatius, and the *Shepherd of Hermas*) in the first two centuries, and by other second-century church leaders (i.e., Tatian, Theophilus of Antioch, Irenaeus, and Clement of Alexandria). The apostolic father Papias knew of this Gospel and wrote about its author. Tatian wrote, in AD 170, his own harmony of the Gospels—he clearly taught that Matthew, Mark, Luke, and John were the only four Gospels accepted by the second-century church.[63]

Archaeological evidence also exists for the antiquity of John's Gospel—a very early fragment of John's Gospel. The John Ryland's fragment of John chapter 18 has been dated by some scholars to about AD 130. However, papyrologist Carsten B. Thiede has persuasively argued that this fragment of a copy of John's Gospel should probably be dated earlier—as early as AD 100. In fact, Thiede adds that there is no reason why it could not have originated in the late first century.[64] Since this fragment was found in Egypt, the original of John's Gospel would have had to be written considerably earlier; for, the Gospel did not immediately spread to Egypt from Israel.[65]

The author of John's Gospel refers to himself as "the disciple whom Jesus loved" (John 21:20, 24). The internal evidence of the Gospel of John shows the author to be a Palestinian Jew who had knowledge of Jewish feasts and customs, as well as an eyewitness perspective of the events he records.[66] He was the disciple who leaned on Jesus' chest during the Last Supper (John 13:23–25). Hence, he was one of Jesus' inner circle. The other Gospels reveal this inner circle to be Peter, and the two sons of Zebedee—James and John (e.g., Matt 17:1). But, Peter was not the author; for, the author of John's Gospel speaks about Peter talking to "the disciple whom Jesus loved" (John 13:23–25). James, son of Zebedee, could not be the author for he was martyred before this Gospel was written, in the early to AD mid-forties (Acts 12:1–2). Hence, by process of elimination, the Apostle John was the author of the Fourth Gospel.

Many scholars reject the Apostle John as the author of the fourth Gospel. They point to Papias's statement which seems to indicate a different John was the author, not the Apostle John. Papias wrote:

> I would inquire about the discourses of the elders—what was said by Andrew, or by Peter, or by Philip, or by Thomas or James, or by John or Matthew or any other of the Lord's disciples, and what Aristion and the elder John, the disciples of the Lord say. For I did not think that I could get so much profit from the contents of books as from the utterances of a living and abiding voice.[67]

---

62. Thiessen, *Introduction to the New Testament*, 162–64.
63. Ibid., 162–65.
64. Thiede, *Rekindling*, 10–11, 26–27.
65. Ibid., 122.
66. Thiessen, *Introduction to the New Testament*, 167–69.
67. Eusebius, *Hist. Eccl.* 3.39.3–4; Lightfoot and Harmer, *Apostolic Fathers*, 528.

I agree with those scholars who argue that Papias is not talking about two distinct Johns; instead, he is speaking about two different ages—the age of the original apostles and the age of the elders. The Apostle John was an original apostle; but, he also outlived the rest of the other original apostles. John lived into the age of "the elders." The "elders" were leaders in the early church who personally knew Jesus, but were not necessarily of the original twelve apostles. The Apostle John was the one person who was both a leader in the age of the apostles and a leader in the age of the elders.

During the age of the apostles (i.e., when most of the apostles were still alive), their colleagues were called "elders." This can be seen in the Jerusalem church at the time of the Jerusalem Council (Acts 15:2, 22, 23). The phrase "the apostles and the elders" is repeated numerous times. Hence, the early church was led by the apostles and the elders. When all the apostles had died, except for John, then John and the elders led the church. At this time, the "age of the elders" began.

Some of the elders may have been members of Jesus' seventy disciples (Luke 10:1). They followed Jesus and were appointed positions of leadership by him while the apostles were alive. However, many of them outlived the apostles—they were probably less likely to be martyred. Hence, John lived through the age of the apostles (in fact, he was one of the apostles) on into the age of the elders. This is why he identifies himself, later in life, as "the elder" (2 John 1 and 3 John 1).

The age of the apostles roughly ran from AD 30 to about 70. Most of the orignal apostles had been martyred by AD 70. Then, the age of the elders would have extended from AD 70 to about 95. With the death of the last elder, the age of the eyewitnesses would have ended. Next, came the age of the apostolic fathers. The apostolic fathers led the church from AD 95 to about 156, ending with the death of Polycarp (the last living pupil of the apostles).[68]

If the above speculation is sound, then it makes sense that Papias would include the Apostle John in two separate lists: first with the original apostles, later with the elders. Hence, he does not mention two Johns. Instead, he mentions two ages: the age of the apostles and the age of the elders. John was an abiding voice in both ages.

If the Apostle John did not write this Gospel, then it is inexplicable as to why the author never mentions the Apostle John by name. This is especially true in that the Apostle John plays such a prominent role in the other three Gospels. The most reasonable conclusion is that the Apostle John wrote the fourth Gospel. This is the most prevelant view throughout the history of the church. Irenaeus and Clement of Alexandria both accepted John the Apostle as the author of this Gospel, as have most Christian thinkers before the advent of higher criticism.[69]

However, even if someone rejects the Apostle John as the author, and instead believes John the Elder is a different person from the Apostle, it is still clear that the

---

68. Some of the writings of the "apostolic fathers" were actually written well before AD 95 and were written during the "age of the elder.

69. Thiessen, *Introduction to the New Testament*, 164–65.

author ("the disciple whom Jesus loved") is an eyewitness who knew Jesus. This is the view of leading New Testament scholars such as Martin Hengel and Richard Bauckham.[70] They deny the author was one of the original apostles; still, they acknowledge the author was an eyewitness of Jesus and one of his most beloved disciples.

We must now attempt to answer the question as to when this Gospel was written. Due to early fragments of copies of this Gospel and many quotations found in the writings of the leaders of the second-century church, it is no longer acceptable to date the composition of this work to the second century. It is unambiguously a first-century document. Most conservative scholars (and even some liberal scholars) date John's Gospel to around AD 85 to 95.

Still, a minority of scholars entertain the possibility that the Gospel of John may have been written even earlier. John A. T. Robinson dates John's Gospel from AD 40 to 65.[71] James Charlesworth of Princeton, due to his research on the Dead Sea Scrolls, is open to the possibility that John's Gospel may have been authored as early as AD 50.[72] The hypothesis that John's Gospel has a pre-AD 70 date is strengthened by the fact that John speaks of the temple grounds in the present tense in John 5:2. This would not be the case if John's Gospel were written after AD 70.

Those who argue for the later date of AD 85 to 95 for John's Gospel usually assume that a considerable amount of time is needed for the development of the theology found in John's Gospel. But, this is not necessarily the case. For Paul's theology is highly developed even in his earliest letters—Galatians and 1 Thessalonians. If Paul's theology was this developed by the late AD forties or early fifties, then there is no reason why John's theology could not be this developed at that point in time as well. And, if the other three Gospels (i.e., Matthew, Mark, and Luke) were already written in the AD thirties and forties, then the theology of John's Gospel would not be too advanced for the AD mid-fifties. Though most scholars prefer the later date, I now lean toward the earlier date—the AD mid-fifties.

There are other good reasons for entertaining the possibility that John wrote his Gospel before the temple was destroyed in AD 70. In John's Gospel, the enemy of the church is not the Roman Empire, but the Jewish religious leaders (John 7:1; 8:48, 52; 10:31; 12:9–11). There is no hint in the Gospel of John of any opposition to the church coming from the Roman Empire. This implies that the Gospel was written before Nero's persecution of Christians in the AD sixties.

The theological thought forms in John's Gospel, rather than being too developed for first-century literature, are actually very consistent with that found in the Dead Sea Scrolls.[73] Also, John emphasizes salvation through faith in Jesus more than the other three Gospels (John 1:12–13; 3:16–18; 5:24; 6:35, 47; 10:26; 20:30–31; etc). Could it

---

70. Bauckham, *Testimony of the Beloved Disciple*, 73–91.
71. Robinson, *Redating the New Testament*, 352.
72. Thiede, *Dead Sea Scrolls*, 181.
73. Thiede, *Dead Sea Scrolls*, 181.

be that John's Gospel is the only Gospel written after the Jerusalem Council of AD 49? If this is the case, John had the motive to emphasize salvation through faith in Jesus while clearly showing that salvation is not earned through the works of the Old Testament Law. John stated his reason for writing his Gospel: "Therefore many other signs Jesus also performed in the presence of the disciples, which are not written in this book; but these have been written so that you may believe that Jesus is the Christ, the Son of God; and that believing you might have life in His name" (John 20:30–31).

Hence, John wrote this Gospel to encourage people to believe in Jesus for salvation. His specific reasons for writing his Gospel may have been: (1) to more explicitly declare the deity of Christ, (2) to more clearly proclaim salvation through faith in Jesus, and (3) to show that Jesus, and not John the Baptist, is the Jewish Messiah (or, to at least show John the Baptist's disciples where the Baptist fit in the Messianic scheme of things—he was the forerunner of Messiah).

Both Irenaeus and Clement of Alexandria say that John wrote his Gospel after the other three Gospels had already been written.[74] John may have wanted to supplement the material found in the other three Gospels (assuming he was aware of these writings). If this is the case, he may have chosen to include Jesus' most unambiguous claims to be God (John 5:17–18, 22–23; 8:23–24, 58–59; 10:30–33; 14:9; 17:5). And, since John writes after the Jerusalem Council, he may have decided to clearly annunciate Jesus' teachings about salvation through faith in him. Christ's deity and salvation through faith in Jesus were already taught in Matthew, Mark, and Luke. Still, John may have wanted to emphasize these teachings more than the other three Gospels.

Irenaeus tells us that John wrote his Gospel while in the city of Ephesus.[75] Even in the AD mid-fifties, the teachings of John the Baptist were still popular in that city (Acts 18:24—19:7). Could it be that John wrote his Gospel in the AD mid-fifties while in Ephesus, and that one of his reasons for writing was to remind the Jews in Ephesus that John the Baptist was not the Messiah and that the Baptist's ministry pointed to Jesus, the true Jewish Messiah (John 1:6–8)?

John's Gospel goes to great lengths to argue for Jesus' full deity (John 1:1, 14; 20:31; etc). This may be because he wanted to refute the Ebionite heresy. This heresy argued that, though Jesus was the Jewish Messiah, he was not God. Ebionism was one of the earliest christological heresies that confronted the church.[76]

Many scholars argue that John's Gospel could not have been written in the AD mid-fifties, since the final chapter of John's Gospel implies that the Apostle Peter has already died (John 21:18–23). Since Peter died around AD 67, John's Gospel had to be written after that date. But, it is also possible that the first edition of the Gospel of John was completed in the AD mid-fifties, and that it contained only the first twenty chapters. John 20:30–31 do seem like a plausible ending for this Gospel. Then, after Peter's

---

74. Thiessen, *Introduction to the New Testament*, 172–73.

75. Ibid., 173.

76. Erickson, *Word Became Flesh*, 42–44.

death, John may have added chapter twenty-one to dispel the rumor that Jesus had promised that he would return before John the Apostle died. John may have felt the need to include this final chapter to set the matter straight (see John 21:18–23). Still, it is also possible that the final chapter of John's Gospel was not a later interpolation, and that it was written while Peter was aging, though still alive. This is also consistent with an AD mid-fifties date. A rumor that John would still be alive when Jesus returns could have started while Peter was still alive. Whatever the case, John felt the need to set the record straight by clarifying what Jesus said, as well as what Jesus did not say, concerning the matter.

John's Gospel may explain why one of Jesus' greatest miracles (i.e., Jesus raising Lazarus from the dead) is not mentioned in the first three Gospels. For John tells his readers that the Jewish religious leaders desired to kill Lazarus after Jesus raised him from the dead (John 12:9–11). Why would Matthew, Mark, and Luke fail to mention this powerful miracle? Could it be that Lazarus was still alive when they wrote their Gospels, and that mentioning him in their Gospels would place his life in danger? Maybe Lazarus had finally died a second time before John wrote his Gospel?

Whatever the case, John does seem to indicate that the temple is still standing when he writes his Gospel (John 5:2). This indicates a pre-AD 70 date for his Gospel. During the writing of this Gospel, many of the disciples of John the Baptist are probably still ministering throughout the Roman Empire (John 1:6–8, 15, 19–37; Acts 18:24—19:7). John had to clearly identify the Baptist's role in the Messianic movement—does anyone really think John would have to clarify this as late as the close of the first century? John refutes the Ebionite heresy which denies Jesus' deity—he does not emphasize disproving the Docetist heresy which denies Jesus' humanity. The Docetist heresy did not become popular until later in the first century; whereas Christ's deity was opposed from the inception of the church. Also, in John's Gospel the main opposition of the church comes from the Jewish religious leaders, not the Roman authorities. This also indicates an pre-AD 70 date for John's Gospel. Hence, I favor an AD mid-fifties date for the composition of John's Gospel.

## CONCLUSION

This chapter has argued that evangelical apologists should not blindly accept the dates given to the four Gospels by liberal critics. Instead, we must ask the question, "How early could the four Gospels have been written?" It has shown that Matthew could have been written as early as AD 35 to 42, while Mark could be as early as AD 45. Evidence lends support to an AD 45 to 50 date for Luke's Gospel, whereas John's Gospel may have been written in the AD mid-fifties. Though I do not believe these dates are definitive, evangelicals should be open to the possibility of these early dates for the Gospels.

Chapter 30

# Misinterpreting J. I. Packer on Inerrancy and Hermeneutics

## WILLIAM C. ROACH AND NORMAN L. GEISLER

On August 7, 2014, Justin Taylor of Crossway posted J. I. Packer's review of Harold Lindsell's book *The Battle for the Bible*.[1] Some Neo-Evangelicals, however, are using Taylor's article to misinterpret Packer's views on inerrancy and hermeneutics by isolating this article from the full corpus of his published literature, in particular, Packer's expressed views in the Chicago Statement on Biblical Inerrancy and Chicago Statement on Hermeneutics (both of which Packer was a founding member and drafter).

Taylor cites Packer responding to the question: Is inerrancy a revealed truth belonging to the catholic Christian heritage? "YES—*but* . . . the questions of inerrancy and interpretation *must* be kept separate."[2]

On the one hand, evangelical readers should be thankful Taylor brought this timely article by Packer to the forefront of our attention. On the other hand, present-day evangelicals should not draw any false implications from this article that Packer never drew; namely, that because "inerrancy and interpretation must be kept separate," one can remain a consistent inerrantist while utilizing a hermeneutic that denies the historicity of any part of the biblical narrative. This position can be made in the following points.

First, present-day evangelicals should notice that Packer later included this article in a much larger work titled *Beyond the Battle for the Bible*, published by Cornerstone Books in 1980. This book serves as a treatise to introduce a faithful hermeneutic

---

1. See "J. I. Packer's Critique of Harold Lindsell," on the Gospel Coalition blog.
2. See ch. 9, where Geisler addresses the relationship between inerrancy and hermeneutics, "'It's Just a Matter of Interpretation, Not of Inerrancy': Examining the Relation between Inerrancy and Hermeneutics."

## Part 2—Inerrancy Defended

into the debates concerning biblical inerrancy. Packer's article also predates the ICBI statements on inerrancy and hermeneutics (Summit II Conference). That being said, two implications can be drawn:

(1) This single article does not capture all that Packer has said on the topic of hermeneutics and inerrancy (namely, it was one section of much larger book, *Beyond the Battle for the Bible*, which critiques Neo-Evangelical views; there are also his numerous other publications, one being *"Fundamentalism" and the Word of God*).

(2) Neo-Evangelical interpretations fail to note that Packer affirmed the Chicago Statement on Biblical Hermeneutics (1982), which by way of theological and historical purview, condemned the prevalent Neo-Evangelical views of Scripture and interpretation (in particular, any hermeneutical method used to dehistoricize the biblical narrative).

The first implication disproves any notion that Packer favors the interpretive beliefs of present-day Neo-Evangelical views on inerrancy and hermeneutics. This is not to say he does not recognize the debates concerning the distinction between inerrancy and hermeneutics. Take for instance, in *Beyond the Battle for the Bible*; Packer makes the following points about inerrancy and interpretation. Packer writes: "Recently the so-called 'battle for the Bible' has switched evangelical interest back to inspiration and the inerrancy which was traditionally held to be bound up with it, though hermeneutics is still the main concern of the rest of the church."[3]

The point being, Packer and other classic evangelicals rightly understand there is a separation (or the better term would be distinction) between inerrancy and hermeneutics, however, not a *total* separation (more on this below). In other words, as a classic evangelical and signer of the CSBI statement, Henry Blocher said to Baptist Press on November 9, 2012, "It is thus possible to talk of Scripture's supreme authority, perfect trustworthiness, infallibility and inerrancy and to empty such talk of the full and exact meaning it should retain by the way one handles the text."[4]

Second, Neo-Evangelical theologians who use Packer to justify their hermeneutical practices, overlook the fact that Packer's answer to the question of whether inerrancy is part of the catholic (universal) heritage is "Yes . . ." So, contrary to the claims, Packer has always affirmed that inerrancy is the belief of the historic universal church.[5] Neo-Evangelicals also overlook the fact that Packer wrote a critical review of Rogers and McKim's book *The Authority and Interpretation of the Bible: An Historical Approach* in *Beyond the Battle for the Bible*.[6] There, Packer, reaffirms that inerrancy is the historic position of the church, not the invention of rationalistic or Enlightenment philosophy and methodology. In many places, Packer notes how Rogers and McKim misrepresent the history of biblical authority and inerrancy. So much

---

3. Packer, *Beyond the Battle for the Bible*, 9.
4. See Roach, "Licona Appeals to J. I. Packer's View."
5. See Hannah, *Inerrancy and the Church*.
6. Packer, *Beyond the Battle for the Bible*, 146–51.

so, Packer concludes his assessment with these words: "Now I saw in my dream, that when Rogers and McKim got to heaven they found two shining ones waiting arm in arm, with something to say to them. The name of the one was Calvin, and the name of the other was Warfield. I saw that the new arrivals were freely and heartily forgiven; and I was glad. So I awoke, and behold it was a dream."[7] What were they forgiven for? Misrepresenting their (numerous Christian theologians throughout history) views because the book was "unhelpful . . . to dwell on philosophical and methodological differences between men as to cloud the fact that in their view and use of the Bible, and their understanding of the message of the gospel, they were substantially at one."[8] Contrary to the Neo-Evangelical belief that inerrancy is a modern phenomena, Packer believes that despite their methodological differences, each orthodox theologian down through the ages affirmed the classic view of inerrancy (despite their methodological differences). Whereas present-day Neo-Evangelicals not only operate according to a different methodology, they also affirm a different view of inerrancy.

Third, the qualification given that inerrancy and interpretation are to be separated is misinterpreted by Neo-Evangelical theologians. While it is true that inerrancy and interpretation can be separated (once again, the better term is distinguished), they cannot be *totally* separated. Much like we can distinguish between inspiration and inerrancy, we can distinguish between inerrancy and hermeneutics; however, we can never make a complete or total separation between the two. This was such an important point to the framers of the ICBI, they declared, "We *affirm that the text of Scripture is to be interpreted by grammatico-historical hermeneutics*" (art. XVIII). Further, article XVIII also declares that "we deny the legitimacy of any treatment of the text or quest for sources lying behind it that leads to relativizing, *dehistoricizing*, or discounting its teaching, or rejecting its claims to authorship" (emphasis added). Namely, this is another way of affirming with Blocher, "It is thus possible to talk of Scripture's supreme authority, perfect trustworthiness, infallibility, and inerrancy and to empty such talk of the full and exact meaning it should retain by the way one handles the text."

In addition, in *Beyond the Battle for the Bible*, Packer cites at length the official commentary on article XVIII.[9] The implications being: First, since at least 1979 (or 1980 depending whether you cite the article or its presence in the later published book) it has been the practice of framers of the CSBI to cite the official commentary in order to properly interpret the statement. Second, the commentary rightly states, "History must be treated as history, poetry as poetry, hyperbole and metaphor as hyperbole and metaphor . . . and so forth." However, Neo-Evangelicals wrongly treat "*history* as poetry, hyperbole and metaphor." Lastly, Packer (along with the CSBI and

---

7. Ibid., 151.

8. Ibid., 150–51, emphasis added.

9. Ibid., 57–58.

ICBI framers) rightly notes that the Bible utilizes genres, however, they do not fall prey to genre criticism (unlike present-day Neo-Evangelical theologians).

True, Packer also said, "But now it really is important that we inerrantists move on to crystalize an *a posteriori* hermeneutic which does full justice to the character and content of the infallible written word as communication, life-embracing, and divinely authoritative." However, we must not forget that shortly after the publication of this article, Packer participated in the 1982 conference on Inerrancy and Hermeneutics (Summit II Conference) in which he affirmed emphatically, "We deny that generic categories *which negate historicity* may rightly be imposed on biblical narratives which present themselves as factual" (emphasis added). In fact, Packer considered the Council on Biblical Hermeneutics (1982) an attempt to "crystallize an *a posteriori* hermeneutic"!

But this is precisely what Neo-Evangelical's do not want to highlight about Packer's views. Mainly because their views of inerrancy do to biblical texts (namely, denying the historicity) exactly what the ICBI and Packer forewarned. By way of historical purview, I (Norman Geisler) being one of the ICBI framers with Packer, can testify to the fact that we consciously had Robert Gundry in mind when we penned these words. For Gundry had just denied that sections of the Gospel of Matthew (like the story of the Wise Men—Matt 2) were historical. Eventually, Gundry was asked to resign from the Evangelical Theological Society in 1983, by an overwhelming majority of the society for these declarations. Note again, the Summit II Conference took place in 1982, predating Gundry's actual resignation in 1983. The point being, the Summit II Conference was to prevent Gundry-like approaches, not a reaction to the ETS decision on Gundry-like approaches.

Taylor also cites Packer, saying: "Is inerrancy really a touchstone, watershed and rallying point for evangelicals, and did Lindsell do well to raise his voice about it?"

Here again, this citation can easily be misinterpreted by Neo-Evangelical theologians, when in fact, Packer actually gave a positive answer, saying, clearly, "YES . . ." ; but adds only that Lindsell would have gained by "re-angling" his work. Of course, most everything could gain by "re-angling." The point is that Packer said, "Yes"; inerrancy is a "touchstone, watershed" issue! But this is the very thing that the Neo-Evangelical theologian's deny.

Packer has made it very clear, contrary to the claims of Neo-Evangelical theologians and their view of inerrancy, that he does not approve of any hermeneutic which denies the historicity of the biblical narrative (the Gospels in particular). For example, when he was asked whether Mike Licona's hermeneutic, which denies the historicity of the resurrection of the saints in Matthew 27 by declaring them as legend and factually inaccurate, was in accordance with the classic doctrine of inerrancy, Packer wrote: "As a framer of the ICBI statement on biblical inerrancy who once studied Greco-Roman literature at advanced level, I judge Mike Licona's view that, because the Gospels are semi-biographical, details of their narratives may be regarded as legendary and factually erroneous, to be both academically and theologically unsound."[10]

Packer is not alone in his judgments, for even R. C. Sproul declared: "As the former and only President of ICBI during its tenure and as the original framer of the Affirmations and Denials of the Chicago Statement on Inerrancy, I can say categorically that Mr. Licona's view are not even remotely compatible with the unified Statement of ICBI."[11]

In summary, the classic doctrine of inerrancy has served as the orthodox position of biblical authority since the advent of the church. Our shared hope with Taylor is that Packer's writings will continue to influence the views of present-day evangelicals in their approach to theological doctrines. Taylor's reintroduction of Packer's article would have benefited present-day evangelicalism more if it presented the entire corpus of Packer's thoughts, publications, and interactions to prevent any misinterpretations of Packer (even though it never intended to do so). Nevertheless, without taking these thoughts into consideration it will continue to provide Neo-Evangelical theologians a platform to falsely claim their position is in agreement with the orthodox theologians of the church and the central figures of evangelicalism. We hope and pray this article will serve as a corrective to the prevalent misrepresentations of Packer, so that evangelicals will both understand properly the doctrine of inerrancy and interpret correctly the writings of J. I. Packer.

---

10. Letter to Norman L. Geisler, May 8, 2014.
11. Letter to Norman L. Geisler, May 22, 2012.

# Chapter 31

# Can We Still Trust New Testament Professors?

## BOB WILKIN

In his book *Can We Still Believe the Bible?*, New Testament professor Craig Blomberg (Denver Seminary) says that the Bible is still trustworthy. He says we can still believe the Bible, but only if we learn to distinguish between inspired fiction and inspired history.

If that sounds a bit puzzling to you, good. It should. In Blomberg's book, he criticizes Evangelical scholars whom he considers to be "over conservative [and] judgmental."[1] He specifically names Drs. Norm Geisler, Robert Thomas, David Farnell, and William Roach.

### WHY ARE SOME EVANGELICALS "OVERLY CONSERVATIVE AND JUDGMENTAL"?

What is their problem? Blomberg sees two major flaws in their thinking. First, as mentioned above, they fail to adequately distinguish between what the Bible presents as fictional stories and what it presents as actual history. Second, they apply an anachronistic view of what errors are to the writings of Scripture. Let's consider each of those points.

---

1. Blomberg, *Can We Still Believe*, 217.

## INSPIRED FICTION VERSUS INSPIRED HISTORY

First, let's consider fiction versus history. We all know that the Bible has parables in it. While we might not think of parables as inspired fiction, that is essentially what they are. That is, they are nonhistorical stories that convey important lessons for us.

Some of the things which Blomberg considers to be fictional stories in Scripture might shock you as coming from someone teaching at a fairly conservative seminary. Blomberg favorably cites Old Testament professor James Bruckner (North Park Theological Seminary) who says that Jonah is "a unique parable about a real prophet."[2] He gives the impression he agrees. Yet later Blomberg turns around and says, "I suspect that Jonah really intended to recount a miracle that really did happen."[3] I suspect? So Blomberg is not certain. In addition, what does he mean when he speaks of "a miracle"? There are at least six miracles in Jonah: the storm suddenly comes up to stop Jonah's ship, the lot falls on Jonah, the storm stops the moment Jonah is thrown overboard, the great fish saves Jonah from drowning, the plant grows up in minutes to shade Jonah, and the plant suddenly wilts to cause Jonah discomfort and hopefully to lead him to compassion for the Ninevites. Is all of that historical? Blomberg does not say.

What about Adam and Eve and the six days of creation? Blomberg believes that "Genesis 2–3 cannot be pure fiction."[4] That is comforting. At least there is some kernel of truth there. Blomberg considers Genesis 1–3 to be fiction with a little bit of history underlying the fiction. In his view there were two people named Adam and Eve. But they were not directly created by God. They were chosen out of a group of humans who lived at that time. The universe was not created in six days. But it was created in some fashion. Blomberg says, "The genre of much of Genesis 1–11 remains a puzzle; historical narrative as the ancients would have recognized it begins in earnest only with the call of Abram in Genesis 12."[5] Later Blomberg makes this statement: "I would support an old-earth creationism and opt for a combination of progressive creation and a literary framework approach to Genesis 1."[6] What does that mean, other than he doesn't believe in a young earth or in six literal days of creation and that he considers much of Genesis 1–3 to be a literary creation (i.e., fiction) and not to be historical?

Does that mean that there was no universal flood? Blomberg doesn't directly address that issue, but presumably, in light of his indication that "historical narrative ... begins in earnest only with the call of Abram in Genesis 12," the flood as recorded

---

2. Ibid., 160.
3. Ibid., 177.
4. Ibid., 154.
5. Ibid.
6. Ibid., 177.

in Genesis 6–9 is more inspired fiction (though presumably there was really someone named Noah who had three sons).

What about Job? It too is inspired fiction, though there might have been an actual person by that name.[7]

Blomberg says the account of the rich man and Lazarus in Luke 16:19–21 is a parable, though it is not called a parable by the Lord. The events described never happened. The fact that no other parable lists the specific names of people (this one mentions both Lazarus and Abraham by name), and that it is not called a parable, should not confuse us. This is inspired fiction.[8]

Remember the amazing account in Matthew 27 of departed saints in Jerusalem who rose from their graves when Jesus rose from the dead? Matthew says, "The graves were opened; and many bodies of the saints who had fallen asleep were raised; and coming out of the graves after His resurrection, they went into the holy city and appeared to many" (Matt 27:52b–53). Blomberg says that Matthew included this account because of "the desire to maintain that Jesus's bodily resurrection from the dead guarantees the coming bodily resurrection of *all* God's people from throughout human history."[9] He then continues, "But does that mean that Matthew 27:52b–43 must reflect simple history? Or could the text, too, narrate symbolically what Paul phrases more prosaically [in 1 Cor 15:20]?"[10] In his view it is not "simple history." His point seems to be that this never happened, but that Matthew included it to show that all will rise one day. He even defends a scholar named Michael Licona (Houston Baptist University) who wrote concerning Matthew 27:52b–53: "It seems best to regard this difficult text in Matthew as a poetic device added to communicate that the Son of God had died and that impending judgment awaited Israel."[11] Later Blomberg indicates, "I have yet to be persuaded by Licona's initial views of Matthew 27:51–53 but would love to see additional comparative research undertaken."[12] In other words, he is not yet convinced that Licona is right. But he is open to the fact that Matthew has given us a fictional account of bodily resurrections.

Licona went on to wonder, "If some or all of the phenomena at Jesus's death are poetic devices, we may rightly ask whether Jesus's resurrection is not more of the same."[13] He goes on to suggest that the answer is no. Jesus really rose from the dead. However, if one adopts the views of Blomberg and other New Testament scholars like him, it would seem that just about anything reported in the Bible might be considered to be inspired fiction.

7. Ibid., 155–57; see also 177.
8. Ibid., 150.
9. Ibid., 174, emphasis original.
10. Ibid., 174–75.
11. Licona, *Resurrection of Jesus*, 553.
12. Blomberg, *Can We Still Believe*, 177.
13. Licona, *Resurrection of Jesus*, 553.

## HOW DO WE DECIDE WHAT WOULD BE AN ERROR IN THE BIBLE?

Second, let's now consider Blomberg's other contention. He believes that overly conservative Christians are too narrow in what they consider errors in the Bible. Blomberg writes: "Sadly, some extremely conservative Christians continue to insist on following their modern understandings of what should or should not constitute errors in the Bible and censure fellow inerrantists whose views are less anachronistic."[14]

What he is saying is that there are errors in the Bible *based on our modern understanding of the reporting of history*. However, Blomberg says that the people of the first century did not view historical reporting as we do. They felt it was not an error to present miracle stories as history, when in fact they were fiction created by the Gospel writers to express their faith in Jesus.

Blomberg would have us believe that the New Testament authors had a very low view of reporting history. Hence, Matthew can include a resurrection that might never have actually occurred (Matt 27:52b–53).[15] John can report that Jesus cleansed the temple at the start of his ministry (John 2:13–20), when in fact, according to most New Testament scholars today, he only cleansed the temple once, at the end of his ministry.[16]

Blomberg and his non-anachronistic friends like Bock and Harris believe that at Jesus' baptism the Father did not say, "This is my beloved Son, in whom I am well pleased," as Matthew reports (Matt 3:17). Instead, he supposedly only said, "You are my beloved Son, in whom I am well pleased" (Mark 1:11; Luke 3:21–22).[17] If anyone suggests he said both, one to Jesus and one to John the Baptist and the crowd, then he is called "ultraconservative"[18] and "far right."[19] Surely Matthew's readers knew not to think that the Gospel writers reported what was actually said or done. According to Blomberg, the Gospel writers made things up, but that's OK because they viewed the reporting of history much differently than we do today.

Did Jesus really walk on water, feed the five thousand, heal the sick and raise the dead? I thought he did. But after reading Blomberg, maybe I should wonder if some or all of those events might be inspired fiction designed to teach me important truths, but not to tell me what was actually said and done.

---

14. Blomberg, *Can We Still Believe*, 10.
15. See Blomberg, *Can We Still Believe*, 174–78.
16. Blomberg does not discuss this incident specifically.
17. See n3. Bock and Harris specifically say that the Father did not say, "This is my beloved Son." Blomberg does not mention this incident.
18. Blomberg, *Can We Still Believe*, 176, 214.
19. Ibid., 120.

Part 2—Inerrancy Defended

## INERRANCY IS NOW A VERY FUZZY CONCEPT

Where do we draw the line? Ah, that is the beauty of the Christian faith and academic freedom. You can draw the line anywhere you want and still teach at leading evangelical seminaries and Bible colleges. As long as you can affirm there are no errors in the Bible, it does not matter what you mean by that.

Can we still trust New Testament professors? No, we cannot trust most New Testament professors. At most leading evangelical seminaries most of those who teach the New Testament hold Blomberg's views. He mentions some of his friends who are New Testament scholars and who, like him, have been criticized for supposedly abandoning inerrancy. Blomberg speaks of "such evangelical stalwarts as Darrell Bock [Dallas Theological Seminary], D. A. Carson [Trinity Evangelical Divinity School], and Craig Keener [Asbury Theological Seminary]."[20]

So, if you believe that Adam and Eve, Noah's flood, Jonah, Job, and the creation account are all meant to be history, get your head out of the sand.[21]

I was at Dallas Theological Seminary from 1978 through 1985. I received both my ThM and PhD degrees there in New Testament studies. Back then we were taught that inerrancy meant that the Bible had no errors in it *based on our current view of what constitute errors*. Today the term *inerrancy* is, for most of the New Testament faculty, essentially meaningless at leading conservative schools, including Dallas Theological Seminary.[22] Almost anything in the Bible could be made up. That includes the creation account, the universal flood, and even the very words of Jesus.

I am grieved that the views expressed by Blomberg are now widely accepted and are even considered conservative. If what he believes passes for inerrancy, then inerrancy no longer has meaning.

---

20. Ibid., 120.

21. When I first wrote this some thought I was saying that Blomberg, Bock, Carson, Keener, and others do not believe that these events are *in any way* historical. That is not at all what I meant. I was writing tongue in cheek. What I meant is that most New Testament scholars today only consider these events to be historical in a very limited sense, in ways that fit their understanding of science. For example, Carson says, "I hold that the Genesis account is a mixed genre that feels like history and really does give us *some historical particulars* [emphasis added]. At the same time, however, it is full of demonstrable symbolism. Sorting out what is symbolic and what is not is very difficult" (Carson, *God Who Is There*, 15). Similarly Keener says, "Apart from some Israelite parables, nowhere else in the Bible do we read anything like this: a talking serpent convinces Man and Life to pluck a fruit that is Knowledge. Not surprisingly, *many biblical scholars, including evangelical biblical scholars* [emphasis added], suspect some figurative language here. Modern questions aside, is it possible that this way of reading the narrative is closer to how it was meant to be read?" (Keener, "Is Young-Earth Creationism Biblical?").

22. For more on DTS and inerrancy see the DTS Cultural Engagement Chapel on "Discrepancies in the Gospels," by Drs. Darrell Bock and Hall Harris, https://www.youtube.com/watch?v=C651fVKKehg. Also see, "Toward a Broad View of Ipsissima Vox," ETS 1999, Dan Wallace; and see my response, "Toward a Narrow View of Ipssisima Vox," available at http://www.faithalone.org/journal/2001i/wilkin.html.

## WE CAN NO LONGER TRUST NEW TESTAMENT PROFESSORS

If your son or daughter wants to go to Bible college or seminary, you would be wise to check out the schools, and particularly the New Testament departments, very carefully. Most schools do not believe in inerrancy.

If you think that there are no errors in the Bible based on the highest standard of what an error is, then you can't trust New Testament professors today.

The Southern Baptist Convention turned the tide when those denying inerrancy were seeking to take it over. They even rid their flagship seminary, Southern Seminary in Louisville, of all the professors who did not believe in inerrancy.

Some of the faculty at Biola and Talbot Theological Seminary left to teach at The Master's College and The Master's Seminary. While I do not agree with the Lordship Salvation stance of the president of those schools, I am pleased by their high regard for the inerrancy of Scripture. Drs. Robert Thomas and F. David Farnell, both New Testament professors there for many years, are among those highly criticized by Blomberg as being "overly conservative [and] judgmental."

If it could happen for the SBC and some seminaries, it can happen elsewhere. But until it does, I will not be sending students or any financial donations to any school which fails to teach a high view of inerrancy. If enough of us withdraw our support, the schools will make changes. As Blomberg says, if the schools determine that their faculty no longer agree with their doctrinal statement, then many will freely move on to other less-conservative schools and some will be fired.[23]

## WHY THIS HAS DIRECT RELEVANCE TO THE PROMISE OF LIFE

If Jonah never really was in a fish for three days, then why did Jesus say, "As Jonah was three days and three nights in the belly of the great fish, so will the Son of Man be three days and three nights in the heart of the earth" (Matt 12:40)?

The Lord Jesus also considered the following to be actual history: the creation account (Matt 19:4; Mark 10:6; 13:19) the universal flood (Matt 24:38–39; Luke 17:27), the burning bush (Mark 12:26; Luke 20:37), and the manna in the wilderness (John 6:49, 58).

If I cannot believe that what the Lord said about Jonah, the creation account, and the flood is true, then it is hard to see how I can be sure that what he said about everlasting life is true. The promise of John 3:16 hinges on the trustworthiness of the Lord Jesus Christ and of the Word of God.

The Lord (Matt 5:18), Paul (2 Tim 3:16), and Peter (2 Pet 1:19–21) all taught that the Bible is without error, that it is God-breathed.

While belief in inerrancy is not a condition of everlasting life, that belief surely moves a person in the direction of believing the promise of life. The one who does not

---

23. Ibid., 120.

## Part 2—Inerrancy Defended

believe in inerrancy must somehow become convinced that John 3:16 is true even if other parts of Scripture are not true.

Call me overly conservative and judgmental if you wish. But I am convinced that any seeming discrepancies in the Bible are not actual discrepancies, whether I can explain everything or not. God does not err. Therefore neither does his Word.

Chapter 32

# Did Roman Christians Detect the Influence of Roman Historiography in Matthew 27:45–54?

## CHRISTOPHER T. HAUN

Precisely what was Matthew *really* trying to say about all those unusual events that coincided with the death and resurrection of Jesus? Was he saying that the light of the sun was *really* eclipsed totally by something for three hours during the day? Was the thick fabric of the great veil of the Second Temple *really* torn completely in half? Did the earth *really* shake so fiercely that boulders were split and stone tombs were broken open? And were the bodies of several saints *really* raised back to life from the dead such that they could walk a few miles and provide a witness to the inhabitants of Jerusalem? At face value it seems Matthew recording these events as historical fact. But could it be, as a few have theorized, that Matthew styling his reporting after the Roman historians who liberally mixed fact and fiction? Such a Roman influence theory could be tested if any of the Christian citizens of the Roman Empire wrote about these events in a way that showed awareness of a stylistic emulation.

But if the critics are right, Matthew is the only historian who mentioned these events and our testing ends before it begins. James Crossley concludes that the reporting of the saints being raised from the dead was "quite obviously a human invention . . . the first Christians were inventing stories about resurrection[s]." Why? Because Josephus did not mention it and it is "not mentioned elsewhere."[1] Similarly, Michael Bird asserted confidently that "Matt 27:51–53 is a strange story that is reported nowhere else in Christian or non-Christian literature."[2] But fortunately for those who

---

1. Crossley, *Was Jesus Raised from the Dead?* Minutes 38–40.
2. Bird, "Michael Licona on the Resurrection of Jesus."

"examine everything carefully" (1 Thess 5:21) there are around thirty references to these contested events.

The testing should include references to any of the events in Matthew 27:45–54. The reluctance of some apologists to defend the literal interpretation and the historical reality of this account tends to focus mostly today on the raising of the dead saints (v. 52b) and their subsequent appearance in Jerusalem (v. 53). Some harbor less reservation over the other events clustered together with them between verses 45 and 52a. But each of these events has received a significant amount of skeptical criticism.[3] Given the cohesive nature of the cluster of events (nothing grammatical in the text sets any of the nine events apart from any of the other events), any attempt to separate one from another seems contrived. Moreover, since a sequence of multiple events clustered together is needed in the first place to form the pattern that can supposedly be recognized in the reporting of Matthew (in comparison with Virgil, Plutarch, Philo, and Dio Cassius)[4] the references use references for any of the events. It would seem inconsistent to use six or so of the nine events to recognize the pattern that leads one to interpret nonliterally and then proceed to only interpret two of the nine events nonliterally.

## The Cluster of Nine Unusual Events

|   |   | Mt 27 | Mk 15 | Lk 23 |
|---|---|---|---|---|
| 1 | three hours of total darkness | v. 45 | v. 33 | vv. 44–45 |
| 2 | temple veil being torn | v. 51 | v. 38 | v. 45 |
| 3 | earth shook | vv. 51, 54 | | |
| 4 | rocks were split | v. 51 | | |
| 5 | stone tombs were opened | v. 52 | | |
| 6 | bodies of dead saints raised from the dead | v. 52 | | |
| 7 | raised saints left tombs after Jesus arose | v. 53 | | |
| 8 | raised saints appeared to many in Jerusalem | v. 53 | | |
| 9 | Centurion vindicates or worships Jesus | v. 54 | v. 39 | v. 47 |

Arguably the most formidable objection to the recommendation to interpret any of these events in a less-than-literal way is the fact that there is nothing stated clearly in words by Matthew in the text of Matthew 27 that indicates that part of it should be interpreted any differently (nonliterally) than the rest of the historical narrative of Matthew. There are no obvious clues left by the author to shift the reader into nonliteral mode like there are, for example, when Jesus analogized believing in him to eating

---

3. For a discussion of the controversy over the tearing of the temple veil, e.g., consider Plummer, "Something Awry in the Temple?," 301–16.

4. Licona, *Resurrection of Jesus*, 552. Also Garland, *Reading Matthew*, 276.

his flesh and drinking his blood (John 6:47–66). Nor is there even a faint clue here like there seems to be in Matthew 11:14–15 where Jesus seems to say that John is not literally a reincarnation of Elijah. All we supposedly have in the text of Matthew 27:45–54 is a pattern that supposedly can and should be recognized by those who are familiar with ancient trends in ancient Latin historiography.

| Matthew 27 | Virgil | Plutarch | Dio Cassius |
|---|---|---|---|
| The Lord Jesus was executed | Emperor Julius Caesar assassinated | Emperor Julius Caesar assassinated | Death of Emperor Claudius |
| Three hours of total darkness in daytime | The sun became less radiant | The sun paled for one year | |
| The temple veil torn in half | Pagan temple idols wept / images sweated | | Jupiter's temple opened |
| The earth shook | The Alps rocked with earthquakes | | |
| Rocks were split | | | |
| Stone tombs were opened | | | |
| The bodies of dead saints were raised | | | |
| Raised saints left tombs after Jesus arose | | | |
| Raised saints appeared to many in Jerusalem | Phantoms were seen | One phantom spoke to Brutus | |
| Centurion vindicates/worships Jesus | | | |
| | Animals spoke with human words | | |
| | Wolves howled, dogs barked | | |
| | Bad omens in entrails | | |
| | Birds behaved strangely | | Bees swarmed |
| | Great lightning without any clouds | | |
| | Comet's glare caused alarm | Great comet seen for 7 days | Comet seen |
| | Blood flowed from water wells | | Rained blood |

The first part of the pattern, to the best of my ability to discern it, is the main subject of the report. When the Roman historians were writing about the death of a great leader (such as the assassination of Emperor Julius Caesar or the death of Romulus) or the end of a great epoch, they reported *that part* literally and factually. Matthew was writing factually about the main subject here—the execution and resurrection of Jesus. The second part of the pattern consists of events that were unusual—but not absurd—disturbances in the natural world. Examples of this might include mighty earthquakes, volcanic eruptions, and disturbances among the sun and stars.

A third part of the pattern consists of events that are just plain unbelievable or absurd to enlightened thinkers today but which would have impressed superstitious people of old as "bad omens." Examples of this could include idols in temples weeping, blood flowing from wells that once produced water, animals speaking in human languages, and phantoms (spirits without material bodies) appearing and communicating with the living.

It is possible to note a resemblance in the accounts of events that were triggered by the execution of Jesus and the accounts of events that supposedly occurred after the assassination of Julius Caesar. But is the resemblance strong enough to warrant ironclad categorizations of genre which can then be used to impose an external meaning upon what Matthew wrote? Or is this resemblance and the theory built upon it just another case of "parallelomania"[5] that scholars sometimes fall into? Was the resemblance strong enough to cause any ancient Romans to interpret some of Matthew 27 symbolically? It is one thing for a modern scholar to imagine the correlation; it is quite another for ancient Romans to make it.

Michael Licona mentioned four Roman test cases that he considered before publishing his Roman influence theory. He describes them as "a number of sources [that] may report that these were real persons who were raised by Jesus."[6] He lists Ignatius, Quadratus, and *The Acts of Pilate*, but then dismissed them due to ambiguities or questions of authenticity. He also briefly considered a reference to the eclipse by Thallus. We start with a reexamination of those four cases before proceeding to consider additional test cases.

Ignatius was a leader of a Roman-Syrian church in the second century. Licona cites his letter to the Magnesians, which says, "Even the prophets . . . rightly waited [for Christ] raised them from the dead."[7] Licona does not put much weight on this as an interpretive precedent however because, "it is uncertain how this report was intended to be interpreted." It is unclear which prophets Ignatius is talking about and it is unclear when they were raised. But regardless of whether the references to the raised prophets refer specifically to the saints mentioned in Matthew 27, to other people Christ raised to life before his arrest, or to a combination of both, these remain witnesses to the fact that Jesus did raise many from the dead. Matthew's account of raised saints should not be interpreted as fiction because it seems unusual.

Licona does not mention Ignatius's letter to the Trallians which does clearly echoes Matthew 27: "For says the Scripture, 'Many bodies of the saints that slept arose,' their graves being opened. He descended, indeed, into Hades alone, but he arose accompanied by a multitude."[8] The noteworthy objection has been raised that

---

5. Sandmel, "Parallelomania," 1–13.
6. Licona, *Resurrection of Jesus*, 551.
7. Lightfoot et al., *Apostolic Fathers*, 115.
8. Roberts et al., *Ante-Nicene Fathers*, 1:70.

this may not have actually been written by Ignatius.[9] It is found in the long recension of Ignatius letters (which contains material that is probably not genuinely written by Ignatius) and is not found in the shorter recension. While this makes it less valid for corroborating the historicity of the event, it still legitimately sets another precedent for a literate Roman Christian (although not Ignatius himself) interpreting Matthew 27 literally.

Quadratus of Athens was a Greco-Roman. He was also one of the first Christian apologists. He provides an early (AD 125) attestation for Jesus raising several from the dead. Eusebius conveys his view as follows:

> After Trajan had reigned for nineteen and a half years Ælius Adrian [Emperor Hadrian] became his successor in the empire. To him Quadratus addressed a discourse containing an apology for our religion, because certain wicked men had attempted to trouble the Christians. The work is still in the hands of a great many of the brethren, as also in our own, and furnishes clear proofs of the man's understanding and of his apostolic orthodoxy. He himself reveals the early date at which he lived in the following words: But the works of our Saviour were always present, for they were genuine:—those that were healed, and *those that were raised from the dead*, who were seen not only when they were healed and when *they were raised, but were also always present; and not merely while the Saviour was on earth, but also after his death, they were alive for quite a while, so that some of them lived even to our day*. Such then was Quadratus.[10]

Licona rightly points out that this reference should not be pinned specifically to the saints Matthew mentions. For the dead mentioned by Quadratus were raised from the dead before Christ was arrested while the dead Matthew mentioned were raised on the same day that Jesus arose. However, in a general sense this does give further evidence that Jesus really did literally raise several people. The idea of Jesus raising people is not an odd one. And this would not necessarily exclude the saints mentioned by Matthew. Quadratus (and presumably Eusebius) clearly interpret these events literally and present them as historical realities. The fact that several saints were literally raised was an argument that the genuineness of the amazing, enduring, and verifiable works of Jesus Christ.

The apocryphal book *The Acts of Pilate* which Licona mentioned is perhaps better known today as *The Gospel of Nicodemus*. This book should not be considered a reliable witness to any records that Pontius Pilate may have written about the events surrounding Jesus' trial, execution and resurrection. Licona understandably dismisses this account as having historical value because "the authenticity of this source has long been questioned." But his second objection ("it is likewise possible that this was

---

9. Peters, "Fathers Know Best?"
10. Eusebius. *Hist. eccl.* 4.3.1–2, emphasis added.

a reference to one of Jesus's activities during his earthly ministry"[11]) is unpersuasive considering the many details which Pseudo-Nicodemus shares with Matthew:

> And it was about the sixth hour, and *darkness* was upon the face of the whole earth until the ninth hour. And while the sun was *eclipsed*, behold the *veil of the temple was rent* from the top to the bottom; and the *rocks also were rent*, and the *graves opened, and many bodies of saints, which slept, arose*. . . . Have ye seen the *miracle of the sun's eclipse*, and the other things which came to pass, while Jesus was dying? That while they were guarding the sepulcher of Jesus, there was an *earthquake*; and we saw an angel of God roll away the stone of the sepulcher.[12]

> And Joseph rose up and said to Annas and Caiaphas: Truly and well do you wonder, since you have heard that Jesus has been seen alive from the dead, ascending up into heaven. But it is more to be wondered at that *he is not the only one who has risen from the dead: but he has raised up alive out of their tombs many others of the dead, and they have been seen by many in Jerusalem.* And hear me now, that we all know the blessed Simeon, the great priest, who took up with his hands Jesus, when an infant, in the temple. And Simeon himself had two sons, full brothers; and we all were at their filling asleep, and at their burial. Go, therefore, and *see their tombs: for they are open, because they have risen*; and, behold, they are in the city of Arimathaea, living together in prayers. And, indeed, they are heard crying out, but speaking with nobody, and they are silent as the dead. But come, let us go to them; let us conduct them to us with all honour and respect. And if we adjure them, perhaps they will speak to us of the mystery of their resurrection.[13]

> After we had crucified Jesus, not knowing that he was the Son of God . . . we deliberating among one another about the miracles which Jesus had wrought, we found many witnesses of our own country, who declared that they had seen him alive after his death . . . and *we saw two witnesses, whose bodies Jesus raised from the dead*, who told us of many strange things which Jesus did among the dead, of which we have a written account in our hands.[14]

Since this book may have been composed around AD 425 by a Roman, and since it may contain material written by other Romans that goes back to AD 300, it still could serve our purpose of testing how the ancient Romans were inclined to interpret Matthew's events. Despite the fact that Pseudo-Nicodemus was probably (but not necessarily) inventing historical details to harmonize with and fill in some gaps with the apostolic Gospel accounts, the fact remains that there is no hint that he was interpreting Matthew less than literally. Nor is there any hint in his text that would make us expect that he expects his readers to take his account less than literally.

11. Licona, *Resurrection of Jesus*, 552.
12. Hone, "Gospel of Nicodemus," in *Lost Books of the Bible*, 73–75.
13. Ibid., 79.
14. Ibid., 89–90.

If we only had these three test cases, the test results would be weak. While they may be irrelevant as to the question of historicity, they remain relevant as interpretive test cases from real Romans. Besides, there are more test cases to be considered. For the sake of determining how literate Romans interpreted Matthew, we will consider any echoes of Matthew made by any Romans up into the fifth century (when the Latin half of the Roman Empire was overcome by Germanic tribes) and beyond (the Greek half of the Roman Empire continued on until Constantinople was conquered by the Turks in the sixteenth century).

Sextus Julius Africanus (third century AD), citing both Thallus (whom Licona mentioned) and Phlegon, refers to the darkness, the earthquake, the splitting of rocks, and the resurrection of the saints:

> On the whole world there pressed a most *fearful darkness*; and the *rocks were rent by an earthquake*, and many places in Judea and other districts were thrown down. This darkness Thallus, in the third book of his History, calls, as appears to me without reason, an eclipse of the sun. For the Hebrews celebrate the Passover on the 14th day according to the moon, and the passion of our Savior fails on the day before the Passover; but an eclipse of the sun takes place only when the moon comes under the sun. And it cannot happen at any other time but in the interval between the first day of the new moon and the last of the old, that is, at their junction: how then should an eclipse be supposed to happen when the moon is almost diametrically opposite the sun? Let that opinion pass however; let it carry the majority with it; and let this portent of the world be deemed an eclipse of the sun, like others a portent only to the eye. Phlegon records that, in the time of Tiberius Caesar, at full moon, there was a *full eclipse of the sun* from the sixth hour to the ninth–manifestly that one of which we speak. But what has *an eclipse in common with an earthquake, the rending rocks, and the resurrection of the dead, and so great a perturbation throughout the universe*? Surely no such event as this is recorded for a long period. But it was a *darkness* induced by God, because the Lord happened then to suffer. And calculation makes out that the period of 70 weeks, as noted in Daniel, is completed at this time.[15]

Julius read Latin, wrote in Greek, travelled the Roman world, and studied in Alexandria. He gives no hint whatsoever of wondering if any of these elements really happened. He takes the three hours of darkness so literally that he makes an argument that the eclipse must have been caused by something other than moon. Following Matthew's list of events perfectly, he is certainly referring to the raised saints of Jerusalem when he mentions "the resurrection of the dead." And showing his eschatological fascination, he spends the next several paragraphs (not quoted here) working through historical dates to calculate the literal fulfilment of prophecies in Daniel. He makes no foray into notions about nonliteral apocalyptic symbols. The modern Roman

---

15. Roberts and Donaldson, "Writings of Julius Africanus."

influence theory fails the tests offered by Julius Africanus quite miserably. It also fails the test with Thallus and Phlegon. Thallus was a Roman historian who wrote around AD 52 and tried to dismiss the literal darkness as a literal solar eclipse by the moon. Phlegon was a non-Christian, Roman historian who wrote in the first century and who was clearly fascinated by Jesus Christ. In the ninth century, the Roman-Byzantine historian George Syncellus cites Julius positively in his discussion of these events.[16]

Celsus was a Roman pagan who was antagonistic to the Christian faith. Early in the third century he argued that the earthquake and the darkness at the time of Jesus' death were inventions rather than actual happenings. Origen gave an answer to Celsus's criticism. Origen was a scholar in Alexandria, the greatest center of scholarship (Christian and otherwise) of the Greco-Roman world. He had access to the greatest library in the world and was one of the best-read scholars in the world. With Neo-Platonic predilections, Origin had earned a reputation for attempting to transcend the literal sense of a text (or Bible passage) and seeking out its supposed deeper, spiritual, higher, nonliteral sense. It is no stretch to say that if anyone would have been inclined to interpret the Matthew 27 cluster in a nonliteral way, it would have been Origen. It is also difficult to imagine that Origen was not acquainted with Virgil and Plutarch. If the Roman influence theory is right, we should expect Origen to say that these events were spiritual rather than carnal events. But instead Origen surprises us by defending the literal historicity of the event. He wrote:

> And with regard to the *eclipse* in the time of Tiberius Caesar, in whose reign Jesus appears to have been crucified, and the *great earthquakes* which then took place, Phlegon too, I think, has written in the thirteenth or fourteenth book of his Chronicles. [ . . . ] Celsus [ . . . ] imagines also that both the *earthquake and the darkness* were an invention, but regarding these, we have in the preceding pages made our defense, according to our ability, adducing the testimony of Phlegon, who relates that these events took place at the time when our Saviour suffered. . . . Now to this question, although we are able to show the striking and miraculous character of the events which befell Him, yet from what other source can we furnish an answer than the Gospel narratives, which state that 'there was an *earth quake*, and that the *rocks were split asunder*, and *the tombs were opened*, and the *veil of the temple was rent in twain* from top to bottom, and the *darkness prevailed in the day-time*, the sun failing to give light. . . . But if this Celsus, who, in order to find matter of accusation against Jesus and the Christians, extracts from the Gospel even passages *which are incorrectly interpreted*, but passes over in silence the evidences of the divinity of Jesus, would listen to divine portents, let him read the Gospel, and see that even the *centurion*, and they who with him kept watch over Jesus, on seeing

---

16. Syncellus, "Chronography."

the earthquake, and the events that occurred, were greatly afraid, saying, "This man was the Son of God."[17]

It seems that Origen (a defender of the Christian faith) and Phlegon (a pagan historian of the second century AD) interpreted the Matthew 27 cluster events literally. Even Celsus who denied that the events happened at all was responding to the account as if he interpreted it literally (Christians said it literally happened and Celsus was saying it literally did not happen). I detect no hint of any attempt to salvage their credibility by removing them from the sphere of real history and placing them into a realm of symbol and type. The Roman-influence theory fails these rounds of testing.

Irenaeus, an early Roman church leader, may have been writing of the raised saints Matthew mentions when he wrote about "those souls aloft that followed His ascension," and "the many souls ascended and were seen in their bodies."[18] If the objection is raised that Irenaeus was not the actual author, the point still stands that an ancient, literate Roman set no precedent for interpreting the raising of saints less than literally. And if someone were to be raised that these specific raisings might not refer to the raised saints of Matthew 27, one runs into the difficulty of identifying which other group of raised saints Irenaeus might be referring to. In the four Gospels there are only three other examples recorded of Jesus raising someone from the dead: a widow's son (Luke 7), Jairus's daughter (Matt 9, Mark 5, Luke 8), and Lazarus (John 11). Perhaps John opens the door to the possibility of additional groups of the dead being raised by writing, "Therefore many other signs Jesus also performed in the presence of the disciples, which are not written in this book" (John 20:30–31 NASB). The simplest explanation would be to associate them with the saints Matthew wrote about.

Along with Phlegon, Eusebius, a Roman and Christian historian, took the darkness and earthquake literally saying:

> Indeed Phlegon, who is an excellent calculator of olympiads, also writes about this, in his 13th book writing thus: "However in the fourth year of the 202nd olympiad, an *eclipse of the sun* happened, greater and more excellent than any that had happened before it; at the sixth hour, *day turned into dark night*, so that the stars were seen in the sky, and an *earthquake in Bithynia* toppled many buildings of the city of Nicaea." These things the aforementioned man [says].[19]

John Philoponus (Philopon) of Alexandria, echoing Phlegon, writing in the sixth century AD, treats the eclipse as having literally happened.

> Phlegon mentioned *the eclipse* which took place during the crucifixion of the Lord Jesus and no other (eclipse); it is clear that he did not know from his

---

17. Roberts et al., *Ante-Nicene Fathers*, 4:444–46.
18. Ibid., 1:573.
19. Jerome, *Chronicle*.

sources about any (similar) eclipse in previous times . . . and this is shown by the historical account of Tiberius Caesar.[20]

John Malalas, a Greco-Roman historian writing in the sixth century AD, offers:

> And the *sun was darkened*, and there was darkness upon the world. Concerning which darkness, Phlegon, that wise Athenian, writes thus: "In the eighteenth year of the reign of Tiberius Caesar, there was a *great eclipse of the sun*, greater than those that had been known before: and it became night at the sixth hour of the day, so that the stars appeared."[21]

Maximus the Confessor, a Byzantine scholar in the seventh century AD wrote,

> Phlegon, the Gentile chronographer, in the thirteenth book of his Chronography, at the two hundred and third olympiad, mentions this *eclipse, saying that it happened* in an unusual manner: but does not say in what manner. And our Africanus in the fifth book of his Chronography, and Eusebius Pamphili likewise in his Chronicle, mention *the same eclipse*.[22]

Clement of Alexandria very well may have been talking about the same raised saints as Matthew when he wrote, "But those who had fallen asleep descended dead, but ascended alive . . . many bodies of those that slept arose—plainly as having been translated to a better state."[23] Even if Clement was talking about a set of raised bodies that is not the same set Matthew was talking about, there is still some indirect relevance to Matthew's set.

Tertullian, an early and influential Roman and Christian, clearly affirmed the literal interpretation of several of the Matthew 27 events: "And the sun grew dark at mid-day; and when did it shudder exceedingly except at the passion of Christ, when the earth trembled to her centre, and the veil of the temple was rent, and the tombs burst asunder?"[24] He again wrote about the darkness and the earthquake in *The Apology*:

> And yet, nailed upon the cross, he exhibited many notable signs, by which his death was distinguished from all others. At his own free-will, he with a word dismissed from him his spirit, anticipating the executioner's work. In the same hour, too, *the light of day was withdrawn, when the sun at the very time was in his meridian blaze. Those who were not aware that this had been predicted about Christ, no doubt thought it an eclipse.* You yourselves have the account of the world-portent still in your archives. Then, when his body was taken down from the cross and placed in a sepulcher, the Jews in their eager watchfulness

20. Philopon, *De Opificio Mundi*, 2:21.
21. Malalas, *Chronographia*.
22. Maximus the Confessor, *Scholia*.
23. Roberts et al., *Ante-Nicene Fathers*, 2:491.
24. Ibid., 3:170.

surrounded it with a large military guard, lest, as he had predicted his resurrection from the dead on the third day, his disciples might remove by stealth his body, and deceive even the incredulous. But, lo, *on the third day there was a sudden shock of earthquake, and the stone which sealed the sepulcher was rolled away*, and the guard fled off in terror: without a single disciple near, the grave was found empty of all but the clothes of the buried One.[25]

Cyril of Jerusalem clearly paralleled Matthew as if the events literally occurred:

> But it is impossible, someone will say, that the dead should rise; and yet Eliseus twice raised the dead,—when he was alive and also when dead . . . and is Christ not risen? . . . But in this case both the Dead of whom we speak himself arose, and many dead were raised without having even touched him. For many bodies of the Saints which slept arose, and they came out of the graves after his Resurrection, and went into the Holy City, (evidently this city in which we now are,) and appeared to many.[26]

Jerome touched on several of the events in a literal way:

> As Lazarus rose from the dead, so also did many bodies of the Saints rise again to shew forth the Lord's resurrection; yet notwithstanding that the graves were opened, they did not rise again before the Lord rose, that he might be the first-born of the resurrection from the dead. It is not doubtful to any what these great signs signify according to the letter, namely, that heaven and earth and all things should bear witness to their crucified Lord.[27]

Gregory of Nazianzus also seemed to take the events literally when he wrote, "He lays down his life, but he has the power to take it again; and *the veil rent*, for the mysterious doors of Heaven are opened; the *rocks are cleft, the dead arise*."[28] Similarly, Chrysostom wrote, ". . . and *come out of the graves after his resurrection, and went into the holy city, and appeared unto many*."[29] Remigius adds, "But someone will ask, what became of those who *rose again when the Lord rose*. We must believe that they rose again to be witnesses of the Lord's resurrection. . . . We ought therefore to believe without hesitation that they who *rose from the dead at the Lord's resurrection* ascended also into heaven together with him."[30] Hilary of Poitiers harmonizes well saying, "The *graves were opened*, for the bands of death were loosed. And *many bodies of the saints which slept arose,* for illuminating the darkness of death, and shedding light upon the gloom of Hades, he robbed the spirits of death."[31] Augustine of Hippo mentioned

---

25. Ibid.
26. Ibid., 7:98.
27. Aquinas, *Commentary on the Four Gospels*, 1:964.
28. Ibid., 6:309.
29. Ibid., 1:963–64.
30. Ibid., 1:964.
31. Ibid., 1:963.

several of the disputed events as if they happened literally: "As at the time of Christ's passion *many bodies of the saints arose*, and after his resurrection *appeared*, according to the Scriptures, *to many in the holy city*," and "Matthew proceeds thus: 'And the *earth did quake, and the rocks rent; and the graves were opened; and many bodies of the saints which slept arise, and come out of the graves after the resurrection, and went into the holy city, and appeared unto many*.' There is no reason to fear that these facts, which have been related only by Matthew."

There a few more apocryphal accounts worth considering. Pseudo-Dionysius, a Greco-Roman writing around AD 532, was no historian. But even this Neo-Platonist managed to write as if he took one of Matthew's events literally:

> What have you to say about the *solar eclipse* which occurred when the Savior was put on the Cross? At the time the two of us were in Heliopolis and we both witnessed the extraordinary phenomenon of the moon hiding the sun at the time that was out of season for their coming together. . . . We saw the moon begin to hide the sun from the east, travel across to the other side of the sun, and return on its path so that the hiding and the restoration of the light did not take place in the same direction but rather in diametrically opposite directions.[32]

There are a few letters written as a correspondence between Pontius Pilate, King Herod, and Emperor Tiberius Caesar. They show up in some sixth-century Syriac manuscripts and mention several of the contested events.

> And when [Jesus] was hanged supernatural signs appeared, and in the judgment of philosophers menaced the whole world with ruin.[33]

> [Jesus] raised the dead. . . . There is another very mighty deed which is strange to the gods we have: he raised up a man [Lazarus] who had been four days dead, summoning him by his word alone . . . so did he go forth from his tomb.[34]

> Now when he was crucified, there was darkness over all the world, and the sun was obscured for half a day, and the stars appeared, but no lustre was seen in them . . . the dead appeared rising again, as the Jews themselves bore witness, and said that it was Abraham, and Isaac, and Jacob, and the twelve patriarchs, and Moses, and Job, who had died before. . . . And there were very many whom I myself saw appearing in the body. . . . And the terror of the earthquake continued from the sixth hour of the preparation until the ninth hour . . . walked in the body among the dead that were raised. . . . He that raised up all the dead and bound Hades . . . Others saw the apparition of men

---

32. Luibheid, *Pseudo-Dionysius*, 268.
33. Hone, "Epistle of Pontius Pilate to Tiberius Caesar," in *Lost Books of the Bible*, 273.
34. Hone, "Report of Pilate," 273–74.

rising again whom none of us had ever seen. . . . I have written what I saw at that time.[35]

> [Jesus] raised from the dead one Lazarus, who had been dead four days. . . . Now when he was crucified darkness came over all the world; the sun was altogether hidden, and the sky appeared dark while it was yet day . . . in all the world they lighted their lamps from the sixth hour until evening. . . . And on the first day of the week . . . the mountains and hills were moved, and the rocks were rent, and great chasms were made in the earth, so that the very places of the abyss were visible. And amid the terror dead men were seen raising again, so that the Jews who saw it said "We beheld Abraham and Isaac and Jacob, and the twelve patriarchs . . . and we beheld Noah clearly in the body." And all the multitude walked about and sang hymns to God with a loud voice, saying, The Lord our God, who hath risen from the dead, hath made alive all the dead, and Hades he hath spoiled and slain.[36]

> . . . through the transgression of Pilate, the darkness and the earthquake had happened to all the world . . . and verily his records are true; for even I myself was convinced by his works that he was greater than all the gods whom we venerate . . . they compelled Pilate to crucify a certain god called Jesus, through which great transgression of theirs the world was darkened and drawn into ruin.[37]

*The Lost Gospel according to Peter* may have been written in the second century by a Greco-Roman. It may still have value in showing how yet another early Greco-Roman writer interpreted the gospels which he plagiarized from and expanded upon.

> And it was noon, and *darkness* came over all Judea; and they were troubled and distressed, lest the sun had set, while he was yet alive: it was written for them, that the sun set not on him that hath been put to death . . . and many went about with lamps, supposing that it was night, and fell down. . . . And in that hour the *veil of the temple of Jerusalem was rent in twain*. And then they drew out the nails from the hands of the Lord, and laid him upon the earth, and *the whole earth quaked*, and great fear arose. Then the sun shown, and it was found the ninth hour.[38]

---

35. Ibid., 274–75.
36. Hone, "Report of Pontius Pilate," 276–77.
37. Hone, "Trial and Condemnation of Pilate," 277–78.
38. Hone, "Lost Gospel of Peter," 284.

## Part 2—Inerrancy Defended

| | Writer | Year | Sun Eclipsed | Veil Torn | Mega Earth Quake | Rocks Split | Tombs Broken Opened | Centurion Vindicates Jesus | Dead Saints Raised | Risen Saints Appear | Lazarus Raised |
|---|---|---|---|---|---|---|---|---|---|---|---|
| 1 | Matthew | 55 | Y | Y | Y | Y | Y | Y | Y | Y | |
| 2 | Mark | 56 | Y | Y | | | | Y | | | |
| 3 | Luke | 57 | Y | Y | | | | Y | | | |
| 4 | John | 60 | | | | | | | | | Y |
| 5 | Thallus | 109 | Y | | | | | | | | |
| 6 | Ignatius of Antioch | 117 | | | | | Y | | Y | | |
| 7 | Publius Cornelius Tacitus | 117 | Y | | | | | | | | |
| 8 | Phlegon of Tralles | 137 | Y | | Y | | | | | | |
| 9 | Gospel of Peter | 175 | Y | Y | Y | | | | | | |
| 10 | Celsus | 177 | Y | | Y | | | | | | |
| 11 | Clement of Alexandria | 200 | | | | | | | ? | | |
| 12 | Irenaeus of Lyons | 202 | | | | | | | Y | Y | |
| 13 | Quadratus of Athens | 220 | | | | | | | ? | ? | |
| 14 | Tertullian | 222 | Y | Y | Y | | Y | | | | |
| 15 | Hipolytus | 235 | | | | | | | ? | | |
| 16 | Sextus Julius Africanus | 240 | Y | | Y | Y | | | Y | | |
| 17 | Origen | 284 | Y | Y | Y | Y | Y | Y | | | |
| 18 | Lucian | 312 | Y | | | | | | | | |
| 19 | Eusebius of Caesarea | 340 | Y | | Y | | | | | | |
| 20 | Hilary of Portiers | 357 | | | | | Y | | Y | | |
| 21 | Cyril of Jerusalem | 386 | | | | | | | Y | Y | |
| 22 | Gregory of Nazianzus | 389 | | Y | Y | | | | Y | | |
| 23 | Chrysostom | 407 | | | | | | | Y | Y | Y |
| 24 | Jerome | 420 | ? | | | | Y | | Y | | Y |
| 25 | Gospel of Nicodemus | 425 | 3 | Y | | | Y | 2 | Y | 3 | 2 |
| 26 | Augustine | 430 | | | Y | Y | | | Y | Y | Y |
| 27 | Pseudo-Dionysus | 532 | | | | | | | | | |
| 28 | Remigius | 533 | | | | | | | Y | Y | Y |
| 29 | John Philoponus | 570 | Y | | | | | | | | |
| 30 | John Malalas / Malelas | 578 | Y | | | | | | | | |
| 31 | Letters of Herod and Pilate | 600 | 3 | | 2 | 2 | Y | | 5 | 5 | 2 |
| 32 | Maximus the Confessor | 600 | Y | | | | | | | | |
| 33 | George Syncellus | 800 | Y | | | | | | | | |

After examining thirty references to various events that fit with Matthew's account, it seems the Roman influence theory has nothing going for it and everything going against it. Not a single Roman betrayed any hint of a need to interpret these events in any way that was less than fully literal and fully factual. Those who are favorable toward the nonliteral, nonfactual interpretation of any of the events Matthew 27 are then favoring an interpretation that is alien to Matthew (in so far as he did not follow the alleged pattern) and to early Roman Christians of the first several centuries. To the chagrin of this theory, even the Neo-Platonists, the plagiarists, and the critic Celsus seemed to take Matthew's events literally. For this and other reasons,[39] this Ro-

---

39. Even if the first premise of the Roman influence theory could have managed to pass this round of testing, its second premise would have failed the next test. The theory also stands on the supposition that just as the Roman authors did not intend for their readers to take everything they said literally, so too Matthew did not intend for his readers to take everything he wrote seriously. And therefore we should not take everything Matthew (or Virgil or Plutarch) wrote as factual. The theory assumes to know the unstated intentions of the minds of these authors. But such attempts at retroactive clairvoyant psychoanalysis can never transcend the confines of unverifiable speculation. While agreeing that many (perhaps even most) of the ancients flavored their historical reporting with

man influence theory deserves the genre categorization of "worldly and empty chatter and the opposing arguments of what is falsely called knowledge" (1 Tim 6:20–21).

This is not just about one little section of Matthew's narrative. The discussion of the relationship of various books of the Bible to other ancient literature is at the forefront of scholarly evangelical discourse. The Matthew 27 controversy is just one intrusion of the New Hermeneutic and New Historicism[40] into the biblical studies of what some have dubbed the New Evangelicalism. As the New Evangelicalism is pried away by the wedge of postmodern methodologies from traditional Evangelicalism on what might seem like little things—things like the raising of some saints in Matthew 27 or the raising of Lazarus in John's Gospel[41]—further concerns about the same wedge eventually creating discontinuity in the big things (like the interpretation of Jesus' resurrection in Matthew 28) are not unwarranted.

---

fiction, we cannot know what the unstated authorial intentions of Virgil, Plutarch, Matthew, etc., were. We only know what they thought and wrote, not what they thought but did not write. Besides, is it not more reasonable to imagine that Virgil and Plutarch really did intend for their superstitious Roman readership to interpret their extraordinary tales of bad omens in the heavens and on the earth as literally true?

40. There is room to question whether or not the term "New" here is coterminous with "Postmodern." The subtitle of Licona's book, *New Historiographical Approach*, shows its connection to the methodology of New Historicism. This movement (or school of thought) applies a variety of philosophies (rooted in some of the ideas of Stephen Greenblatt, Lynn Hunt, Michel Foucault, and Karl Marx) to the interpretation of literature and history. The New Historical methods are influenced by pre-modern, modern, and postmodern philosophies. Dr. Licona holds that his new historiographical work should not be classified as postmodern. Postmodernism denies that the truth of history can be known. Licona does not. He believes strongly that many important historical truths can be known with confidence. While his book should not be classified as a purely postmodern work, it is not absolved from the charge that it remains influenced by postmodernism. In her treatment of the history of historicism, Dr. Davaney, citing Veeser and Colebrook, contends that "the 'New Historicism' that has emerged in literary studies demonstrates the fluid relationship between a diffused postmodernism and new forms of historicism" (Davaney, *Historicism*, 185). Davaney also pointed out that "a number of contemporary thinkers see postmodernism as either an outgrowth of the more radical implications of earlier historicisms or, alternatively, contemporary historicism is interpreted as one mode of a larger, more diffused postmodern shift. . . . In theology, postmodernism has taken a number of forms and, in its varied forms, has expressed all of the above stated relations to historicism" (ibid., 132). The fluidity and diffusion factors at work here do not remove postmodernism from the equation; they make it more difficult to pin down. The fact remains that Licona's interpretive method clearly leads to skepticism about several narratives in the Gospels. He himself admits that using this method leaves one in doubt of "where history ends and legend begins" (Licona, *Resurrection of Jesus*, 34).

41. John's report of the raising of Lazarus is similar to Matthew's account of raised saints and suffers similar attacks. See Hunter, "Contextual and Genre Implications," 53–70, and Lea, *Reliability of History in John's Gospel*, 387–402. Note also James Hamilton's anemic conclusion in the attempt to defend it: "It appears to be at least possible that the raising of Lazarus is historical and took place in the way John has recorded it"; see Hamilton, *Did Jesus Really Raise Lazarus from the Dead?*

# Epilogue

# Historical Criticism vs. Grammatico-Historical
## *Quo Vadis* Evangelicals?[1]

### F. DAVID FARNELL

#### THE ASSAULT OF HISTORICAL CRITICISM ON THE ORTHODOX DOCTRINE OF INERRANCY

In 1998, *The Jesus Crisis*[2] sounded a warning to Neo-Evangelicals about their drift toward historical-critical ideologies. While many evangelicals ignored the warning, others directed significant hostility toward it. Bock claimed that the book "displays a lack of discernment about Gospels study.... The book should have given a more careful discussion of difficult details in the Gospels and the views tied to them, especially when inerrantists critiqued by the book are portrayed as if they were denying the accuracy of the Gospels, when in fact they are defending it."[3] In the day it was written, evangelicals were in "crisis" and now—fifteen years later—they are "searching" to find Jesus. The Gospels are now "probability" based. Inerrancy is being redefined or submerged into a historical-critical philosophical morass. Subsequent history since its writing has proved *The Jesus Crisis* accurate even if some evangelicals will not admit it. The drift has continued unabated at the cost of the historical integrity of the Gospels,

---

1. This article is reprinted and adapted from the article by Farnell, "Historical Criticism vs. Grammatico-Historical: *Quo Vadis* Evangelicals?," in *Jesus Quest*.
2. Thomas and Farnell, *Jesus Crisis*.
3. Review of *Jesus Crisis*, by Darrell Bock, 232.

the only documents that testify to the true life of Jesus. Bock's recent summary book on searching, *Who Is Jesus?*, accepts the German philosophical distinction between *historie* (what actually happened) and *geschicthe* (history as imagined through the eyes of faith). The crisis we warned of at the end of the twentieth century has become a full-fledged reality in the twenty-first.

## TWO ROADS FACING EVANGELICALISM: GRAMMATICO-HISTORICAL OR HISTORICAL-CRITICAL INTERPRETATION?

A large portion of evangelicals, especially those who now call themselves "critical-evangelical scholars," now march toward the acceptance of some form of historical-critical ideology rather than the time-tested grammatico-historical approach that has dominated sound scholarship throughout church history and upheld the integrity of God's Word among Bible-believing people. Many of the more recent evangelical works discussed in this book, like Craig Blomberg's *Can We Still Believe the Bible?* (2014); Michael Licona's, *The Resurrection of Jesus* (2010); John Walton's and D. Brent Sandy's *The Lost World of Scripture* (2013); John Walton's *The Lost World of Adam and Eve* (2015); and Christopher Hays's and Christopher Ansberry's *Evangelical Faith and the Challenge of Historical Criticism* (2013)—to name only a very, very few—now show a shocking departure from orthodox views of inerrancy held throughout church history. Clear also, the battle fought in the years leading up to the International Council on Biblical Inerrancy (ICBI) and Hermeneutics appears of little consequence to these historical-critical evangelical scholars who somehow must think that they are immune or wise enough to avoid any negative influence on their thinking by historical criticism. But *Vital Issues in the Inerrancy Debate* stands with ICBI as a firm witness against such thinking and shows the devastating impact historical criticism is now having among these evangelicals. Even more importantly, *church history stands as the firmest witness against them*, for it reveals that every time the church departed from the plain, normal sense of Scripture, the grammatico-historical sense, disaster has always ensued among God's people. Disaster is now the watchword once again.

One must now repeat Harold Lindsell's warning herein from his books *Battle for the Bible* (1976) and *The Bible in the Balance* (1979). Lindsell, who helped in the founding of Fuller Theological Seminary, catalogued what he perceived was an alarming departure from the doctrine of inerrancy among evangelicals. Around this same time, Francis Schaeffer had argued, "Holding to a strong view of Scripture or not holding to it is the watershed of the evangelical world."[4] Lindsell catalogued departures from inerrancy by the Lutheran Missouri Synod, the Southern Baptists, and other groups. He listed what he perceived as deviations that resulted when inerrancy is denied as well as how the infection of denial spreads to other matters within evan-

---

4. Schaeffer, *Great Evangelical Disaster*, 51.

gelicalism. Because Lindsell was one of the founding members at Fuller Seminary, he especially focused on what he felt were troubling events at Fuller Seminary regarding the watershed issue of inerrancy.[5] Most strategically, Lindsell attributed the "use of historical-critical method" as a foundational cause of the destruction of inerrancy among denominations. He noted, "There are also those who call themselves evangelicals who have embraced this [historical-critical] methodology. The presuppositions of this methodology . . . go far beyond mere denial of biblical infallibility. They tear at the heart of Scripture, and include a denial of the supernatural."[6] In *The Bible in the Balance*, Lindsell dedicated a whole chapter to historical criticism, labeling it "The Bible's Deadly Enemy":

> Anyone who thinks the historical-critical method is neutral is misinformed. . . . It appears to me that modern evangelical scholars (and I may have been guilty of this myself) have played fast and loose with the term because they wanted acceptance by academia. They seem too often to desire to be members of the club which is nothing more than practicing an inclusiveness that undercuts the normativity of the evangelical position. This may be done, and often is, under the illusion that by this method the opponents of biblical inerrancy can be won over to the evangelical viewpoint. But practical experience suggests that rarely does this happen and the cost of such an approach is too expensive, for it gives credence and leads respectability to a method which is the deadly enemy of theological orthodoxy.[7]

Many more than Lindsell sounded the alarm over historical criticism, but that alarm helped lead up to ICBI on inerrancy (1978) and hermeneutics (1982). *The alarm must be again sounded.*

Instead, these historical-critical evangelicals now more closely resemble the thinking and approach of Jack Rogers's and Donald McKim's work, *The Authority and Interpretation of the Bible* (1979).

Orthodox views of inerrancy, such as those expressed by the hundreds of Bible-believing scholars from all walks of evangelicalism who formed the International Council on Biblical Inerrancy and Hermeneutics, go ignored, challenged, or summarily dismissed by these critical evangelical scholars. Either these historical-critical evangelicals were too young to remember the battle that these hundreds of scholars who gathered in Chicago fought or think that somehow they are immune from the negative presuppositions and influence of Spinoza's method. The evidence, however, from *Vital Issues* is clear: critical-evangelical scholars who are attempting to interpret the Bible with historical-critical principles, either by advocating their usage or

---

5. Lindsell, *Battle for the Bible*, 23.
6. Ibid., 204.
7. Lindsell, *Bible in the Balance*, 283.

blending historical criticism into some hybrid with grammatico-historical, end up in a destructive assault against the plain, normal sense of Scripture.

*The Jesus Crisis* (1998), *Defending Inerrancy* (2011), *The Jesus Quest* (2014), and *Vital Issues in the Inerrancy Debate* (2016) have been not only prescient in seeing this tsunami wave disaster developing among evangelicals, but also correct in their assessment that a horrific crisis regarding the inerrant reliability of the Gospel documents exists among these critical-evangelical scholars who differ little from liberal New Testament critical scholarship as a whole.

Furthermore, Jesus in now lost among many of these critical evangelical scholars! They now search for a myth called the "historical Jesus." Books like Darrell Bock's and Robert Webb's *Key Events*[8] constitute strong evidence that *The Jesus Crisis* sounded the correct warning. Many evangelical scholars apparently no longer accept the Gospels at face value, but now must apply rules of critical scholarship (i.e., postmodernistic historiography) to demonstrate "probability" that the Gospels might have a core of historicity in them by applying criteria of authenticity, the same criteria that liberals in the Jesus Seminar used to dismiss the foundations of the Gospels. For them, demonstrating this kind of scholarship is even their priority. Why? Because this is what critical scholars do.[9] Evangelicals previously recognized the ruinous bane that "searching" for a myth called "the historical Jesus" was. They refused to participate in such an assault on the Gospels during the first and second quests. Now this generation of historical-critical scholars pursue the third search as if there was virtue in a pursuit that promotes doubt and uncertainty of the eyewitness testimony of the Gospels (Luke 1:1–4; John 21:24).

The term "historical Jesus" is a historical-critical fiction as well as aberration that is now being normalized among these evangelicals. It posits a heretical position that the Jesus of the Gospels and the Jesus of history are somehow different—*they are not*. It is best perhaps termed the "existential Jesus," since a close examination of the questing reveals that the "historical Jesus" is whatever the quester *a priori* determines Jesus to be or wants to make him as somehow significantly distinct from the biblical documents. After an arbitrary *a priori* decision has been made on a preconceived concept of Jesus, criteria of authenticity which stem from tradition criticism, are applied to the Gospels so that their preconceived concept of Jesus is affirmed. Since the criteria are subjective and conflicting, other criteria can be invented and applied to ensure the desired outcome. The critical weakness of these criteria, in addition to their inherent subjectivity, lies in the fact that the *same* criteria can be applied or countered with different criteria to ensure whatever view has already been assumed by the quester. If critical evangelical scholars can utilize these criteria to affirm "probability," while their more liberal counterparts use them to negate "probability" and even discredit the Gospel material, then these principles have no real value. Instead, they are acutely

---

8. Bock and Webb, *Key Events*; Bock, *Who Is Jesus?*
9. For a full delineation, see Geisler and Farnell, *Jesus Quest*.

subjective. In reality, these evangelicals have proved nothing. Like some kind of scholarly jujitsu, evangelicals' critical counterparts can apply equally negating arguments to fend off any evangelical assertions. The loser again, however, is the Gospels and their integrity.

"Questing" or "searching" for the "historical" Jesus is as a *philosophically-motivated historical-critical* construct which assumes that the Jesus presented in the Gospels is not the same or not to be identified fully with the Jesus who actually lived in history. Underlying the questing is the assumption that "scientific" research has shown that the Jesus of history was different from the Christ of Scripture, the creeds, orthodox theology, and Christian piety. These evangelicals have bought into philosophical systems that are inherently hostile to God's Word without due consideration of their destructive nature. One cannot overstress that the rise of modern *philosophical* ideologies inherent in historical criticism generates such distinctions between Jesus as he is presented in the canonical Gospels and any conceptualizations of how he is alleged to have actually existed in history. Hostile philosophical underpinnings of the ideology in terms of a virulent *anti-supernaturalism* are a major factor in creating these hypothetical distinctions. True to Spinoza's original design for historical criticism, *the overarching intent in these searches is the destruction of the influence of the Gospels, as well as the church, over society*. Evangelicals now are unwittingly participating in the destruction of the Gospels by normalizing such principles in research.

A simple question should be asked: beyond themselves, who among critical scholarship have these evangelicals convinced of the wisdom of their approach? I would doubt that any true opponents of the Gospels have ever been convinced by these methods. What has resulted is the subjecting of the historicity and reliability of the Gospels to the shifting sands of the "one-upmanship" of those who can beg the question in applying these principles by assuming what they are trying to prove.

The ICBI Statements of on Inerrancy (1978) and Hermeneutics (1982) arose as hard-won documents from previous decades of attacks on the trustworthiness of the Bible. Significantly, these documents affirm "grammatico-historical" rather than "historical-critical" hermeneutics as employed by these critically-trained evangelicals. Why? Because the authors and those who signed their affirmation to these documents knew the ruinous impact that historical-critical ideologies had upon God's Word in church history. However, these British and European critically-trained evangelicals who now advocate the adoption of some form of historical criticism have effectively annulled these two hard-won documents because they have forgotten history. Article XVIII reads:

> We affirm that the text of Scripture is to be interpreted by grammatico-historical exegesis, taking account of its literary forms and devices, and that Scripture is to interpret Scripture. We deny the legitimacy of any treatment of the text or quest for sources lying behind it that leads to relativizing, *dehistoricizing,*

or discounting its teaching, or rejecting its claims to authorship. (emphasis added)

What is the true essence of this term "historical criticism" which arose from the days of Spinoza? It is the ingredient that is used to make the Bible say whatever the researcher wants it to say. It is the dissolvent that destroys the plain, normal sense of Scripture and, in turn, can make the Bible reflect any prejudice of the interpreter that is imposed on the text. When Bible "scholars" want to make the Bible say something that it does not naturally say, they apply judicious and generous portions of historical criticism to accomplish that magic! When Bible "scholars" are offended by something in Scripture, i.e., find it unacceptable to them for a variety of their own prejudices, it allows the scholar to remake anything in Scripture to his or her own liking—either by negating it entirely or manufacturing an entirely different sense or meaning for a particular portion of Scripture. It allows the Bible to be *remolded* into something acceptable to the critical scholar's whims. The philosophical pedigree of historical criticism guarantees the magic of transforming the Bible into something more acceptable to the modern, critical mind. This has been most prominent in "historical Jesus" research in which historical-critical criteria are the tools that German- and British-trained critical scholars use (borrowed from Spinoza) to find a Jesus that they have already decided on in order to determine how they think he must really, truly be—a Jesus they find acceptable to them. These authenticity criteria tools are the "solvent" that allows critical scholars to dissolve the canonical Gospels and the information therein in order to find a Jesus that they prefer through the genius of historical criticism. *However, no two critical scholars agree on the same list of criteria or their exact definition and nature—proof positive that great evangelical confusion exists over terminology and the practice of interpretation.*

In contrast, the goal of the grammatico-historical method is to find the meaning which the authors of Scripture expressed in Scripture which the readers can discover (not create) by proper exegesis of the text. Special allowance/provision is made for (1) inspiration, (2) the Holy Spirit, and (3) inerrancy. It may be understood as the study of inspired Scripture designed to discover under the guidance of the Holy Spirit the meaning of a text dictated by the principles of grammar and the facts of history.

The "grammatico-historical" method, advocated by the both the Reformers as well as the signers of the ICBI statements of 1978 and 1982, allows the Bible to say what it naturally says plainly and normally without an *a priori* agenda as with historical-critical ideologies. As more recent evangelicals receive their education from schools that advocate some form of historical criticism, an unstable blending of these two approaches is occurring. Much confusion exists in current evangelical circles regarding grammatico-historical and historical-critical approaches to exegesis.[10] These two hermeneutical disciplines are distinct and must not be confused by evan-

---

10. Thomas, "Current Hermeneutical Trends," 241–56.

gelicals. In contrast to the Reformation roots of the grammatico-historical method, the historical-critical hermeneutic has its roots in deism, rationalism, and the Enlightement. Edgar Krentz, favorable to the practice, readily admits in his *Historical-Critical Method* that "Historical method is the child of the Enlightenment."[11] Gerhard Maier, opposed to historical criticism, argued, "historical criticism over against a possible divine revelation presents an inconclusive and false counterpart which basically maintains human arbitrariness and its standards in opposition to the demands of revelation."[12]

Because of its distinct philosophical differences and developments, the grammatico-historical method is open to the supernatural and miraculous, while the historical-critical is inherently hostile to such ideas. It assumes the Scriptures are true regarding their assertions and posits the idea that God can and does intervene in human history. The historical-critical method, however, assumes Troeltsch's ideological principles of (a) criticism or methodological doubt—history achieves only probability, nothing can be known with any certainty; (b) analogy (somewhat like the modern idea of Uniformitarianism) that present experience becomes the criteria of probability in the past (hence, if no supernatural events occur today, they do not occur in the past either); and (c) correlation or mutual interdependence that postulates a closed-continuum of cause and effect with no outside divine intervention.[13] Therefore, anytime evangelicals dehistoricize the Gospels or the Scriptures as a whole, they practice a form of historical-critical, not grammatico-historical hermeneutics. Grammatico-historical exegesis does not shift the burden of proof upon the Scriptures to demonstrate their truth, reliability, or historicity as do historical-critical ideologies like source criticism. The goal of the grammatico-historical approach is to understand the Scripture as was intended by the original author, not what is desired by the critical scholar.[14] It seeks single, not multiple, layers of meaning, while emphasizing the perspicuity of Scripture. In contrast, the historical-critical approach does not attempt to understand the Scripture as was necessarily intended. It pursues a deductive approach that *a priori* assumes an interpretation and forces Scripture into that mold. It often practices an allegorizing hermeneutic that sees multiple layers of meaning.[15] At root, philosophy

11. Krentz, *Historical-Critical Method*, 55.

12. Maier, *End of the Historical-Critical Method*, 25.

13. See Krentz, *Historical-Critical Method*, 55; Troeltsch, "Historical and Dogmatic Method," 11–32.

14. Terry, *Biblical Hermeneutics*, 173.

15. Evangelical drift from the single-meaning principle is alarming. Wallace, reflecting the evangelical drift into multiple layers of meaning, argues: "One of the reasons that most NT grammarians have been reticent to accept this category [plenary genitive] is simply that most NT grammarians are Protestants. And the Protestant tradition of a singular meaning for the text (which, historically, was a reaction to the fourfold meaning employed in the Middle Ages) has been fundamental in their thinking. However, current biblical research recognizes that a given author may, at times, be *intentionally* ambiguous. The instances of double entendre, sensus plenior (conservatively defined), puns, and word-plays in the NT all contribute to this view. . . . Tradition has to some degree prevented

controls the exegetical approach of historical-critical approaches like source, form/tradition, and redaction criticism. The grammatico-historical method of interpretation has been the safeguard in hermeneutics, because it downplays subjectivity and emphasizes the need for Spirit-guided objectivity in exegeting Scripture.

The grammatico-historical method has a required spiritual dimension that is entirely lacking in historical criticism: the interpreter *must* be indwelled by the Holy Spirit to interpret Scripture properly (which involves acceptance and understanding—Rom 8:3; 1 Cor 2:6–16). Certain areas of meaning will be hidden to the natural man because he will lack the necessary spiritual guidance to use the exegetical data properly. As Paul warned, "But a natural [unsaved] man does not accept the things of the Spirit of God, for they are foolishness to him, and he cannot understand them, because they are spiritually appraised" (1 Cor 2:14).

In spite of this, critically-trained evangelicals now apparently advocate a blending, or acceptance, of historical-criticism with grammatico-historical approaches. They maintain, of course, that some form of modification of any elements in historical criticism that are hostile to the supernatural is possible. For example, I. Howard Marshall argued, "The study of any narrative which purports to convey historical information in order to determine what actually happened and is described or alluded to in the passage in question" and "conservative scholars may often seem unduly reactionary in their refusal to accept hypotheses which depend on the presence of errors and contradictions in the NT."[16] Likewise, Robert Guelich said, "For many to whom the Scriptures are vital the use of these critical tools has historically been more 'destructive' than 'constructive.' But one need not discard the tool because of its abuse."[17] Evangelical Darrell L. Bock thinks that the current generation of evangelicals is intelligent and wise enough to overcome the bane of historical-critical approaches, "In the hands of a skilled exegete who uses the tools of interpretation in a way that fits what they are capable of, Form Criticism can be a fruitful aid to understanding and to exposition."[18] A recent generation of evangelicals produced *New Testament Criticism & Interpretation* that included the following in the editor's preface: "For many years American evangelicals assumed that a high view of Scripture was incompatible with the employment of higher-critical methods. While Moses Stuart, the great nineteenth-century scholar, actually served as the pioneer introducing American Christians to the field of biblical criticism, it was the work of Ned B. Stonehouse and George Eldon Ladd that paved the way for recent discussions among American evangelicals. . . . One thing, however, is certain: If American evangelicals are to have an impact in the academy and in the church, they must enter into dialogue

---

Protestants from seeing this"; see Wallace, *Greek Grammar*, 120n134.

16. Marshall, "Historical Criticism," 126–38 (quotes from 126 and 133).

17. Guelich, *Sermon on the Mount*, 23.

18. Bock, "Form Criticism," 192.

with contemporary scholarship."[19] The preface continues, "To deny that the Bible should be studied through the use of literary and critical methodologies is to treat the Bible as less than human, less than historical, and less than literature."[20]

Immediately apparent is the startling blindness, or intentional overlooking, of the hostile presuppositions and historical antecedents in the development of historical criticism by these contemporary evangelicals who are now training pastors and teachers in evangelicalism.[21] Somehow these evangelicals believe that they are immune to historical criticism's biases. The roots of historical criticism are the same roots as those of biblical errancy—there is no essential, qualitative difference.[22] As Geisler noted, "It is often näively assumed that because contemporary theologians are evangelical in doctrine and practice they somehow are immune from adverse philosophical influences. . . . Often in the history of Christianity some of the most philosophically unorthodox writers believe themselves to be defending and preserving 'true' Christianity."[23] A very telling remark about how quickly historical criticism negatively overshadowed the gains of grammatico-historical methods espoused in the Reformation is also noted by Geisler:

> Within a little over one hundred years after the Reformation the philosophical seeds of modern errancy were sown. When these seeds had produced their fruit in the church a century or so later, it was because theologians had capitulated to alien philosophical presuppositions. Hence, the rise of an errant view of Scripture did not result from a discovery of factual evidence that made belief in an inerrant Scripture untenable. Rather, it resulted from the unnecessary acceptance of philosophical premises that undermined the historic belief in an infallible and inerrant Bible.[24]

Stephen Davis, far from espousing fundamentalist views, confirms this:

> What leads them to liberalism, apart from cultural and personal issues, is their acceptance of certain philosophical or scientific assumptions that are inimical to evangelical theology—e.g., assumptions about what is "believable to modern people," "consistent with modern science," "acceptable by twentieth-century canons of scholarship," and the like.[25]

---

19. Preface to *New Testament Criticism & Interpretation*, 13.

20. Ibid., 14.

21. For the history and presuppositional developments of historical criticism, see Farnell, "Philosophical and Theological Bent," 85–131.

22. See Geisler, *Biblical Errancy*.

23. Ibid., 7.

24. Ibid., 11. This excellent work presents a variety of articles that trace the underpinnings of historical-critical methodologies to baneful philosophical methodologies. Unfortunately, Geisler's warning has not been heeded by evangelicals who continue their connections with Historical Criticism.

25. Davis, *Debate about the Bible*, 139. What is refreshing about Davis's statement is the outright candor of the remark compared to some evangelicals who refuse to admit the philosophical basis of

Many of the evangelical historical-critical writings cited in this work as well as *The Jesus Crisis* in 1998 constitute demonstrable proof that these evangelicals who have advocated such a blending of historical criticism with grammatico-historical criticism now operate very similar to their liberal counterparts and are using the same ideologies. Not only has inerrancy been diminished in importance, but now Neo-Evangelicals display in works like *Key Events* such terminology as "core historicity," "probability," "possibility," or "essential historicity" of these "footprints," "surviving traces," or "historical traces," all showing the reduction of the value of inerrancy since they openly invite the speculation that some parts may not be accurate. Bock and Webb argued,

> The goal was to see the extent to which a study of key events might provide an overall framework for understanding Jesus. Once these key events had been selected, each essay was to do three things: first, it was to set forth a case for the probable historicity of the event using the criteria of authenticity. The focus was to, first, establish the probable historicity of the event's core rather than concerning itself with all of the details. Second, explore the socio-cultural contextual information that contributes to understanding the event in its first-century context. Third, in light of this context, to consider the significance of the event for understanding Jesus. Thus, each study would have both macro and micro concerns, being both analytic and synthetic.[26]

Importantly, these types of concessions by evangelicals to historical criticism show just how negative the impact has been upon the Gospels as well as biblical literature as a whole. Any evangelical attempts at modifying historical criticism have failed to arrest the negative impact upon Scripture research by these evangelicals, for these chapters have catalogued numerous ways in which the Scriptures, especially the Gospels, have been brought into suspicion as reliable documents. The *key question* remains unanswered in all of the works of these critically-trained evangelicals: will the more radical (i.e., tradition liberal critics of Scripture) accept these evangelical modifications of historical criticism or will they say that these evangelicals have not gone far enough in their adoption of historical criticism? So far, none have warmly embraced these evangelical modifications, for they say, evangelicals have not gone far enough! These critically-trained evangelicals play to a very small audience—themselves.

## CONCLUSION TO QUO VADIS

In 2007, Andreas Köstenberger edited a work entitled *Quo Vadis Evangelicalism?* The work consisted of a highly selective choice of presidential addresses of Evangelical Theological Society scholars who, in the history of the society, favored the move in the

---

such crucial issues.

26. Bock and Webb, introduction to *Key Events*, 5.

society toward historical-critical ideologies. No presidential addresses that warned against historical-critical ideologies were allowed. The work related that ETS has been "polarized" into two camps, one represented by Eta Linnemann and Norman Geisler who warned against historical-critical ideologies and the other by Darrell Bock and others who heartily embrace "the judicious use of a historical-critical approach."[27] The book was extremely prejudiced toward one side and hardly objective. Köstenberger never stated what a "judicious" use of historical criticism was or whose version would be accepted. He did note, however, that "the pendulum [at ETS] seems to have swung toward the side of the latter ['judicious use'] group."[28] It actually constituted a personal vanity toward praising a direction that the editor apparently embraced. He concluded his preface by noting "speaking personally, reading and digesting these presidential addresses—spanning a half-century and delivered by some of evangelicalism's most distinguished leaders—has given me, a third-generation scholar in the ETS, a much fuller and deeper appreciation for the history of the evangelical movement and my place within it."[29] He concluded, "In my judgment the present volume offers great hope for the future of a movement whose best days, by God's grace and abundant mercy, may yet lie ahead."[30] The writer of this chapter had a rather aged church history professor during his days at Talbot Seminary who issued a warning that he has not forgotten to this day. He would say that church history teaches consistently that by the third generation of any Christian group, the original intent of the organization was lost (Harvard, Yale, Princeton, etc.), and the loss in these organizations is always away from a steadfast trust in the Word of God and being faithful to it. What is noticed here is that Köstenberger admits that ETS is now in its third generation. The new third generation is in charge of ETS.

Long ago, Harold Lindsell, the scorn of much of these younger scholars today, said this about his own day that is worth repeating again:

> Anyone who thinks the historical-critical method is neutral is misinformed. Since its presuppositions are unacceptable to the evangelical mind this method cannot be used by the evangelical as it stands. The very use by the evangelical of this term, historical-critical method, is a mistake when it comes to describing its own approach to Scripture. The only way he can use it is to invest it with a different meaning. But this can only confuse the uninformed. Moreover, it is not fair to those scholars who use it in the correct way with presuppositions which are different from those of the evangelical. It appears to me that modern evangelical scholars (and I may be guilty of this myself) have played fast and loose with the term because they wanted acceptance by academia. They seem too often to desire to be members of the club which is

27. Köstenberger, *Quo Vadis Evangelicalism?*, 18.
28. Ibid.
29. Ibid., 26.
30. Ibid.

nothing more than practicing an inclusiveness that undercuts the normativity of the evangelical theological position. This may be done, and often is, under the illusion that by this method the opponents of biblical inerrancy can be one over to the evangelical viewpoint. But practical experience suggest that rarely does this happen and the cost of such an approach is too expensive, for it gives credence and lends respectability to a method which is the deadly enemy of theological orthodoxy.[31]

Church history stands as a monumental testimony against this third generation of ETS evangelicals who have thought that they are somehow special, endowed with exceptional abilities, and able to overcome historical criticism's negativity that no one else in church history has been able to accomplish.

A warning is sadly necessary: evangelicals have wrongly blended or used grammatico-historical and historical criticism as synonymous. History and philosophy are being ignored, overlooked, or disdained. Evangelicals must always remember or be reminded of three essential axioms in scholarly activity:

## The First Axiom:

Grammatico Historical
$\neq$ (does not equal and cannot be equated with)
Historical Criticism

## The Second Axiom:

A bad methodology/ideology always leads to bad theology

## The Third Axiom:

Lordship always over scholarship

"When pride comes, then comes dishonor, but with the humble is wisdom" (Prov 11:2) or, stated more bluntly in another way in the warnings of the New Testament: "It is required of stewards [of God's Word] that one be found trustworthy" (1 Cor 4:2); "The things which you have heard from me in the presence of many witnesses, entrust these to faithful men who will be able to teach others also" (2 Tim 2:2); "For the time will come when they will not endure sound doctrine; but wanting to have their ears tickled, they will accumulate for themselves teachers in accordance to their own desires, and will turn away their ears from the truth and will turn aside to myths" (2 Tim 4:3–4).

---

31. Lindsell, *Bible in the Balance*, 283.

# Appendix
## Statements on the Importance of Inerrancy from Prominent Christian Leaders

In 2014, DefendingInerrancy.com went on the web to defend *the inerrant Word of God* against the current onslaughts against its timeless truth and historicity. As the men and women who formed the Chicago Statements took their bold stance for God's inerrant, infallible Word, so also did the editors of this site.

As of the writing of this book, almost fifty thousand individials have signed the petition in support of inerrancy and the Chicago Statements. The following Christian leaders offered their support to us.

*Praise the Lord* for Gideon's army! Judges 7:2—"The LORD said to Gideon, 'The people who are with you are too many for me to give Midian into their hands, for Israel would become boastful, saying, "My own power has delivered me."'" If anything is accomplished by DefendingInerrancy.com, the editors of the site give all praise to the Lord.

Our prayer is that the Lord will raise up an army who faithfully hold to his Word, for Zechariah reminds us all: 4:6—"'Not by might nor by power, but by my Spirit,' says the LORD of hosts."

### INERRANCY QUOTES

Notable scholars, pastors and theologians are speaking out concerning the modern erosion of inerrancy. Will you add your name to our list?

### Billy Graham—Evangelist

"The Bible has stood the test of time because it is divinely inspired by Almighty God, written in ink that cannot be erased by any man, religion, or belief system. Through the many dark ages of man, its glorious promises have survived unchanged. That is because God's Word is pure—the beginning and the end. His written word has survived every scratch of the human pen."

# Appendix

## Franklin Graham—President & CEO, Samaritan's Purse and Billy Graham Evangelistic Association

"To demonstrate trust in the inerrant Word of God is to exhibit faith in the One who spoke life into existence. History and human nature prove the truth of the Bible every day, but the greatest evidence is seen in changed lives that cannot be denied. This infallible Book is its own great commentary: 'The entirety of your word, Lord, is truth' (Psalm 119:160)."

## Ravi Zacharias—President, Ravi Zacharias International Ministries

"The Bible is the Word of God, and God cannot err. So, to deny inerrancy, rightly understood, is to attack the very character of God. Those who deny inerrancy, soon enter the dangerous terrain of denying all Scriptural authority for both doctrine and practice."

## Norman Geisler—Co-founder, Southern Evangelical Seminary and Veritas Evangelical Seminary

"The inerrancy of Scripture is the foundational doctrine in which all other doctrines rest, and the Psalmist rightly said, 'If the foundation be destroyed, then what can the righteous do?'"

## John H. Munro—Senior Pastor, Calvary Church, Charlotte NC; World-Wide Bible Teacher of Back to the Bible

"If I did not believe in the inerrancy of Holy Scripture I would resign as a preacher and teacher of the Bible which is the Word of God written. I can authoritatively say, 'Thus says the Lord' when I preach the Bible as it comes from a God who cannot lie. 'Let him who has my word speak my word in truth' (Jeremiah 23:28). To question the inerrancy of Scripture inevitably leads to weak and confusing preaching with disastrous consequences!"

## John Warwick Montgomery—Distinguished Research Professor of Philosophy, Concordia University; Director, International Academy of Apologetics

"The inerrancy of Holy Scripture is the watershed theological issue in the church today–as it has been in every generation since the rise of modern secularism and rationalistic biblical criticism. Every single denomination, theological seminary, and Christian college that has departed from it has begun an inexorable decline and loss of biblical witness. The saving gospel itself cannot be sustained apart from a trustworthy

Scripture. Any other position displays appalling naïveté and ignorance of the history of the modern church both in Europe and in America."

## David Limbaugh—Attorney, Author, and Social Commentator

"I have never quite understood the tendency of so many Christians to pick and choose from Holy Scripture. Biblical inerrancy was not only affirmed unambiguously by Jesus Christ, but is foundational to our firm reliance on God's promises and revelations contained in the Bible. It seems to me that an attitude of dismissiveness toward inerrancy amounts to intellectual and theological laziness and is ultimately destructive to the faith."

## John Ankerberg—Founder and President, The John Ankerberg Show

"The Bible provides the foundational beliefs of Christianity. Biblical inerrancy, properly understood, affirms Scripture's accuracy in every area it addresses. God's Word records the history of humanity, the teachings of our Savior, numerous fulfilled prophecies, and the principles of our faith. Despite numerous attacks by skeptics and opponents, its words continue to stand true and change lives today."

## Mark L. Bailey—President, Dallas Theological Seminary

"Both the incarnation of Jesus and the inspiration of the Bible, as products of the Holy Spirit, can and must be without error or we have challenged the ability and impugned the character of Almighty God to do what his Word says he did (2 Tim 3:16; 2 Pet 1:20, 21; 1 Cor 2:9–16). If an omnipotent God by his Spirit can take a human agent and conceive his perfect Son, that same omnipotent God can use human agents through whom his Spirit can communicate his mind to humanity though the Holy Scriptures."

## Paige Patterson—President, Southwestern Baptist Theological Seminary

"The inerrancy of Scripture is an essential and not optional doctrine for the church. Otherwise we are cast on a raging sea of subjectivism with a high priesthood of scholars who assume the position of God, telling what we should and should not believe."

## Al Mohler—President, Southern Baptist Theological Seminary

"Inerrancy is nothing less than the affirmation that the Bible, as the Word of God written, is totally true and totally trustworthy. When the Bible speaks, God speaks.

This is the Bible's own testimony about itself, and it is the historic faith of the Christian church."

### Richard Land—President, Southern Evangelical Seminary

"The inerrant Scripture is our fixed, North Star by which we can be led by God to a saving knowledge of him and his plan and purpose for our lives. Once you surrender the objective, infallible, inerrant nature of God's revelation of himself to us, all you are left with is each interpreter's subjective, autobiographical, idiosyncratic God, who may bear little or no resemblance to the one, true, immutable God with whom we must all deal ultimately."

### Walter C. Kaiser, Jr.—President Emeritus, Gordon-Conwell Theological Seminary

"The Inerrancy of the Bible seeks to represent the claims of the Biblical text that all it says is true and accords with the actual and the real in life and history as it was intended by the writers of Scripture. The total truthfulness of Scripture is claimed because this is what Scripture teaches and without it we are left to our own devices to try to figure who God is and what he has said."

### Daniel L. Akin—President, Southeastern Baptist Theological Seminary

"The doctrine of inerrancy is ultimately an issue of Christology. Jesus clearly affirmed the complete truthfulness and reliability of Scripture. Matthew 5:17–18; Luke 24:25–27; John 10:35, 17:17 make this abundantly clear. To live under his Lordship is to hold his view of the Word of God."

### Elmer L. Towns—Co-Founder, Liberty University

"I believe inspiration guarantees the accuracy of every word in the original language, therefore we should study every word, translate it properly, and understand its meaning and live by it. I also believe that inspiration means the Holy Spirit breathed His presence into every word of scriptures, therefore we ought to read it daily, memorize it, meditate on it and let the life of the Spirit control our life."

### Erwin W. Lutzer—Senior Pastor, Moody Church, Chicago, IL

"I'm thankful for this website dedicated to the inerrancy of Scripture which is the bedrock of our faith. At a time when subtle attacks against the Bible continue (even from

*Statements on the Importance of Inerrancy from Prominent Christian Leaders*

those who profess to believe it), it is refreshing to know that there are fine scholars who are able to respond to these challenges with thoughtful arguments and an appreciation for logic. I hope that it has a wide-spread impact in these confusing times."

## Joseph M. Holden—President, Veritas Evangelical Seminary

"Inerrancy is the fundamental of the fundamentals. Only divinely inspired and inerrant Scripture guarantees the truth and authority of the doctrines that flow from them. Only then can the church rest assured that when the Bible speaks, God speaks."

## F. David Farnell—Professor of New Testament, The Master's Seminary

"The importance of inerrancy generates from the very perfections of the character of God himself who cannot lie. To say that his Word errs or is imperfect is to blaspheme God himself who is the Author of his Word."

## Thomas A. Howe—Professor of Bible and Biblical Languages, Southern Evangelical Seminary

"Jesus said to Nicodemus, 'If I tell you of earthly things, and you do not believe, how will you believe if I tell you of heavenly things?' If we cannot trust the Word of God in earthly matters, matters that we can verify or falsify because they are down here with us, how can we trust the Word of God when it speaks of heavenly and spiritual matters, matters that we cannot verify or falsify because we have not ascended to heaven?"

## William C. Roach—Adjunct Faculty, Southeastern Baptist Theological Seminary

"Methodologically and strategically, the axiom of inerrancy is both an article of faith and a guideline of biblical interpretation to safeguard the belief that in all the inspired texts, whatever their literary genre and style, God still speaks His mind to humanity through the agency of human writers, culminating in the communication of errorless, cognitive-propositional revelation."

## Grant C. Richison—Vice-President, Advancing Indigenous Missions

"Without inerrancy there is no clear and final word from God. If there is ambiguity in what God said then the burning conviction of what he said is not as imperative."

# Appendix

## Bruce Little—Senior Professor of Philosophy and Director of the Francis A. Schaeffer Collection, Southeastern Baptist Theological Seminary

"Inerrancy is entailed in our understanding of inspiration and without it, divine promises would give no assurance and divine commands would require no obedience."

## Forrest S. Weiland—Professor of Biblical Studies, Veritas Evangelical Seminary

"There is a real sense in which 'inerrancy' is the most important doctrine of the Bible, for every other major (and minor) doctrine is derived from that one source, whether it be the Trinity, the Deity of Christ, or salvation by faith alone in Christ alone. Inerrancy is taught throughout the Bible, but the words of Psalm 19:7 powerfully crystallize the teaching, 'The law of the Lord is perfect.'"

## Phil Roberts—International Director for Theological Education, Global Ministries Foundation

"There is no greater encouragement to the evangelist, proclaimer or teacher of God's Word than to know that the Bible they use is totally trustworthy, reliable and inerrant. Such truth is as wind to the sailing ship. "I, the Lord, speak the truth.' Isaiah 45:19."

## Ross Rhoads—Chaplain, Billy Graham Evangelistic Association

"The inerrancy of the holy Scripture in the Old Testament and New Testament is the foundation for the sole authority in all theology and in obedience to the faith."

## Mark Hanna—Professor of Philosophy and Religion, Veritas Evangelical Seminary

"The importance of holding to the inerrancy of Holy Scripture is that it focuses the authority on the divinely inspired Scriptures of the Old and New Testaments and not on the fallible human judgment that decides which parts should be accepted as the word of God and which parts should be rejected. Both inductive evidence and deductive theological entailment provide unequivocal support for that conclusion."

## Ron Rhodes—President, Reasoning from the Scriptures Ministries

"John Calvin once said, 'Our faith in doctrine is not established until we have a perfect conviction that God is the author [of Scripture].' Let us be clear: It is *only* because the Bible is inerrant that we can trust what it says about God, Jesus Christ, the gospel of salvation, and all other doctrines."

*Statements on the Importance of Inerrancy from Prominent Christian Leaders*

## Phil Fernandes—Founder and President, Institute of Biblical Defense

"The basis of our evangelical faith is an inerrant Bible, grounded in real history. Once evangelicals begin to deny inerrancy and remove biblical miracles from space-time history, reducing them to mere metaphors, then these interpreters cease to be evangelical."

## Kenny Rhodes—President, Scofield Seminary

"Inerrancy is the epistemological rationale for all theological knowledge, a sublime first principle; without its ground and defense, fallen man is left as both arbiter and judge of what God hath really said. Inerrancy is grounded in the nature and character of God. God cannot err, therefore, God's 'breathed-out' word, in the original autographs, cannot err."

## Elliott Johnson—Professor of Bible, Dallas Theological Seminary

"There are certain foundational beliefs for life and godliness. One of those is believing as true what the Bible claims of itself: God speaks and what he says is true. The Scripture is the expression of that truth and its messages are true."

## Ed Hindson—Dean and Distinguished Professor of Religion, Liberty School of Religion

"No one defended the inerrancy of the Scriptures more than Jesus. He quoted biblical passages in responding to his disciples (Matt 16:21), his critics (Matt 22) and the devil himself (Matt 4:4, 7, 10). He referred to almost every controversial story in the Old Testament including: Noah, Jonah, Elijah, Elisha, Isaiah, and Daniel. He emphasized technical details of interpretation (Ps 110:1) and dared to claim the entire Old Testament message was all about him (Luke 24:44). We are ultimately left with one of two choices: poor dumb Jesus or poor dumb scholars. I'll stick with Jesus every time."

## Ramesh Richard—President, Reach Ministries; Professor, Dallas Theological Seminary

"Unless the Bible is free of error, the Christian faith is minimized to an intriguing phase in human moral development. That reduction carries christological, salvific, even eternal consequence. Further, the epistemological conviction and missiological confidence needed to reach spiritually lost people, and especially those who hold to the inerrancy of their own Scriptures, are rendered vacuous at best and void at worst."

Appendix

## Win Corduan—Past President, International Society of Christian Apologetics

"Only by holding fast to the actuality that God has revealed himself without error in all matters that the Bible affirms can we avoid substituting the uncertainty of human inventiveness for the assurance of salvation."

## Ray Comfort—Founder and President, Living Waters Publications

"To forsake the inerrancy of Scripture is to snuff humanity's only candle of truth. Inerrancy is the ship's rudder, the traveler's compass, the lamp to our feet and light to our path."

## Steve Collins—Dean, Distinguished Professor of Archaeology, College of Archaeology & Biblical History, Trinity Southwest University

"As an archaeologist who deals with material evidence along with Ancient Near Eastern cultures and texts, and who is also an evangelical Christian, I often find the debate about biblical inerrancy puzzling, if not irritating. For me, the concept of inerrancy is tied to divine intent. It is clear to me that Scripture has come to us as God's unique representation of reality, an aggregate of authentic ancient records and eyewitness accounts driven by divine selectivity toward the ultimate goal of bringing forth the final record of the New Covenant through Messiah, Jesus. Because it is self-evident that God does not superintend error, 'doctrinal' inerrancy is axiomatic. Further, on the pragmatic side of the issue, my 45+ years of examining biblical texts in the light of archaeology and history (and vice versa!) have given me unequivocal confidence in the Bible's 'inductive' inerrancy; i.e., I have yet to identify anything in it that I would consider to be in error. In my mind, an errant Scripture is an affront to logic, science, and faith."

## Robert P. Lightner—Professor Emeritus of Systematic Theology, Adjunct Professor of Theological Studies, Dallas Theological Seminary

"Both the Written Word and Christ the Living Word embraced the total inerrancy of the Word of God. Christ's statement in Matthew 5:17–18 and in a number of other passages claim inerrancy for the entire Old Testament. And he promised the ministry of the Holy Spirit in the work of New Testament inspiration (John 14:26; 15:26–27)."

*Statements on the Importance of Inerrancy from Prominent Christian Leaders*

## Arnold Fruchtenbaum—Founder and Director, Ariel Ministries; Adjunct Professor of Old Testament, Veritas Evangelical Seminary

"If the doctrine of inerrancy is not true, then the Scriptures become an untrustworthy document. To claim that it is inerrant in areas of faith and practice but errant in other areas is simply a self-contained contradiction. Furthermore, it is now the interpreter who determines what in the Bible is true and what is not and therefore it all becomes subjective and the Scriptures become just another 'holy book' but not a reliable document. Inerrancy provides the believer an objective standard that enables him to determine truth from error in all subjects the Bible addresses."

## Randall Price—Distinguished Research Professor, Executive Director, Center for Judaic Studies, Liberty University

"Since the basis for the authority of Scripture is its nature as divine revelation, if this revelation can be claimed to be errant through comparison with the limited data from history, archaeology, science, and the like, it cannot maintain its status as divine revelation and becomes simply a man-made message. Consequently, if Scripture is not totally inerrant with reference to the things of this world, it has no authority to command men in the world of men and has no claim above any other religious texts produced by mankind."

## Richard Howe—Professor of Philosophy

"The Bible is the Word of God. God cannot err. Therefore, the Bible cannot err. If the Bible errs, then either in some sense it is not the Word of God or in some sense God can err. The logic is undeniable."

## Donald T. Williams—President, International Society of Christian Apologetics

"Some doubt whether inerrancy makes a practical difference. The difference it makes is this: Without it, authority is inevitably transferred from the Text to the 'Expert,' whether it be the critic, the scholar, the pastor, or the individual. For now someone other than the Apostles and Prophets has to tell you what to believe."

## Emir Caner—President of Truett-McConnell College in Cleveland, TN

"The inerrancy of Scripture is the key doctrine as it pertains to the character of God and how he relates to man. What is on the line is no less than the souls of men and women. Thus, an affirmation of his Word is an affirmation of his love for mankind, a love that is best seen in the sacrifice of Christ on the cross."

# Appendix

## Perseus Poku—President of AYCE Apologetics

"The Scriptures are a direct reflection of its author (God). As a result, it is void of error and can be trusted in all its affirmations as well as negations."

## David Chadwick—Pastor, Forest Hill Church; Host, The David Chadwick Show

"Biblical inerrancy is essential for the proper, bold proclamation of the Gospel. How can a preacher hope to change the world with his preaching if he doubts the absolute truth of God's Word. Otherwise, it's mere human opinion. Believing inerrancy is the only way to bring people to faith. It is the only way for their faith to grow and produce holiness and obedience. As Jesus prayed, 'Father, sanctify them with your truth. Your Word is truth' (John 17:17). The Word of God is truth."

## The Honorable Phil Ginn—Senior Resident Superior Court, Western North Carolina

"In these last days, Satan himself is attempting to undermine the very foundation of true Christianity. It is no wonder that his arrows have attacked the Word of God more than anything else; for if the foundation is compromised, then the building will surely fall. In the coming battle, count me on the side of God's Holy Word, inerrant, infallible, and the authority for my faith in Christ as my true and only Savior and Lord. As in Luther's day, 'Here I stand, I can do no other!'"

## Paul K. Hoffman—Attorney at Law, JD

"The inerrancy of scripture goes to the very power of God. Embracing its purported errors goes to the 'wisdom' of men. Yet our faith is to rest, 'not on the wisdom of men, but on the power of God' (1 Cor 2:5). Resting upon the power of God, I do not reject out-of-hand all specific claims of error but confidently analyze each allegation. This analysis is no small matter, for in so doing I recognize, first, that my Lord undeniably affirmed the perfection of Scripture and, second, that if error is conclusively determined, I must abandon my faith in him. There really is no middle ground."

## Ron Susek—President, Susek Evangelistic Association

"If God did not reveal himself with word-by-word precision, then he has placed the revelation of truth into the incompetent hands of fallen man. That would prove hopelessly imbecilic. He who revealed himself with exactness in 'natural' creation chose the precise words, sentences, and paragraphs to compile one Book in which we have his perfect Word."

*Statements on the Importance of Inerrancy from Prominent Christian Leaders*

## H. Wayne House—Distinguished Research Professor of Theology, Law, and Culture, Faith Evangelical College and Seminary

"The doctrine of inerrancy is foundational to all other Christian doctrines, and can never be set aside without great peril to the church. Without Scripture being without error, an interpreter of Scripture could never be sure what teaching of the Bible should be believed. In accepting the teaching of the Word of God on inerrancy, we can be confident that what God has revealed to us is in fact truthful and reliable regarding what we believe and how we live."

## Robert Wilkin—Executive Director, Grace Evangelical Society

"Option 1: The Bible is God's Word and is absolutely true in every detail.
Option 2: God never errs and neither does his Word.
Option 3: Men's ability to find fault with God and his Word is about to run out.
Option 4: God's Word is 100 percent true from Genesis to Revelation."

# Bibliography

Allen, Ronald B. "A Response to Genre Criticism—Sensus Literalis." In Radmacher and Preus, *Hermeneutics, Inerrancy, and the Bible*, 193–203.

Appleby, Joye, et al., eds. *Telling the Truth about History*. New York: Norton, 1994.

Aquinas, Thomas. *Commentary on the Four Gospels Collected out of the Works of the Fathers*. Oxford: John Henry Parker, 1842.

———. *Commentary on the Four Gospels*. Vol. 1, part 3, *St. Matthew*. Oxford: John Henry Parker, 1841.

———. *The Literal Exposition on Job: A Scriptural Commentary Concerning Providence*. Translated by Anthony Damico. Oxford: Oxford University Press, 1989.

———. *Summa Theologica*. Complete English ed. Bellingham, WA: Logos, 2009.

———. *Summa Theologica*. Edited by O. P. Gilby. New York: McGraw-Hill, 1966.

Aristotle. *The Metaphysics*. Translated by Hugh Lawson-Tancred. London: Penguin Classics, 1999.

Augustine. *Confessions and Letters of St. Augustin, with a Sketch of His Life and Work*. Nicene and Post-Nicene Fathers, 1st ser., vol. 1. Buffalo, NY: Christian Literature, 1886.

———. *On the Gospel of St. John*. Nicene and Post-Nicene Fathers, ser. 1, vol. 7. Grand Rapids: Eerdmans, 1979.

"Averroism." In *The Oxford Dictionary of the Christian Church*, edited by F. L. Cross and E. A. Livingstone, 116. Oxford: Oxford University Press, 2005.

Baird, William. *The History of New Testament Research: From Deism to Tübingen*. Minneapolis: Fortress, 1992.

———. *The Quest of the Christ of Faith*. Waco, TX: Word, 1977.

Barr, James. *Beyond Fundamentalism*. Philadelphia: Westminster, 1984.

———. *Escaping from Fundamentalism*. London: SCM, 1984.

———. Foreword to the American edition of *Fundamentalism*. Philadelphia: Westminster, 1977.

———. *Fundamentalism*. 2nd ed. London: SCM, 1981.

———. *The Semantics of Biblical Languages*. London: SCM, 1961.

Bauckham, Richard. *Jesus and the Eyewitnesses: The Gospels as Eyewitness Testimony*. Grand Rapids: Eerdmans, 2008.

———. *The Testimony of the Beloved Disciple*. Grand Rapids: Baker, 2007.

Beilby, James K., and Paul Rhodes Eddy, eds. *The Historical Jesus Five Views*. Downers Grove: InterVarsity, 2009.

Bible Conference Committee. *God Hath Spoken (Hebrews 1:1–2): Twenty-Five Addresses Delivered at the World Conference on Christian Fundamentals*. Philadelphia: Bible Conference Committee, 1919.

Bird, Michael F. "Beware the Dangerous Heresy of Michael Bird!" Patheos.com. Euangelion blog. Posted April 23, 2014. http://www.patheos.com/blogs/euangelion/2014/04/beware-the-dangerous-heresy-of-michael-bird.

———. "An Evangelical and Critical Approach to the Gospels." Patheos.com. Posted March 7, 2012. http://www.patheos.com/blogs/euangelion/2012/03/an-evangelical-and-critical-approach-to-the-gospels.

———. "Inerrancy Is Not Necessary for Evangelicalism Outside the USA." In Merrick and Garrett, *Five Views on Biblical Inerrancy*, 145–73.

———. "Michael Licona on the Resurrection of Jesus." *Patheos*. Posted September 14, 2011. http://www.patheos.com/blogs/euangelion/2011/09/michael-licona-on-the-resurrection-of-jesus.

———. Review of *Can We Still Believe the Bible?*, by Craig Blomberg. Patheos.com. Euangelion blog. Posted March 24, 2014.

Black, David Alan, and David S. Dockery, eds. *New Testament Criticism & Interpretation*. Grand Rapids: Zondervan, 1991.

Blomberg, Craig L. "Can the Biographies of Jesus Be Trusted?" In *The Case for Christ*, edited by Lee Strobel, 19–36. Grand Rapids: Zondervan, 1998.

———. *Can We Still Believe the Bible? An Evangelical Engagement with Contemporary Questions*. Grand Rapids: Brazos, 2014.

———. "A Constructive Traditional Response to New Testament Criticism." In Hoffmeier and Magary, *Do Historical Matters Matter*, 345–65.

———. "The Globalization of Biblical Hermeneutics." In *Evangelical Hermeneutics*, edited by Michael Bauman and David Hall, 31–51. Camp Hill, PA: Christian, 1995.

———. "The Globalization of Biblical Interpretation: A Test Case John 3–4." *Bulletin for Biblical Research* 5 (1995) 1–15.

———. "The Historical-Critical/Grammatical View." In *Biblical Hermeneutics Five Views*, edited by Stanley E. Porter and Beth M. Stovall, 27–47. Downers Grove: InterVarsity, 2012.

———. *The Historical Reliability of the Gospels*. 2nd ed. Downers Grove: InterVarsity, 2007.

———. "The Implications of Globalization for Biblical Understanding." In *The Globalization of Theological Education*, edited by Robert A. Evans et al., 213–28, 240–45. Maryknoll: Orbis, 1993.

———. Interview by Justin Taylor. The Gospel Coalition blog. Posted March 26, 2008. http://thegospelcoalition.org/blogs/justintaylor/2008/03/26/interview-with-craig-blomberg.

———. *Matthew*. New American Commentary. Nashville: Broadman & Holman, 1992.

———. "New Testament Miracles and Higher Criticism: Climbing Up the Slippery Slope." *Journal of the Evangelical Theological Society* 27 (1984) 425–38.

———. "The Past, Present and Future of American Evangelical Theological Scholarship." In *Solid Ground: 25 Years of Evangelical Theology*, edited by Carl R. Trueman et al., 310–19. Leicester: Apollos, 2000.

———. "Where Do We Start Studying Jesus?" In *Jesus Under Fire*, edited by Michael J. Wilkins and J. P. Moreland, 17–50. Grand Rapids: Zondervan, 1996.

Blomberg, Craig L., and Stephen E. Robinson. *How Wide the Divide? A Mormon and an Evangelical in Conversation*. Downers Grove: InterVarsity, 1997.

Bock, Darrell L. "Abandon Studying the Historical Jesus? No, We Need Context; A Response to 'The Jesus We'll Never Know.'" *Christianity Today*, April 9, 2010. www.christianitytoday.com/ct/2010aprilweb-only/24-51.0.html.

## Bibliography

———. "Craig Blomberg's Can We Believe the Bible—Chapter 4." Bock's blog. March 16, 2014. http://blogs.bible.org/bock/darrell_l._bock/craig_blombergs_can_we_believe_the_bible-_chapter_4.

———. "Do Historical Matters Matter to Faith? A Critical Appraisal of Modern and Postmodern Approaches to Scripture." Bock's blog. March 31, 2012. http://blogs.bible.org/bock/darrell_l._bock/do_historical_matters_matter_to_faith_a_critical_appraisal_of_modern_and_postmodern_approaches_to_scripture.

———. "Editor's Thoughts." Amazon.com review of *Key Events in the Life of the Historical Jesus: A Collaborative Exploration of Context and Coherence*. http://tinyurl.com/9p7r99j.

———. "Faith and the Historical Jesus: Does a Confessional Position and Respect for the Jesus Tradition Preclude Serious Historical Engagement?" *Journal for the Study of the Historical Jesus* 9 (2011) 3–25.

———. "Form Criticism." In *New Testament Criticism & Interpretation*, edited by David Alan Black and David S. Dockery, 175–96. Grand Rapids: Zondervan, 1991.

———. "The Historical Jesus: An Evangelical View." In *The Historical Jesus Five Views*, edited by James K. Beilby and Paul Rhodes Eddy, 249–81. Downers Grove: InterVarsity, 2009.

———. "Precision and Accuracy: Making Distinctions in the Cultural Context That Give Us Pause in Pitting the Gospels against Each Other." In Hoffmeier and Magary, *Do Historical Matters Matter*, 367–81.

———. Review of *The Jesus Crisis*. *Bibliotheca Sacra* 157 (2000) 232–55. ———. *Studying the Historical Jesus: A Guide to Sources and Methods*. Grand Rapids: Baker, 2002.

———. *Who Is Jesus? Linking the Historical Jesus with the Christ of Faith*. New York: Howard, 2012.

Bock, Darrell L., and W. Hall Harris. "Discrepancies in the Gospels." Video, 46:38, posted April 3, 2013. https://www.youtube.com/watch?v=C651fVKKehg.

Bock, Darrell L., and Robert L. Webb, eds. *Key Events in the Life of the Historical Jesus*. Grand Rapids: Eerdmans, 2009.

Bockmuehl, Markus, and Donald Hagner, eds. *The Written Gospel*. Cambridge: University Press, 2005.

Bovell, Carlos R. *Rehabilitating Inerrancy in a Culture of Fear*. Eugene, OR: Wipf & Stock, 2012.

Boyd, Gregory A. *Cynic Sage or Son of God?* Wheaton, IL: Victor, 1995.

———. "Is the Jesus of History the Same as the Jesus of Faith?" In *The Case for Christ*, edited by Lee Strobel, 110–27. Grand Rapids: Zondervan, 1998.

Brannan, Rick, trans. *The Apostolic Fathers: Greek-English Interlinear*. E-book. Bellingham, WA: Logos Bible Software, 2012.

Bray, Gerald. *Biblical Interpretation: Past & Present*. Downers Grove: InterVarsity, 1996.

Bromiley, G. W. "The Authority of Scripture." In *The New Bible Commentary*, edited by F. Davidson et al., 15–23. London: IVF, 1954.

Brown, Colin. *Jesus in European Protestant Thought, 1778–1860*. Durham, NC: Labyrinth, 1985.

———. "Quest of the Historical Jesus." In *Dictionary of Jesus and the Gospels*, edited by Joel B. Green et al., 718–56. 2nd ed. Downers Grove: InterVarsity, 2013.

Brown, D. Mackenzie. *Ultimate Concern: Tillich in Dialogue*. New York: Harper, 1970.

Brown, Raymond. "Eschatological Events Accompanying the Death of Jesus, Especially the Raising of the Holy Ones from Their Tombs (Matt 27:51–53)." In *Faith and the Future: Studies in Christian Eschatology*, edited by John Galvin, 43–73. New York: Paulist, 1994.

*Bibliography*

Bultmann, Rudolph. *Kerygma and Myth*. New York: Harper & Row, 1961.
Burridge, Richard A. *Four Gospels, One Jesus? A Symbolic Reading*. 2nd ed. London: SPCK, 2005.
———. *What Are the Gospels? A Comparison with Graeco-Roman Biography*. 2nd ed. Dearborn, MI: Dove, 2004.
Bush, L. Russ, and Tom Nettles. *Baptists and the Bible*. Nashville: Broadman & Holman, 1999.
Byron, John, and Joel N. Lohr, eds. *I (Still) Believe: Leading Bible Scholars Share Their Stories of Faith and Scholarship*. Grand Rapids: Zondervan, 2015.
Cairns, Earl E. *Christianity through the Centuries*. Grand Rapids: Zondervan, 1981.
Calvin, John. *Calvin's New Testament Commentaries*. Translated by A. W. Morrison. Edited by David and Thomas Torrance. Grand Rapids: Eerdmans, 1972.
———. *Institutes of the Christian Religion*. Translated by Henry Beveridge. Peabody, MA: Hendrickson, 2007.
Carson, D. A. *The Gospel according to John*. Grand Rapids: Eerdmans, 1991.
———. "Matthew." In *The Expositor's Bible Commentary*, vol. 8, edited by Frank E. Gaebelein et al. Grand Rapids: Zondervan, 1984.
Carson, D. A., and John D. Woodbridge, eds. *God and Culture: Essays in Honor of Carl F. H. Henry*. Grand Rapids: Eerdmans, 1993.
Charlesworth, James H. *The Historical Jesus: An Essential Guide*. Nashville: Abingdon, 2008.
Clarke, Adam. *The Miscellaneous Works of Adam Clarke*. Atlanta: Emory University Digital Library Publications, 1836.
Cooperman, Alan. "Evangelical Leader Returns to Catholicism." *Washington Post*, May 12, 2007. http://www.washingtonpost.com/wp-dyn/content/article/2007/05/11/AR2007051101929.html.
Copan, Paul. *Will the Real Jesus Please Stand Up? A Debate between William Lane Craig and John Dominic Crossan*. Grand Rapids: Baker, 1999.
Copleston, Frederick. *A History of Philosophy*. New York: Doubleday, 1960.
Cowan, Steven B. "Is the Bible the Word of God?" In *In Defense of the Bible*, edited by Steven B. Cowan and Terry L. Wilder, 429–63. Nashville: Broadman & Holman, 2013.
Craig, William Lane. "Dr. Craig Acknowledges That the Resurrection of the Saints in Matthew 27 Is a Legendary Story!!" Video, 8:23, posted December 19, 2012. http://www.youtube.com/watch?v=3SNuhjRZZI4.
———. Interview on Guards at the Tomb by John Ankerberg. May 25, 2010. Transcribed from video. http://www.youtube.com/watch?v=b8UMb7NlxkU. Video no longer unavailable.
———. *Reasonable Faith*. 3rd ed. Wheaton: Crossway, 2008.
———. "Resurrection and the Real Jesus." In *Will the Real Jesus Please Stand Up?*, edited by Paul Copan, 156–69. Grand Rapids: Baker, 1998.
———. "What Price Biblical Inerrancy." Posted July 2, 2007. http://www.reasonablefaith.org/what-price-biblical-errancy.
Credo House Ministries. "Michael Licona Response to Norm Geisler." Press release, September 8, 2011. http://www.reclaimingthemind.org/blog/2011/09/press-release-michael-licona-response-to-norm-geisler.
Crossan, John Dominic. *The Historical Jesus: The Life of a Mediterranean Jewish Peasant*. San Francisco: HarperOne, 1993.
Crossley, James. "Was Jesus Raised from the Dead?" Video, posted May 17, 2012, 1:55:47. https://youtu.be/_tDZQagVoMY.

## Bibliography

Dallas Theological Seminary. "Records of the International Council on Biblical Inerrancy." N.d. http://library.dts.edu/Pages/TL/Special/ICBI.shtml.

Davids, P. H. "Authority, Hermeneutics, and Criticism." In *New Testament Criticism & Interpretation*, edited by David Alan Black and David S. Dockery, 19–37. Grand Rapids: Zondervan, 1991.

Davis, Stephen T. *The Debate about the Bible: Inerrancy versus Infallibility*. Louisville: Westminster John Knox, 1984.

Dayton, Donald W. "'The Battle for the Bible': Renewing the Inerrancy Debate." *Christian Century*, November 10, 1976, 976–80.

———. "The Church in the World: The 'Battle for the Bible' Rages On." *Theology Today*, April 1, 1980, 79–84.

Denver Seminary. "Final Report on the Globalization Project at Denver Seminary." Denver: Denver Seminary, 1993.

Dockery, David S. *Christian Scripture: An Evangelical Perspective on Inspiration, Authority and Interpretation*. Eugene, OR: Wipf & Stock, 2004.

———. *New Dimensions in Evangelical Thought: Essays in Honor of Millard J. Erickson*. Downers Grove: InterVarsity, 1998.

Dungan, David L. *Constantine's Bible*. Minneapolis: Fortress, 2007.

———. *A History of the Synoptic Problem: The Canon, the Text, the Composition, and the Interpretation of the Gospels*. New York: Anchor, 1999.

Dunn, James D. G. *Jesus Remembered*. Grand Rapids: Eerdmans, 2003.

Ehrman, Bart D. *Forged and Counterforgery: The Use of Literary Deceit in Early Christian Polemics*. Oxford: Oxford University Press, 2012.

———. *Forged: Writing in the Name of God—Why the Bible's Authors Are Not Who We Think They Are*. San Francisco: HarperOne, 2012.

———. *Jesus, Interrupted: Revealing the Hidden Contradictions in the Bible (And Why We Don't Know about Them*. San Francisco: HarperOne, 2010.

———. *Misquoting Jesus: The Story behind Who Changed the Bible and Why*. HarperOne, 2007.

Ehrman, Bart D., and Michael Licona. Debate at Southern Evangelical Seminary, Charlotte, NC, April 2, 2009. https://vimeo.com/35235544.

Enns, Peter. "Inerrancy, However Defined, Does Not Describe What the Bible Does." In Merrick and Garrett, *Five Views on Biblical Inerrancy*, 83–116.

———. *Inspiration and Incarnation: Evangelicals and the Problem of the Old Testament*. Grand Rapids: Baker, 2005.

Erickson, Millard J. *The Word Became Flesh*. Grand Rapids: Baker, 1991.

Eusebius. *Ecclesiastical History*. Translated by G. P. Gould. Edited by Kirsopp Lake. 2 vols. Loeb Classical Library. Cambridge: Harvard University Press, 1926, 1932.

———. *Ecclesiastical History: Complete and Unabridged*. Peabody, MA: Hendrickson, 1998.

Evans, C. Stephen. *The Historical Christ and the Jesus of Faith*. Oxford: Oxford University Press, 1996.

Evans, Craig. "In Appreciation of the Dominical and Thomistic Traditions: The Contribution of J. D. Crossan and N. T. Wright to Jesus Research." In *Resurrection of Jesus*, edited by Robert B. Stewart, 48–57. Minneapolis: Fortress, 2005.

Farmer, William R. *The Gospel of Jesus: The Pastoral Relevance of the Synoptic Problem*. Louisville: Westminster John Knox, 1994.

———. *The Synoptic Problem: A Critical Analysis*. Macon, GA: Mercer University Press, 1976

Farnell, F. David. "The Case for the Independence View of Gospel Origins." In *Three Views on the Origins of the Synoptic Gospels*, edited by Robert L. Thomas, 226–309. Grand Rapids: Kregel, 2002.

———. "Form and Tradition Criticism." In Thomas and Farnell, *The Jesus Crisis*, 185–232.

———. "Historical Criticism vs. Grammatico-Historical: Quo Vadis Evangelicals?" In Geisler and Farnell, *The Jesus Quest*, 503–20.

———. "How Views of Inspiration Have Impacted Synoptic Problem Discussions." *The Master's Seminary Journal* 13 (2002) 33–64.

———. "Philosophical and Theological Bent of Historical Criticism." In Thomas and Farnell, *The Jesus Crisis*, 85–131.

———. Review of *Can We Still Believe the Bible: An Evangelical Engagement with Contemporary Questions?*, by Craig Blomberg. *The Master's Seminary Journal* 25 (2014) 99–104.

———. Review of *Do Historical Matters Matter to the Faith?*, edited by James K. Hoffmeier and Dennis R. Magary. *MJS* 24 (2013) 149–57.

———. Review of *The Lost World of Scripture: Ancient Literary Culture and Biblical Authority*, by John H. Walton and D. Brent Sandy. *The Master's Seminary Journal* 24 (2014) 121–29.

———. "Searching for the 'Historical' Jesus: Does History Matter to Neo-Evangelicals?" In Geisler and Farnell, *The Jesus Quest*, 421–66.

———. "Searching for the 'Historical' Jesus: Evangelical Participation in the Third Search." In Geisler and Farnell, *The Jesus Quest*, 361–420.

———. "Searching for the 'Historical' Jesus: The Rise of the Three Searches." In Geisler and Farnell, *The Jesus Quest*, 361–420.

———. "The Synoptic Gospels in the Ancient Church: The Testimony to the Priority of Matthew's Gospel." *The Master's Seminary Journal* 10 (1999) 53–86.

———. "Three Searches for the 'Historical Jesus' but No Biblical Christ, Part 1: The Rise of the Searches." *The Master's Seminary Journal* 23 (2012) 7–42.

———. "Three Searches for the 'Historical Jesus' but No Biblical Christ, Part 2: Evangelical Participation in the Search for the 'Historical Jesus.'" *The Master's Seminary Journal* 24 (2013) 25–67.

Farnell, F. David, and Norman L. Geisler. "A Critical Review of Don Hagner's 'Ten Guidelines for Evangelical Scholarship.'" *Journal of the International Society of Christian Apologetics* 6 (2013) 179–205.

Feinberg, Charles L., ed. *The Fundamentals for Today*. Grand Rapids: Kregel, 1958.

Fernandes, Phil. *The God Who Sits Enthroned*. Maitland, FL: Xulon, 2002.

———. *No Other Gods*. Maitland, FL: Xulon, 2002.

Frame, John M. *The Doctrine of the Word of God*. Phillipsburg, NJ: P & R, 2010.

Franke, John R. "Recasting Inerrancy: The Bible as Witness to Missional Plurality." In Merrick and Garrett, *Five Views on Biblical Inerrancy*, 259–87.

Fuller, Daniel P. "Benjamin B. Warfield's View of Faith and History." *Journal of the Evangelical Theological Society* 11 (1968) 75–83.

———. "The Resurrection of Jesus and the Historical Method." *Journal of Bible and Religion* 34 (1966) 18–24.

Funk, Robert, et al. *The Five Gospels: The Search for the Authentic Words of Jesus*. New York: Macmillan, 1993.

Gadamer, Hans-Georg. *Truth and Method*. 2nd ed. London: Continuum, 2004.

*Bibliography*

Galli, Mark, and Ted Olsen, eds. *131 Christians Everyone Should Know*. Nashville: Holman, 2000.

Garland, David E. *Reading Matthew: A Literary and Theological Commentary on the First Gospel*. Macon: Smyth & Helways, 1999.

Garrett, Stephen M., and J. Merrick. "Opening Lines of Communication." Conclusion to Merrick and Garrett, *Five Views on Biblical Inerrancy*, 309–26.

Geisler, Norman L. *Baker Encyclopedia of Christian Apologetics*. Grand Rapids: Baker, 1999.

———. *Beware of Philosophy*. Matthews, NC: Bastion, 2012.

———, ed. *Biblical Errancy: An Analysis of Its Philosophical Roots*. Grand Rapids: Zondervan, 1981.

———. *Biblical Inerrancy: The Historical Evidence*. Charlotte: Bastion, 2013. ———. "A Brief History of the Evangelical Theological Society on the Discipline of Its Membership." In Geisler and Farnell, *The Jesus Quest*, 349–57.

———. *Chosen but Free: A Balanced View of God's Sovereignty*. Grand Rapids: Bethany House, 2010.

———. *Christian Apologetics*. Grand Rapids: Baker, 1976.

———. *Christian Apologetics*. 2nd ed. Grand Rapids: Baker, 2015.

———. "The Concept of Truth in the Inerrancy Debate." *Bibliotheca Sacra* 137 (1980) 327–39.

———. "The Early Fathers and the Resurrection of the Saints in Matthew 27." http://defendinginerrancy.com/early-fathers-resurrection-saints.

———, ed. *Inerrancy*. Grand Rapids: Zondervan, 1978.

———. "Licona's Denial of Inerrancy: The List Grows." December 22, 2011. http://www.veritasseminary.com/LiconaListGrows.pdf.

———. "Methodological Unorthodoxy." *Journal of the Evangelical Theological Society* 26 (1983) 87–94.

———. "Mike Licona Admits Contradictions in the Gospels." https://www.jashow.org/articles/bible/mike-licona-admits-contradiction-in-the-gospels.

———. *Miracles and the Modern Mind*. Grand Rapids: Baker, 1992.

———. "The Philosophical Roots of Modern Biblical Criticism." In Geisler, *Biblical Errancy*, 65–85.

———. *Systematic Theology*. 4 vols. Minneapolis: Bethany House, 2002–2005.

———. *Systematic Theology: In One Volume*. Minneapolis: Bethany House, 2011.

———. *Thomas Aquinas: An Evangelical Appraisal*. Eugene, OR: Wipf & Stock, 2003.

———. "What Did the Early Fathers Say about Matthew 27's Risen Saints?" http://normangeisler.com/the-early-fathers-and-the-resurrection-of-the-saints-in-matthew-27-2.

———. *When Critics Ask: A Popular Handbook on Bible Difficulties*. Wheaton, IL: Victor, 1992.

———. "Why I Resigned from the Evangelical Theological Society." http://normangeisler.com/why-i-resigned-from-the-evangelical-theological-society.

Geisler, Norman L., and F. David Farnell. "The Erosion of Inerrancy among New Testament Scholars." http://normangeisler.com/the-erosion-of-inerrancy-among-new-testament-scholars-a-primary-case-in-point-craig-blomberg.

———, eds. *The Jesus Quest: The Danger from Within*. Maitland, FL: Xulon, 2014.

Geisler, Norman L., and Thomas Howe. *The Big Book of Bible Difficulties: Clear and Concise Answers from Genesis to Revelation*. Grand Rapids: Baker, 2008.

Geisler, Norman L., and Shawn Nelson. *Evidence of an Early New Testament Canon*. Matthews, NC: Bastion, 2015.

Geisler, Norman L., and Ron Rhodes. *Conviction without Compromise: Standing Strong in the Core Beliefs of the Christian Faith*. Eugene, OR: Harvest House, 2008.

Geisler, Norman L., and William C. Roach. *Defending Inerrancy: Affirming the Accuracy of Scripture for a New Generation*. Grand Rapids: Baker, 2011.

———. "Defending Inerrancy: Response to Methodological Unorthodoxy." *Journal of the International Society of Christian Apologetics* 5 (2012) 61–87.

Geisler, Norman L., and R. C. Sproul. *Explaining Hermeneutics: A Commentary*. Oakland: International Council on Biblical Inerrancy, 1983.

Georgi, Dieter. "The Interest in Life of Jesus Theology as a Paradigm for the Social History of Biblical Criticism." *Harvard Theological Review* 85 (1992) 51–83.

Gerhardsson, Birger. *The Reliability of the Gospel Tradition*. Grand Rapids: Baker, 2001.

Green, Michael E. *The Message of Matthew*. Downers Grove: InterVarsity, 2001.

Grant, Robert M. *The Apostolic Fathers: A New Translation and Commentary*. New York: Nelson, 1964–1968.

Grenz, Stanley. *A Primer on Postmodernism*. Grand Rapids: Eerdmans, 1996.

Grudem, Wayne. *Systematic Theology: An Introduction to Biblical Doctrine*. Grand Rapids: Zondervan, 1994.

Guelich, Robert. *The Sermon on the Mount: A Foundation for Understanding*. Waco, TX: Word, 1982.

Gundry, Robert H. *Matthew: A Commentary on His Handbook for a Mixed Church under Persecution*. 2nd ed. Grand Rapids: Eerdmans, 1994.

———. *Peter: False Disciple and Apostate according to Saint Matthew*. Grand Rapids: Eerdmans, 2015.

———. "Peter: False Disciple and Apostate according to St. Matthew." Lecture given October 6, 2014, at Westmont College. Video, 51:42, posted October 8, 2014. http://www.youtube.com/watch?v=QloN9EuOGXE&feature=youtu.be.

———. *Sōma in Biblical Theology: With Emphasis on Pauline Anthropology*. Cambridge: Cambridge University, 1976.

Habermas, Gary R. *The Historical Jesus*. Joplin, MO: College, 1996.

Habermas, Gary R., and Michael R. Licona. *The Case for the Resurrection of Jesus*. Grand Rapids: Kregel, 2004.

Hagner, Donald A. "An Analysis of Recent 'Historical Jesus' Studies." In *Religious Diversity in the Graeco-Roman World*, edited by Dan Cohn-Sherbok and John M. Court, 81–106. Edinburgh: T. & T. Clark, 2005.

———. *The Jewish Reclamation of Jesus*. Eugene, OR: Wipf & Stock, 1997.

———. *Matthew 1–13*. Word Biblical Commentary. Grand Rapids: Zondervan, 2015.

———. *Matthew 14–28*. Word Biblical Commentary. Grand Rapids: Zondervan, 2015.

———. *The New Testament: A Historical and Theological Introduction*. Grand Rapids: Baker, 2012.

———. "The New Testament, History, and the Historical-Critical Method." In *New Testament Criticism & Interpretation*, edited by David Alan Black and David S. Dockery, 73–100. Grand Rapids: Zondervan, 1991.

———. "Ten Guidelines for Evangelical Scholarship." Baker Academic blog. Posted March 12, 2013. http://blog.bakeracademic.com/don-hagners-ten-guidelines-for-evangelical-scholarship.

Hague, Dyson. "The History of the Higher Criticism." In *The Fundamentals*, edited by R. A. Torrey et al., 9–42. Grand Rapids: Baker, 1972.

Hamilton, James. "Did Jesus Really Raise Lazarus from the Dead? A Test Case for Harmonization between the Synoptics and the Fourth Gospel." Bible.org. July 20, 2004. https://bible.org/article/did-jesus-really-raise-lazarus-dead.

Hamilton, William. *A Quest for the Post-Historical Jesus*. London: Continuum, 1994.

Hannah, John, ed. *Inerrancy and the Church*. Chicago: Moody, 1984.

———. *An Uncommon Union: Dallas Theological Seminary and American Evangelicalism*. Grand Rapids: Zondervan, 2009.

Hansen, Collin. "ETS Resignation Triggers Tradition Discussion." *Christianity Today*, May 9, 2007. http://www.christianitytoday.com/ct/2007/mayweb-only/119-32.0.html.

Hanson, R. P. C., and A. T. Hanson. *The Bible without Illusions*. London: SCM Press, 1989.

Harris, Murray. *Raised Immortal: Resurrection & Immortality in the New Testament*. Grand Rapids: Eerdmans, 1985.

Harrisville, Roy A., and Walter Sundberg. *The Bible in Modern Culture Theology and Historical-Critical Method from Spinoza to Käsemann*. Grand Rapids: Eerdmans, 1995.

———. *Pandora's Box Opened: An Examination and Defense of Historical-Critical Method and Its Master Practitioners*. Grand Rapids: Zondervan, 2014.

Hasel, Gerhard. *New Testament Theological: Basic Issues in the Current Debate*. Grand Rapids: Eerdmans, 1978.

Hays, Christopher M., and Christopher B. Ansberry, eds. *Evangelical Faith and the Challenge of Historical Criticism*. London: SPCK, 2013.

Helm, Rudolf. *Eusebius Werke*. Vol. 7, *Die Chronik des Hieronymus, in Die Griechischen Christlichen Schriftsteller der ersten Jahrhunderte*. Berlin: Akademie-Verlag, 1956.

Hemer, Colin J. *The Book of Acts in the Setting of Hellenistic History*. Edited by Conrad H. Gempf. Winona Lake, IN: Eisenbrauns, 1990.

Hengel, Martin. "Eye-Witness Memory and the Writing of the Gospels: Form Criticism, Community Tradition and the Authority of the Authors." In *The Written Gospel*, edited by Markus Bockmuehl and Donald A. Hagner, 70–96. Cambridge: Cambridge University Press, 2005.

Henry, Carl F. H. "The Bible and the Conscience of Our Age." In *Hermeneutics, Inerrancy, & the Bible*, edited by Earl D. Radmacher and Robert D. Preus, 915–21. Grand Rapids: Zondervan, 1984.

———. *Carl Henry at His Best: A Lifetime of Quotable Thoughts*. Portland: Multnomah, 1989.

———. *God, Revelation, and Authority*. 6 vols. Waco, TX: Word, 1976–1983.

———, ed. *Jesus of Nazareth: Savior and Lord*. Carol Stream, IL: Tyndale, 1967.

———. "The Uses and Abuses of Historical Criticism." In Henry, *God, Revelation, and Authority*, 4:385–404.

Hill, David. *The Gospel of Matthew*. New Century Bible Commentary. Grand Rapids: Eerdmans, 1972.

Hodge, Archibald A., and Benjamin B. Warfield. *Inspiration*. Philadelphia: Presbyterian Board of Publication, 1881.

Hoffmeier, James K., and Dennis R. Magary, eds. *Do Historical Matters Matter to Faith?* Wheaton, IL: Crossway, 2012.

Holden, Joseph M., and Norman L. Geisler. *A Popular Handbook of Archaeology and the Bible: Discoveries That Confirm the Reliability of Scripture*. Eugene, OR: Harvest House, 2013.

*Bibliography*

Homer. *The Iliad*. Translated by Richard Latimore. Chicago: University of Chicago Press, 2011.

Hone, William. *The Lost Books of the Bible*. New York: Bell, 1979.

Howe, Thomas. "Does Genre Determine Meaning?" *Christian Apologetics Journal* 6 (2007) 1–19.

———. *Objectivity in Biblical Interpretation*. Longwood, FL: Advantage, 2004.

Hume, David. *Enquiries concerning Human Understanding and concerning the Principles of Morals*. Edited by L. A. Selby-Bigge. 3rd ed. Oxford: Clarendon, 1975.

———. *An Inquiry concerning Human Understanding*. New York: Liberal Arts, 1955.

Hunter, W. Bingham. "Contextual and Genre Implications for the Historicity of John 11:41b–42." *Journal of the Evangelical Theological Society* 28 (1985) 53–70.

International Council on Biblical Inerrancy. "The Chicago Statement on Biblical Inerrancy." 1978. http://library.dts.edu/Pages/TL/Special/ICBI_1.pdf.

———. "The Chicago Statement on Biblical Hermeneutics." http://library.dts.edu/Pages/TL/Special/ICBI_2.pdf.

Jeanson, Nathaniel. "Did Adam and Eve Exist? Genetic Clocks Sharpen the Origins Debate." *Christian Apologetics Journal*, 12 (2014) 56–58.

Jerome. *Chronicle*. The Tertullian Project (website). http://www.tertullian.org/fathers/jerome_chronicle_03_part2.htm.

Jewett, Paul K. *Man as Male and Female: A Study in Sexual Relationships from a Theological Point of View*. Grand Rapids: Eerdmans, 1990.

Johnson, Alan F. "Historical-Critical Method: Egyptian Gold or Pagan Precipice?" *Journal of the Evangelical Theological Society* 26 (1983) 3–15.

Kantzer, Kenneth, ed. *Applying the Scriptures*. Grand Rapids: Zondervan, 1987.

———. "Rhetoric about Inerrancy: The Truth of the Matter." *Christianity Today*, September 4, 1981, 16–19.

Kantzer, Kenneth, and Carl F. H. Henry, eds. *Evangelical Affirmations*. Grand Rapids: Zondervan, 1990.

Käsemann, Ernst. *Essays on New Testament Themes*. Philadelphia: Fortress, 1982.

Keating, Karl. *What Catholics Really Believe*. Ann Arbor, MI: Servant, 1992.

Kee, Howard Clark. *Jesus in History: An Approach to the Study of the Gospels*. New York: Harcourt Brace Jovanovich, 1977.

Keener, Craig S. "Is Young-Earth Creationism Biblical?" *Huffington Post*, June 8, 2012. http://www.huffingtonpost.com/craig-s-keener/is-young-earth-creationism-biblical_b_1578004.html.

Keith, Chris, and Larry W. Hurtado, eds. *Jesus among Friends and Enemies: A Historical and Literary Introduction to Jesus in the Gospels*. Grand Rapids: Baker, 2011.

Keylock, Leslie R. "Evangelical Scholars Remove Robert Gundry for His Views on Matthew." *Christianity Today*, February 3, 1984.

Klauck, Hans-Josef. *The Religious Context of Early Christianity: A Guide to Greco-Roman Religions*. Translated by Brian McNeal. Minneapolis: Fortress, 2003.

Köstenberger, Andreas J., ed. *Quo Vadis Evangelicalism?* Wheaton, IL: Crossway, 2007.

Krentz, Edgar. *The Historical-Critical Method*. Philadelphia: Fortress, 1975.

Kümmel, Werner Georg. *The New Testament: The History of the Investigation of Its Problems*. Translated by S. MacLean Gilmour and Howard Clark Kee. Nashville: Abingdon, 1972.

Ladd, George E. *The New Testament and Criticism*. Grand Rapids: Eerdmans, 1967.

———. "The Search for Perspective." *Interpretation* 25 (1971) 41–62.

## Bibliography

Lea, Thomas D. "The Reliability of History in John's Gospel." *Journal of the Evangelical Theological Society* 38 (1995) 387–405.
Lewis, C. S. *The Best of C. S. Lewis: Five Best Books in One Volume*. New York: Iversen, 1969.
———. *Miracles*. New York: Collier, 1960.
———. *Miracles: A Preliminary Study*. San Francisco: HarperOne, 2015.
Lewis, Gordon, and Bruce Demarest. *Challenges to Inerrancy: A Theological Response*. Chicago: Moody, 1984.
Licona, Michael R. "Michael Licona Discusses What Makes a Bible Contradiction." Video, 20:59, posted November 23, 2012. https://www.youtube.com/watch?v=TJ8rZukh_Bc.
———. "On Chicago's Muddy Waters." RisenJesus.com. Posted June 2, 2014. http://www.risenjesus.com/chicagos-muddy-waters.
———. *The Resurrection of Jesus: A New Historiographical Approach*. Downers Grove: InterVarsity, 2010.
———. "When the Saints Go Marching In (Matthew 27:52–53): Historicity, Apocalyptic Symbol, and Biblical Inerrancy." Paper presented at the Evangelical Philosophical Society, San Francisco, November 2011. http://www.risenjesus.com/wp-content/uploads/2011-eps-saints-paper.pdf.
Lightfoot, J. B. *Essays on the Work Entitled Supernatural Religion*. London: Macmillan, 1889.
Lightfoot, J. B., and J. R. Harmer, trans. *The Apostolic Fathers*. Grand Rapids: Baker, 1984.
Lightfoot, J. B., et al., trans. *The Apostolic Fathers: Greek Texts and English Translations of Their Writings*. 2nd ed. Grand Rapids: Baker, 1992.
Lindsell, Harold. *The Battle for the Bible*. Grand Rapids: Zondervan, 1976.
———. *The Bible in the Balance*. Grand Rapids: Zondervan, 1979.
———. "The Strange Case of Fuller Theological Seminary." In Lindsell, *The Battle for the Bible*, 106–21.
Linnemann, Eta. *Biblical Criticism on Trial*. Grand Rapids: Kregel, 1990.
———. *Historical Criticism of the Bible: Methodology or Ideology?* Grand Rapids: Kregel, 1990.
Luibheid, Colm. *Pseudo-Dionysius: The Complete Works*. New York: Paulist, 1987.
Luther, Martin. *Word and Sacrament*. Parts 1 & 3. Luther's Works 35 & 37. Minneapolis: Fortress, 1960.
Machen, J. Gresham. *The Christian Faith in the Modern World*. Grand Rapids: Eerdmans, 1936.
———. *Christianity and Liberalism*. Grand Rapids: Eerdmans, 1946.
———. *The Virgin Birth of Christ*. 2nd ed. New York: Harper, 1932.
———. *What is Faith?* Grand Rapids: Eerdmans, 1946.
Maier, Gerhard. *End of the Historical-Critical Method*. St. Louis: Concordia, 1977.
Malalas, John. *Chronographia*. http://straightforward.wikidot.com/phlegon-roj.
Marsden, George M. *Reforming Fundamentalism: Fuller Seminary and the New Evangelicalism*. Grand Rapids: Eerdmans, 1987.
———. *Understanding Fundamentalism and Evangelicalism*. Grand Rapids: Eerdmans, 1991.
Marshall, I. Howard. *A Critical and Exegetical Commentary on the Pastoral Epistles*. International Critical Commentary. Edinburgh: T. & T. Clark, 1999.
———. "Historical Criticism." In Marshall, *New Testament Interpretation*, 126–38.
———, ed. *New Testament Interpretation: Essays on Principles and Methods*. Grand Rapids: Eerdmans, 1977.
Martin, Ralph P. *New Testament Foundations*. 2 vols. Grand Rapids: Eerdmans, 1975–1978.

## Bibliography

Massaux, Édouard. *The Influence of the Gospel of Saint Matthew on Christian Literature before Saint Irenaeus.* Translated by Norman J. Belval and Suzanne Hecht. Edited and introduction and addenda by Arthur J. Bellinzoni. Macon, GA: Mercer University Press, 1990.

Maximus the Confessor. *Scholia.* http://straightforward.wikidot.com/phlegon-roj.

McArthur, Harvey K. *The Quest through the Centuries: The Search for the Historical Jesus.* Philadelphia: Fortress, 1966.

McCall, Thomas H. "Religious Epistemology, Theological Interpretation of Scripture, and Critical Biblical Scholarship: A Theologian's Reflection." In Hoffmeier and Magary, *Do Historical Matters Matter,* 33–54.

McCallum, Dennis, ed. *The Death of Truth.* Minneapolis: Bethany House, 1996.

McDowell, Josh. *Evidence That Demands a Verdict.* San Bernardino, CA: Here's Life, 1979.

McKnight, Scot. "The Jesus We'll Never Know, Why Scholarly Attempts to Discover the 'Real' Jesus Have Failed. And Why That Is a Good Thing." *Christianity Today,* April 2010, 22–26.

McKnight, Scot, and Grant R. Osborne, eds. *The Face of New Testament Studies: A Survey of Recent Research.* Grand Rapids: Baker, 2004.

Merrick, J., and Stephen M. Garrett, eds. *Five Views on Biblical Inerrancy.* Grand Rapids: Zondervan, 2013.

Meyer, Stephen C. *Signature in the Cell: DNA and the Evidence for Intelligent Design.* New York: HarperOne, 2009.

Miller, Robert. "When It's Futile to Argue about the Historical Jesus: A Response to Bock, Keener, and Webb." *Journal for the Study of the Historical Jesus* 9 (2011) 85–95.

Mohler, R. Albert, Jr. "The Devil Is in the Details: Biblical Inerrancy and the Licona Controversy." AlbertMohler.com. Posted September 14, 2011. http://www.albertmohler.com/2011/09/14/the-devil-is-in-the-details-biblical-inerrancy-and-the-licona-controversy.

———. "When the Bible Speaks, God Speaks: The Classic Doctrine of Biblical Inerrancy." In Merrick and Garrett, *Five Views on Biblical Inerrancy,* 29–58.

Montgomery, John Warwick, ed. *God's Inerrant Word.* Minneapolis: Bethany, 1974.

Moore, G. E. *Some Main Problems in Philosophy.* New York: Collier, 1962.

Moore, John. "The Quest for the Historical Jesus." In *The Conspiracy to Silence the Son of God,* edited by Tal Brooke, 171–88. Eugene, OR: Harvest House, 1998.

Morris, Henry M. *Men of Science, Men of God.* El Cajon, CA: Master, 1988.

Morris, Leon. *The Gospels according to Matthew.* Pillar New Testament Commentary. Grand Rapids: Eerdmans, 1992.

Murray, Iain H. *A Scottish Christian Heritage.* Edinburgh: Banner of Truth, 2006.

Nash, Ronald H. *Evangelicals in America.* Nashville: Abingdon, 1987.

Neff, David. "Q&A: Francis Beckwith." *Christianity Today,* May 9, 2007. http://www.christianitytoday.com/ct/2007/mayweb-only/119-33.0.html.

Neill, Stephen, and Tom Wright. *The Interpretation of the New Testament 1861–1986.* Oxford: Oxford University Press, 1988.

Neusner, Jacob. "Who Needs 'The Historical Jesus'? An Essay-Review." *Bulletin for Biblical Research* 4 (1994) 113–26.

Noll, Mark A. *Between Faith and Criticism: Evangelicals, Scholarship, and the Bible in America.* 2nd ed. Vancouver: Regent College Publishing, 1991.

———. *The Scandal of the Evangelical Mind.* Grand Rapids: Eerdmans, 1994.

## Bibliography

Oden, Thomas C., and Christopher A. Hall. *Mark*. Ancient Christian Commentary on Scripture. Downers Grove: InterVarsity, 1998.

Orchard, Bernard, and Thomas R. W. Longstaff. *J. J. Griesbach: Synoptic and Text-Critical Studies, 1776–1976*. Cambridge: Cambridge University Press, 1978.

Orchard, Bernard, and Harold Riley. *Order of the Synoptics: Why Three Synoptic Gospels?* Macon, GA: Mercer University Press, 1987.

Origen. *Against Celsus*. In *The Ante-Nicene Fathers*, edited by Alexander Roberts, 4:440–45. Grand Rapids: Eerdmans, 1976.

———. *De Principiis*. In *The Ante-Nicene Fathers*, edited by James Donaldson, 4:341–42. Grand Rapids: Eerdmans, 1976.

Osborne, Grant R. "The Evangelical and Redaction Criticism: Critique and Methodology." *Journal of the Evangelical Theological Society* 22 (1979) 305–22.

———. "The Evangelical and *Traditionsgeschichte*." *Journal of the Evangelical Theological Society* 21 (1978) 117–30.

———. "Genre Criticism—Sensus Literalis." In Radmacher and Preus, *Hermeneutics, Inerrancy, and the Bible*, 163–90.

———. "Historical Criticism and the Evangelical." *Journal of the Evangelical Theological Society* 42 (1999) 193–210.

———. "Redaction Criticism and the Great Commission: A Case Study toward a Biblical Understanding of Inerrancy." *Journal of the Evangelical Theological Society* 19 (1976) 73–85.

Packer, J. I. *Beyond the Battle for the Bible*. Wheaton, IL: Crossway, 1980.

———. *"Fundamentalism" and the Word of God*. Grand Rapids: Eerdmans, 1958.

———. "J. I. Packer's Critique of Harold Lindsell on Inerrancy and Interpretation." The Gospel Coalition blog. Posted by Justin Taylor, August 7, 2014. Excerpted from Packer's 1979 *Crux* (Regent College journal) review of *The Bible in the Balance*, by Lindsell. http://thegospelcoalition.org/blogs/justintaylor/2014/08/07/j-i-packers-critique-of-harold-lindsell-on-inerrancy-and-interpretation.

Perrin, Norman. "Against the Current." Review of *Jesus and the Kingdom: The Eschatology of Biblical Realism*, by George Eldon Ladd. *Interpretation* 9 (1965) 228–31.

Peters, Nick. "Fathers Know Best?" *Deeper Waters* (blog). June 18, 2014. https://deeperwaters.wordpress.com/2014/06/18/fathers-know-best.

Petrie, C. Steward. "The Authorship of 'The Gospel according to Matthew': A Reconsideration of the External Evidence." *New Testament Studies* 14 (1967) 15–32.

Philopon. *De Opificio Mundi*. Cited at http://straightforward.wikidot.com/phlegon-roj.

Pinnock, Clark. *The Scripture Principle*. San Francisco: Harper & Row, 1984.

Plotinus. *The Enneads*. Translated by Elmer O'Brien. Indianapolis: Hackett, 1964.

Plummer, Robert L. "Something Awry in the Temple? The Rending of the Temple Veil and Early Jewish Sources That Report Unusual Phenomena in the Temple around AD 30." *Journal of the Evangelical Theological Society* 48 (2005) 301–16.

Popkin, Richard. *The History of Skepticism from Savonarola to Bayle*. Rev. ed. Oxford: Oxford University Press, 2003.

Quarles, Charles L. Review of *The Resurrection of Jesus: A New Historiographical Approach*. *Journal of the Evangelical Theological Society* 54 (2011) 839–44.

Radmacher, Earl D., and Robert D. Preus, eds. *Hermeneutics, Inerrancy, and the Bible*. Papers from ICBI Summit II, November 1982, Chicago. Grand Rapids: Zondervan, 1984.

## Bibliography

Reasoner, Vic. *The Importance of Inerrancy: How Scriptural Authority Has Eroded in Modern Wesleyan Theology*. Nicholasville, KY: Fundamental Wesleyan, 2013.

Reimarus, Hermann Samuel. *Apologie oder Schutzschrift für die vernünftigen Verehrer Gottes*. 2 vols. Im Auftrag der Joachim Jungius-Gesellschaft der Wissenschaften Hamburg herausgegeben von Gerhard Alexander. Frankfurt, Surhkamp, 1972.

———. *Fragments*. Edited by Charles H. Talbert. Translated by Ralph S. Fraser. Philadelphia: Fortress, 1970.

Reu, Johann M. *Luther and the Scriptures*. St. Louis: Concordia, 1980.

Rhodes, Ron. *Reasoning from the Scriptures with Mormons*. Eugene, OR: Harvest House, 1995.

Riches, John K. *A Century of New Testament Study*. 2nd ed. Cambridge: Lutterworth, 1993.

Riley, William B. "The Great Divide, or Christ and the Present Crisis." Bible Conference Committee, *God Hath Spoken*, chapter 1.

Roach, Erin. "Licona Appeals to J. I. Packer's View." *Baptist Press*. Posted November 9, 2011. http://www.bpnews.net/36523.

Roberts, Alexander, and James Donaldson. *The Writings of Julius Africanus*. Edinburgh: T. & T. Clark, 1867.

Roberts, Alexander, et al., eds. *The Ante-Nicene Fathers*. Vol. 1, *The Apostolic Fathers with Justin Martyr and Irenaeus*. Buffalo, NY: Christian Literature, 1885.

———. *The Ante-Nicene Fathers*. Vol. 2, *Fathers of the Second Century*. Buffalo, NY: Christian Literature, 1885.

Robertson, A. T. *A Grammar of the Greek New Testament in the Light of Historical Research*. 4th ed. Nashville: Broadman, 1934.

———. *Word Pictures in the New Testament*. 6 vols. Nashville: Broadman, 1930.

Robinson, James M. *A New Quest of the Historical Jesus*. Studies in Biblical Theology 25. London: SCM, 1959.

Robinson, John A. T. *Redating the New Testament*. Eugene, OR: Wipf & Stock, 2000.

Rogers, Jack. *Biblical Authority*. Waco, TX: Word, 1977.

———. *Confessions of a Conservative Evangelical*. Philadelphia: Westminster, 1974.

Rogers, Jack, and Donald K. McKim. *The Authority and Interpretation of the Bible: An Historical Approach*. New York: Harper & Row, 1979.

Ross, Allen P. *Creation and Blessing*. Grand Rapids: Baker, 1997.

Ross, Tim. "Ageing Church of England 'Will Be Dead in 20 Years.'" *Telegraph*, July 12, 2011. http://www.telegraph.co.uk/news/religion/8633540/Ageing-Church-of-England-will-be-dead-in-20-years.html.

Ross, Tim, et al. "Former Archbishop of Canterbury: We Are a Post-Christian Nation." *Telegraph*, April 26, 2014. http://www.telegraph.co.uk/news/religion/10790495/Former-archbishop-of-Canterbury-We-are-a-post-Christian-nation.html.

Ryrie, Charles. *Basic Theology: A Popular Systematic Guide to Understanding Biblical Truth*. Chicago: Moody, 1999.

Sacred Sandwich. "If Paul's Epistle to the Galatians Was Published in Christianity Today." *The Sacred Sandwich* (website). Posted February 20, 2009. http://sacredsandwich.com/archives/2781.

Sanday, William. *Inspiration: Eight Lectures on the Early History and Origins of the Doctrine of Biblical Inspiration*. 2nd ed. London: Longmans, Green, 1894.

Sandeen, Ernest R. *The Roots of Fundamentalism: British and American Millenarianism 1800–1930*. Chicago: University of Chicago, 1970.

## Bibliography

Sandmel, Samuel. "Parallelomania." *Journal of Biblical Literature* 81 (1962) 1-13.

Scaer, David P. "A Response to Genre Criticism—Sensus Literalis." In Radmacher and Preus, *Hermeneutics, Inerrancy, and the Bible*, 207-16.

Schaeffer, Francis. *The Complete Works of Francis Schaeffer*. 5 vols. Wheaton, IL: Crossway, 1985.

———. *The Great Evangelical Disaster*. Wheaton, IL: Crossway, 1984.

Schaff, Philip, and Henry Wace. *Nicene and Post-Nicene Fathers*. 2nd series. Grand Rapids: Eerdmans, 1976.

Schoedel, William R., trans. *Polycarp, Martyrdom of Polycarp, Fragments of Papias*. Vol. 5 of Grant, *The Apostolic Fathers*.

Schweitzer, Albert. *The Quest of the Historical Jesus: A Critical Study of Its Progress from Reimarus to Wrede*. New York: Macmillan, 1968.

Silva, Moisés. "Can Two Walk Together Unless They Be Agreed? Evangelical Theology and Biblical Scholarship." *Journal of the Evangelical Theological Society* 41 (1998) 3-16.

Sparks, Kenton. *God's Word in Human Words: An Evangelical Appropriation of Critical Biblical Scholarship*. Grand Rapids: Baker, 2008.

Spinoza, Baruch. *A Theologico-Political Treatise*. Translated by Samuel Shirley. Indianapolis: Hackett, 2001.

Sproul, R. C. *Explaining Inerrancy: A Commentary*. Oakland: International Council on Biblical Inerrancy, 1980.

Sproul, R. C., and Norman L. Geisler. *Explaining Biblical Inerrancy: Official Commentary on the ICBI Statements*. Matthews, NC: Bastion, 2013.

Stanton, Graham N. "Presuppositions in New Testament Criticism." In Marshall, *New Testament Interpretation*, 60-71.

Stewart, Matthew. *The Courtier and the Heretic: Leibniz, Spinoza, and the Fate of God in the Modern World*. New York: Norton, 2006.

Stonehouse, Ned Bernard. *J. Gresham Machen: A Biographical Memoir*. Edinburgh: Banner of Truth, 1987.

———. *Origins of the Synoptic Gospels: Some Basic Questions*. Grand Rapids: Eerdmans, 1962.

Streeter, Burnett H. *The Four Gospels*. London: Macmillan, 1924.

Strimple, Robert B. *The Modern Search for the Real Jesus*. Phillipsburg: P & R, 1995.

Strobel, Lee. *The Case for Christ*. Grand Rapids: Zondervan, 1998.

Swanson, Dennis M. "The Downgrade Controversy and Evangelical Boundaries: Some Lessons from Spurgeon's Battle for Evangelical Orthodoxy." In Geisler and Farnell, *The Jesus Quest*, 229-98.

Syncellus, George. "Excerpts from 'The Chronography.'" The Tertullian Project. http://www.tertullian.org/rpearse/syncellus.

Talbert, Charles. *What Is a Gospel? The Genre of the Canonical Gospels*. Philadelphia: Fortress, 1977.

Terry, Milton S. *Biblical Hermeneutics*. 2nd ed. Grand Rapids: Zondervan, 1974.

Thiede, Carsten B. *The Dead Sea Scrolls and the Jewish Origins of Christianity*. New York: Pelgrave, 2000.

———. *Rekindling the Word*. Valley Forge, PA: Trinity, 1995.

Thiessen, Henry C. *Introduction to the New Testament*. Grand Rapids: Eerdmans, 1987.

Thiselton, Anthony C. *The Two Horizons: New Testament Hermeneutics and Philosophical Description*. Grand Rapids: Eerdmans, 1980.

Thomas, Robert L. "Current Hermeneutical Trends: Toward Explanation or Obfuscation?" *Journal of the Evangelical Theological Society* 39 (1996) 241–56.

———. "The 'Jesus Crisis': What Is It?" In Thomas and Farnell, *The Jesus Crisis*, 13–34.

———. "Redaction Criticism." In Thomas and Farnell, *The Jesus Crisis*, 233–67.

Thomas, Robert L., and F. David Farnell, eds. *The Jesus Crisis: The Inroads of Historical Criticism into Evangelical Scholarship*. Grand Rapids: Kregel, 1998.

Thompson, Mark D. "The Divine Investment in Truth: Toward a Theological Account of Biblical Inerrancy." In Hoffmeier and Magary, *Do Historical Matters Matter*, 71–97.

Thornbury, Gregory A. *Recovering Classic Evangelicalism: Applying the Wisdom and Vision of Carl F. H. Henry*. Wheaton, IL: Crossway, 2013.

Tillich, Paul. *Ultimate Concern: Tillich in Dialogue*. San Francisco: Harper & Row, 1965.

Torrey, R. A., ed. *The Fundamentals*. 4 vols. Grand Rapids: Baker, 1972.

Torrey, R. A., and Charles L. Feinberg, eds. *The Fundamentals: The Famous Sourcebook of Foundational Biblical Truths*. Updated ed. of *The Fundamentals for Today* [1958]. Grand Rapids: Kregel, 1990.

Tosh, John, ed. *Historians on History*. 2nd ed. Harlow, UK: Pearson, 2009.

Troeltsch, Ernst. "Historical and Dogmatic Method in Theology (1898)." In *Religion in History*, translated by James Luther Adams and Walter F. Bense, 11–32. Minneapolis: Fortress, 1991.

Urquhart, John. *Inspiration and Accuracy of the Holy Scriptures*. New York: Gospel, 1904.

Vanhoozer, Kevin J. "Augustinian Inerrancy: Literal Meaning, Literal Truth, and Literate Interpretation in the Economy of Biblical Discourse." In Merrick and Garrett, *Five Views on Biblical Inerrancy*, 199–235.

———. *The Drama of Doctrine: A Canonical Linguistic Approach to Christian Theology*. Louisville: Westminster John Knox, 2005.

———. *First Theology: God, Scripture and Hermeneutics*. Downers Grove: InterVarsity, 2002.

———. "Lost in Interpretation? Truth, Scripture, and Hermeneutic." *Journal of the Evangelical Theological Society* 48 (2005) 89–114.

Wallace, Daniel B. "An *Apologia* for a Broad View of *Ipsissima Vox*." Paper presented to the Fifty-First Annual Meeting of the Evangelical Theological Society, Danvers, MA, November 18, 1999.

———. "The Gospel according to Bart." Review of *Misquoting Jesus: The Story behind Who Changed the Bible and Why*, by Bart D. Ehrman. Bible.org. Posted April 24, 2006. https://bible.org/article/gospel-according-bart.

———. *Greek Grammar beyond the Basics*. Grand Rapids: Zondervan, 1997.

———. "Who's Afraid of the Holy Spirit? The Uneasy Conscience of a Non-Charismatic Evangelical." Introduction to *Who's Afraid of the Holy Spirit? An Investigation into the Ministry of the Spirit of God Today*, edited by Daniel B. Wallace and M. James Sawyer, 1–14. Dallas, TX: Biblical Studies, 2005.

———. "The Problem with Protestant Ecclesiology." Wallace's blog. Posted March 18, 2012. http://danielbwallace.com/2012/03/18/the-problem-with-protestant-ecclesiology.

———. Review of *Defining Inerrancy: Affirming a Defensible Faith for a New Generation*, by J. P. Holding and Nick Peters. Wallace's blog. Posted June 1, 2014. http://danielbwallace.com/2014/06/01/review-of-defining-inerrancy.

Walton, John H., and D. Brent Sandy. *The Lost World of Scripture: Ancient Culture and Biblical Authority*. Downers Grove: InterVarsity, 2013.

Warfield, Benjamin B. *The Inspiration and Authority of the Bible*. Grand Rapids: Baker, 1977.

*Bibliography*

Weaver, Walter P. *The Historical Jesus in the Twentieth Century: 1900–1950*. Edinburgh: T. & T. Clark, 1999.

Webb, Robert L. "The Historical Enterprise and Historical Jesus Research." In *Key Events in the Life of the Historical Jesus*, edited by Darrell L. Bock and Robert L. Webb, 9–93. Grand Rapids: Eerdmans, 2009.

Wenham, John. *Redating Matthew, Mark, and Luke: A Fresh Assault on the Synoptic Problem*. Downers Grove: InterVarsity, 1992.

Wesley, John. *The Bicentennial Edition of the Works of John Wesley*. Nashville: Abingdon, 2005.

———. *Explanatory Notes upon the New Testament*. London: Epworth, 1950.

———. *The Works of John Wesley*. Edited by Albert C. Outler. Nashville: Abingdon, 1984.

Westerholm, S. "Pharisees." In *Dictionary of Jesus and the Gospels*, edited by Joel B. Green et al., 609–14. Downers Grove: InterVarsity, 1992.

Westminster Assembly. *Westminster Confession of Faith*.

Westmont College. "Gundry to Unveil Peter as False Prophet." Westmont College website. Posted September 22, 2014. http://blogs.westmont.edu/2014/09/22/gundry-to-unveil-peter-as-false-prophet.

Wilkins, Michael J., and J. P. Moreland, eds. *Jesus Under Fire*. Grand Rapids: Zondervan, 1995.

Windschuttle, Keith. *The Killing of History*. New York: Encounter, 1996.

Woodbridge, John D. *Biblical Authority: A Critique of the Roger/McKim Proposal*. Grand Rapids: Zondervan, 1982.

Wright, N. T. *The Contemporary Quest for Jesus*. Minneapolis: Fortress, 2002.

———. "Jesus, Quest for the Historical." In *Anchor Bible Dictionary*, edited by David Noel Freedman, 3:796–802. New York: Doubleday, 1992.

Yarborough, Robert W. "The Future of Cognitive Reverence for the Bible." *Journal of the Evangelical Theological Society* 57 (2014) 5–18.

———. "God's Word in Human Words: Form-Critical Revelations." In Hoffmeier and Magary, *Do Historical Matters Matter*, 327–43.

# Person and Subject Index

This index is not exhaustive but rather deals with the subjects and individuals when they are dealt with in-depth. Subjects that are discerned from the table of contents are not listed individually, the subject of *inerrancy* does not receive a listing, since in some manner every page would require notation.

2015 Shepherds' Conference on Inerrancy, 99ff

Acts (dating and authorship), 481ff
Albright, William F., 467
American Inerrancy Tradition (AIT), 86ff
Ankerberg, John, 531
Aquinas, Thomas, 29, 85, 116, 382
Arminism(ists), 111ff
Atkin, Daniel L., 532

Bacon, Francis, 30
Bailey, Mark L., 531
Barr, James, 168ff
Barth, Karl, 88, 115, 119, 148, 180, 181, 213
Beck, W. David, 25
Bible Difficulties (dealing with), 80ff
Bible Institute of Los Angeles (BIOLA), 146ff
*Biblical Authority and Interpretation of the Bible: A Critique of the Rogers/McKim Proposal*, 86, 167ff, 219ff
*Bios, Bioi* (literary form), 192ff, 325ff
Bird, Michael, 60ff
Bird, Michael, 403ff
Blomberg, Craig, 25, 170ff, 186ff, 204ff, 208–239, 272ff, 288ff, 367, 388ff, 410ff, 452, 494ff
Bock, Darrell, 72, 74, 189ff, 209, 212, 227, 229, 252, 255, 288ff, 308ff
Boyd, Gregory, 454
Brigham Young University, 191
Byron, John, 42

Calvin, John, 85, 94, 109ff, 382

Calvinism(ists), 109ff
*Can We Still Believe the Bible?*, 211ff, 272ff, 410ff, 494ff
Caner, Emir, 537
Carson, D. A., 14, 114ff
Chadwick, David, 538
Chancellor, James, 25
Cheater Beatty Papyri, 475ff
*Chicago Statement on Biblical Hermeneutics*, 3, 14, 19, 130, 220ff, 282ff
*Chicago Statement on Biblical Inerrancy*, 3, 11, 14, 22, 37, 46, 61ff, 97ff, 102ff, 213ff, 220ff, 282ff, 365ff, 490
Clement of Alexandria, 378ff
Clement of Rome, 27, 473
Collins, Steve, 536
Comfort, Ray, 536
Corduan, Win, 536
Craig, William Lane, 25, 132ff, 198ff

Darwin, Charles, 30
Davids, Peter H., 290
Deductive Reasoning, 132ff
Descartes, Rene, 447ff
*Do Historical Matters Matter?*, 181ff, 193, 288
Dunn, James D. G., 51ff

Eddy, Mary Baker, 117, 123
Ehrman, Bart, 32ff, 75, 136, 138, 195ff, 202ff
Enns, Peter, 60ff
Ethics, 87ff
Evangelical Theological Society (ETS), 2, 5, 10, 62ff, 90ff, 123, 180ff, 241ff, 297ff, 347, 362
Evans, Jermey A., 536

559

*Person and Subject Index*

ExtraBiblical Data, 72ff

Farnell, F. David, 468ff, 533
Feinberg, Charles L., 157
Feinberg, Paul, 237, 244
Fernandes, Phil, 535
*Five Views on Biblical Inerrancy*, 60ff
Franke, John, 60ff
Fruchtenbaum, Arnold, 537
Fuller Theological Seminary, 46, 115, 124, 234ff
Fuller, Charles, 234ff

Geisler, Norman L., 3, 5, 7, 814, 17, 19, 21, 23, 25, 27, 29, 31, 33, 35, 37, 39, 41–43, 46, 51, 53–54, 79, 81, 83, 87, 89, 91, 93–95, 97, 99–101, 103, 105, 107, 109–111, 113, 115, 127–129, 133–135, 137, 139–141, 143, 145, 147–151, 153, 155, 157–162, 164, 169, 184, 188–189, 191, 195, 198–199, 227, 229–230, 232, 235, 236, 241, 245, 248, 250, 255, 259–261, 274, 281, 282, 286, 292, 293, 296, 302, 320, 341–342, 366, 368, 369–373, 379–381, 383, 386, 389, 391, 393, 395, 397, 399, 401, 403, 405–407, 411, 415–420, 425, 427, 434, 437, 442, 447, 449, 451, 453, 455, 457, 462, 463, 466, 507, 511, 513, 537, 542, 544, 548, 562, 565, 567, 573
Genre, 6, 74, 135, 420ff
Gerhardsson, Birger, 47
Ginn, Phil, 538
Graham, Billy, 234, 369, 529
Graham, Franklin, 161, 387, 548
GrammaticoHistorical Hermeneutics, 6, 143ff
GrecoRoman Genre, 136ff, 501ff
Green, Michyael, 201ff
Grudem, Wayne, 58
Gundry, Robert, 76, 92ff, 115ff, 124, 170, 297ff, 326ff, 339ff

Hagner, Donald A., 45ff, 201ff, 290ff, 348ff
Hague, Dyson, 147ff
Hanna, Mark, 534
Hannah, John, 86
Harmonization (gospels), 330ff
Harris, Murray J., 400ff
Hebermas, Gary, 25
Henry, Carl F. H., 63, 66, 102ff, 162, 229, 248ff
Hermeneutics, 7, 74, 102ff, 115ff, 516ff
Hindson, Ed, 535
Historical Criticism, 279ff
Historical Jesus Studies, 300ff, 448ff
Hobbes, Thomas, 30
Hodge, A. A., 110

Hoffman, Paul D., 538
Holden, Joseph M., 533
House, H. Wayne, 538
Howe, Richard, 537
Howe, Thomas A., 533
Hume, David, 30, 56
Hume, David, 448ff

*I (Still) Believe*, 42ff
Ignatius, 377ff
Inductive Reasoning, 132ff
Infallibility, 20, 68
Inspiration, 20, 25ff, 116ff
Institute of Biblical Research, 178, 310ff
International Council on Biblical Inerrancy (ICBI), 3, 22, 37, 61ff, 74, 107, 110, 134, 167, 210ff, 240ff, 282ff, 367ff, 388ff
Irenaeus, 378ff

Jewitt, Paul, 124ff
John, Gospel of (dating and authorship), 483ff
Johnson, Elliott, 535
*Journal of the Evangelical Theological Society*, 171
Justin Martyr, 28

Kaiser Jr., Walter C., 532
Kantzer, Kenneth, 22, 92, 141
Keener, Craig S., 25

Ladd, George Eldon, 163ff, 179, 236, 260ff
Land, Ricahrd, 532
*Lausanne Covenant Statement on Inerrancy*, 369
Lessing, Gotthold E., 449ff
Licona, Michael, 23, 24ff, 33, 37, 67, 75, 95, 141ff, 215ff, 242ff, 365ff, 375ff, 496, 504ff
Lightner, Robert P., 536
Limbaugh, David, 531
Lindsell, Harold, 27, 46, 90, 165ff, 204, 209, 266, 363, 526
Linnemann, Eta, 184ff, 204, 470, 526
Little, Bruce, 534
Lohr, Joel N., 42
Luke Gospel of (dating and authorship), 481ff
Luther, Martin, 85, 94, 109ff
Lutzer, Erwin W., 532ff

MacArthur, John F., 99, 263
Machen, J. Gresham, 178, 188, 191, 278, 284, 304, 312, 380
Macroevolution, 438ff
Mark, Gospel of (dating and authorship), 479ff
Marshall, I. Howard, 287

## Person and Subject Index

Matthew, Gospel of (dating and authorship), 476ff
McKim, Donald K., 167ff, 218, 490ff
McKnight, Scot, 57ff, 178
Mentoring, 39ff
Midrash, 136
Miller, Robert, 179ff
Mohler, Albert, 60ff, 264
Montgomery, John Warwick, 161, 548, 530ff, 570
Moo, Douglas J., 25
Moreland, J. P., 25
Morris, Leon, 202
Munro, John H., 530

Nicole, Roger, 92

Osborne, Grant, 171ff

Packer, James I, 61, 119, 142, 489ff
Patterson, Paige, xiv, 7, 14, 106ff, 124–126, 129, 161, 282, 549
Paulus, H. E. G., 450ff
Perrin, Norman, 179, 452
Pinnock, Clark, 65, 97, 242
Poku, Perseus, 538
Preparation, Day of, 141ff
Preus, Robert, 22, 129, 243, 247, 407, 442, 559, 567, 571, 573
Price, Randall, 537

*Quo Vadis Evangelicals?*, 516ff

Radmacher, Earl, 22, 129, 232, 243, 247, 258, 407, 442, 559, 567, 571, 573
Reimarus, Hermann S., 449ff
Rhoads, Ross, 534
Rhodes, Kenny, 535
Rhodes, Ron, 534
Richard, Ramesh, 535
Richardson, Grant, 533
Roach, William C., 533
Roberts, Phil, 534
Robinson, James M., 308ff
Roger, Jack, 115, 133, 166, 219, 490ff
Roman Catholicism, 97

Sanday, William, 151
Sandy, D. Brent, 295ff, 430ff
Schaeffer, Francis, 104, 208
*Sensus Literalis*, 122

Silva, Moises, , 171
Smith, Wilbur, 234
Southern Baptist Convention, 106ff
Southern Evangelical Seminary, 117
Sparks, Kenton, 77
Spinoza, Benedict, 30, 129, 448ff, 459ff
Sproul, R. C., 3 , 4, 11, 47, 61, 65, 76, 111, 119, 120, 122, 142, 209, 213, 214, 220, 221, 225, 226, 227, 240, 243, 285, 286, 366, 386, 392, 398, 401, 405, 409, 416, 424, 444, 493, 548, 555
Struss, David F., 450ff
Susek, Ron, 538

*The Battle for the Bible*, 165ff, 209, 266
*The Fundamentals*, 145ff, 258, 265
*The Jesus Crisis*, 171ff
*The Jesus Quest*, 260ff
The Master's Seminary, 99, 256
Thiede, Carsten B., 475ff
Tillich, Paul, 117
Torrey, R. A., 165, 173, 176, 178, 276, 278, 486, 567, 574
Towns, Elmer L., 532
Trinity Evangelical Divinity School, 92, 212

Vanhoozer, Kevin, 60ff, 230
Vassady, Bela, 162
von Harnack, Adolph, 451ff

Wallace, Daniel B., 25, 194ff, 248
Waltke, Bruce, 50ff
Walton, John D., 295ff, 430ff
Warfield, Benjamin B., 21, 63, 110, 490
Warren, William, 25
Webb, Robert , 308ff
Weiland, Forrest S., 534
Wenham, John, 467ff
Wesley, John, 111ff
Wiersbe, Warren W., 158
Wilkin, Robert, 539
Williams, Donald T., 537
Woodbridge, John, 86, 168ff
*World Conference on Christian Fundamentals*, 158ff

Yamauchi, Edwin M., 25
Yarborough, Robert, 184ff, 205ff

Zacharias, Ravi, 530

# Scripture Index

This index is also not exhaustive. Only references that are dealt with in some detail are listed, individual references and citations used in support are not listed.

## Genesis

| | |
|---|---|
| 1 | 72ff, 281ff, 495ff, 432ff |
| 1–3 | |

## Deuteronomy

| | |
|---|---|
| 20 | 83ff |

## Joshua

| | |
|---|---|
| 6 | 83ff |

## Matthew

| | |
|---|---|
| 5 | 83ff |
| 5:18 | 26 |
| 10:25 | 39 |
| 17:27 | 187 |
| 26 | 341ff |
| 27:51–53 | 24ff, 47ff, 115ff, 200ff, 215, 244, 375ff, 501ff |
| 28:27 | 23 |

## Mark

| | |
|---|---|
| 2 | 33ff |
| 16:7 | 328ff |
| 16:57 | 23 |

## Luke

| | |
|---|---|
| 1:14 | 135 |
| 5:32 | 196 |
| 24:47 | 23 |

## John

| | |
|---|---|
| 3:12 | 140 |
| 34 | 175ff |
| 10:34–35 | 26 |
| 20:11–14 | 23 |
| 19:35 | 135 |

## Acts

| | |
|---|---|
| 9 | 81ff, 437ff |
| 17:26 | |
| 22 | 81ff |

## 1 Corinthians

| | |
|---|---|
| 15 | 126 |
| 15:17 | 140 |

## 2 Timothy

| | |
|---|---|
| 3:16 | 26, 195 |

## 1 Peter

| | |
|---|---|
| 2:23–25 | 26 |

## Jude

| | |
|---|---|
| 3 | 113 |

www.ingramcontent.com/pod-product-compliance
Lightning Source LLC
Chambersburg PA
CBHW081142230426
43664CB00018B/2776